Monash

Monash

GRANTLEE KIEZA

ABC
Books

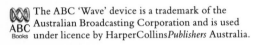 The ABC 'Wave' device is a trademark of the Australian Broadcasting Corporation and is used under licence by HarperCollins*Publishers* Australia.

First published in Australia in 2015
by HarperCollins*Publishers* Australia Pty Limited
ABN 36 009 913 517
harpercollins.com.au

HarperCollins*Publishers*
Level 13, 201 Elizabeth Street, Sydney NSW 2000, Australia
Unit D1, 63 Apollo Drive, Rosedale, Auckland 0632, New Zealand
A 53, Sector 57, Noida, UP, India
1 London Bridge Street, London, SE1 9GF, United Kingdom
2 Bloor Street East, 20th floor, Toronto, Ontario M4W 1A8, Canada
195 Broadway, New York NY 10007, USA

National Library of Australia Cataloguing-in-Publication data:

Monash : the soldier who shaped Australia / Grantlee Kieza.
  ISBN: 978 0 7333 3353 8 (hardback)
  ISBN: 978 1 4607 0314 4 (ebook)
  Includes bibliographical references and index.
  Monash, John, Sir, 1865–1931.
  Australia. Army – Officers – Biography.
  Generals – Australia – Biography.
  Engineers – Australia – Biography.
  Australia – History – 20th century.
355.0092

Index by Michael Wyatt
Typeset in 12/15pt Bembo by Kirby Jones
Printed and bound in Australia by Griffin Press
The papers used by HarperCollins in the manufacture of this book are a natural, recyclable
product made from wood grown in sustainable plantation forests. The fibre source and
manufacturing processes meet recognised international environmental standards, and carry
certification.

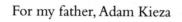
For my father, Adam Kieza

Chapter 1

BUCKINGHAM PALACE, LONDON, 27 DECEMBER 1918

*I would name Sir John Monash as the best general on the Western
Front in Europe; he possessed real creative originality, and the war
might well have been won sooner, and certainly with fewer casualties,
had Haig been relieved of his command and Monash appointed to
command the British armies in his place.*
FIELD MARSHAL BERNARD MONTGOMERY, CHIEF OF THE IMPERIAL
GENERAL STAFF 1946 TO 1948[1]

*I am convinced that there are no troops in the world to equal the
Australians in cool daring, courage and endurance.*
JOHN MONASH, WRITING TO HIS WIFE FROM GALLIPOLI[2]

THE KING'S CONQUERING HERO stands outside the
most magnificent palace in the world, and rubs a forefinger
across his thick salt-and-pepper moustache. He sticks out his
aristocratic jaw and takes a deep gulp of the cold, crisp night air.
Ever so slowly, Lieutenant General Sir John Monash breathes
in the stunning sight before him, both the tranquillity and the
splendour, as the biting breeze on this cold London night slaps
him hard across the face.

A man of medium height with a large nose, swarthy skin
and dark penetrating eyes, he has lost the businessman's paunch
of younger days and now, at 53 and dressed in the uniform of

Australia's supreme military commander, he looks as fit as he did when he cut a swathe through the fashionable young ladies of Melbourne 30 years earlier. His boots gleam with a mirror finish and his peaked officer's cap covers his thinning, tawny-grey hair. His face is heavily lined and creased, but that only adds to his reputation as an intellectual. Ever since he was a small boy herding goats in the Australian bush, this son of German-speaking Jews has dreamed of such glory for himself, such public reward for his hard work and sacrifice. Now he has played a leading role in the destruction of the German Army and is about to dine with the King and Queen of England, the President of the United States and some of the most famous figures in history. For so long, all through the horrors of the past few years, Monash has had a furrow carved deep into his brow, but on this cold night, as his breath escapes in a cloud of vapour, his face displays only wide-eyed awe.

Four years earlier, having never seen a shot fired in anger, he was sitting behind a desk at his engineering firm in Melbourne, the years of hard work and struggle having at last opened the door to a comfortable life in one of Melbourne's grandest homes. Swept up in the bloody whirlpool of the Great War, his first taste of military action was the massacre at Gallipoli – yet now he is being lauded as the greatest living Australian, and one of history's most astute military tacticians.

It takes a few moments for Monash to comprehend the magnificence of the occasion and the opulence of the royal residence, surrounded as it is by a carpet of white frost. Golden lights in every window make the enormous building glisten like a treasure chest. As he enters Buckingham Palace, Monash nods towards Winston Churchill and Rudyard Kipling among the other dinner guests drinking in the moment.

He speaks briefly to some of the assembled dignitaries, the Prime Ministers of Britain, South Africa and Australia. The guttural vowels that once betrayed his German ancestry have long gone. Monash's world has been one of mud and blood and death ever since he landed at Anzac Cove in 1915, to first experience a war that became the first truly global conflict. He has risen from weekend soldier to command more than 200,000 Australian, British, Canadian and American troops, and British Prime Minister David Lloyd George says he has become the most resourceful general in the entire British Army.[3]

Seventeen million lives, among them 62,000 Australian, have been lost in the fighting, and another 20 million men, women and children have been left mutilated and maimed. In less than half a decade, ancient kingdoms have crumbled, empires have been destroyed, dynasties toppled. Within 10 years, war has changed from hand-to-hand combat to aerial bombardment and artillery fire that can destroy targets more than 100 kilometres away.

No wonder that when the Armistice was signed in a railway carriage in a French forest just six weeks ago, on 11 November 1918, men and women around the globe danced in the streets, waving flags and hats, free at last from the shackles of fear.

Now, in Monash's home city of Melbourne, department stores are revelling in the post-war euphoria as a populace giddy with excitement and optimism ticks up sales records.[4] This has been the war they say will end all wars,[5] and there is exhilaration everywhere now that the bloodletting and the bloodlust are over.

Monash knows, though, that the end of hostilities has only brought about a fragile peace. Famine and pestilence strain at the leash and political unrest bubbles.

The Spanish flu, accelerated by massive troop movements and the close proximity of soldiers weakened by malnourishment and war, has already started to infect 50 million people. It will soon kill twice that number.[6] In Germany, children are still dying from starvation and disease as a result of the Allied blockade. The lingering resentment over Germany's humiliation will fester in the minds of conquered soldiers such as Lance Corporal Adolf Hitler. Reports out of Russia say Bolsheviks are dismembering their opponents alive. Communism looms as a threat to the rest of the world.[7]

But these are all problems to be addressed at a later time. For now, Monash steps out of the cold London night and into the grandeur of the palace.

He strides forth with the same resolute air, the same forceful bearing that have propelled him past all the other career army officers to command the Australian Corps on the Western Front. Throughout his life he has been as impervious to opposition as the tanks so instrumental in his victories: a great rumbling machine that sweeps aside all before him. He has picked himself up from every blow aimed at him, whether from a jealous husband or from the most powerful army ever assembled. Now Monash marches towards the new rulers of the world with the confident bearing of a military commander who has destroyed all opposition at Hamel, Amiens, Mont St Quentin and the Hindenburg Line.

Yet here in the palace even Monash has to shorten his stride, agog at what he regards as the 'unsurpassed brilliancy' of this State banquet.[8] He walks into a spacious corridor leading to the State Rooms and reacquaints himself with many of the 117 invited dignitaries who are making small talk about the biggest decisions ever considered on earth. The Ministers of the Cabinet, the Ambassadors of France, Italy, the United States, Spain and Japan, all dressed in top hats and tails, stand chatting about the Peace Conference at Versailles that is due to start in three weeks and which will apportion the crushed remains of the conflict among the victors.

The other military men are all in uniform. Monash greets one of his greatest supporters, Field Marshal Douglas Haig, commander-in-chief of the British forces, who is standing with two of his generals, William Robertson and Henry Wilson, and Admirals John Jellicoe, David Beatty and Rosslyn Wemyss.

Nearby are Randall Davidson, the Archbishop of Canterbury, the Indian statesman Satyendra Sinha and the Maharaja of Bikaner, Ganga Singh, the only non-white member of the British Imperial War Cabinet. Billy Hughes is here too; the Prime Minister of Australia and self-styled 'Little Digger' has always been wary of Monash's astonishing rise.

The King's guests mingle for 10 minutes before costumed officers of the palace lead them into the White Drawing Room. Here, amid the breathtaking luxury, wait King George V, Queen Mary and some of their children, Princes Henry and George[9] and Princess Mary, as well as the King's elderly aunt Princess Christian, his grey-bearded uncle, the Duke of Connaught, and the Duke's daughter Princess Patricia. With them is the tall, haggard, bespectacled figure of American President Woodrow Wilson, accompanied by Edith, the widow he married three years ago. The Wilsons arrived in London yesterday to tumultuous cheering from crowds estimated at 2 million,[10] but America's involvement in the war has taken a hard toll on the President. After his speech in Congress committing troops to the fighting in Europe 20 months earlier, Wilson returned to the White House, buried his head in his arms and sobbed like a child because he knew thousands of Americans would die.[11]

Monash waits his turn to shake hands with the President and the King. It was only four months ago, near Villers-Bretonneux in France, that he knelt before His Majesty as the King placed a sword upon Monash's shoulder and invested him with his knighthood. He was the first soldier to be given this honour on the battlefield in two centuries.

George V is a slight, middle-aged man with slicked-down, thinning hair and a greying beard, but in this room, surrounded by this finery and these great men, he stands in all his regal pomp, basking in the Allied triumph and the vanquishing of his cousin, the Kaiser. Monash bows and warmly shakes the King's hand and is then presented to President Wilson, standing on the King's right. Next he moves on to meet the towering and imposing figures of Queen Mary and Mrs Wilson.

It seems as if hardly any time has passed since Monash was clambering up the steep ravines of Gallipoli, dodging sniper bullets or looking out over the muddy, bloody killing fields of France, but now he and the other guests are ushered along a brilliantly lit corridor full of glorious masterpieces and lined on both sides with bearded Yeomen of the Guard, in their traditional black, gold and crimson Tudor uniforms. The guardsmen stand at attention like statues as the guests enter the banquet hall, which has been richly decorated in white and gold, and where six great crystal chandeliers spread a dazzling electric light such as Monash has never seen before.

Yeomen stand stiffly all around, the light gleaming off the sharp steel points of their pikes. All of the royal gold plate has been brought to Buckingham Palace from Windsor Castle and the light is reflected from it in a halo effect. Large gold flower bowls overflow with scarlet and crimson azaleas.

The female guests look stunning in full evening dress with sparkling diamond coronets and necklaces, but Monash is at this event alone. Vic, his wife of 27 tempestuous years, is back in Melbourne, and he dare not appear at such a politically delicate evening with his lover Lizzie Bentwitch.

The guests quickly take their appointed places at the table, which is arranged in a giant horseshoe shape. The royal party enters, ushered in by uniformed officers of the palace household walking backwards. The band strikes up a fanfare, followed by 'The Star-Spangled Banner' and 'God Save the King', as the President leads in the Queen who is arrayed in gold cloth and wears magnificent diamonds on her corsage, including the Koh-i-Noor and Cullinan diamonds. The King follows with Edith Wilson, with the rest of the royal family close behind.

Seated opposite Monash is Louis Botha, a one-time enemy of the British as a guerrilla leader in South Africa. Next to Botha is the jowly Winston Churchill, who by sheer coincidence was captured by Botha's men during the Boer War, when Churchill was a gung-ho war correspondent.[12] Much has happened since their first meeting near Pretoria in 1899. Now, two days after Christmas 1918, Botha is Britain's ally as South Africa's first prime minister, while Churchill is still trying to salvage his reputation as a soldier and politician. He was sacked from his role as First Lord of the Admiralty for ordering the disastrous invasion of Gallipoli in 1915, in which 44,000 Allied soldiers died, including almost 9000 Australians.[13] Churchill went back to battle in France as a lieutenant colonel in an attempt to atone in some way.

Monash was seen as a very different kind of commander by his troops. To him the welfare of his men was paramount; they were not cannon fodder, but flesh and blood, husbands and fathers, sons and brothers. To them he was a paternal leader who fought to save their lives as much as he fought to save the Empire.

Seated on Monash's left is Lord Burnham, owner of Britain's *Daily Telegraph*, who believes the Australian soldiers are second to none.[14] On Monash's right is Kipling, the Nobel-Prize winning writer, sad-eyed and balding with a walrus moustache and round, rimless spectacles. Monash first met him almost 30 years ago in Melbourne, and back then even souvenired Kipling's autograph.

At the outbreak of hostilities Kipling was quick to lend his name and fame to Britain's war effort, writing propaganda speeches and encouraging young men to fight for King and Country. The only good Germans, he suggested, were dead ones.[15]

Kipling urged his 18-year-old son John to join the war effort, and even pulled strings to get him to the frontline despite the boy's poor eyesight. John Kipling died at the Battle of Loos in 1915, his face torn apart by an exploding shell. He was last seen stumbling blindly through the muddied battlefield screaming in agony. His body was never found among all that mud and death, and Kipling has been haunted by the loss ever since.

Kipling and Monash are the same age but have emerged from the Great War with vastly different outcomes. Still, the celebrated author of *The Jungle Book* and 'Gunga Din' tries his best to be good company. He entertains fellow guests seated nearby with apocryphal tales about Monash that he has heard from Australian soldiers on leave. Monash tells him of how he asked for Kipling's autograph all those years ago, when fountain pens were a novelty, and Kipling adds his signature again to the little autograph book Monash carries in his breast pocket. It already contains the signatures of the King and Queen and of Alfred Deakin, the former Australian prime minister, whom Monash befriended as a teenager.

George V is scheduled to address this distinguished gathering soon, but first Monash has his own stories to tell the guests surrounding him. He can spin tales as fascinating as any Kipling has ever dreamed up. He has been talking himself up since boyhood, and in the past four years he has been the strongest advocate Australia and Australian fighting men have ever had. This gentle, theatre-going engineer, whose first words were in German, is the grandson of a man who printed Jewish prayer books and the nephew of a celebrated Jewish historian.

He was first attracted to the military because teenage girls loved his uniform, and as one commentator will remark, Monash resembles Napoleon in his confident bearing, his imposing personality, his forceful manner and the way in which he has become the author of his own legend.[16]

He has always had an overwhelming desire to prove himself in the face of what he calls the handicaps of race and religion, a Jew born to German parents. Yet he has always had to work hard at the confidence, forcing himself to speak in public at times when the butterflies in his stomach felt like Zeppelins. He possesses a wonderfully elastic mind and brilliance at organisation. Above all, whether it is commanding one of the great armies of history or chasing a love interest, Monash's driving force is his relentless ambition.

At just 17 he wrote in his diary: 'Is it true that Ambition is a vice? Surely then it is a vice common to all mankind; for how can a man live without ambition? ... The sole thing that bears up my failing spirits is this ambition.'[17]

He is an extraordinarily complex man: a man who writes tender love letters to his wife while carrying on an affair with one of her oldest friends; a man who sees himself as devoted to the welfare and success of his countrymen while advocating the firing squad for cowards and deserters.

Monash has been fashioning his own astonishing tale from boyhood, when he claimed to have met a big-bearded horse thief named Ned Kelly at the colonial outpost of Jerilderie. Now Monash is one of the most important soldiers in the world.

How proud his grandfather would have been, back in the synagogue he built in Prussia.

Chapter 2

KROTOSZYN, IN WHAT IS NOW
WESTERN POLAND, 1801

Lord Kitchener recently sent me a certain amount of nasty correspondence about [Monash] from Australia with reference to his alleged German proclivities, but I told [Kitchener] I am not prepared to take any action in the matter.

LIEUTENANT GENERAL SIR WILLIAM BIRDWOOD, COMMANDER OF THE AUSTRALIAN AND NEW ZEALAND ARMY CORPS, 1915[1]

IN THE YEAR WHEN John Monash's grandfather cries the first of his many tears, Napoleon takes control of continental Europe[2] and Thomas Jefferson becomes the third president of the United States.

It is 1801, and in an unremarkable house in an unremarkable Polish town of cobblestone streets, within the shadow of a Gothic castle, Leibush[3] and Maria Monasz welcome their new son, Dov Baer.[4] They pray that the God of Israel will bless him, that Baer will enjoy a long life full of peace and prosperity here in the town of Krotoszyn, about 100 kilometres south of the city of Poznan.

The Monasz family are most likely descendants of Manasseh, the grandson of Jacob, also known as Israel, who was the grandson of the patriarch Abraham, a man so blessed he was called the 'friend of God'.[5]

Leibush is a kindly, mild-tempered schoolmaster and teacher of the Talmud, the most important text of Rabbinic Judaism. His wife is a kindred spirit who will never lose her sunny outlook even though she will lose all but three of her 13 babies.[6]

The countryside around Krotoszyn is mostly flat farmland given over to the growing of grain, but the political landscape of Poland, a nation caught between the Prussians on one side and the Russians on the other, has always been rocky. By the 19th century, it has long been a safe haven for Jews escaping persecution, so much so that it is known in Latin as *Paradisus Iudaeorum*, 'Paradise for the Jews'.

Three-quarters of all the Jews in Europe were said to be living in Poland by the middle of the 16th century,[7] yet they weren't always safe. The Jewish settlement in Krotoszyn was almost wiped out by Polish soldiers in 1656, when 350 of 400 families were murdered,[8] but by the time Baer is born, there are about 2000 Jews among the 6000 inhabitants of his town.

Until he is 12, Baer is an only child, all his siblings having died in infancy. Since he is small, frail and sickly, Leibush and Maria spoil him with affection. He is named after a fierce animal, the bear, but he has no aptitude for fighting and no interest in warfare except to run out onto the streets to see Russian troops or Napoleon's French soldiers in their vivid uniforms marching to the stirring music of military bands as they make their way through Krotosyzn to fight the many battles that take place in Prussia during Baer's childhood.

His parents hope that Baer might become a rabbi, like many of the Monasz men before him, and Leibush instructs him in the biblical and rabbinic writings, teaching him to observe all the Jewish holy days. He teaches his son to read and write German, the language that has replaced Polish in most of Krotoszyn now that the Prussians have control. To many Poles the German tongue is guttural and harsh, but the Prussians have already changed the name of Krotoszyn to Krotoschin. Poznan is now Posen and Wroclaw, the home town of Baer's mother, has become

Breslau. As a young man Baer knows little Polish and prefers to write and speak Yiddish, the language of his father, but in time he will sign his works in German as Baer-Loebel Monasch, 'Baer, the Son of Loebel'.

Leibush supplements his teaching income with work as a bookbinder, and Baer stays up late with him as they toil by lamplight. When Baer is 14 his father takes him to the town of Milicz, about 25 kilometres from Krotoszyn, to begin a year-long apprenticeship in bookbinding under Master Drebs, a short-tempered Gentile who eventually beats him and sends him packing.

It takes time for Baer's emotional wounds to heal, but in the meantime he becomes more proficient as a bookbinder, working all day from a small bedroom in his father's home and then taking lessons from him in the Hebrew scriptures.

When Baer is 18 he suffers his first great setback. An itinerant bookseller defrauds him of 80 marks, all the money he has saved. Prone to depression, Baer calls this the beginning of the 'red thread of misfortune' that cuts through his entire life. The stress makes him deathly ill for several weeks, but Leibush comforts him with the biblical story of the patient Job and asks Baer to trust in the one who created heaven and earth. 'My father's words made a deep impression on me', Baer will later write. 'I wept bitterly and he kissed me and dried my tears.'[9]

When Baer is 22 he meets Mathilde Wiener, whose ancestors, a family of scholar-rabbis, fled persecution in Vienna in 1684.[10] Baer and Mathilde marry in 1823 and Baer sets to work building a future for his family. If he has no bookbinding to do, he makes hat boxes. Until his delicate physique and weak constitution curtail it, he travels to country fairs, hawking prayer books, mirrors, briefcases, handbags and other fashionable goods.

Nine months after their wedding, Mathilde gives birth to a daughter, Julie, the first of their 13 children.[11] A second daughter, Marie, arrives in 1826 but the bliss of the young family ends abruptly the following year when their home and their synagogue are among 160 buildings destroyed by the greatest fire Krotoszyn has ever seen. Baer has a key role in rebuilding the synagogue and occasionally leads prayers there.

His first son Isidor is born in 1829 and two years later Baer and Mathilde welcome a second son, Louis, who will become the father of Australia's greatest soldier. Baby Louis will show his fighting qualities from birth, surviving Krotoszyn's great cholera epidemic.

When Louis is two, Baer expands his bookbinding business and becomes a printer and publisher, using a creaking wooden press and purple-black iron-gall ink. His first two small volumes in German fail to sell, but Rabbi Jaffe, from the village of Zduny, hires Baer to print a book in Hebrew. Baer finds some old Hebrew fonts in Wroclaw, and also finds his calling.

Hardly has the book been completed than Rabbi Urbach from Lenschütz commissions another major work of 120 pages. Next Baer begins work on his Pentateuch,[12] the five books of Moses, translated by the esteemed German Jewish scholar Dr Joseph Johlsohn.[13] Soon the businesses B.L. Monasch & Co or B.L. Monasch und Sohn, when Isidor is helping him, have four printing presses and 36 employees.

One of Baer's major assignments is the printing of local copies of the *Monthly Magazine for the Science and History of Judaism*, the world's leading Jewish journal.[14] With the financial support of his cousin Moritz Monasch, a Wroclaw bookseller, Baer also prints a 12-volume Bible, a Hebrew edition of the Jerusalem Talmud, and the Torah in 18 volumes, translated into Yiddish and German.

He never becomes a rich man, though, and is forever preoccupied with providing dowries for the five daughters who make it to adulthood. His own ill health, his wife's nervous breakdowns, the continuing political turmoil in Europe and several unsuccessful projects will have an impact on his business for the rest of his life.

He is so busy he cannot follow his father's example and participate in the religious education of his children. Instead, he sends them to the local high school, and for two years also pays a tutor 60 marks a year with free board and lodging to teach his sons Hebrew and Jewish learning and religion.

Baer thinks Louis might become a scholar, and at considerable expense sends him to board at a prestigious high school in Glogau, 100 kilometres away. But Baer is already short of funds and after a year Louis comes home to finish his education.

By then Baer has found a match for 18-year-old Julie – striking, as he says, while the iron is hot and she is in the flower of youth.[15] He marries her off to a young book dealer named Ben-Zion Behrend, who repays the favour by almost sending Baer broke, investing in a timber business as it is about to crash.

With Behrend's help, Baer's second daughter, Marie, strikes a match with Dr Heinrich Graetz,[16] who is on his way to becoming one of the world's foremost Jewish historians, but Baer and Mathilde lose another daughter, Klara,[17] to consumption.

As their sons Louis and Julius find work at a trading house in Berlin, another outbreak of cholera tears through Krotoszyn in 1852 and takes two of their other daughters, one-year-old Helene and her 15-year-old sister Hanchen.

Louis sends 200 marks home to his father to help the family and tells Baer he wants to do much more for his parents.

When six ships bearing 8 tons of Victorian bullion sail up the Thames[18] in April 1852, gold fever erupts throughout Europe. Men and women from around the world, from noblemen to navvies, set off to chase their fortune.

Louis writes to his father from Berlin that he has made a life-changing decision. He plans to try his luck among all the fortune-hunters heading to Victoria. He will return to Krotoszyn after five years, having not only restored the family fortunes but also established his own.

His bosses at the trading company offer Louis 2000 marks' worth of goods on credit to take to Australia so he can establish a business selling 'fancy goods', stationery, cutlery, brushes, leather goods, glassware, embroidery, jewellery, electroplated toys, baskets, perfumes and tobacco.[19]

Louis makes a farewell visit to Krotoszyn, then in October sets sail from Hamburg with a certain degree of style in cabin class, aboard the 38-metre-long barque *Johann Cesar*.

The journey to Melbourne takes the best part of four months and Louis arrives with 61 other passengers on 29 January 1854. Between 1852 and 1855 about 300 Jewish families from London and Poznan arrive in Melbourne,[20] boosting the congregation of the synagogue first established there in 1841.[21]

The Melbourne of 1854 that greets Louis is the fastest growing and most expensive city in the world. The population has swelled from 29,000 to 76,560 in just three years, and 1500 more migrants arrive every week. Nearly a quarter of a million people are trying to make a go of it in Victoria[22] and the colony is in chaos. Lieutenant Governor Charles La Trobe presides over a regime in shambles and a workforce downing tools to rush to the goldfields. Yet Melbourne is also a city exploding with possibilities – even for a man with a thick German accent. Louis forms a business partnership with another German immigrant, Louis Martin, to act as commission agents and general merchants.

Great public works are either in the pipeline or already built: the Princes Bridge across the Yarra, a train terminus, a marvellous public library, a town hall and a telegraph service. Melbourne University is about to open under its first chancellor, Redmond Barry, an aristocratic judge who has a soft spot for the ladies,[23] and who in January 1855 presides over the treason trials of some of the 13 rebels from Ballarat's Eureka Stockade.

In March, work begins on a new synagogue to house 650 of the Melbourne faithful. Louis begins to advertise his new business on the front page of the *Argus* newspaper, telling readers it is operating from 45 Flinders Lane West.[24] The business is called Martin and Monash, Louis having dropped the 'c' from his surname to make it less jarring to the predominantly Anglo-

Celtic population. Many of his relatives in Australia and America will follow his lead.

The following year, on 25 April – a date that will eventually loom large in the history of the Monash family and of all Australia – Louis reverts to the German spelling as 'Louis Monasch, merchant, native of Prussia' stands before Judge Barry and undergoes a naturalisation ceremony, promising to 'establish himself for life' in the new colony of Victoria.

At the time Louis pronounces his surname MOH-NARSH. He and his son will eventually use MOH-NASH but later generations will adopt MON-ASH.[25]

Louis writes home to his parents often, and in one letter in 1856 promises 500 marks towards the marriage of his sister Charlotte, though Baer later complains that Louis sends no assistance at all.

Louis has other things on his mind.

Soon he is adding his name to the list of political supporters for William Foster Stawell, Redmond Barry's old schoolfriend from Trinity College, Dublin, who is about to be elected as a representative for Melbourne in Victoria's first Legislative Assembly.[26] Louis also becomes secretary of the local German Association,[27] and one of his first tasks is organising the 1857 annual ball at Melbourne's newly built Exhibition Building on William Street.[28]

He and Louis Martin move their business to 10 Little Collins Street West[29] and start importing fancy goods and toys from Frankfurt and Nuremburg, as well as concertinas, flutinas, beads, cutlery and stationery.[30] By 1861, when Australia's first stock exchange opens in Melbourne, there are 10,418 German-born residents of Victoria.[31]

Louis wants to do his bit to increase those numbers. He writes home, asking Baer to send Louis's 16-year-old brother Max Monash to help him. Max is in his second year at the local high school but thinks Victoria will provide him with all the education he needs. Louis and Max's 16-year-old nephew Albert

Behrend, the son of Julie and Ben-Zion, decides to make the voyage as well.

The eager teenagers sail to Liverpool, where they board the steamer *Great Britain* on 18 October 1861 and set off down the Mersey towards the Great South Land.

On Christmas Eve Max and Albert steam into Melbourne, and look on in stunned awe as 10,000 people greet the ship with a tumultuous welcome of shouts and hurrahs.[32] Louis Monash is in their midst, dressed in the fine apparel of a wealthy young businessman.

Max and Albert look at each other in astonishment, asking other passengers: '*Was geschieht?*' ('What is happening?'). The magnificent welcome, of a kind rarely seen in Victoria, is not for the two callow German teenagers, though, but for England's first cricket XI to travel to Australia. They have been brought to Melbourne for a series of matches after the owners of the Café de Paris in Bourke Street have failed to entice the author Charles Dickens to come out for a lecture tour and decided on a cricket promotion instead. The first match, featuring an England XI against the city's best 18 players, is due to be played in a week at the Melbourne Cricket Ground, with its new 6000-seat grandstand.[33]

While the cricketers make their way through Melbourne in a magnificent carriage towed by eight grey horses, Louis and Max Monash and Albert Behrend travel anonymously to Little Collins Street West, where Louis lives at his shop with his lodger, the sculptor Emil Todt, who has recently made a name for himself with his masterpiece *The Gold Diggers*.[34] Soon it all gets a bit crowded, and the following year the four men move to a villa in St Kilda.

Louis, though, is looking for some female company. He is 32 and keen to find a wife – not among the new Australians, but a nice Jewish girl from the old country.

He sails home.

Baer is now an old man but he cries like a baby when the most enterprising of his 13 children returns after a decade abroad. The Passover feast of 1863 is about to begin, and Baer and Mathilde feel truly blessed. Louis is now a darkly handsome, debonair businessman. His arrival seems like a ray of hope for Baer, as his other sons Isidor and Julius have been dragging him towards financial ruin. Julius has even spent time in the debtors' prison.

During Louis's visit, as he and Baer walk to the Jewish cemetery on Ostrowskiej Street to put flowers on the graves of Louis's grandparents and his sister Hanchen, Baer reveals the critical state of his finances. Louis promises to send him a monthly allowance of £3. 'I thank God that he has given me such a son', Baer later writes.[35]

Louis wants a son of his own, and with that in mind he travels 400 kilometres north to the Baltic Sea port of Szczecin[36] to romance his 21-year-old sister-in-law, the buxom, sensual, dark-eyed Bertha Manasse, one of six children born to Jacob Manasse and his wife Charlotte Benjamin. Her sister Emilie is married to the perpetually broke Julius Monasch.

Louis is smitten with just one look into those big, soft, dark eyes. He writes to his brother Max, who is looking after his interests back in Melbourne, telling him that Bertha plays the piano like an angel and that he has fallen in love. He describes Bertha as his 'black-eyed Xanthippe', a reference to the spirited, tempestuous wife of Socrates.[37]

Bertha is Jewish, but her town of Dramburg has no synagogue and her family have long embraced the secular world, rather than the religious. To her family, Louis is an 'odd Australian' from an orthodox family threatening to drag their daughter back into the old Jewish customs, and to a land as remote as Mars. When Louis goes away to source goods for his business, Bertha's family forbids her to correspond with him.

Too late. She has already resolved to follow him to the ends of the earth. 'What do I care', she writes, 'if they believe Australia is a desert, where I am in danger of being eaten for dinner one day by savages?'[38]

Louis's siblings act as go-betweens. Ulrike,[39] Louis's baby sister, is about the same age as Bertha, and her confidante. She writes to Louis, 'You may feel *quite* sure of her. She commissioned me to send you a multitude of greetings and kisses … be of good cheer, for all will come right, when you once come back again.'[40]

To appease both families, the couple go through both a civil marriage and a Jewish ceremony in Szczecin on 15 November 1863. Baer makes the long train journey to attend but Mathilde is too frail. A week after the wedding the young couple visit Krotoszyn to say goodbye. Bertha has promised her family she will be back in five years but they never see her again.

Bertha and Louis honeymoon in Paris for a week and spend a few days in London before Louis buys two one-way tickets to Melbourne. He intends to book passage on a fast clipper called the *Star of Peace*, but English names confuse him and he and his new bride end up sailing out of Liverpool on the *Empire of Peace*, a vessel he calls 'a miserable tub'. Bertha spends much of her time trying to improve her English after her fellow travellers mock her accent. There are only eight other passengers in cabin class and 259 in steerage. It takes 124 days of claustrophobia and caustic comments from what Louis calls the 'rogues, thieves and drunks on board escaping English law' before they finally reach Melbourne. When the ship anchors in Port Melbourne, Max and Albert row out to meet the newlyweds who are let down in big baskets amid 'derisive screams from those on board'.[41]

The Monashes set up home in St Kilda, where Bertha is an instant hit among the Jewish community with her splendid piano playing and charming conversation. But things are not so happy back in Krotoszyn. Isidor becomes bankrupt and Mathilde dies in September 1864, six days after the Jewish New Year.

Ninety kilometres away in Kruszewnia, just outside Poznan, Klara Ludendorff, wife of a reserve cavalry officer, is pregnant with the third of her six children. Their boy, Erich Ludendorff, is born on the small family farm on 9 April 1865. He and John Monash will one day have the future of the world in the palm of their hands as they face each other at the head of opposing forces on the battlefields of the Western Front.

In Melbourne, Louis and the heavily pregnant Bertha move out of the St Kilda villa and into a house called Richhill Terrace at 58 Dudley Street, West Melbourne, on the north side of the Flagstaff Gardens. Louis knows it will be tough for a new mother in a new country, even with the established German Jewish community of Melbourne as support, so he writes home begging Baer to send Ulrike to Melbourne and promising to 'marry her well'. He guarantees her travelling expenses and a trousseau, the clothes, linen, and other belongings collected by a bride for her marriage.

On 27 June 1865, Louis and Bertha become proud parents of a baby boy, forgoing Polish and German names in their new country to call him John Monash. The birth is reported with a minimum of ink in the next day's newspaper:

BIRTHS.
MONASH – On the 27th Inst., at her residence, the wife of L. Monash, Esq., of a son.[42]

Louis registers the birth with the government registrar and at the East Melbourne synagogue, though the date of birth is incorrectly noted as 23 June. When Louis gives his address as Richhill Terrace, his thick accent causes the place of birth to be recorded as 'Rachel Terrace'.

A week after John's birth, Baer and Ulrike set off for Berlin. Julius has decided to travel to Australia with his sister, too, and Baer will see his precious daughter and his troublesome son for the last time.

Ulrike and Julius arrive in Melbourne in September 1865, and before long Albert Behrend's sister Hilda and her husband Moritz Brandt arrive. John Monash will grow up surrounded by an extended family of Polish–German Jews who dote on him.

Ulrike lives with Louis and Bertha until 1868, when she marries Max Roth from Berlin, a storekeeper in Deniliquin, just over the Murray River in New South Wales. Louis hires a maid named Emma Arnott, who wheels John in his pram through the Flagstaff Gardens. Tante (Aunt) Ulrike will later recall that he drew railway engines from the age of two, fascinated by the West Melbourne rail yard, past which Emma takes him on daily outings.

Then there is a crash. The financial collapse in Britain, known as the Panic of 1866, is felt all the way to the Australian colonies.

Louis's partner Louis Martin suffers a stroke and is forced to return to Germany, and dies soon afterwards.[43] Judge Redmond Barry declares Martin and Monash insolvent on 25 March 1867.[44] Louis keeps trading, and though money is tight, he can still hire a photographer to capture his little boy on his third birthday dressed like a young prince.

As he stares confidently at the camera, John Monash's expression, his protruding bottom lip, dark eyes and round face convey a wisdom far beyond his years.

Louis still sends Baer £3 every month, even though the Insolvency Court suspends him from trading for 12 months from 27 March 1868 because he cannot pay creditors.[45] The young family moves to a succession of small rented cottages. At first they live at Victoria Parade, East Melbourne, and early the following year they spend three months with Ulrike and Max Roth in Deniliquin. Max Monash travels with them. They come back to a home in Church Street, Richmond, where on 18 October 1869 four-year-old John is presented with a sister, Mathilde.

Louis and Bertha speak German to their children but Bertha reads bedtime stories to John in English. Yiddish is never spoken, though John will learn Hebrew and attend the East Melbourne Synagogue on the corner of Little Lonsdale Street and what is now Exhibition Street. He will speak with a slight German inflection until adulthood, when after considerable work he is able to stop what he describes as 'pronouncing the gutturals in a distinctly Teutonic accent'.[46]

John is barely walking when Bertha starts imparting to him her love of the piano and taking him to Liedertafel concerts for male choirs. Before he is six, John is able to bring a little joy into his father's increasingly miserable financial plight by playing a short piece for Louis's birthday.

Despite their money problems, in 1871 the Monashes save enough to move into a five-room house in Clifton Street, Richmond Hill, and name it Germania Cottage. It is just 450 metres from the bluestone St Stephen's Church of England School on top of the hill, where John begins his education and where he will impress his teachers with his intelligence and hard work. 'Industry seems to be his chief characteristic', declares his report card after three years' schooling. 'Conduct excellent.'[47]

His schoolmates include George Dethridge, later chief judge of the Arbitration Court, and Arthur Cocks, future Lord Mayor of Sydney.[48] The little boy with the funny accent keeps his friends amused with caricatures and sketches and a mind that never rests.

Monash's earliest surviving letter is written to his mother when he is seven, and has been staying overnight at the house of a friend:

My beloved Mamachen
Papa went with me to the ferry and kept watching me till I reached the other side and I found the house without problem ... Then I played a lot with Karl in the sand. At 10 o'clock I went to bed [and] in the morning I got up at a quarter past seven and had a bath.

I hope that you and Mathilde are quite well. Kiss Papa and Mathilde for me.

Your loving son
Johnny.[49]

Louis and Bertha write their own letters home to Prussia. They tell of the Mercantile Society that Louis and Albert Behrend have helped to form,[50] and their joy surrounding the birth of another daughter, Louise, at Germania Cottage on 5 August 1873. They write lovingly of little Mathilde as well and tell their families about the prodigy that is John Monash, how he plays the piano beautifully and how in the second form at St Stephen's he has even won first prize for schoolwork.

At age eight, John receives a birthday letter written by an old man in a Prussian town.

Dov Baer Monasz, known for so long as Baer-Loebel Monasch, is now 72 and infirm. Most of his children have moved to Australia or America.

As the light grows dim on his life, he lives with his daughter Rosa and has given her his printing works as a dowry, delighted that she is marrying a typesetter who can carry on his work. Baer has paid off his debts and believes he will go to his reward having walked a straight path all his days, owing nothing except to the God of his forefathers.

He takes his steel nib and writes to 'Mister John Monash (sic),' a little boy in a land far away, a little boy he will never meet but for whom he wishes nothing but the very best.

John Monash will keep the old man's letter all his life.

'I am glad to hear that you are doing well at school', Baer writes in German to his Australian grandson. 'If you go on like that you will become a great, good and famous man.'[51]

Chapter 3

*Louis Monash brought over to the Post Office … an old rusty
revolver [but] householders seemed disinclined to identify themselves
in any way with providing firearms, fearing that some of the outlaws'
sympathisers roaming the town might be likely to inform on them
when the gang returned.*

EYEWITNESS ACCOUNT OF LOUIS MONASH'S REACTION TO THE KELLY
GANG RAID ON JERILDERIE[1]

WHEN JOHN IS NINE, Louis is forced to trade his smart
office in Little Collins Street West for the lurching coach-
wheel and the creaking bullock-chain of the Australian bush. Louis's
finances, precarious since the crash of 1866, have at last been sunk by
'terrible losses',[2] and he will never again know peace and prosperity.
The fancy goods he imports from Europe have become passé.

His brothers Max and Julius have headed into the vast
Australian interior looking for opportunities and Louis decides
to uproot his wife and children and take them to a place in a
different colony, 330 kilometres away, where birds do not sing but
screech and squawk; a place where huge flocks of sulphur-crested
cockatoos and pink and grey galahs dominate cloudless blue skies.

John's contented Melbourne childhood, full of music, books
and drawings, is broadsided.

The wrench from Melbourne is also painful for Bertha, who has cultivated many friends. She has even received life governorship from Melbourne Hospital for her work in assisting with a fundraising bazaar. The maid Louis has hired to help her with the children regards Bertha as a 'noble lady',[3] but there is no longer money to pay her. The neatly manicured lawns and the European-themed gardens of Richmond Hill must give way to mile upon mile of dried-out, drought-ravaged earth and the 'everlasting sameness of the never ending plains'.[4]

Since 1869 Max has been in the Riverina district of New South Wales, where he came to mine gold at Cowabbie, about 45 kilometres north of the village of Narrandera.[5] Naturalised in 1871,[6] he has now abandoned the goldfields and opened a general store in Narrandera, running Max Monash and Co. with another young immigrant, Albert Jonsen, from Cologne. Their store is first housed under calico,[7] but they have grand designs, taking out large newspaper advertisements, declaring their humble outlet as 'The Bushman's Store' and promoting their company motto of 'Small profits and quick returns'. They advertise huge sales and 'Great Reduction in Prices'.[8]

Julius has opened a similar business at Wanganella, 250 kilometres south-west of Narrandera, and Louis has decided to try his luck – however bad that now seems to be – as a shopkeeper somewhere between the two points. He goes ahead of his family, and early in 1875, Bertha and the three children, John, nine, Mathilde, five, and one-year-old Lou, head for Jerilderie, 45 kilometres north of the Murray. As the steam engine lurches and rattles through the harsh Australian bush from Melbourne to Wodonga, Bertha nurses the baby and wonders where under Gott's heaven her husband is dragging her now.

Melbourne is 16,000 kilometres from her birthplace, but at least its prosperity and growing grandeur remind her of the elegance and order of home. Out here in the scrub, as the train billows smoke and steam and bumps and shakes her children, there looks to be nothing but sunburn and sweat.

When the Monashes arrive in Wodonga, they traverse a bridge across the Murray to Albury then travel in a horse-drawn coach for 160 kilometres to Jerilderie and the great sheep runs of the southern Riverina.

Situated between Wagga Wagga and Deniliquin, on a wide, flat, empty plain beside Billabong Creek,[9] Jerilderie is home to about 500 people[10] living in a succession of ramshackle wooden houses, more like huts than the homes of Richmond Hill.

Louis opens a branch of Max's business[11] on Jerilderie Street, in premises that had been occupied by storekeeper Herman Levy.[12] A big, bearded, 21-year-old horse thief named Ned Kelly, who has already done long prison stretches for assault and horse stealing, spends a week at Jerilderie's Royal Mail Hotel, just down the street from Louis's store,[13] scouting out buyers for nags he is rustling on the Victorian side of the Murray. Kelly has been at war with authorities ever since his father, an Irish-born convict, died a broken man nine years ago.

Jerilderie has been a dangerous place since Mad Dan Morgan, a crazed bushranger and murderer, frequented the town in the 1860s,[14] and the Monashes have arrived at a time of hostility between the battling settlers and the wealthy pastoralists. Drought is everywhere and the once-lush plains are littered with the carcasses of livestock. The adversity hardens young John for greater conflicts ahead.

Louis quickly becomes a leading light in this small rural community, joining the Progress Association and backing the struggling locals in the Farmers and Traders Association as they wage a campaign against the pastoralists monopolising water frontages. The selectors boycott the Jerilderie show of 1876, ensuring it is a dismal failure.[15]

Louis also joins the board of the local school, where teacher William (Bill) Elliott,[16] an ambitious Irish-born 24-year-old, has just been posted.

Elliott was born at Enniskillen, County Fermanagh, in the north-west of Ireland, and was brought to Sydney by his parents as an infant in 1854, growing up around the Hunter River.[17] He started his teaching career at the prestigious Fort Street Model School in Sydney, and in 1874 journeyed by train to Goulburn, then the southern railhead, before spending the next 430 kilometres on a Cobb and Co stagecoach[18] to reach Jerilderie.

The town already had eight hotels, but no one had bothered to rebuild the public school that had burned down in 1872. Elliott opened a classroom in a shed that attracted 44 pupils, many of whom had never attended a school before.[19]

By the time John Monash arrives in Jerilderie, wide-eyed at the kangaroos and wallabies bounding around its edges, the school has moved from the shed to a new building on Bolton Street and has about 70 students. For the young teacher tasked with educating them, the new boy from Melbourne is a revelation.

John is soon made his assistant, tutoring some of the younger children and the slower learners. He is placed in the second class on his arrival but within two years is promoted to the sixth. Elliott teaches John all the mathematics he has learned and finds he has an insatiable appetite for knowledge. Along with three other boys, Elliott takes John for extra lessons on a Saturday afternoon, teaching them material outside the curriculum in Latin, higher mathematics, English literature and geography.[20]

John and his schoolteacher form a friendship that will last the rest of their lives. Years later Monash writes to Elliott of 'the happy recollections that cling about every corner of the place, every bend of the creek',[21] and half a century later credits Elliott with laying 'the foundation of my career'.[22] In his old age, Monash will still be able to draw a map of the town as he remembers it for his daughter, marking the bend of the Billabong Creek where he says a bunyip dwelled, the place where an old man lived in a haunted hut and the spot where he and the sister he called 'Mat' built mia mia huts. He marks another place where 'I used to see the blacks spearing Murray cod'.[23] He acquires a waddy club from the local Indigenous people, but, lacking the political correctness of later times, remembers them as 'a miserable set of wretches'.[24]

He supplements his formal education by reading *The Australasian* newspaper and tackling the word and maths puzzles in the widely popular *Australian Town and Country Journal.* In his spare time he immerses himself in music and rides a little bay mare alongside his mother's big chestnut.[25] Sometimes he hitches a ride on a bullock wagon to explore the countryside. He and his friends collect bottles for a penny a dozen, and John and Mat sell sets of clothes for toys. He teaches Mat much of what he has learned about reading, writing and arithmetic, and even some rudimentary French. He often plays pranks. He has little time for the roughhouse games of the farm children who are his schoolmates and prefers textbooks and piano to sports, but he has an aptitude for hard work and regimented order.

His organisational abilities are first tested marching hundreds of goats from the common – located immediately south of what is now the town's airstrip – across the Wangamong Creek at milking time.[26] 'Every farm kept goats,' Monash will later recall, 'and the duty of driving those gregarious creatures in from the plains at milking time ... devolved upon us youngsters. We loved doing it. We copied the drivers of bullock-teams, swimming our charges across the waist-deep river. We rejoiced over any kids to the flock. We organised goat races. And sometimes we made goat-carts, decking the harnessed goats with red ribbons, and driving proud little brothers and sisters down the main street.'[27]

Back in Prussia, young Erich Ludendorff is also growing up in a rural background, learning all the mathematics that his maternal aunt can teach him. Like Monash, he has a flair for figures and an insatiable appetite for knowledge.

Bertha Monash isn't having such an enjoyable time, however. She and Louis, a mild-mannered man with sad eyes and a gentle disposition, quarrel constantly over their harsh surroundings. Louis is stuck there, trying to make a go of his store, but early in 1876 the more forceful Bertha takes the children back to Melbourne. The Monashes don't have much money but Bertha will do all she can to make sure her children are given every opportunity.

John, now 10, is enrolled in the privately owned South Yarra College, in Darling Street. It is run by 51-year-old Reverend Henry Plow Kane, who emigrated as a young man from Britain to Launceston and in 1854 was granted a Lambeth Master of Arts degree by the Archbishop of Canterbury. Like Louis Monash, Kane is an enterprising businessman whose enterprises have gone bad.

John attends classes for only six weeks before Bertha decides it is best for everyone if she returns to her husband, even if it means living in the middle of nowhere. The Reverend Kane, faced with missing out on a year's school fees, writes to Bertha saying he is 'very sorry to lose your boy as he is one of our most promising scholars. In every way he has given me satisfaction and has gained the goodwill of all − masters and pupils alike − I only wish you could make arrangements for him to remain.'[28] His words go unheeded and John leaves Melbourne with his mother and sisters.

Back in Jerilderie, Louis takes over the sole ownership of his store after his partnership with brother Max and Albert Jonsen is dissolved,[29] and John continues his studies under Bill Elliott. He works hard, sometimes too hard, and Elliott later writes to him: 'I had always grave fears that you were having too much study when you were with me what with German French Hebrew and Music at home in addition to the schoolwork. I thought it was too great a strain on your mind and that your health would suffer.'[30]

Bertha and Louis have noticed this too, and are often at the schoolhouse talking to Elliott about John's potential. After John spends 18 more months in Jerilderie, Elliott tells the Monashes what they have long suspected: the boy genius is going to waste at this bush school.

Elliott recommends his previous institution, Fort Street in Sydney: 'the best school in New South Wales,' he declares, and the perfect platform for progression to university. Louis agrees to send him there, but Bertha has no desire to break the close connection with her boy. Elliott then recommends the Presbyterian school Scotch College, opposite the Fitzroy Gardens in East Melbourne.[31] Bertha wants John to become a doctor, an honourable profession for a good Jewish boy, but Elliott says: 'Put him to engineering, for the aptitude he is showing in mathematics he will make his mark in that profession and if he has time at his disposal let him also study law.'[32]

At the time John is studying the third book of Euclid, the ancient Greek writer often called the 'Father of Geometry'. As a thank you for fostering his talent as a youngster, John will later give Elliott 10 volumes of *Chambers's Encyclopaedia*. Elliott will write of his young friend: 'He was of a quiet, kind and gentle disposition, with a studious turn of mind, and a staunch friend. Even in those early days he was marked out by all who knew him as one who would make his mark in the world later on ...'[33]

Bertha and the children again return to Germania Cottage on Richmond Hill but Louis stays in Jerilderie running his general store, now one of three such businesses struggling to survive in the town.[34] John will be the man of his house for the next five years, until he is 17, living with his mother and two younger sisters.

Bertha is certain that the boy she calls 'Johnnychen' will become a great man. While the family's Germanic background is important to her, she resolves that John will grow up as an Australian, a loyal subject of Queen Victoria. Over the next few years Bertha cultivates influential and stimulating friends, both German and Anglo-Australians. Surrounded by older people with sharp intellects and a wide array of opinions on the world, 'Johnnychen's' confidence and poise blossom. Visitors to Germania Cottage include Wilhelm Alexander Brahe, the Hawthorn-based consul for the newly federated German Empire,[35] and the writer and publisher Hermann Püttmann Junior, founder of the Association for German Schools (Deutscher Schulverein) of Victoria. Hamburg-born Charles Troedel is also a frequent guest as he builds up a lithographic printing business that will employ apprentices such as the emerging artist Arthur Streeton. There are also the importer and mining speculator Richard Hodgson, his wife Margaret, and their eldest son Richard Junior, who is bound for Cambridge University and international fame for his research into the supernatural.

Bertha is a great fan of Chopin. The sounds of 'Fantasie' and the 'Minute Waltz' regularly waft down Clifton Street. She forms a strong friendship with Catherine (Katie) Deakin, another talented pianist and the older sister of the brilliant young lawyer and journalist 'affable' Alfred Deakin, who will become Australia's second prime minister. Even though John is 15 years younger than Katie, he is seconded to help her with calculations from Books One and Two of Euclid as she prepares to teach at the Presbyterian Ladies' College in East Melbourne. Monash is 'a born teacher,' his sister Mat says. 'He could explain everything.'[36]

Bertha promotes a spirit of familial pride and unity among her three children, and once writes to John while he is away on holidays to tell him: 'You just wait and see, dear Johnny, you will eventually be just as proud of your sisters as they are of their brother. May God keep you all in good health and make good people of you!!' She concludes another letter by telling him: 'Now, dear son farewell, stay happy and good, take care with your riding; you know how dear your life is to your parents. Keep loving your mother Bertha.'[37]

John and his sisters are encouraged to read to Bertha every night, and while not yet a teenager John delights in the *Tales of the Arabian Nights*, *Chambers's Miscellany*, Jules Verne, Alexander Dumas and *The World of Wonders*. He is enthralled by Charles Dickens, Walter Scott, George Eliot, William Makepeace Thackeray and the thrillers of Edward Bulwer-Lytton, the English politician who first said the pen was mightier than the sword,[38] coined the opening line 'It was a dark and stormy night' and gave the world such expressions as 'the almighty dollar' and 'the great unwashed'.[39] John keeps sketching too, and places in an album of keepsakes his first painting of a flower taken from a greeting card. He also delights in showing off his talent in reading both German and French, and is entertained and amused by the satirical illustrations in London's *Punch*.

On 9 October 1877, John is enrolled at Scotch College, given the number 162 and placed in the upper third of students. The headmaster is an imperious Scotsman, Dr Alexander Morrison, 48, a tall, bearded, magisterial disciplinarian and graduate of Aberdeen University with a propensity to wield both the thick strap known as the tawse and the whippy cane.

'Dr. Morrison was a powerful personality', the *Argus* later recalls. 'He was famous for his habit of lining up all boys with bad records once a week, and setting out to cane them all. He usually gave in after the first dozen, and forgot the remainder. Under his guidance the school buildings grew, and were improved, and the attendances increased swiftly.'[40] Morrison is also a canny Scot. 'The Doctor', as he is known, sailed from Scotland to take charge of the college 20 years ago and was given an almost free rein over its growth, development and curriculum. His wage is tied to the school's success and he has turned the collection of grey Gothic buildings into the biggest private school in Australia, attended by 340 boys. Morrison's brother Robert, who has a Master of Arts from Edinburgh University, spends 35 years as vice principal there, and another brother, George, becomes the first headmaster of Geelong College.

When John Monash arrives at the school, The Doctor is just back from a year overseas and is encouraging the study of German. Morrison has just opened the first science laboratory in an Australian school and is busy making preparations to open the school's own cricket ground.

The Doctor assures Bertha that there will be no prejudice towards John on account of his faith, as there are 30 Jewish boys already enrolled. The school also teaches Hebrew, and Jewish students are excused from Christian prayers. An orthodox Jew named Moses Moses is in charge of the post–matriculation class.

John Monash's accent and his faith, even his delicate features and lack of enthusiasm for sport, will make him an outsider, but at Scotch he will never be alone.

The Doctor will teach John history and geography and Robert Morrison will teach him maths and science. Yorkshireman Frank Shew, with a Master of Arts, will instruct him in the classics. John Nelson will take drawing classes and Edmund Augustus Samson, graduate of King's College, London, will sharpen John's elocution, helping him overcome his shyness before crowds and working, with only some success, on eradicating the guttural vowels.

Dr Morrison has modelled Scotch on his own school, the Elgin Academy near Inverness, and is determined to turn out Victoria's future leaders: self-reliant young men, free of class divides, who will climb to the top of professions and business based on merit and hard work. Nearby, the daughter of another Scot, 16-year-old Helen (Nellie) Mitchell, is coming to the end of her schooling at Melbourne's Presbyterian Ladies' College. She will later become known as Dame Nellie Melba.

After the school year of 1877 finishes, John heads back to Jerilderie to holiday with his father, and while there, apparently has an experience he will keep recounting all his life. He will recall it as being as profound as meeting all the world's leaders at Buckingham Palace.[41] We have only his word for it that he had a long meeting with one of Australia's most colourful and infamous criminals, but he will recite the story so many times that it acquires the flavour of truth.

Early in 1878, Ned Kelly is not yet a bushranger but his horse-stealing racket is in full swing as he partners his young American stepfather George King in raids in north-eastern Victoria and across the border into New South Wales.

Police suspect that a pair of Prussian farmers and vintners, William and Gustav Baumgarten, from Barnawartha on the Victorian side of the Murray, are receiving some of the stolen horses and selling them on.[42] Kelly's teenage friend Steve Hart, a noted bush jockey around Beechworth and Wangaratta, is also a frequent visitor to Jerilderie, and at one time has a very public feud with the town's auctioneer, Michael Curtin, over Hart's dubious ownership of some horses.

According to Monash's later accounts, his father is in need of a new horse and buys four white ponies from young Kelly; Ned even takes them to the Monash home. Louis is said to have boasted that he even managed to trick Kelly out of his money.[43] John Monash will later tell audiences that Kelly gave him a shilling to hold his horse. Kelly and his gang, he says, would have made good soldiers.[44]

Back home at Germania Cottage, John writes regularly to his father in German and to Bill Elliott in English. He enjoys this correspondence, but later complains over the way his mother also makes him write in German to so many aunts and uncles that he has never met back in Prussia.[45]

The aunts and uncles in Australia are a different story. They often accompany him and Bertha and his sisters on outings, and he tells his father of visits to family friends in Melbourne – the Troedels, Wischers and Meiers – of picnics in the Botanic Gardens and Royal Park, of circuses and pantomimes and even catching a bag of lollies tossed by a clown. There are trips to Melbourne's beaches and an organ concert in the Town Hall. He has quite a stamp collection going and asks his father to keep sixpenny New South Wales stamps for him. He tells Louis that he can 'translate already several things' from Hebrew.[46] He is mesmerised by *Struck Oil*, a hit play starring American actor J.C. Williamson and his wife Maggie Moore that ignites John's lifelong love for the theatre. He will spend hour upon hour reprising the scenes with Mat.

As John approaches his teens Melbourne is home to about 3000 Jews, the largest population in Australia.[47] Half of the Jewish migrants are British but German-speaking Jews are the next largest group, though they quickly assimilate into the British culture of Melbourne where religious freedom and tolerance are promoted. Jews such as Jonas Felix Australia Levien, said to be the first Jewish baby born in Victoria, and the British-born Edward Cohen, Sidney Ricardo, Nathaniel Levi and Ephraim Laman Zox all become prominent members of Victoria's Legislative Assembly. While most Jews identify themselves as such culturally, Melbourne has a shortage of women and many Jewish men marry outside their faith. Many Jewish shopkeepers keep their doors open on the Saturday Sabbath, dietary laws are often ignored and Hebrew studies become unfashionable. Even Jonas Levien raises his children as Anglicans.[48]

Most of Melbourne's Jews rarely visit the synagogues on Bourke Street or in St Kilda, or the new temple on Albert Street, East Melbourne, where John and his family worship. The East Melbourne temple is presided over by Edinburgh-born Freemason Rabbi Moses Rintel, but is largely frequented by Jews with Polish and Germanic backgrounds.

The synagogue is about 400 metres beyond Scotch College, to which John walks each day on a 3-kilometre journey from Germania Cottage. Usually he will escort his sisters to the Yarra Park State School in Punt Road, then walk past the Melbourne Cricket Ground, which has just hosted the very first Test match between Australia and England.[49] On weekends he will sometimes pay a penny to ride the train from Richmond Station to Flinders Street, or take a horse bus to Flinders Street from Bridge Road.

In 1878 John joins the East Melbourne Synagogue choir, which sang magnificently at the synagogue's recent opening.[50] The choir is led by eccentric 23-year-old Louis Pulver, the headmaster of the East Melbourne Hebrew School and a talented musician and composer. Tall, with thick spectacles and a full jet-black beard, he is generous in giving out biscuits or threepennies to spend at the fruiterer's for good work, and once rides his tricycle from Sydney to Melbourne and back.[51] Just like Bill Elliott in Jerilderie, Pulver will have a strong hand in shaping Monash's resolve to do his best in life.[52] Pulver is just one of the many musicians who visit Germania Cottage for impromptu concerts with Bertha and the children, and John makes many friends among both Jews and Gentiles.

George Jackson, who lives nearby, is one close pal, and Arthur Hyde another. John goes on long walks with a third friend, Victor Wischer, to Ivanhoe and Doncaster. Their friendship survives an argument when they are 12 over the fact that when the Wischers come to visit one day Victor discovers John is probably the only boy in Melbourne without a cricket bat. When the Wischers return for another visit John has the necessary hunk of willow, and they play not only cricket but draughts as well, and together they watch an eclipse of the sun.[53]

In 1878, John studies mathematics, in which he tops his class at Scotch College, as well as elementary physics, Bible studies, English, electricity and magnetism, Latin and French. In March he outlines his weekly routine in a letter to his father:

> Monday, getting up 7, practising till 8, breakfast till 8.30 walk to school, school and walk back home till 1 o'clock dinner, walk to school, school til 4 o'clock, 4.30 to 6 at Mr. Meiers', till 6.30 walk back home, tea till 7, homework till 9.30 and then to bed. Tuesday is the same only from 7 to 8.30 I am at the choir and back home at 9.30. Wednesday morning I do my home-work and have my piano lesson at night, Thursdays are the same as Wednesdays, on Friday I do not go to Mr. Meiers' and come home at 4.30 then I do my school-work before tea and after tea I have German lessons. Saturday morning I go into the synagogue and come back at 12 noon and then I have the afternoon to myself, perhaps we are going out or I read something to Mama. Sunday mornings I go to the choir again and come home at 1 o'clock. In the afternoon I have my piano lesson. So you see that I only have Saturday afternoons to myself.[54]

Louis questions John over why, with his great brain, he is not doing better in English, Latin, geography and history. He asks him to think about entering the school essay prizes and to keep working hard at his piano lessons, and to play some sport for its health benefits, even though John cares little for cricket or football. He sets John little assignments, household chores and exercises in German, and asks him to measure Melbourne's temperature twice a day. Again and again he drives home the point that he and Bertha have done so much for the boy and he must repay them with application.[55]

It is quite extraordinary, though, that in July 1878, a few days after John's 13th birthday, Louis is not at the synagogue for John's bar mitzvah, the Jewish coming-of-age ritual. The ceremony is presided over by a young Pole, Reverend Isidore Myers, who has a career in Hollywood beckoning.[56] Bertha, the girls, some of John's uncles and his pals Victor Wischer and Arthur Hyde are all there to celebrate but John's father misses one of the most important occasions in the life of his only boy. Still, John will write to Louis of his delight over the gifts presented to him: 'things I had wanted for a very long time'.[57] His parents give him a microscope, a collection of Shakespeare's plays and an autographed French translation of the landmark work *History of the Jews*, written by his uncle Heinrich Graetz. Uncle Max gives him a gold watch and Tante Ulrike gold studs. His cousin Albert Behrend, 20 years his senior, gives him a chemistry set, and there is also a stamp album, a knife and the sheet music for Haydn's sonatas for him to practise.[58]

On reading John's report of the occasion, Louis still urges him to remember the sacrifices his parents have made so that John might one day become 'something extraordinary'.[59] It is left to Albert Behrend, and not John's father, to remind John of the importance of the bar mitzvah to his Jewish faith. Albert writes his young cousin a long missive calling on him to respect their Jewish traditions and stand by his vows to the God of Israel. Liars are cowards, Albert writes, and only weaklings lose their temper.[60]

Just three months after John's coming of age, Judge Redmond Barry, who presided over Louis's naturalisation ceremony in

Melbourne 22 years earlier, is in the northern Victorian town of Beechworth, hearing a variety of criminal cases at the local court. An embezzler is given two and a half years in jail, a child molester receives three years and three whippings of 20 lashes each, and another child rapist receives four years and three sets of 25 lashes. William Baumgarten, the Prussian immigrant suspected of assisting Ned Kelly in his horse-stealing endeavours, is given four years.[61] Ned Kelly's mother, Ellen, with a baby daughter at her breast and an isolated bush hut full of small children waiting for her to come home, then stands in the dock, accused of aiding and abetting Ned in an attempt to murder the notorious Constable Alexander Fitzpatrick,[62] a drunk and habitual liar. There are serious questions over Fitzpatrick's testimony but Judge Barry gives Ellen Kelly three years in Melbourne Gaol. The fuse of Ned's explosive temper is lit.

Two weeks later, beside a narrow stream called Stringybark Creek near the Victorian town of Mansfield, Kelly, his brother Dan and their mates Steve Hart and Joe Byrne ambush and kill three policemen. The Kelly Gang, as they become known, are outlawed, with a price on their heads, dead or alive.

On 10 December 1878, two months later, the gang robs the National Bank at Euroa in northern Victoria. The news does not interest John as much as seeing his name in Melbourne's *Argus* newspaper for winning his class maths prize at the Scotch College speech night.[63]

But Ned Kelly will loom large in the life of the Monash family soon enough. Even though police are guarding the major crossings on the Murray River, the four outlaws find an isolated, unguarded place halfway between Mulwala and Tocumwal on 7 February 1879, and wade their horses through water up to their saddle flaps.[64] They head towards Jerilderie, the town Ned and Steve Hart know well, with a plan to murder the two policemen stationed there, then rob the Bank of New South Wales.

At sundown the next evening they reach Mrs Davidson's Woolpack Inn,[65] about 3 kilometres from the township. Ned gives the barmaid, Mary Jordan — better known as 'Mary the Larrikin' — a tip of a florin (two shillings) because she does as she is told and stops serving Joe Byrne whisky.[66] After a short ride the four gunmen surround Jerilderie's rudimentary police barracks and call out that there has been a murder at Davidson's. When the two policemen, Senior Constable George Devine and Constable Henry Richards, come out to investigate, they are taken prisoner along with Devine's wife Mary and their three children. Mary Devine pleads for the life of her husband.

The Kellys march the policemen into the log-cabin watchhouse and lock Mary and the children inside their home, threatening to burn them alive if they try to escape. Over the next two days, disguised in police uniforms, the gang gradually capture 30 Jerilderie residents, almost all of them well known to John Monash, who is safe at school in Melbourne. The Kellys menace some of the men, again threaten to execute the police officers and subject their prisoners to long harangues about the evils of Australia's lawmen.

The Jerilderie branch of the Bank of New South Wales is housed in a room in the eastern portion of the Royal Mail Hotel, where Ned has previously stayed. He knows the layout well. On Monday, 10 February, the gang bail up bank manager John Tarleton, his teller Edwin Living and James Mackie, his junior.

Onto the scene walks unsuspecting Bill Elliott, who has dismissed Monash's former classmates at 12.30 and was planning to deposit the takings from the collection plate of Methodist missionary Reverend John Gribble. As Elliott walks into the bank, Joe Byrne levels a revolver at his head.

Ned tells Elliott and Byrne to hold open a sugar bag and orders Tarleton to throw the contents of the safe into it: chamois leather bags of coins and rolls of notes, property deeds, mortgages, bills of sale and jewellery; even precious family heirlooms and keepsakes from dead loved ones.[67]

Sensing something is very wrong in the town, with these four new policemen wandering about and behaving suspiciously, the local newspaper editor, Samuel Gill, heads to the police barracks to quiz George Devine. He knocks at a window and sees the distressed Mary Devine and a crying child huddled in a corner. Mary is too scared to speak but finally blurts out: 'Run, for your life is in danger!'

Gill bolts down Jerilderie Street and into the Monash store, where he breathlessly tells Louis and his assistants what he's seen. Louis is dumbfounded by the consternation but the store assistants dismiss Gill's claims, saying he's exaggerating.[68] Confused and in a panic, Gill charges off to a homestead 10 kilometres out of town, hoping to get a message to police at Deniliquin.

Gill's flight derails Kelly's plan to have copies made of his 8300-word diatribe, hand-written on 56 pages by Joe Byrne. It is full of rage and irrationality but he hopes it will explain the shootings at Stringybark Creek. The document will become known as the 'Jerilderie Letter'.

Kelly gives the pages to Edwin Living instead and makes him promise that it will be printed and published. It isn't. The police confiscate the letter, and although small sections appear in print it will not be published in full for 51 years.[69]

The Kellys order telegraph poles in Jerilderie to be cut down and send some of their captives into the store of Louis's business rival James Rankin, where they grab a new axe from manager Albert Brasch. Communication with the outside world having been disabled, the gang warn their captives not to repair the telegraph lines because they will be coming back to kill anyone who has disobeyed them. Ned puts on a display of horsemanship before riding off with about £2100 in cash and a good supply of gold and jewellery.

The moment the bushrangers are out of sight the freed captives swing into action. Four men begin restoring the telegraph line while Louis and others hunt around for firearms, ready for a shootout when the bandits return. Many of the townspeople are reluctant to produce weapons because they fear Kelly sympathisers in Jerilderie, but Louis procures a rusty old revolver.[70] He brings it over to the post office and then starts chasing around for ammunition. James Rankin does even better, producing four double-barrelled, breach-loading shotguns and plenty of cartridges. A carpenter lends Bill Elliott his shotgun and a couple of pounds of shot and the new recruits stand guard in the post office as the alarm is finally sent down the telegraph line. By then the Kellys have vanished like ghosts.

Elliott will later tell John that there was a lot of the 'Don Quixote' about Ned Kelly. In his view, Kelly would have liked to be a military commander at the head of a hundred followers, but 'the leader of the outlaws was also a bit of a lunatic, or rather, a dreamer ... a desperate man, driven to desperation by his imaginary wrongs'. His 'Jerilderie Letter', Elliott says, was 'little better than emanations of wild fancies from a disordered brain'.[71]

Louis's excitement over the Kelly raid is tempered by the news of Baer's death in Krotoszyn. The bookbinder and publisher of Hebrew texts is buried next to his wife and children in the Jewish cemetery, under a tombstone with inscriptions in both Hebrew and German.[72]

Still, life goes on. Max Monash travels down from Narrandera to the synagogue on Albert Street to marry his niece, Helene Behrend.[73] Louis sells the Jerilderie store to his rivals, Joseph and Hyman Harris,[74] and Albert Behrend, having failed to succeed in Melbourne, decides to return home. He will spend the next six years in Europe. Louis's brother Julius has already moved back to Prussia, and soon Max and Helene Monash will join him. Louis elects to take over Max's store in Narrandera, and after a visit there John describes it as 'a most curious conglomeration of all that appertains to man ... a shelf with Scott's novels under which is placed a barrel of tar, a heap of moleskin trousers piled on top of a sugarbin'.[75]

The life of a rural storekeeper is not for this boy.

John begins his writing career at 13, critiquing a concert at the local church hall. He has visions of writing a book set in England during the Civil War and jots down an outline. He pens two pages of a play before abandoning the idea. In his earliest surviving notebook, he makes notes in Pitman's shorthand, jottings on Latin translations, maths calculations, notes on Horatio Nelson and the Duke of Wellington and the beginnings of an essay entitled 'How I Spent My Holidays'. In 1879 he is placed in the matriculation class, and in June begins his first diary, outlining the schedule of a busy and productive teenager:

> Home at 4.30, rest till 4.45. Practise piano 4.45–5.45. Get tea ready 5.45–6.15. Tea till 6.45. Collect books together till 7 o'clock. Euclid etc. till 7.30. English till 8.30. Latin till 9 o'clock. Maps etc. for Wednesday till 10. Bed at 10 or after.[76]

He has little interest in the pastimes of the other schoolboys, football, boxing and cricket – 'he took no part in games or appeared to be in any way athletic', his great pal George Farlow will recall[77] – although he still considers himself a physical youth, as he has spent a good amount of time in the bush, acquiring experiences and skills foreign to many of the city lads. In the main John is quiet and studious, determined to meet and perhaps even exceed the academic expectations of Bertha and Louis. He never feels the sting of the strap or the cane. Not that he is always the perfect student. He has a quick temper and will sometimes wag school to visit Cole's Book Arcade in Bourke Street, where he reads penny-dreadful adventures featuring action hero Jack Harkaway.

He does not yet match Harkaway's derring-do in real life. Although George Farlow, a tough scholarship boy from a battling Brunswick family, is always there to back him up, John's chief means of defence in quarrels are his sharp mind and rapier tongue. He prefers to disarm rivals with ridicule and logic. He will never recall being the target of anti-Semitism or bullying and will always regard Scotch and its teachers with a great degree of affection.

He is wise beyond his years. At 14, John fares well in the matriculation and civil service examinations for the October term of 1879 as only one of five candidates from a list of several hundred to pass in nine subjects – arithmetic, algebra, Euclid, English, Latin, French, German, history and geography. He also wins a prize for an essay on Australian explorers, and is part of Louis Pulver's Hallelujah chorus at the opening of Melbourne's first ever Jewish bazaar at the Town Hall on 30 December 1879, to raise funds for the Melbourne and East Melbourne congregations.[78]

The following night, New Year's Eve, the Victorian Engineers military unit ushers in a new decade with a stunning display of electric lighting before a huge crowd in Melbourne's Botanic Gardens. The upper lawn is 'brilliantly illuminated by two self-adjusting electric lamps' supplied from a couple of dynamo-magnetic machines from the German company Siemens, and another electric light shines like the sun across the garden lake.[79]

Since Louis's arrival in Melbourne in 1854, the city's population has grown from less than 80,000 to 280,000, and within a decade will nudge half a million.[80] It is the biggest and richest city in all the Australian colonies, bigger and richer than many European capitals. Grand buildings are being erected everywhere, and none more stunning than the new Exhibition Building to house the eighth World's Fair, which opens on 1 October 1880. It attracts almost as much attention and press in Melbourne as the hanging six weeks later of Ned Kelly, after Kelly is sentenced to death by Redmond Barry.

In 1880, John completes his additional studies in the post-matriculation year under teacher Moses Moses. He comes second in mathematics and logic, fifth in French and sixth in Latin. Top of the class in all three is Jim McCay,[81] who pronounces his surname to rhyme with 'sky'. He is the son of a Presbyterian minister and will be John's lifelong friend and rival. McCay wins just about every prize on offer at the Scotch College speech day on 16 December 1880 at the Melbourne Athenaeum on Collins Street. The hall is crowded to overflowing with proud parents and friends. The Victorian Governor, the Marquess of Normanby, stands to address the assembly. Dressed in his regal uniform, the Queen's representative is a commanding figure as the light bounces off his shiny bald head, and what he says next will resonate with John Monash all his life.

'I do not know anything more satisfactory in this great colony,' he tells his audience, 'than the attention that is paid to education. Education is of vital importance in a young country, which, like this, is endowed with free and liberal institutions. In fact, there is no post in the colony which is not open to any of her citizens provided they sufficiently prepare themselves for it.'[82]

John is preparing himself well. Although McCay is wearing out the floorboards walking to the stage and back to accept his many awards, John receives prizes for mathematics and is runner-up for the Sir James McCulloch Prize for English composition for an essay on the poet John Milton. Dressed in a new suit tailored by the Goldberg Brothers of Flinders Lane, he is presented with *The Wealth of Nations*, written by the Scottish economist Adam Smith.

With an eye to beginning his Bachelor of Arts degree at Melbourne University in January 1881, even though he is just 15 and a half, John starts studying Greek and Latin at night with his friend Arthur Hyde.

The Scotch headmaster, though, has other ideas. Early in the New Year Dr Morrison sends a letter to 'My dear Monash' asking for his help.[83] Morrison is locked in battle with his rivals at Wesley College to be Melbourne's pre-eminent high school and he needs as much heavy artillery as he can muster. Morrison wants Monash back for another year. John writes to his father in Narrandera that the valuable prizes on offer for the school year will more than cover the fees. The deal is done.

Before returning to Scotch, John enjoys a week in Sorrento with Tante Ulrike and his cousins. The steamer ride down

Port Phillip Bay makes him seasick but he can still tell his father that he 'had a lot of fun and went for a swim twice or three times each day ... and was positively delighted with the environment'.[84]

John prepares a roster for his homework that will see him hitting the books from 7 p.m. to midnight Monday to Saturday, but soon realises the schedule is too taxing even for a young man of such energy. He spends weeks preparing an essay on *Macbeth*, lifting passages verbatim from the commentary in the 1873 New Variorum edition of the play, published in New York. He borrows heavily from the analysis of Shakespeare's dark murder tale, safe in the knowledge that there are few copies of the New Variorum edition in circulation in Melbourne. His work contains many original ideas as well, but his lack of credit for the source betrays a brilliant, and occasionally devious, mind.[85]

He maintains his impressive stamp collection and practises rudimentary carpentry in the backyard. He sketches and paints when he has time.

Although he still eschews sports, he stays fit, at one stage taking a long hike through the Dandenongs, 30 kilometres west of Melbourne, and up through the lush rainforest of Ferntree Gully. His mind is ever open to new experiences, and he joins the Wesley Church Mutual Improvement Society, one of many such working-class societies set up for members to debate ideas, discuss literature and art, listen to lectures and develop skills in public speaking. To his sisters John is the life of the party, organising games when other children come to visit, setting up fireworks and charades, always 'full of pranks and energy'.[86]

Melbourne is abuzz with news that electricity is coming to the city as more than just a sideshow, and in July the Eastern Market is lit up with six electric lights for the first time by the Victorian Electric Company, which is soon refloated as the Australian Electric Company Limited,[87] with the delightfully eccentric William Charles Kernot as its chairman. Kernot is a balloon enthusiast, who years earlier built a velocipede, an early bicycle, and holds the record for the fastest penny-farthing ride to Geelong.[88]

It is an astounding year for John, too. Back at the Athenaeum Hall on 16 December 1881, with wealthy pastoralist and parliamentarian Francis Ormond as guest of honour, John shares the five guineas for Dux of Scotch College with James Thomson, who is bound for medical school, and another prize of five guineas with Patrick McEachran,[89] who will soon take up arts at the Melbourne University college that bears Ormond's name. John also shares the James McCulloch Prize for the best essay of the year for his *Macbeth* entry, thanks in large measure to the 1873 book no one else at the school seems to have read. He is top of his class in logic and mathematics and the combined study of French and German. He spends his cash prize on scholarly works: Gibbon's *Decline and Fall of the Roman Empire*, Froude's *History of England* and Walter Scott's collection of *Waverley* novels.

His first published work appears in a short-lived weekly journal, *Town Talk*. His entry for a competition putting together 50 words starting with 'f' begins: 'Four flimsy farthings ... furnishes fun for fascinating females.'[90]

At the public examinations, which decide both university or civil service acceptance and offer financial aid for tuition, John wins the mathematics exhibition with first-class honours and gains a first in French and German. He is holidaying at Portsea with his relatives in January 1882 and about to visit Louis in Narrandera when his mother writes to him with delight that Scotch has trumped every other school.

At Narrandera on 27 January he seconds in his diary that he has submitted a newspaper report on the 'entertainment last night' and a fire that has engulfed Junee Railway Station. He also notes that he 'first tasted whiskey today'.[91]

Soon after he writes to his cousin Leo Monasch,[92] a printer, in Minnesota of his stay in Narrandera that 'this was the first time in my life that I have been left to go on my own "hook" and I enjoyed it thoroughly … But such short stays are always unsatisfactory. You make a few acquaintances, chum with everybody you meet then leave the place, and probably never meet them again in your life.'[93]

Back in Melbourne, Bertha can hardly contain herself over her son's scholastic success. He is now the talk of Richmond Hill and a long way beyond. The gasman had stopped to congratulate her on raising such a genius, she writes to her son, and their relative Moritz Brandt has called around to sing his praises. The postman has taken a break from his rounds to marvel at such a mind. Their friend Hermann Püttmann is beside himself.

'From everywhere they congratulate me', Bertha writes. 'I have to tell you from Miss Deakin: you realised fully and entirely her expectations. Mrs Bourke wants to let you know that … she loves you for being such a good son and she respects you for being such a clever boy. Mr and Mrs Koch send their kindest congratulations, so do Saul and Louis Pulver.'[94]

On 8 February John leaves Narrandera on the horse-drawn coach, bound for the train at Wodonga. He is heading for Melbourne University, and what everyone tells him will be a glorious future.

He is only 16 and a half, but already a master of the art of winning friends and influencing people.

Chapter 4

My stores of energy are unlimited and now at last am I finding a field
for their application. I have taken up an important position in my
University, one of its leaders in actual fact.
MONASH DIARY[1]

MONASH is becoming his own man faster than his parents
like. They fear he is losing his religion and running amok
as he feels his first stirrings of sexual attraction. The soft and
delicate-featured schoolboy is growing into a lean and darkly
handsome charmer with a sizeable ego.

His childhood has been heavily influenced in the synagogue
by Louis Pulver, Rabbi Myers, Moses Moses and his pious cousin
Albert Behrend. But in the three years since his bar mitzvah,
John's ears and eyes have been opened to many conflicting
opinions, to many opposing intellectual thoughts. His parents
still respect Jewish tradition but are no longer orthodox, and
John begins to reject the religious guidance of his Jewish teachers
as bunkum. Louis and Bertha let him make up his own mind
when it comes to a belief in the Almighty and Monash gradually
rejects the concept, influenced as he is by Darwin's theory of
evolution and the growing tide of intellectual opposition to a
Judeo-Christian God that is starting to take root in Melbourne.

He studies the new book *Some Mistakes of Moses* by the American agnostic Robert Ingersoll.

He is living in momentous times, and a world that is rapidly evolving. America is still struggling to recover from its civil war and militarism is rampant across Europe and Asia. There have been major conflicts in France, South Africa, Spain, Russia and Turkey. Trade unions are changing the political landscape in much of the developed world. Germany has become unified and established its Second Reich.

Monash is enthralled by the emergence of the telephone, electric light bulb, phonograph, steam drill and coaxial cable. The only miracles that interest him are those created by man's ingenuity. 'I can hardly help looking upon the falsity of the Bible as others do its truth',[2] he declares, and later tells a girlfriend that it would be 'far better for the peace of mankind to completely disassociate itself from … the direction of superstitious beliefs'.[3]

Monash enrols in the arts program at the University of Melbourne with a plan to then take engineering. He comes to the university at a time of radical ideas. After a quarter of a century under the conservative chancellorship of Redmond Barry, the university is the premier educational facility in the colony and has finally allowed women, such as the feminist arts student Bella Guérin, to study for degrees.[4] There are about 450 students at the university when Monash arrives and it is dominated by the 150-strong medical faculty. His will soon be a loud, conflicting voice.

Monash has won £25 from his mathematics exhibition, which will cover his university fees and textbooks. While Louis can scrounge together £1 a month in Narrandera to help his son, Monash will have to pay his own way for the most part. His friend Tom Hodgson finds him a matriculation student needing a tutor in French. He will begin his journey as a university student by taking the train from Richmond to Flinders Street then walking 2 kilometres to the campus. Not that he will do it every day.

He starts with the classics, mathematics and logic but by the end of the first term is looking for something more exciting. He has worked so hard for so long on his studies at Scotch that he decides to exploit his new-found freedom. He is no longer a boy under the stern gaze of an authoritarian headmaster; what does it matter if he wags class now and again to read his favourite thrillers? He is 16, after all, with a head full of knowledge and a sense of intellectual superiority after having won academic prizes and seen his name in the papers. He has become practised at deception, too, not just of the kind used in his oft-quoted *Macbeth* essay, but also in telling his mother that he is off to important lectures, when more often than not he is off to the latest stage production.

He assures himself again and again that he will become a big man in Melbourne. He's not sure how or why he'll do it, but his ultimate goal, he tells himself, is to be famous and admired. His mother's acquaintance with a wide circle of friends allows him to rub shoulders with Melbourne's best and brightest. Only a few weeks into his university studies he first speaks to Katie Deakin's famous brother, the 25-year-old Alfred, who is now the Liberal member for the rural electorate of West Bourke, which takes in Melton and Keilor.[5] The young icon of Melbourne's upwardly mobile youth promises Monash 'his assistance and advice whenever required'. Monash swoons and calls it 'one of the most beautiful evenings I have ever spent'. He describes Deakin's soon-to-be wife Pattie Browne as 'the most beautiful woman I know'.[6]

Bertha complains to her absent husband about John's defiant behaviour and Louis gives him a few written clips over the ear in a series of forceful letters from Narrandera, telling him to show more respect and gratitude to his mother, to control his temper, watch his manners and be more patient in teaching Mat. He warns Monash that he will halt the £1 a month if he gets more bad reports[7] and tells him to keep up his piano practice and to make twice-weekly visits to the German gymnasium[8] the Turn-Verein, on La Trobe Street East, for the sake of his health. Monash replies that he is sick of having to write back in German,[9] a point that will continue to rankle as he begins to identify himself as a true Australian son rather than a European. His faith in Judaism has evaporated but he still follows the advice in Ecclesiastes that 'Whatever thy hand findeth to do, do it with thy whole might',[10] even if it is having a good time. He will make the quotation one of the first listed in his Commonplace Book of important sayings. He begins compiling intimate diaries to document his innermost passions and spends Sundays copying all his correspondence for future reference. There is order and structure in the life of this teenager going places, but disorder at home and an increasingly chaotic attitude towards formal education.

His revolt against religious teaching is soon followed by a retreat from the secular as well. He decides to educate himself through experience and voracious reading. Every couple of days he commits to memory and paper his thoughts on the books he devours, critiquing Dr Samuel Johnson's hundred-year-old biography of John Milton as 'a strange mixture of sarcasm, irony, censure, criticism, spite, praise and enthusiasm'.[11] His eclectic reading takes in the Koran, which he finds fascinating, making plans to read from Islam's holiest book every day.

While he claims to have jotted down more than a hundred 'glaring errors' in the Bible, he nevertheless attends the Wesley Church Mutual Improvement Society to develop his public-speaking abilities through discourses and debates, usually with Bertha and the girls in the audience. He lectures on Robin Hood, Joan of Arc, Shakespeare, the Saracen and the Islamic ruler Harun al-Rashid. He reads his *Macbeth* essay to rapturous applause and revels in the praise for its dazzling originality. At the same time he exposes a prominent Methodist layman for reading a plagiarised essay and earns a rebuke from Louis Pulver, his former choirmaster, for bad manners.[12]

On 30 April, Monash is among the overflowing crowd at the Melbourne Opera House to hear a free 7 p.m. lecture by the Englishman Thomas Walker, a disgraced former spiritualist now doing his best to debunk the idea of a God.[13] A correspondent for *Australasian Sketcher* describes Walker as a charlatan and reports with a hint of dismay that 'audiences, as large, probably, as that assembled at any church in Melbourne, are contented to come, Sunday after Sunday ... to listen to these unintellectual repetitions of arguments and sarcasms directed against Christianity'.[14] Walker, though, has found a believer in Monash, who attends at least 10 of his talks and writes in his diary that Walker has 'put into words and speech my very thoughts'.[15]

In May Monash attends his first ball, at the Püttmanns' home in Lisson Grove, Hawthorn, and makes small talk with most of the nine Püttmann sisters. The following month he is at the Sanders family ball, dancing and making the first of so many after-dinner speeches. He escorts three girls home as though he is walking on air.

He celebrates his 17th birthday on 27 June 1882 with 'the most pleasant day that I have spent as long as I can remember'.[16] He follows his father's instructions over the next few weeks and helps Mat with her homework, and stays active by walking with her as far as Doncaster and back, a round trip of 30 kilometres. On 26 July he witnesses snow falling in Melbourne for the first time and, in a buoyant mood after such a rare event, has a few drinks five days later, admitting: 'I was never in my life nearer being drunk than today.'[17]

When he is not at the Wesley Church, winning arguments and losing faith, Monash spends nights exercising at a gym or goes to the theatre with Victor Wischer. He twice sees Gilbert and Sullivan's new hit *Patience* at the Theatre Royal and is so taken with the German operetta *Boccaccio* he sees it five times at the Opera House. 'I have fortunate capacity for great risibility and can enjoy even the broadest fun',[18] he will say later, admitting that his tastes stretch from the most highbrow art to 'sensational trash'.[19]

He skips classes to attend sessions of parliament, watches criminal trials, studies paintings in the National Gallery, watches construction work and keeps an eye out in city streets for celebrities such as the British actress Jennie Lee, starring in *Jo* at the Princess Theatre, and the journalist John Stanley James, who writes under the pen name The Vagabond.[20]

He forgoes lectures to read at the State Library and peruse bookshops. He and Tom Hodgson go on long walks, dig for fossils at Brighton Beach, sail on Albert Lake and occasionally go fishing, though Monash admits, 'I cannot conceive where the enjoyment lies'.[21]

He misses weeks of lectures, and when he does turn up for the 10 a.m. classes he often walks in late because he's been up all night. He laments:

> My whole time is taken up in dreams of the future, that is the distant future, and then I feel generally happy and buoyant; but when I reflect on the near future a restlessness comes over me ... I cannot submit to settle down to drudgery like my fellow students – my mind is too much engaged on other things. I am never in the same state of mind for two consecutive days. Once it is an overmastering desire for literary studies, then it is philosophical discussions, then a roving restless, unsettled feeling, then an ardour for living with the world, but most often a fitful, self-extinguishing, self-expiring eagerness in the pursuit of 'fame'. Is not life one great longing, yearning, hoping and desiring?[22]

He is taken by the adulation shown to 'Demon' fast bowler Fred Spofforth and the Australian XI after they score a remarkable seven-run win in a Test cricket match in England that results in a mock obituary on 2 September in England's *Sporting Times*:

In Affectionate Remembrance

of

ENGLISH CRICKET,

which died at the Oval

on

29 August 1882,

Deeply lamented by a large circle of sorrowing

friends and acquaintances

R.I.P.

N.B.–The body will be cremated and the

ashes taken to Australia.

Though Monash has never shown a great interest in team sports before, he pastes two accounts of the match into his scrapbook. There is such overwhelming interest in the Australian victory that Monash can't help but be swept along by the waves of enthusiasm.

In September and October, with exams looming, he begins to study harder but still spends most of his nights in the city, drawn like a moth to the gas lights of the entertainment district with its sensual delights.

'Avoid temptation lest you may not be able to resist it', he warns himself in his diary. 'The anticipation of a pleasure is better than the enjoyment thereof.' At another time he says he 'strolled about streets, without success, till 11.30', looking for girls to chat up.[23]

Monash normally sleeps late, but on 6 October he and sister Mat are up early at Burnley Park to see the Great Comet of 1882, perhaps the brightest comet ever seen.[24]

For Monash, though, the most startling event that month is news that his father is finally selling out of Narrandera after eight years and moving back to Melbourne.

Louis will not be happy with John's attitude to university.

His results in Latin, Greek and upper mathematics are a disaster, and while he passes lower mathematics, logic, chemistry, mineralogy and botany, he fails his first year. Latin in particular will continue to haunt him.

He is mortified. Not game enough to break the news to Louis and Bertha, he and his co-failures go out drinking, toasting 'better success next time', though the plonk tastes like poison and Monash becomes decidedly unwell trying to convince himself that the whole catastrophe has been an important learning experience.

The next day, when he finally summons the courage to tell Louis and Bertha and manages to get the words past the lump in his throat, there is 'great mourning' from his family and he becomes so forlorn he feels like drowning himself.[25]

He realises that while he thought he knew it all, putting the stage before his studies has been his biggest mistake. He seeks out the Morrison brothers and other masters at Scotch for advice. On 28 November 1882, he writes down a solemn oath in his diary that from now on he will be 'putting forth all my energies to redeem the time and opportunities lost by my present failure'.

Just two days later he is swept up in the excitement that grips Melbourne when Spofforth and the Australian cricketers return from England after what will become known as the 'Ashes' triumph. He and his sisters are among the thousands present on the night of 30 November as 700 firemen form a torchlight parade and the victorious Australians are paraded on two drays down Collins Street and all the way out to the Melbourne Cricket Ground.[26] Monash sends a report to the *Jerilderie Herald*, writing that the Australians have brought home 'the championship of the world in the manliest of British games'.

He reads and reads, book after book, and often aloud as he practises his enunciation to rid himself of those guttural vowels. No work so affects him as Bulwer-Lytton's *Kenelm Chillingly*. The story of a young man who doesn't seem to fit resonates with Monash, the rebellious Jewish student with no faith in God, who sees himself in the author's description of a square peg being forced into a round hole.[27]

He also writes continuously. Bill Elliott's stories of the Kelly Gang's raid on Jerilderie inspire him to flesh out the bones of a novel. It is set in an Australian bush town and Monash describes it as a 'sensational love and murder tale'.[28] After a few thousand words, though, it reaches the same full stop as another of his stories about a criminal and a bush telegraph operator. He is miffed when his offer to write a column on Melbourne news for the *Narrandera Argus* is rejected by editor Samuel Gill, who has moved there from Jerilderie. Monash makes a few shillings for a couple of 'Melbourne Gossip' columns in the *Jerilderie Herald*, which Bill Elliott will soon buy.[29] The *Bendigo Independent*, where his friend Arthur Hyde is now working, publishes his report of a railway collision near his home on 2 December; the article reveals a talent for exaggeration that will come in handy years later.

Monash is again caught up in cricket fever, and spends two days watching many of the victorious Ashes players compete on opposite sides in a much-ballyhooed five-day inter-colonial match, which New South Wales finally wins against Victoria on 30 December.

Still stung by his academic failure, he has not stayed repentant for long, writing in his diary on the last day of 1882:

Upon the whole, I candidly think that my character leans to virtue's side ... though I do not always act up to my principles I am not so foolish as to condemn myself as irresolute; I feel that, if I once set myself a task, I can accomplish it; that I could conquer the world ... I have spent one year as a student, am told that I thought too lightly of the work attendant thereon and so, as I failed to comply with a ridiculous condition of passing what is called an 'examination' I am doomed to atone for my lost time by sacrificing my recreations. But was it 'lost time'; most emphatically no; never was my time so well spent.[30]

Congratulating himself for doing just as he damn well pleases, on one hand, he nevertheless confesses that his university results have made him 'generally miserable, decidedly suicidal ... stagnating'[31] and complains that his studies have given him 'combined attacks of headaches, overwork, and . . . ennui'.[32]

While there had been domestic friction between John and his mother when he first left high school, and she had complained often about his rebellious behaviour, Monash comes to realise that Bertha is his rock. He understands now that he can talk to her about anything, safe in the knowledge that her love is unconditional, secure in the confidence she has always had in him. She encourages him not to give up on his education.

Louis is hardly back in Melbourne when Bertha and the children are uprooted again. Louis has bought a block of land in Yarra Street, Hawthorn, 3 kilometres east of Germania Cottage, and has plans to build a bigger house, designed by Hamburg-born architect John Koch, the former mayor of Richmond. Monash has his 'first venture into the engineering craft'[33] early in February 1883, discussing alterations and witnessing his father's signature on the contract with the builder.

His time is spread thin. He is still a regular at the Wesley Church, sometimes giving recitals with Mat, and on 11 February 1883 he is elected Secretary of the Mutual Improvement Society after what he calls 'a stormy and exciting committee meeting'. Two days later he writes to a friend, 20-year-old Will Steele – who also failed first-year arts and is now a teacher at Warrnambool – telling him that the Melbourne University students should form a union to help each other.[34]

Then, in a change of heart, he considers giving university away altogether, and is backed by Arthur Hyde, who has also failed first-year arts. Hyde tells Monash to 'send the University to the devil and take up the press'.[35] Hyde proposes they start a journalists' agency together to supply country newspapers, but Monash rethinks his circumstances and decides to remain a student. He tells himself on 28 March 1883: 'Tomorrow, I am going to make a fresh start. I have become a wiser and, let me hope, a better man.'

He finds another student to tutor and a few weeks later spends three guineas taking the exam for a clerkship at the Mint, where his old friend George Farlow works, but Monash is not offered a job there. In vain, he asks around for some part-time journalism work, and teaches classes for extra money at Mrs Howe's Ladies' College in West Melbourne.

The university has just appointed William Kernot as its first professor of engineering, and graduates will now receive a degree rather than a certificate. Kernot is still Chairman of the Australian Electric Company and he will soon light a fire in Monash's brain.

Monash's burgeoning personal library is further expanded in April when an uncle in Prussia sends him the complete works of Goethe – 30 volumes – as well as the complete 16 volumes of Gotthold Lessing's writings. He takes art lessons and copies sketches from magazines at the public library. He goes to parties at the homes of other German families, but just like his religion, his ardour for all things Prussian is fading. He writes to his cousin Leo Monasch in Minnesota:

> Your 'mother-tongue' is not mine. I do not exactly perceive the great desirability of preserving ... this 'mother-tongue' by those to whom it is such no longer ... What, beyond the fact that correspondence with my relatives must be carried on in German – what, beyond this, is there to induce me to cling to the German language and German customs, or to saturate myself with a German spirit? To what country and people do I owe the most? To that which I have never seen ... or to that in which and among whom I was born, have grown up, where I have learned all that I know, to which I owe all the happiness that I have experienced? ... it is my native land.[36]

The two cousins have lively debates about their shared background and youthful patriotism. They are both 'grandsons of one of the devoutest followers of Judaism that ever lived',[37] but Monash tells his cousin that he has become an 'Infidel of the very blackest type, an atheist and a materialist', and has been so 'as long as I have been able to reason, and ... I shall continue to be so as long as I remain in my senses'.[38]

Monash is busy moving into the new family house in July, and he practises his rudimentary carpentry on a kitchen dresser and a bookcase before laying out the garden for his mother.

He is stunned one morning to find Louis and Bertha going through his diary, and has to do some fast talking to explain away the drinking, the temptations and the lost faith. For a while, until he feels the coast is again clear, his diary entries drop off and he keeps his most intimate thoughts to himself.

In the classical lecture room in the middle of 1883, 'a note passed from hand to hand'[39] suggests students should form a university union, an idea Monash has had in mind for some time, even before expressing it to Will Steele. He sees such a union as a potential springboard for a prominence that he is not achieving academically.

Monash is also a member of the student committee, which arranges an Arts Students Conversazione at Gunsler's Café Hotel on Collins Street on 14 August, and he seconds a motion by the 33-year-old Presbyterian minister and arts student John Mathew to form a student 'association of a literary and social character'.[40] Monash is hoping to be the first secretary but in the end has to be content with a spot on the committee.

He continues with his debates at the Mutual Improvement Society and has great success with ample preparation and rehearsal. But one night, trying an off-the-cuff argument, he freezes and has a 'complete breakdown'.[41] It is an important lesson for him in planning. The following month, having 'drawn all the good for myself that I could from the Association', he decides to walk away.[42]

He fares much better in the university examinations of 1883 than he did the previous year. He passes in five subjects, but receives only a third-class honour after expecting a first, and admits with melodramatic melancholy: 'I despair of the realisation of the smallest of my dreams. My mental equilibrium is rapidly becoming disorganised and I am becoming indifferent of everything. A little longer and I will be lost for good and all.'[43]

But not quite. About this time Monash has taken to carrying 'a knobby walking-stick', and though privately he may be racked with self-doubt, outwardly he is a commanding presence 'of strength and energy', as his friend from university Jim Lewis later remembers.[44] His self-assertive manner did not always make him popular, Lewis recalled, but when there was a job requiring brains and hard work, even Monash's critics knew he was the best man for the task. Jim Lewis's sister Kate remembered him as a young man who liked to tease the girls but who was 'a tower of strength and resourcefulness' when needed. He emboldened everyone he met, with his own resolute bearing[45] and she recalled, once, how after a University Engineers boating picnic many of the girls seemed too afraid to face the boat trip home in the dark until Monash led each one by the arm 'down the slippery, dark track to the landing ... his word was enough ... we felt perfectly safe'. In March that year Monash takes another walking tour up Ferntree Gully, this time over two days. While he has never been much on organised sports, he is now 19 and an impressive physical specimen of 174 centimetres, with an athletic build.

His searching mind peers into every facet of learning. Not only is he a voracious reader and theatre patron but he has already begun what will be an enormous collection of memorabilia, correspondence and souvenirs that he will maintain all his life. Early in 1884 he gains another odd curiosity, a hair from the head of the 'Baby Farming Murderess' Frances Knorr, taken from the knot after her hanging at the Melbourne Gaol. The execution of the woman who had strangled two infants in her care fascinated Melbourne and Monash was captivated by the grisly memento.

His career as a big man on campus gains momentum when, on 2 June 1884, his long-cherished dreams of a university union reach fruition. He is at the Athenaeum Hall in the presence of Alfred

Deakin and Dean Macartney, the 85-year-old Bishop of Melbourne, for the inaugural meeting of the Melbourne University Union. J.S. Elkington, Professor of History and Political Economy, is chairman and 150 union members are gathered together.[46] His ambitions as a writer receive a sizeable boost when he is put in charge of the *Melbourne University Review* and tasked with offering encouragement 'to the exercise and expression of original thought'.[47] He dives into the role with the same enthusiasm that he has for the university's growing contribution to the defence of Australia.

The mid-1880s is a time of fervent nationalism in the Australian colonies. It has been a decade since two British officers, Major General William Jervois[48] and Lieutenant Colonel Peter Scratchley, first arrived in Australia to advise the colonial governments on defence. In 1883, Queensland works with the other colonies to annex parts of New Guinea amid fears of Germany's expansion in the South Pacific. Over the following two years, Australia's colonial defence force increases from 8000 to 22,000 men.

Schools and universities as well as rifle clubs are quick to take up arms to practise war against any number of perceived invaders, and Monash too becomes carried away by what he calls 'the storm of enthusiasm'.[49] As Dr Morrison and the Scotch College boys wait to receive their shipment of 120 Lancaster rifles in order to establish their schoolboy cadet corps,[50] Monash becomes one of the first 11 tertiary students in Victoria to join the new University Company – D Company, 4th Battalion, Victorian Rifles – on 8 July 1884. They will become soldiers under the withering command of the hard-driving Sergeant Sullivan.[51]

Just three days later Monash has his first drill, an experience so taxing that one of the recruits faints. Soon the company will have 60 volunteers,[52] and though they will have to wait some months for uniforms, Monash plans to be the best soldier he can be.

Sergeant Sullivan drills his troops every day but Monash still finds time to immerse himself in university life. He produces his first issue of the *Melbourne University Review* on 26 July 1884, with a self-congratulating editorial. Since universities develop a nation's leaders and produce its greatest thinkers, he says, 'no available means should be spared for affording every opportunity for the exercise of the literary abilities and mental faculties of the individual members of such a powerful institution'.[53]

He revels in student activities and in carousing with the medical students. After joining a group of 200 students at a performance of *Lady Macbeth* at the Theatre Royal on 9 August he admits: 'I contributed more than my share in the shape of vociferous bawling, and as a consequence lost my voice.'[54]

George Farlow will recall that if ever Monash appeared when his friends were chatting to girls, 'it was a foregone conclusion that all the young ladies became more interested in his conversation and escort than all the others of us put together'.[55] In August 1884 he rides the train with Mat and her friend, 16-year-old Clara Stockfeld, into the city from Elsternwick Station and confides that 'Clara has been somewhat excited about me since last Saturday, and told Mat so in confidence. Poor little thing.' Clara gives Monash two small flowers, which he places in his diary. 'Oh the innocence of it', he writes.[56] When Clara becomes a country governess they correspond with each other often; she calls him 'Jack'o' and signs herself 'Queen of Hearts'.

Monash has found his mojo again. He writes in his diary that month:

Again do I find myself on the upward path, gaining in social position, moral and physical character, and most of all in self esteem ... My stores of energy are unlimited and now at last am I finding a field for their application. I have taken up an important position in my University, one of its leaders in actual fact ... and one of the fountain heads of the largest movement of Union that ever manifested itself within our walls, the mainstay and practical conductor of the first genuine Students Paper ... rising rapidly through exertion of a little push, through tier after tier of the strata of society ... extending my acquaintanceship in advantageous directions, taking part in all movements likely to benefit myself in time to come.[57]

The answer to all melancholy is 'Throw yourself with energy into something', he tells Will Steele on 12 October. 'Find something to do, and stick to it with what energy you may – activity is the antidote of despondency.'[58] It is a mantra that will sustain Monash through tough economic times and the greatest conflict mankind has seen. He will become known as a man able to master any task, confident of scaling any obstacle, no matter how great, and almost always managing to remain unflappable in the midst of adversity.

Monash is pushing himself to the limit, working with the University Union, producing the *Review* just about every month, drilling with the university militia every day, tutoring pupils and preparing for his own exams. He confesses that the workload constitutes 'a strain upon my mental and physical powers which I can scarcely bear', but that despite his stress he is 'enjoying the most perfect content and peace of mind'.[59]

Two days after this diary entry, on 14 October, he receives his first military promotion, to corporal, and although some of his fellow recruits call him 'Corporal Potash', he tells himself that it will be the first of many promotions.

A few weeks of cramming later and Monash gets through the examinations of 1884, passing in advanced mathematics, natural philosophy II, French, German and practical chemistry, but is judged only equal 14th in second-year arts, once again hardly the first-class honours he expected. He also passes the prerequisites for engineering – surveying and levelling and practical mensuration. His friends suggest he would have done much better had he not had so many competing interests.

He isn't about to slow down, though. Not only is he revelling in the importance others place in his work, but it also takes his mind off troubles at home.

For so long Bertha has encouraged him, guided him and given him the confidence to move among the colony's elite. The Monashes have never been a wealthy family, but thanks to her, John has been well connected from a young age.

Now the light in Bertha's eyes has dulled. She complains of abdominal pain and fatigue and is often gripped by fever. Louis is trying to make a go of a new career as a moneylender, in partnership with Ulrike's husband Max Roth, but like most of his endeavours it goes badly.

John senses dark days ahead and cheers himself by making friends of both sexes. He becomes great mates with Jim Lewis, whose mother, a deserted woman raising eight children, runs a Carlton boarding house. He goes on a picnic in the Dandenongs with seven girls and stays for three days with Mat and her friend Selina Hooper. He and one of his students Fyffe, James, walk from Box Hill station over Mount Dandenong and back, more than 70 kilometres, and 'got well drunk on the way home'.[60]

His interest in chess is piqued when the 'Black Death', Joseph Henry Blackburne, arrives in Melbourne at the end of 1884. Monash watches the English master play 20 consecutive games. 'I should much like to perfect myself in the art of chess playing,' he writes, 'but I am much afraid that I am endeavouring to push forward in too many directions. One occasionally does hear, however, of men who have many irons in the fire at once, and yet do not dissipate their energies. I cannot help wishing that the hours of a day might be doubled; yet I find that much can be done by due economy of time.'[61] He duly takes the lead in organising the University Chess Club, playing for Arts against Medicine and takes on the Turn-Verein and the Victoria Club.

On 17 January 1885 he is among the 250 revellers at the German Society of Victoria's picnic at Mordialloc, celebrating the 14th anniversary of the German Empire. Hermann Püttmann, the society's president, explains to the guests lunching in Bloxsidge's Hotel that the festivities have no bearing on the struggle between British and German interests over Pacific territories.[62]

In the afternoon Monash has a starring role in the running contests. All the parade ground drilling under Sergeant Sullivan is paying off. He also proves to be a nimble dancer at the picnic, declaring that he has 'succeeded in rendering myself universally pleasant, without any maladvertence to overshadow it ... The conditions [were] most favourable for rapturous enjoyment ... I believe to have detracted nothing and added much to my reputation today.' But 'The chiefest pleasure' of the afternoon is the long ramble he takes with 18-year-old Hermine 'Franzchen' Püttmann, Hermann's daughter and 'a tender, good-hearted, contemplative-minded girl', who communicates 'passive appreciation of my attention to her, as to lead me to flatter myself that I am held in considerable favour by her. Time will show how much I am deceived.'[63]

The regimented discipline of military training is also a tonic. Nine days after the picnic, on 26 January 1885, in the university's Wilson Hall, there is a special parade of the militia volunteers as they are presented with their helmets and uniforms.[64] Monash is delighted with his new attire and he knows Bertha and Louis will beam at the sight of him in his vivid red tunic, even if he has not done as well in his examinations as he should have. 'My appearance in this gaudy outrig has caused no little astonishment,' he writes, 'and some amount of admiration among my friends.'[65] There are also plenty of critics. Not only does Corporal Potash cop a ribbing from some classmates but, borrowing a line from Bulwer-Lytton, he also complains that his appearance in the streets in uniform is the 'signal for the display of all the wit of which unwashed Melbourne seems possessed'.[66]

On the same day as Monash is presented with his militia uniform, on the other side of the globe in the besieged Sudanese city of Khartoum, British Major General Charles Gordon is being hacked to death by rebel forces. The news of his death outrages the British Empire. Subscriptions begin pouring in for a Melbourne memorial to the fallen hero,[67] and Premier James Service makes an offer (in vain) to send a Victorian legion to gain revenge.[68]

Monash, though, is not ready for a fight just yet. His mother's condition has worsened. She has had surgery, but it provides no relief and she becomes bedridden. John will have to help care for Bertha, cook and clean for her and play her favourite pieces on the piano – Chopin's 'Polonaise' and 'Fantasie' and Franz van Suppé's 'Poet and Peasant'. He hardly attends a lecture for the rest of the year. Bertha's illness haunts him night and day; he calls her cancer 'the darkest recollection of all … too omnipresent to need more than reference'.[69]

He keeps his pain to himself, but Bertha's illness shapes his thoughts about the future. He writes in his diary, 'Clearly my circumstances render it impossible for me to go [to war], and in view of this impossibility my inclination does not seem to lean in that direction either. I am fully aware that remaining behind will be far from pleasant, much less will be the comparison with the returned troops; further I consider the whole movement a mistake of misdirected enthusiasm. I should much prefer to see it displayed in the formation of a national army … and in any case the colonies will derive no material advantage from the business.'[70]

He and his comrades undergo their first taste of war games, and two months later, in April 1885, Britain's war in Afghanistan and the 'rumoured approach of a Russian fleet' towards Australia's east coast[71] put Australia's threadbare defence forces on high alert. With cries around Victoria that 'The Russians are coming', Monash lines up on parade at an Easter training camp in Frankston. He has 'a rough and vulgar time' at what he calls 'a paragon of mismanagement', and at other military activities condemns the 'childish misbehaviour of some of the men who seem to have nothing beyond schoolboy impulses'. To him the Williamstown rifle range is a place of 'utter bleakness and heathlike ghastliness'.

Away from these war games, the piano continues to be a comfort for him and his mother and he plunges further into his studies of classical music. By June he is regularly practising on Sunday mornings with Albert Behrend, just back from Vienna after six years abroad. Starting on 25 June 1885, Monash attends the three Town Hall concerts of violin maestro Johann (John) Kruse, back in Melbourne after 10 years in Europe.[72] Kruse is supported on the stage by the young soprano Nellie Melba. Soon Monash is performing regularly at University Union socials and at a union concert in the Temperance Hall. He also plays at private houses, and after one recital basks in the adulation: 'I was kept at the piano almost continuously, and had to listen to endless compliments and expressions of appreciation, which though undeserved and of little value, I feel intense gratification in hearing.'[73] He still craves adoration, and longs to be famous and loved. But he also recognises that such a craving can be dangerous, and presents a paradox for someone who needs always to be busy. 'Activity brings unpopularity, and popularity is the object of my life, pursuit of it my greatest vice', he writes on 15 June.

Monash has started to visit the lovely Blashki sisters – Minnie, Jeanette, Rose and Eva. They are the daughters of Phillip Blashki, a devout Jew who was born Favel Wagczewski in a place called Blaszki, Poland, in 1837, and who has established a jewellery and watchmaking business at 120 Bourke Street. The shop has six rooms attached for his large family, which at one stage numbers 15 surviving children.[74] Monash is often around there, showing off his militia uniform, along with the beginnings of a moustache – a 'sort of lion',[75] as he describes himself, or perhaps more like a peacock – playing the piano and writing verses for 17-year-old Eva. He flirts with 20-year-old Minnie, the 'prettiest and most amiable' of the sisters, but has strong competition in Albert Behrend, more than double his age and able to charm Minnie with exotic tales of cosmopolitan Europe.

Meanwhile, Monash finds the younger Eva a 'bright, intelligent, fairly-read, warm-hearted sympathetic girl – the sort of girl a fellow could lose himself to'. He continues, 'She flattered me by an urgent wish to read my famous prize essay on "Macbeth" ... I look forward with expectation to my closer acquaintance with these girls.'[76]

On Monash's 20th birthday, on 27 June 1885, Clara Stockfeld sends 'Jack'o' a 'neat piece of handwork', which he calls 'an attention and kindness which I do not well know how to meet'.[77] But he has a lot on his mind and takes some of the load off it by telling Clara that they should just be friends. He does not want to break her heart.

Early in July Monash is the first in the University Company to pass the exam for sergeant, while his talent at the *University Review* is not going unnoticed. Alfred Deakin, now Victorian Solicitor-General and Minister of Public Works, sends him congratulations on the 'sustained quality' and 'improved appearance' of the publication and assures him that 'all things are possible to the young and earnest'.[78]

Monash is the life of every party and he practises cards and magic tricks to ensure he is always the centre of attention. He is a frequent lunch guest at the home of John Springthorpe, Vice President of the University Union and the first Australian graduate admitted to membership of the Royal College of Physicians.[79] At the Blashki house he tries to be as dazzling as the gems in Phillip's shop window. He takes Mat to Franzchen Püttmann's 19th birthday dance on 26 August 1885, and while rejoicing that his sister is becoming a success in social circles, he readily reacquaints himself with many 'old lady friends'. He dances in 'all but the waltzes with them – the Staubels, Miss Anderson, Dora Sander and Olga Arnold, which latter's offered advances I readily accepted'.[80]

Along with George Farlow and Tom Hodgson, Monash applies to the Captain of the University Company, his physics professor Henry Andrew, for another promotion. He is made a colour sergeant on 4 September, writing in his diary: 'I have scored a great triumph, and the fact gives me unlimited and unalloyed satisfaction ... now I feel that all my self-sacrifice in the interests, ostensibly of the company, but really of myself have been repaid in full – a lesson to the crowd of weak-headed fellows who are fond of ridiculing me ... A rise from a recruit to absolute seniority is not a bad year's work. With so much accomplished in one direction, and so much gained, I feel encouraged and instigated to a fresh start in the race for a position in the world.'

Monash regularly takes out his uniform to admire it, and on the night of his promotion pays a visit to the Blashkis. The budding romance with Eva is thwarted by the family's 'strictness in religious observance', which 'greatly amuses' him: 'Matters are beginning to assume altogether too definite a shape for my liking', he laments.[81] He loves being with Eva but not enough to share her family's thoughts of marriage.

He can be hard on himself but is even harder on Eva. 'I am now of an age when questions of heart and home are of importance if not ever present ... But I ask myself to pause, before I do harm to [Eva] or myself. Her character is after all the question on which everything turns, and incidents, which I cannot easily forget ... have warned me of the possible existence of grave anomalies and unamendable deficiencies.'[82] Some days later he concludes: 'The comedy is, I think, for the present played out ... She is as raw as possible and quite uneducated as to feelings and sentiments ... the defects of her nature seem radical.'[83]

Still, despite all the faults he finds in Eva, he remains close to the sisters. As his mother is racked by ever greater pain and he realises the inevitable must soon come to pass, he visits the Blashki girls often, especially Eva and Rose, posing questions on the meaning of life and imploring Eva to allow him to become her mentor. How could a girl *not* benefit from such a worldly-wise and educated man, after all?

He continues to drink with his militia friends, but he now looks at them with a more critical eye. He and some of the other non-commissioned officers meet at the Port Phillip Club Hotel in Flinders Street, and while Monash finds some of them 'decent and agreeable' his critical eye decides they are of 'a low intellectual standard ... I met an old army Major ... who displayed a soldier like propensity for beer and "baccy". As a consequence I came home very late.'[84]

Early in October 1885 he takes the Blashki sisters to a union lecture and then escorts them to the university sports day, in which he competes in the office-bearers' race. At another party, 'the choice of the company was all that could be desired, and the interesting part of it – the girls – was excellent … Lily Damman is a lively girl but knows how to take care of herself. We broke up at 3.30 and I suffered correspondingly the next day.'

Monash has gone back to lectures, but with a financially crippled father and a bedridden mother, he too is broke. He makes about £50 a year as a part-time tutor but he still has to pawn his watch and can't get it out of hock. He can't pay the exam fees and resolves to skip university until February 1886.

He still believes in his own drive and talent, though, and he advertises them shamelessly. The fact that he is from an ethnic minority and a struggling family only makes his determination stronger. Jim Lewis suggests that even though Monash is without a degree they could still go into partnership together and chase engineering projects.[85]

Yet Bertha's desperate illness casts a pall over everything.

She has lingered for months in great pain,[86] realising that her condition is terminal and that soon her husband and children will face life without their driving force. Monash later recalls the time as 'terrible' and 'horrible'. As Bertha clings to life in her bedroom at Yarra Street, she turns to the boy she has tried to make a great man, and implores him to be a good soldier and perform one last duty. She asks him to watch over and cherish his sisters.[87]

Bertha dies on 18 October 1885 from abdominal cancer.

The 23 words marking her passing in one of the Melbourne papers cost Louis two shillings and sixpence.

MONASH.– On the 18th inst., at her residence, Yarra street, St. James's Park, Hawthorn, Bertha, wife of Mr. Louis Monash, aged 44 years.[88]

'I have lost the dearest and most sympathetic friend I ever had', John tells 18-year-old Rose Blashki. 'My mother was far more than that and now I feel utterly, utterly alone. Outwardly I may seem no different ... but I have great self-control, and were I not to tell you, you might not believe how much of the brightness of life has been taken away. I feel like a wandering unit with no place in the world ...'[89]

Monash will spend the next few years in a mental fog, bobbing around like a cork in the ocean and fighting hard to regain his direction and equilibrium. Bertha's death has not only knocked him off his course to the glittering academic prizes he craves, but it will also force Mat, Dux of Presbyterian Ladies' College in 1886, to forgo university herself to care for her younger sister Lou and to keep the Monash household going.

More than that, Bertha's death sends the already fragile Louis crumbling.

John Monash will have to grow up fast. He will have to find a job, and somebody to support him on life's journey.

Chapter 5

*The gorgeous uniforms and all the pomp of officership bear for me
sufficient attraction to make their attainment a matter of fierce desire.*
MONASH ON THE PROSPECT OF MILITARY ADVANCEMENT[1]

LIKE JOHN MONASH, David Munro is a man of boundless
energy and ambition. Gold enticed his blacksmith father to
bring his young family from Scotland to Victoria in 1854, and
now David is the 41-year-old self-made monarch of Victorian
industry. Balding, with a neatly trimmed beard and an aura of
audacity, he is one of the colony's biggest employers. An army
of thousands toils in his engineering workshops, construction
projects, granite and basalt quarries and sawmills. His company
trademark is a phoenix rising from the fire, and it sums up the
way Munro has strode confidently through the business world,
dragging a large part of Victoria's workforce with him – brushing
off bankruptcy early in his career, plunging headlong into bold
new ventures and forging a business empire. More than just
about anyone in Melbourne he has benefited from the massive
building and railway boom of recent years, and from the need for
machinery and farming equipment.[2]

As the winter of 1885 comes to a close the business giant is
in a bubbly mood. In the Queen Street office of David Munro

and Company, 'engineers, boiler makers, contractors, machinery merchants, and importers of machinery of every description',[3] he has good reason to be celebrating after securing the biggest project in Melbourne: a new thoroughfare to replace the narrow 34-year-old Princes Bridge across the Yarra River, linking Swanston Street with St Kilda Road.

Munro has won the tender with a bid of £136,098[4] and sees the bridge as a magnificent steel and stone ornament for his city. It will be 100 metres long and 30 metres wide, and Munro will need to employ even more engineers, stonemasons, teamsters and navvies. Not only will they build the bridge but they will also reconstruct the southern approach, and widen the Yarra at the point of crossing to prevent the floods that have blighted the capital for so long.

John Monash sees the new bridge as a lifeline for his family. His mother's death and the family's parlous financial situation have made him increasingly worried. Melbourne is Australia's largest city and the second largest in the British Empire, its magnificent city buildings a testament to its wealth and prosperity. Yet the Monash family has been left behind.

The *Australasian Sketcher* gives readers an insight into the super-sized structure. The bridge 'somewhat resembles the Blackfriars' bridge, London'. The arches will each consist of 10 wrought-iron ribs, the outer ribs covered with ornamental castings. There will be 1100 tons of wrought iron and 200 tons of cast iron. The largest stones in the cutwaters (wedges at the base of the piers) will weigh upwards of 12 tons, and the granite columns on the piers 20 tons each.[5] It has been designed by British-born architect and civil engineer John Grainger, who, at a home in North Brighton, has a domineering wife named Rose and a musical toddler named Percy.[6]

Work begins in September 1885. A gang of labourers starts excavating on the Yarra's south bank opposite Flinders Street Station. For the construction of the piers and the widening of the river, large cofferdams (temporary enclosures) are prepared with corrugated iron, and three huge steam cranes run side by side for the whole length of the bridge.

George Higgins, the recipient of the *Argus* Scholarship in 1879, and the brother of judge Henry Bournes Higgins, is in charge of the project, backed by fellow Melbourne University men Jim Lewis and Charles Stewart.

Monash plans to study part-time and take a job to keep his family functioning. Lewis manages to talk Higgins into giving Monash a start at the end of 1885.

But David Munro has not become rich through philanthropy. He extracts every bead of sweat he can for each penny paid. Monash signs on for just 30 shillings a week, less than a ditch-digger earns.[7] It is the first rung on a long ladder he is determined to climb.

Twenty years old and about to earn his first real pay cheque, Monash is nervous and uncertain. As he surveys the footings for the new bridge, his confident outward appearance is an illusion resting on a teetering foundation. 'I was in great fear of my applicability to the new order of things,' he confides to his diary, 'and troubled Lewis extremely by persistent applications to him for advice and assistance.'[8]

The challenge is both daunting and empowering, and Monash is determined to be a leader, not a follower. Charles Darwin's ideas of natural selection, frequently discussed at the university, now affect all his relationships. Even when socialising with his friend and one-time protector George Farlow, Monash makes it his 'especial business to show him that I still [hold] the upper hand'.[9]

Rather than be crushed by responsibility, Monash embraces it. He deflects the grief over his mother's death by immersing himself in a project that has the whole country talking. 'The first work which was given me ... is usually entrusted to men of great experience and requires both time and care', he writes in his diary. 'It was the drawing out of a complete set of courses for the masonry ... upon my drawings the whole of the masonry has been cut and will finally stand.'[10]

He has many deep conversations about the meaning of life with his soulmates, the Blashki girls, in person and through correspondence. Their father is a pillar of Melbourne's Jewish community and has just moved his family into a new home on Lansdowne Street, East Melbourne, near the synagogue.

Monash looks for this 'supreme joy' at every opportunity. At the end of the year he fits in a brief holiday with Mat, now 16, and Will Steele's family at Goldsborough near Dunolly, 220 kilometres north-west of Melbourne. He has a brief dalliance with 23-year-old Jane 'Jennie' Walls, the sister of Dunolly's Scottish-born blacksmith, Archibald Walls, who, on his anvil 16 years earlier, broke up into manageable pieces the world's largest alluvial gold nugget, the Welcome Stranger. Jennie later writes to the young engineer to complain he has led her on and has trifled with other girls behind her back. She returns his letters and demands he return hers.

Back in Melbourne and no longer a full-time student at the university, Monash joins the Deutscher Verein von Victoria, the German Club, at their newly opened home in Albert Place off Collins Street East,[11] in January 1886. Cousin Albert is the secretary. A sizeable minority of the members are Jewish and most of the conversations are in German. There are always plenty of fräuleins, and while members rarely paint the town red, Monash occasionally gets plastered at the smoke nights and staggers home in the early hours. He attends dozens of the German Club's social functions, sometimes as MC, and also frequents the smoke nights for the Metropolitan Liedertafel, occasionally joining in the performances with the all-male choristers.

His fears are realised as Albert Behrend and Minnie Blashki become an item. Monash bristles every time he sees them holding hands, Minnie looking so young and lovely and Albert – old enough to be her father, blast him – going on and on with all that palaver about Vienna and Berlin and Hamburg. It's a different Albert from the one Monash knows, yapping and nagging him about the Torah, 'an iceberg to his nearest and dearest' with an 'overmastering will'.[12]

Monash takes aim at Minnie's sisters Eva and Jeanette, and revels in being the cat among the pigeons. He is quite the young philosopher and sparks considerable debate between them over religion and his lack thereof, though he tells Rose Blashki that 'No sane man can believe in nothing'.[13]

Starting in March 1886, Monash and Jeanette Blashki become very close. She is a year older than him but not as worldly-wise, and she falls prey to his red tunic and silver tongue. She calls him 'Dearest Jack' as he looks deep into her dark eyes and whispers to her again and again that she is just made to be 'petted and cuddled'.[14]

Monash begins recording his life in even more intricate detail, itemising everything: his successes, his failures, his foibles, his vanities. He calls his diary 'a most trusty and confidential friend', a sort of living conscience, a second self to which he can turn – for consolation when he is broken down with disappointment, for reproof when he is about to break his resolutions, and for encouragement and vigour when he feels dispirited by failure.[15] For the rest of his life, the diary will be a 'vivid recollection of bygone joys and sorrows, struggles, triumphs and failures',[16] and while he is disarmingly honest about his life – even the darker aspects of his character – his amorous adventures are revealed only in the chaste framework of Victorian morality. Nothing more than a kiss and cuddle is ever committed to paper.

At work he is a diligent employee for David Munro, whose huge project still dominates Melbourne life. Its importance is reinforced on 6 July 1886, when two elderly Scotsmen, Sir Henry Loch, the new governor of Victoria, and John Nimmo, the Commissioner of Public Works, make an inspection tour, watching the steam crane removing logs from the Yarra.[17] For the next two years as the bridge comes together, Monash helps in the planning of piers, retaining walls and abutments. He works closely with government officials and once even interviews Nimmo himself, doing his best to curry favour.[18]

He feels inspired to hit the textbooks again and prepare for the end-of-year examinations,[19] and whenever he can he trains with the University Company militia. Attendance on the parade ground has dwindled now that the Russians are not coming after all, but Monash's ardour for soldiering has been accelerated by his discovery that so many women love a man in uniform.

He tries to win a commission with the Victorian Engineers militia unit but after missing out decries the volunteer army as a 'wretched business ... a fraud [that] bristles with mismanagement', and says he has little heart to bother about it further.[20] Others agree. Such is the poor attendance for the University Company's training that it is disbanded on 23 July. Monash's red tunic is temporarily retired.

Instead, he spends weeks practising his dancing – 'a necessary evil', he calls it – and becomes the must-have partner at balls and parties. He is already a veteran campaigner on the social scene but on 31 July 1886 he dances the first waltz of his life 'outside of a dancing class' with a girl named Ethel Jones. His piano playing reaches a crescendo too, and he makes a list of a dozen pieces that will become his oeuvre. He has long believed that 'once you have mastered the principle of high class music, the effect upon the character is wonderful'.[21] 'Mendelssohn's great concerto is my present hobby', he writes at one point, though he gladly receives many compliments, especially from young women, for the duets he plays with Albert Behrend, a family friend named Max Joseph, members of the Levy family and the Püttmann and Krakowski sisters.[22]

Monash is quite the catch, and the tension is building between Eva and Jeanette Blashki. Eva is strictly orthodox in her faith and she asks Monash just where he stands on the question of God. His written reply stretches for several thousand words. The Bible, he says, is a collection of folklores, though the Ten Commandments are a 'succinct and complete basis for all systems of ethics'. Culturally, he still identifies himself as Jewish, but he does not believe in any of the gods or deities of the major religions. He accepts the moral teaching of the Bible as part of the 'Universal Good' that permeates all things, but Goethe and Lessing have convinced him that God is not a deity but everywhere around him in nature.[23] The loss of his mother has wounded him and the sermons at Christian and Jewish funerals promising an afterlife are 'meaningless form' and 'bitter farce'.[24] 'We emerge from the Unknown,' he says, 'rush across the astonished earth, then plunge again into the Unknown.'[25] He envies 'the happiness of ignorance' and 'the bliss of a mere physical existence of the lowest men ... Youth is all a hope, age is all a regret, and we must be content to take the few moments of supreme joy as a counterpoise to years of trouble and sorrow.'[26]

Many of the volunteers from the disbanded University Company transfer to the North Melbourne Battery of the Metropolitan Brigade of the Garrison Artillery. Their cannons defend Victorian ports. Monash, still angry at not becoming an officer, hesitates at joining them, but in August 1886 admits his 'long cherished hope for military advancement' is uppermost in his mind.

'I can scarcely understand why this wish is so intense within me', he admits. 'Nevertheless the gorgeous uniforms and all the pomp of officership bear for me sufficient attraction to make their attainment a matter of fierce desire.'[27] He does not want a full-time military career, though. Monash is too independently minded to spend his life saluting superiors but the Victorian Militia Force, which offers its 5000 volunteers a small wage in return for service of a few days each year, provides him with social status and professional contacts. After the British garrison left Australia in 1871, each colony had raised its own forces for defence but there are only about 300 permanent soldiers in Victoria.

Two of Monash's schoolfriends, part-time soldiers George Farlow and medical student Joe Miller, already have commissions with North Melbourne, and Monash asks them for a recommendation to their commanding officer, 47-year-old newly promoted Major Jacob Robert Yannasch Goldstein. He is a native of Cork, Ireland, with Polish, Jewish and Irish heritage. Goldstein works as a contract draughtsman and has been a part-time officer in the Victorian Garrison Artillery for 19 years.[28] He has abandoned his Jewish heritage in favour of the Unitarian faith and is deeply involved in charitable works, though he can be 'irascible, domineering and opinionated'[29] and is always at loggerheads with his feminist wife Isabella. Their daughter Vida Goldstein was a schoolmate of Mat's at Presbyterian Ladies' College. Monash feverishly awaits[30] the outcome of his request for promotion but Goldstein makes him wait. And wait.

On the domestic front, Eva has 'practically declared herself': 'Heaven knows where this will end. I am beginning to have my doubts', he writes, admitting he is starting to get cold feet about Jeanette as well, given their father's devout faith.

Monash loves literature, classical music and the theatre, but he also has a bawdy side, and he and Farlow and other young volunteers sometimes engage in banter, using hints and double entendres about potential conquests for their 9-inch guns.[31] Soon Monash's diary will feature more than 50 names of girls he fancies. Most of them are not Jewish. The comely Berrie Rennick, for one, has 'an eager ear to amorous whisperings, and is not easily offended by too much boldness of speech'.[32]

He is soon documenting the secrets of his success with women.

[I] devote myself solely to the cultivation of the esteem and, be it admitted, admiration of the lady guests. I endeavour to gauge rapidly the character of my partners and act accordingly. Sometimes this bears me flattering satisfaction and sometimes it is mere waste of energy, but in most cases my immediate aim is accomplished ... It is my aim to convince each in turn of my own great personal importance, wonderful depth of knowledge and outstanding versatility of acquirements, a task very easy to the most shallow character. In all earnestness I find I can easily take up any possible line of conversation, and approach skilfully any possible topic.[33]

He meets Rosie Schild at a dance and finds her 'outrageously flirty'.[34] She is from a prosperous Footscray family and the sister of John Schild, a sergeant in the Garrison Artillery. At a dance in September 1886 Monash is enchanted by Evie Corrie, who he calls 'a poem in white muslin, with fine expressive eyes, and a frank, innocent manner'.[35] Evie will be on Monash's arm at three successive Melbourne Cups, occasions he relishes though he is not a gambler. He maintains a long friendship with Evie and her elder sister Amy.

Monash's name is starting to appear in the papers as one of Melbourne's bright young things. George Higgins and Jim Lewis give him more and more responsibility on the bridge. He plans excavations for the foundations of the machinery used to set the stone. He runs a supply yard and opens a quarry 16 kilometres out of Melbourne.

He looks forward with great eagerness to the laying of the foundation stone – only to be 'deeply hurt by being excluded altogether from the list of recognised guests'[36] when, under threatening skies, the Lady Mayoress Amelia Stewart arrives at the southern side of the bridge to perform the honours, along with David Munro, Alfred Deakin (now Victorian Chief Secretary) and the Jewish parliamentarian Ephraim Zox. Streamers and flags flutter from the wooden framework of the bridge and bright bunting is all around. A band provided by the New Brewery keeps the 500 invited guests entertained.

Deakin tells the crowd of his pride in Melbourne and in the geniuses creating such a magnificent structure. 'Forty years ago Melbourne had 12,000 inhabitants,' Deakin says, 'and the colony as a whole had only a population of 33,000. To-day, Melbourne has 365,000 inhabitants, and the colony has a population of more than a million within its borders.'

Loud cheering breaks out.

'Such a change in so short a space of time, I suppose has not been witnessed in any other part of the world.'[37]

Even though Monash hasn't made the official guest list, his work on such an important project is noticed in high places. He catches the eye of another Polish–Prussian, the enterprising journalist Maurice Brodzky, who writes in his new weekly *Table Talk*:

> I am always glad to chronicle the successes of Australian youths when opportunity occurs. It is therefore pleasing to me to find that the whole of the civil engineers and other professional men engaged on the new bridges and works in connection with them are of purely Colonial training. Mr. Higgins C.E., who has charge of the works at the Princes and Falls new bridges, and his assistant (Mr Monash) are both Melbourne University men. The fact that over a quarter of a million of money is being expended in the work proves that considerable confidence must be reposed in those under whose supervision it is being carried out.[38]

It is just the kind of flattering attention Monash needs to push hard academically.[39] After work, by the light of a gas lamp, he studies long into the night to pass third-year arts.

His workload on the bridge is staggering and he also has to cope with much angst in his personal life. He tries to let Jeanette Blashki down gently by telling her that he's too young to marry and that she would be much happier with someone else.[40] He can't help but wonder what might have happened between him and Minnie Blashki if Albert Behrend hadn't been around. Monash is asked to help with their wedding ceremony but is soon dismissed from the role for being overbearing and officious, and Jeanette takes his part on 27 October at the synagogue in Bourke Street, as a young Londoner, Rabbi Dr Joseph Abrahams, performs the wedding ceremony. Albert, eldest son of Ben-Zion Behrend and Julie Monasch of Krotoschin, is 41. Minnie is 20 years younger.[41]

There is great rejoicing all around, except from Monash, who is grinding his teeth and watching with a degree of disbelief as his ageing cousin heads off to his honeymoon with his young bride.[42] Monash mopes and his exams the following month are a 'most miserable time ... I did not know my work and hoped to scrape through ... I felt deeply my complete failure as a student.'[43]

He still feels that he's the intellectual superior of the girls he meets, and is keen to prove it at a ball in the middle of December 1886 when he is 'all knocked of a heap by the smart attacks and really first class wit' of a certain Miss Jess Robinson. Determined to 'lower her flag', he reduces her to silence and gains her 'sympathetic attention': 'I am conceited enough to think she feels she has found her match. We had a few dances together and became very good friends.'[44]

He has a final showdown with Jeanette just before Christmas. Her mother Hannah is putting out feelers and lets it 'be very clearly understood that she would not object to me as a son-in-law'. The way Monash tells it, his father Louis, 'an open but shrewd man', informs Mrs Blashki that his boy won't be marrying anyone any time soon. Hannah Blashki twists the tale, so that Jeanette and the other girls all turn on Monash.

Jeanette corners him in a fury, demanding, 'What did you mean by getting your father and aunt to tell my mother it was no use her trying to get you for one of her daughters as you had better prospects elsewhere?'

Monash grows 'very hot tempered'. Believing that a counter-attack is the best defence, he hits back 'with some very warm things', and through her tears Jeanette tells him that he and all the other Monashes are just a bunch of liars.

'I told her she was no better,' Monash admits, 'and I have not seen, spoken or written to her since.'[45]

He tries to forget his girl troubles from an almost permanent seat at the theatre, a sanctuary that makes him feel 'elevated morally'.[46] Dressed in a top hat that has his friends scoffing behind his back, he becomes a fixture at the new Alexandra Theatre[47] in

Exhibition Street, where he sees Martin Sorenson's Royal Italian Opera Company perform repeatedly.

Monash is hopeless at the new craze of tennis and admits he is too timid to take up the fad of roller-skating. He lives near the Melbourne Cricket Ground but never goes there any more, having little interest in the cricket and Australian football games played there, though he did read something in the papers about Geelong's winning the premiership that year.

At Christmas he and George Farlow, struggling with his work at the Mint and part-time law studies, make the first of their annual treks through the Victorian bush. Monash is a skilled bushman, who knows how to look after himself in unfamiliar territory. Marching with Farlow through the Gippsland villages of Warragul, Drouin and Poowong, he looks all about for engineering opportunities,[48] studying the way people live and how their lives could be improved.

'We strolled through the country … as wandering minstrels,' Monash writes, 'I playing and he singing whenever we came across a piano. The whole trip cost us about 15 [shillings] as the people were glad to give us tucker and a shakedown in return for our entertainment.'[49]

Farlow notices that Monash has a tendency to exaggerate both distances covered and incidents along the way.[50] He is a natural storyteller.

Back home in Hawthorn on New Year's Day 1887, at a quarter past midnight, Monash ponders the year ahead. He is rising fast professionally, but wants his progress to accelerate. He notes in his diary that he must 'guard against any false slip which might ruin my career'. He is acutely sensitive to the slightest criticism and says he is mostly disliked and even 'personally ridiculed' but has been able to 'compel submission' – even admiration – from others.

My vanity has been flattered by the clear demonstration that
I possess the capabilities of rising above my surroundings.
Repeated successes have implanted in me a feeling of

superiority present or future over those with whom I come in contact ... In the militia, I left many behind me, and I have made a magnificent start in my profession ... I feel that I will always possess the self-confidence engendered by actual success over other men, or with the consciousness of my power.[51]

He tries to concentrate on his studies and the complex work for Munro, but the unpleasant break-up with Jeanette clouds his mind and he is still befuddled by the time he sits for a supplementary university exam in February. He performs 'ignominiously', passing three subjects but failing geology.

At least his request to Munro for a pay rise after 12 months is successful and he is now earning £2 a week: no mean feat, considering that during a temporary slump in work the hard-driving construction boss cuts his labourers' wages from seven shillings a day to six shillings and sixpence, telling protesting workers that their union officials are 'vermin to be squelched'.[52]

Monash helps plan the employees' picnic, and there is a finance committee meeting at Young and Jackson's Hotel, where he finds that his lofty opinion of himself is not shared by his co-workers. Monash is never shy about self-recommendation and his relentless ambition and obvious vanity often make workmates bristle. It's their loss, he reasons, because 'these fellows do not seem to appreciate my fraternisation with them as much as they ought'.[53]

He helps organise the annual German picnic on 5 February at the Royal Horticultural Society's 10-hectare site on the Survey Paddock at Richmond,[54] where, under leaden skies and despite his constant protests that he's no athlete, he carries off 200 cigars for winning a foot race.

A few days later he has 'an interesting flirtation with [Dolly Phelps], a striking but mysterious girl from Adelaide'. 'I spoke to her in all the languages I know, English, German, Latin and, of course "love". I played my hand boldly, and I think she found her match.'

Two weeks later Monash is one of 100,000 people crammed into Melbourne's streets for the annual torchlight procession of the fire brigades,[55] and he says the girls are like a moth to his flame. 'Standing in the crowd, I by slow degrees found a pretty girl in my arms; I don't know and scarcely can recollect her, but the attraction was mutual and perfectly strong.'[56]

There is no stopping Monash on the job site either. Lewis calls him 'embarrassingly curious' and says Monash wants to know every minor detail about the project. Monash's 'restless energy' drives even the ambitious Lewis to 'greater endeavour' just to keep up.[57]

His military push is back on the offensive as well. Major Goldstein finally relents and Monash is formally attached to the North Melbourne Battery on 3 March 1887. Monash later claims that a descendant of Johann Sebastian Bach[58] puts him through his first drill and now Monash realises 'a combination of military and engineering professions is a possibility that is before me'.[59]

A few days later, Monash is back at his office working late after dinner when two women arrive, noisily demanding the pay of one of their husbands. 'They had made havoc within. One of them Miss Ricardo Josephine Burt was a girl with unbridled behaviour. I escorted them home, and she went back with me to the office where we remained locked in each other's arms for nearly two hours. She left as a keepsake some verses which I could not have believed any woman capable of writing.'[60]

Two days later Monash and the wild Miss 'Ric' Burt get together again. She tells him she is the 'unmarried wife of a bigamist' and that she had a daughter, Violet, who died four years ago, aged six months. Monash is intrigued rather than shocked.[61] He takes Ric to the works picnic, saying, 'I don't intend to give her up awhile as I may get what I want from her yet. At any rate her acquaintance will be an amusing episode.' They go to the theatre together and he visits her lodgings in St Kilda, where she greets him in her nightdress. He praises his own great 'self-control and calmness', although they spend 'three hours in ardent love making'. 'I think that I may do her a little moral good, she needs it', he declares, and yet what Ric offers is tantalising.[62]

He passes the exam for a militia commission and becomes a probationary lieutenant on 5 April 1887. His success makes the papers, and 'after many a weary and anxious day, the fulfilment of one of my most ardent hopes has been consummated ... I was gazetted today, and go down in full regalia'.[63]

He tells himself that he looks magnificent in his officer's tunic, and what young woman could resist his appearance or intellect? The pittance he earns in the militia hardly pays for his uniform but he would serve for free. Being an army officer is a much higher rung on the social ladder than a junior engineer and it gives him an immediate social status that his German-Jewish background, which he will later call 'very solid handicaps',[64] and those guttural vowels have stymied in a society that is predominantly Anglo-Celtic and where most government officials are of British origin.

Some of his enemies mock him with 'sneers and reproaches' and call his strutting about in uniform a 'silly game of soldiering',[65] but he tells them he will have the last laugh. If things don't work out at university, if the bridge workload and his studies become too burdensome, there is now the chance to become a full-time military commander.[66] He even imagines himself commanding the garrison at Fort Nepean that guards the entrance to Melbourne at Port Phillip Bay. He has holidayed with Tante Ulrike and her family at nearby Sorrento and can see himself saving Victoria from a naval attack.

On 8 April, at the annual Easter military camp at Queenscliff, Major Goldstein leads his 64-strong North Melbourne Battery to Fort Nepean for instruction on the cannons. The following day, Good Friday, Monash takes part in war games under the supervision of the Victorian governor, Henry Loch, and Victoria's military commander Colonel Henry Studholme Brownrigg, an Afghan war veteran.

Monash has a hard time of it. His ego, vanity and ambition betray him and he makes more enemies, displaying an 'utter want of tact'. 'These fellows are not like our old boys [in the University Company]', he complains, 'and when I took up my work with manifested zeal, they saw only a desire to put myself forward, and assume unnecessary officiousness. I gained little of that additional entree among the higher men which I expected.' He is temporarily ostracised by many of his fellow artillery officers and ends up spending most of his time with 'the Torpedo men' instead. Still he isn't about to change his bearing or demeanour, saying, 'I have fought down much opposition in the past, and feel able to do so again.'[67]

Ric is driving him mad with desire. One Thursday he takes her to lunch and then they laugh themselves silly at the Arthur Pinero farce *The Magistrate* at the Princess Theatre. 'I had prepared myself to see her home and return myself late,' Monash admits? 'I shall never forget May 5, 1887. I am not sorry for what has happened.'

At the bridge site, the great granite columns from Harcourt, near Castlemaine, are shored up and the bluestone from Malmsbury near Kyneton is laid for piers. Monash is vain enough to feel he is indispensable to the project, even though at one stage he makes a serious miscalculation, which fortunately is soon rectified. He watches closely when the cofferdam fails and has to be rebuilt.

His relationship with the Blashki sisters is still in tatters. On a visit to Albert and the now pregnant Minnie at their house in Sherwood Street, Richmond, he finds Jeanette and Eva sitting in the parlour, stony-faced despite Minnie's excitement over approaching motherhood.

'Jeanette was there but we completely ignored each other', Monash says. 'With Eva I exchanged but two words "good evening" and to Rosie I had little more to say.' Monash is tempted to call a truce but there is a lot of bitterness still bubbling. 'Minnie is the incarnation of selfish and ingratitude,' he whines, 'first impressions are often follies.'[68]

He has no such confusion with the adventurous Ric. She knows what she wants and so does he. Yet something unsettles him.

Monash tries to get his studies back on course, attending the commencement in April followed by drinks at the Clyde Hotel. A few weeks later he meets Nellie Daley, 'a bright little flirt … bristling with sparkly fun and mischief',[69] and flora, 'zany and as frisky as lamb'. In July he attends a University Union social where his old friends give him a rousing welcome and he experiences none of the unpopularity he once suspected. He finds another flame, Agnes Murphy, a great intellect.[70]

He is still not so popular with his fellow soldiers, and they are not afraid to tell him he is pompous, arrogant and aloof. He is a good soldier, though. Major Goldstein asks him to prepare illustrated charts for the drill room and he becomes secretary of the Battery ball.[71] He also begins a lifelong involvement with the Pipeclay Club, an officers' association first presided over by Colonel Robert Rede, the man who provoked the rebels at the Eureka Stockade and supervised Ned Kelly's hanging.[72]

George Farlow advises Monash not to worry about what the other volunteers think of him. He has a job to do. 'You are not yet popular with the men', Farlow counsels, '… the first aim is to be firm even to severity so as to make men jump at an order. Cultivate your popularity afterwards.'[73]

Monash incurs 'the serious anger of Colonel Brownrigg' himself for his surliness, and Brownrigg complains about the young upstart to Goldstein. Monash misses the mark with his shooting as well, performing badly on the range with both rifle and revolver.

He is lucky that Goldstein is supportive, 'confidential and not aggressive', and at one stage takes him out for a meal of oysters. Monash sees him as a model for military success: a man with a similar Jewish-Polish background making it in Anglo-Australian society.[74] He remains circumspect, though, when it comes to dealing with Goldstein's second-in-command Captain John Stanley, a brusque 36-year-old from Lancashire, whom Monash regards as a 'brainless idiot'.[75] Stanley can't abide Monash's prickly personality and Monash grows to hate him more and more.

On 22 June 1887, Monash attends a fancy-dress ball at Government House, and a few days later, after a night of 'intense fun ... never to be forgotten', he takes command of a parade by himself. He is so delighted with his success that he calls it a 'little sensational'.[76] Monash is an unabashed social climber, and after another vice-regal function writes that while there were few girls there to chat up he is 'toady enough to like to boast that I was there'.[77]

Meanwhile, his relationship with Ric Burt is deteriorating. After many nights sitting with her by the fireside and hoping for much more, he visits again in late July and is instead greeted in the doorway by a muscular young giant. Ric rather nervously introduces the big lump as 'Gilchrist'. She asks the man to give her and Monash a little privacy and Gilchrist sulks off with a scowl.

'Then she melted into extravagant fondness,' Monash says, 'and wept a good deal.' Amid the tears Ric tells him that Gilchrist is her husband.

The news is almost as astonishing as that which greets Monash back home when Louis, now white-haired and looking much older than his 56 years, does his best to console his gobsmacked son. Louis tells him of his own misadventures with women before he had met Monash's mother. 'My father astonished me by informing me of his cognizance of certain facts,' Monash writes in his diary, 'and forthwith he told me many of his early experiences which still more astonished me.'[78]

The Princes Bridge is taking shape as a thing of beauty, but it's a dangerous workplace for the men whom Munro drives hard.

As night begins to fall on Tuesday, 26 July 1887, Monash watches on as a stone weighing about half a ton is being hoisted into position, with a gathering of men heaving and huffing and groaning underneath it. Then, with a shattering of exploding metal, it bursts from its chains and crashes into a young labourer named Hugh Golden.

Had it fallen directly on him he would have been killed, but instead his ribs are broken and his shoulder and one of his hands are crushed. As quick as he can Monash readies a horse and cart and dashes off with his stricken worker to Melbourne Hospital, on the corner of Swanston and Lonsdale Streets.[79] The horror of the wretched man's broken body 'mangled by a stone' is etched on Monash's consciousness, but he does not forget the demarcation between management and the workers. 'It has considerably affected me,' he says, 'simple minded slave that he was.' Golden survives, but every worker on the bridge knows he will have to watch his step. Even Monash takes a tumble on site. Afterwards he experiences a 'fit of depression' that lasts several days.[80]

Then, on the evening of 15 August, 54-year-old John Bell, an inspector of works at the bridge and one of the pioneers of the Eight Hours Committee that in 1856 won better working conditions for all, loses his footing on some scaffolding and plunges 8 metres into the cofferdam. He suffers massive head injuries and dies two days later.[81]

Monash is spared the sight of it. He is in Bendigo that night, acting as best man and master of ceremonies for a workmate named James Blair, a young surveyor and budding architect. On the way back from St Paul's Church in Sandhurst, Monash makes his move on the two bridesmaids, who look irresistible in their white and blue satin bodices and white lacy skirts.[82] He says they accept his 'caressing advances as a matter of course',[83] and why wouldn't they!

Back home he is now smitten with 20-year-old Ada Krakowski, but also keeping company with John Schild's sister Rosie. He plays Chopin for Rosie at her family's Footscray home and delights her with his card tricks. She is not a very pretty girl, Monash complains; her eyes lack any expression and she has an odd habit of talking to the air in front of her rather than to the handsome young officer in her company. But she is pleasant and he will pursue a friendship with her, aiming to make it more than that.

He also spends time with the Rosenhain and Huntsman families, who hold regular literary evenings, though their ardour for all things German and Jewish wears thin. To make matters worse, he is roped into attending the circumcision ceremony for Minnie and Albert's new baby, Philip. Monash calls it his own 'initiation into this mystery', and while a beaming Albert makes special mention of his cousin in his speech, Monash hides himself in a corner and hopes no one is looking at him.[84] He's had enough of Tante Ulrike and the Roths too and, 'perhaps unworthily', admits that 'truly I am ashamed of my relatives'.[85]

Yet he is proud of his heritage. He has many long, deep conversations on Jewish history with Joel Fredman from the West Melbourne Hebrew School and attends meetings and lectures at the Jewish Literary Society in the Albert Street synagogue. He listens with rapt attention to a lecture on 'Jewish talents and their application' delivered by Theodore Fink, an ambitious young lawyer about to buy the Melbourne *Herald*. Monash tells Fink that 'perhaps some day' he will also give 'these good folk' something worth talking about.[86]

Monash has already urged himself to get his books together 'for a fresh start' at studying, and declares, 'I mean to do it this time.'[87] 'I have no fear of coming exams,' he writes on 7 September 1887, 'and hence a heavy load that has been on my mind for months is removed ... Mathematical problems, which I used to shun, I now court and fight with successfully.' He would give five years of his life to gain the mathematical scholarship on offer in February 1888.[88]

Major Goldstein has long been telling Monash about his beautiful daughter Vida, and Monash has heard a lot about her from Mat, yet 'having looked forward to such an opportunity' for such a long time he is displeased when he finally meets the opinionated 18-year-old feminist.

'I was much disappointed', Monash writes of the girl who will become the first woman in the British Empire to stand for election in a national parliament. 'I found her all too self-possessed and affected, and she plainly did not like me.' Still, he's willing to back his charm over her lack of interest: 'if I can get an uninterrupted half-hour with her, I doubt not I can put myself on a satisfactory footing'.[89]

Instead, with two young boys as chaperones, he goes for an outing with Rosie Schild to her family's rural retreat in leafy Mooroolbark, 35 kilometres west of Melbourne. Nestling by the fire, he tells Rosie how much he respects and cares for her, and soon learns how to play what he calls 'the delicate keyboard of her soul'. Yet Rosie remains cautious, staring deep into his eyes and telling him: 'If I thought you were only playing with my feelings, I should never trust another man.' That stops Monash in his tracks, and he says from that moment she becomes 'sacred' to him.

The next night they take a romantic stroll arm in arm down a lush gorge covered in ferns, and though they are ankle-deep in mud, Monash feels enveloped in the 'most romantic experience' of his life. Rosie stares lovingly at him, kisses him tenderly and tells Monash, 'I loved you from the moment I set eyes on you.'

Next morning he bids Rosie farewell and heads for the station at Ringwood. They are 'satisfied with each other' and Monash is glad that nothing serious happened between them 'for which I could be sorry'. He misses the train and has to walk on to Box Hill, 13 kilometres away. He doesn't mind, though. The day is 'glorious' and he is walking on air. Yet he can't help but feel pangs of regret. He asks himself: 'How long can this last I wonder? … I feel very flattered at the conquest … but vanity what a curse you are … These women are strange cattle without exception.'

In letters to him she calls herself 'Little Tempter' and 'Little Black Devil', and writes of the sand on the back of her dress when he comes to visit. Yet his stirrings for Rosie and their occasional tiffs distract him from work for both his military and university exams. He must put thoughts of her away and fall in love with his studies instead.

As work on the Princes Bridge nears completion, rumours are rife that Monash will be rewarded with control of another Munro project, the Queens Bridge, a few hundred metres away. Monash is so elated by the idea that he can't shut up about it and begins planning the masonry work.[90]

He takes leave to study and late in October 1887 passes his military exams. In November his commission is confirmed. 'At last I may feel safe in the possession of a magnificent prize, the reward of many years of aspiration and hard struggle ... Very little more effort will now be required to ensure my advancement in my military function. Most of my brother officers delighted me by their demonstrative congratulations on my success.'[91]

Being a military officer makes him feel 'quite a man',[92] and Goldstein now becomes a good friend, 'a very smart man with a justifiable amount of humbug'.[93] Only that 'brute Stanley superciliously ignores' Monash's achievement.[94]

His application to his university studies reaps rewards too. He has always been fascinated by mathematics and physics, 'the wonderful process of analysis, of the sense of law, order and sequence in all things physical',[95] and finds that 'as if by inspiration, all the difficulties of conception of the higher mathematical work' vanish with 'a little steady application'.[96]

To inspire himself further he visits the National Gallery, housed inside the State Library on Swanston Street. The Grosvenor Gallery art exhibition is on loan from London and is designed 'to have an educational effect upon Australian taste'.[97] Among the masterpieces on display is Holman Hunt's *The Triumph of the Innocents*. 'I am no judge of art,' says Monash, who is still painting occasionally, '... yet some of these paintings delighted me'.[98]

He passes his five third-year arts subjects. George Farlow and Will Steele also pass and 'thus three friends finish together'. Monash still has to sit for Latin, so long his nemesis, before he can complete his final studies in engineering and enter his profession with what he calls 'full éclat'.[99]

His next examination in February hangs over his head, but for now he is in 'a continuously contented frame of mind': 'Success, and promise of further success attend me. My military position is secure, my University degree within reach and my confidence in my ability and powers of self-restraint are greater than ever before ... Daily my vanity is pandered to on all sides.'[100]

He spends Christmas 1887 with Rosie Schild and her family at a large party at Mooroolbark, and his old flame Jess Robinson is there too. Three's a crowd and there is friction between Monash and Rosie. He is starting to find her volatile and she is irritated by his desire to plan and organise everything, including their regimented walks.

On Christmas morning he decides he'll go walking with Jess Robinson down to a nearby creek, and something happens that he can only hint of in his memoirs: 'an incident ... such as one often hears of but not often realises'.

He patches things up with Rosie and two days later tells her: 'I spent with you the happiest time that I can remember ... Rosie, I do believe you are about the best dose I could recommend to a fellow down in the dumps, your bright spirits are simply irresistible ... I hope you will forgive any ill behaviour or disagreeableness that I have been guilty of. I know I am one of the most unreasonable, selfish wretches on the face of this fair earth.'[101]

Soon after, he and Farlow go walking in the Yarra Ranges, 50 kilometres west of Melbourne, from Lilydale to Fernshaw via Healesville and back, a trip of about 70 kilometres. Out in the bush, the two mates talk of their hopes and desires for the year ahead.

At work, Monash has earned praise and greater responsibility from Munro and he tells Farlow it is 'a genuine pleasure' for him to perceive his '"savoir faire"' in these matters rapidly growing'.[102] He admits he can be high-maintenance, with an innate desire for superiority, and it troubles him that he is still on the outer with many of his co-workers.[103] But how can he inspire confidence if he doesn't display it? Inwardly, he confesses, he is beset by 'moroseness, depression and the blackest pessimism' and is disgusted by his 'own egotistic ... self'.[104]

For a while in early 1888 Monash even falls out with Jim Lewis. Higgins, too, becomes not so much a boss as a rival for praise and position. Monash says he will one day be as good an engineer as Higgins, 'and much else besides', and that though he has a good working relationship with his manager he finds him 'strangely unsympathetic' to his interests. Monash plans to make Higgins fear him and does not think it will be hard.

He even speaks strongly to Higgins about James Blair, the man for whom he was best man in Bendigo. He has no hesitation in talking about his friend behind his back. 'Blair has been taking to himself a lot of credit for my work', Monash fumes. 'I hope Blair won't hear of this treachery – but after all each for himself.'[105]

As far as this young go-getter is concerned, all is fair in business and war. Monash wants the glory for himself.

Chapter 6

There had been some cause for gratification latterly at the manner in which some of my old varsity acquaintances, who used to affect ridicule of me and my efforts, now come forward with apparently sincere congratulations and envious recognition of my success. Pardon the vanity which prompts these expressions.

MONASH, AGED 22, ON THUMBING HIS NOSE AT HIS DETRACTORS[1]

THE SMELL OF GUNPOWDER stings Lieutenant Monash's nostrils on a warm summer's afternoon, even though he is well used to the acrid scent. Six separate parties of the North Melbourne Battery are at rifle practice on the Williamstown range, blasting away at targets 720 metres away. The range is the home of the Victorian Rifle Association, but on Saturdays the militia uses it, employing some of its workers as markers to display hits on the targets.

As the guns bark around him Monash has a lot on his mind. With so many irons in the fire and job opportunities apparently just waiting to be accepted, he has decided against chasing maths honours while working full-time, though Latin has become 'pleasing rather than irksome' and he is full of confidence about his upcoming exams to progress to engineering.

It has not been a good day for the militia, though. Accidents are frequent out here, and there seems scant regard for health or safety for the markers. There is a lot of yelling and consternation after a marker named John Hart suffers superficial wounds from bullet ricochets as Monash's comrades blast away with their breech-loading Martini-Henry rifles. Hart has grazes on his thighs and abdomen, but since there is no first-aid room at the range, the garrison doctor patches him up in the lavatory before sending him home to Bourke Street East.[2]

Captain Stanley is in command but he leaves the range and hands over to Monash, who, deciding to put other men through drills, hands the shooting detail over to Sergeant John Schild. The roar of rifle shots assaults Monash's ears but he takes little notice of the proceedings until one of his soldiers shouts that another man has been hit. It is 42-year-old John James Carter from North Melbourne.[3] Carter has been earning pennies by recording hits and misses on the Number 6 target when a lump of hot .450-calibre lead cuts through his groin and lower abdomen and explodes out of his back below the left shoulder blade. He collapses in a screaming heap. Blood is soaking into the dirt around him as Monash and the others run to his aid. Monash has never seen a man shot before.

The garrison doctor calls for a stretcher, but the only one that can be found is broken and one of the men has to cut a piece of wood to repair it. All this time Carter is moaning and screaming in agony. There is no pillow for the stretcher so the soldiers toss their tunics onto the tattered canvas. Carter is carried into the rifle club pavilion 800 metres away, but there is no casualty room.

Blood gushes from the man and the doctor suspects a ruptured femoral artery. He doesn't want to dress the wound in the lavatory, so he puts Carter on a horse wagon and races with him to North Williamstown Station to wait for the train to Melbourne Hospital.

Monash, fearing the damage to his personal reputation and that of the North Melbourne Battery, immediately reports the tragedy to Captain Stanley. But Stanley tells him to shut up about what's transpired, and under no circumstances is he to appear before any hearing. He also tells him to make sure that everyone knows it is not Stanley's fault.

Carter makes it to Melbourne Hospital but the wound is fatal. There is hell to pay, and Monash complains that he is being bullied at the hands of Colonel Brownrigg's assistant, 37-year-old Englishman Major Peregrine Fellowes,[4] who is demanding answers. Monash is so stressed that he has trouble 'preserving' his 'presence of mind'.[5]

He calls Stanley's behaviour 'cowardly' and 'unfriendly', but follows his advice to stay away from the first day of the inquest. He is then summoned to appear before the Victorian Coroner, 66-year-old Dr Richard Youl, who has made it known many times that he favours flogging, the death penalty and punishing parents who do not control their children.[6]

Monash frets about what he's in for when he takes the stand on Wednesday, 22 February 1888. He tells the coroner that he was in charge of six parties at the range, with five firing and the other group going through drills. 'I had no control over the markers,' he says. 'The Rifle Association engaged them.' He goes on to explain that there are frequently minor accidents at the range such as the injuries caused to John Hart from bullet 'splashes', and these cannot be avoided 'even if the regulations are strictly observed'.[7]

Youl gives him a sharp look. 'Do you think, Lieutenant Monash, that if the markers belonged to the forces, instead of taking Tom, Dick, and Harry, it would be safer?'

'It would be advantageous,' Monash replies. 'Because the officer in charge would then have control over them.' And then, in a statement that is hardly a comfort to Carter's widow, Monash adds, 'And possibly the markers would be a better class of men.'

The jury finds that Carter was accidentally shot.

Monash is relieved that the coroner has been surprisingly 'gentle' on him, and he tells friends that in the end the publicity has 'been a good thing' for his career.[8]

His studies have been totally derailed by the anguish, though. He heads to Dandenong to clear his head and decides not to sit the February exams. Instead he attends the sobering melodrama *Drink* at the Theatre Royal, and as the central character ends up chained in a madhouse for his intemperance, Monash ponders the lesson in what he calls the play's 'severe admonition against infirmity of purpose and weakness of character'. He admits he has once again taken the wrong course, and will not work on his degree again for two and a half years.[9]

He wins another athletics prize 'as usual'[10] – he says – at the annual German picnic, but he is starting to be disturbed by the way other club members are placing pride in their old country above that in their new one. It contributes to the return of his low mood. On 8 March he notes: 'I have not been in the best of health, nor have my spirits been good ... I half fear that I am losing some of the faculties on which I used to pride myself. My music has gone by the wall nor have I the same address in social gathering as formerly.'[11]

Five days later he perks up. The engineering firm Graham and Wadick wins the tender for Melbourne's Outer Circle railway line with a bid of £125,016. They plan to complete work by 30 September 1889.[12] Half in jest, Jim Lewis suggests Monash apply for the job running the construction,[13] even though his lack of experience and the absence of an engineering degree hardly qualify him to oversee the 17 kilometres of track linking Fairfield in Melbourne's north with Oakleigh in the south.

Yet Monash has never shied away from an opportunity and puts forward his application, waiting with 'intense anxiety' for the next few days as a victim of his 'promiscuous confidence'. He lets everyone he meets know that he's in line for the job.[14] It is a massive job too, almost as expensive as the Princes Bridge, and involving not only the building of the rail line but also 25 kilometres of roadworks, a 180-metre-long viaduct over the Yarra at Fairfield, and 16 iron and timber bridges.

But why shouldn't he get it? he reasons. Victoria is undergoing a period of prosperity not seen since the first gold strikes 40 years ago and huge building projects are underway all over Melbourne. Engineers are in huge demand.

Late in March 1888, while he waits on news about his application, Monash is also eagerly looking forward 'to the time when I shall be a commanding officer, with everything in my own way'. With that indefatigable spirit of optimism he heads off with his militia comrades to the Easter Camp at Langwarrin, 40 kilometres south of Melbourne, 'with good health, high spirits and great expectations'.[15] The camp provides him with 'much pleasure and a fair proportion of pain'.[16] He is in his element at the 9-inch cannon drill, commands a guard for the first time, and is captivated by a mock gunboat attack. Yet he quarrels with some of the other officers, who find him a pompous prat and tell him he is not welcome among them. For the second year in a row he goes home with the torpedo men. He writes a letter to one of the officers with a 'circumstantial apology', but adds that 'if however you really wish to quarrel with me, I can't help it having done all on my part that I honourably can'.[17] The apology is accepted.

Monash begins smoking heavily and drinking whisky to wash away his troubles,[18] carousing with his fellow engineering students after their exams and ending up blotto one night at the City Club Hotel. He remains anxious about the Outer Circle job, knowing he isn't really qualified but also realising Melbourne's massive construction boom is his golden opportunity to shine. He tells himself that he has made many valuable contacts through the military, and it's not always what you know but who …

How many other applicants have attended military functions at Government House? Surely his civic duty in defending the colony must count for something.[19]

Whatever the reason, Graham and Wadick decide to put the precocious youngster in charge of one of the biggest engineering assignments in the colony. Monash is overjoyed.

In 'one leap', he says, he has been put 'years ahead of most' of his former colleagues.[20] The pay is £7 a week, more than four times what he was earning when he signed on with Munro just three years ago. He has to pay for his own instruments and for a clerk, but he calculates he will still make £200 a year: a huge pay rise. He will be on three months' probation with a contract for 12 months after that.

Monash hands Munro his resignation, and even though the construction giant has given him his start and then two pay rises, Monash gives Munro a good, swift kick as a parting gift. The tycoon might not have lost such a talent, Monash admonishes, if he been more generous and prompt with recognition and promotion.

'I should have hesitated to take the step,' he tells the autocrat, 'had I had any prospect of speedily bettering myself with you.'[21]

Munro explodes with wrath, telling him: 'I am so much struck with the ungratefulness of your behaviour that I … require you forthwith to leave my employ.'[22]

Monash starts his new job with 'much hesitation and many misgivings', but he is not about to let his bosses or his subordinates know that – projecting an air of confidence, asserting himself at all meetings, taking the credit for any success and striking up a friendship with the government inspector of works. The responsibility emboldens him and he quickly shows Graham and Wadick that he is more than up for the task. He prepares the plans for the works, calculates and directs the earthworks, designs the temporary structures and staging, purchases machinery and negotiates with all the sub-contractors. He assures Professor Kernot that he will be back at the university soon to finish his degree, but he has far more pressing matters at hand.

He attributes his administrative skills on the job site to his military experience, crediting his training in 'the arts of organisation and management of bodies of men'. 'The engineer in charge does not often come into personal contact with the workmen', he explains. 'He deputises all the duties of direct supervision to the different gangers and foremen which answer the non-commissioned officers of the military service and it is in close supervision of these gangers that lies the chief part of my duties.'[23]

Though he revels in the 'position of administrative power', he quickly realises there is little prospect that the company will make any profit from the contract. He has a few conflicts with Graham and Wadick, but they trust his judgment and he is given a free hand. He makes close friends of two junior assistants, Jack Grey and W.B. Shaw, a first cousin of the writer George Bernard Shaw.

For the first time in his life, and only a few years after failing at university because of his wayward behaviour, he feels he is working at full capacity. There is no more idling at the theatre, or practising Mendelssohn or spending all his time reading Bulwer-Lytton or any of the other new novels that had taken his fancy including Fergus Hume's *The Mystery of a Hansom Cab*. No. Monash is now a steamed-up engine working 'at the greatest pressure that I am capable of',[24] and he is finding the work, the responsibility and the praise a 'perfect delight'. Watching the rail line take shape he says is not so much work as almost like a 'perpetual holiday'.[25] Giving orders all day and constantly taking command give him an 'irritability of temper' but the role is a magnificent triumph over the 'blockheads and the envious'. His is the survival of the fittest and the cleverest. The great new responsibilities focus his mind like nothing else has in his 23 years. He admits to friends that in the past he has been nothing but a 'paltry dabbler' and 'nothing that I did was well done'. Now … 'latterly with the narrowing of my sphere and the concentration of energies I am doing each thing better of its kind'.[26]

He strives to be a better person but there are structural weaknesses lurking under his own surface. In his confessional diary on 6 May he admits that he has some serious character flaws: his 'absurd vanity and brutal self-assertion' not only give him 'growing cause for anxiety' but also make him 'ashamed of and disgusted' with himself.

But he fights on, taking pride in his professional achievements and seeing that he is becoming a productive member of society and of commerce. 'I want to try to give the best qualities of my nature the very best opportunities for emphatic development',[27] he writes, remarking later that 'I feel a new sense of dignity and importance as a tangible factor in the production of wealth'.[28]

Monash has never felt so confident, yet his personal life remains turbulent and unsettled. He loves being intimate and amorous with women but is not yet ready to settle down and marry. Most of his girlfriends are Gentiles and he is not about to be pressured into marrying a Jewish girl just for the sake of custom. Morals of the time still frown upon pre-marital sex and he is often in a dilemma about how far to take his liaisons with respectable young women.

He corresponds often with that pert, flirty little temptress Rosie Schild, but not often enough for her liking. Occasionally he dwells upon making a life with her but her temper is unpredictable, she is more mercurial even than him, and after she blows up like a 'barrel of gunpowder' at him for not writing more often, his ardour for her cools once and for all. By April he feels tired of her 'as of all the rest of her sex'.[29] But his weariness over women does not last long.

Soon after starting his new job on the Outer Circle, Monash falls head over heels for a pretty little Ballarat girl named Annie Gabriel. Sexually she is more experienced than him and she is bold and adventurous, 'a pleasant plucky little woman'.[30] Soon he loves her 'fully and deeply', and she is making Monash 'a better man than ever I hoped to be'.[31]

Annie Gabriel becomes the sole object of his life; she pushes all his thoughts of work and a military command to one side. Every chance he gets he is in her arms, kissing her passionately, loving her and telling her of the wonderful life they will share together.

Monash is almost delirious with joy. Annie Gabriel's husband is furious.

Chapter 7

Her praise, applause, and subjugation to my will, which my soul
craves for, she does not give me …
MONASH COMPLAINING ABOUT THE FAULTS OF HIS FIANCÉE
VICTORY MOSS[1]

A NNIE GABRIEL excites Monash more than any other
woman has ever done. She is petite with light brown hair
and her piercing eyes bore straight through his outer shell to his
heart, exposing all his vulnerability and helplessness. In public
he presents a picture of emotional detachment: the intensely
professional, if occasionally volatile engineer; the tightly buttoned
and ambitious artillery officer. Yet in private Annie makes Jack go
weak at the knees.

She is a few weeks older than Monash, the first of John and
Lavinia Hill's children born in Australia after they arrived with
eight older children aboard the *Royal Family* from Derbyshire
to settle in Hope Street, Geelong, in 1863. John Hill took a job
driving an engine in a gold mine near Ballarat, and in 1884 Annie
married Londoner Fred Gabriel with Wesleyan rites at her father's
house.

Just days after Monash is given the reins to drive construction
of the Outer Circle railway he gives Fred a job as his clerk. Fred,

Annie and their two-year-old son, Gordon, take a house near the construction site at Hartwell, about 5 kilometres from the Monash home in Hawthorn. Monash asks to use a room in Fred's house as his site office, but he has more than trains on his mind. As he does whenever he meets an attractive woman, Monash immediately sets out to create a favourable impression on Annie – and she welcomes the attention.

Being close to this good-looking young woman becomes a constant temptation for him, but he assures himself that he only has to turn on his charm to be triumphant in any campaign.

Within a few weeks Monash has been drawn into what he calls 'an altogether novel and embarrassing relationship'.[2] He and Fred keep working together, with the latter seemingly unaware of the developments going on behind his back.

Each day Monash draws up a work schedule, compiling a list of tasks and crossing each one off as it is completed, before finally drawing a vertical line through the whole list when each phase of the project is complete. Meanwhile, he works overtime on Annie.

Despite the conflict he knows is brewing over his love affair, Monash is experiencing 'mental calm' and has developed a 'proud self-respect which makes me altogether happy, and allows me to feel that I am living a full life'. He tells himself that his 'conquest over my tendencies to evil, has been complete'.[3] Of his militia activities, he tells Farlow that he now has 'a very firm footing in the battery both with juniors and seniors'. 'The Major and I are the best of friends,' he explains, 'and I have at last gained that passive influence over him, which you will remember I set myself as an aim to acquire.'[4]

He is gaining more than a passive influence over Mrs Gabriel too, and Fred is becoming increasingly wary of the way his boss and his wife behave around each other: the stolen glances, the nervous discomfort.

One cold winter's day in July 1888, Fred catches them keeping warm by huddling together on the bank of the Yarra at Hawthorn. Fred charges up to them, taking them by surprise.

He's a little terrier and looks ready to bite. But the two young lovers manage to placate his fury by explaining that they were just having an innocent conversation. And it *is* awfully cold.

All of his senses tell Fred they're lying, but he gives them the benefit of the doubt. He tells himself to watch everything they do.

Monash gains a sneaking joy, not just from the comfort that little Annie brings him, but also from the knowledge that he is outwitting her husband. The chess master is taking Fred's queen. Monash and Fred keep working in the room at Hartwell with Annie watching on in silence. She and Monash communicate with gestures behind Fred's back and Monash is aroused by the delicious excitement. As Monash and Fred work late into the night Annie is never far away, taking more interest than ever in their work and especially in everything Monash has to say.

They pass notes like schoolchildren, and in August Monash begins to express his feelings in passionate love letters. Annie watches with furtive pride as he marches, so upright and proud, in that smart uniform at the opening of Melbourne's Centennial Exhibition on 1 August 1888.

Monash thinks Fred is a good worker but self-assertive and obviously not particularly bright or observant. Fred likes a drink too, and one night when he has drunk himself into a stupor, Annie and Jack sneak off together.

They become careless. Fred finds one of Monash's love letters. He attacks Annie. He threatens to keep Gordon for himself and 'send her adrift' – back in disgrace to her parents in Ballarat.

Annie is terrified of losing her son and begs Monash to do something. As much as it pains the young military man, he swallows his pride. He humbles himself 'deeply' before Fred 'for her sake' and stands before him 'on the evidence' that he and 'Annie concerted between us'.

'I am less than a rogue,' he tells the aggrieved husband, who holds himself back from punching Monash in the face. 'I am a fool and a brainless idiot.' Monash doesn't believe that for a second but he tells Fred what he wants to hear: that their brief tryst was all

Monash's fault, that Annie is utterly blameless and that he repents of the terrible wrong he has done to both of them.[5]

Fred agrees that Monash is a fool but he says his wife is even worse. He has to think long and hard about his marital situation and the breaking of trust. Eventually he calms down. Monash is such a charming fellow, after all. And also his boss. Fred says Annie can stay but she's on her last warning.

Monash ponders his dilemma. He could, he supposes, turn off the charm, but why should he when he's so irresistible to women?

'Shall I repel her for her own good?' he asks himself in his diary. 'Or shall I risk worse hereafter?' He risks worse.

Slowly the tension between the three is released. Fred begins to trust his boss again. He enjoys his job and now that the misunderstanding over Annie is behind them he finds Monash easy company.

They agree to share the expenses of taking over Hartwell House, an abandoned estate in the area, as their headquarters, and to rent out a paddock for agistment and to run poultry for market. But while Fred seems to have forgiven Monash, he takes out his frustration on Annie and is frequently abusive. She plans to flee the whole sordid mess and race back to Ballarat.

To Monash, Fred has become nothing more than a 'bully and coward', and he wants not only to protect the love of his life from a man he sees as a thoughtless oaf, but also to keep her for himself no matter how messy the situation. He is guided by his own principles and his own desire.

He begs Annie to stay, making all sorts of promises from the heart. 'I would not be surprised if I shall keep. For I have won from her all that I ever desire in my life.'[6]

He re-establishes 'a perfect mutual understanding' with her and together they wait for an opportunity. When Fred, ignoring what has previously happened in his absence, journeys to Ballarat to buy poultry, Monash and Annie make hay together for 'two happy days – and nights'.

Monash seems to have the answer to any crisis. When Annie fears she is pregnant he takes advice from his old pal Joe Miller, now a doctor.

On 7 October he writes in his diary: 'Firmly established and content in my professional position, successful in my work, secure in my military rank, and with gradually improving financial condition I have little cause for anxiety. Morally I have made a greater advance in the few months than in all the years that preceded. With every evil tendency allayed or checked, with the thirst for applause gone ... I am living through happy days of work and love.'

He is reunited with Jeanette Blashki on the anniversary of their break-up, and even though he has been busy for months stealing another man's wife he complains that Jeanette made 'the most indiscreet advances' and told him, 'Jack, your only fault is that you make people like you, without thinking of the consequences.'

He can think of no reply except to say, 'How very true.'[7]

Later that month, as Fred naively heads to Sydney for a week, Monash and Annie become like man and wife, reaching a point of 'mutual confidence' beyond anything Monash has ever dreamed of. They hit the town together arm in arm, Monash in his bright red tunic and Annie the most wondrous creature he has ever met. He experiences 'the greatest happiness I have known, a happiness so great that I cannot hope ever to meet the like again'.[8]

When Fred returns and realises he's been duped yet again, he can't control his rage. Annie's mother comes to Melbourne and takes her back to Ballarat. Fred lets Monash know he wants to kill his boss but Monash is only worried about his sweetheart. 'I little realised how my love had grown upon me', he confesses.[9]

He writes passionately to Annie: 'What have I to live for if your love is gone? ... Night after night, I have lain awake thinking, thinking – calling up one by one all the moments of happiness you have brought me ... hearing the sound of your voice, feeling the touch of your lips ... and my whole soul went out to you ... Annie, my love, my darling – come back to me – be mine again.'[10]

Each day he rides home from Hartwell to Hawthorn at lunchtime, hoping to find an adoring reply in the mail. Once when thinking of his darling he 'absent mindedly' crashes into a dray and falls over the front of his own trap.[11] He is perpetually sour and anxious in Annie's absence, and he and Fred avoid each other for some time.

In November, the labourers on the Outer Circle go on strike in vain for higher pay, and Monash is brutal in his assessment of them. Growing up in Jerilderie he saw hardship aplenty, but now he thinks himself above all that. The workman of Melbourne, he says, 'goes on the false doctrine that there is strength in numbers only. Thus he collects himself into a crowd and says "We don't like work, we prefer to loaf, let us have a strike" ... so he throws down his shovel, and rages about the country, clamouring, getting drunk, and fighting and when all his money is gone ... he begins to feel what a fool he has made of himself, he gets sober ... and humbly begs to be allowed to work again.'

Monash believes there is a recognised price for labour and when money is tight the wages should go down rather than up.[12] He has no sympathy for the striking workmen, telling Will Steele: 'Today I stopped at one of the cuttings at noon owing to the blinding dust. By 4 o'clock the place was strewn with drunken beasts, lying in the hotels and public roads. You lose all respect for them as men. If you tried any reforming influences they would only laugh at you.'[13]

Annie returns to Melbourne in mid-December, after a few weeks' convalescence, and she and Fred work on some sort of reconciliation. Monash and Fred agree to continue working together, though the relationship is strained to the limit by Fred's suspicions – well-founded, as Monash is not one to give up without a fight.

His love for Fred's wife has never waned and he writes so many secret letters pouring out his heart to Annie – 115 of them, amounting to 200,000 words – that she feels like she is being stalked. She tries to pour cold water on his desire by reminding him that she is a married woman, after all, and that Fred might actually have meant what he said about killing Monash if he caught them together again. Occasionally Monash convinces Annie to see him for a brief rendezvous, but their time together is brief, unsatisfying, fretful.

'If I lost your love ...' he gushes, 'I would die morally – go downhill and be utterly lost ... the sole object of my life ... my love, my mate, my wife in all but name ...'[14]

She reminds Monash every time that she has her little son, Gordon, to worry about. What will he think, years down the track, and what will her parents say? Still, just having her nearby brightens Monash's mood, and he remains hopeful that she will leave Fred so they can be together, forever. Fred watches Monash and Annie constantly, so much so that Monash despairs that 'he can see and hear through stone walls' and makes 'the shrewdest guesses'.[15]

Monash explains to her new legislation regarding divorce and the prospects of starting a new life together. To give her time to think things over, he undertakes another long walk with George Farlow. As they trek 80 kilometres through the Yarra Ranges from Healesville up to Marysville and then down to Warburton, Monash talks about Annie non-stop.

It has been an eventful year and the stress on his physical condition is telling. He walks at a slow, deliberate pace of about 5 kilometres an hour and needs frequent stops.

On the last day of 1888, Monash writes in his diary that Annie's return has meant a 'happy close' to a happy year. 'My material advancement has been rapid, and I can look back with ecstatic self-satisfaction on exceptional difficulties and obstacles overcome ... I have learned to bear worry and anxiety more easily, and to look boldly into the face of a difficulty. In my moral nature too, I have gained much that is worth gaining – increased self-respect and consciousness of power, increased strength of will, and ease of self-denial – and have lost much that was harmful – much of my old brutal selfishness of purpose, and personal egotism.'[16]

Monash has never been able to master his Bar-Lock typewriter, and continues to write thousands and thousands of words by hand to Annie, swearing his undying love. He tells her that she can help him realise his full potential. He has 'stores of energy' within him, he announces, and 'great ambitions' taking shape. He promises her that 'the best efforts of my life will be devoted to doing what I can for my native land and its people. Just wait a few years, till my early struggles are over, and see what I will do.'[17] One day when he becomes a great man, she can tell others it was because of her love and inspiration. How could any woman resist such a chance?

He is elected to the Naval and Military Club in January 1889 and tells Farlow that his commission is 'a pleasant and most enviable possession ... It gives a man social position and tone and is an excellent advertisement.'[18]

At work he and Fred circle each other mentally. Monash suspects Fred has 'some deep plot maturing' but is confident he can outsmart him.[19]

He is not prepared for Fred's surprise attack.

He and Annie are again in each other's arms at Studley Park in Kew on 16 March 1889, unaware that Fred has followed them. As they canoodle, Fred comes hurtling over a hill above them like a charging cavalryman. Monash is sent tumbling as the two men grapple over Monash's walking stick. Annie screams in terror but Fred drags her down to the Johnston Street bridge. Monash follows from a distance, yet does not try to rescue her, he explains later, for fear of making the scandal more public. However, as Fred, 'very violent in his language', pushes Annie onto a tram, Monash jumps on as well, and the three combatants go at it hammer and tongs in a furious row, startling passengers, until all three jump off at Smith Street, Collingwood, 5 kilometres away.

Annie manages to escape Fred's clutches, but he tracks her down the next day. He asks her father to help him scare off Monash, and John Hill sends the young artillery officer a furious letter.

Fred takes Annie to the train station to send her back to her parents, away from temptation, but Monash is lurking in the shadows watching her departure. He jumps into a horse-drawn cab, tells the driver to 'Follow that train', and races across town to North Melbourne. His plan to leap upon the non-stop express as it rushes by is thwarted when he stumbles and falls on his face.[20]

Yet the battle has just begun.

Fred furiously hands in his notice and warns Monash that he's serious about causing him great harm if Monash goes near Annie one more time. Instead, Monash dashes off a note to her in Ballarat, telling her he will help her pursue a legal separation.

Fred, fed up with Annie and the whole sorry mess, approaches Louis Monash to say he'll leave Victoria without his wife for the right price. Louis does not respond. Monash mopes, and says Annie's love 'will leave its mark on me for the rest of my life'.[21]

He writes to her to say that when he took the Outer Circle job he was so lonely that he only wanted to bury himself in hard work, to be like a machine, like all the other working men. That was until Annie came along: 'a woman who looked into my soul and understood me.'[22]

> There came into my life ... a love which I soon knew was to be the great passion of my life, and then ... came back with a rush, all my old ambitions, all my old incentives and motives, and with them all a new motive greater than all the rest – the motive to try to be a good man worthy of the love and the trust of a good woman – I learned to be kindly in word and deed, to be pure in thought, unselfish in action ... Annie ... I want to be allowed to care for you, support you, help you bring up your boy, help you always to have a comfortable home and want for nothing.[23]

The letter has the desired effect, and six days later, with Fred none the wiser, Annie and Monash spend the day together in Ballarat and Buninyong, where 'all passed off splendidly'.[24] They cannot risk such a meeting again for more than nine weeks.

But Monash's 'undying' love gets untracked during the absence. He is not one to sit around idly waiting. He keeps going to dances and says a girl named Lizzie Smith falls in love with him almost 'at once'. Evie Corrie becomes jealous at the way he waltzes with Jeanette Blashki. He can offer no argument whatsoever when Evie's sister, Amy Corrie, tells him, 'No one can see much of you without loving you.'

Evie whispers in Monash's ear that they should have a 'love affair', and after a nano-second to think about it he heartily agrees. She says they should 'set a voluntary limit' to their ardour, but while it lasts 'throw aside all constraint, and enjoy a passionate love making'.

Monash accepts, though he tells himself that it's 'more for her sake than my own, for though the touch of a beautiful girl's lips is enticing to a young man, yet I cannot love two women at once'. Annie is still uppermost in his mind, but at a party two weeks later he enjoys himself 'fully' with Evie for hours, hidden away from prying eyes in a dark staircase, admitting that he just cannot 'deny myself the pleasure of [Evie's] adoration'.

'That dark-haired Devil' Rosie Schild is tough to fend off too, and they spend an evening at his office in Camberwell. He tells her that as a Jew he has 'a racial disability to marry her' but they can still have some fun. It's a handy escape clause. Monash has not worried about upsetting his family in his relationship with Annie or any of the other Gentiles. And as far as Rosie is concerned, who said anything about marriage? 'I am not afraid of harming Rosie,' he admits; 'she is well scorched and a woman of the world.' Monash revels in his appeal to women. He is educated, well-spoken, polite, confident and has promising careers in engineering and the military. The smart officer's uniform doesn't hurt his prospects on the dance floor, either.[25] Kitty Lunday, a waitress at the Victoria Coffee Palace, calls him her 'dear soldier boy'.

*

At the end of May, Fred brings Annie back to Melbourne. She tells him she now realises her place is with her husband and son, but Fred is taking no chances. He forbids Annie to approach or communicate with Monash.

To no avail. Monash is soon getting notes to Annie, telling her they should be together. Rosie becomes his accomplice, willing to do anything to please him. He has her running messages for him and keeping Fred occupied while he chases Annie.

Meanwhile, Monash keeps all options open and remains a regular on the social circuit. He has passed his captain's exam and is pushing for another promotion. He makes a formal submission to Major Goldstein, asking for more money for the Garrison Artillery, and calling for more and longer drills. He wants practice of up to a day's duration in Victoria's forts under war conditions, pay incentives for the men and greater status for non-commissioned officers.[26] He receives no response but he makes a start at throwing his increasing weight around in military affairs.

Even though his ties to the German Club are fraying because his sympathies are becoming 'too English' for the other members, he heartily agrees with a lecture by Rabbi Isidore Myers that the younger Jews of Melbourne have to take action 'to prevent the extinction of purely Jewish feeling'.[27]

It is at a German Club dance on 22 June that Monash meets 20-year-old Jewish girl Hannah Victoria Moss. She calls herself 'Victory'. Monash calls her Vic. He met her and her older sisters Sa[28] and Belle[29] seven years earlier, in 1882, while on holiday at Portsea, but at this dance his 'attention is particularly engrossed by Vic. Moss'.

'I sought an introduction – a thing I seldom do – and found my name was very familiar to her,' he says. 'In a very few moments we were excellent friends ... she made a striking impression on me, and I am longing to meet her again.'[30]

Vic is a striking young woman, almost as tall as him, dark and elegant, with an hourglass figure. She shares Monash's love for classical music. Her late father was the London-born Moton Moss, who came to Australia as a young man in the 1820s and became a prosperous merchant, mining investor, gold broker, insurance agent and landowner. By the 1870s he was a property investor with hotel interests and a 'well known money lender' of 3 Alfred Street, Carlton.[31] One newspaper calls him a ruthless 'Modern Shylock', claiming that while most 'Melbourne Hebrews ... are to the fore in every work of charity and mercy' Moss is 'almost a solitary exception'. 'There is scarcely a Jew in Melbourne that cares to own Moss as one of the race.' After he petitions a court to sell the furniture of a widow to repay a loan to him, *Punch* says Melbourne's Jews are now 'more ashamed of him than ever'.[32] When he was 53 Moss married 25-year-old Rebecca Alexander in Sydney. Moton was 69 when Vic was born and 79 when he died of a stroke. Vic has older brothers but has been raised by her two sisters from the age of 13 after their mother died in 1882, and in the last couple of years has developed into one of the most stylish of Melbourne's smart young set. She is also combustible.

Soon after their first meeting, Monash and Vic dance again at a German Club social, where Monash attaches himself to Vic and her chaperone, making 'much advance in their good graces'.[33]

He puts on a show of cool composure for Vic, but has confided in his diary that the 'total collapse' of his 'close companionship with Annie' has caused him merely to exist rather than to live.[34] His father has been ill and in a low mood, and Monash complains that Louis 'is too absorbed in his own broken hearted nature to care much' for his son's misery.[35]

He tells Annie he thinks about shooting himself because he misses her love so much[36] – even though he has never really contemplated such a thing. But his pathetic pleas melt Annie's heart. She and Monash rekindle their affair.

Yet now, when Monash is with Annie, he can't stop thinking about Vic, his 'new goddess'.

Just two nights after his first passionate embrace with Annie in oh so long, and while she is with Fred and young Gordon at their lodgings in Abbotsford, Monash trips the light fantastic with Vic at another dance at the Town Hall.

'I bespoke her for several dances, and she signalised her pleasure in my company by stealing a few more. I thus had an opportunity of studying her more carefully. But she is almost too clever for me, and nearly turned the tables completely on me, by making me disclose myself to no purpose. She is a woman far beyond her years – and has a disposition startlingly akin to my own.'[37]

Somehow, despite his busy social life and tangled relationships, Monash still finds time for work and intellectual pursuits. And the military. He has improved his relationship with his fellow officers thanks to 'a little circumspection of manner', and has become such a friend of John Stanley that this former enemy details all his marital woes to Monash in 'a most appalling and extensive confidence of his own domestic unhappiness … which evoked my genuine and fervent pity … Here again is another household with a skeleton.'[38]

In July, Joe Miller is promoted to captain and Monash becomes the senior subaltern. At Stanley's suggestion he has started work on his 'first piece of mechanical design', a wooden practice model of the new breech-loading 5-inch cannon that replaces one of the big old muzzle-loaders guarding Victoria's ports. Monash hopes his ingenuity will lead to a rapid promotion, but he will have to be patient.

On 29 July 1889 he lectures at the Jewish Literary Society on one of his pet subjects, 'Mohammedanism', and afterwards in his diary is not backward in praising 'the great change that a few years have wrought in the nervous boy of former times': 'To my military life I owe much of the change. I got through my subject, listened with gratification to the flattering comments, made my brief reply and all was over. I was the gainer in the esteem of many people, and gained an advertisement by brief reports (written by myself at the German Club in company with Isidore Myers and the secretary Marks) in the morning papers.'[39]

Two days later, on 1 August, he is supervising the positioning of heavy stones on bridgework at Fairfield when a rope snaps, and a huge stone crashes down inches from his head: 'I seemed to live over all my life in a flash ... By good luck I was paralysed with a moment's hesitation; had I moved a step it would have been all over with me.' Monash escapes injury but a mason has his hand crushed, and it takes nearly an hour to stop the bleeding before Monash can race him to hospital.[40]

The accident sets off a chain of calamitous events that will change the direction of Monash's life.

He is soon convinced that Vic is 'very much in love' with him but he wonders about 'her inner nature'. 'I doubt if she has much softness, or any of that womanliness, which Annie possesses in such a degree. Our conversation [has been] mainly by way of fencing – each waiting for the other.'[41]

Yet he begins writing to Vic, and soon is finding his affair with Annie, the woman he could never live without, 'a little oppressive'. He and Mat are invited to the Moss home, where he plays the piano beautifully and astonishes everyone with his card tricks, yet he senses that Vic 'cannot understand the full force of my character'.[42]

The strain of his torn love begins to show. He develops a heavy cold. His father becomes dangerously ill and Monash has to administer a catheter. He has more women in his life than he can handle, and in doing his best to douse Evie's designs on him, fobs her off by saying he is in 'a very miserable, discontented state of mind' and that the 'illness in our house' revives memories of his mother's death.[43]

While Monash weighs up his options, Annie rocks his world on 23 August by suddenly agreeing to leave Fred and run off with Monash to begin a new life together:

> ... her sudden offer of willingness to come to me staggered me, and like a coward I pretended not to understand. Yet the idea has taken root, and although I know that such a

step means for me the ruin of my whole future, yet I would sooner take it with all its terrible risks and dangers than break my faith with Annie. Since meeting Vic – who fulfils in my estimation all the requirements of a suitable wife to me – dim visions of a home life, and a finality to all my present struggles have been assuming a prominent place in my thoughts. The two possibilities that are before me I have been vainly trying to reconcile.[44]

He feels 'the most real, and harmful mental agony' he has ever known, an agony compounded two days later when Vic and her elder sister Belle come to his home and Monash once again runs a critical eye over Vic, assessing their prospects as a couple, and comparing her with Annie.

Vic seems eager to please, but Monash says he doubts she 'could subjugate herself' sufficiently to suit his temperament. Annie is his first love, 'my true love and I think the only love of my life'.[45]

All his relatives urge him to forget the married Mrs Gabriel and pursue a marriage with Vic. Monash spends the next few sleepless nights weighing up 'Annie and infamy' against a 'reputable home of my own'.[46]

'If there is such a thing as love in my cold, calculating, material and unidyllic temperament [Annie] has it all,' he tells Will Steele, '[but] I have met … a young girl – of surpassing beauty … a girl altogether of my liking – and deeply in love with me to boot.'[47]

On 28 August he meets with Annie to plan their escape but second thoughts cloud his mind. He is 'fearfully agitated' because 'the real risks and dangers have never been so plain'. He is prepared to take the plunge but fears he will sink forever because of it.[48] His feet are cold. He tries to convince himself that he's doing the right thing but admits to himself that he is now 'half-hearted'. He puts on a brave face for Annie but tells her how dangerous it will be, secretly hoping that his warnings 'may affect the strength of her determination'. His nerves are in a tangle.

Then Annie tells him she's pregnant. To Fred.

What more can go wrong? He dashes off a secret note, the most important words he has ever put on paper.

'This is the crisis of our lives,' he tells Annie, 'if you are prepared to trust yourself and your child to me for the rest of your life, come now at once to Hawthorn … Decide now once and for all. Everything depends on your present decision.'[49]

He gets no reply. Fred has foiled him again. Ever watchful, Fred has intercepted the note and spirited Annie away. Monash suspects it might be for the best. He hopes Annie is sick of the stress as well.

'The end, or what is very near it, has come at last', he writes on 6 September. 'There has been a great collapse, and a complete downfall of my pretty castle of cards … If she does return, I have perfected plans to help her to what extent she chooses; if she does not choose, then she can go for good and all, and I can feel I have come out with unbroken faith, and much the injured party.' Yet he promises himself that if Annie still wants him he will go away with her even if it means his 'ruin'.[50]

The next night Monash takes Vic to the theatre.[51]

Finally Annie decides. She chooses Monash. He doesn't know whether to laugh or cry. He hopes that writing down his emotions will help him think more clearly, and on Friday, 13 September he notes he is now 'face to face with a great crisis in my life'.

He will turn his back on his family, on centuries of Jewish heritage, on all that he has worked for, to run off with a married woman and her son. Has he gone mad?

The more he dwells on what he is about to do, the more he realises the pain it will bring him. Yet a promise is a promise. He spends most of the day making plans for their escape.

That night, with Fred away on an errand, Monash takes his buggy to Annie's lodgings to collect her and her bags for their mad dash into an uncertain future. As quickly as they can, they drive on to collect her son, Gordon, staying with a friend, looking over their shoulders the whole time.

They make it to South Yarra Station with freedom just a train ride away. Then, 'like a thunderbolt the ubiquitous Fred', with a bigger head of steam than the waiting locomotive, appears out of nowhere and punches Monash fair in the face. The attack is so sudden Monash is 'straight away robbed of every resource'.

A big crowd of onlookers soon gathers to witness the commotion. As Monash tries to clear his foggy head, Fred drags his screaming wife away and pushes her roughly into a waiting horse cab. Monash grabs the reins and tries to stop the horse and driver, but too late.

Annie's white face becomes a mask of terror. 'Save me, Jack, save me,' she cries as the horse gallops away.

'All will be right, Annie,' Monash calls out. 'You know what to do!'

As soon as Annie is out of sight, Monash realises he is seriously hurt. His vision is blurred and one of his eyes is beginning to swell badly. He's groggy, but despite offers of assistance from the onlookers he wanders up and down the street in 'aimless despair'.

Yet even in the midst of this tumult something tells him it will be for the best. 'My first feelings were those of intense relief' and 'the resolve, there and then to dismiss all from my mind'.[52]

So Monash looks up Rosie Schild. The following afternoon, on the banks of the Yarra, she kisses his black eye better, and while he is the subject of much mirth and gossip at work and at home over his behaviour and his humiliating defeat, within a few days he is celebrating the end of the affair.

He writes long notes in his diary detailing every aspect of his relationship with Annie and Fred. He suspects somehow that he has been predestined for greatness and he wants every aspect of his life, the triumphs and the shame, documented for posterity.

'My great longing for her is gone', he writes, adding that he would open his arms to her if she came back, 'yet I care not if I never see her again'.[53]

Fred takes Annie and Gordon to Sydney and makes a new home for them in Marrickville. Annie writes to Monash, castigating him for not staying in contact. Monash apologises for everything, for failing to keep her from Fred's clutches and for not following through with his promise to rescue her. He invents a story that he was confined to bed for several days after the incident at the station and was not able to pursue them. He arranges with Karl Roth, now living in Sydney and down on his luck, to help Annie escape if she wants to, but in December she writes a 'Dear John' letter to Monash, saying she has come to her senses and will stay with her husband.

Their daughter Dora Madeleine Gabriel is born in Marrickville in 1890. Fred and Annie will remain together for more than 40 years.[54]

Meanwhile, Monash has his own future mapped out.

Now that Eva Blashki has realised she can do without Monash's love she marries a German-born Fitzroy dentist named Siegfried Pincus. Rabbi Dr Joseph Abrahams performs the ceremony at her father's house on 18 September 1889 and Monash is especially charming with Vic by his side, even though his black eye is still a little puffy and he has to quash the rumours Vic has heard about its cause. He confides to her that he can be a bit full of himself and that he has a 'strange knack of repelling people'.[55]

The next night Monash and Vic play piano duets of Haydn symphonies. They make beautiful music together; Monash feels he can relax in her company and does not need to pretend. He tells Vic, 'there is something about you that banishes from my manner the least attempt at artificiality, and I only appear to you as my own clumsy natural self'.[56] He wants to make their arrangement permanent and yet the very next day visits Evie Corrie, admitting 'how great a temptation there is for me here'.[57]

No challenge seems too great for him now. Soon after Eva's wedding, he is the centre of attention inside the North Melbourne Garrison's orderly room when he lectures for 45 minutes on gun-laying – the aiming of artillery pieces – to Melbourne's three metropolitan batteries. He has hardly done any preparation for the talk but is regarded by senior officers as an expert. He later describes the moment he stepped forward to speak as 'a supreme one in my life. I was buoyed into full power by the importance of the occasion and felt a perfect rapture in the sense of perfect self-possession.'[58]

The new commander of the Victorian Artillery forces, Lieutenant Colonel Douglas Dean Pitt,[59] tells Monash 'it was one of the best lectures on Elementary Artillery I have ever heard'. Monash tells Vic the audience came 'to scoff but remained to praise'.[60]

Vic shows little interest when Monash proudly shows her the Princes Bridge and all the work he performed on one of Melbourne's great structures, yet 'the touch of her fingers' caressing him makes his 'blood go a little faster'.

'If she can awaken a real live spark of love,' he tells himself, 'it will soon blaze into a flame that will astonish her.'[61]

On 4 October she calls him 'Jack' instead of 'John' for the first time when they go to a German Club ball. Monash has to fend off a rival suitor who becomes all too familiar with his girl, and that night he makes up his mind to pop the question.

'I will throw myself entirely on her mercy — tell her my position and leave her to judge for herself.'[62]

The next day he proposes. She accepts.

Yet as they stroll by the Yarra arm in arm, he wonders already if he has done the right thing. Vic shows 'little emotion of any kind, her frigidity laid chains on my tongue, and I felt full of all kinds of doubts and misgivings'.[63] Vic is not as exciting as Annie Gabriel and she is always nagging him about all the other women he has kissed.

Which brings Monash to his next crisis.

He has a variety of social events on the calendar and has to 'resort to all sorts of devices and subterfuges' to prevent Vic from meeting his many past girlfriends.

He does not take her to the North Melbourne Battery Ball because Evie and Amy Corrie will be there, though Vic later learns that Monash and Evie have shared many dances. At the same ball Monash clashes with the now 'very rude' Jeanette Blashki, firing back at her attacks with 'severe retaliation'.[64]

Table Talk runs the engagement announcement of 'Miss Victory Moss, of South Yarra to … Lieutenant Monash, of Hawthorn',[65] yet they are hardly a happy couple. Vic hears all the rumours about the other girls and about his fling with Annie.

Monash takes Vic to the 1889 Melbourne Cup, where they watch an apprentice jockey named Jack Anwin steer Bravo to victory over the mighty Carbine. The excitement of the great upset and of being among 85,000 racegoers pressed into Flemington seems to bring Monash and his fiancée much closer. 'In the new light of passionate love,' Monash writes, 'my whole nature warmed towards her in an altogether new degree.'[66]

She is not perfect, he reasons, but he assures himself that with hard work he can mould her into the ideal submissive wife for an officer and a gentleman.

'I tried to let her feel, in a gentle way, that much was wanting in her nature', he says. Vic tells him that she will watch and learn the ways of the world from him. But is she being sarcastic? He's not sure.[67] They have a powerful physical attraction to each other but are very different people. He is a student with a hunger for knowledge, whose hard work helps keep his extended family fed. She has inherited money to live on and has wealthy relatives. She likes going to parties and being the belle of the ball. He devours books, makes lists, works incessantly. She tells him she doesn't like reading but prefers to learn from observation. Still he promises to 'persevere until I wake up in her the thirst for light'.[68]

Monash goes hiking again with George Farlow, covering 200 kilometres of rugged mountain country from Toongabbie up to Walhalla and across to Healesville. Walhalla is the most beautiful place Monash has ever seen, yet all the way his mind is clouded with doubts about Vic.

When he gets back to Melbourne he subtly suggests, in the nicest possible way, that Vic should be more of a shadow for him than an equal. He is uncomfortable with her boldness and flirtatious manner with other men. Her independent streak makes him nervous.

Little wonder that he is soon complaining about her 'ruthless faultfinding'. He is cautious with his savings; she is 'frivolous'. Their love is turning to war. There is no way Vic will play the subordinate to this part-time lieutenant with a runaway ego.

'In Vic I see the outward embodiment of my physical ideal. But in her moral nature I have been bitterly deceived and disappointed. These feelings lie in the great and perhaps irredeemable deficiencies in her nature. She is no mental companion for me … she is most difficult to lead and instruct, and repels all my attempts to do so. I have battled with her now for three months, and nightly leave her side, disappointed, defeated, miserable.'[69]

In April 1890 he tells her that it might be best if she is left to 'seek her pleasure alone' so he can spend his spare time in 'pursuits more congenial to me than gadding about, or listening to her rebukes'.[70]

He earns more favourable treatment from the military and the press, who praise his design for the model practice cannon. After an introduction from Stanley, who Monash now reckons will become 'a rattling good CO', he has shown his design to 'a very interested' Colonel Frederick Sargood, the former defence minister, and on 22 April 1890, Monash is again the focus of attention when he unveils his model at the North Melbourne drill room for a team of dignitaries that includes James Bell, the Minister of Defence, General Alexander Tulloch, Victoria's military commandant, and Colonel Dean Pitt.

Monash is chuffed that the top brass 'saw the new model gun in work, and expressed themselves perfectly satisfied with it'. They plan to place a copy of the new practice gun in every garrison artillery drill room in the colony.

'Its conception is due to Major Stanley', one newspaper reports. 'He … entrusted the working out of such an idea to one of his officers, Lieutenant J. Monash, C.E., whose professional qualifications enabled him to approach the task with a due regard for both military and mechanical requirements. The whole design, and all the details of construction, were left entirely in the hands of the latter.'[71]

Despite the praise, Monash is disappointed that he receives no patent or bonuses for his design, no royalties, and just £140 to cover his expenses. 'Such is the gratitude of the paternal state', he laments, but at least he has enhanced his reputation among the senior officers.

Stanley leaves the battery for a position as a staff officer, and while Monash encourages Joe Miller to apply for the new command so that Monash might also be elevated to captain, the top job goes to postal official Frank Outtrim, brother of the ambitious politician Alfred Outtrim. Monash feels Frank is 'an indulgent and kindly man' but 'quite unfit for military command'.[72]

Monash's command on the Outer Circle powers ahead despite repeated alterations and on 30 May 1890 the Oakleigh to Camberwell section of the track opens.[73] His relationship with Vic is in danger of derailing, though, and by July he is sick of the constant fighting. She is too.

He tells Vic that if she wants to break off the engagement that's fine by him.[74] They make up but in August she demands to go to the theatre without him and he tells her sarcastically that she is obviously seeking 'any form of distraction rather than incur the tediousness of a few hours alone' with him. He can no longer imagine a quiet home life with her.[75]

He tries to put all of this domestic wrangling into the back of his mind when invited to read his paper 'The Superintendence of Contracts' to the Engineering Students' Society at Melbourne University on 22 August 1890. Despite not yet having his degree, he is a commanding speaker on the subject, telling the final-year students that the buck stops with them, and that they alone will carry the can if a project does not work out. They must have confidence in their abilities and, while having complete administrative control, should be guided by 'expert foremen, without any sacrifice of dignity or loss of prestige'.

He details all the hazards and harassments the engineer will face from government inspectors, from pointing out that 'some bridge or culvert five miles away is being built upside down', to fickle weather, reluctant labourers and know-all employers who have to be handled carefully to prevent them from blundering into trouble. He gives insights into how to delegate and how best to work with site managers, accountants, storekeepers, foremen, navvies, messengers and watchmen. He advises the students to keep meticulous records, just as he does, copying every letter and document, to always carry a notebook and to keep all records until a contract is complete so as to resolve any disputes. His lecture will soon be published as a pamphlet.[76] Professor Kernot insists that now, more than ever, Monash must finish his course.

The following night he and Vic quarrel 'over a trifle'. 'How selfish I have grown', he says, seeing his fiancée 'writhe' under his sneers.

He hates himself for the way he behaves, but that doesn't stop him. He and Vic go at it again in September. Monash writes her a 'hot and bitter letter' and Vic tells him the wedding is off. She wants him out of her life.

'The quarrelling of the last few months,' she explains, 'has told on me more than you think.' He has damaged her self-confidence and she says they should go their separate ways to both 'endeavour to live a peaceful life'.[77]

Monash backs off. He gives her space. He promises never again to utter a 'word of reproach or complaint'. He says that if she really wants to break off the engagement he will leave Melbourne forever and take the blame for everything. They make up again.

On 18 October Vic shows off her latest outfit at the Caulfield Cup despite Monash's insistence that she stay home to honour the fifth anniversary of his mother's passing. They then fight over how much time they should each spend visiting their sisters, and on 30 October Vic refuses to dance with him at the Naval and Military Ball, organised by John Stanley, now a major. The cream of Melbourne society has gathered for a night of vice-regal style, courtesy of the Governor, Lord Hopetoun. Monash is furious with Vic and says if not for the scandal it would cause, he would 'send her about her business at once'.

By Tuesday, 4 November they are arm in arm again as they watch Carbine win the 1890 Melbourne Cup. Monash is on his best behaviour and later admits that he trotted after Vic 'like a little dog by her side all day'.[78]

At least he is the boss on the Outer Circle. Alterations have pushed the finishing date to well beyond the original deadline of September. Monash watches the testing of the Fairfield Bridge in pouring rain as locomotives are rolled over it and declares 'the sight of the heavy engines galloping along' to be 'magnificent'.[79]

It is far more edifying than the sight that greets him early in December after Vic refuses to go out with him. Walking through the city, he comes face to face with her and another man.

Cousin Albert warns him that Vic is becoming the subject of gossip around town and Monash tells her that he's now ready to call off the wedding. She calls his bluff and he quickly retreats, apologising profusely and asking Vic to 'pity' him. He needs her to boost his confidence and to help him through more personal crises.

'Help me to be a man,' he begs, 'help me to be great and win fame and fortune.'[80]

Meanwhile, life at Hawthorn has grown tougher. Mat does not approve of Vic and Monash will sometimes stay in his room all day rather than talk to his sister. He falls out with Albert and Minnie Behrend and has to 'kick up an awful row' to retrieve £100 he's lent to Tante Ulrike's husband Max Roth.[81] He refuses to lend his cousin Karl Roth £3, saying he needs every penny for his wedding, but finally relents after Karl threatens to sever all ties with him. Monash eventually has to sool lawyers onto his wayward cousin to retrieve the money.[82]

At Christmas he takes off with Farlow to clear his head in the wilderness on a nine-day hike from Beechworth in Victoria's north. They climb Mount Buffalo, where Monash is filled with 'feelings of awe, and admiration of nature', and they walk over Feathertop to Mount Hotham, Omeo and finally Bairnsdale, where they board the train for home.

Yet, all the time that the beauty of the Australian Alps enlivens him, Monash is drowning in self-doubt. He is to be married in three months but has developed a 'deep despondency and irritating anxiety'.

'Very shortly I shall be married to Vic,' he writes, 'and I have the secret fear that I am entering upon years of toil and anxiety.'[83]

Chapter 8

Vic pretended to think I had really struck her, and swore and raged.
MONASH AFTER ANOTHER HEATED ROW WITH HIS WIFE[1]

VIC HAS SIX BRIDESMAIDS and George Farlow is best man when Rabbi Abrahams marries Lieutenant and Mrs Monash at Melbourne's Freemasons' Hall. The newlyweds spend their first night together at Melbourne's Federal Hotel then take the train to Sydney, staying at the Grosvenor, walking through the botanic gardens to the art gallery and riding the steam tram to Bondi to visit the aquarium and the immensely popular Cyclorama, where among 'an undiminished stream of visitors'[2] they see a display of the Battle of Gettysburg, a military milestone that has Monash enthralled.

They visit the theatre and Monash puffs out his chest, declaring that he is cutting 'a dash with my beautiful wife'.[3] They spend a week cocooned in the grandeur of the Blue Mountains and gaze in wonder inside the Jenolan Caves. Monash is convinced Fred Gabriel is watching him at Central Station when they arrive and when they leave.

Back in Melbourne the Monashes move into a rented house in Lennox Street, Richmond, but tremors shake their marital home.

At the prompting of Professor Kernot, Monash completed his engineering degree a few weeks before the wedding. He complained that he was 'almost overpowered by the great strain of my studies, the military, the contract, my own finances and my unhappy state of mind about Vic'.

He was in such mental disarray that the night before he was to hand in his last paper he gave up on cramming, went to a military dinner and came home drunk at 2 a.m. Even though he was in a 'very seedy condition' he managed to do 'extremely well' in his final subject, and 'an anxiety which has been pursuing me for years is set aside at last. I can now look to the future with a clear conscience, for I have done all I can for my future success.'[4]

Yet he wars continually with his new wife.

He wants a nurturing comforter like his mother was – a shoulder to cry upon, a friend to lift his spirits. Bertha was a wonderful hostess but Monash finds Vic materialistic, showy, flirtatious, strong-willed and independent-minded: a social butterfly fluttering about, seemingly unconcerned about the lofty ambitions he has for himself. He promises to make her rich so she can surround herself with luxuries but he stresses that she must play a more subordinate role, as it is 'absolutely necessary to our success and happiness'.[5] Gradually Monash will develop a more enlightened view, but as a proud and preening young man used to directing subordinates about on the parade ground, he wants order and regiment at home. For a man who prides himself on routine, Vic's independent attitude threatens him with chaos. He begins to fret.

His sense of losing control has been exacerbated by military disappointments. He was put in charge of the garrison for the annual competition between artillery batteries at Fort Gellibrand at Williamstown on 7 March. Six batteries took turns firing their 5-inch cannons at a sheet of canvas representing the side of a ship 2 kilometres away. But while the watching reporters said that, overall, the accuracy of the guns proved that an enemy would receive a 'warm reception' if they came within the firing range of the battery, Monash's team might as well have stayed at home. Though his selection to be their leader for the day had been met with spontaneous applause from the men, he was humiliated when a local newspaper reported: 'The North Melbourne [batteries], under Lieutenant Monash, were the last to fire. It was expected that they would make a very fair stand, but their performance was a great disappointment. No direct hits were recorded ... while the time was the second slowest of the day.'[6] Monash complained that his 'men behaved execrably. Many things went wrong and I felt sorely disappointed and ashamed.'[7]

A week before the wedding he was presented with his Bachelor of Civil Engineering and won the *Argus* Scholarship for Engineering with a high second-class honour.[8]

Vic and Monash argued over details for the wedding and Vic won.

John gave her a gift of a gold watch, but there was no dowry; instead, Vic appointed Max Simonson, husband of her sister Sa, as the trustee of her property, which included an interest in the International Hotel in Victoria Street.

Just a few weeks after they arrive back from their honeymoon, Monash tells Vic she will have to recognise his 'authority' or leave.[9] She says that's fine by her. He says, 'As soon as such a step is financially possible we shall separate.' 'Good,' she says. Then he says, 'Don't go.' She stays. He says they are 'very happy together'.[10] Soon, though, they are back at each other's throats.

They are both social climbers with a love of music and the stage. On 30 May at the Princess Theatre, Sarah Bernhardt, the most famous actress in the world, opens a month-long run in Melbourne that will see her star in *La Dame aux Camélias*, *La Tosca*, *Théodora*, *Cleopatra* and *Fedora*. Mr and Mrs Monash go to see her three times. They join the Austral Salon of Music, Literature and the Arts, a new club 'founded by the women of Melbourne chiefly in the interests of intellectual culture'.[11] They are regulars at the Melbourne Town Hall for concerts by George

Marshall-Hall and his orchestra. Monash tries to educate Vic in literature, and although she finishes Dickens's *Our Mutual Friend*, she quickly tires of Walter Scott's *Ivanhoe*.

Three months after the wedding, Dr Joe Miller suspects Vic may be tubercular and recommends a holiday in the country. She and her sister Belle head to Beechworth for some mountain air, but over the month of her recuperation Vic makes far too many friends for Monash's liking. Even though husband and wife write each other affectionate letters, Monash is unsettled about her absence as he pores through 18 hours of exams for a new qualification with the municipal surveyor's course. When Vic returns she infuriates Monash by creating a social whirl with her new friends, dining at the Café Anglais in a private den. He accuses her of 'gadding about town', 'running after men' and reading his diary, which reveals to her his innermost concerns about their future together. He threatens to physically 'discipline her' but doesn't, even though he says it's 'his right and duty', considering what he regards as childish behaviour that is embarrassing him publicly.[12]

Money problems make things worse.

An escalating financial crisis around Australia has dried up Vic's investment income, and Louis is so broke that his furniture is taken away until his son can raise £100.

Monash keeps working for the Outer Circle railway, off and on, until the paperwork is finally finished in September, even though construction ended three months before his wedding.

There are a million people in Victoria by the early 1890s but the great economic boom has gone bust. Unemployment skyrockets, migration dwindles and many businesses go under. Property prices in Melbourne crash and even the mighty contractor David Munro goes belly-up, owing £158,000.[13] Prices for wool, wheat and metals sink. It is becoming impossible to raise loans in England for building railroads and other civic projects. Jim Lewis, who was making £700 a year on the Princes Bridge project, is now unemployed and almost penniless. The violent Australian maritime dispute has given way to the Great Shearers' Strike and armed stand-offs in Queensland between the army and Australian workers.

Monash has poured £100 – much of his life savings – into a quarter share in a new shearing appliance being designed by one of the Outer Circle employees and it is money down the drain. He predicts hard times for Australia and that 'soon it will be a hard struggle to live at all'.[14]

Well-paying engineering jobs are now as fanciful as the flying machine that Monash talks about building with Jim Lewis after they hear about experiments in Europe. A lack of capital, and a lack of faith in Lewis's business acumen, stop Monash going into business with him, or entering a design in the contest for the new Spencer Street bridge crossing the Yarra to join Clarendon Street, South Melbourne.[15]

The craze of bicycle riding infatuates Melbourne too, though Monash and Vic remain unimpressed. Even if they could afford a bicycle Monash would be unlikely to ride one despite the genius of its engineering.

Monash refuses a loan of several hundred pounds from Vic's older brother, Dave,[16] a 34-year-old London-based executive who has a senior role with the Equitable Life Assurance Society of the United States and a conviction for false pretences over some of his insurance sales techniques.[17] Monash tells Dave he will wait for the good times again and a 'big public position',[18] but he warns Vic that they will have to tighten their belts. He has promised her that he could earn £20 a week as a fast-rising engineer, but they will have to make do on less than £7 because 'any amount of other men are willing to do so' in these hard times.

'Perhaps you will be content after all to share a life with me on a lesser scale than we at first hoped for,' Monash offers while she is away on one of her frequent country breaks, 'after all, things may improve and our first ideal of a rapid social rise and a brilliant career in our youths may yet be realised.'[19]

Monash has a cracking résumé. He calls in favours. He asks Alfred Deakin to take a little time out from planning a federated Australia to honour his old promise to provide 'assistance and advice whenever required'.[20] Monash seeks references from his former boss George Higgins from Graham and Wadick, (now) Colonel Goldstein and Professor Kernot. He applies to be the superintending engineer on the sewerage works for the new Melbourne and Metropolitan Board of Works, and the shire engineer of Seymour and of Camberwell; he offers to lecture on hydraulic engineering at the university, draws up plans on spec for the Benalla water supply and the East Boort Irrigation and Water Trust works, and enters a design competition for the new Pyrmont Bridge across Sydney's Darling Harbour.[21] He scores only a few days' work here and there. He thinks about trying his luck in Western Australia, where new goldfields are opening up and where the new Great Southern Railway offers promise.

At Kernot's suggestion, Monash lands a job at the Melbourne Harbour Trust in November 1891. It's mundane work,[22] but it pays the bills, and he is already planning on bettering himself through education and influential contacts.

In 1879 Monash's friend Theodore Fink became the youngest member of the Yorick Club, aged just 24. He has cultivated close friends such as the writers Marcus Clarke and Jules Archibald. In November 1891 the Yorick Club and the Austral Salon host functions for Rudyard Kipling, who is travelling through New Zealand and Australia. The fountain pen is still something of a rarity, but such a pen is produced, and though autograph hunters are anathema to the owlish author, he is fascinated by the latest writing instrument and scrawls his signature a dozen times across a menu card.[23] The card is later dissected and the pieces clamoured over. Never one to miss an opportunity, Monash seizes his.

He enrols as a student at the Supreme Court. He sees an opportunity for an engineering expert in legal disputes. Earning a law degree is becoming tougher in Victoria, with new legislation recently introduced, and Monash predicts that with his qualifications he will be 'absolutely without competition ... for many years at least'.[24]

He is so busy that he and George Farlow spend only four days on their annual Christmas trek, journeying up Mount Buffalo for two summer nights in a tent.

In January 1892 Monash goes back to university for the water supply engineers' exams under lecturer J.T. (Josh) Noble Anderson, a 36-year-old Irishman who has been in Victoria for two years and has worked on the Laanecoorie Weir near Bendigo. Anderson gives his students the text of the exam papers in advance, and, 'with a severe moral twinge' Monash scores 100 per cent on his first three papers and 95 per cent on the fourth.[25]

In March Monash misses out after applying for a better job at the Water Supply Department, even though Professor Kernot recommends him. Still, he busies himself at work, designing Victoria's first swing bridge for the crossing of the Saltwater River (now called the Maribyrnong) at Footscray, and designing sheds, roads and drainage at the recently excavated Victoria Dock. Work is a refuge from troubles at home.

A promotion at the Harbour Trust has seen the Monashes move to a bigger house called Rydal in Caroline Street, South Yarra, but the bickering has followed them.

His mood is not improved at the 1892 Easter training camp at Queenscliff when Lieutenant Colonel Dean Pitt abuses and frequently insults him.[26] Even though Dean Pitt has a high regard for Monash's capabilities at other times, Monash still cannot gain his promotion to captain. He thinks perhaps it is because he is a Jew.

Monash is not long back from the military manoeuvres when he and Vic have a heated row. Monash says Vic 'pretended to think I had really struck her, and swore and raged'.[27] She storms out and heads for the protection of Sa and Max Simonson, who cools the situation by talking it over with Monash. Vic comes home two days later.

She soon falls pregnant. Monash is overjoyed: some peace between husband and wife at last! He chases every dollar he can, because soon he will have three mouths to feed, plus his father and sisters who rely on his help. He starts coaching students who are taking the water supply exams.

In May he gets a break. He is made Chief Draughtsman at the Harbour Trust on £260 a year, more than double the average working man's wage.[28] It is enough to pay for a servant to do the housework while Vic is socialising.

Monash takes leave from the trust to use his legal training as an advocate for Graham and Wadick as they fight for £30,700 from the Railway Department over the Outer Circle Line. After hearing evidence for 21 days, the arbitrators award the firm £13,022.[29] Monash charges Graham and Wadick five guineas a day – five times his usual salary – plus his lost wages.

He briefly falters in his legal studies, but with encouragement from a barrister friend named Leo Cussen,[30] he starts to attack them so relentlessly that he is soon sick from 'overstrain'. He has previously written to Vic during one of her holidays: 'Strange isn't it, that I can't work well unless I am very busy and hard pressed for time.'[31] He manages to spend a day at a picnic organised for the university students by Josh Anderson and calls it 'one of the jolliest amusements I've had for a very long time'. He and Anderson become firm friends, and combine the students they are privately coaching for government exams into one class.

By December Monash has passed the subjects of property, obligations and Roman law, and constitutional and legal history. He writes on the first day of 1893 that he is proud of his wife and 'settled' in his home life. The hard work and overstrain has unsettled him momentarily and in something of a low mood he says he is 'no genius' and predicts he will 'only attain a moderate success', even with very hard work. But he *has* worked hard, he reassures himself, keeping up 'in what I think is a remarkable degree the resolves, methods, and discipline of my earlier life. I am pleased to feel I am living an earnest, kindly and contented life.'[32]

Three weeks later, on 22 January 1893, Monash becomes a father when Vic delivers a baby girl they name Bertha. Mother and daughter are doing splendidly, but in keeping with the mores of the time Vic gets very little credit when the announcement appears in the newspapers:

MONASH. – On the 22nd inst, at Rydal, Caroline-street South Yarra, the wife of John Monash, C.E. – a daughter.[33]

Monash is ecstatic at the birth but refuses to attend the synagogue for the naming ceremony. He might have been married by a rabbi but that's as far as he wants to go with religion for now. The little family has a three-week holiday in Daylesford, but the climate is no good for Vic's lungs and back in Melbourne she clashes with Mat, who is a frequent visitor to Caroline Street and will always be Monash's best friend.

The air throughout Victoria is filled with tension. Public works have dried up, most of the engineers Monash knows are unemployed.

And then there is the crash.

The Victorian Cabinet meets secretly on Sunday, 30 April 1893, and at 1 o'clock the following morning Premier James Patterson declares that the banks have suspended payments and will close for five days.

Thousands of people, driven by fear, gather angrily outside the buildings where their money is locked. Melbourne is gripped 'in a panic of unbelief',[34] Monash writes. He goes to work that morning not knowing what to expect and is told he will likely lose his job soon.

Two weeks later, after a long illness, Max Roth dies in debt at his home in Grattan Street, Prahan,[35] and Monash has to handle his affairs as executor. Max's boys will have to support Tante Ulrike and their sisters, though they will not do a good job.

Monash manages to find a little work for Jim Lewis at 10 shillings a day, but people are being laid off at the Harbour Trust and salaries are slashed. Monash appeals to one of the Harbour Trust commissioners, Ephraim Zox MLA, a shining light of the Jewish community, to help him keep his job.[36]

He hopes for some military advancement and in July Major Outtrim gives him a glowing report, as does Colonel Goldstein. His revolver-shooting has improved to the extent that he sometimes tops the score for marksmanship, and his expertise in the science of warfare has won him attention throughout the colony. On 21 August General Tulloch is part of 'a large audience, notwithstanding the inclement weather' packed into the Biology School at Melbourne University to hear Monash deliver a talk called 'Implements of War'. With the help of slides projected by lantern onto a white screen, Monash speaks about applying science to war, and 'the great advances which have characterised the nations during the last half-century in the perfecting of the weapons of warfare … the discovery of explosives, and the uses of gun cotton and gunpowder, and their relative forces'. He ignites a small quantity of explosive to demonstrate its power. He explains the nature and uses of modern arms, including the heavy fortress guns, the lighter field guns, the quick-firing guns with which the Australian auxiliary fleet has been armed, the machine-gun, and the rifle. His audience is fascinated and he receives a hearty vote of thanks.[37]

Monash must bide his time for promotion. He now has a Master's Degree in Engineering and finds more work in the courtroom. In June 1893, he gives evidence for David Syme, proprietor of the *Age* newspaper, against libel action from Richard Speight, a stocky little Englishman sacked as Chief Commissioner of Railways following the paper's campaign against him. Speight is suing for £25,000 damages.

Privately Monash is on Speight's side, calling the case *Speight v Slime*, but the young father needs money. James Purves QC, representing Syme, blames the depression on men like Speight who have wasted public money, and says the *Age* reports were 'fair comment' about a man who is 'too thin skinned'.[38] Monash is called to back up that claim. In preparation for his appearance he walks the Glen Iris and Outer Circle Lines and documents every place where money was ill spent, calculating that there have been 127,000 cubic yards of excess earthworks on the Outer Circle Line and that 28 per cent of the total cost has been unnecessary.

Although there is some raising of eyebrows at the youth of the *Age*'s expert witness, Monash tells the court he is 28, and that he received his master's degree earlier in the year and his bachelor's two years ago. He says he was solely responsible for carrying out the plans given to him on the Outer Circle Line by the Railways Department.

Alfred Deakin, assisting Purves, guides Monash through other evidence that is damning for Speight. There are railway stations needlessly close together, 'great quantities of material' wasted, extravagant bridges and unnecessary fencing, embankments unnecessarily wide.[39]

The hearing takes 98 days and there is an appeal lasting 86 days. Monash is called again when the case is reheard and earns £40 for his two appearances combined.

The final verdict is for Syme on nine counts and Speight on one. Rather than the £25,000 Speight has sought, he receives just one farthing in damages.[40]

Although Monash has supported the *Age* in court, he is opposed to the protectionist policies of Syme and Purves, telling cousin Leo in his regular missive to Minnesota that economic growth in Victoria relies on each individual who is starting 'off on the road to his personal support and enrichment'.

By August the only professional men still employed at the Harbour Trust are Monash, the Chief Engineer and two inspectors. Though businesses are going bust and the prospects of Monash and his young family have become precarious, he tells Leo that he has not lost faith 'in this land; the wealth is there; but instead of garnering it we have been living for the last 10 years on artificial and speculative enterprises'.[41]

Monash begins a rush on his legal studies in September, six weeks before the exams. Farlow lends him £10 towards the fees, Will Steele transcribes old exam papers to help him and another friend, Jack Mackey, gives him his lecture notes and lends him books.

On 3 October he takes a break from cramming to address the opening of the annual gunnery course of the Metropolitan Garrison Artillery on the basis of coastal defence, 'ranging from the loading of the gun to the impact of the projectile, with a description of the different natures of guns and their mountings, ammunition, and the effect of the various natures of fire upon armour plating'.[42] By the next day he is in a 'nervous overwrought state' and feels 'quite ill'[43] over his workload, but he passes all his subjects – wrongs, and equity and procedure, international law, and finally, in December, Latin, the subject that has given him so much trouble over the years. Monash has already obtained a master's degree in engineering and now he has qualified for a Bachelor of Arts and a Bachelor of Laws. But he will not formally graduate for two years until he can finally pay the university fees.

Vic continues to make fashion news, earning a mention from social writer 'Queen Bee' in the *Argus* for her ivory silk Melbourne Cup gown with lace insertions.[44] The same paper praises Monash's 'first-rate style' when he delivers another lecture to military officers in the North Melbourne Battery rooms, telling them at considerable length, without the use of extensive notes, how improvements in their construction of cannons by the use of steel coils instead of solid metal allow the 'gun to be lightened and lengthened, while the charge of explosives was increased, thus getting greater penetration'.[45]

But this man cannot live on praise alone. And Vic is finding it increasingly hard to live with him.

She accompanied him to Government House not long after their wedding but is always angry when he is invited there solo. After a function for visiting Austrian officers he comes home drunk. Vic goes to dinner with other men, usually in the company of her sister Belle, but Monash has his suspicions and at one point receives an anonymous note warning him about her behaviour.

In December 1893 she is pregnant again, but because her health is so fragile, doctors induce a miscarriage. Monash offers little sympathy, such is the rancour between them.

As the daughter they call Bert approaches her first birthday, Vic tells Monash they should separate. Forever.

Max Simonson appeals to them to patch up their differences. Privately, he tells Monash that it is time to treat Vic 'firmly and unbendingly'. He persuades Monash to let her have a few weeks in the fresh air of Christmas Hills, north of Melbourne.

Monash hopes money might grease some of the friction between them and applies to be the contractor for the main Hobsons Bay sewer. He misses out, and starts writing letters to the Harbour Trust commissioners, pleading for them to keep him on.

In March 1894, General Tulloch asks Monash if he would like to go to England for an artillery course with the Royal Artillery, at Shoeburyness on the mouth of the Thames, but Monash will have to pay for everything except his passage. He can't afford it.

His frustration is exacerbated by the constant feuding with his wife. Vic is not long back from Christmas Hills when she leaves Monash for four days, until the Simonsons persuade her to return again.

Monash faces losing his wife and job at the same time. On 20 March 1894, he writes another letter to Zox asking him to support 'the only Jewish engineer in good practice in Victoria'.[46] It doesn't help. The Harbour Trust gives him notice three weeks later.

In July he applies to be a consulting engineer on the Saltwater bridge he has designed. He has an interview with another Harbour Trust commissioner, Nathan Thornley, a wealthy Member of the

Legislative Council, who, rather than interviewing Monash for the position, interrogates him over what he calls 'disloyalty to the chief engineer'. He accuses Monash of overstating his qualifications. Then the trust amends his design for the bridge by adding extra bracing and Monash declares that it is not only dead weight but also 'atrociously disfiguring the symmetry of the design'. He tells the trust he could have saved them money if he had kept his job.[47]

He applies for a municipal post at St Arnaud, the roles of Surveyor and Town Clerk of Brunswick and a position in Tasmania as a hydraulic engineer, but misses out on all of them, even though he has the support of Deakin and Major Outtrim's politician brother Alfred.

So 'guided more by necessity than by choice', Monash decides to accept his former lecturer Josh Anderson's proposal that they open a private consulting firm. Vic and Anderson's wife Ellen are friends, so the deal is sealed.

'I have greatly improved my business connections and reputation,' Monash tells Anderson. 'We combine an excellent array of qualifications.'[48] At the same time as he and Anderson try to build their business, Monash will also pursue his own career, trying to procure as much work as he can as an engineering expert in legal cases and advocate for construction companies.

Landlords are desperate to rent properties cheaply, and Monash estimates he and Anderson will at least be able to pay their own expenses.[49] So it is that in June 1894, Monash & Anderson – claiming they have overseen projects worth a total of more than £1 million – open their doors for business. Their office is in the magnificent 12-storey Australian Building at 49 Elizabeth Street, at 53 metres Australia's tallest structure.[50]

Monash has similarly lofty ambitions. The company letterhead describes him and Anderson as 'Consulting Civil, Hydraulic, and Mechanical Engineers, and Surveyors; Licensed Patent Agents; Municipal Surveyors and Engineers of Water Supply'.[51] Almost immediately they find work designing a cable tramway for the Strzelecki Consolidated Colliery at Korumburra in Gippsland.[52]

The affable Anderson will be responsible for securing new businesses because he 'has a much better first impression' than Monash, who declares himself 'far superior in all practical details'. He complains that Anderson 'cannot work hard, continuously or accurately',[53] but at least Anderson's amiable nature procures them plenty of work.

Monash needs it.

His financial woes and the constant fear that Vic will leave him make him socially withdrawn for the first time in his life; the unbridled confidence of his youth is replaced with a certain awkwardness. While Vic is always the centre of attention, he now confesses that he feels small among 'great men', and at Government House balls becomes something of an outsider.

Once he couldn't wait to show off his card tricks or play the piano, but criticism of him as a show-off has curtailed all that. He now carries a notebook containing poems by Kipling in case he is called upon to recite something at parties. His notebook also contains rude limericks and the outlines of jokes to help him if he gets stuck for conversation. He becomes so self-conscious that he will only stand for election on the Engineering Students' Committee if he is unopposed.

Finally, the guillotine falls on his personal life.

Monash has taken little interest in politics outside of election time, when he always votes conservative, but in September 1894 he helps Jack Mackey run as a Liberal Free Trader in the seat of Melbourne South. One night he even stands guard with a gun outside Mackey's committee room.

He comes home after midnight and he and Vic get into another slanging match. He later says he caught her hand to stop her striking him; she says he had his hands around her neck.

After three stormy years, Vic walks out of the marriage.

She leaves with the baby to stay at the Simonsons' and starts proceedings for a legal separation.

Forlorn, Monash dismisses the servant and moves back with his father and sisters at Hawthorn.

He begs Vic to come home. He promises there will be no more trouble, but he only inflames things when he tells her that he knows the law and will pursue all avenues, warning Vic that she can present no good reason for deserting him.

He visits Bert twice, but then Vic stops the visits, and after three weeks of not seeing his daughter, Monash and his now aged and frail father go over to the Simonsons' to set things straight.

They find Max Simonson on the veranda and sit down for a chat. Bert is brought out and Monash cradles her in his arms. After three generations of the Monashes sit with Max for 10 minutes or so, old Louis, white-haired and slow, hobbles to the gate and in his thick German accent hails a horse-drawn cab. It clip-clops to the front of the house.

Monash then turns to his brother-in-law, who has always been the peacemaker between the warring husband and wife, and says: 'I am going to take the child away with me.'

Max says he objects to 'any kidnapping' but Monash says he has a right to take his own flesh and blood.

'Well, I will have to tell Vic,' Max says, and as he gets up to do so, Monash, still holding Bert, canters down to his father waiting in the cab. The two abductors flee as Vic comes barrelling out of the house and, forgetting her social graces, races after the cab as fast as her long skirts will let her, yelling at them to come back.[54]

Bert is then entrusted to the care of Monash's sisters, with the help of a nurse. Vic is allowed to visit but there is plenty of security to prevent a re-abduction.

Monash wishes Vic would stay longer when she visits, and he is broken-hearted as he awaits the inevitable divorce. Every day he comes home for lunch hoping his wife, that vision of loveliness he was once so smitten by, will come through the front door and reconcile with him. He adores his idealised vision of Vic. He tells himself that if she just gives him another chance – and does as she's told for once – they can have a happy life together. He must be the commanding officer, of course, but his whole being craves the responsibility of taking care of a wife and family. He sees it as his duty.

On her next visit Vic arrives with Sa and both are stony-faced.

Monash takes the baby into the front room and tries to kiss his wife. She turns away.

'Please come back home, this is where you belong,' he says.

'No I don't,' she replies. 'I feel sorry for you, Jack, I really do. But I just want a rest.'

'When will you be back, then?' Monash asks her.

'Never,' she says.[55]

Chapter 9

My success here is one of my only comforts in the midst of much grave trouble.

MONASH ON HIS MILITARY ADVANCEMENT AMID MYRIAD BUSINESS
AND PERSONAL WOES[1]

THREE MONTHS AFTER Vic leaves her marriage, she decides to leave Australia. Monash is devastated. The dreams and aspirations of so many other ambitious, educated men have been shattered as Victoria splutters under the financial squeeze, and now Monash feels *his* family life has been crushed as well.

He has been working tirelessly to make a go of things for his daughter and for his father and sisters, who all depend on him, and now the future seems black.

While Mat, increasingly shy and withdrawn, teaches languages for a short period at University High School, she mostly stays at home, advertising her services as a private tutor 'with an exhibition in modern languages, 1st class honours in mathematics, also matriculated in English subjects'.[2] The Monashes have to watch every penny.

Lou has finished her schooling at Presbyterian Ladies' College and will also learn shorthand and typing. Occasionally she helps

Monash in his office but her passion is to become a physical education teacher, and she studies at the Melbourne Ladies' Gymnasium run by Miss Harriet Elphinstone-Dick.

In the first week of December 1894 Monash has just returned to Yarra Street from Gippsland, where he and Anderson have been making a feasibility study on widening the harbour at Inverloch and building a railway from the coalmines to the coast.[3] Monash learns that his wealthy brother-in-law, Dave Moss, has arranged for Vic and Belle to sail for London to stay with his family at their big Kensington house, complete with three servants. Even though he has all but abandoned his faith Monash seeks out Rabbi Abrahams to help him win back Vic's love. He confesses to Dave Moss that he is 'oppressed with grief both at the loss of my wife and home, and the dreadful conduct of the wife I have loved and cherished so much'.[4]

He says Vic has started to make unfounded accusations about him, lashing out with pain over the loss of Bert, and that her friends are spreading lies. He tells his cousin Karl Roth, who has just been married in Sydney, that 'the husband must be master',[5] but he still begs Vic to see reason before her ship sails.

On 9 December, the night before Vic and Belle are due to leave Melbourne, Monash arranges to have a letter specially delivered to her, telling her he is desperate to have her back, while still standing firm.

He blunders and blusters: 'The statements which you have made about me to many people you must know in your heart are utterly false, and I know that, apart from this, seeming friends of yours have helped to poison your mind.'

He says she is making a terrible mistake; that she might be only 25 but as she gets older she will find 'that pursuit of pleasure, sacrifice of every good emotion, will lead you to an abyss of mortification'.

Monash virtually commands her to 'take counsel with yourself, sit down and think, think hard' and be a 'good, sensible woman and come back'.

'You say you never loved me,' he pleads, 'but I have made a home and name for you, of which you were proud.'

If that might have worked, he shoots down any chance of a reconciliation by suggesting Vic ponder their life together 'honestly and fairly', and admit that as a wife and mother she has been 'selfish, jealous, truthless ... and neglectful'.

Vic is unmoved. She and Belle set sail for London the next day. Monash begs them to get off at Adelaide or Albany, and asks the captain of the ship to make sure Vic behaves herself, but he fears that his wife is gone for good.

Monash is in a deep funk for the next few days. His father is in low spirits too. Monash asks Joe Miller to give Louis a check-up.

On 15 December, after Mat sends an urgent telegram to the Naval and Military Club, Monash rushes home and finds Louis unconscious. He runs to find a doctor, but by the time he returns with one, the life that began in Krotoszyn 63 years before has gone.

Officers of the Melbourne Hebrew Congregation are summoned to perform the last rites and Monash visits the synagogue the next day for the first time in however long. At the insistence of Tante Ulrike and Albert Behrend, Yiddish prayers are said in the Hawthorn house for the next four evenings.

Monash is racked with grief, and plagued by feelings that somehow his marital strife has contributed to his father's death.

He has to wind up Louis's estate, and although there are assets worth more than £4000, much of it is in heavily mortgaged real estate and it all seems 'hopelessly insolvent'. Monash does his sums and finds Louis's balance sheet is £1500 in the red. Some of the properties, including a derelict farm at Moe, are unsaleable forfeited securities from his money-lending business that no one wants. Some at Jerilderie and elsewhere are sold over time.[6]

Just as in the months after his mother's death, Monash grieves over the loss of his wife and father by losing himself at the theatre and by drinking at the Naval and Military Club and the Yorick Club, where Goldstein and Kernot have nominated him as a man with an intellect worthy of membership. Many times Monash staggers home after daybreak.

He officially graduates as a Bachelor of Laws in 1895. He now has three bachelor's degrees and a master's: yet another reason to drink up. Sometimes he'll go out with a female friend or visit the Card and Krakowski families or the O'Haras, and while he becomes very fond of Ada Krakowski, he never pursues any woman seriously.

He renews his interest in chess, sketching and carpentry. Sometimes he will give artillery lectures and voice his conservative political views. At one such talk in Port Melbourne he finds himself 'among a den of ill-bred ungrammatical socialists'.[7]

When he closes his eyes to sleep Vic will sometimes appear in his dreams, and they will be friends again just like they were when they first met. Alas, the dreams are fleeting, and he wakes up alone and broke. The mortgagee forecloses on Louis's home in Yarra Street and Monash, his daughter and two sisters move to rented accommodation. He is now skint, having borrowed almost the whole value of his life insurance policy.

The military is his only real source of joy. In 1894, he joined the United Service Institution of Victoria, an organisation promoting the security of the colony, and a few months later drew up plans for a grand public display of the latest in defence innovations. On 2 May 1895, a two-day Naval and Military Conversazione opens at the Town Hall, and is attended by a huge crowd and proclaimed a roaring success — because, the *Argus* reports, 'of the energy and enthusiasm of Lieutenant Monash, who has been mainly responsible for the classification and arrangement of the exhibits'.[8] Monash is made Secretary of the United Services Institution.

Yet often Monash stares forlornly at his teetering world through the distortion of a glass. He is lonely and almost without hope for the future.

Then something marvellous happens.

Monash does not believe in miracles but on 13 July 1895 a letter arrives on his doorstep that will change the course of his life again. Ten months after walking out on him, Vic writes to say she is back in Australia and wants to see him and Bert.

Elation surges through Monash along with a sense of vindication and triumph. Then he begins to wonder what he is letting himself in for. He now faces what he calls a 'terribly difficult position'.[9]

Twelve days later husband and wife are reunited, but only for preliminary talks. Both agree to make their relationship nothing more than a casual acquaintance for now.

After the initial euphoria Monash feels at seeing Vic again, they share a hesitant embrace. Monash has all sorts of feelings clashing inside him. He confesses to a degree of bitterness, and while he resolves to be fair with Vic, he plans also to be firm. Vic still refuses to play by his rules.

For a while they eye each other cagily, and after what seems like an eternity of silence, Monash asks imperiously: 'Well, what has brought you back?'

'I am willing to confess that I had more regard for you than I thought,' she replies.

Monash cannot help admiring her elegance and independent spirit, but is still suspicious of her motives, admitting later that 'I doubted her sincerity'. He suggests 'guarantees' for their relationship but Vic laughs at him.

Their reunion is brief. They say their goodbyes coolly, each careful to disguise any desperate longings.

The next day they meet again. Monash does most of the talking and tries to lay down some ground rules for their marriage 'logically and fairly'. Vic refuses to admit that she has been entirely in the wrong but Monash is satisfied when she 'again promises to make amends'. He explains that the constant strain of fearing she might take off again will only damage the career he is trying to build for both of them.

He has waved a red flag.

'Well maybe I should go for good,' she snaps. 'Would that make things better? Bert is happy, and does not want me. You no longer love me. Sorry I've again come into your life. I will go out of it again. Goodbye.'

Monash is about to beg her to stay. But no. He will not give ground.

'I let her leave,' he says later, 'but was so deeply moved, that the same evening I wrote asking her to see me again.'

He spends another sleepless, fitful night fretting, and the next morning is too stressed for work.

All morning he paces around his rented home, anxiously wondering if Vic will return for more peace talks.

She finally comes through the gate at 2 p.m. and their discussion is much more pleasant than he anticipated. It is even more pleasant the following day, 28 July.

Monash says that Vic 'seems greatly changed and her warm affectionate manner, if sincere, augurs for future well-being'.[10]

That night he jots down some lines of verse that begin:

It was dreary and dark, and all joy had fled
And I lost your face in the shadows falling

And conclude with:

I am kissing you over and over
I am holding you close to my heart
As of old, we'll be lover and lover
And live in a world apart.[11]

Monash knows that for a long time he will have to endure gossip and whispers about his marriage, and about what happened during their long separation, but he is happy just to be back with Vic. Her return also increases the family income through her investment earnings now that the worst of the Depression is over, and within a week they take a house on the corner of Coppin and Isabella Groves in Hawthorn at £5 a week. They call the house Bertmont after their daughter, and Monash, Vic,

Bert, Louise, Mat and a maid all move in – along with a brewing storm.

The fighting resumes. Vic once more refuses to accept his authority, spends money they don't have and is off to the theatre or the races without consulting him.

Once more Monash finds some refuge in his work.

He and Anderson secure their first really big contract, worth £1201, to build an 'aerial tramway' in Gippsland at the Landy's Dream goldmine, 10 kilometres from Walhalla. The tramway will transport quartz 2 kilometres from the mine for crushing on the Aberfeldy River. It is an exciting and potentially profitable venture after a year of struggle. Much of Monash & Anderson's work has been for mining companies, and they are consultants to the Coal Creek company.[12]

Through a letter-writing campaign to the *Age*, Monash advocates for the industry as a whole. Yet many of their clients are slow to pay, and Monash and Anderson often labour just for their expenses in the hope that a good report will lead to paying work. When they do submit an invoice their fee is two guineas a day, three for country work: the lowest allowed by the Institution of Civil Engineers in London.

Monash and Anderson arrange to sell clay from Moorooduc on the Mornington Peninsula. Through this venture they meet John Gibson, a tall, handsome industrial chemist from Scotland who manages the cement works owned by David Mitchell, father of Nellie Melba. They join a syndicate hoping to salvage a sunken ship, make a feasibility study on navigating the Barwon River and apply for work with the Mount Lyell Co. in Tasmania. They also consult for Healesville and Cranbourne Shires.

Monash still finds time to advance his military career, and on 18 October 1885 is promoted to captain in the same week as he serves as an aide at the reception for the new Victorian governor, Lord Brassey. Monash asks his friend, the journalist Donald MacDonald, to place a paragraph in the *Argus* noting his promotion, but his application to immediately sit for promotion to major is rejected and his business takes a hit too.

Landy's Dream looked like an El Dorado. But just like Monash's marriage it is troubled from the start.

The company has not cleared the land for the tramway properly, the ropes ordered from England are late and too stiff,[13] and the ironwork does not arrive on time. The company then changes the routes for the tramway, which delays completion.

Monash spends three weeks at the mine in January 1896, camping in a bark hut beside the Aberfeldy. He lives rough but is glad to get out of the house. He and Vic had been arguing so viciously that on New Year's Day Monash 'left the house distracted and spent a terrible night'.[14] Three weeks away from Vic allowed the friction to go off the boil and finally, over time, there is a gradual ceasefire. Over the next few months, Monash's sisters both move out of the house, leaving Vic as the unchallenged queen. Husband and wife slowly make some compromises and learn to live with each other more amicably. The heated rows cool. Their mutual love for Bert is the glue that ensures they stick together and they slowly begin to tolerate and understand each other's personality. Monash works harder and harder to give his family a strong financial base.

Anderson & Monash wins another contract from a fledgling company called Golden Fleece, to move 28 tons of machinery from Daylesford to beyond Walhalla and to erect an ore-crushing plant and a dam.[15] They find a good long-term foreman for their business in Chris Christensen, a former ship's carpenter. But Anderson submits a woefully underestimated tender and Monash has the embarrassment of having to submit a revised one. The stress brings on diarrhoea and haemorrhoids.

On 16 March, he almost has apoplexy when he reads a report in the *Argus* that a trial of the aerial tramway at Landy's Dream has proved a 'failure'.[16] Monash quickly informs the paper that no trial has yet taken place but that it will probably occur that week.

It doesn't. Work is constantly delayed. The shareholders are angry and Monash tells Anderson that he feels 'like a marked man'.[17] The pair are in heavy debt but their bank advances them a £100 overdraft, and Monash and Anderson use their inside knowledge to trade shares in the Landy's Dream company as prices fluctuate wildly.

On 12 May the directors rescind Monash's contract and demand possession, just as Monash is telling the company that the tramway is about to work splendidly. With Farlow briefing their counsel, Monash and Anderson take the case to court.

A month later the Golden Fleece project is stalled, with Monash and Anderson unable to pay their carrier. After the matter is finally resolved there are more arguments and legal threats over final payments.

The case against Landy's Dream begins in August, with Monash & Anderson claiming £499. The case lasts 10 days and Monash spends three of them in the witness box before a judge and jury of four. They find in favour of Monash but Landy's Dream appeals and finally in December Monash and Anderson give back £190 of the £442 they were awarded.[18]

They work on improving the steam tramway they built for the Strzelecki Colliery and they pick up the occasional legal case, but the work is piecemeal and Monash is often dodging debt collectors. He can't even afford five guineas to continue his subscription to the Institution of Civil Engineers.

But he is rich when it comes to influential friends. Lieutenant Colonel W. Henry Hall, a London-born State school headmaster in command of the Metropolitan Brigade, takes Monash under his wing. Major Outtrim grooms Monash to take command of the North Melbourne Battery, since he and Joe Miller are retiring. The Militia Garrison Artillery (Coastal) is made up of two brigades: the Metropolitan in Melbourne and the Western District in Geelong. The Metropolitan, under Hall's command, contains three batteries: North Melbourne, Williamstown and Harbour Trust. All up, with the inclusion of some permanent forces, the coastal artillery has just on a thousand men operating from seven forts.

Outtrim tells Monash to bide his time and the promotion is his. But Monash is impatient. He suggests Outtrim take three months' leave so that Monash might acquire such 'a vested interest in the battery it would be hard to shake'.[19] Outtrim tells him to settle down, but Monash is relieved when he and Vic are among the dignitaries at a party hosted by Lady Holled-Smith, wife of Victoria's military commandant, at the Holled-Smith home, Linden, in Williams Road, Windsor.[20]

Vic remains a social butterfly, the papers reporting her regal presence at a reception for the Mayor and Mayoress of South Melbourne on 28 May, and at the Old Scotch Collegians' Club Ball the following night at the Masonic Hall, where she looks magnificent in 'a beautiful gown of pink brocade, the shoulder straps and edge of the skirt showing a row of beaver',[21] and with silver sequins brightening the bodice. A few weeks later she is back at the Masonic Hall, 'handsomely gowned in yellow satin with passementerie trimming',[22] at a dance in aid of the library fund for the Jewish Literary Society.

On 1 June Monash uses his powerful connections to secure the Governor, Lord Brassey, to lecture the United Service Institution at the Town Hall on the subject 'Our Naval Position and Policy'. Brassey is an expert on the subject as editor of the *Naval Annual*, 'the most valued authority … in connection with the British Navy'.[23] The Governor has just been inspecting a marvellous innovation by which all the doors of railway carriages can be closed simultaneously as the train is about to start and every door can be opened when the train stops.[24]

Even though Monash has largely cut his ties with his German roots, Mat and Albert and Minnie Behrend all sing at the German Reading Club at Gracepark House in Hawthorn on 21 July, and their friend Clara Rosenheim plays Chopin's *Fantaisie Impromptu*.[25] Monash earns life membership from the Turn-Verein after he donates his collection of more than 400 German novels. He has no further use for them, later telling a cousin that while German 'in a sense' is his mother tongue and he can still read it fluently, he can no longer write or speak the language 'except in the plainest and most infantile terms'.[26]

While Vic usually attends the synagogue on Yom Kippur, a day of fasting and prayer, Monash steadfastly refuses, staying in his office all day out of sight and telling her that the only time he fasts is between lunch and dinner. From 1896 he stops paying his dues to the Melbourne Hebrew Congregation where Vic's family are members. His religious scepticism rages. Religion has done nothing to ease the pain over the loss of his mother and father. It has given him no comfort, and full of conflicting philosophies about the origin of man, he is sometimes critical of others of the faith he once shared. At one time he refers to a group at a party as 'a crowd of Jews – few of them to my taste'[27] and to others as 'a brood of better class Jews'.[28] Later, though, he will begin to again find pride in his Jewish heritage if not, so much, its teachings.

In July 1896 Outtrim finally steps aside and joins the military reserve, paving the way for Monash to be made acting commander of the North Melbourne Battery Garrison Artillery.[29] He complains that 'poor old Outtrim let things drift terribly' with the garrison and that it will take 'many good days' before he can have 'everything fixed to my liking'. But he adds, 'My success here is one of my only comforts in the midst of much grave trouble.'[30]

Monash immediately shows himself to be an inspiring commander, with Farlow later recalling that 'his orders were models of conciseness and at the same time completeness. Nothing appeared to be overlooked.' Monash has the ability to make suggestions that men will adopt as their own ideas and 'be proud of such'.[31]

Monash passes his exams to make major with 99 per cent for drill, 98 per cent for coast artillery tactics and 87 per cent for regimental duties. He fails his riding exam but is standing tall as he passes overall.

He and Vic celebrate with their last summer holiday for eight years, spending a few days in what he calls the 'glorious amphitheatre of the Great Australian Alps', at the Mount St

Bernard Hospice on the Alpine Road, about 13 kilometres north-west of Omeo. Like a pair of lovebirds, they carve 'J&V Monash 31/12/96' on a survey cairn.

Things have settled down at home and the children's parties the now-happy couple throw in Hawthorn are worthy of newspaper reports. On the occasion of 'Bertie's' fourth birthday, 'Captain and Mrs. Monash' turn 'their residence Bertmont' into a children's playground. That becomes a regular occurrence for many years to come. 'The young found much enjoyment in the entertainment provided for them,' *Table Talk* reports, 'which included a magic lantern show and a fireworks display. About 70 were present and included the Masters and Misses Simonson, Valentine, Mount, Meyrick-Rainsford, Browne, Williams, Slade, Dean, Clemence, and Roxburgh.'[32]

At home Monash is finally reaching a degree of peace and contentment that has been foreign to him for so long. His military career is finally starting to flourish as well. His promotion to major is announced on 2 April 1897. It should be a time of great personal triumph but Monash has little time to celebrate. Just as he reaches a long-awaited military milestone, he finds the demands of his growing business give him less and less opportunity to spend in uniform.

Soon he will be waging battles right across Australia.

Chapter 10

*I will have to choose sooner or later, between my military work and
my business career. One of the chief attractions which the military has
for me is the social opportunities. You can't imagine how it grieves me
but there is simply nothing for it.*

MONASH ON HAVING TO GIVE UP HIS MILITARY AMBITIONS TO
SUPPORT HIS FAMILY[1]

MONASH IS 32 but he feels 20 years older. He wishes he
could spend more time with his four-year-old daughter
Bert, but he hardly sees her now as he travels all over Australia
picking up advocacy and engineering jobs, hoping that one day
his heavy workload will reap dividends for his young family.
His weight climbs and his clothes become tighter. He often feels
nauseous. Joe Miller tells him to stop drinking.

Vic has her own circle of friends, including the young and
flighty Lizzie Bentwitch,[2] whose father Morris has a thriving
tobacco store at 172 Swanston Street.[3] Lizzie is a lot of fun even if
Vic thinks her dress sense is too showy, but Vic's friends can amuse
her for only so long and she yearns to have her husband back.

Monash writes home to say that while he misses her and Bert
desperately he is making good money on the road and that it can

only help all of them down the track. Vic says she misses him so much that it would now be impossible for her ever to live without him. Their brief reunions are passionate and intense.

As a young man marching through the wild bush of Victoria, Monash delighted George Farlow by studying the faces and lives of the people he met, always on the lookout for engineering opportunities. From the middle of 1897 Monash begins to spend weeks and then months away from home, captivated by the endless potential and personality of this wide brown land. Between 1897 and 1899 he travels constantly, accompanied by haemorrhoids, biliousness, diarrhoea, depression, nervous tension, nervous exhaustion, rashes, frequent bouts of influenza and heavy colds, brain fag, heat, flies and courtroom cross-examinations. He is sometimes so exhausted he feels like lying on his back 'for a month'.[4] He visits Queensland four times, New South Wales six times and Western Australia twice.

He still has to watch every penny. He earns a little in rent from his father's bush properties, and he and Josh Anderson each declare £298 profit from their partnership for 1897. They earn £90 less the following year. Both men also have private consulting work. Monash needs plenty to pay his hefty expenses, including a servant for his wife.

In May 1897 he is in Portland, 360 kilometres west of Melbourne, representing the Austral Otis Engineering Co. against the Portland Freezing Co. The next month he takes the train to Queensland, and between hands of euchre with other first-class passengers, expresses his astonishment at the rich farmland of the Darling Downs. The firm of Baxter & Saddler retains him for their claims against the Queensland Government over a section of the 130-kilometre railway line they've built from Rosedale, near Bundaberg, to Gladstone. Monash spends two weeks travelling by ballast engine to the bush camp of the contractors.

From Queensland he heads to Jerilderie for the first time in 20 years to start work in July on a case for a group of farmers, graziers and townspeople against the wealthy Irish-born brothers

David and Samuel McCaughey, who have been damming water in the Billabong and Colombo Creeks to irrigate their properties. He appears before the Land Board at Urana and at the Land Appeal Court in Sydney. Back in Melbourne, briefly, he sees his first motion picture in August at a show by comic singer Harry Rickards at the Opera House, where the highlights of Queen Victoria's Diamond Jubilee, including footage of English and colonial troops, are 'projected by the latest and most perfect cinematographie' and 'marvellous realism' amid a variety of other attractions including a 'long-legged Comedian and Kockney Komic', a 'world-renowned whistling ventriloquist' and a quick-change artist.[5]

He returns to Queensland in September, preparing to make 20 claims against the railways totalling £25,465 and tells Vic the case 'is the chance of a lifetime'.[6] If he wins, it will be his biggest achievement and his name will be made across the country.

While Monash charges Baxter & Saddler five guineas a day, Anderson works on a deal that will ultimately make their company much more than that.

Anderson strikes up an agreement with Frank Moorhouse Gummow, a Sydney contractor and civil engineer. His firm Carter, Gummow and Co. has acquired the Australian patent rights for a system of reinforced construction developed by a French gardener named Joseph Monier, who was sick of having his flowerpots fall apart. Monier reinforced his concrete tubs with a latticework of iron rods. His patented invention costs builders about the same as timber and far less than iron or steel. Monash says it can be moulded to 'any form of beauty'.[7]

Anderson negotiates a temporary agreement for Monash & Anderson to become Gummow's Victorian agents, and soon Anderson is overseeing the use of Monier construction on three major bridge projects: the 90-metre-long Anderson Street Bridge across the Yarra, near Melbourne's Botanic Gardens; the 80-metre Fyansford Bridge across the Moorabool on the Ballarat Road at Geelong; and the 45-metre Wheeler's Bridge near Creswick. For the bridge across the Yarra, Anderson persuades Carlo Catani, then Chief Engineer of the Public Works Department of Victoria, and William Davidson, the Inspector-General of Public Works, to use three 30-metre Monier arches constructed by Gummow: the largest Monier project Gummow has attempted.

Back on the Jerilderie water-supply case, Monash finds himself in Narrandera trying to help the desperate Chinese community after a bedroom lamp starts a fire that eventually destroys 32 houses and wipes out the town's whole Chinese quarter. Monash has respect for the often unpopular immigrants, enjoys conversing with them and has a high regard for their mining skills, saying, 'they can do almost anything with water power as on the Ovens River'. Yet he is also prone to the prejudice of the time, telling Vic of the victims of the great fire: 'it was the most pitiable yet the most excruciatingly funny performance I ever witnessed … Nothing could be done to save the buildings, though we pulled down 2 houses in an effort to make a fire break. I will not soon forget the poor Chows with their goods, josses and womenfolk. There were the most ludicrous scenes.'[8]

On Melbourne Cup day, 2 November 1897, Monash is amid the hoi polloi in Sydney, where the festive mood is infectious. As he looks around at the eager throng crowding into a bookie's shop in a right-of-way off George Street, he remarks how 'our great Cup Race' is so 'far reaching and Australian in its character'. Monash is among a crowd of several hundred men and women pushing their way into the lane, carried along by a stream of sweating humanity eager to place bets on a horse race a thousand kilometres away.

He finds himself in a long, low room like 'a warehouse basement' where all along one side is a long counter and behind it seven young men, coatless, collarless and reeking of sweat, with stains on their chests and under their arms. Feverishly, they yell the odds until their throats are dry. Coins are passed over the counter – farthings, pennies and shillings 'by the shovelful'. Monash stands there in amazement for half an hour watching the old men, clerks, spivs, 'out at elbow vagrants', factory girls, men in top hats and boys in short pants battling the bookies. At 3.50 p.m. he marches along with the huge crowd to King Street, opposite the telegraph office, to witness the latest in modern communications. When the Sydney Post Office clock begins to chime 4 p.m., a deathly hush falls across the crowd as they all look at their betting tickets.

A day's train journey away, at Flemington, two full brothers, Gaulus and The Grafter, have gone neck-and-neck, charging to the finish line in the great 2-mile (3200-metre) race.[9] Inside the telegraph office a senior operator receives word from Melbourne and flashes up a large sign in the front window: 'GAULUS'. The name is instantly repeated by thousands of voices, some in hushed excitement and others in shocked dismay. Hats are thrown into the air or crushed in desperate hands. 'There were not a few curses,' Monash recalls, 'but business for the day was done.'[10]

Eight days later, on 10 November, the railways case opens at Brisbane's Arbitration Court. It lasts 10 weeks. Monash often works past midnight preparing his evidence. In the cloying heat of a Queensland summer he starts wearing a pith helmet, porous cellular shirts and Assam silk suits. He tells Vic he has become 'quite a bananalander', existing mostly on fresh pineapples and other fruit, though he sweats so much that he goes through three collars, two sets of underwear and three cold showers a day.

He turns the heat up even higher in court, performing splendidly against the railways counsel Arthur Rutledge, a prominent political figure and leader of the Queensland Bar. Monash tells Vic he is in line for a healthy bonus and that soon he will be earning £2000 a year. He even lets her buy the Behrends' piano for 55 quid.

He catches the steamer *Burwah* south for Christmas. Bert is now nearly five and Monash dotes on her, reading to her what he now considers fairytales from the Bible, teaching her to write and encouraging her to take up the piano.

'I have been successful – very – yet a long way short of my early ambitions', he writes on New Year's Day 1898. 'I have had many griefs – death and time have torn away great gaps in the past which I still cherish so fondly. I am happy in my domestic sphere and try to do my duty to my dear wife and darling daughter, and I feel they love me. My sisters too are cared for ... I fear I am as self-conscious as ever, yet I have grown sober – more contented and single of purpose.'[11]

Yet there are some rough passages ahead.

The railways case resumes on 13 January and Monash checks into Brisbane's plush Gresham Hotel.[12] He is compelling during the four days of his final address, but the outcome is a disappointment. Baxter & Saddler are awarded just £7722,[13] a third of what they were chasing, and after costs there is no bonus for Monash. He is doubly grieved when a bushfire scorches his father's land at Thorpdale in Gippsland.

Vic becomes seriously ill in February and travels to the warmer climes of Sydney to convalesce, but Monash hardly has time to kiss her. Soon he is working even harder because now, with her ill health, she says she needs a second servant back at home. In March 1898 Monash is in the Riverina again surveying the Yanco Creek, across from Wanganella up to the Murrumbidgee,[14] as he prepares to advise barrister Sir Julian Salomons in the Jerilderie water-stealing case of *Blackwood v McCaughey* at the Supreme Court in Sydney. The McCaugheys' mouthpiece is the 53-year-old former New South Wales attorney-general John Henry Want.

During an adjournment Monash takes time to visit Gummow's Sydney works to learn everything he can about the Monier system from Gummow's chief designer, Prussian-born William Baltzer.[15] He is back in court in late May as *Blackwood v McCaughey* nears its completion. Tante Ulrike and Vic join him in Sydney as he wades into the great courtroom showdown.

Jack Want goes on the attack, rising to his imperious height, the court's lights reflected on his shiny forehead and his long drooping moustache draped around his mouth like a lizard. He toys with his watch-chain as he lectures the jury in a sonorous[16] voice and dismisses Monash as 'this gentleman from Victoria'. During the lunch break Monash confronts his learned opponent with fire in his eyes. Want merely pats his young rival on the back and invites him for a drink saying, 'It's all in the game.'

Monash wins.

One of the jurymen later tells him that Want's summing-up was 'a fool of a speech' and the court awards £2000 damages. Samuel McCaughey is so impressed by Monash that he suggests future work for him in his employ, and even suggests Monash run for the New South Wales Legislative Assembly to steer through Monash's ideas on damming the Murrumbidgee.

Meanwhile, Josh Anderson has also brought new business into the company with works at Mildura and the installation of machinery at the Ballarat Woollen Mills.

But Monash has no time to spare.

In July 1898, at the request of V.J. (Valentine) Saddler, Monash heads to Perth representing Baxter & Saddler again, this time in their case against the West Australian Government over the 320-kilometre rail line between Geraldton and the Murchison goldfields. Monash expects to stay five weeks but ends up staying a year.

His voyage to Perth aboard the RMS *Peninsular* is reported in the West Australian newspapers on the same day as the uncovering of a plot to assassinate the Austrian Emperor, Franz Joseph. Monash's voyage, though, is without incident, apart from the fact his mouth is constantly watering as Saddler and his rich friends talk of immense projects and massive profits.

Work on the case is delayed as Baxter goes on a huge punting spree at the races, but eventually Monash travels north from Perth to inspect the rail line and gets down to work on the case, supported by a staff of nine, including a secretary who takes dictation.

He is welcomed by the wealthy mining and pastoral families of the west. He dines at the exclusive Weld Club, at a function attended by the explorer brothers John and Alexander Forrest. John is the Premier of Western Australia and Alexander the Mayor of Perth. Old Dick Speight, now a railway boss on the west coast, is there too, and has no hard feelings towards Monash for acting against him in the *Age* case.[17] Monash writes home of his delight at meeting the 'ruling caste' of the west – six families, 'the Forrests, Venns, Lee-Steeres, Stentons, Hammersleighs and Leakes' – and jokes that the people in this 'Sassiety' are 'all intermarried in the most bewildering and interminable confusion'.[18] The wealth dazzles Monash, and he is all ears as Saddler offers him further projects, including oil works in New South Wales and the Zeehan–Strahan railway line in Tasmania.

Monash needs money more than ever. He is now supporting Vic, Bert and his sisters and occasionally lending money to his cousins, the Roths.

Mat raised Lou after their father's death but becomes increasingly socially withdrawn, working as a private tutor from home. Lou is now 25 and keen to teach fitness classes to girls. When Monash suggests Lou work as a governess, Mat says such a life would be a 'slow death' for their sister, who has 'a thirst for excitement.' She has spent the last year writing to her sweetheart Walter Rosenhain. He is a German-born metallurgist whose parents brought him to Melbourne as a small boy so that he would never have to fight in a war. Like Monash, Rosenhain has a civil engineering degree from Melbourne University, but he is now at St John's College, Cambridge.

Monash does not like the Rosenhains. Years ago he clashed with Walter's mother Friederike, a rabbi's daughter, who claimed he had insulted her own daughters. Monash thinks Walter is 'a little prig' and delighted in beating him at chess. Walter seems to make Lou happy, though, even from 16,000 kilometres away.

In Perth Monash invests £200 in a quarry with W.B. Shaw, his friend from the Outer Circle Line. He convinces Josh Anderson, under protest, to throw in £100 of their combined funds – but before long the quarry manager absconds with the cash.

Monash renews his friendship with his old flame Ada Krakowski, who has moved to Perth with her husband Samuel, a leather merchant. Monash thinks it prudent not to mention their reunion to Vic. He starts playing the piano again with an amateur orchestra. The trappings of high society delight him but he also realises that the wealthy have often had to fight to make their fortunes. In September 1898 he laughs out loud at the sight of Saddler punching on with another elderly business rival at the Perth railway as captains of industry and knights of the realm are embroiled in a melee when commercial negotiations take an ugly turn.

Back in Melbourne, Vic consoles her friend Lizzie Bentwitch, whose father has died suddenly in Russell Square, London, while on a holiday.[19] Lizzie's brother Norman organises prayers at the East Melbourne synagogue and Lizzie soon will pack her things and move to London permanently to pursue an artistic life. The Monashes will stay in close touch.

Monash's long periods away from the militia have almost curtailed his military career, and in October 1898 he writes to Vic that he will soon have to swallow the bitter pill and choose between his business career and the militia, a much-loved hobby of 15 years. 'You can't imagine how much it grieves me,' he writes, 'but there is simply nothing for it.'[20]

He visits Kalgoorlie and in November begins preparing the case for Baxter & Saddler against the railways. Realising he is in it for the long haul, he sends for Vic and Bert to join him, regardless of the cost. They stay in Perth for six months and Vic immediately becomes the belle of every ball she attends, even though Monash has become weary of social galas, confessing that 'when men get rotund in bulk, and just a little balder – they wonder how they used to find pleasure in the mazy dance'.[21]

Vic has no such qualms. When Monash rushes back to Melbourne for three weeks for the 1899 Easter military camp, Vic writes to tell him that she wore her 'pink and blue' and looked 'awfully well' at the mayor's reception. 'As I entered,' she says, 'there was a buzz and the men simply rushed me.'[22]

She is sent a diamond ring in the post, anonymously.

With Monash and Farlow calling the shots at the 1899 Easter Camp, the North Melbourne Battery triumphs in the shooting competition at the Queenscliff forts.[23] North Melbourne has been increased to 186 men and divided into two companies, each with a captain and sergeant major. The No. 2 Company sets a record for Australasia, scoring 12 hits out of 16 shots at a ship-sized piece of canvas nearly 2000 metres away that is being towed at 12 knots. Monash says the success shines a brilliant light on his command. 'Both my companies were classed as "First-class shooting Companies",' he says; 'a cruiser would have had a very poor show against us.'

The Baxter & Saddler case finally begins in Perth in late April 1899. Monash makes a claim of £151,000 to the arbitrator, Charles Yelverton O'Connor, an Irishman who is Western Australia's engineer-in-chief and who has a disdain for money-hungry entrepreneurs. Monash works with barrister Walter James, soon to be Western Australia's fifth premier, while the distinguished politician Septimus Burt represents the government. O'Connor awards £15,000 on 42 of the 46 claims, while the others are referred to the Supreme Court before a private settlement. By July Monash manages to extract upwards of £45,000[24] for his clients and earns about £1000 for the year.

He returns to Melbourne that month as skirmishes break out between British settlers and the Boers in South Africa. Queensland Premier James Robert Dickson offers to send 250 troops to support any military action by Her Majesty's forces[25] and Britain soon requests mounted troops from New South Wales and Victoria.

But Monash is more concerned with his business interests.

Two weeks after he returns from the west he is standing alongside his old tutor Professor Kernot, William Davidson and other engineering experts from Victoria and New South Wales to see his company's latest engineering project take shape. The

30-metre spans of the Anderson Street Bridge are put to a test that is 'thorough in the extreme'. A 15-ton steamroller belonging to the Melbourne City Council is run across the bridge and back again. Hundreds of tons of earth are trucked onto the bridge, 'giving a pressure of 100lb to the square foot'. The *Argus* reports that experts gave the 'keenest attention to the trial' and 'declared the result to be all that could be desired'. Monash tells the newspaper Monier construction offers 'cheapness, durableness, lightness, and simplicity'. The bridge has cost £6000,[26] and while Monash and Anderson earn £125 from the deal they take great pains to explain that they neither designed nor built the bridge, but only acted as 'representatives of the patents'.[27] Yet the names Monier and Monash become so intertwined that it will soon be a popular misconception that 'Monier' is derived from Monash's name.

Two weeks later a 160-foot (49-metre) span for Monash & Anderson's North Mount Lyell railway in Tasmania, 'said to be the largest single span steel structure of its kind yet manufactured in Victoria',[28] is unveiled in the yard of the builders Dorman, Long, and Co. of South Melbourne. The railway will cross the King River between Crotty and Linda Valley.[29]

Meanwhile, the fighting escalates in South Africa. On 11 October 1899 Boer soldiers advance into Natal and Cape Colony. Ten days later the first Australian mounted troops to fight in South Africa defeat the Boers at Elandslaagte. Two hundred and fifty Victorian mounted troops are quickly brought together in Melbourne, along with 84 from Tasmania,[30] and Monash is among the thousands farewelling them before they board the *Medic* bound for Cape Town. 'There has been a growing conviction,' the *Australasian* newspaper declares, 'to show our unity with the Empire, not in words only, but in deeds.'[31]

Two weeks after New Year's Day 1900, Monash leads his North Melbourne Garrison in a parade of more than 4000 militiamen as 'immense crowds'[32] line the streets of Melbourne to farewell a second Victorian contingent of 265 mounted troops under the command of the straight-shooting Colonel Tom Price. A decade earlier, when faced with protesting trade unionists, Price told his men that if there was any trouble to 'fire low and lay the bastards out'.[33]

Most of the soldiers heading to the war believe it will soon be won, but older heads fear that with the 'strength of the Empire … menaced … blood and treasure' will be freely poured out.[34]

The Empire needs men who can ride and shoot and wage hand-to-hand guerrilla warfare, not desk-bound businessmen with expanding waistlines, so instead of heading to the veldt, just a week after the soldiers' farewell Monash is at the Town Hall for the civic farewell for Alfred Deakin, off to London with other colonial representatives Edmund Barton and Charles Kingston to oversee the passage of Australia's Federation Bill through the British Parliament.

The Boer War will rage for two more years. The British implement a scorched-earth policy, burning farms to starve the enemy and confining huge sections of the local populace in concentration camps, where more than 40,000, half of them children, die from hunger and disease.[35]

Monash, meanwhile, pours his energy into a campaign imploring the Victorian Government to do more to fund higher education, lest it become 'only a rich man's ambition', and he sees himself as having a pivotal role in building the nation from the ground up.

He and Anderson see enormous potential in selling Monier pipes and have already convinced the Melbourne and Metropolitan Board of Works to undertake trials.

Monash buys an investment cottage in Port Melbourne in Vic's name, putting down £40 on the £140 purchase price. He still has to economise, because struggling shire councils are so slow to pay.

Work on the Fyansford Bridge stalls several times over payment delays from the Shires of Bannockburn and Corio. Finally, on 16 February 1900, the £5500 bridge passes its test under the load of an 18-ton steamroller. Carlo Catani, from the Public Works Department, calls it 'an excellent piece of work',[36] yet Monash and Anderson will have to wait more than a year and undergo costly court battles before the business is finished. Their contract for £4507 is paid but the shires refuse to meet the final sum of £6142, which includes new work. The shires say the bill is fraudulent.

The struggling engineers have their capital tied in a knot that threatens their business and forces staff retrenchments. Monash is so jaded that he now assumes 'every man a rogue till he is proved honest – a sorry maxim for humanity, but, I believe, a necessary one'.[37] 'My experience is that the dishonest man never carries his hallmark in view.'[38]

Nothing ever seems to run smoothly. Anderson comes down with typhoid. Monash starts fighting with Vic again and his cousin Louis Roth, a lowly paid 27-year-old bookkeeper, is charged with embezzling £93 18s from the shipping firm of McIlwraith, McEacharn & Co. Apart from Monash's charity, Louis is the sole support for the widowed Tante Ulrike. Monash pays for George Farlow to defend Louis, but although Rabbi Abrahams gives a glowing character reference to the court, Monash's cousin is still sent to Castlemaine Prison for 18 months.

For Tante Ulrike and her daughters, Sophie and Mathilde, the sentence is even more heartbreaking than the headlines that call it 'The Roth Embezzlement Case'.[39] Monash sticks by Louis, though, helping him get back on his feet as an accountant at Katanning in Western Australia after his release. He also pays the mortgage and the rates for his aunt, but Ulrike's other two sons are no help. His childhood companion Karl has failed as a pharmacist in Maitland, New South Wales and become an itinerant, indigent hawker, while Herman Roth will be banished from the family after being caught with his hand in the till while working for Monash & Anderson. Herman fails to register a number of patents, causing one irate client to insist on a heavy financial settlement that cost Monash & Anderson more than £100, as well as the damage to their reputation.

Albert Behrend takes Minnie and their now-large family to Austria in the hope of improving their lot. Monash writes to tell him that things are equally grim in Melbourne and that he is feeling severe strain from 'constant work, and the responsibility for keeping up two households'. 'In younger days I strove and drove to make a position,' he says, 'and now the position drives me ... there is fearful competition in contracting work ... and the nett result is a bare comfortable livelihood for those for whom I am responsible, and for myself a steady continuous grind and mental strain week in, week out.'[40] Albert returns to Melbourne a year later and asks Monash for a loan.

On 30 March 1900, just outside Creswick, 130 kilometres west of Melbourne, the Victorian Minister for Public Works, George Graham, watches two traction engines being rolled back and forth over the two 22-metre spans. He then declares Wheeler's Bridge open and calls it both 'a highly creditable piece of work' and 'a distinct era in municipal engineering practice'.[41] But it isn't all it's cracked up to be, and within a month the walls of the bridge start bulging outwards. Monash and Anderson blame inferior cement and interference from the staff of the Kingston Shire but agree to contribute just over half the cost of repairs.[42]

A 440-foot (134-metre) wooden truss bridge across the Tambo River at Bruthen, in Gippsland, causes Monash and Anderson more headaches after they win the tender for £8290.[43] The original concept of four 92-foot (28-metre) Monier arches proves unfeasible and on 28 May, Monash, Chris Christensen and three workmen travel by train to Bairnsdale and then by horse coach to Bruthen to begin work on a timber structure. Christensen's brusque manner irritates the local inspectors and when it is found that his calculations make the bridge 5 feet 6 inches (1.68 metres) too short, they demand he be sacked. Monash tells Christensen, 'this matter has caused us very grave anxiety, and an immense amount of trouble'.[44]

Monash eventually wins the dispute but he is careful not to come on too strong as he negotiates a £6967 deal to build eight

Monier bridges in Bendigo, where a concrete channel has been devised to avoid flooding of the Bendigo Creek.[45] The engineers will source their cement from David Mitchell and from Richard Taylor's Fyansford works.

Monash makes headway with his scheme to manufacture Monier pipes after Mitchell, through his manager John Gibson, offers Monash land next to his works in Burnley Street, Richmond, provided that Monash uses his Emu brand cement.

On New Year's Day 1901 Monash is in Sydney with Gummow for the inauguration of the Australian Commonwealth. A jubilant crowd of 150,000 swarms around the Federation Kiosk at Centennial Park for the swearing in of Lord Hopetoun as the first governor-general and for the singing of 'God Save the Queen' and 'Advance Australia Fair'.[46] Monash negotiates a deal in which Gummow sells his rights to the Monier process in Victoria for £500, with the money being repaid as royalties from a new company formed by Monash, Anderson and Mitchell: the Monier Pipe Company.

Just three weeks after Australia becomes a nation, her first Queen, Victoria, lame, and her eyes clouded by cataracts, dies at 81 after reigning for 63 years. Her body is clothed in a white dress and her wedding veil as two of her sons, Prince Albert Edward and Prince Arthur, the Duke of Connaught, along with her eldest grandson Kaiser Wilhelm II of Germany, help lift her into her coffin, which is decorated with an array of mementos from family, friends and servants.

Australia hosts large public displays of its collective grief, and Monash attends the non-denominational service at Melbourne's Exhibition Building on the afternoon of Sunday, 27 January, where the metropolitan and naval forces join the Indian and imperial troops visiting Australia.[47] He is at the Melbourne Cricket Ground the following night for 'the grand sacred concert'[48] and at Parliament House the next day for the proclamation declaring Prince Albert Edward as the new King Edward VII.[49]

Then it's back to work.

At Bendigo he has 22 bridge-builders starting work at daybreak and knocking off at 3.20 p.m. Dressed in a dusty suit and an old black bowler hat pushed down hard on his head, he is a picture of grim concentration, smoking furiously and completely absorbed in his work as he directs operations in the building of the eight bridges,[50] with the largest, the King's Bridge, being built 'on the acute angle of 40 degrees, in order to meet the trend of the creek and the formation of the roadway'.[51]

On 9 May 1901, Monash and Vic attend the opening of the first Federal Parliament at the Exhibition Building, seeing for the first time the Duke of Cornwall and York, who within a decade will be crowned King George V.

Five days later, at 4.20 p.m. on 14 May 1901, Monash, Bendigo's City Engineer, Joseph Richard Richardson, and a team of council employees assemble to conduct the load test on the 28-metre span of the King's Bridge. A roller and a traction engine are parked on it so Monash can take photographs. Council workers take their positions under the bridge to record how much the span flexes under the heavy loads.

A fine crack appears on the bridge surface and there are other signs of distress. Richardson and Monash examine the bridge but decide the cracks are only superficial and that the load is far greater than the bridge will experience under normal use. Richardson says it's safe to continue with the heavy examination.

The roller and traction engine are brought close together near the middle of the span, concentrating 25 tons in a small area, while men standing under the arch take measurements.

Suddenly the bridge starts to warp.

Pieces of concrete fall off and splash into the water.

Monash and others cry out, 'Get away, get away!' as desperate men try to save themselves. The men on the traction engine jump clear but most of the spectators on the bridge, including Richardson, come crashing down in a rain of concrete, bricks and flailing arms and legs.[52] The steamroller remains perched on the edge of the section of bridge still standing, but the traction engine teeters and falls in a crash of belching, spitting steam. Pinned underneath it is 37-year-old husband and father Albert Edward Boldt, one of the engine's co-owners.[53] His left leg and arm are severed and he is disembowelled. His mangled corpse is retrieved and laid on the water's edge. Bags are placed over his torn body.

Horrified, Monash immediately does a roll call to make sure none of his men are buried under the rubble. He is covered in mud and dust and his face is clouded by shock. With a look of stunned disbelief he stammers at a local reporter: 'I'm totally bewildered ... I have nothing but the greatest regret ... the loss of life ... such harrowing circumstances.'[54]

It is not just the carnage of the loss of life amid the collapsed structure. Monash's whole career seems to have come crashing down along with the bridge.

Things are as bad as they've ever been. All Monash can do is face the battle squarely.

Chapter 11

CORONER'S COURT, BENDIGO HOSPITAL,
15 MAY 1901, 2 P.M.

*A child of one's own links one strangely both to the past, and the
future and one both starts life afresh and lives one's childhood and
youth all over again.*

MONASH TO HIS SISTER LOU, WHO IS ABOUT TO
EXPERIENCE MOTHERHOOD[1]

THE BRIDGE COLLAPSE and the horrific death of Albert
Boldt take a heavy toll on Monash and Anderson. The
inquest begins at the Bendigo Hospital the following afternoon as
large crowds come to gawk at the nearby death scene.

Two days later, Monash writes to the Bendigo City Council
to express his company's deep regret over the 'loss of life, a loss
which is, unhappily, beyond recall'. He and Anderson offer their
'utmost assistance to a searching inquiry into all the circumstances'
and promise to continue with the work at their own cost, and
to complete the contract 'in a manner which will be thoroughly
satisfactory to the council, and will undoubtedly inspire complete
public confidence'.[2]

George Farlow, representing Monash & Anderson, has
Professor Kernot show the court on a blackboard just how much

the skewed angle of the bridge, as demanded by the council, has contributed to the unique stress on the structure.

'For the first time in the history of Monier Bridge building, a section gave way,' the court hears. 'The expert evidence does not suggest that there was bad workmanship or lack of supervision.' Kernot says he has selected a sample of cement and tested it, finding that it was slightly stronger in quality than several specimens of similar cements tested by the Melbourne and Metropolitan Board of Works.

At the end of May a seven-man jury rules Albert Boldt's death accidental.[3]

Despite the favourable trial outcome, the tragedy costs Monash and Anderson a great deal of anxiety, which they have in abundance, and a great deal of money, which they completely lack.

The following month, June 1901, Justice Sir Hartley Williams, in civil sittings of the Supreme Court, awards them £1902 plus costs in their claim over the Fyansford Bridge, declaring there is not a 'tittle of evidence'[4] to support the 'scandalous charge' of fraud made by the two shires. But Monash still can't get his money. With their lawyers urging them to fight on, the shires appeal to the Full Court, and Monash and Anderson then take the extraordinary step of having the bailiff seize office furniture, books and road rollers from both councils to sell at auction.[5]

Construction on Bendigo's new King's Bridge begins in August 1901, following key recommendations by Kernot that the brick parapets be replaced by light iron, that the central pier be carried down to rock and that weep holes be provided in the pier for drainage.

Monash manages to scrape together enough money to pay his sister Lou's fare in cabin class on the steamer *Weimar* bound for England via Bremen. Her lengthy correspondence with Walter Rosenhain has culminated in the long distance lovebirds' decision to marry. The Monashes farewell Lou on 24 September[6] and she arrives in Southhampton seven weeks later but the generosity leaves Monash so strapped for cash that he can't afford to send her a telegram when she finally marries Walter in Maida Vale, London, on 4 December 1901. He hopes, though, that his little sister can avoid the marital minefield he is again treading after Vic storms out of the house and leaves him for a week, complaining that he treats her like a child.

She suspects he is involved with other women, though she has no evidence. He complains that she has no interest in the demanding work that puts food on their table and pays for her servants, that she spends money they don't have – sometimes donating it to bookmakers – and that her flirtatious manner causes much gossip and innuendo.

For all that, things are calmer than they once were. Years later, though, Monash will write to Walter Rosenhain and say that while his own married life for a long time was 'irksome and almost intolerable' and involved 'several years of severe suffering', a gradual change came and his domestic affairs finally 'reached smooth waters'.[7]

His financial troubles, however, still weigh heavily on him, and even though he and Vic cut a fine figure at government balls and at the theatre every couple of weeks, Monash's perilous financial straits humiliate him. Attending the balls is essential for social advancement and Vic is his perfect assistant, dancing with the commanding general and other dignitaries, but Monash is sometimes months behind with his rent and life assurance payments. He deftly sidesteps letters of demand. Yet he still has a charitable heart, and records in his diary that he found an old woman in the gutter on his way to the Varsity Club and took her home. He is a gregarious companion who enjoys the company at the Old Scotch Collegians' Club and the University Club, moving the founding motion. He becomes a regular at the Yorick Club but struggles to pay the fees despite a turn as club auditor.[8] He tries his hand at photography but does not have time to become really proficient.

He is under constant stress. His belly gets bigger and his hair thinner.

He and Anderson score minor jobs and Monash spends some time on an inquiry into the Melbourne and Metropolitan Board of Works, alongside his old friend Jack Mackey. He apologises to Mat when he can't afford a birthday present, but scrapes together enough pennies during the lean years to buy a set of the *Encyclopaedia Britannica*, a *Library of Famous Literature*, a set of the *Arabian Nights* costing nine guineas, and the *Masterpiece Art Portfolio*. While he frittered away his first few years as a student following his mother's death, education is now his foundation for the future. To him knowledge and success are all by-products of study, hard work and relentless application.

The Bendigo Council, which has considered cancelling Monash's bridge contracts, insists another of his bridges at High Street be tested under the weight of 30 tons. A crowd of 600 gathers to see the potential carnage on 3 October 1901, but they have assembled in vain, for the bridge passes muster.[9]

Over Christmas and New Year, Monash is away from home again, camping out at Hells Gates at Macquarie Harbour in Tasmania's west, where he is working on an arbitration case at Strahan. He finds the area as wild and unpredictable as the depiction in Marcus Clarke's *For the Term of His Natural Life*.

The rebuilt King's Bridge is tested satisfactorily in January 1902, though once again there is a protracted battle over final payment.

Back in Melbourne, Monash is delighted with the progress of eight-year-old Bert at the Stratherne Ladies' College in Hawthorn, where she is among the prizewinners of 1901. He takes her bushwalking and bird-watching and plans a bright future for her, following his sisters at Presbyterian Ladies' College and perhaps even at a finishing school in Europe if he can ever raise the extra money.[10] He writes to Lou when she is about to experience motherhood, telling her: 'You will soon find out what a different aspect life will assume ... and the joys, tempered also by troubles, which are their outcome.'[11]

Early in 1902 he makes a few pipe sales to the Public Works Department and to the Prahran municipality, but the Board of Works and the railways, potentially big customers, refuse to commit.

In February he and Anderson, represented by Leo Cussens, are in the Court of Appeal, arguing their case against the shires over the Fyansford Bridge payment. Edward Mitchell, a former cabinet minister, and Isaac Isaacs, the most famous Jew in Melbourne, are in the other corner. Judgment is deferred for seven months, and while Monash and Anderson are seeking damages and costs totalling £4000, they finish with just £725. Justices Holroyd, Hodges and a'Beckett rule that Monash & Anderson were hard done by, but that there had been ambiguity in the contracts and the law is on the side of the shires.[12]

Cussens wants to take the matter to the Privy Council in England, and Mat starts typing up the proceedings for the Lords of Appeal on the typewriter her brother still cannot master. The potential expense scares Monash out of further action, and he and Anderson finally settle with the shires for a slightly increased payout in April 1903. Monash calculates that the case has cost him and his partner £3000. They owe creditors, including Gummow and Mitchell, at least another thousand. He is furious with Farlow over his hefty legal fees.

Struggling to support his large family, Anderson accepts a job in Dunedin, New Zealand, running the city's sewerage system. He and Monash remain partners, but Monash is left to deal with the mess in Melbourne. Faced with insolvency, Monash begins fighting his way out of trouble, telling Gummow that he and Anderson aim to work their way out of debt and pay their bills within two years. He begins to echo the lugubriousness of his grandfather back in Krotoszyn.

On 20 September 1902, Monash and Bert are among the crowd at Spencer Street Station to welcome home Nellie Melba from Europe with 'a tremendous ovation' as her own special railway carriage glides to a halt.[13] The next month Monash takes Madame Melba around the pipe factory he has built with her father's money, but the strain of his many commitments and family responsibilities shows on Monash's lined face.

In Germany, though, Erich Ludendorff is making all the right moves and is now a senior staff officer with V Corps HQ, working under Field Marshal Count Alfred Graf von Schlieffen,[14] who is devising a bold plan to one day overrun France.

While Ludendorff wonders how many more steps he must take to become a general, Monash struggles with an oppressive workload and an uncertain future.

He writes to Lou that 'latterly it is all I can do to keep pace with the really important current work. I find too that I can work neither as fast, nor so long as I used to, and require more regular and longer sleep.'[15]

He suffers another blow when his old friend and physician Joe Miller dies suddenly of acute septic poisoning after eating tinned salmon. 'So great was the respect entertained for the deceased gentleman,' the next day's paper says, 'that thousands of people lined Sydney Road to pay their last respects to the doctor.' Monash calls Miller 'my almost constant companion since my school days' and leads the garrison in salute at his military funeral.[16]

He drinks away the sorrow a couple of weeks later at Jack Mackey's buck's night, surrounded by lawyers and politicians. Monash has become a brilliant engineering lecturer, able to enthral his students for long periods without notes. He believes that to inspire confidence in others he must display it himself but often he has to force himself to take charge. He is still uncomfortable when asked to make speeches off the cuff and he still carries his book of poems and limericks in case he gets stuck for something to say in social settings. Still mourning Miller, he is no mood for frivolity at Mackey's do. His usually confident bearing is deflated. When asked to propose the toast to the groom he tries to wriggle out of it at first by saying, 'This is not much in my line.'[17]

He tells Lou in England that his fortune has still not materialised, despite his labours, but the company negotiates to build some smaller bridges: one in East Ballarat using a T-shaped beam structure rather than an arch, another across Ford's Creek at Lancefield, and one over the spillway of the Upper Coliban Reservoir, near Kyneton. Anderson's brother Jack is the foreman there, though he is eventually dismissed after one bender too many.

Monash makes a small amount as a patent agent, though he says he has never yet known an inventor to make sixpence from any of the more than 100 patents he has organised. He also advises the Dunlop Pneumatic Tyre Company on updating its machinery. But preliminary work on an electric tramway in Essendon goes nowhere, and requests to Deakin to be made commissioner for the investigation of sites for Australia's new national capital fall on deaf ears.

He duels with Isaac Isaacs in court again in 1903, appearing for a Russian woodcarver named John Kannaluik in his fight with the Hawthorn Council over the constant flooding of his house. Monash plays on the winning team and Isaacs says Monash always 'came to the Court with a perfect grasp of the points at issue, a perfect understanding of the rights and wrongs of the dispute, a perfect power of expressing with lucidity the opinions he held'.[18]

Monash's business affairs have become all-consuming and he 'has to almost entirely neglect military matters', admitting that he has only been able to retain his 'position of command by the assistance of my subordinate officers, and the goodwill of my seniors'.[19] Devon-born Major General 'Curly' Hutton[20] is now Chief of the Australian Military Forces and is busy uniting the six colonial militias into one national army. From July 1903, Monash's battery becomes No. 3 Victorian Company, Australian Garrison Artillery.

Vic's bronchitis and asthma force the Monashes to leave the dampness of their Hawthorn home for more comfortable lodgings at the Bungalow, a boarding house in East Melbourne, on the corner of Gipps and Powlett Streets. Monash begins walking to work as he did as a schoolboy through the Fitzroy Gardens. He takes a three-month post at the university to lecture on hydraulic engineering and becomes a member of the faculty, borrowing notes and a cap and gown. He tells every public official and engineer he can about the superiority in cost and durability of Monier reinforced concrete over wrought iron, brick and ordinary concrete. With the aid of lantern slides he lectures to the Royal Victorian Institute of Architects on the principles.[21]

His Monier Pipe Company receives orders in various sizes from the Board of Works, Department of Public Works and local councils and by the end of 1903 Monash has made enough from the business to pay his establishment costs, including the rights fee to Gummow.

But his engineering business still struggles. With a bid of £9472 – other bids range up to £14,000 – Monash wins the tender to build a 270-foot (82.3-metre) bridge across the Murray between Koondrook, near Kerang in Victoria, and Barham in New South Wales.[22] The bridge will be made of wood and metal from the Eureka Ironworks in Ballarat and will have a tilting span in the middle to allow steamers to pass through. But the project hits rough waters early. Delays by the Public Works Department in New South Wales force the Bank of Australasia to remind Monash of his alarming accounts. His overdraft has gone beyond its limit of £120. He promises that payments from other projects will see him through and that the cheques are in the mail.

Saddler, who agreed to bankroll the new bridge deal, pulls out, realising that Monash has underestimated the costs. Another backer, A.G. Shaw, steps in, lending Monash £520 to pay the deposit on the deal in return for six per cent per annum interest on all outstanding monies.

The interest piles up as unusually heavy rains raise the level of the river. Work stops for months. By 1904 the cofferdam is leaking heavily and Monash has to apply for a six-month extension on the deadline for completion. Two carpenters suffer from infections or 'poisoned hands' and Christensen clashes often with the New South Wales inspector, J.B.A. Benyon Reed. Christensen's mood has soured because Monash has been forced to garnish his wages to pay the foreman's deserted wife and children.

The bridge finally opens in October 1904 with a revised cost of £10,345.[23] Monash makes next to nothing, but at least has a little extra money to pay for Vic to take up shooting with the Commonwealth Ladies' Rifle Club. She becomes a crack shot but the novelty soon wears off.

Monash at last has the funds to join the Victorian Institute of Engineers as well, and at a meeting there on 7 September, when his membership is confirmed, Professor Kernot presents a paper called 'Introductory Notes on Motor-cars'. Kernot has spent months experimenting with a steam-powered automobile, testing it for more than 500 kilometres – chugging it up 'the noted steep hill of Heidelberg from the lower road past the Incurable Hospital' and letting it rip up Curly Hill at Keilor. He tells his audience that the motor-car will not mean the death of the horse, 'that useful friend of man through thousands of years', but that it will take the heavy and exhausting work from this 'beautiful and gentle animal' and 'terminate much hardship and cruelty that at present distresses every kindly and sympathetic mind'.[24]

Monash listens intently as the institute's president George Turner says there is 'no class of machinery at present demanding such perfect workmanship and materials' as the motor-car, and that after enjoying a trip in Professor Kernot's steam car, he considers 'it infinitely more comfortable to ride in than the petrol-motor'. The major drawback for steam, though, Kernot admits, is that 'the steam car requires about 15 minutes in which to raise steam. If, after lying unused for some hours or days, it is urgently needed for some sudden emergency, it is not ready at once; the petrol car is.'[25]

That December, with Kernot supervising, Monash conducts his own tests on reinforced concrete beams and presents his findings to the institute. He performs tests on T-beams and is so sure of his construction principles that he challenges a formula developed by a leading Austrian expert.

By March 1905 Monash has spent 20 years in the Victorian Militia and qualifies for his long service medal. His old school rival Jim McCay, though, once again has left him behind and is now the Federal Minister for Defence under Prime Minister George Reid.

Erich Ludendorff, meanwhile, joins the Great General Staff in Berlin, responsible for the Mobilisation Section. The plan of Ludendorff's mentor, the ancient Count von Schlieffen, calls on Germany to find another 100,000 professional troops and 100,000 militiamen for a war with France that has been brewing all of the count's long life.

Monash is a long way from the top of the Victorian militia. He is still only a part-time soldier, a reservist, with the yearly Easter manoeuvres the highlight of his military calendar. But he is well regarded by his seniors and has won widespread backing from Victoria's volunteer soldiers by supporting better pay for non-commissioned officers, instructors and specialists. He realises that to get the best out of his men a pat on the back is more effective than a kick in the pants – but he can kick when called upon, dismissing employees who let him down and fighting tooth-and-nail in court for his fair shake.

Yet he suspects a prominent place in the Australian military has passed him by. The failure of his business to maintain its early advance has forced him to relegate his militia involvement to that of a hobby.

He is 40 now and, despite his education and involvement in major projects, still has little to show from his relentless pursuit of the pound.

Monash & Anderson ceases to exist in April 1905. Monash claims his old tutor was largely responsible for the Fyansford debacle and resents having to chase and perform most of the work to pay off the company's debts while Anderson is in New Zealand.

He gives Anderson a discharge of his liability calculated at £2372 that also means Anderson will have no share in any future profits from Monier construction.

The split will cost Anderson dearly as Monash at last begins to make headway.

Monash moves his family out of their lodgings at the Bungalow to a rented house at 74 Gipps Street, East Melbourne, and becomes good friends with his landlords, the Cathie family.

He restructures his business as the Reinforced Concrete & Monier Pipe Construction Co., with Monash and David Mitchell having 40 per cent each, John Gibson 19 per cent and the company secretary, Edward Newbigin, one per cent.

Gummow gives Monash patent rights in two more States, South Australia and Western Australia, and early in 1905 Monash completes a flat reinforced concrete roof for a ballroom at Raveloe, home of the family of Mabel Emmerton,[26] in Domain Road, South Yarra.

With his future starting to brighten, Monash turns his attention back to the militia, hoping to take command of the Garrison Artillery from Henry Hall, who moves to another post in 1906. In his exams to become a lieutenant colonel, Monash finishes first out of five candidates in two subjects and second in the other. But Major John James Hanby, eight years Monash's senior, is given the position.

Monash is staggered.

He suspects there is now little prospect of advancement for a portly middle-aged man whose field of expertise in coastal artillery is so specialised. The stress of long hours and heavy financial burdens has weighed heavily on him and the siren call of still-elusive affluence makes him work harder 'and with less relaxation than ever'.[27]

Concerned over his health, he eventually writes for advice to Eugen Sandow, the world-renowned bodybuilder who left Prussia to escape military service and is now based in London, dispensing fitness routines around the world by mail order.

Monash gives Sandow the bad news about his own physique and lifestyle. He is a heavy pipe smoker and overweight, with a sedentary lifestyle and a fondness for 'starchy and fatty foods, because I find that vegetable diets such as fruits, raw and cooked give digestive trouble'. He has recovered from many of the earlier complaints that plagued him during his travels around Australia and tells Sandow that 'with the exception of a tendency to bilious or dyspeptic aches (not severe)', his health is 'excellent – never had a serious illness, quickly shake off a cold'.

He puts on the best possible front for Sandow, disregarding all the times he'd staggered home blotto as a younger man to say that most of his habits are 'very temperate, but not a total abstainer'. He drinks tea at every meal and takes a cold shower every day, all year. Only one-fifth of his time is spent travelling now, but the only exercise he gets is 'five to ten minutes stretching and light dumbbell exercises every morning after bath, before breakfast'. He is fairly supple and sleeps well. He needs spectacles for reading.

His neck is 16½ inches. His 'chest empty' is '40½ in, expanded 43 in'. His 'normal' waist is 43 inches. When he sucks in his gut as hard as he can, he can squeeze it down to 41 but he knows that's still not good.[28]

Major Monash is starting to think of himself as a fat old has-been.

Chapter 12

OFFICE OF THE REINFORCED CONCRETE CO., 12TH FLOOR, AUSTRALIA BUILDING, MAY 1905

Gummow in Sydney, and I in Victoria have simply and boldly been the pioneers of a new era in engineering. We are the precursors of a new development in the Engineering profession.

MONASH EXPLAINING THE REASONS FOR THE TURNAROUND
IN HIS FORTUNES[1]

I am afraid that in some subtle way our poor mother's early death gave me the idea that one became old at 40 ... my experience is that the calming down of youthful exuberance brings with it a much stronger, much more real and solid sense of vigorous living.

MONASH ON HIS SECOND LEASE OF LIFE[2]

BOOM. After years of crumbling fortunes in the building game, everyone in Melbourne is now talking about the way property values are going through the roof. Almost overnight, it seems, tradesmen can charge what they want because of the demand for new buildings and renovations.[3] Large parts of the city are being torn down to make way for bigger and better buildings. There are so many structures in Brunswick being ripped apart for rebuilds that it resembles the earthquake-ravaged San Francisco.[4] Monash, who was facing ruin after the bridge collapse in Bendigo only a few years earlier, has weathered a financial storm to emerge into the glorious light. He had promised his creditors that he would work his way out of trouble and he has. He can barely keep up with the building contracts and orders for supplies pouring into his office.

Before long Monash's Reinforced Concrete Co. is erecting bridges in Elwood, Staughton Vale near Geelong, Sunbury, Lancefield, Elsternwick and a site near Kilmore.

Even more lucrative are his building contracts, with his reinforced concrete being used in a seven-storey block of offices and apartments for the National Mutual Life Association in Bank Place.

Monash becomes engaged in a fierce contest with the Building Surveyor's Department over approval for the project, which is his first building with a reinforced concrete structural frame.[5] The City Building Referees believe his proposal does not conform to existing regulations, but Monash emphasises reinforced concrete's resistance to fire and the fact that his floors are stronger than both stone and plain concrete slabs.

He dashes off a letter of delight to Gummow after the referees finally give him the green light, telling Gummow: 'the whole of the footings, columns, floors, joists, girders, stairs, partitions, lintels and flat roof are to be of reinforced concrete, totalling in value, roughly £3500'.[6]

Soon, Monash has contracts to provide reinforced concrete for the stores of Australian Mercantile Land & Finance in the suburb of Kensington, a five-storey block of offices for the same company in William Street, Melbourne's Dental Hospital, the City Abattoirs in Kensington, two buildings for David Mitchell in the city, the Central Telephone Exchange and an extra floor and roof for the BATC (British Australasian Tobacco Co.) Building. Then there are concrete tanks, culverts, the university dissecting room, additions to the Government Printing Office and a £26,000 contract for the Preston No. 2 Reservoir. Interstate there is the Commercial Bank in Launceston and, in South Australia, renovations at city buildings, a railway bridge across the

Hindmarsh River at Victor Harbor, the Holland Street Bridge in Adelaide and a wharf at Port Adelaide.

Monash pays off his debts at £1000 a year. With a dozen major projects on the go at any one time, he finally feels that his business is out of danger after three years of 'a rough passage', when 'it was touch and go, and an undue pressure of an impatient creditor would have smashed the thing to splinters'.[7] Monash says he will forever be in the debt of David Mitchell, 'who befriended me when I needed help so badly',[8] and he sends a gift of £250 to John Gibson, Mitchell's manager, as a way 'to express in a tangible form my sense of the many obligations I am under to you in the assistance you have generously given in rebuilding my shattered fortunes'.[9] Monash is still rotund, but the weight of extra funds makes him feel lighter and younger than he has in years; indeed, he has a feeling of 'immense juvenility'.[10]

Vic's nerves are still unpredictable and her asthma plays up. Every year from 1906 she takes a break from her husband to holiday on her own in Sydney or Adelaide.

While Monash barely made £200 in partnership with Anderson in 1898, he is earning 10 times that by 1907. He is so confident of making even more money that he rejects an offer to become the Chief Commissioner of the Victorian Police from Jack Mackey, now a member of Thomas Bent's Victorian Government. Instead, Monash branches out and forms the South Australian Reinforced Concrete Co. Ltd in an equal partnership with Mitchell, Gibson and the wealthy pastoralists Edward Howard Bakewell and Charles Howard Angas.

By 1909 his annual income is £7000: about $2 million in 2015 terms. He has personal assets of £3146 and is on his way to amassing a property portfolio of more than 20 suburban houses.

While he has personally rejected the teachings of Judaism, the influence of his relatives and the desire to have a religious and cultural foundation for his family prompts him to rebuild bridges with Melbourne's Jewish community. He wants Bertha to grow up with the heritage of his parents and his many relatives living in Melbourne. He is able to regain his seats at the Melbourne Hebrew Congregation, where Vic's family were members, after they were forfeited in 1905 for unpaid fees dating back nearly a decade. He donates small amounts to Jewish charities, the Austin Hospital and the Salvation Army, but as always saves his biggest donations for the family he has supported all his working life.

He holidays occasionally at Lorne with Vic and Bert, and over the Melbourne Cup weekends of 1906 to 1908 leads walking parties of six or eight, including Dave Bevan, Farlow and Gibson, to Mount Buffalo, camping out under the stars. Sometimes they explore the underground creeks and caverns using ropes. Monash earns the nickname 'Thunder Roars' for his snoring, which is said to echo through the alps.

He makes many good friends during this prosperous time. One of them is another Old Scotch Collegian, lawyer and Boer War veteran Julius Bruche,[11] who was born in Melbourne eight years after Monash to parents who had also migrated from Germany. John Stanley, now the Victorian Commandant, is also Monash's close confidant despite the rocky start to their friendship, and Stanley's eventual successor John William Parnell, a former university colleague, also becomes a close mate.

Monash wants Mat to have close friends and experience good times as well. She has hardly made the most of her intellectual gifts, having achieved first-class honours in Modern Languages all those years ago in the university matriculation examination. In an age when few women had careers, she had stayed home to look after Lou, while her brother gained three university degrees and his first footings in the corporate world. Monash feels a sense of guilt over Mat's situation. She has not had the opportunities to thrive as he has, and while constantly cheering on her brother's success, she has become more and more socially withdrawn, tutoring students from home. Long ago Monash had helped her draft a letter fobbing off a potential suitor but no other prospective husbands have arrived in the interim. So instead, Mat becomes involved in charity work and eventually translates 207 books into

Braille. Monash wants her to see the world. She is living with Tante Ulrike and her cousins Mathilde and Sophia in Tivoli Place, South Yarra, in what Monash calls 'poverty stricken, not to say squalid surroundings'. Shy and awkward, she is becoming increasingly reclusive, slow to make friends and wallowing in a 'pathetic loneliness'.[12] Just as he sent Lou to England to marry six years earlier, Monash pays for Mat to travel to England to broaden her outlook on life. She sets off in February 1907 to stay with Lou and Walter, who is now the Superintendent of the Department of Metallurgical Chemistry at the National Physical Laboratory at Teddington, in south-west London.

There is initial friction between the sisters over the way Mat raised Lou following their mother's death. Monash describes it as 'a delusion' of Lou's that she was badly treated by her siblings and a 'failure to recognise' just how much Mat did for her, or that Monash did his best to support her financially when he was all but skint himself.

'I have the satisfaction of knowing that during all the time I was solely responsible for her material welfare, I did the best I could for her', he writes, '... so far as emotional troubles are concerned – they are almost wholly of our own making ... if people allow themselves to really suffer from such things as jealousy, wounded pride or ingratitude they have themselves to blame more than those who cause such feelings'.[13]

Mat finds her younger sister nervous, skittish, self-absorbed and lacking friends, and suspects that Walter is jealous that his brother-in-law is making so much money. She also admits she is envious of the love the Rosenhains have for each other and their children, a love she has never known.

Lou finds her older sister 'moody and morbid',[14] but eventually Mat proves a great help to the Rosenhains as a babysitter. She starts to make long trips to the Continent and talks about staying in London permanently. Monash promises her she can visit Europe every two or three years on his tab, because 'Gummow and I are unquestionably at the very top of the profession and ...

are looked up to as leaders of scientific thought … since you left my standing and influence and power have grown enormously'.[15] Mat makes the most of her first trip abroad and ends up staying away for more than 18 months. On her return she becomes a member of the Alliance Francais and Melbourne's Lyceum Club, an organisation restricted to women university graduates or other women who have distinguished themselves in arts, music, literature or public service.

Even as she visits Europe, though, there are dark clouds over much of the continent.

Germany now leads the world in the production of weapons and Erich Ludendorff, the army's chief of mobilisations, is preparing for war.

In Melbourne, Monash's increasing success in business sparks a stunning turnaround in his military fortunes as well.

Having believed himself to be all but finished in his trajectory as an artillery officer, he is suddenly in big demand. Even though Lieutenant Colonel Hanby has command of the Garrison Artillery, Monash applies the same principles in the militia as he does in business, believing that perseverance and hard work will pay off eventually. Making good contacts along the way hasn't hurt either. He attends a course of instruction in staff duties taught by Colonel Hubert Foster, the Director of Military Science at the University of Sydney, and takes another course two years later.

In December 1907, Monash's old schoolmate and one-time arch-rival, Colonel Jim McCay, takes command of the newly created Australian Intelligence Corps and he makes Monash an offer he can't refuse: to command its Victorian section.

The driving force behind the corps is the tall, slightly built, Scottish-born Colonel William Throsby Bridges,[16] four years Monash's senior and a Boer War veteran. The corps's main role is to collect information about the topography and military resources of Australia and surrounding countries, especially in the Pacific, and use it to prepare strategic maps and defence plans.

When it comes to military maps Australia's cupboard is bare, and Monash immediately realises the importance of the work. He accepts the position, but insists on a promotion in rank, pointing out that while he is still a major, 32 men once junior to him have now been made lieutenant colonels, even though he passed his second exam for promotion in January. He suggests Farlow take over his role with No. 3 Garrison.

Eventually McCay and Monash both get what they want, and on 7 March 1908, Monash becomes a lieutenant colonel, tasked with testing the efficiency of Australia's coastal warning systems against invasion. In January 1909 McCay and Bridges run a week-long school for the State's commanding officers at Melbourne's Victoria Barracks. They do most of the talking, but on 22 January Monash lectures his fellow officers on 'The Use of Existing Data for the Making of Military Maps'.[17]

When Professor Kernot dies suddenly after a stroke at his home on Royal Parade, Parkville, on 14 March, Monash is put in charge of organising the university tributes. Eerily, the tramway cables that run past Kernot's house stop just as Kernot's life leaves him.[18]

Monash, though, has never felt more alive. The tough times have not destroyed him, only made him stronger. He says he has developed a 'calmness of spirit which makes life ever so much more enjoyable' and that because of his ambition and application he can 'enjoy the fruits of a first rank position fairly won – doubtless by much hard work, but then work which I have keenly enjoyed'.[19]

At the 1909 Easter Camp, involving more than 5500 men[20] swarming around Langwarrin, Monash plans the attack and defence of the camp so well for the war games that neither of the respective commanders, Colonel Hall and Colonel Robert Ernest Williams, can gain the upper hand.

In August 1909,[21] Monash, along with John Stanley, is on the founding committee of the Victorian branch of the Australian Aerial League, newly formed in Sydney by a *Bulletin* cartoonist named George Taylor. Lawrence Hargrave, the world-renowned aviation expert who has famously conducted numerous experiments with box kites, chairs the first meeting of the group in Sydney on 28 April 1909. A month after the Victorian branch is formed, George Taylor opens Australia's first aeroplane factory in Brumby Street, Surry Hills, Sydney, and in October Lawrence Adamson, the headmaster of Melbourne's Wesley College, imports the first powered aircrafts into Australia: a Wright Model A, which costs him £1500, and a Blériot that costs £800.

Monash's primary involvement is to see how this new technology can be applied to military purposes. He is fascinated by it, and corresponds with Walter Rosenhain to keep abreast of the latest progress in Britain. In October he is also among a group of officers mulling over Bruche's secret defence and mobilisation plans. Monash has a high regard for this 36-year-old major and two years earlier had given him a fulsome, if unsuccessful, reference when Bruche had applied for the position as Victoria's chief commissioner of police. Monash wrote that Bruche was 'the one real live and up to date man among our Victorian permanent officers', 'young and energetic' with a 'magnetic personality ... vigour and force of character ... a cultured mind ... and a loyal temperament'.[22]

Monash is now so well thought of by the military that he is put in charge of mapping the Seymour–Avenel area for a series of manoeuvres to be held before the man hailed as the Empire's greatest soldier,[23] Field Marshal Kitchener,[24] who has been invited to Australia by Prime Minister Alfred Deakin to inspect Australia's defences. The looming threat of Germany's colonisation in the Pacific and the growing might of Japan after its destruction of the Russian fleet at the 1905 Battle of Tsushima have caused considerable concern in Melbourne (the current seat of the Federal Government). Deakin has already introduced a bill providing for compulsory military training in peacetime.[25]

Kitchener's visit is akin to a royal tour, and Monash works with his customary zeal to make sure the field marshal sees that Australian troops are the finest in the world. For three weeks, aided by the Victorian section of the Australian Volunteer

Automobile Corps, which ferries him over all sorts of terrain, Monash goes on reconnaissance – planning, mapping and taking field notes as long as daylight lasts.[26]

Not that Monash is successful in every battle.

Convincing architects to use his reinforced concrete is often a hard sell but Monash reads papers on its use to the Victorian Institute of Engineers, the Royal Victorian Institute of Architects and the Society of Chemical Industry of Victoria. He leads parties of dubious architects around his different works in progress and gives them examples, supplied by Walter Rosenhain, of great projects using the construction method in England: 'nothing talks so strongly with the profession and State Departments in this country as to be able to quote English practice. America is regarded as unreliable and speculative, while anything savouring of being "Made in Germany" is unwelcome as a precedent.'[27]

Despite the success of his own engineering business, he constantly faces opposition from the building establishment. The Reinforced Concrete Co.'s Preston No. 2 Reservoir contract sends the Master Builders' Association into a fury, as does Monash's plans for the domed roof of the Reading Room in the Melbourne Public Library.

In April 1906, Henry Gyles Turner, as library chairman, declares that the trustees wish to erect a 'great central reading room ... octagonal [in] design, like the Congressional Library at Washington'.[28] Prahran architect N.G. (Norman) Peebles, from the firm Bates, Peebles and Smart, draws up plans. Monash works on structural details with Peebles, who becomes a good friend and joins the annual trek to Mount Buffalo. Monash and his assistants prepare calculations and drawings and in May 1908 submit a quote of £18,692.

The Master Builders' Association tears into the deal, and into the reservoir project, saying that neither of them has involved a fair tender system; both are more like private arrangements between friends. They add that while Monash's company embraces 'in its methods the cleverness and ingenuity of the smartest of American combines ... here is a private company designing and carrying out buildings and other constructions ... usurping the positions of architects and builders; eliminating that element of check that is the sole protection of the client'.[29]

When the reservoir is completed, photographs of cracks and minor defects are taken to discredit Monash. The Board of Works takes him to arbitration over the final payment, but Monash triumphs, with the court deciding that a supposed deflection in the wall is only due to the elasticity of the material.[30]

Monash is not so successful in the dispute over the library dome. The Master Builders demand the library trustees rewrite specifications for the dome to allow open tendering and the *Age* backs their claims, saying, 'The public money is being spent, and no firm has a right to any preference.'[31] Monash is livid when, without hearing his proposals and his explanation as to why his method of construction is superior, the trustees award the tender to Swanson Brothers, who sign the contract on 17 May 1909, backed by the Trussed Concrete Steel Co. of England.

Monash writes an angry letter to Peebles, who advises his friend to take a holiday. 'The idea of a man of your vast intellect and attainments, unimpeachable honour and social standing being in any way affected or disturbed by fancied humiliations and the puerile calumnies of a few of the members of the Master Builders' Association is simply preposterous,' Peebles writes, 'as is also your anxiety with regard to the future of your business affairs.'[32]

Perhaps Monash is still churlish over a scathing attack on his portly appearance in Melbourne *Punch* a few weeks ago. It said of the '*Intelligent* Corps' that 'its [lieutenant] colonel and his adjutant' looked 'like two comic characters out of a pantomime or a music hall. The colonel is inclined to be large. His waist measure cannot be a day under 60. He is not tall either, and his girth makes him look short. When he wears the candle-extinguisher helmet of the Intelligent Corps he is strongly reminiscent of a large mushroom.'[33] Monash has the last laugh, though, as one of the leading military officers in Victoria.

Lord Kitchener arrives at Spencer Street Station on Tuesday, 11 January 1910 after stops in Brisbane, Toowoomba, Newcastle, Sydney and Bathurst. The streets are thronged with cheering crowds as the field marshal is lauded for his 'great work' in South Africa,[34] though the press does not mention his signing of the death warrants for the Australians Breaker Morant and Peter Handcock, nor the Boer War concentration camps. Kitchener is charismatic and charming, a confirmed bachelor though the regal bearing and handlebar moustache are a hit with the ladies.

Monash and Vic are high up on the guest list for receptions for Kitchener at the Town Hall and State Parliament. 'He looks just lovely,' Vic says in a letter to Monash during another of her holidays out of town. 'How some woman has not stolen, drugged and married him, I don't know.'[35] Monash feels even more self-conscious about his extra pounds.

Three days later Kitchener is at Seymour overseeing the manoeuvres Monash has helped to plan. Having seen his fill of skirmishing and surprise attacks by small parties in unexpected places, Kitchener asks to see a fight in the open so he can watch brigade formations. Monash, John Stanley and Julius Bruche get their heads together and submit a scheme to his Lordship. 'That will do excellently,' says Kitchener, as he takes his binoculars to watch the whole force go on the attack.[36]

The field marshal's report on his visit to Australia is submitted a few weeks later and supports the introduction of compulsory military training, as put forward in Alfred Deakin's bill a year earlier. The recommendation is implemented in 1911.

Monash comes out of Kitchener's visit with a glowing report and the *Argus* calls his map work 'a marvel of detail and accuracy':

Never before, probably, has any corps of citizen officers performed such a work, and certainly never before have citizen officers accomplished such a huge task in such a remarkably short space of time. It is scarcely a month since the Seymour district was definitely selected for the

Kitchener camp. The only maps, which existed then, were parish plans, which were so inaccurate as to be more of a hindrance than a help … The work would have been a creditable performance on the part of a permanent corps. The fact that it has been accomplished by militia officers enhances its merit a hundredfold, and goes far to show what militiamen can do when properly led and organised.[37]

Monash has turned his fortunes around dramatically in the past few years. Even though the patents for his reinforced concrete are about to expire, he is unconcerned. He has become one of Melbourne's most prominent citizens and most lauded military men. He is nearly 45, and now sets out to conquer the world – or at least see as much of it as he can.

For years he has wanted to travel with Vic and Bert, to see for himself and show them the land of his ancestors; to view the great industrial centres and engineering feats of the world. Until now he has been too busy squirrelling away assets for the future, but now, with Bert graduating from Presbyterian Ladies' College, he feels the time is right to make a move.

He plans out his voyage of discovery like he is plotting a military campaign. He writes to the Rosenhains in London and to Leo Monasch in Minnesota to let them know of his intentions, to seek their advice on the best way of seeing all the sights of their respective countries and to set up meetings with as many relatives as he can. He plans to be away from March to November 1910 and sounds out Thomas Cook's travel agency before settling for 12 weeks on the European continent, eight weeks in Britain and two weeks in America. He takes letters of introduction, itemises every piece of clothing among the family's 17 pieces of luggage and makes lists of everything to be carried, from handkerchiefs to toothpicks to pipe cleaners.

At different times Monash has employed junior engineers, including Samuel James Lindsay and John Albert Laing, but he leaves the business in the hands of his most trusted aide, Percy

Fairway, who he feels is bright and resourceful enough to handle any problems while he is away. Mat becomes the rent collector for all his properties and John Gibson is given power of attorney. Monash even leaves code words for McCay, who might be able to give him command of the Intelligence Corps should McCay be elected to the senate.

Monash plans the trip as a 'preliminary canter', preparing him for what he envisions will be a pattern of long holidays on the Continent every two or three years as he settles down to a life of luxury, finally enjoying the fruits of all his hard labour.

World events, though, will soon play him a different hand.

Chapter 13

*His memory was a marvel ... It was a flexible, steel-trap
memory. A slow reader going over every page as if studying
it, putting his finger on the passage when interrupted as to be
sure to find the place — reading was a study. What he read was
never forgotten.*

JOHN RUSSELL YOUNG ON HIS FRIEND ULYSSES S. GRANT, US PRESIDENT
AND CIVIL WAR GENERAL[1]

In truth, life for him was one great job after another.

DR FELIX MEYER ON MONASH, HIS LIFELONG FRIEND[2]

JOHN MONASH IS STANDING amid a forest of gravestones
and tombs in the Jewish cemetery in Krotoschin. He's
studying the German and Hebrew epithets on the graves of his
grandparents Baer and Mathilde Monasch, paying his respects
to them and the generations of rabbis who preceded them and
who are interred nearby. The cemetery covers half a hectare, with
some graves dating back 300 years. Monash is at last a prosperous
businessman in the New World but he still respects the bonds
that tie him to the birthplace of his mother and father in central
Europe. He does not share their devout religious faith, but he does
share their heritage and he believes he has become the good man

that his grandfather envisioned. He still hopes one day to seize the greatness that Baer also wished for him.

Just as Monash has savoured every sight, smell, taste and feeling that he can on his long treks with Farlow through the Australian bush, so he plans to soak up every experience the wider world has to offer on his tour of the globe alongside Vic and Bert.

Their journey began on 23 March 1910 as the newly built HMS *Otranto* sailed out of Port Phillip Bay. Monash tried out the deck chairs but couldn't relax completely as the ship cruised along the Victorian coast towards South Australia. His company was tendering for £25,000 of work to reconstruct the 550-metre Ocean Steamers' Wharf in Port Adelaide, and knowing that the ship would be calling in there on Good Friday, two days later, he had already sent his original notes and calculations to his chief engineer in South Australia, Herbert Gordon Jenkinson, telling him: 'This is by far the largest proposition we have ever tackled. It is … the largest work you are likely to have to carry out for a long time. Hence it must be approached by you in no light spirit.'[3]

Monash takes a canny businessman's approach to his family's great voyage. He wants a degree of comfort, telling Vic and Bert that he's earned some luxury but, ever the pragmatist, he is not about to waste money either. It will be first class for the long ocean voyage and second class on the shorter train journeys.

He is restless on the ship, since he has never been one for idleness, but gradually he settles down, puts his feet up and starts to read some George Meredith novels and make friends with the other first-class passengers. On board is Monash's lifelong friend, the Melbourne obstetrician and gynaecologist Felix Meyer, and his wife Mary, a well-known painter. Like Monash, Meyer is the son of a Prussian-born Jew. He and Monash are both members of the Yorick Club and the Monashes and Meyers regularly attend university functions together. At Naples they all disembark to take in the sights.

The Monashes spend a few days marvelling, photographing, discussing and embracing the sights of Rome, Florence and

Venice before taking the train to Paris, where Monash is delighted that his French can be plainly understood by the locals. They dine at Maxim's. Monash souvenirs a toothpick from the world's most famous restaurant and adds it to the 468 souvenir items he lists on his detailed inventory for this grand European adventure, detailing all expenses, tips, newspapers, cups of tea and coffee, and stamps purchased. He studies weekly expenditure and makes a comparative analysis of hotel bills, spending 15 minutes a day on a flow chart to see where the money's going and what benefit is being derived. He is meticulous in planning everything. Vic and Bertha can hardly keep up, and often let him go solo as he rushes around inspecting every major engineering feat in each city.

Monash also makes sure he gets himself noticed in London on 20 May during one of the Empire's great events of the decade. As Big Ben tolls 9 a.m., Monash attends the funeral for King Edward VII, taking a place at the Horse Guards Parade in the stand of the 'Colonial Office for distinguished citizens from the Dominions'.[4] He has managed to score an invitation from Victorian Agent-General Sir John William Taverner, a former coach driver who has served as President of the Victorian Board of Land and Works and knows Monash well.

Monash and Vic stand solemnly as the glass carriage carrying the King's widow, Queen Alexandra, leads the funeral procession to the New Palace yard, where Edward's favourite horse and his fox terrier await. Two weeks ago Alexandra allowed the King's hysterical mistress Alice Keppel[5] to farewell him on his deathbed in Buckingham Palace.[6]

Kaiser Wilhelm, back in England less than a decade after burying his grandmother Queen Victoria, kisses Alexandra and pays his respects. He escorts her into Westminster Hall for the funeral service of his uncle, who lies there in state, shafts of light shining onto his coffin through the Gothic windows, like streams of gold.

Wilhelm is dressed in the uniform of a British field marshal, but Monash knows where the German Emperor's heart really lies.

Wilhelm's ally, Archduke Franz Ferdinand, ruler of the Austro-Hungarian Empire, is by the Kaiser's side. In all there are nine kings present, and royalty representing Russia, Norway, Greece, Spain, Bulgaria, Denmark, Portugal, Turkey, Belgium, Japan, Italy, Romania, the Netherlands, Egypt, Sweden, Montenegro, Serbia and France. Seventy countries have sent distinguished mourners, and Monash is entranced by the vivid spectacle of the most famous men and women on earth in their robes and plumed helmets. Soldiers ride by against a backdrop of the great buildings of London, draped in black, purple and violet. It is the greatest assemblage of royalty and rank ever gathered in one place, and with the world about to implode and reshape, it will be the last funeral 'of its kind'[7] ever held.

The previous night, at a dinner given for the visiting mourners by the new King, George V, the Kaiser sidled up to the French Foreign Minister Stéphen Pichon and suggested that if Germany were ever at war with England he would count on the support of the French.[8]

Monash has been in Europe only a few weeks but he has already assessed the Continent as a powder keg. As a senior officer in the Intelligence Corps, the guise of a corpulent Australian tourist travelling with his family presents the perfect opportunity for him to see Germany's war preparations with his own eyes. The Germans have been provoking the French in Morocco and there are escalating tensions between Russia and the German–Austro-Hungarian alliance over its control of the Balkans. England and Germany are engaged in massive armament programs and rapid development of the new technology to control a war in the skies. The speed, heavy armour and massive firepower of England's warship HMS *Dreadnought*, and the class of ships named after her, have made all previous battleships seem obsolete.

Monash journeys back to Paris and takes Vic to the Moulin Rouge and the Folies Bergère, though he is underwhelmed by the Paris nightlife despite its reputation. He likens it to 'the stage beauty ... all wig, and paint and powder ... That is just what midnight Paris is – a hollow sham.'⁹

Brussels follows, then Waterloo, Cologne, Berlin, Dresden, Breslau, Vienna and Munich. Monash is astounded by the busyness of industry in Germany; the Germans seem to be increasing productivity with much greater haste than England.

From Berlin, the Monashes travel 140 kilometres north to Stettin. His mother's family are all dead but he pays his respects at the grave of her mother Charlotte Manesse in Dramburg. How different things would have been if they had stopped Bertha from marrying Louis Monasch, and stifled her dream of travelling with him to the ends of the earth!

The Monashes return to Berlin, then take another train for 350 kilometres south-west to Breslau. Monash leaves the weary Vic at a hotel and journeys 100 kilometres north to Krotoschin. During his travels he meets his father's siblings Rosa, Adolph, Julius and Max, and many Prussian cousins who have not prospered as he has. They speak to him in German and Yiddish.

He visits the home where his grandparents lived and died. He collects leaves from their graves to take back to Melbourne. Max Monash's son Bruno, himself an engineer, asks Monash in vain to help him gain British citizenship to avoid military service with the Germans or Austrians. The printing business of Monash's grandfather is about to close down after 75 years, but Monash gets to study Baer's presses and inspect the fonts of type he first used to print Jewish prayer books nearly 80 years ago.

From Wroclaw the Monashes travel on to Vienna, then the Alps of France and Switzerland, breathing in the crisp summer air and hiking around Chamonix and Mont Blanc, Lucerne and the Matterhorn at Zermatt. Every time he can, Monash checks the construction of tunnels and the railway bridges arching across the rivers and valleys. The family then heads back to Britain for a month and a half, going to the theatre on more than a dozen occasions and spending a week with Lou and Walter Rosenhain on the Isle of Wight.

Monash has developed a deep affection for his sister and the brother-in-law he once found so irritating, and he calls them by the single nickname 'Walterlou'. After some early frostiness, which Monash puts down to their taking his '(reputed) dignity for pompousness', he came to find them both 'most charming'.[10] He calls their seven-year-old, Mona, 'very clever' and four-year-old Nancy 'the dearest, sweetest little girl'.

Later he tells Walter that he considers him a true friend, and that their parting has been 'a tragic experience' for him. 'Perhaps I am rather too emotional,' he says, 'for a hard-headed businessman.'[11] Monash and Vic also catch up with Vic's old friend Lizzie Bentwitch, now living in Piccadilly,[12] and part of a thriving community of Jewish-Australian expats in London. Lizzie is a little ditzy, and not the buxom beauty Vic was in her glory days, but there is something about her ...

The Monashes next spend a week in Scotland, where the inquisitive engineer adds a piece of the stonework from Edinburgh Castle to his souvenir inventory.

From Scotland they journey to New York, catch up with old friends from Melbourne, Alice and Arthur Card, and are transfixed by the huge fingers of cement, stone and steel pointing towards the sky, particularly the new 47-storey Singer Building and the 50-floor Metropolitan Life Insurance Company Tower, which has just surpassed the Singer as the world's tallest building. Express lifts are fast, safe and convenient. Monash is able to see the magnificent Queensboro and Manhattan Bridges, which have just been completed, while massive excavations continue ahead of the reopening of the Grand Central Terminal. Monash describes Penn Station as 'the last word' in construction and is dazzled by the bright lights and electricity running through Times Square. What his Reinforced Concrete Co. could do here! He is able to telephone anywhere in America from his hotel room and make toast in a General Electric device sitting on the breakfast table.

The family visits Grant's tomb in New York, then travels on to take in the natural wonder of Niagara Falls, with its adjacent hydro-electricity plants, and then after a train ride to Chicago, Monash is equally spellbound by regimented rows of automobiles travelling in opposite directions up and down the streets. He calls the precision and order of the passing traffic a 'superb sight' and predicts that soon American 'brain power' and business enterprise will dominate the world.

The Monashes meet many distant relatives in the Windy City and then travel on to Minnesota to spend five days with Monash's cousin Leo and his uncle Isidor, Baer's 81-year-old firstborn, who long ago worked the printing press in Krotoschin. From there, the train takes them to Banff and the Canadian Rockies and then on to Vancouver, where they board the three-deck steamer SS *Marama* for the trip home via Honolulu, Suva, Brisbane and Sydney, arriving back in the first week of November.

After more than seven months abroad, Monash finds Melbourne dwarfed by the magnificence of Manhattan, and everything appears 'shrunken and dingy'. Compared with New York's grandeur even London and Berlin are 'put in the shade'.[13] Everything around him now seems 'provincial' as his 'sense of proportion' has been adjusted with 'a vengeance'.

'It is not so much the achievements of the people – great as they are – that made such an impression on me,' he tells Walter, 'but the altogether new and vigorous and arresting attitude of mind towards life in all its activities.'[14]

By the end of 1910 Monash estimates his net worth at £14,097: about 100 times the average annual salary.

The tender for the Ocean Steamers' Wharf in Port Adelaide has failed and business activity has declined in his absence. The patents on the Monier process are expiring, ending his monopoly, along with his formal agreements with Gummow, but Monash remains in high spirits, refreshed and re-energised by his world tour. He says he is ready to 'enjoy all the excitement of the chase and the battle' of business.[15] For as long as he can remember, his parents' lives and his own have mostly been a 'struggle to barely carry on in very modest comfort',[16] but now he is a self-made man at the top of his profession.

'Naturally this state of affairs is reacting very beneficially upon my health,' he tells Lou, 'plenty of leisure for physical exercise, and sleep; no overwork, no brain fag; no serious worries; with the result that I feel extremely well, and full of energy.' Vic is also enjoying excellent health, putting on weight to a Rubenesque 70 kilograms. 'With increased good looks and weight, and the better dressing which she can now afford,' Monash gloats, 'she is really as much admired as she is admirable.'[17]

Work pours in throughout 1911, among the bigger contracts £7040 for work on the State Savings Bank head office in Melbourne's Elizabeth Street, £7700 for the headquarters of the Gippsland & Northern Co-operative Selling Co. in Flinders Lane, £4900 for six floors of the Centre Way Arcade in Collins Street, £8736 for Queensland House, a six-storey office block in William Street, and more than £10,000 for additional storeys for the Patterson, Laing & Bruce Warehouses in Flinders Lane. In Adelaide there is £4700 for six floors of the Verco Building on North Terrace and £6300 for work on Fowler's Building on King William Street after it is gutted by fire.[18] There are bridges at Flemington and Janevale in Victoria and Mitcham in South Australia, and huge demand for pipes for building the Trans-continental Railway and from the Board of Works.

In February 1911, Monash agrees to chair a committee to end the internal fighting in Victoria's Boy Scouts movement and as a result becomes Vice President of the Imperial Boy Scouts, an organisation that reminds him of his days at Jerilderie, and which he sees as a beneficial prelude to military training.[19]

The arms race escalates in England and Germany. Australian newspapers are now warning of a potential 'Armageddon' in Europe[20] and that Germany has designs on 'the deepest interests of England'[21] and a plan to swallow up Holland.[22]

Monash is the subject of a large feature article in *Punch* magazine on 9 March 1911 that describes him as the finest citizen officer in the Commonwealth, and says that Australia will have to depend on men like him if ever she finds herself at war, highlighting his 'superb quickness of figures and accurate mental calculations, which astound those who deal with him'. Few engineers in the world, the article says, have more daring, ability or skill.

But to the writers of *Punch*, he is still a Jew, and despite now following a diet eschewing bread and sugar and eating more fish he is described as 'stout and ruddy, with the typical Hebrew mouth and the typical Hebrew eye'. Monash complains that the article is 'anything but a satisfactory advertisement'.[23]

The Intelligence Corps concentrates on mapping work, compiling an inch-to-the-mile map of the Kilmore area for the 1911 Easter Camp. Monash's military workload grows and grows; he will soon be appointed to the District Defence Officers' Promotion Board and will have to conduct exams. He is made Chairman of the District Inventions Board, showing 'infinite patience in examining any idea put before him' and kindness towards inventors even when their ideas are useless.[24]

Erich Ludendorff has also become a colonel in the German Army and is appointed the regimental commander in Düsseldorf. He is immersed in testing Germany's invasion plan, gaining intelligence on the dozen forts defending the Belgian city of Liège.

In July 1911, after frequent prodding from Vic, Monash places an order with the German-born automobile-builder Ernest Schultz of Stanley Street, West Melbourne, for a four-cylinder French-designed Berliet, producing 15 to 20 horsepower and seating eight in three rows. The purchase price is £575 and Monash orders the car with 18 coats of paint in green and black vertical stripes, dark green upholstery, brass lamps and the gilt monogram 'JM'. The car is delivered in September and Monash hires a chauffeur, but he still tries to manoeuvre the confounded thing himself. Even though Bertha is able to acquire her driving licence, Monash gives up on getting his without much effort, refusing to do anything badly. Vic is the picture of regal elegance being driven to the races, and tells Monash, 'I do hope I have not overdone it but it is such a temptation.'[25]

From 1 November, Monash and Vic attend every first night of Nellie Melba's Grand Opera season after Monash arranges with J.C. Williamson – the American actor turned Australian theatrical manager – for permanent first-night dress-circle seats. They are regulars at Gregan McMahon's Melbourne Repertory Company, which first performed at the Turn-Verein.

Monash continues his social ascent. Since 1906 he has been Vice President of the Old Scotch Collegians' Club and over the next few years becomes a member of the Wallaby Club for bushwalkers, the Stock Exchange Club, the Victoria Racing Club, the Victoria Amateur Turf Club, the Melbourne Cricket Club, the Royal Society of Victoria and the Royal Geographical Society of Australasia. He advises the university on a successor to Professor Kernot and backs the successful applicant, Henry Payne. He is made chairman of the university's graduates' association, becomes President of the Victorian Institute of Engineers and represents the engineers on the Melbourne University Council. This last is an honour he prizes as one of the great achievements of his life, telling Mat that he is now among the great professional dons, 'those revered deities of our youth',[26] and thanking George Higgins, his old boss on the Princes Bridge, for not only introducing him to the profession and guiding his 'first faltering steps' but also for nominating him for the Institution of Civil Engineers in London and the Victorian Institute of Engineers.[27] He helps Higgins build what may be Victoria's first reinforced concrete house in Beaumaris.[28]

In April 1911 Andrew Fisher's Australian government, still based in Melbourne, announces an international contest to produce a design for the new national capital in Canberra. After the decision on 23 May 1912 that the Chicago architect Walter Burley Griffin has won from 137 entries, Monash writes to his cousin Leo that he hopes the government lays out a 'Capital worthy of the nation'.[29]

He is also moving home. Despite his wealth and his portfolio of real-estate investments, his family still rents in East Melbourne, and Monash complains that their inability to entertain on a grand scale is 'a serious bar to our social advancement'.[30]

He advertises in the *Argus* and the *Age*, offering to rent or lease a modern house, preferably in fashionable Toorak. He is then given the option to buy Iona, the run-down single-storey mansion of the Hamburg-born businessman Friedrich Wilhelm Prell, who has died in April. It is situated on almost an acre (4000 square metres) at 33 St George's Road, though Monash exaggerates its position to Mat by saying it is 'absolutely the highest point in Toorak – the very pick of the suburbs'.[31] While Iona's architect had 'scanty aesthetic ideas', Monash is satisfied with its big rooms, basement, gas and electric lighting and heating. The grounds are a mess of thistles and weeds but with plenty of work it could become a 'really sumptuous home'.[32]

Six weeks after paying £4750, the Monashes move in with a maid and a cook, though sadly most of their stored crockery and glassware is broken in the move and rats chew many of Monash's diplomas, books and letters. He begins to rebuild an impressive library and buys many of Prell's artworks at auction for a fraction of their value, including a Carrara marble statue of Ruth, standing more than 2 metres tall, and several European paintings including *Snake Charmer in the Harem* by the Greek artist Théodore Ralli. Monash's friend Ernest Wright is called in to redecorate and the front garden is replanted with 200 roses, the back with an assortment of vegetables next to a tennis court, a glasshouse, concrete incinerator, chook pen, clothes hoist and workshop where Monash can 'potter about' as he did in his youth. A reinforced concrete drive is created for the Berliet. Soon the Monashes have joined a film library and are showing silent movies at home and entertaining with a new rosewood Rönisch baby grand piano.

Monash restructures the Reinforced Concrete Co., making Gibson an equal partner with Mitchell and himself. (He previously tried to buy Mitchell out by threatening to walk out of the business,[33] but Mitchell called his bluff.) Monash moves the office out of the Australia Building and into nine rooms in Collins House, which he has just finished constructing for William Lawrence Baillieu, the financier and politician, and his enterprising brothers. Collins House accommodates 50 companies,[34] and will be a towering symbol of Australian capitalism for more than six decades.[35] Jim McCay's legal office is just across the hallway from Monash's rooms.

In 1912 Monash treats Mat to another overseas trip, though she quarrels with Lou when she gets to London. He gives Sophie Roth a break from caring for Tante Ulrike by sending her on a vacation to Ceylon. He gives Max Simonson's daughter Vera a diamond ring, helps her brother Karl financially and assists another brother, Eric, with his engineering course, telling him education is better than money or influence.[36] Other members of his extended family also share in his success. When he learns that his old flame Annie Gabriel is ill in Sydney, he writes frequently to her son Gordon, asking him to pass on his love.

Monash reads everything he can on military history from the previous century: how Napoleon marshalled his troops at Austerlitz and how Wellington turned them back at Waterloo. The book *Stonewall Jackson and the American Civil War* by the British military historian Colonel G.F.R. Henderson becomes his favourite, and he uses it to set tests for the men under his command. It also forms the basis of his essay 'The Lessons of the Wilderness Campaign, 1864', which wins the army's Gold Medal competition and is published in the *Commonwealth Military Journal* of April 1912. Monash writes of the similarities between the American and Australian citizen armies, 'bred in an atmosphere of personal liberty and independence, well qualified physically ... and well skilled in bushcraft and horsemanship'. He argues that the most successful commanders of the American Civil War 50 years ago were well-educated graduates of West Point, and that Grant's success was facilitated by a lack of political interference.

While the strategies of past battles intrigue him, Monash is very much a modern commander, and he is just as absorbed by the ominous warnings in the new book *The Aeroplane in War*, penned by the British aviator Claude Grahame-White and the world's first aviation correspondent, Harry Harper of the *Daily Mail*. Of aerial reconnaissance, they write: 'The use of a well-trained corps of military airmen will revolutionise the tactics of war. No longer will two Commanders-in-Chief grope in the dark. They will sit, so to speak, on either side of a chessboard, which will represent the battlefield. Each will watch the other's moves; nothing will be concealed.'[37]

Grahame-White has recently established a flying school and aircraft factory at Hendon Aerodrome in London, and is running a national campaign called 'Wake Up, England!'[38] to whip up an increase in spending on military aircraft. Monash finds claims that England lags badly behind Germany and the rest of Europe in air power[39] 'very startling and suggestive'.

On 15 June 1912 Monash is on the Federal Government parade ground in Melbourne alongside 1000 Victorian boy scouts to welcome the founder of the movement, Robert Baden-Powell.[40] The Melbourne University Chancellor and Chief Justice Sir John Madden, Rear Admiral Sir William Creswell, the Minister for Defence, Senator George Pearce,[41] and the Boer War hero Lieutenant Colonel Harry Chauvel[42] are also honoured guests.

Meanwhile, Jim McCay's military career is going down in flames. McCay has become an irritant to his superiors and is on bad terms with the Military Board.[43] He quits his post as head of the Intelligence Corps and heads overseas, but hardly has his back been turned when, despite Monash's protests, the post is abolished and a restructuring proposed in which the corps will be under the control of the General Staff, rather than a separate entity.

Monash, fearing his own military career is also under attack, has a rush of blood and confronts the universally popular and avuncular Major Cyril Brudenell White,[44] the newly appointed director of military operations at army headquarters, Melbourne.

'It seems to me, Major,' Monash says, puffing out his chest as he is inclined to do, 'that, under the proposed organisation, you are not going to have any suitable place or duty for a senior Lieutenant Colonel like myself.'

'No,' White replies as coolly as a sniper, 'I do not suppose we will.'[45]

Monash is 'a good deal disgusted' at his 'shabby' treatment. He now fears he has no future in Intelligence and will have to face either 'the prospect of going out of active duty, or of looking for some soft place to fall'.[46]

Still it's not all bad. The army wants full-time soldiers doing the intelligence work, rather than part-time militia men and White suggests there's a good chance Monash will be given command of an infantry brigade if he applies and exercises a little patience. Monash's acting command of the Intelligence Corps is terminated on 5 December, though he remains in charge of the Victorian section for another six months of work that he finds 'very dull'.

Other diversions are more exciting. The great focal point of Melbourne leisure becomes Luna Park, the brainchild of touring Canadian movie man J.D. Williams. The amusement park has been built at St Kilda at a cost of £40,000 in the style of New York's Coney Island.[47] Huge crowds turn out for the opening on 13 December 1912 and Monash, Vic and Bert are there every week along with thousands of others enjoying the Palais de Folies, River Caves of the World, the Ferris Wheel, the American Bowl Slide and the Scenic Railway. The motor-car also provides scenic highlights for the Monashes, and at Christmas 1912 they enjoy a five-day drive, chugging through Marysville, Yea, Woodend and Ballarat.

Soon afterwards, J.D. Williams leaves for Hollywood to sign Charlie Chaplin to the first million-dollar movie deal and form a company that will eventually become Warner Bros. Three American brothers – Herman, Henry and Leon Phillips – form a new company to run Luna Park with Monash as chairman. He is in big demand for other companies as well, joining the board of Wiltshires, who make Worcestershire sauce, and the board of another company making automatic postage stamp machines.

He sees Australia as ripe for development if only there were more enterprise, and calls on senior engineers to travel abroad more often and bring home the latest ideas so that Melbourne's trams and trains can be modernised, harbour facilities improved, country roads bettered, provincial centres sewered and hydro-electricity developed.

In 1913 the Metropolitan Gas Company employs him to give evidence before George Higgins's brother Henry, now President of the Commonwealth Court of Conciliation and Arbitration, in their fight with the Federated Gas Employees' Industrial Union.

Monash argues that nine shillings a day is too high a wage for coke shovellers and that they do fairly 'comfortable work which never [becomes] exceptionally arduous'.[48] After months of haggling, a compromise is reached, with labourers receiving eight shillings and sixpence a day and stokers ten and six.[49]

Monash is earning much more than that, and he boosts his art collection with works by E. Phillips Fox, Norman Lindsay, Hans Heysen, Jessie Traill, Dora Messon and J.J. Hilder. The beauty of the works captivates him, but nowhere near as much as Vic's words when she writes to him from one of her holidays, after 22 years of marriage: 'I have come to the conclusion that there is no man alive … that can compare with you in any way.'[50]

He has good reason to be well pleased with his achievements and station in life. He is employing an impressive team of engineers, including Thomas Haynes Upton and Clarence Sexton, and has a wide circle of influential friends including his next-door neighbour Robert Garran,[51] head of the Attorney-General's Department since Federation, and the man who organised the first Federal election in March 1901. He has developed close friendships with Walter Rosenhain, Bruche and Gibson to replace those who have drifted from his life, such as Arthur Hyde, Jim Lewis and the tragic Will Steele, who, after Monash helped him overcome suicidal thoughts, died a recluse in 1912. Steele's heart was broken long before that, when his father forbade him to marry his beloved.

Monash now estimates his net worth to be about £30,000, and even if he never works another day in his life he and his family can live in luxury for the rest of their days. He has come so far in a short time, climbing through a mountain of debt that had almost buried him at the start of the century to now be at the peak of a thriving business. He has combined his great work ethic with patience, discernment and unwavering faith in the power of his ambition. Still he remains a man unsatisfied, still trying to prove himself at every turn.

Monash sees his life as a triumph of hard work over adversity, and is most likely writing about himself when he pens an editorial for the *Varsity Engineer* at the end of the year saying that the engineer must be 'a man of broad education and outlook, free from petty bias and prejudice, full of sober commonsense, of human sympathy and understanding, in nothing an extremist, and in nothing a faddist. He must understand men, because he has to organise, direct and lead men ...'[52]

It is akin to being a military general.

Monash spends what little spare time he has translating the German cavalry journal *Kavalleristische Monatshefte* (Cavalry Monthly) for the General Staff, and with the support of Bruche and Stanley is given the command of the 13th Infantry Brigade on 1 July 1913. Nearing 50, he guesses this will be his last hurrah and is thrilled to receive the 'pick of all commands'. He has to mount a fierce fight to finally gain promotion to colonel in September.

The following month he lectures his officers, telling them they are soldiers preparing for the possibility of war rather than social prestige. Monash stresses that the 13th Brigade must be a unified force based on co-operation and discipline. The officers must be men with character strengthened by self-control, self-confidence, the courage of their convictions, firm decisions and practical views. They have to be cool in a crisis and dignified when dealing with the men under their command. They have to be prepared to back their own judgment in a conflict or when the chain of command is broken, and be patient with men of varying intelligence. And at a time when troops are often seen as mere numbers, Monash tells his officers to keep their men informed of everything that is happening.[53]

He makes notes on '3 principles of Arrangements for Battle', and is already thinking of campaigns in the same way as Grant or Lee approached the Civil War:

1. When battle imminent, always be ready to fight quickly on suitable front; this helps you to decide on disposition for approach.
2. Envelopment is more effective than frontal attack; this helps you to select your main objective.
3. Keep control as long as possible, i.e. don't throw in all at once; this helps you to concentrate on decisive point.[54]

Always stressing that education is paramount in all endeavours, Monash distributes his advice in a pamphlet, *100 Hints for Company Commanders*.

Late in 1913 the threat of a large-scale war continues to bubble in Europe as nations flex their military muscles. The Balkans are at a flashpoint, having been torn apart by local wars and skirmishes that have left more than 200,000 dead. Russia pledges support to Serbia in any future conflict.

A world away in Melbourne, Monash begins preparations for his brigade's first large-scale manoeuvres, to be held over eight days during the following February in Lilydale. They will be the first manoeuvres to be reviewed by the lean and spare cavalry veteran General Sir Ian Hamilton,[55] Inspector-General of the British Overseas Forces. Monash seeks medical opinions on how far young soldiers should march in hot weather.

He is getting medical opinion on the personal front as well, helping to arrange the affairs of Max Simonson, who is going blind, and he tries to make life as comfortable as he can for Sa, who has a heart condition.

Three weeks into 1914, Monash takes the salute for the Australian Boy Scouts' Rally at the Church of England Grammar School grounds, where more than 1000 scouts are on parade.[56]

On 8 February he leads 2500 men of his brigade into Lilydale on special trains, as dust and flies meet them with a frontal attack[57] and nearby bushfires make the air hot and thick with smoke for their eight days of manoeuvres. On 12 February, the day before Hamilton is to inspect them, Monash stages a full dress rehearsal of their mock battle and the next day the real thing goes splendidly, with Hamilton, Governor-General Thomas Denman and the army's senior officers nodding approval.

Hamilton, dressed in field-service khaki, the left breast of his tunic almost hidden by a mass of war ribbons,[58] is an expert horseman and has seven specially trained chargers at his disposal, tiring out three of them as he dashes about the bush watching Monash's men practising the art of war.

The men are 'tired, dusty, hot, and hungry', but happy that their work has been appreciated by one of the most distinguished soldiers of the Empire. They trudge back to camp after the exercise, which has covered 32 kilometres of hard country, 'the manoeuvres involving a great deal of hill-climbing in broiling sun and crouching in awkward positions behind undergrowth and in creek beds'. Water-carts follow each battalion, but it is still a struggle to cool the parched throats.[59]

Hamilton describes Monash as an 'outstanding force of character'[60] and says he has the makings of a first-rate commander. Some of the British officers have tears in their eyes at the commitment of the Australian citizen soldiers.

Monash rewards himself by taking Vic and Bert to Tasmania for two weeks: their first real holiday since going abroad. They drive from Burnie to Launceston and then down the coast road to Hobart.

But controversy follows their every move. The *Age* attacks Monash viciously for having overworked his men[61] on the manoeuvres, but he is adamant that they are 'training for war and not for picnics'.[62]

On the other side of the world, in Belgrade, the wounded heart of the Balkans, a terror cell called the Black Hand is training a group of sickly youngsters for a suicide mission they believe will help free their people from the hated rule of the Austro-Hungarian Empire. The Black Hand is preparing to kill the heir to the Austro-Hungarian throne, Archduke Franz Ferdinand.

Monash is fighting a personal war after being involved in the expulsion of Boer War veteran Major T. (Timothy) Marcus McInerney from the Naval and Military Club. McInerney, the President of the Celtic Club and a loyal son of Erin, has breached military etiquette by criticising Field Marshal Earl Roberts over the Troubles in Ireland. Monash says he threw McInerney out because he was a 'disloyalist', but McInerney has powerful friends. They seize upon the fact that Monash and two of his comrades behind the expulsion did not volunteer for the Boer War. McInerney did.

At a smoke social in McInerney's honour attended by about 300 people at the Cathedral Hall in Fitzroy on 3 July 1914, Dr William Robert Maloney, the Labor member for the Federal seat of Melbourne, slams Monash and co. as 'lick spittle little puppies'. McInerney likens the three colonels behind his expulsion – Monash, Frederic Hughes and James Burston – to 'sewer rats ... ready and willing to avail themselves of the opportunity to spit their venom and express their violence and hostility to freedom'. The actions of the Naval and Military Club, he continues, are 'worthy of the barnacles of bigotry, the sycophants of society, and the parasites of party and privilege'.[63] He would 'have thought that centuries of persecution would have seared tolerance into the heart of a Jew'.[64]

A letter to the editor of the *Argus* claims Maloney's attack is an attempt to 'arouse prejudice'[65] against Monash, though one of McInerney's defenders is quick to say the Irish have always been friends of the Hebrews – 'both persecuted races' – and 'no such act would be countenanced at any gathering whereat Irishmen preponderated'.[66]

Monash fobs off the attacks because he can afford to.

By the middle of 1914 he estimates that even if he never did another day's work he could make about £3000 a year, 15 times the average wage, just from his investment income. The years seem to be passing by more rapidly than he would like, and he is now in a 'rather passive, unenergetic frame of mind so far as money-making activity is concerned. I have worked so hard for so many years, that I feel a yearning for more quiet and peace …'[67]

He agrees to lend Walter Rosenhain £200 to help bring his family out for the meeting of the British Association for the Advancement of Science in July and August. It will be the 84th annual meeting of the venerable body but the first to be held in Australia, and Monash is made a member of the Victorian executive committee and of the scientific business sub-committee.

Not that he's looking for more work.

Instead, he is hoping to make another long trip abroad, starting in March 1915, stopping in Japan on his way to America and then travelling to Europe to attend the World Engineering Congress. He wants to immerse himself in studies of art, literature and history. His library is overflowing with the classics, law books and encyclopaedias and he is at the theatre every chance he gets. But, oh, what he could study and learn if work did not get in the way. Travel is the best way he knows to broaden the mind. However, history is about to open a dark chapter in Europe, and the World Engineering Congress will go ahead without him after being postponed for six months and moved to San Francisco.

The rumbling volcano of Europe in 1914 is ready to blow on the summer morning of 28 June 1914, when Franz Ferdinand accepts an invitation to look over army manoeuvres outside Sarajevo, the capital of Bosnia.

Franz Ferdinand has few admirers apart from his wife and three children. Pompous, arrogant and opinionated, he has absolute belief in the absolute power of kings. He loathes Hungarians as 'infamous liars' and regards southern Slavs as sub-human, referring to the population of Serbia as 'those pigs'.[68]

As he arrives for his inspection tour, six young men – five Serbs and one Bosnian Muslim – and their handler wait for him along a wide Sarajevo avenue called the Appelkai (Appel Quay).

Between them they have six hand grenades and four pistols. Three of them have tuberculosis. Each also has a cyanide pill to end his life when the mission is accomplished.

Twenty-one years ago the Archduke made a trip to Narromine and Mullengudgery in western New South Wales, shooting kangaroos, emus, pelicans, turkeys, ibis, koalas and platypuses.[69] It is said he has shot 300,000 animals during his 50 years, but now he is the target.

At 9.28 a.m., Oskar Potiorek, Governor of Bosnia and Herzegovina, meets the archduke and his wife Sophie with a motorcade of six automobiles. The royal couple climb into the back of an open-top Gräf & Stift Double Phaeton sports car. Potiorek rides in the back with them, while their security officer Lieutenant Colonel Count Franz von Harrach sits up front next to the driver.

The archduke is dressed in the uniform of an Austrian cavalry general: blue tunic, gold collar with three silver stars, black trousers with red stripe and a helmet with green peacock feathers.[70] He is wearing a corset to harness his paunch. Around his neck he has seven amulets of gold and platinum to ward off evil, and high on his left arm is a tattoo of a Chinese dragon in every colour of the rainbow.[71] Sophie, his wife of 14 years, is radiant in a white hat and veil, a long white silk dress with red and white fabric roses tucked into a red sash, and an ermine stole on her shoulders.

After a brief review of the troops at 10 a.m., the motorcade heads along the Appelkai towards the Sarajevo City Hall. Those loyal to the empire, or just trying to curry favour, turn on a warm welcome: there are flags fluttering and displays of flowers, some shop windows display the archduke's photograph, and there are cheers of '*Zivio*' – 'Long may he live'.[72]

As the motorcade approaches the first two assassins, they have a change of heart and keep their grenades in their pockets, but further along, at 10.10 a.m., Nedeljko Cabrinovic, a 19-year-old compositor, takes his grenade from his long black coat and tosses it at the royal car.[73] The grenade bounces off the folded-back hood of the Double Phaeton and explodes underneath the car behind, injuring two of the archduke's officers and more than a dozen bystanders. Sophie's face is cut by a small piece of shrapnel.

Cabrinovic swallows his cyanide pill and dives into the Miljacka River to drown himself, but the cyanide mix is old and only makes him vomit, and the water is so shallow he barely gets wet. He is dragged out, beaten and arrested.

Franz Ferdinand's driver puts his foot to the floor, and the Double Phaeton races to the City Hall. The car speeds past the other three assassins, and is moving too fast for the sickly 19-year-old student Gavrilo Princip to fire a shot.[74] Princip decides to stop in front of Moritz Schiller's café on Franz Joseph Street for the archduke's return journey.

The royal car screeches to a halt at the City Hall, where the city's religious leaders, the bishops, mullahs and rabbis, greet Franz Ferdinand as planned.[75] The archduke then demands to be taken to the hospital to see the soldiers wounded by the grenade.

The chauffeur, however, has not been told of the change of plans and heads back along the published route along Franz Joseph Street. Governor Potiorek orders him to stop and turn the car around just as they get to Schiller's café.

Princip, racked by tuberculosis and nationalist rage, steps from the cheering crowd and draws his pistol.

The first shot hits the archduke near the jugular vein. Princip then takes aim at Governor Potiorek, but as Sophie tries to protect her husband, the second bullet tears through the car door, blasts through Sophie's corset and into her abdomen.[76] As blood bubbles from beneath her white dress Franz Ferdinand gasps, '*Sopherl! Sopherl! Sterbe nicht! Bleibe am Leben für unsere Kinde!*' – 'Sophie, Sophie, don't die, stay alive for our children!'

Princip places the muzzle of his pistol against his own head but the gun is wrestled from him before he can pull the trigger. The archduke's car speeds across the Latin Bridge towards the governor's residence so that the royal pair can receive emergency medical treatment, but Sophie is dead by the time the car arrives. Franz Ferdinand is carried inside but dies a few minutes later.[77]

The murders provide the perfect excuse for the Austrian Government to whip up violence against the Serbs. Diplomatic wrestling ends with Austria-Hungary declaring war on Serbia on 28 July. The following day, Russia, alarmed that the Austro-Hungarian Army is about to increase its strength in the Balkans, begins mobilising its own troops.

Germany, with its finger poised on the trigger, is about to enter the conflict too, and Monash will be soon fighting against the people of his father's homeland.

The first shot will be fired in his own backyard.

Chapter 14

PORT PHILLIP BAY, MELBOURNE, THURSDAY
30 JULY 1914

*With the help of many fine men who are going to serve under me, I
hope to be able to sustain the honour of Australia, of British arms,
and not the least, of the Jewish community.*

MONASH IN A LETTER TO RABBI JACOB DANGLOW OF THE
ST KILDA SYNAGOGUE[1]

THE MOST VIOLENT AND DESTRUCTIVE STORM
mankind has ever seen is about to be unleashed across
Europe as Captain Wilhelm Kuhlken sails the newly built 6000-
ton German cargo steamer SS *Pfalz* into the safe harbour of Port
Phillip Bay on 30 July 1914. The *Pfalz* has only been sailing for
a year, bringing lager and other goods to Australia from Bremen
and returning with Tasmanian apples and South Australian pears
in its state-of-the-art refrigerated hold.[2] Kuhlken and his crew
berth the Nordeutscher-Lloyd steamer at No. 2 Victoria Dock,
offloading the cargo bound for Melbourne and keeping a close
eye on the reports of a flashpoint at home. Kuhlken only has a
small load of coal and plans to buy more on the return journey, in
Sydney, where it is cheaper.

With the kingdoms of Europe poised to fall like dominoes,
Kuhlken knows he will soon be in hot water if he lingers too long

in Port Phillip Bay. He fears that if war is declared his ship will be confiscated by the Royal Australian Navy, and who knows what will happen to him and his crew?

On 1 August Germany declares war on Russia, and is soon also at war with Luxembourg, France and Belgium. Great Britain delivers an ultimatum to Kaiser Wilhelm to keep Belgium neutral, and in Melbourne, Prime Minister Joseph Cook's Federal Cabinet, about to be swept out in the national elections, votes to offer Great Britain the Australian fleet and 20,000 men if needed.[3]

News of Britain's ultimatum has been relayed to Australia but the German response remains unknown. Captain Kuhlken decides to make a run for a safe haven in South America. He dumps the cargo that was destined for Sydney, and on the night of 4 August takes on 200 tons of coal. The Federal Government has given orders to the army and navy that German ships must not leave port, but there is nothing the Australian forces can do to prevent the *Pfalz* from taking off until war is actually declared.

At 7.45 a.m. on Wednesday, 5 August, an hour and a quarter before war is declared in London[4] the *Pfalz* casts off, and under the guidance of Captain Montgomery Robinson from the Port Phillip Pilot Service on board, steams towards Port Phillip Heads and freedom. There is congestion in the Yarra but Kuhlken has the ship pushing her top speed of 13 knots as they pass Williamstown, the Germans cheering their good fortune.[5]

In London, British Prime Minister Herbert Asquith finally announces 'that a state of war exists between Great Britain and Germany'.[6] Australia is also now at war, but that news has still not made it down the telegraph line to Melbourne. Kuhlken slows down to half speed to conserve coal for the long voyage awaiting them just around the heads, but at about 10 a.m. the *Pfalz* arrives off Portsea.

An officer and two seamen from the Naval Board Examination Service arrive on the launch *Alvina* and climb on board the *Pfalz* with a rope ladder. They take as much time as they possibly can to examine the ship's papers, until they eventually run out of excuses to delay Kuhlken any longer.[7] The *Pfalz* is allowed to proceed at 12.30 p.m. and German consular officials emerge from below deck to stand on the bridge and heartily congratulate Kuhlken on his mission accomplished.[8]

Almost instantaneously Lieutenant Colonel Augustus Henry Sandford, in command of nearby Fort Queenscliff, receives the telephone instructions he had been anxiously anticipating: '*PFALZ* MUST BE STOPPED OR SUNK.'

The command is quickly transmitted by telephone via an underwater cable and the flashing light of a heliograph to Lieutenant Charles Morris on the opposite side of the heads at Fort Nepean. Midshipman Stan Veale, on board the *Alvina*, hoists a flag signalling that the *Pfalz* must be stopped. Signalmen at Fort Nepean hoist flags telling the *Pfalz*, 'HEAVE TO OR BE SUNK.'[9] The gun crews, which have practised for so long with Monash, load the 6-inch Mark 7 naval gun known as F1 with 55 kilograms of cordite and a 45-kilogram projectile. They take aim, planning a warning shot across the bow: a delicate task, because the current is flowing fast and they know if the aim is just a little too high or wide they might hit people on the other side of the bay.

Pilot Robinson is so busy negotiating the *Pfalz* into the rip current of the open sea that he doesn't notice the warning flags, and no one else on board bothers to tell him.

Lieutenant Morris waits a minute or two and then shouts, 'FIRE!' Gunner Sergeant John Purdue presses the electric trigger and the 45-kilogram shell explodes on its trajectory.

The British Empire's first shot of World War I roars out from Gun Placement No. 6 of the Point Nepean Battery and the massive shell screams across the bow of the *Pfalz*, splashing into the water 50 metres off the stern. Robinson almost jumps out of his skin, and looks up to finally see the signal flags. He telegraphs a message to the engine room: 'Full speed astern.'

'*Nein!*' shouts an agitated Captain Kuhlken, so close to his escape. 'Full speed ahead!'

Robinson knows the next shot from Fort Nepean won't miss, and he and Kuhlken start wrestling desperately for control of the ship's telegraph system. One of the Germans pulls out a Luger pistol and aims it at Robinson's head. Robinson pleads for the Germans to see reason.

At Fort Nepean, the aim of the huge cannon is adjusted for a direct hit on the German steamer. Lieutenant Morris orders Sergeant Purdue to prepare to sink her.

Robinson desperately tries to get across his point that the artillery won't miss again, and after some furious shouts and wild gesticulating commonsense eventually prevails. The *Pfalz* is turned around and Robinson steers her back to Portsea, where Kuhlken and his crew, all German naval reserves, are arrested. They will be interned at Berrima, south of Sydney, for the duration of the war. Inspection of the *Pfalz* reveals preparations have already been undertaken to convert her into a merchant raider, with deck plates drilled to take 4-inch guns stored in the hold.[10]

Recruiting for the war begins immediately in Australia, with promises that the whole thing will be over by December after the Kaiser is put back in his place. Australian propaganda highlights the merits of British imperialism and the value of frontiersmen who can ride and shoot. The rush to enlist is like a stampede, and a stigma quickly surrounds those not in uniform. The Australian Army offers six bob a day, three times the pay of British soldiers, and though it is still below the average wage, enlistment is promoted as a paid adventure, the government subsidising the travel of so many young men to foreign shores they might not otherwise see.

On 2 August the Australian Government had recalled McCay to duty as its chief military censor, and he establishes a headquarters in Melbourne, with offices in the other State capitals.

Monash's American cousins Leo and Gustav Monasch write to say they are very much on the side of Germany, but Monash leaves no doubt about his loyalties, declaring: 'you must not fail to remember that I am Australian born, as is my wife and daughter, that my whole interest and sympathies are British ... and that every man who can, and is able to do so, must do his best for his country.'[11] To Karl Roth he explains that their country must 'help the Empire to crush a peril which may mean the end of Australia as a free country'.[12] The childless 45-year-old Karl is now a tiny, decrepit, balding deadbeat ravaged by alcoholism. His wife, Mary, has just died in Charleville, Queensland,[13] and with not much left to live for, Karl soon volunteers to fight, understating his age in the process.[14]

Expecting to be called up to the militia at any time, Monash is going hell-for-leather. He shelves his work in preparation for the British Association meetings and awaits the arrival in Melbourne of Walter and Lou Rosenhain and their family, which has now grown to three daughters.

On 9 August, McCay calls Monash, asking him to take over as Chief Censor. McCay had been offered the command of a brigade in the Australian Imperial Force. Monash agrees to take temporary charge of what becomes 'a most worrying, anxious and strenuous job' monitoring all wireless broadcasts and communications from German businesses and private citizens. After a week of making the Rosenhains comfortable and getting other affairs in order, he starts work on 17 August. He warns his own family not to send letters to anyone in Germany or Austria and begins an unpopular crackdown on the press, suppressing any reports that are unofficial, critical, alarmist or likely to offend fractious allies such as Japan. Monash calls the job 'a grievous and deplorable necessity of war' and is glad to hand pass it to Colonel Henry Hall four weeks later.[15] He is given a much more important role that will take him to the other side of the world.

Europe is on fire.

Kaiser Wilhelm himself presents Erich Ludendorff with the Blue Max,[16] Germany's highest military honour. On 22 August Ludendorff is one of the German leaders who take the Belgian city of Liège.

The German High Command also recalls 66-year-old Prussian general Paul von Hindenburg from retirement to lead the 8th Army on the Eastern Front. Together with Ludendorff, his new chief of staff, Hindenburg orchestrates stirring victories in what is now north-eastern Poland, destroying the Russian 2nd Army at the Battle of Tannenberg and crushing the Russian 1st Army at Masurian Lakes.

Hindenburg and Ludendorff are soon the most honoured men in Germany, pushing the Kaiser into the background. But a few weeks later the Germans, retreating from the First Battle of the Marne in north-eastern France, suffer massive casualties around the Aisne River. Australian newspapers report that German blood is being spilled like water in a valley of death,[17] and the fighting is soon bogged down in trench warfare. The Germans rape Belgium, murdering thousands of civilians, destroying villages and towns and burning 300,000 medieval books in the University of Leuven.

The first battle around the Belgian city of Ypres becomes known in Germany as the *Kindermord bei Ypern* (Massacre of the Innocents), with approximately 40,000 German troops killed in just 20 days.

Out of 250 men in the 1st Company of the 16th Bavarian Reserve Infantry Regiment just 42 survive. One of them is an eccentric loner, a failed Austrian artist with a deep hatred of Jews, Bolsheviks and Democrats. His name is Adolf Hitler.

Australia suffers its first casualty in what is to become the Great War on 26 August 1914. Just three days after arriving in France with the East Lancashire Regiment, 22-year-old Lieutenant Malcolm Chisholm, a former Sydney Grammar student, is wounded in the stomach in the Battle of Le Cateau, near the Belgian city of Mons. He dies the next day.[18]

Two weeks later, after New Zealand troops have taken German Samoa without a fight, volunteers from the hastily raised Australian Naval and Military Expeditionary Force land in

German New Guinea on 11 September. They plan to capture a radio station at Bita Paka, on the island of New Britain in the Bismarck Archipelago. The station is in direct communication with Vice Admiral Maximilian von Spee's[19] German East Asian Cruiser Squadron. An Australian party of about 40 men immediately meets armed resistance from Melanesian and German forces. As the Australians advance down a jungle road, a shot roars out from a coconut plantation and tears through the body of Able Seaman Billy Williams, from Melbourne. The bullet rips through his right breast and out his left side.[20]

Army doctor Captain Brian Pockley, a graduate of Sydney University, realises Williams needs to be evacuated immediately. Pockley gallantly ties his Red Cross armband around the white hat of Leading Stoker William Kember, as protection from snipers, and tells him to carry the wounded man to safety. Not long afterwards, Pockley is also shot through the chest and he and Billy Williams die together that afternoon on board HMAS *Berrima*:[21] the first soldiers killed fighting in Australian uniforms. Three days later the Australian submarine *AE1* disappears near Rabaul with the loss of 35 lives.

Back in Australia, the race to volunteer for war is unprecedented. From Melbourne to Mandurah, from the ocean to the outback, men clamour for a chance to shoot at the Hun. Recruiting officers turn back boys in short pants and bare feet as young as 13, and men as old as 71. Some who are rejected stumble away in tears.[22]

Three brigades are formed for the First Australian Imperial Force (AIF) force under William Bridges, and his chief of staff, Major Brudenell White. Bridges is promoted from brigadier to major general on a salary of £1500 a year and 15 shillings a day field allowance.[23]

Initially Monash is in no hurry to enlist, reasoning that while his services are 'at the unreserved disposal of the government' if they want to call on him, his business and academic interests will be disadvantaged by his absence in a war. He remains in charge of four large companies in Victoria and South Australia, is on the University Council and several committees, and is chairman of several scientific bodies. Still, he can't help but be swept up in the tidal wave of enthusiasm for the fight, and throwing in the censor's job, he finally applies for a command on 10 September.

Five days later, and with recruits pouring in, he is appointed to lead the 4th Infantry Brigade of the Australian Imperial Force, bound for the war in seven weeks. Colonel James Gordon Legge,[24] the Chief of the General Staff, tells Defence Minister George Pearce that he preferred 49-year-old Monash to the other candidate, the extremely capable 56-year-old Gerald Campbell from Sydney, largely because Monash is the younger man.[25] Kitchener's praise for Monash while the field marshal was in Australia does no harm either.[26]

Monash celebrates with a reception for Walter and Lou at Iona, attended by a couple of dozen prominent guests, including Legge. Vic is suitably impressive, with one reporter saying she was, 'most artistically frocked in soft ivory satin crepe'.[27] Walter tells Monash, only half in jest, that he will be a knighted major general before long. It turns out he is underestimating what his brother-in-law will achieve.

The 4th Brigade is formed from four infantry battalions: the 13th, raised from New South Wales, the 14th from Victoria, the 15th from Queensland and Tasmania, and the 16th from South Australia and Western Australia.

Hardly before he has given an order, Monash comes under attack from the very people he has sworn to defend. A hate campaign begins and Monash blames a 'clique' that supports his old adversary Marcus McInerney.[28] One newspaper reports that Monash's past has been 'raked over by some ecstatic patriots who have discovered that though born and bred in this country, he had German parents'.[29] A petition is started to force the government to dump him. His enemies send letters to Pearce and Kitchener. Rumours circulate that Monash can't speak English properly; that he only got the brigade command because the wives of Monash and Pearce are related. (They aren't.) Other officers with foreign backgrounds such as Bruche also come under suspicion.

Pearce later writes that if he had listened to 'gossip and slander' as he was urged to do, 'Monash would never have gone to the war'.[30] Yet some of the mud sticks and the Military Board eventually stops commissioning officers of foreign origin. Already there is talk of establishing internment camps for enemy aliens,[31] and Monash fears for the Behrends and Tante Ulrike, who still prefers to speak in German. Yet he ploughs on, buoyed by encouragement from the Melbourne University Vice Chancellor, John MacFarland, who tells him, 'God has given you a good nervous system' and hopes it wears well.[32]

The thought of leading a brigade in an actual war, after 30 years of pretend battles, is overwhelming at first, but the more Monash studies his task, the more confident he becomes. Confidence soon turns to enthusiasm. He appoints Paddy McGlinn,[33] a tubby lines engineer with the Post Master General, as a brigade major, and makes Carl Herman Jess,[34] son of a German painter, a staff captain. They both dine with Monash at Iona, and over the port make plans for great victories.

The departure of Monash's brigade is delayed for several weeks, allowing him a quick trip to Mount Buffalo before his Victorian troops assemble at Broadmeadows, in Melbourne's north, in October.[35] The *Hebrew Standard of Australasia* gives him a prominent position in its list of Australian Jews 'in the volume of defenders of the Empire',[36] while Vic cuts a dash on Caulfield Cup day in a 'putty-coloured gabardine suit … and smart sailor hat of black taffeta'.[37]

Monash's brigade is still being put together on 1 November 1914, when the 1st Australian Imperial Force and the New Zealand Expeditionary Force leave King George Sound off Albany, bound for England and the war in Europe, although many will never make it that far. William Bridges is the commander.

There are 38 vessels carrying 30,000 men in total. Eventually 331,814 Australians will be deployed overseas to fight in what will become known as World War I.

The convoy stretches for 12 kilometres and the Japanese cruiser *Ibuki* is one of several warships enlisted to give the transports safe escort. Just eight days into the voyage, HMAS *Sydney* forces the surrender of the German raider *Emden* in the Cocos Islands.

By then Britain has begun a naval blockade to starve the German populace and Russia has declared war on the Ottoman Empire, with Russia's allies France and the British Empire following suit. Fighting is already being waged throughout Europe, Africa, Mesopotamia, the Pacific and the Middle East. The Turks, under advice from the Germany military, have closed the narrow straits of the Dardanelles to Allied shipping and have started attacks on Russia's Black Sea fleet, declaring a *jihad*, or holy war. The Germans are said to have 5 million soldiers waging war on both fronts in Europe – in the west against the French and British and in the east against the Russians – and another million 'who can easily be put into the field'.[38]

Monash visits Sydney, Brisbane and Adelaide to inspect the battalions being raised there for his brigade. Vic visits Flemington for Melbourne Cup, the Derby, the Oaks and the Steeplechase. Monash makes an appeal to the racing men and women of Melbourne to lend their binoculars to his troops, as there is a desperate need for field glasses. It is thought that the trouble in Europe will not last long.[39]

Monash's interstate forces begin arriving at Broadmeadows in late November and soon there are '10,000 men under canvas'.[40] He distributes more copies of *100 Hints for Company Commanders.*

On 25 November, Winston Churchill, now England's First Lord of the Admiralty, suggests a plan to the British War Council to divide and conquer the Germans. He reminds them that the Central Powers – Germany, Austria-Hungary and Turkey – are fighting primarily on two fronts, western and eastern. He says creating another front in the south against an under-strength Turkish Army will require German reinforcements from the rest of Europe and weaken German defences in all areas. An attack on the Dardanelles will also open the vital supply route for grain and military supplies between the Mediterranean and Russia. The operation is conceived as a naval assault and the plans for the AIF to join the fight in Europe undergo a rethink.

On 3 December, the first troops of the AIF land in Egypt. The majority are young men who have never been overseas before. They are intoxicated by the wonders of the Nile Valley: the sights, the smells, and the women. The 1st Division establishes a camp at Mena, near Cairo, practising drills, polishing their weapons and trying on their new slouch hats with the Rising Sun badge.

In Melbourne 10 days later, Monash momentarily shelves his scorn for all things religious to take his place in the warden's seat inside the packed St Kilda Synagogue along with 80 or so other Jewish military men. It is at a special ceremony organised because of the 'large number of Jewish members of a second Australian Expeditionary Force, who are about to proceed to the front'.[41]

The choir sings 'Baruch Haba', the hymn of welcome. Chanukah candles are lit, and a reading is given from the Books of the Maccabees, highlighting the bravery of a Jewish rebel army, 'Israel's lion-hearted sons', 2000 years earlier.[42] Monash opens the synagogue's ark to remove the Torah; a prayer is given on behalf of the soldiers now in Egypt and another for the King and Royal Family. The choir sings the 23rd Psalm about walking through the valley of the shadow of death, yet fearing no evil.

Then, London-born Rabbi Jacob Danglow, a tall, dark and handsome 34-year-old,[43] addresses the congregation, dressed in the crisp uniform of an army chaplain:

Against the shadow of the darkest calamity which has ever befallen this world, there is a just God judging in the world, who will not allow might to crush right, who will not permit militarism to override morality. We Jews of the Empire will share with our fellow citizens of other creeds, even as we have done at all times of national peril, as one people, grief and gladness, joy and pain beneath the British flag with its imperishable traditions. Never has the patriotism of His Majesty's Jewish subjects been more wholehearted, never their loyalty more devoted than it is today, at this season of grave national peril. It is a matter of pride and gratification to our community that the command of the 4th Infantry Brigade of the Second Australian Expeditionary Force has been entrusted to an esteemed co-religionist, Colonel Monash, who, we are sure, will prove himself fully worthy of the great honour and high responsibility which his country has bestowed upon him. We Jews, like all our fellow citizens, will follow with bated breath the progress of this fateful struggle. As Jewish members of the defensive forces of the Commonwealth, your Faith looks to you to comport yourselves in all circumstances as true patriots. May you prove yourselves worthy Jews, rising to the full height of your manhood during the many trials which await you.[44]

At 7 a.m., eight days before Christmas and just a few hours after the German fleet begins shelling Scarborough and Hartlepool in northern England, Monash climbs upon his horse Tom at his Broadmeadows camp and surveys the formation of his khaki-clad soldiers, transport wagons and packhorses. They form a line that stretches for all of 4 kilometres.[45] He orders them to 'forward march' down the dusty Sydney Road towards Melbourne, 18 kilometres away, in their first test as a combined military unit.

Just on noon, Governor-General Ronald Munro Ferguson, wearing his decorative uniform as Commander-in-Chief of the Commonwealth Military Forces and standing proudly under the Union Jack on the Parliament House stairs, salutes Monash as he and his long line of men approach.[46]

Company after company rolls round the Collins Street corner after the long march. Gleaming bayonets form a sparkling crest on what looks like a slow-flowing khaki river.[47] Munro Ferguson says that 'the troops are magnificent. Nothing could have been finer',[48] and that he is proud to think 'that such fine troops are going from Australia'.[49] Privately, he calls Monash 'a competent Jew'.[50]

The soldiers' mess tins are packed with jam sandwiches, and after a lunch shared with thousands of supporters, families, friends and busy pie-men in Royal Park, the troops march back to Broadmeadows, arriving at about 7 p.m. Monash issues a proclamation expressing his 'complete satisfaction' with the way all tasks have been performed.[51] Gibson treats him to a function with the directors of Luna Park and Wallaby Club members, and Monash calls on Annie Gabriel, now living with Fred and the children at Balaclava.

Monash had stayed in touch with 'the love of his life' over the years, and visited her and Fred in Sydney a month ago, just before the Gabriels' move to Melbourne. When Annie heard he was sailing for the war she wrote to him in secret, asking: 'Will you write to St Kilda P.O. the same name as usual ... It is awful to think you have to go.'[52]

On 21 December, about 100 tenants and clerks of Collins House gather to wish Monash well on his march to the war and present him with a travelling kit bag and camper's dining outfit as though he is off on holidays. Monash is the third tenant of Collins House to lead a brigade, following Jim McCay, who is already in Egypt commanding the 2nd Infantry Brigade, and Colonel Frederic Hughes, Director of the Dunlop Rubber Company, who has been given command of the 3rd Light Horse. Monash is praised at the function for his 'slogging qualities and exceptional brain power' and his co-tenants look forward 'confidently to a brilliant career for him at the front'.[53] Monash tells his audience that after 30 years of military service he has the honour to command 'the best fighting material which has yet been gathered together in Australia'. The whole Empire, he says, including Australia, 'is in an absolutely jeopardous condition', and it infuriates him to think that anyone could openly question that a native-born Australian, such as himself, even with German parents, could fail to do his utmost for King and Country in such a crisis.[54]

On the same day as Monash's farewell, British Major General Sir William Birdwood,[55] a small, thin, nervy 49-year-old with a stammer, takes command of the Australian and New Zealand units in Egypt. He served as Military Secretary to Kitchener in the Boer War. His troops are formed into two divisions: the 1st Australian Division under William Bridges, and the New Zealand and Australian Division under the tall, regal and pompous Alec Godley,[56] who played international polo for England before becoming Commandant of the New Zealand Military Forces.

The next day, 22 December, Monash says his goodbyes to Vic and Bertha, promising them he will be back before they know it, as the Germans are already on the run. Rabbis Danglow, Joseph Abrahams and Jacob Lenzer send a telegram to Monash saying: 'On behalf of the Victorian Jewish Community we wish you and your brigade *bon voyage*, successful expedition, and safe return.'[57]

Eleven trainloads of troops singing 'Australia Will Be There' make their way from Broadmeadows to Port Melbourne from 11 a.m. Most have never been on a ship before; indeed, many are seeing salt water for the first time.[58] Secrecy has been urged, but such a great moving mass of men can't help but draw a crowd, and there are 4000[59] well-wishers to cheer Monash, the Senior Military Officer, when he boards His Majesty's Australian transport ship *Ulysses*, a 15,000-ton cargo vessel leased by the Commonwealth from the China Mutual Steam Navigation Co. It is one of 17 ships transporting Monash's men to rendezvous with a New Zealand contingent off King George Sound. Charles Brewis, the principal transport officer in the Royal Australian Navy, and a man 'of peculiar temperament'[60] who has helped chart the coast of Western Australia and the South Pacific, is commanding the ships.[61] Monash's three horses Tom, Dick and Harry are also making the voyage.

While the Australian Government initially promised Britain 20,000 men, 52,561 have enlisted by the end of 1914 and many more will soon join the fight. After waiting hour after hour in the scorching sun, 'sweethearts and young wives, mothers and sisters', many of whom have journeyed from remote country towns or interstate, are gathered at the side of the ships wishing 'in secret that their men should not go',[62] but knowing that their wishing will do no good and praying, instead, that they will soon be home safe. To the accompaniment of 'Auld Lang Syne', *Ulysses* is the last of the ships to leave the dock, at 8 p.m.

'It was a beautiful send off,' Monash writes to Vic, 'a never to be forgotten sight – the shore, the pier, the red ribbon, the cheering crowd, the towers and lights of the city gradually sinking back into the background and into the night ... a splendid ship, a splendid table, am most comfortable in a roomy cabin with both steward and batman to wait on me hand and foot.'[63] After so many years of service, so many Easters playing at war, Monash is now on his way to fight in the real thing. More than once he had thought his military career was going nowhere but now he is heading to the greatest cataclysm the world has known. And thousands of lives are in his care.

On Christmas Day, as they sail across the Great Australian Bight, the troops dine on ham and eggs for breakfast and for dinner roast pork, plum pudding and Christmas cake. As dinner is being served, Monash walks among his troops, wishing the men merry Christmas and a happy New Year. The Presbyterian Chaplain, 47-year-old Edinburgh-born Captain Andrew Gillison, a father of four with a mop of greying hair, gives a sermon about peace on earth and goodwill to all men, but tells the troops on the flagship that sometimes man must *fight* for this peace. Christmas carols are sung on deck by hundreds of soldiers. When there is a rendition of 'Home Sweet Home', some of the younger lads brush tears from their eyes before their mates can notice.[64]

By Boxing Day several cases of measles and appendicitis have developed, and some soldiers are transferred to hospitals in Albany when the convoy arrives late on the night of 27 December.[65] Monash spends three days making final preparations during a gale, frantically trying to sort out a bureaucratic mess that has seen men and provisions on wrong ships, naval officers defying his orders, his own officers disobeying him and a tug-masters' strike. Finally, on 31 December, 14 Australian ships[66] and three New Zealand vessels leave King George Sound, heading for Egypt. There are 10,500 Australian soldiers and 2000 more from across the Tasman.[67] With the *Emden* having been run aground, the Australian convoy has only submarine *AE2*, under tow of the *Berrima*, as protection.

Monash has an upset stomach and a nervous obsession about falling overboard. But when calm is eventually restored after the frantic events surrounding their departure, he stands on the bridge of the flagship, and marvels at the magnificence of the occasion, and the spectacle of the convoy, all under his command. In single file the ships stretch for more than 30 kilometres. He cannot help but feel proud of his achievements, of rising from his days as 'Corporal Potash' to become a commander of such importance; of seeing his indefatigable ambition finally rewarded with such a position. He asks Vic to keep the newspaper cuttings about him 'as it will be an interesting souvenir in years to come'.[68] 'I feel it is something to have lived for,' he tells Vic, using what will become one of his favourite expressions, 'to have been entrusted by one's country with so magnificent a responsibility.'[69]

On deck the men box, wrestle, practise fencing and engage in rough-and-tumble. Those not on duty dress as they please. 'Some of the toffs have bought themselves white duck suits, others have their blue dungarees cut down into short knickers, with the sleeves cut out of the jackets. Others wear pyjama trousers and putties … For headdress we have wideawake hats, uniform peak caps, woollen night caps, white caps and khaki fatigue caps.'

As the convoy sails towards the Ceylonese capital of Colombo, Vic and Bert enjoy the fresh air of Clifton Springs for a few weeks[70] and one night dine there with Australian Attorney-General Billy Hughes[71] and his wife Mary. Hughes is a 52-year-old scrapper, who, born poor in London and raised in Wales, has climbed his way through life from umbrella repairman to union powerbroker. He is now deputy leader of Australia's ruling Labor Party and his sharp eye is on the top job.

Hughes presents Bert – who will work throughout the war as a nursing aide – with a copy of his 1910 book *The Case for Labor*, compiled from his weekly columns in Sydney's *Daily Telegraph*. Vic calls him a 'dear' and says he is awfully hard of hearing. She has been busily forming a branch of the Purple Cross Service, a charity for troop horses, and is elated that 26,500 bandages have already been sent to headquarters, along with 'comforts' such as linseed meal, oatmeal, arrowroot, salt, absorbent wool, flannel tape, poultice boots and molascuit, a fodder made from molasses and sugar-cane fibre.[72] She is also involved in helping Lady Mayoress Minnie Hennessy and her Patriotic League organise a Belgian Flag Day fundraiser.

In order to get his way, Monash has to direct, advise, scold, bully and criticise his officers, and stamp his command of the convoy with what the *Argus* war correspondent Charles Smith calls 'his powerful personality and impregnable sense of justice' in such a way that 'there is not a man on board who would not follow him to the ends of the earth with perfect confidence'.[73]

Monash approaches his new role with the same practical work ethic he embraced as an engineer. He sacks one officer because he is feuding with the captain of his ship, but every officer demands Monash's time and none is disappointed. 'His real merits as an administrator are disclosed when everyone is on the rush and believes that his own little piece of business is all important.'[74]

Monash writes that he seems impervious to inoculations, a pain that makes others squirm. They are administered to every soldier, but despite this precaution, the first of 11 deaths on the voyage occurs at 8 a.m. on New Year's Day 1915,[75] when 20-year-old ambulance man Private Benjamin Acreman, a sawmill worker from Brisbane, succumbs to typhoid on the troopship S.S. *Borda*. His body, in full uniform, is bound in his hammock and he is buried at sea three hours later while a bugler plays the 'Last Post'. During the service every man in the expeditionary force stands at attention for five minutes.[76] Monash now regrets not bringing nursing staff with him.

The convoy arrives at Colombo at 8 a.m. on 13 January. Monash finds the place 'full of hard work and trouble'.[77] He observes all the diplomatic courtesies, lunching with the governor and showing him over the *Ulysses*. But on the second morning in port, as dozens of small local craft surround the convoy, hundreds of Monash's men unwind like compressed springs. Ignoring their orders, they dive off decks or shimmy down anchor chains and ropes to be carried into the bars or waiting arms of Ceylonese women. Monash sends 50 soldiers and three officers to corral them, and with help from the local European garrison, the convoy eventually leaves Colombo with all but 20 of the revellers.

Monash will have to defend himself against official complaints from the Ceylonese authorities and rumours back home. He admits the Colombo debacle to George Pearce but says it won't happen again: 'Our Australian relatives and friends have been asked to believe that at every port of call … the soldiers committed to my charge landed in considerable numbers and indulged in drunken and immoral orgies … the exact contrary … has been the case … no one could wish to command a finer and more earnest, more worthy, and well behaved body of men … for the sake of our parents, our wives and our children [do] not allow our good name to be tarnished in Australia.'[78]

For a week, as they head towards Aden, near the Suez Canal, the men loll about on board the transports, waiting for something to happen. Some practise with their machine-guns or learn a language or play deck cricket, but most are already sick of sea life and confinement. Monash complains to Vic that he is already 'horribly homesick'. This whole blasted war business has been a 'rooting up of everything in which I have any interest … I suppose the only thing to do is set one's teeth and go straight ahead.' He tells her that the Australians will likely be based in Egypt and could be there until the end of the war, 'that is of course unless the war goes on over next spring and summer'.[79]

While his troops are at sea, the war council agrees to Churchill's attack on the Dardanelles. British troops in Egypt are put on alert and the travel plans of the Australians heading to Britain are quickly changed.

Monash's convoy arrives off Aden on 20 January but Monash and Captain Brewis, wary of the frenzy at Colombo, anchor more than 6 kilometres off shore. Monash gets wind of intelligence about Turkish snipers at the Suez Canal. He has reinforcements and bags of flour, chaff, bran and potatoes brought on deck as makeshift armour for the bridge of the *Ulysses* as the steamer finally navigates the more than 100 kilometres of narrow waterway. The Australians are cheered for much of the way by friendly forces on both banks: Kiwis, Sikhs, Gurkhas, Bengal Lancers − 'splendid fellows' − the Egyptian Camel Corps, the Lancashire Territorials and the King's Own Scottish Borderers.[80]

The troops finally arrive at Alexandria in Egypt on 31 January and set up their base 8 kilometres from Cairo at the Aerodrome Camp near the modern city of Heliopolis,[81] complete with palatial buildings, wide asphalt streets and a Luna Park of a similar size to the one in St Kilda. Their base is about 25 kilometres from the 1st Division at Mena. A fast electric train carries the men to Cairo when off duty.[82]

Monash has a high fever and feels seedy, but the warm welcome from the foreign soldiers lifts him, and Birdwood and Godley greet him warmly. He dines with Birdwood, 'a fine dapper little chap, with whom I am sure I will get on very well' although on first impressions Birdwood and his stammer leave much to be desired in a military commander.[83]

*

Monash's 4th Brigade, Harry Chauvel's 1st Light Horse Brigade and the New Zealand Infantry Brigade and Mounted Rifles will all be under Godley's command. In turn they are under Birdwood's umbrella command as part of the Australian and New Zealand Army Corps, or ANZAC.

To Monash, Birdwood is an unimpressive figure on first sight, small, thin and 'rather nervy' but he has a 'perfectly wonderful grasp of the whole business of soldiering'. Monash and Birdwood spend hours together, talking to everyone from buglers to brigadiers, and 'every time he left the man with a better knowledge of his business'.[84] By contrast, Godley – whom Monash at first describes as 'elegant, graceful, genial and expansive' – will gradually make himself hated by all the New Zealanders because of his 'violent temper' and 'pernickety and selfish nature'.[85]

Both the generals inspect Monash's men at church parade on their first Sunday in camp. Birdwood defends Monash to the hilt over the suspicions surrounding his German leanings. Yet he tells Australian Governor-General Munro Ferguson that while the well-known engineer is 'an exceptionally able man on paper, observant – and with knowledge', he doubts his ability to apply that textbook knowledge in the field because he is not much on horseback.[86] Godley disputes Birdwood's opinion and says Monash will do well, calling him 'energetic and capable … an excellent officer' and 'very ready to act upon all suggestions and orders'.[87]

Monash feels very much a stranger in a strange country, calling his surroundings a land of 'sand, sin, sorrow and syphilis'. Everything is dirty, squalid, smelly and repugnant to 'any refined sense', he complains to Vic. The wind, dust and cold are 'highly unpleasant', and after a trip to the ancient city of Memphis, 20 kilometres south of Cairo, his lasting impression is not of the ruins but of 'a yelling screaming crowd of dirty, smelly, Arabs, donkey boys, Bedouins, Dragomans, donkeys, camels and mules, whirling along in a pandemonium of confusion, noise, shouting and muddled arrangements'.[88]

The 4th Brigade goes through its first training exercise on 11 February and Godley praises Monash's men for their 'punctuality, precision, steadiness and thoroughness'.[89] Four days later Godley tells Monash that he and Birdwood consider his to be the best Australian brigade in Egypt, and while the praise causes some degree of resentment among other commanders, Monash laps it up.[90]

He is visited by a deputation headed by the elderly Grand Rabbi of Cairo, Moroccan-born Refael Aharon ben Shimon, who is arrayed like the ancient Joseph in robes of many colours. The two Jews converse in French. Monash promises to gather as many Jewish officers as he can for the Purim service on 28 February. Ben Shimon begs Monash to recapture Jerusalem from the Turks and, eager as always to make a big impression, Monash promises to use his 'great influence' with King George and Kitchener 'to that end'.[91]

Monash leads his brigade on intensive training, much of it night work, and holds up well despite being 'in the saddle from 7.50 to 6.15pm'.[92] He writes *Operation Standing Orders* as a guide for his brigade and speaks to each of his four battalions separately, imploring them to develop self-sacrifice, patience and endurance for the hard road ahead, and to discipline those among them who are slackers and wasters.

'I have confidence you will do your level best for the sake of your manhood,' he says, 'for the sake of Australia and for the sake of the British Empire.'[93]

Every second day the men march 30 kilometres and engage in mock battles, against the East Lancashires, the New Zealand Mounted Brigade and the New Zealand Infantry. They relax with games of football.

Monash has already established a good relationship with his staff – McGlinn and Jess; veterinary officer Cyril Robert

Seelenmeyer, an Australian Rules football star with (Melbourne) University, and William Locke, a 20-year-old 'charming, gentlemanly lad' who has just graduated from Duntroon Military Academy.[94] McGlinn and the *Argus* reporter Charles Smith, who is starting to love Monash like a father,[95] begin to socialise in Cairo, along with the lanky, red-haired Charles Bean,[96] who is now the official war correspondent for the AIF.

Bean is a 35-year-old Bathurst-born, English-educated barrister and *Sydney Morning Herald* writer. He was chosen as the AIF's official correspondent by the Australian Journalists Association just ahead of the 29-year-old Keith Murdoch,[97] the Melbourne political correspondent for the Sydney *Sun*. Bean writes that Monash 'has been recognised as one of the ablest citizen soldiers' in Australia and is already well respected for the 'methodical, painstaking thoroughness with which he worked out every detail of the activities of his brigade, and the extreme lucidity with which he could explain to his officers any plan of coming operations'.[98] Bean feels the need to stress that Monash is 'Jewish by race and religion'.[99]

Like Bean and the others, Monash makes the most of the travel opportunity this war has given him and visits the attractions of Cairo: the museums and even the belly dancers. On St Patrick's Day, 17 March, McGlinn 'and all the other Paddys in the Brigade' take him to a Greek Catholic service in Heliopolis,[100] and a week later he and a dozen fellow passengers take a two-day trip to see the temples of Thebes at Luxor and the nearby pyramids, 'by far the most wonderful and impressive sight I have seen anywhere'. He is astonished by the sarcophagus of 'Amenhotep the Second, the great Pharaoh of Joseph's time, where he has lain asleep, undisturbed for over 4000 years', and by a culture that 'flourished 2000 years before Rome was heard of and 3500 years before Westminster Abbey was built'. The engineering feats of the ancient world astound him and he hopes that some day he and Vic can see them together.[101]

*

Contrary to Monash's assurances to Senator Pearce about the behaviour of his men, tanked-up Australians and New Zealanders run riot among Cairo's brothels on Good Friday, 2 April, on a street called Haret el Wasser. Several brothels are torched and firefighters assaulted. The riot becomes known as the Battle of the Wazzir. Many seek revenge for having caught the venereal disease that will be officially logged on their service records forever. Some are just angry that their beer has been watered down, with what many fear is not really water. As many as 2500 Australians and Kiwis take part, though most later claim only to have been spectators.

Monash is part of a court of inquiry under Colonel Fred Hughes. Fifty witnesses are interviewed. It is hard to get a straight story from any of them and the court's report is inconclusive. Monash finds the whole case 'very disagreeable', and after inspecting the damage calls it 'a sickening, revolting and disgusting spectacle', writing, 'Phew! I'm glad it's all over.' He turns his nose up at the 'revolting black women' in Cairo who, in the aftermath, curse the Australians with 'filthy abuse'.[102]

If Monash himself is tempted by the female attractions of the Nile, as so many of the other men are, he never lets on. Temptation, however, will come soon enough.

He writes to his family every few days and they reply in kind. Whenever he feels the going getting tough, with battles looming or worries that there has been no business news from Gibson, the little reminders from home cheer him. On 8 April he is in the middle of a busy Cairo street surrounded by what he describes as 'newspaper vendors, chocolate merchants, bootblacks and people' who are assuring him that they have '*vair gude ohranges*' when he rips open a parcel from Vic. Inside is a cherished memento from home: a locket containing miniature portraits of his wife and daughter.

He assures them both that his health is 'robust' and 'thoroughly good' even when it isn't. In keeping them abreast of everything that is happening he breaks all the censorship rules he once administered, guessing that every one of the flock of Egyptian spies in Cairo can already work out exactly what the Australians are planning.

In barely concealed code, he writes that 'Mr Hamilton … the same gentleman who came to see me at Lilydale' has just arrived in Egypt and is about to start some business at a place across the water.[103]

The place across the water is Gallipoli.

Chapter 15

*There have been scenes of awful slaughter, with heaps of dead and
wounded and ghastly wounds and long lines of stretcher-bearers with
their gory burdens, but men march cheerily past and take up positions
for attack or defence with the certain knowledge that many of them
will share the same fate.*
MONASH, WRITING FROM GALLIPOLI[1]

*On the cold grey dawn of that fearful day when the Australians leapt
on to Gallipoli through a storm of shrapnel and machine-gun fire …
the spirit of Australian nationality was born … This new spirit of
Australian nationality which had been born in the day of Anzac has
permeated every atom of our being.*
PRIME MINISTER BILLY HUGHES ON THE SPIRIT OF ANZAC[2]

THE THIRD CONTINGENT of 10,000 Australians arrive
in Egypt on 14 March 1915, with their horses in splendid
condition,[3] but it is the arrival four days later of General Sir Ian
Hamilton that sets Monash and most of the young men under his
command on the path to their first bitter taste of war. Hamilton has
been appointed commander of the newly created Mediterranean
Expeditionary Force: 70,000 men, including the Australians and
New Zealanders in Egypt, as well as British and French troops.

On the same day as Hamilton's arrival in Egypt, the French battleship *Bouvet* and the British battleships *Irresistible* and *Ocean* are sunk by mines, with the loss of hundreds of lives, after a failed campaign to shell Turkish forts guarding the Dardanelles. As a result, Hamilton decides on a land assault at Gallipoli, even though men such as Birdwood's chief of staff 'Hooky' Walker,[4] with his cap always tilted over one eye, declare the plan doomed.[5]

Monash, though, is thrilled.

'We got the first order issued today by General Sir I.S.M. Hamilton', he tells Vic in a letter home on 8 April. 'What a wonderful compliment to Australia and New Zealand to be included in this great expedition, which I feel pretty sure will exercise a decisive influence upon the whole war.'[6]

It's springtime in Egypt, with the fruit blossoms out and the trees covered in new green. Flies are everywhere and occasionally hot desert winds whip up the sand into clouds that shroud Cairo. One soldier has died from a fall off a pyramid, and more, breathing in mouthfuls of dust, have died from pneumonia. Thousands of others sharpen their bayonets and grease and polish their Lee-Enfield .303 rifles. There is a final overhaul of kits, each man making sure he has everything that is needed and nothing more; the shoes on the horses are checked, revolvers tested, forage loaded, tents and stores packed.

On 11 April, the brigade marches from Heliopolis to Helmia Railway Station for a short journey to Alexandria, where the harbour is choked with all manner of ships: steamers, warships, transports, troopships, colliers – Egyptian, French, British, Australian and even two American ships that also visited Australia.

The Australians are in high spirits, and Monash is confident they will succeed in whatever operation they face. They board more transport ships on 13 April and Monash opens his sealed orders, to reveal that on this glorious, sunny day they will be heading across the blue waters of the Aegean to the port of Mudros[7] on the Greek island of Lemnos, 1000 kilometres to the north. Members of the 3rd Brigade have already been there for a month preparing for the invasion of Gallipoli.

Monash is with the 1000 men of the 14th Battalion as they sail aboard the Chinese tramp steamer *Seang Choon* between Rhodes and Karpathos and, further on, past the almost 3000-metre-high Mount Olympus, tipped with sparkling gold as the sunlight bathes its snow-clad peaks. The rest of his brigade are on an assortment of other vessels.

Monash thinks it strange to be cruising along in 'this beautiful sea and mild fragrant air, and yet to know that so near to us is the centre of epoch-making clash of arms'.[8] To the starboard are the ancient battlefields of Troy.

At Mudros Harbour there are more than 200 vessels being readied for the greatest sea invasion in history. Monash sketches them to relax as he waits for orders. Sketching lets him think. Over the next few days he supervises his men as they practise climbing down rope ladders with heavy packs and jumping into boats in readiness for the land assault.

In the sky 100 kilometres away, Wing Commander Charles Samson of the Royal Naval Air Service spies on the southern half of the Gallipoli Peninsula while planes from the world's first aircraft carrier, HMS *Ark Royal*, cover the northern sector.[9] The Anzacs will land on a 300-metre pebbly shoreline under the rise of Ari Burnu. The troops call it Z Beach. A few kilometres away, 15,000 Turkish soldiers are stationed in the village of Bigali. The Turks have cannon fireballs that explode in the air and burn everything beneath.

On 21 April, rough weather off Mudros prevents Monash from attending a conference with other commanders, but he writes his first operation order 'without a tremor', so calmly he might have been back at Lilydale preparing for peacetime manoeuvres. The next day the Anzacs go through a full dress rehearsal for their invasion, climbing from the troopships into seven destroyers assigned to take them close to shore. The troopships will steam towards the entrance of the harbour, where the men will leap into lifeboats and row towards the beach as fast as they can.

On board the *Seang Choon*, most of the 14th Battalion, now
known as 'Monash's Bodyguard', sleep on deck to avoid the rats
and cockroaches below.[10] Ballarat-born Private Alfred Herbert
Love, who has been listed as a 28-year-old 'plummer' (sic) on his
enlistment form, takes the stub of an indelible pencil and picks up
the diary he is keeping for his wife Glenora and their baby Essie
back home in Brunswick.

'Still on Board the Seeang [sic] Choon at Lemnos Island,' he
writes, 'nothing doing much only more boats coming in from
Egypt – There is a Terrible lot of Boats here now and yet more to
come – still feeling well.'[11]

Birdwood sends his orders telling the Anzacs that 'in
conjunction with the Navy, we are about to undertake one of the
most difficult tasks any soldier can be called upon to perform',
and that 'it will go down to history to the glory of the soldiers of
Australia and New Zealand'.[12] Alf Love writes in his diary: 'Fri
Apr 23rd The Warships are getting ready for the fray now – all
getting steam up – Some Transport (7) and 4 Battleships have
gone out tonight – soon to be our turn now I hope – getting tired
of the ship.'

Monash is overjoyed to receive mail from Vic and Bert on
the eve of his first taste of war – yet he also realises that with
15,000 Turkish troops waiting above the cliffs at Gallipoli he
may never see his loved ones again. Early the next morning,
24 April, he composes farewell letters, keeping them brief because
the emotions bubble over even for a seemingly unflappable
commander. He tells his 'Dearest Wife':

In the event of my going out, you are to believe that I do so
with only one regret, which is, the grief that this will bring
to you and Bert and Mat. For myself, I am prepared to take
my chance ... to win through safely would mean honour
and achievement, on the other hand to fall would mean an
honourable end. At best I have only a few years of vigour
left, and then would come decay and the chill of old age,

and perhaps lingering illness. So, with the full and active life I have had I need not regret the prospect of a sudden end with dismay. I am sure you know how deeply I have always loved you ...[13]

Monash takes a 90-minute ride – 'rough and perilous' – in a little cutter from the *Seang Choon* to meet with other commanders 8 kilometres off Mudros. He is wet through with spray, but later writes that he is about to take part in 'great events which will stir the whole world' and which will go down in history 'to the eternal glory of Australia'. The men, he says, are whistling and singing, cracking jokes.[14]

Hamilton tells the Australians that before them 'lies an adventure unprecedented in modern war'. He says they are about to force a landing upon an open beach, against positions that the enemy believes are impregnable. But he assures them that the landing will be 'made good by the help of God and the Navy'. The positions *will* be stormed, he says, and the war brought one step nearer to a 'glorious close'.[15]

Privately, he knows Gallipoli will be taken only with an enormous loss of life. 'Death grins at my elbow,' he writes in his diary, 'I cannot get him out of my thoughts ... only the flower of the flock will serve him now, for God has started a celestial spring cleaning, and our star is to be scrubbed bright with the blood of our bravest and our best.'[16]

Each Australian soldier has 200 rounds of ammunition, and each wraps two sandbags around his entrenching tool, which he will need to dig a place to shelter from the bullets. The soldiers fill their water bottles, and stuff rations for three days into linen bags which are tied onto their backs. They each have tins of bully beef, tea and sugar, Oxo meat cubes, some hard army biscuits and three sticks of firewood. Each pack weighs 36 kilograms and most of the men will have to carry more than half their body weight as they run through a storm of burning lead.

The dawn landing is to be carried out in waves by 4000 men of the 3rd Brigade under Edinburgh-born Lieutenant Colonel Ewen Sinclair-Maclagan.[17] The second phase, involving about 8000 men from the 1st and 2nd Brigades, will follow shortly afterwards, and by 9 a.m., it is expected that 12,000 Australian and New Zealand troops will be sending the Turks scurrying for cover as they take the high ground at Chunuk Bair and Hill 971, the highest points of the Sari Bair Ridge. Monash's 4th Brigade is to follow later in the day.

The Anzacs are ordered to leave their slouch hats behind and to hit Gallipoli wearing round British field service caps.[18] The idea is to create confusion among the Turks over the identity of their attackers and their numbers.

Alf Love writes: 'Sat Apr 24th A lot more Troops left today – the Battle starts tomorrow morning in earnest at DayBreak.'[19]

The first wave of the attack at Gallipoli will involve 1500 men, 500 from each of Sinclair-Maclagan's 9th, 10th and 11th Battalions, storming Z Beach, soon to be known around the world as Anzac Cove. Another 2500 will be close behind.

At 2 a.m. on the 25th, Turkish patrols watching with binoculars and telescopes from the rugged shore report seeing many enemy ships nearby. The Australians are arriving aboard seven destroyers. They climb into rowboats which will be towed close to the shore by small steamboats. By 2.35 a.m., as the Turks gather in force, the first wave of Australian rowing boats is full, and at 3 a.m. the moon sets, making everything intensely black.

At 3.30 a.m., in the ghostly quiet of that dark, still night in the Aegean Sea, the steamboats start their journey due east, towing the rowboats and the soldiers behind them like a line of wriggling snakes. The throbbing of the small engines keeps time with the pounding of the men's hearts. The first 1500 soldiers head for what Lieutenant Ivor Margetts, a tall, wiry 23-year-old Hobart schoolteacher with a kind face, will recall as their 'first baptism of fire'.[20] In the quiet and the darkness their anxiety festers.

As the boats near the shore at 4 a.m., the first faint glow of a lemon-coloured dawn allows the men to distinguish between hills and sky. The smooth, calm sea glistens like a sheet of oil, but the silhouette of a man on the skyline of the plateau above them sparks carnage.

A voice calls out from the land.[21] German General Otto Liman von Sanders,[22] the son of a Jewish nobleman, is in charge of the Ottoman Empire's forces. He has appointed the tenacious local Lieutenant Colonel Mustafa Kemal[23] to lead the Turkish 19th Division on Gallipoli. The Turks have cocked their weapons as the invaders come into range. 'I don't order you to attack,' Kemal tells his men. 'I order you to die. In the time which passes until we die other troops and commanders can take our place.'[24]

From the top of the Ari Burnu headlands a rifle muzzle flashes. A hot bullet whistles over the rowboats and lands in the Aegean with barely a splash. There is a brief pause and then four or five shots, as if fired from a group of soldiers.

The men row as hard as they can. Their lives depend on it. But more shots ring out and some men are killed where they sit in the boats.

Near land the Anzacs scramble into the water as bullets splash all around them. Most jump into water up to their hips, some up to their chests, but others misjudge the depth and drown under the weight of their 36-kilogram packs.

Joseph Stratford and Duncan Chapman, both from the 9th Battalion, are among the first Anzacs to reach land. Stratford, a canecutter from Lismore, dumps most of his heavy equipment when still waist-deep in the Aegean. He charges across the coarse pebbles and kills two Turks with his bayonet before a barrage of bullets cuts him down.[25] Chapman and others fare better, tearing along the beach as bullets strike sparks off the stones all around them. They fling themselves down in the shelter of the sandy bank below the cliffs and wait to make their next move.

At 4.30 a.m. the Royal Navy begins its covering fire, the thunder roaring for miles all around, but the British landing at Cape Helles, further along the peninsula from Z Beach, is a disaster. The steamer *River Clyde*, a converted collier, is deliberately run aground so that 2100 British troops can storm out of holes cut into the sides. But the Turks are waiting and some of the Tommies don't even make it through the hatches before the bullets strike.

At 7.30 a.m., three hours after the shooting starts at Z Beach, Padre Gillison stands on the bow of the *Seang Choon* and leads Monash's 14th Battalion in prayer.[26] He knows that soon he will be leading funeral services for many of these boys.

Shortly before 8 a.m. 'Hooky' Walker is the first of Birdwood's staff to land on Gallipoli, preparing the New Zealand Infantry Brigade for an assault on what becomes known as Walker's Ridge. By 9.30 a.m., Monash and the 14th Battalion join the long queue of ships in the open sea waiting for the chance to enter the fight. Two and a half hours later they are still not within sight of land when Monash hears the distant thunder of naval guns.

Like most of the men on this boat, he has never experienced battle before, never seen a real war, yet he tells himself he is not afraid, that he feels nothing but 'the keenest expectation ... the thought of the world stirring drama in which we are taking part overshadowing every other feeling'.[27]

By noon most of Sinclair-Maclagan's 3rd Brigade, the first to hit the beach, are dead or incapable of fighting on. The landings cease temporarily at 12.30 p.m. as the Australians gather their wounded.

By 2 p.m. Monash and the 14th Battalion pass the entrance to the Dardanelles and Monash watches the bombardment of the Turkish defences at Achi Baba and the Turks shelling Cape Helles. The smoke on the distant hills reminds him of a raging bushfire, with thunder coming from the cannons of the *Queen Elizabeth* and other British battleships. Many of the men think the battle is all but finished; surely nothing could survive such an all-out assault. Yet they underestimate Mustafa Kemal and the spirit of the Turks.

The survivors from the 9th and 10th Battalions are scrambling up the Ari Burnu slope through heavy green scrub and prickles, dragging themselves along the ravines and steep ridges by grabbing on to gorse branches as though they are grappling hooks. Others dig their bayonets into the ground for traction. The command of 'forward march, no matter what' has been drummed into their heads.[28] All the time bullets rain down. Soldiers reach Plugge's Plateau only to find the Turks have moved to better vantage points. Men from the 9th and 10th Battalions also reach the bottom of 400 Plateau. The 11th and 12th Battalions fight their way up Walker's Ridge and Russell's Top, while others dig in on a piece of high ground called the Nek.

Captain Joe Lalor, the grandson of the Eureka Stockade rebel leader Peter Lalor, is leading his men of the 12th Battalion up a hill called Baby 700 when a Turkish bullet kills him. Lalor's commanding officer Lancelot Clarke suffers a similar fate. They are among the 754 Australians and 147 New Zealanders to die here this day.

As the men of the 11th approach Chunuk Bair, machine-gun fire from the Turks reduces the dwarf oak trees to chaff that flies under the collars of the Anzacs and runs down their backs.

At 4 p.m. the *Seang Choon* nears Gaba Tepe and Anzac Cove, and Monash sees the Turks firing from the ridges in the distance. The men have just eaten a hot meal of bully beef to sustain them for the fight ahead. The commander of the 14th Battalion, Lieutenant Colonel Richard Courtney, a Castlemaine-born solicitor, instructs two platoons of A Company to go ashore. In addition to their packs, each man is given 100 rounds of extra ammunition. They will land at about the same time as the Wellington Battalion. Soldiers from Otago are to follow half an hour later.

One of Monash's men, Bert Jacka,[29] a pugnacious 22-year-old forestry worker from Wedderburn near Bendigo, is anxious to get into the fight. Jacka volunteers with about 30 others from the 14th Battalion's D Company to go ashore and help with the wounded. He and Alf Love and the others wade through the water and then scramble along the beach as bullets and shrapnel whiz around them like swarms of bees. Dead bodies dot the hillsides and ridges. Some of the dying men are still quivering and some of the dead are pushed down the sides of the hills or rolled down back towards the beach to be collected later. The sight does little to inspire the other men trying to make it to higher ground, but onward they crawl.

Lying flush against the ground under whatever cover he can find, Alf scribbles in his diary: 'Reached the scene of action at 5 p.m. and landed and dug ourselves in under fire.'[30]

The chaos on shore has scrambled the plans of the rest of the 4th Brigade, and while Monash's 16th Battalion goes ashore at about 6 p.m. on 25 April, Monash himself will not land until the next day.

Godley sends the 16th to take Pope's Hill, a razorback ridge named after their commander, Lieutenant Colonel Harold Pope, a 41-year-old London-born former railway administrator from Perth. By sunset some of the 15th are at a place called Courtney's Post.

At 7 p.m. the first boatload of wounded men, covered in blood and many dying, comes alongside the *Seang Choon*. More than 700 wounded Anzacs are taken aboard, and more than 2000 in total will be ferried from the battle that night.

An English-born stretcher-bearer, Jack Simpson,[31] has found a donkey and is carting some of the wounded to the shore, where rain falls on row after row of them, as they die caked in blood and dirt.[32] Soon Simpson and the donkey will be dead too.[33]

'Private Simpson and his little beast earned the admiration of everyone,' Monash says. 'Simpson knew no fear and moved unconcernedly amid shrapnel and rifle fire, steadily carrying out his self-imposed task … and he frequently earned the applause of the personnel for his many fearless rescues of wounded men from areas subject to rifle and shrapnel fire.'[34]

Even though there have been massive casualties and the Anzacs have failed in their initial objective to cut the Turks' lines of communications, they form a beachhead – a secure position from which they can launch more attacks – by nightfall. Many of the soldiers are still out in the wilderness, clinging on desperately both to cliff faces and to their lives.

Bridges and Godley ask Birdwood to come ashore at 9.15 p.m. They tell him the position is dire, and that evacuation is the best course. Birdwood is aghast, but he trusts their instincts. He dictates as Godley writes a note for Hamilton, saying they fear the men 'are thoroughly demoralised by shrapnel fire to which they have been subjected all day after exhaustion and gallant work in morning. If troops are subjected to shell fire again tomorrow morning there is likely to be a fiasco as I have no fresh troops with which to replace those in the firing line ... if we are to re-embark it must be done at once.'[35]

When Hamilton reads the note while safe and warm aboard the ship *Queen Elizabeth*, anchored a long way from the fighting, a cold hand clutches at his heart. He consults Admiral Cecil Thursby and Commander Roger Keyes about the possibility of an evacuation and they say it will take days to get the men off the peninsula.

Hamilton writes back to Birdwood, sealing the fate of the men: 'Your news is indeed serious. But there is nothing for it but to dig yourselves right in and stick it out. You have got through the difficult business, now you have only to *dig, dig, dig*, until you are safe.'[36]

Meanwhile, Mustafa Kemal establishes his headquarters high up on Scrubby Knoll, which the Turks will call Kemalyeri, Kemal's Place. He will soon tell his men: 'Every soldier who fights here with me must realise that he is honour bound not to retreat one step ... if you want to rest there may be no rest for our whole nation throughout eternity.'[37]

And so, across these sharp cliffs, steep gullies and mad, craggy hills, the battlelines for a long stay are drawn in blood.

By midnight on 25 April, about 16,000 Anzacs and 42 mules have come ashore. Half the men of Monash's 15th are making their way up 400 Plateau, and in the early hours of Monday 26 April the 13th are sent as reinforcements to Quinn's Post and Pope's Hill and to attack the Turks on Russell's Top.

After the worst night of his life, out in the middle of this barren, Godforsaken hell, Alf Love scribbles: 'Mon Apr 26th Daylight now – The turks are Driven back a mile or two – very heavy losses yesterday for the Australians – about 4 hundred come on one boat last night – we are now ready in trenches and give them hell – We move right up to the firing line in the morning. The Allies are having it pretty rough but we'll win.'

But just in case they don't, Alf scrawls inside the back cover of his diary: 'In the event of my Death I wish this book to be sent to my Dear Wife to let her know that my last thoughts were of her and Essie my darling Daughter. Address Mrs A. H Love 33 Moreland Rd Brunswick Melbourne Victoria Australia.'[38]

Monash and most of his 14th Battalion finally set off in their rowboats for Gallipoli just before 10 a.m. on 26 April.

In Monash's boat are his adjutant, William Locke, and Major McGlinn, who is as portly as his commander. In fact, some of the boys in the 14th call Monash and McGlinn 'Tweedledum and Tweedledee' behind their backs. Monash is sitting next to a young and athletic Ballarat cabinet maker named Ernie Hill and has his field glasses glued to his eyes for the whole 40-minute ride to shore, now less perilous than it was for the first wave of soldiers, since the Turks have moved to higher ground.[39] Hill watches Monash surveying the impact of the naval artillery on the Turkish positions.

'Effective artillery support is going to be vital,' Monash tells McGlinn, who grunts in agreement as he makes notes. The boys in the boat take heart from Monash's calm disposition.[40]

They make it to shore at 10.30 a.m. and reach a temporary camp without cover on the beach. In the afternoon Godley sends Monash to Sinclair-Maclagan to assess how best 'to collect the scattered fragments' of the 4th Brigade, 'which had been distributed piecemeal all over the line'. Monash waddles part way up the hills 'under a hail of shrapnel, and in a chorus of whistling and crackling bullets'.[41] He knows he has to lose some weight.

He has only been in the fight for a few hours when he is struck by a piece of shrapnel that fails to penetrate his skin. It is a curious feeling. He puts the jagged piece of metal in his pocket to study at a later time.

Up on Pope's Hill, Percy Black[42] and his best mate from the West Australian goldfields, 'Mad' Harry Murray,[43] are operating the 16th Battalion's Maxim machine-guns and returning the Turks' fire with heavy interest. The two Australians cut down rows of desperate men trying to defend their homeland. They come under increasingly heavy attack from snipers and artillery men from Russell's Top. Murray is hit but keeps firing, as does Black, who takes shrapnel through his ear and left arm. Black's bicep is ripped apart and his arm flops by his side, useless.[44] As many as 70 shrieking Turks charge Black from their vantage point 80 metres away.

'Here they come,' shouts the big, burly prospector, and then, operating the 27-kilogram (60-pound) machine-gun with just one arm, he spits out bullets at 500 rounds a minute. No Turk gets within 40 metres of him.

'That's the beauty of these guns,' Black tells Lieutenant Colonel Pope, 'you can work 'em with one hand.'[45]

Monash spends the night back on the beach, and at 9.15 a.m. on 27 April leads the 14th through 'fairly heavy fire'[46] into the appropriately named Shrapnel Valley, the main route up from the beach to the frontline on the ridge. The Anzacs call it the Valley of Death.

In a rare moment of ceasefire, Alf Love writes in his diary: 'Tues Apr 27th Arrived at firing line at 10 oclock this morning. having a very bad time of it so far. machine gun played hell on our men. for a start they were getting hit and killed all around me but I escaped so far.' Alf runs out of room for Tuesday 27 April and so scribbles down the margin: 'Thinking a lot of wife and child.'[47]

The rest of his pages remain blank. Alf is killed soon afterwards. His diary, wallet, name tag and letters from his wife Glenora are placed in a brown paper parcel and sent home.

Reverend Gillison says a prayer for Alf as his mates bury him in a rough, shallow grave at Quinn's Post. In Melbourne a clerk stamps his file in red ink: 'DECEASED'. The word is frayed around the edges, as though the rubber has been worn down from overuse.

Monash is called to Plugge's Plateau on the morning of 27 April as, together with Birdwood and Godley, he surveys a second ridge that must be breached. The shrapnel fire eventually sends the three officers scurrying into a trench abandoned by the Turks.

Birdwood sends the New Zealanders out to take Walker's Ridge and Russell's Top, while the 1st Brigade's commander Colonel Henry MacLaurin,[48] a Sydney barrister and son of the Chancellor of Sydney University, is to take the right of the ridge, along with men from the 2nd Brigade led by Jim McCay. General Bridges will direct the operation. Monash's men are to charge up the middle to Courtney's Post, and the whole upper valley will now be called Monash Valley.

Monash returns to the 14th in Shrapnel Gully, sends two companies to help MacLaurin and, under continued fire again, pushes his considerable bulk alongside his men up the steep rise to Courtney's, where his brigade headquarters is established in a rough dugout made with sandbags and a canvas roof in the shade of a gully. Harry Chauvel calls it 'a somewhat dissolute looking rabbit warren … within practically a bomb's throw of the front line'.[49] Telephone lines are rolled out to contact the 14th and 16th Battalions scattered among the ridges.

Early in the afternoon Monash is again summoned to meet with Birdwood and Bridges at MacLaurin's headquarters.

Shrapnel hits Brudenell White, Bridges's chief of staff, but the pellet bounces off his tunic. He laughs it off. The officers discuss their sectors and attack plans.

Mustafa Kemal has his own strategy. 'Of the forces which the enemy brought in his ships only a remnant is left,' he tells his men. 'I presume he intends to bring others. Therefore we must drive those now in front of us into the sea.'[50]

Soon after Monash leaves the leaders' meeting, the 2nd Battalion, backed by men from the Wellington Battalion, make a bayonet charge against Turks coming down Russell's Top. The 2nd is led by 49-year-old Lieutenant Colonel George Braund, a small and slightly deaf Devonshire-born polymath. He's a vegetarian, fitness fanatic, boxing champion, accountant, magistrate and Liberal member for Armidale in the New South Wales Legislative Assembly.

The Turks retreat, but the Anzacs then come under heavy fire from the top of Baby 700. Thousands of Turks in six lines come racing down Battleship Hill, only to be bombarded by the battleships off Anzac Cove. Great clouds of dust and smoke send them into panic. Then 300 or so of them, shooting and waving swords, charge Pope's Hill and Scrubby Knoll only to be turned back by heavy fire.

At Steele's Post, MacLaurin's brigade major, Frank Irvine,[51] a small, 40-year-old veteran of the Royal Engineers and Indian Army, marshals 200 soldiers in disarray from Monash Valley, and is about to send them forward when he receives orders that the immediate need for them has passed. Irvine decides to see for himself and climbs up to Steele's Post. Several of the men warn him that he's a sitting duck but he replies, 'It's my business to be sniped at.'

At Russell's Top, 300 metres away, a Turkish sniper – probably a local farmer used to hunting in the mountains – takes aim at Irvine down the long barrel of a German Mauser rifle and kills him with a bullet just 7.92 millimetres in diameter.[52]

Just a few minutes later, and barely 200 metres away, MacLaurin is standing in his shirtsleeves on the slopes of the ridge that bears his name. Unaware of Irvine's fate, MacLaurin is busy warning his soldiers to keep their heads down when he too is killed by a bullet whistling through the gullies. Possibly the same gun has fired it. No one, from private to general, is safe, observes Trooper Ion Idriess[53] – not even the top brass. The tally of the snipers grows to what Idriess calls grisly proportions.[54]

Charles Smith reports in the *Argus* that Monash's headquarters is always under shellfire. There are hidden vantage points for shooters all along the ridges and ravines, and 'one sniper seems to have accepted it as his particular responsibility' to blow Monash's brains out.

'Throughout the fighting, Colonel Monash has shown the greatest bravery', Smith writes, relating how one morning Monash is called to his field telephone. 'He had scarcely begun his conversation when a signaller sergeant, who was standing beside him was shot through the heart. A few minutes later one of the infantry signallers, who had just come in with a message was hit in the shoulder, and staggered against the brigadier, who steadied him with his right hand. Almost immediately afterwards a third man was struck in the eye. Still [Monash's telephone] conversation went on.'[55]

Carl Jess, watching from nearby, jumps to the rescue, telling Monash, who seems so focused on the conversation that he is oblivious to the death toll around him: 'Your friend the sniper is trying to get you, sir? Brigadiers are much too valuable.' Monash ducks for cover just as another bullet flattens itself against the rock on which his arm has been resting. He later explains that he was concentrating so hard on the job at hand that he had no time to be worried: 'A man as temperamentally phlegmatic as I am, and as occupied as I was then, had small space for consciousness of the fact he was under fire and in personal danger.'[56]

Late on the afternoon of 27 April, the 4th Brigade repels Turkish counter-attacks at Pope's, Quinn's and Courtney's with desperate hand-to-hand combat and liberal use of the bayonet. Sunset heralds a fearful night, with the Turks blowing bugles incessantly, calling on Allah and, according to Lieutenant Ivor Margetts, 'shooting like hell'.[57] They hurl grenades shaped like cricket balls at the narrow trenches the Anzacs are making, but the naval guns keep them from getting too close.

Monash's position at the head of a triangular valley is precarious. The Turks have vantage points at the Nek, Baby 700, Dead Man's Ridge and Bloody Angle. Snipers rarely miss. Even after sandbags are put in place as barricades, movement up the valley remains dicey. Monash confers with Yorkshire-born Fred Skelsey, of the New Zealand Engineers,[58] about erecting defences around Quinn's and Pope's, but by 30 April 1500 of his men are still scattered in the inhospitable terrain, pinned down by Turkish gunmen.

Monash remains a cool head in a crisis. He meets with commanding officers and goes through the list in his notebook of tasks that need to be ticked off: such things as the rotation of the troops on the frontline, placement of Percy Black's and Harry Murray's Maxim guns, bivouac areas, evacuation of casualties and sanitation.

Soldiers on the beach are fashioning rifles with periscopic sights that can be fired from the trenches with less risk. When British marines falter to the right of Courtney's, Monash sends in two companies of the 13th. Then the men at Quinn's come under heavy fire and the 14th and 15th Battalions suffer more heavy casualties.

Suspecting that another big Anzac advance is imminent, Monash tells Godley that the survivors from the 16th have not slept for days and are utterly spent, and that much of his brigade still remains scattered. But, ignoring the advice, Birdwood orders a general advance for 5 p.m. on 1 May.

Monash supports objections to the plan raised by Hooky Walker, and Birdwood modifies it to an attack by Godley's New Zealand and Australian Division after more naval bombardment at nightfall on 2 May. Monash tries to convince Godley to raise further objections over Birdwood's plan but it goes ahead as cannons on the battleships and on land bombard the Turkish positions from 7 p.m. A fusillade of bullets from the Anzac machine-guns and .303 rifles follows.

The bone-weary 13th and 16th Battalions begin their climb towards the ridge on the right of Baby 700, singing 'It's a Long Way to Tipperary' and 'Australia Will Be There'.[59] Their singing is quickly curtailed under another salvo from Kemal's men. Percy Black, his left hand bandaged where the Mauser bullet cut through it, opens fire again with his Maxim gun, one-handed.

The Otago Battalion, which was to charge Baby 700 in support of Monash's troops, arrives 45 minutes late. Yet Godley allows the action to proceed without the reinforcements. A company of the 15th makes it to the Turkish trenches and bayonets many of the enemy, but without support the Anzacs quickly have to withdraw.

By midnight the left side of the Australian defences has fallen apart. Two hours later Monash is given two battalions of British marines – the Portsmouth and Nelson Battalions – to somehow bring together a line of trenches across his front but at dawn on 3 May the marines are cut down by machine-gun fire.

'For many days afterwards on the ugly bare shoulder at the top of Monash Valley their dead lay like ants shrivelled by a fire,' Charles Bean writes, 'until a Marine climbed out at night and pushed them down into the valley, where they were buried.'[60]

Without Monash's knowledge, the artillery is ordered to start blasting the ridge, blowing apart 80 metres of trenches dug by the 16th. Some of the soldiers are forced to retreat along with the surviving marines but the 13th and the rest of the 16th stay in the conflagration.

Brigadier General Charles Trotman of the Royal Marines pulls rank, asking Godley if he can take over Monash's command. Monash is glad to step aside. The battle is already lost and he welcomes a day's spell.[61] Monash calls Trotman 'amiable and helpful', though Birdwood says the marines – young, raw and untrained – were 'nearly useless'. 'They are special children of

Winston Churchill, immature boys with no proper training.'[62] But they die as bravely as anyone else, taking Dead Man's Ridge.

A week earlier the 16th arrived at Gallipoli with a fighting force of 959 men.[63] Overnight, their survivors have been slashed from 637 to 299.[64]

One of the hundreds killed is Private Gordon Fink, son of the *Herald* chairman of directors Theodore Fink, Monash's old friend from the Albert Street synagogue. Gordon is officially listed as 'missing in action', but Monash asks Vic to break the news to his father. 'Young Fink was acting as an observer,' he writes, 'the firing line was running short of ammunition, and young Fink volunteered to carry more out. This he did very gallantly in the face of heavy machine gun fire, but like so many others of this battalion, he did not return.'[65]

The 15th has now been reduced from 934 to just 350 men. From a brigade that numbered more than 4000 when he left Egypt, Monash now has just 1811 able to fight. Three hundred of his men have been killed.[66]

He sends an urgent message to Godley. 'It is imperative that this brigade should be withdrawn for reorganization and the appointment of new staffs and leaders', he says. But there is no withdrawal.

Monash's introduction to war has been a bloody debacle because of orders from British generals. It is a powerful lesson, teaching him that the meticulous planning he took into business is even more important when men's lives are at stake. He is determined for his voice to be heard.

On the afternoon of 3 May, Bean visits Monash at his headquarters, accompanied by Major Tom Blamey,[67] from Lake Albert, New South Wales. Monash seems 'a little shaken',[68] and tells the war correspondent that the battle has been a 'disaster' and that 'they've tried to put the work of an Army Corps onto me'.[69] Bean, who sees Monash as a 'pushy Jew',[70] later writes: 'It was averred against Monash ... that he was seldom seen in the front line ... It was further stated that the disastrous attack by his brigade … had left him unstrung, as well it might, and at higher headquarters doubts were expressed as to how he would "stand up to" heavy strokes of adverse fortune.'[71]

The following day, 4 May, as the 4th Brigade tallies up its dead, Birdwood orders the men to dig in for a long fight. The Anzacs still have a sense of humour. The prevailing thought is that the trenches will have to be extra-wide for Monash to fit through, and extra-deep so that Godley doesn't get the top of his lofty head shot off. Just that morning – at 1 o'clock – Colonel George Braund MLA, the slightly deaf commander of the 2nd Battalion, was walking back to brigade headquarters when the sentry demanded that Braund identify himself. The colonel didn't hear him, so the sentry shot him dead.

Monash receives 500 reinforcements on 6 May. He orders the 13th to hold Pope's and the 14th to hold Courtney's while the savagely depleted 15th and 16th go on 48-hour shifts to hold Quinn's, where tunnels and trenches scar the already tortured landscape. Cape Helles remains the main battleground on the peninsula, but Hamilton orders Godley to continue his attacks so as 'to compel the enemy to maintain a large force in your front'. Despite the opposition to the plan from Monash and all his battalion commanders, Godley wants his men to keep going in numbers against the Turks so the enemy will disclose their positions and strengths.

Monash believes the attacks are suicidal. To clear his head he manages to have a brief swim in the Aegean away from the shooting on 7 May and tries to dissuade Godley from direct attacks when they discuss plans over dinner in a dugout.

Meanwhile the death toll keeps mounting. From a scouting party of five that leaves Pope's to spy on Turkish positions at Dead Man's Ridge on 8 May, one non-commissioned officer is killed and three others badly wounded. The following night, the 15th sustain more than 200 casualties when Lieutenant Colonel 'Bull' Cannan[72] leads them from Quinn's on a charge at the Turkish trenches. The

Turks sustain even heavier casualties and expose their defences, but Monash is still disgusted by the action. Godley 'professes to be very pleased'.[73] When Birdwood visits the following day and asks some of the men of the 15th if they were involved in the attack, a grim-faced Monash tells the general, 'Most of those who were in the charge last night didn't come back.'[74]

On 12 May Colonel Harry Chauvel and his 1st Light Horse Brigade, now being used as infantry rather than mounted troops, take over the left sector to relieve the marines, and on 13 May also replace the exhausted, depleted 4th Brigade. After a heavy bombardment of Chauvel's men, Birdwood and Godley send the 15th Battalion back into action. Of the 60 men who charge the Turks, 46 become casualties, and Monash says Godley has ordered them to their doom. He complains that Chauvel annoys him 'by undue interference with internal administrative matters', and that while Chauvel is always grateful for help 'when he gets into a tangle', he frequently calls Monash for advice on the field telephone during the night.[75]

Chauvel's calls are not the only thing that keeps Monash awake. 'The rattle of musketry and the boom of cannon is incessant.'[76] Gallipoli is abuzz with 'orderlies carrying messages, staff officers with orders, lines of ammunition carriers, water carriers, bomb carriers, stretcher bearers, burial parties, first-aid men, reserves, supports, signallers, telephonists, engineers, digging parties, sandbag parties, periscope hands ... quartermaster's parties and reinforcing troops running about all over the place ... the air is thick with clamour, and bullets and bursting shells, and bombs and flares'.[77]

'We have been amusing ourselves by trying to discover the longest period of absolute quiet,' he tells Vic. 'We have been fighting now continuously for 22 days, all day and all night and most of us think that absolutely the longest period during which there was absolutely no sound of gun or rifle fire ... was 10 seconds. One man says he was able on one occasion to count 14 but none believe him.'[78]

Monash forces himself to stay positive as death hovers all around, even though 'it needed a lot of nerve to keep cool enough … to keep everybody cheerful and hopeful, and to make exhausted men do just that little bit more that turned the scale'.[79]

Already he has started to talk up the Australians at the expense of all other troops. He keeps telling his men that the British officers say the Australians are 'head and shoulders' above all others when it comes to 'physique, dash, enterprise and sublime courage'.[80]

He tries to put Vic and Bert at rest by telling them that bullets passing close by make 'a gentle purring hum', while the Australian rifle fire is 'a low rumble or growl', machine-guns sound like kettle drums and shellfire 'like a gust of wind in a wintry gale'.[81] He also tells them amusing anecdotes, relating the story of a soldier who cursed 'those damn snipers' after being buried by dirt from an 8-inch cannon shell, and of the colonel with a sprained ankle who ran like an Olympic sprinter to dodge enemy fire.[82] He and McGlinn are too weighty to fit through some of the narrow tunnels, but Monash tells his daughter that his long walks with the Wallaby Club have proved excellent training for the 'everlasting tramping about, mile upon mile, up and down these steep hills'.[83]

The first three weeks were 'pretty tough and solid', he says. 'We had nothing but what we stood up in for the first 5 days, then gradually came water, and food, and boxes to sit on, and boxes to burn to boil our camp kettles, then blankets and waterproof sheets, then sandbags to build dugouts and cabins, then tools and timber to make roofs.' He is in danger of being shot like everyone else, yet he always wants to present the best possible appearance. 'By and by came my kit-bag with a change of underclothes,' he tells Bert, 'and so for the past week or two we have been quite comfortable and respectable.'[84]

Monash might sugar-coat the realities of war for his daughter but he admits its horrors to his friend David Masson,[85] the President of the Professorial Board at Melbourne University, telling him that there has already been a 'woeful waste of life'[86] and that there is nothing to be done but to see it through.

Yet McGlinn is an excellent help, 'calm, cool, collected and a man of sound judgment. He works late and early and nothing is too much trouble for him.'[87] His troops are as 'docile and patient and obedient and manageable as children', yet 'full of the finest spirit of self-devotion': 'For the most perilous enterprises, whenever volunteers are called for, every man in sight offers instantly, altho' often it means certain death.'[88]

They are gallant too. After one skirmish, they capture a group of '16 or 17 Turks' and give them biscuits, which the prisoners devour 'ravenously'. The Australians hand out cigarettes, while all the time stretcher-bearers are walking past with dead or wounded Anzacs. Had they set upon these beaten prisoners 'and bayoneted them to death,' Monash says, 'no one could have greatly wondered'. 'It was touching, too, to see the gratitude of the wretched prisoners, who wept copiously and kissed our hands.' One old man falls to his knees and makes a long speech in Turkish 'with many salaams and gestures of homage'.[89]

Monash insists on his people 'exercising reasonable caution' in not remaining stationary in spots that are obviously dangerous. He is seldom in the front trenches himself, yet everyone at Gallipoli is in mortal danger. McCay and all his brigade staff are wounded and Monash has dodged a bullet more than once.

At Quinn's on 14 May, Birdwood is watching the Turks through a periscope when a sniper's bullet crashes into its top mirror. Part of the bullet carves a furrow through Birdwood's scalp and he is momentarily knocked off his feet. Blood erupts from his head. Pieces of the bullet are still in his scalp six months later.

The next day, Saturday 15 May, Birdwood still has a headache but is on his feet when Bridges comes to visit for breakfast.[90] Accompanied by Brudenell White and the wealthy young mining engineer Captain Dick Casey,[91] Bridges is scheduled to meet Monash at 9.15 a.m. at the station where Captain Clive Thompson, the medical officer of the 1st Battalion, dresses the soldiers' wounds.

Monash leaves his dugout and makes his way to the rendezvous, keeping as low as he can and moving as swiftly as possible given his lack of condition, all the time looking at his watch and over his shoulder. Anzac engineers have erected sandbag defences 1.7 metres (5 feet) thick at different points along the track through Monash Valley, and there are also brushwood screens suspended from wire.

Bridges and his men reach the medical station sandbags below Steele's Post and the general stops to light a cigarette. Captain Thompson tells him to be careful and get behind a barricade, but Bridges is not listening as a small piece of nickel-coated lead whizzes down from Dead Man's Ridge and opens a huge crater in his thigh, severing his femoral artery. Blood gushes out of his wound and his suntanned face turns grey just as Monash arrives.

Monash and Thompson carry Bridges behind the sandbags. Bridges tells them not to carry him back down the track because he does not want to endanger the lives of the stretcher-bearers. This time they ignore his orders, get him to the beach and place him upon the hospital ship *Gascon*.

Bridges is too weak to undergo an amputation, but if he doesn't, infection will kill him anyway. The news is conveyed to Buckingham Palace. On 17 May, King George V makes Bridges Knight Commander of the Bath.

The title does nothing to reduce his fever.

Major General Sir William Bridges dies the following day, in agony, at sea.[92]

Chapter 16

*One ought not to hide one's light under a bushel, nor fail to have an
eye to the future and any little discreet publicity may weigh heavily in
the scale when late on it becomes a question for those in authority to
decide on recommendations for the War Honours List.*

MONASH INSTRUCTING HIS WIFE TO SEND ACCOUNTS OF HIS EXPLOITS TO
MELBOURNE NEWSPAPERS[1]

*Australia seems to think that our work began and ended with
that first rush ashore. Why, that was a mere nothing compared
with what followed ... It was during the next three weeks,
when the Turks ... came at us with odds of 5 to 1 ... hurling
themselves upon us like fanatics, in their mad efforts to drive us
into the sea – it was then that the real fine brave steady work was
done by the Australians.*

MONASH WRITING FROM GALLIPOLI[2]

FACED WITH the unyielding determination of the invaders,
General Liman von Sanders makes a serious miscalculation.
He orders General Esad Pasha[3] to mount a full-frontal assault on
the Anzac line at 3 a.m. on 19 May. Four divisions of Turks, as
many as 40,000 men, backed by heavy bombardment that the
Australians call Jack Johnson bombs – after the world heavyweight

boxing champion[4] – come cannoning down the hills like bowling balls, trying to knock over 12,500 Australians.

A huge wave of Turks shouting to Allah washes over Monash's 14th Battalion at Courtney's, throwing bombs into a trench. Bert Jacka leaps in among the enemy, and thrusts his bayonet again and again like it's a locomotive piston. He slams it through one Turk, then twists and withdraws it in one swift motion to attack another and then another. As an enemy soldier thrusts his blade at Jacka, the Australian parries it like a boxer deflecting a punch, kicks his enemy to the ground and slams his razor-sharp weapon through the man's chest.[5] Jacka's .303 rifle has five bullets in the magazine and he kills a Turk with each one. The other Turks in the trench run for their lives, barely escaping his bayonet as he stabs at their retreating backs. When 20-year-old Lieutenant Keith Wallace Crabbe[6] finally makes it in to the trench he finds Jacka surrounded by dead men from both sides, and with three ragged prisoners at his mercy. Jacka has an unlit cigarette dangling from his bottom lip and says dryly: 'I managed to get the beggars sir.'[7]

At about 4.20 a.m. Australian machine-guns repel the Turkish attack on the 15th Battalion at Quinn's, and as dawn breaks hundreds of the enemy are killed by the Anzac riflemen.

Still the Turks fight and fight, dropping like flies around Courtney's until late morning. Liman von Sanders admits that he has made a shocking error of judgment, though it is cold comfort to the families of the 3000 Turkish dead (among 13,000[8] casualties) in that suicidal rush. It will be the last mass attack on the Anzac forces, and just as well, for Monash notes that everybody is exhausted 'with want of sleep and heavy mental strain'.[9]

Harry Chauvel, though, is 'astounded by the coolness and grit' displayed by Monash and the troops. 'I am living cheek by jowl with Monash here,' Chauvel tells his wife Sibyl in a letter, 'and find he is really a very fine soldier. He has been of very great assistance to me the last few days, and very willing indeed considering I have ousted him out of the command of the sector.'[10]

Among the rotting corpses in front of the Anzac line between Russell's Top and Bolton's Ridge, are five lying on top of each other. One Turk dies in a kneeling position, and stays like that for several days until he finally topples over. The Australians have suffered 600 casualties, 160 deaths.

The risk of disease is so great that the Turks, shouting '*Docteur, Docteur!*', make an appeal for a ceasefire. Monash sends two doctors with a Red Cross flag. 'Instantly from all over the place' Turks spring up, 'waving white flags, white rags and red crescent pennants'.[11] A young Turkish officer is brought to Monash to discuss, in French, a brief armistice to collect the wounded and bury the dead. Birdwood agrees for the ceasefire to take place on 24 May.

Heavy rain comes down on the night of 22 to 23 May, and Monash jots down a ditty composed by one of the men to the popular tune of 'Little Grey Home in the West':

> We've a little wet home in a Trench
> Where the rain storms constantly drench
> There's a dead Turk close by
> With his heels toward the sky
> And he gives off a beautiful stench[12]

The Anzacs bombard the Turks that night as a warning of what will come if the terms of the armistice are not adhered to during the ceasefire, and the next day, 24 May, thousands of burials take place in newly designated cemeteries.

Monash spies through his field glasses, about 100 metres away, a Turk breaking the rules by trying to repair one of the Turkish defences. Monash signals to a Turkish officer, pointing out the breach of protocol, and the officer runs over to the man and belts him with a stick. He then returns to Monash and, still in sign language, with a polite salute, expresses his regrets. Then, 'very politely', he asks Monash to stop using the field glasses.[13]

Not that the Australians play by the rules, either. Monash, Birdwood and Godley take the opportunity of the temporary peace to spy out the terrain in front of Pope's, Quinn's and Courtney's. Monash explains to Birdwood a plan to take Baby 700 where so many Australians died a month earlier in the first hours after combat resumes. Birdwood, though, is already formulating his own plan to break the stalemate in this alien land.

At 5 p.m. the ceasefire ends and the two sides are at it again 'hammer and tongs', Monash says; '... now there are several thousand more of their dead to bury'.

Two days later, Hamilton gives Monash a welcome break from the fighting, later remarking that 'he did splendidly at the Dardanelles but was a little old for front line work. I believed I saved his life by pulling him out and making him take a rest.'[14] Hamilton appoints Monash to man his personal bodyguard with 25 soldiers and Monash says it is 'a testimony to the good work done by this Brigade ... no higher compliment could be paid'.[15]

Hamilton sends Monash to rest aboard the *Arcadia* for a couple of days, though Monash refuses to use the ladder when he arrives at Imbros, saying he has 'come for a rest, not to do gymnastics'.[16] He dines with Hamilton over a 'plain dinner', talking about the time the old general came to Lilydale. Monash finds him 'most gracious, charming and considerate'. Monash has seen only a month of fighting but already he's become desensitised to its brutality. He tells Hamilton a story about an Aussie soldier who took a Turkish prisoner to the beach and how the poor old Turk kept going on and on about his wife and children. In the end, the exasperated Aussie shot him. Hamilton 'laughed consumedly' and a King's messenger on the ship finds it so jolly amusing he promises to share it with His Majesty. At last Monash is able 'to get a complete night's rest, with all my clothes off, and a proper bath and clean up for the first time in a month'.[17]

On 28 May, he returns to Gallipoli, and while stopping off at Helles learns that he and about 20 others in the brigade have been mentioned in dispatches. It will only be a matter of time before he becomes a general.

The following morning, at 3.20 a.m., the Turks use tunnels to blow up part of Quinn's Post and then charge the Australian position. A bomb shatters the left elbow of 56-year-old Lieutenant Colonel Granville John Burnage,[18] commander of the 13th. 'The gamest old man', as his troops call him, momentarily staggers from shock and loss of blood. Then, as the bombs and the Turks keep coming, Burnage stands upright as if nothing has happened. Stretcher-bearers arrive but he sends them away. 'Prop me up against the side,' he says, 'I don't want the boys to know I'm hit.'

Finally he collapses. Chauvel rushes up the track to take command from Colonel Pope, who has taken over from Burnage. Monash organises the troops below until the Anzacs regain the upper hand at 8 a.m. Three hundred casualties are added to the Anzacs' grim tally.[19] Despite Burnage's fierce protests, he is eventually carried down Monash Valley and out of the war, to resounding cheers from his troops.[20]

On the hospital ship heading home, though, Burnage hears a rumour that is quickly gaining momentum: that Monash has been executed as a German spy and traitor.[21] The rumours grow hotter.

Hamilton pays Gallipoli a visit on 30 May, viewing Quinn's Post from Monash's headquarters. The next day, 1 June, the 4th Brigade is relieved from Quinn's and Courtney's. Most of his original brigade of 4000 are now casualties, and Monash believes that no other brigade has continuously endured such tough conditions. The men take their leave behind Walker's Ridge, 'out of the eternal rain of shrapnel' – resting, bathing, shaving and, for just about the first time in this hellish campaign, sleeping with both eyes closed.

Monash has his own eye firmly on recognition. He is already worrying about the lack of publicity for the exploits of his men – and himself – even though Vic has had some of his letters published in the *Argus*, extolling the brigade for covering 'itself with glory', and lauding 'the magnificence of our Australian troops'.[22] Monash is furious that Bean has not mentioned the heroics of the mixed Australian and New Zealand division in his early dispatches in the way he has praised the all-Australian 1st Division. He castigates Bean at the first opportunity, ensuring he has at least one enemy for life among the Australian press.

On 2 June, Godley makes a speech to the 4th Brigade in Reserve (Rest) Gully. Monash asks Private Charles Taylor from Boulder, Western Australia, a clerk in the 16th Battalion, to take shorthand notes. Monash has prepared a summary of the brigade's activities for the general and tells him that no group on the peninsula has fought as hard or suffered as much. Godley rises to his great height, all 195 centimetres of it, sticks out his stiff upper lip and congratulates the men on their heroism, announcing that 11 of them will be decorated for valour.

'You have been for five weeks in the trenches, fighting particularly hard the whole time. Never before have troops been subjected to such heavy shell and rifle fire, and very often you have been met with bombs. (*Laughter.*) You [were] pitchforked, I may say, into the middle of the battle. There were many acts of heroism and gallant deeds performed. There were a great many killed and wounded. Yours is a fine record.'[23]

Godley looks at the ragged men, at their hollow faces, at the shock and awe still in their eyes. Already they know that this will not be a war won easily, if won at all. And it will not be long before they are all pitchforked into the fire again.

'I suppose you do not like listening to me speechifying any longer, you no doubt prefer the familiar sound of bullets. I am certain you are wanting to get back, again. (*Laughter.*) I am glad to have taken this opportunity of seeing you, and thanking you, for the gallant work you have done, and on behalf of the Imperial Government for your great work, greater perhaps than you may think to the glory of the Empire.'[24]

Monash calls 'for three cheers for His Majesty the King' and later sends a note to *Argus* journalist Charles Smith that those cheers were 'lustily given from 3000 throats in true Australian style – the echoes rolling from valley to valley and far out to the sea'.[25]

Monash includes the notes of Godley's speech for publication in various Australian papers and is already planning to publicise both himself and his men – the 'Fighting Fourth' as he calls them – as much as possible. Bean reports some of Godley's speech as well,[26] and Monash asks Vic to discreetly get his name into the papers as much as she can.

Later, he begins to fear he will be accused of 'atrocious self advertisement',[27] as McCay and his wife are. Eventually, with the censors prohibiting the publication of names involved in the fighting, letters from Iona to the *Argus* are halted.

Compared with the fighting the men have just experienced, life away from the frontline is heaven, with regular dips in the Aegean and a relaxed dress code. Just about everyone goes about in khaki shorts, often shirtless. On 3 June Birdwood and Monash spend two hours buttressing the morale of the men for a return to action but the soldiers relax as best they can. The sun has made most of them 'blacker in the skin than the Turks or our Hindu muleteer's'.[28] There are impromptu concerts and regular church services.

The Australians celebrate the success of Billy Sing, a 165-centimetre kangaroo shooter from Clermont in central Queensland. Although he is the son of a Shanghai-born drover, recruiting officers have relaxed their restrictions on Asian enlistments because he is the Proserpine Rifle Club champion. Sing is 'a little chap, very dark, with a jet black moustache and goatee beard', according to his spotter Ion Idriess, and 'a picturesque looking mankiller … the crack shot of the Anzacs'.[29] Even Birdwood has a turn as Sing's spotter, and is soon congratulating him on 201 kills.[30] Some estimate his tally at more than 300.[31]

Trooper Tom Sheehan, a farm labourer from Killarney near Warwick in southern Queensland, becomes Sing's spotter for a while, but a bullet from an enemy marksman passes through Sheehan's telescope and mouth before lodging in Sing's shoulder.[32] Sheehan has the tips of some fingers shot off and a gaping wound in his head, and needs surgery in Heliopolis to extract the roots of his teeth sheared off by the Turkish bullet. He is repatriated to Australia suffering severe headaches and nervous tremors. Sing rests for a week as his shoulder mends before taking aim again.[33]

In Reserve Gully, Monash busies himself reorganising his shattered brigade and appointing new officers. The men are even issued with rum on 18 June to celebrate the centenary of Wellington's victory over Nelson at Waterloo.

Much to the angst of Monash, McCay and Chauvel, the Australian Government appoints Colonel Legge,[34] Chief of the General Staff, to replace Bridges as commander of the 1st Division and of the AIF. Two days after Bridges's death Legge is made a brigadier general. Monash complains to Birdwood and Hamilton that while he and his fellow colonels have been human targets for the last few weeks, and know the Gallipoli terrain like the back of their sun-blistered hands, Legge is an unpopular choice. Monash is already hoping he'll be out of the war within a few months, back home with Vic and Bert, and along with McCay he threatens Birdwood that they'll go early. Governor-General Munro Ferguson queries Legge's appointment but approves it after assurances from Prime Minister Andrew Fisher that he's the right man for the job.

Ian Hamilton, who has already sent thousands to their doom, reacts to the news of Legge's promotion by telling Munro Ferguson that a 'commander of men [is] not created so much by education as by birth'. Even Bridges, he says, 'brave soldier as he was … would not have been big enough to command a Corps'.[35]

Legge leaves Cairo bound for Gallipoli on 16 June, but he is no sooner at Gallipoli than he has Birdwood offside, clashing with him over recommendations regarding the Australian base in

Egypt and plans for an Anzac offensive in August. Prime Minister Fisher stands firm on Legge's appointment, though, and he is made a major general on 22 June.

Monash shows reporter Charles Smith around Quinn's and Courtney's, and with New Zealand's Brigadier General Guy Russell,[36] a North Island sheep farmer, treks to 1, 2 and 3 Outposts to the north towards Suvla Bay. It is 'hot and arduous work', and Monash is left limping for a while afterwards with sore joints.

His teeth are still in good shape, despite the attempts by the army to break them with the brick-like biscuits. Yet he realises more than ever that he has to lose some weight. He starts to eat more sparingly, takes some exercise, swims often, and, with many of the men coming down with dysentery, ensures his water is always boiled. He still smokes heavily, though.

Now, in the height of summer, the heat is oppressive between 11 and 4 and he has never seen so many flies, not even on the hottest day in the Australian bush. They fight for his food and swarm around his eyes, nostrils, ears and mouth.[37]

Monash also visits New Zealand's other brigadier general, Francis Johnston,[38] and the headquarters of Legge, White and Lieutenant Colonel Pompey Elliott.[39] With some other senior officers, he spends a day on a trawler visiting Cape Helles, 'an exceptionally thrilling and never to be forgotten experience'.[40] The Turks shoot at them on their way and try to sink them with cannon fire when they arrive.

On 27 June, Monash is woken on his 50th birthday by the sound of the Turks' opening fire on Walker's Ridge, but at 6 a.m. his battalion commanders and their aides gather to shake his hand and 'all day long' officers 'from near and far' come to wish him many happy returns. Lady Godley sends over a cake she's baked in Alexandria; Legge, keen to shore up Monash's support, brings a box of cigars, and the brigade's cooks serve up a 'specially sumptuous' four-course dinner. There is a funeral to attend that day, of course – there always is at Gallipoli – but Monash finishes the day by sharing, with as many officers as he can, a rare bottle of champagne that has been scrounged by someone, from somewhere.[41] More and more he is becoming a commander who inspires respect and admiration. Vic writes to him often and with great affection, signing herself as 'Victory Moss' for good luck and telling him, 'Life is very empty for me and I miss you dreadfully.'[42]

McCay is offered the command of the 2nd Division, currently being formed in Egypt, but breaks his leg jumping a trench and has to be evacuated on 11 July 1915. Birdwood has been at loggerheads with Legge over the planned August offensive, and he seizes the opportunity of McCay's injury to remove Legge from Gallipoli, sending the former Sydney Boys' High School master to Egypt as McCay's replacement. Birdwood takes over the administration of the AIF himself.

Monash complains that the Australian colonels hold lower ranks than British officers of similar responsibilities, and he finally manages to crack the defence at headquarters. On 21 July he receives a cable informing him that, along with McCay, Chauvel and four others, he is being promoted to brigadier general.[43]

It seems all of Melbourne congratulates Vic back home, and Rabbi Danglow gives a sermon about his success. Monash hopes a knighthood is around the corner, and not a Turkish marksman.

The talk of Monash's execution as a German spy has gained traction from London to Melbourne. Some returned soldiers even entertain fellow drinkers with tales of how they have witnessed the German traitor's miserable death.

To mark the first anniversary of the declaration of war, Vic dines at Government House with the wives of Pearce, Legge and Bridges, among many others,[44] but her nervous disposition is soon pushed to the limit by reports that Monash has been forced to resign his commission and is being sent home from Gallipoli in disgrace. One officer tells her that he has suffered a nervous breakdown and is in hospital. Walter Rosenhain writes to Monash from London that there is 'no end of lying reports' from 'all over the place'.[45] An officer in Cairo writes to tell Monash that his enemies there have been stirring up trouble against him, and that 'It may surprise you to know that you have been shot in several places on the peninsula and here in Egypt'. When pressed for the source of the rumour, the officer is met with the reply, 'Oh, everybody is saying it.'[46]

The gossip even makes it into the papers, with the *Argus* reporting: 'In view of persistent rumours which have been in circulation regarding the health of Brigadier General Monash, Mrs Monash recently cabled to General Godley, commanding the Australian and New Zealand troops, as to the accuracy of the reports. A reply has been received as follows – "Rumoured illness of General Monash untrue – Godley."'[47] Monash tells his 'dear old muddleheaded worriers' at home not to believe the gossip of his enemies[48] – though Bert never does, telling her father: 'You are positively the strongest man both mentally and physically, I know.'[49] The Behrend family begin using the surname 'Monash Behrend',[50] and Monash, livid, demands that they stop because their 'openly and deliberately' highlighting his 'connection with a family of German name and origin' could do 'incalculable harm to my interests'. He tells them he has 'many enemies, who are only too glad to seize upon anything that may injure me',[51] and a furious row develops between Mat and Minnie Behrend.

Monash has more than enough to worry about on the peninsula without considering his enemies at home. The rush of adrenaline from those first few days of battle has now died, alongside the thousands of men from both sides. Yet if Monash doubts the Australian cause he never lets on. The loss of his initial enthusiasm just makes him more cautious.

'We have dropped the Churchill way of rushing in before we are ready,' he tells Vic, 'and hardly knowing what we are going to do next, in favour of the Kitchener way of making careful and complete preparations on lines which just can't go wrong.'[52] Of course, they *could*.

While doing his best to appear optimistic in his letters home he can't hide the fact that the 'ample correspondence' is 'absolutely the only brightness is this squalid, weary iron time', and that he longs for the comforts of Iona, his 'home and family and roses and creepers'.[53] Even Paddy, 'Lt-Colonel Joe Beeston's little dog', catches a piece of shrapnel in his chest and after lingering 'for a night and a day' eventually dies, 'the combined efforts of the staff of the fourth Field Ambulance being unable to save him'.[54] Paddy's squeals were piteous 'but he got a soldier's burial'.[55]

Monash's own health has held up well since he has begun to diet and exercise, and he is glad that he is the only 'higher Commander' who has not been given a two- or three-week spell on a hospital ship.[56]

He still wants to go home 'but there is no use in making any forecast' about when that might be. He tells his family: 'It may be as early as three months. It may last another 12 months … It is only a case of hanging on until the job is done. You know I am sure that I am as anxious for all to be over, as you can possibly wish it to be.'[57]

On 12 July Monash and his staff officers Ralph Eastwood[58] and William Locke begin scouting the tawny and green ridges between Outposts 2 and 3 and the following day, with three battalion commanders, Monash boards a destroyer, 'making a reconnaissance of spurs' as it cruises along the Gallipoli coast dodging occasional cannon fire from shore.

Hamilton realises there is no future in continuing the assault on Cape Helles and is now backing Birdwood's long-held plan to break out from Anzac and attack the main range of Sari Bair to the north. Christchurch sheep farmer Major Percy Overton,[59] of the Canterbury Mounted Rifles, was a scout in the Boer War and is one of the men who convinces his senior officers that it will be possible, although difficult, to march a large body of troops on a looping left hook, up through the valleys – or *deres*, as the Turks call them – to take the high positions. From there they could come down behind the Turkish trenches surrounding the Anzac position and begin an advance across the peninsula.[60]

Kitchener has demanded, and received, massive reinforcements from the British Government. They are to land at Suvla Bay, with 25,000 more to be sent on to Anzac. Birdwood will have about 37,000 men and the Turks 20,000 on the high ground. Birdwood's reinforcements will start coming ashore on 3 August and be hidden in dugouts during the day as their numbers swell. Bean describes the dugouts as a cross between a grave and a cave.[61]

The operation is to start with decoy attacks at Helles and Lone Pine on the afternoon of 6 August. The New Zealand Mounted Rifles are to drive the Turks from the foothills to the left of Anzac. The New Zealand Infantry Brigade will form a right-hand column and head for the peak of Chunuk Bair. Monash's 4th Brigade and the 'famous' 29th Indian Brigade[62] – containing one battalion of Sikhs and three battalions of Gurkhas – are to form the column on the left-hand side, going along the coastline before turning into the Aghyl Dere and taking Hill 971 and the twin summits of nearby Hill Q. On the same night, the doddering Lieutenant General Sir Frederick Stopford,[63] 61, but old beyond his years, will guide the 11th Division's attack at Suvla Bay, followed by the 10th Division on the morning of 7 August.

Monash's 4th Brigade will eventually link up with the Suvla Bay force. Five vessels will be off Gaba Tepe providing shellfire support. The plan is to capture the high ground by dawn, take Baby 700 and then charge across the peninsula to trap the Turkish forces.

By the light of a glorious full moon on 25 July Monash writes to tell Vic that for several days he has been expecting a Turkish attack, but that it has fizzled out and is unlikely to happen until the moon begins to wane.

The following day Monash shows General Stopford the Anzac positions. He is rejoicing in the 'grant of the Victoria Cross to

Lance Corporal Jacka, of my 14th Battalion'. Jacka is on Imbros recovering from diarrhoea when the medal is awarded, but Monash is 'jubilant' with 'the first V.C. in this Brigade, and this Division, and I believe in the whole Army Corps'.[64]

Yet there is tension everywhere over the coming storm. Monash asks his four medical officers if his soldiers are fit for battle. Three of them tell him no. They have been cramped up in trenches for weeks, starved of sleep, fresh food, proper hygiene and sanitation, and been easy prey for fly-borne diseases. Most have suffered from dysentery, diarrhoea, paratyphoid, bronchitis, heart palpitations, weight loss and the inevitable stress and nervous tension of war. Still, Monash hopes the excitement of the attack will lift them.

On 1 August, Major General Vaughan Cox,[65] who has spent most of his 35-year military career in India, is given command under Godley of the left assaulting column. Monash calls Cox 'one of the crotchety, peppery livery old Indian officers, whom the climate has dried and shrivelled up into a bag of nerves'.[66]

The next day Monash is on a destroyer with him, Godley and the other brigadiers, dodging shellfire for another look at the country north of the Anzac position. They believe they are gaining an understanding of the terrain but in reality they are wasting their time. The only real way to know the labyrinthine landscape out here is to walk it.

Monash meets with Cox the next night and again on 4 August to confirm the Englishman's plans, going over everything from the artillery timetables to the issuing of extra mules and 15 donkeys, the rationing of a gallon (4.5 litres) of water per man and the sharing of milk cans owing to a desperate shortage of receptacles. On a notice from divisional headquarters stating that Bull Cannan will take over the brigade if Monash becomes a casualty,[67] Monash scratches out Cannan's name and instead recommends Harold Pope. He composes a list of tasks for his men, ticking off each point as he considers and agrees with it: 'Perfect silence, no lights or smoking, fix bayonets when turning into Aghyl Dere [Valley], conserve food and water, vigilance to see orders obeyed, leaders keep cool …'[68]

On 5 August he attends conferences held by Birdwood, Godley and Cox, then runs through a final briefing with his battalion commanders.

Bean visits Monash that night in Reserve Gully, and later writes that the troops were 'perched in dugouts, as in pigeonholes around the great amphitheatre of sandy cliffs'. Monash outlines the battle plan to Bean, who calls it a 'masterpiece of lucid explanation': 'As a clear logical exposition of a scheme of operations, it surpassed any that I had ever listened to.'[69]

Hamilton and Birdwood send rousing messages of encouragement, though they will not be the ones fighting the Turks hand to hand. Godley and Cox address a gathering of 300 of Monash's officers and NCOs[70] sitting on the side of a hill, but do little to inspire the men.

When Monash stands to attention, though, he holds every one of his subordinates in the palm of his hand. His address is 'delivered during a perfect tornado of artillery fire',[71] and it takes some effort to 'keep one's voice steady and an uninterrupted thread to one's remarks',[72] as each man looks at the one next to him and the one in front wondering who among them will soon perish.

Monash tells his audience that he wants to speak to the whole brigade, but there is so little space in their crowded perch that he must rely on them to spread his message down the ranks. The night attack is on a 'gigantic scale', he stresses, with the backing of the whole army corps and the help of several brigades from Kitchener's army and the Indian Brigade, 'which has done such good work at Cape Helles'. The Indians had earned great fame for their extraordinary courage, suffering heavy casualties as they made charge after charge on Turkish machine-gun positions, with soldiers from the Punjab famously leaping barbed wire entanglements as though they were hurdles on a running track and attacking the Turks with bayonets. Monash tells his men that every battalion company and platoon commander must depend on their own initiatives and resources when necessary. He urges his leaders to keep their eye on Hill 971, 'the dominating peak of the whole zone', and if they find an easier route to the top than the present one 'don't keep it to yourself'. He reiterates Birdwood's instruction that they must press forward relentlessly to reach the top, and tells them to give orders in whispers.

Then all of a sudden … *BOOOOOMMM!*

The deafening blast of a shell above the cliffs stops Monash's speech in mid-sentence.

Newly promoted Corporal George Bradley of the 16th, a young farmer from Dowerin, Western Australia, who was shot in the leg in the first two weeks of the campaign, now takes a piece of shrapnel that fractures his right shoulder blade. He is carried away to the hospital ship *Sicilia* as Monash carries on.

There is to be no smoking all night, he stresses, no chasing small parties of Turks, 'who would be running around like rabbits'. The whole objective is to reach the new line on higher ground 7 kilometres away and dig in there. The 4th Brigade has been given the star turn, and they will have to 'fight and fight, good hard and plenty'. The key is keeping their cool, he tells them.

'Every man must make up his mind now, no matter how much clatter there is, to keep calm … a leader who is cool himself will inspire confidence and maintain throughout a grip of his men who in turn will respond to orders in a workmanlike manner, and not as spinning tops.'[73]

Bean says Cox makes a point of being present at Monash's conferences, 'for the sheer pleasure and edification of hearing his expositions'.[74]

The attack begins just after 5 p.m. on Friday, 6 August, with the 1st Australian Division mounting a massive strike on the Turkish line at Lone Pine. It is intended as a diversion, but succeeds in taking control of the Ottoman trench line.

At 9.25 p.m., on what has developed into a black and gloomy night, the 4th Brigade, now numbering 3350 men,[75] begins its march towards enemy territory in the foreboding darkness, leading the left column of 5000 men. Major Cecil Allanson, leading the 6th Gurkhas, says that despite Monash's show of confidence, there is a feeling of 'panic and doubt in the air as to where we were and where we are going'.[76]

They begin their advance by moving out of Reserve Gully, with Monash marching in the middle of the formation. After reaching the enemy position 3 kilometres away, they are to advance another 4 kilometres, but know that the rough terrain will make it seem like 40.

They head north along a newly built beach road and Monash tells the soldiers, 'assuming no halts or checks', they should reach No. 3 Outpost by 10.30 p.m., turn east into the Aghyl Dere at 11.15 p.m., and by 1.40 a.m. reach the forming-up position at the Abdel Rahman ridge for the massed attack on Hill 971. His timetable doesn't include the possibility of getting lost in the dark.

Ralph Eastwood is at the head of the column to regulate the pace.[77] The 4th marches double-time to keep to its schedule; some of those following, including the Gurkhas, break into a jog underneath their heavy packs. The lack of fitness among the troops starts to tell early. Because of the darkness and the need for silence, plans become disjointed, and the tail of the British 40th Brigade falls so far behind time that with the Australians having to wait for them, at one stage three columns of men are moving in parallel along the narrow space between the hills and the sea: Monash's men on the road, and the New Zealand infantry and Kitchener's brigade through the scrub. They are heading into what Cox calls 'mad looking country', where 'there does not seem to be any reason why the hills should go where they do'[78] and where one hill and its adjacent valley look like a dozen others.

Monash feels as though he has walked 'out on a stormy winter's night from a warm cosy home into a hail, thunder, and lightning storm'. They have not gone 800 metres when the 'black tangle of hills between the beach road and the main thoroughfare' comes alive with flashes from rifles, 'and the bursting of shrapnel and star shell'.[79] To the right the hills are brightly lit by a destroyer's searchlight as the beam occasionally dances over Monash and his advancing men. There are yells and shrieks from the enemy and cheers from Monash's men as they return fire and stab with their bayonets.

On their right flank the New Zealand Mounted Rifles are savaging the Turkish positions in the foothills of the range, clearing the path for the New Zealand Infantry Brigade to take Chunuk Bair by first light. Bean calls the New Zealand effort that night 'a magnificent feat of arms, the brilliance of which was never surpassed, if indeed equalled, during the campaign … almost the entire Turkish defence north of Anzac was for the moment swept aside and the way cleared for the infantry to advance up the valleys to Chunuk Bair'.[80]

When the first men of the 4th Brigade reach No. 2 Outpost, they wait for the 40th to catch up. Even though they lie flat, many can't escape the whistling bullets from the hills and men in each column are hit.[81]

After a short, brisk advance the march is reduced to a shuffle as naval shells roar overhead and explosions illuminate the hills again. Gunfire is constant. By 11.30 p.m. the 4th approaches the northern end of the Sari Bair range and begins its vast turning left hook to get completely around the Turks who are defending the mountains and facing the sea.

Their scout, Major Overton, is taking directions from a Greek miller, through an interpreter. Against orders, Overton is persuaded not to lead the men around Walden Point and towards the opening of the Aghyl Dere as planned, but to take a shortcut through the narrow Taylor's Gap instead.

It is a dark, gloomy night, and men can see no further than 10 metres in front of them. The shortcut is so narrow that soon the 13th Battalion, in the lead, have to move in single file,[82] hacking their way through thick scrub as bullets fly at them.

Monash now orders the men at the front of the advance not to load their rifles so the final stages of the march will be as silent and secretive as possible. They manage to drive the Turks away with the bayonets and run through those not quick enough to escape but before long small parties of Australians are shooting it out with Turks hiding in the hills.

Progress is at a funereal pace. Overton's shortcut saves just 500 metres, but delays the advance by three hours, until 2 a.m. Anyone not dead is an exhausted bundle of nerves.

Bean is later caustic in describing Monash's performance on this night, saying that Monash is 'a leader of whom it was already said that he would command a division better than a brigade and a corps better than a division … but in this crisis, he ultimately decided to take personal control'.[83] Monash sends officers including McGlinn ahead to sort out the delay. But then, frustrated by the lack of movement, Monash obtains permission from Cox to make his way to the head of the column, huffing up the narrow gully which is choked with troops, and past the medical staff dressing wounds. Critics will say he should have taken action sooner, although Cox has ordered him to stay in the middle of the attack.

Monash finds Overton, Eastwood and Lieutenant Colonel Les Tilney[84] arguing and unable to decide on the right course.

'What damn nonsense,' Monash thunders. 'Get a move on quick.' He demands they follow their orders and the original route, and puts 'vigour into the advance … by dint of yelling and swearing'.[85]

Monash leads the 13th and 14th across the Aghyl Dere – looking 'rather worried', according to the 14th's Sergeant Major Les Bain[86] – and into a field of stubble that will be called Australia Valley. He supervises the organising of the men into their platoons. He scrambles back to then direct the 15th and 16th as they make a dash, fighting with the bayonet, for 2 kilometres under heavy fire.

In the dark and in unfamiliar, largely uncharted terrain, no one knows exactly where they are. The 15th under Bull Cannan have the worst of it, trying to advance over rough, broken, stony ridges, densely covered with low prickly undergrowth, in which the Turks have taken cover and are 'obstinately disputing every yard'.[87]

The 13th and 14th reach what they believe are their positions to cover the attack by the 15th and 16th, and begin to dig in. Exhausted, and with their commanders Cannan and Pope convinced they can go no further for now, the 15th and the 16th also dig in, still 800 metres from the Abdel Rahman assembly point, and still 2 kilometres from their objective of Hill 971. The New Zealand infantry is within striking distance of Chunuk Bair and Overton, and the Indians head for Hill Q.

Monash establishes his headquarters just as dawn breaks on 7 August. The 15th and 16th have managed to take a Turkish base and Monash has commandeered an officer's folding bed and a copper bath for himself.

He is contemplating how relaxing a good soak might be out here in the war zone when he hears 'slight movement' and spots two Turks hiding in scrub nearby. Monash pulls out his revolver and says he'll shoot if they don't surrender. The frayed soldiers crawl out of a hole and throw up their hands 'quite tamely'.[88]

Two extra prisoners are added to the growing list the Australians are sending down the range. Charles Bean has been shot in the leg by a stray Turkish bullet while following Monash's brigade but refuses to be evacuated.

Most of Monash's men are dead on their feet after a long march and a night of heavy fighting, but Monash still talks himself up at every opportunity. Surrounded by death and disaster, he writes home to Vic knowing that his exploits will almost certainly make it into the papers. He tells her his latest action has been 'brilliantly successful'[89] even though they have not yet conquered the mountain range. He says he had 'the whole brigade going in fine style' and they swept forward in a magnificent dash of 2 miles (3.2 kilometres), and that on the first night he counted 500 Turkish dead and 600 prisoners.

Once again his talent for exaggeration shines. His men have actually suffered horrifically. Of the 4000 soldiers of the 4th Brigade who marched through Melbourne behind Monash eight months ago, scarcely 600 remain. The war has left them a 'ragged, bearded, dirty crew'.[90] Percy Overton is among the many who will die today.

The Turks have been caught by surprise and driven from the ridges, but they still have the highest points. As the morning light becomes brighter, Monash looks out at the dead and mutilated. The 3rd Light Horse Brigade is making a disastrous attack on the Nek as Turkish trenches allow a rain of fire on the Australian positions below. Wave after wave of the light horsemen are cut down by rifle shots and machine-gun fire. At Suvla Bay, General Stopford falls asleep on the HMS *Jonquil* during the attack. Troops wade ashore submerged up to their necks, only to be killed as soon as they reach land. Stopford is sacked, but too late for the 1700 casualties suffered during the first 24 hours of fighting.

Monash believes, in error, that his headquarters in the Australia Valley is bordering the Asma Dere and facing the spur of Abdel Rahman, which leads to Hill 971. He is actually well short of the location. He tells Cox, who is bleeding from a slight head wound, that Cannan's and Pope's men are 'absolutely done and lying and panting instead of digging'.[91] They are in urgent need not only of rest but also of securing their positions. Bean scribbles in his diary that Monash has stopped 'without being stopped … a decision which many weak commanders would make but utterly unjustifiable'.[92] Cox tells Monash to launch an attack on Hill 971 at 11 a.m. They argue heatedly before Cox allows him more time.

Major Allanson, who has a general dislike for Australians – he says they lack discipline and 'their habits are just too disgusting and filthy for words'[93] – arrives at Monash's headquarters with his Gurkhas at 7 a.m. Though no one else ever reports it, Allanson will claim two decades later that he found Monash not with a cool head but in a dreadful panic, 'hopelessly tied up'.[94]

'There were some wounded lying about, but what I mostly saw were men hopelessly exhausted lying about everywhere, all movement and attempt to advance seemed to have ceased ... What upset me most was that Monash himself seemed to have temporarily lost his head, he was running about saying "I thought I could command men, I thought I could command men"; those were his exact words ...'[95] Allanson will claim that Monash told him the whole offensive had become 'a hopeless mess' and that Allanson was 'no use' to him at all.

'I was in reality anxious to get away from Monash as quickly as I could,' Allanson goes on, 'as I felt thoroughly upset by what I had seen.' Others will be thoroughly upset with Allanson, who seems to have taken offence in later years at Monash's failure to give sufficient credit to his Indian troops.[96] Field Marshal Lord Slim, who comes to know Allanson well, will call him an unreliable witness 'who tended to embroider badly' as time went on.[97]

Cox allows Monash and his men to go on with their entrenching on a stifling hot day, but even that becomes a deadly exercise under fire from Turkish snipers and field guns, so that the best many of the men can do for protection is to lie flat on the ground. Closer to the sea, where the 40th Battalion have dug in, soldiers are able to procure water and raid beehives on a nearby farm.[98]

At 6 p.m. on 7 August, Cox ignores Monash's protests at the condition of his troops by ordering the attack to be renewed on the three peaks at 3 a.m. the next day, with the 4th Brigade to hit Hill 971 at 4.15 a.m. following a naval bombardment. Monash writes in his diary: 'Reconnaissance 6 to 7.30. Issue orders to C.Os. at Conference at 8.30. Sleep 10 to 2 a.m.'[99]

Monash tells Cox that his men have been working all day and night burying their dead and digging holes to save their own lives. He needs more reinforcements. Godley provides a battalion from the 38th Brigade, who, together with Monash's 13th Battalion, hold their line, freeing the 14th, 15th and 16th for the charge, guided by Captain Locke, who has reconnoitred the area in the afternoon.

Given his bulk and the difficult climb, Monash decides to stay out of the assault, remaining in touch by telephone with Pope, the de facto brigadier.

The 8 August attack has no hope of success, given the terrain, the state of the men, and the fact that the position is heavily defended. Further, no one has realised that there has been a monumental navigational blunder, and that the 4th Brigade is not on Asma Dere facing Abdel Rahman but on Kaiajik Dere,[100] a spur 650 metres to the west that looks very similar. Godley has said the men must attack with 'loud cheering', but Bean later writes that taking Hill 971 'was never within the range of human possibility'.[101]

At 4.15 a.m., when the bombardment is supposed to cease and the strike force is due to reach Hill 971, the force is disjointed. The 15th Battalion, trapped in an oat field, is virtually defenceless against machine-guns that are being fired with 'tornado-like intensity'.[102] The soldiers are too tired even to run, and Major Charles Dare of the 14th says 'they seemed to wilt away in front of us'.[103] The 14th only escapes decimation by taking cover behind the reverse slope of the spur. Shellfire and a Turkish infantry counter-attack follow.

Monash watches impotently from a high point above his headquarters. His telephone line is cut by a Turkish field gun at the start of the shooting and not repaired until 7.05 a.m. Pope eventually gets a message to him that the attack against the Turkish guns is futile. Monash informs Cox, who orders the column to withdraw to its lines, and the brigade's machine-gun section under New Zealand's Captain J.M. Rose[104] offers a blistering cover for the retreating Anzacs.

Bean calls the machine-gunners 'possibly the finest unit that ever existed in the AIF'.[105] But despite their support, the 15th, already devastated by the previous day's fighting, suffers massive casualties. Seven officers, including Bull Cannan's brother, Major

Doug Cannan, have been killed. Only 280 men of the 15th remain from the 850 who set off with Monash two days ago. The 14th and 16th have each suffered about 500 casualties.[106]

It is one of the darkest days in the young history of the Australian nation. 'Everyone seemed scattered', writes Private Charles Smith. 'Wherever one looked, there were troops, yet no-one seemed to have any fixed objective.'[107]

The field ambulance has not been informed of the attack, and for the first time in the war, Australian soldiers have to abandon those who are hit. 'Very few of the wounded left in Turkish hands survived', according to Bean. 'Some were shot or bayoneted. A German officer, seeing the Turkish soldiers kicking a number of wounded men and preparing to roll them over a cliff on the hillside, stepped in and saved their lives.'[108]

The Anzac retreat finishes at about 8.30 a.m. The 4th Brigade might have taken Hill 971 if the attack from Suvla had worked, but in the end the whole offensive has been a disaster. However, Godley tells Senator Pearce that 'General Monash handled his brigade excellently' and that they 'made a most wonderful night march through the really desperately difficult scrub-covered country, and at the end of it attacked the ridge with the greatest possible gallantry'. That they were not successful, he says, is due 'alone to the extraordinary difficulties of the country, and the fact that they were so enormously outnumbered'.[109] Birdwood and Cox echo those sentiments.

Bean sees it differently, though. He concedes that Monash has brilliant organisational abilities and a powerful intellect, which raises him 'head and shoulders above most of his colleagues', but – and it's a crucial but – Bean is adamant that Monash is 'not a fighting commander' to match Walker, McCay or Chauvel. Bean says the attack on 971 called for 'the touch of a Stonewall Jackson' and the recklessness of Jeb Stuart, Jackson's fellow Confederate in the American Civil War. Of course, what Jackson and Stuart might have done in similar country under similar circumstances against such a well-entrenched enemy is anyone's guess.

As usual, Monash will put the best possible spin on this disaster.

He tells Vic that Captain Reginald George Legge,[110] the major-general's nephew, has been 'shot clean thro' the neck' for the second time in three months but keeps on fighting, and that 'Lt-Col. Pope and Lt-Col. Cannan are still well and in splendid fighting trim, and altho' their battalions have been badly shattered, they are full of go and confidence'.[111]

'The Brigade has done magnificently and we have gained a large amount of new territory.'[112] 'The whole aspect of matters has improved immensely, and except for the fatigue of the men, and the hard conditions of living, I feel very hopeful that another rush will crumple the enemy up.'[113]

Rather than destroy him, he says, the danger and stress have made him feel 'fit and hard and strong, and I never seem to tire'.[114] 'All our operations have been successful.'[115] 'So far I have had no actual defeats in any of my operations.'[116]

Chapter 17

The real cause of the failure is the poor quality of the British troops.
Over and over again they have allowed themselves to be driven out
of positions which have been ... won by the Australian and New
Zealand troops ... they can't soldier for sour apples. They have no
grit, no stamina or endurance, poor physique, no gumption and they
muddle along and allow themselves to be shot down because they don't
even know how to take cover.
MONASH TALKING UP HIS AUSTRALIAN TROOPS AT GALLIPOLI[1]

THE 4TH BRIGADE has been devastated. Although the men are only about 300 metres from the Turkish trenches higher up, their advance has stopped dead. Those who are still walking busy themselves with evacuating the wounded, burying the dead, collecting scattered equipment and munitions, digging wells and sorting out reserves of tools, bombs, arms, sandbags, periscopes and barbed wire.[2]

Less than a year ago, Monash was in his reserved seat at the theatre in Melbourne. Now he is in a living hell, where death and decay is everywhere and where he is encouraging the men to be ruthless killers in order to save their own lives. With his urging, 'all the influences tend to emphasize and bring out the non-spiritual and purely brutal characteristics of the men'.[3]

His brigade has been 'badly (and needlessly) cut up'[4] and is left out of another attack on 9 August, but the 13th, supported by the 15th, have to fight off a Turkish counter-attack. The 16th is called in to relieve a devastated British battalion. Monash's men are forced to sleep out in the open and many are sick with bronchitis, 'worn out after their great exertion'.[5] 'Everybody exhausted and rattled,' he scrawls in his diary, 'but self and Eastwood doing all possible to calm people down.'[6]

The approaching rain makes Monash fearful that soon his ailing forces will be 'mud and clay from head to foot', and he laments that the overall failure of Hamilton's invasion plan has overshadowed 'the many minor successes and the brilliant achievements of the Australian troops and New Zealanders'.[7]

'It is the same old story,' he says, 'insufficient troops, inadequate munitions, attempting more than was possible with the means available ... the Turks have contested our advance inch by inch, and have fought with the greatest bravery and skill ... [their] losses have been enormous – I should say at least 50,000 dead and wounded, but our losses have been heavy too.'[8]

Major Allanson's Gurkhas, with some British reinforcements, advanced to within 70 metres of Hill Q the previous day under heavy shelling. At sunrise the Gurkhas drove the Turks off the hill, but then were bombarded by 'friendly fire' and were forced to retreat. On 10 August Mustafa Kemal leads a counter-attack to take back the entire Sari Bair ridge.

Monash tells Vic that he is 'more than satisfied' with the efforts of his brigade, but is scathing of the British efforts and the lack of training among their soldiers. With most of Britain's regular army slaughtered at Mons, 'the thing we have now is a very poor imitation'.[9]

'They have a willing enough spirit, and plenty of dull stupid courage, but they simply don't know enough to come in out of the wet.' He blames their leaders, complaining that the British officers do not mix with their men as the Australians and Kiwis do, 'but keep aloof and ... appear chiefly concerned in looking after themselves'.[10] He says they are 'so many gentlemen earning their war medals on board luxurious transports, decked all over with gorget patches and arm bands and lace, acting as Deputy-assistant-acting-inspector-general of something-or-other'.[11]

For a month the exhausted 4th continues to fight. Hamilton still plans to link the Suvla landing force with the men from Anzac, and orders an assault on Hill 60 for 21 August. Five hundred of Monash's men from the 13th and 14th are to form the right flank of the attacking force under Cox and Russell, charging across open ground for 200 metres under the cover of artillery fire.

But, like so much that happens at Gallipoli, the artillery cover is bungled. Almost half of the first two charging lines of the 4th are shot down. They suffer more than 200 casualties and are removed the next night. The survivors have to dig for cover. Monash describes it as 'mis-timed, miscalculated and mis-directed', an assault in which 'everybody got rattled'.[12] He and Godley have a falling-out when Monash asks for reinforcements and describes his men as 'survivors'.[13]

Six days later, on 27 August, Cox decides on another daytime assault on Hill 60. Monash and Russell protest, saying a night mission will be far safer now that the men know their terrain, but eventually Russell leads 250 men from what's left of the 4th Brigade on another attack.

Once again the artillery bombardment supposed to be covering the Anzac advance goes awry. The result is what Monash terms 'a considerable loss of life and little gain',[14] and 'a rotten badly organised show ... those who planned it are responsible for a heavy loss to the Brigade'.[15] The organisation of the Allied forces is diabolical, Monash says:

> We give the Turks ample notice of our intention to land a
> military force. We almost tell them in detail the date and

place ... Then we land a force which is adequate *only* to secure a bare landing and hold it defensively ... The latest English papers talk of the whole undertaking as a strategical blunder, and say that the whole future effort should be concentrated on Flanders, which means that the sacrifice of nearly 15,000 magnificent Dominion troops has been useless and to no purpose!! ... during the first 48 hours after the landing at Suvla while there was an *open road* to the Dardanelles, and no opposition worth talking about, a whole Army Corps sat down on the beach while its leaders were quarrelling about questions of seniority and precedence ...[16]

Cox attacks Monash over the 4th Brigade's failure to advance and Monash replies that they could do no more, since every officer involved in the campaign had been killed or wounded; he complains to Godley about Cox's bullying. He also asks for Pope to be rested, saying it would be better for his 'mainstay' 'to recoup now, while I myself am in good going order'.[17]

When Monash marched out of Reserve Gully on 6 August his brigade numbered 3350 men. Now only 1037 are fit to fight.[18]

At the end of August, the 4th Brigade is finally removed from its position and placed on a line of Bauchop's Hill, where the fighting has subsided. The English troops already there make Monash feel decidedly unwelcome, and the brigadier has to sleep out in the open for two nights. Despite the privations and the horrific losses, Monash claims that 'no other troops at the Empire's disposal could have got *and held* a footing on Gallipoli, except the Australians and New Zealanders'.[19] Monash has learned early in the campaign the importance of focus: maintaining an eye on the overall prize of winning the war, even if battles are lost along the way.

He relaxes away from the frontlines occasionally, reading and writing correspondence, catching up with the newspapers and the cuttings his family send him, and requesting that Vic post him more reading material: sixpenny fiction or some classics, or even some monthly magazines, 'without putting you to too much trouble'. He asks her to buy him the works of Rupert Brooke, the young English poet who died from an infection in Greece just before the Gallipoli invasion, and he laments the death of conductor George Marshall-Hall, whose passing is announced in a copy of the Sydney *Sun* that arrives at Gallipoli. 'What a blow to the Ormond school of music [at Melbourne University]', he says.[20]

Even with a war raging around him he has an eye on the state of his fortune back home. Before he left Melbourne, he and Gibson, along with Richard Taylor, formed the Concrete Constructions Co., amalgamating their pipe manufacturing concerns. It is a profitable enterprise, but the Reinforced Concrete Co. has suffered a loss this year, and Monash's business in South Australia is also stalling. Gibson, well aware that Monash has other pressing matters, rarely writes of the business's troubles, so Monash tersely informs him, 'I have faced disaster and defeat before, cheerfully; but it is hard to have to face uncertainty and doubt.'[21] Gibson writes back to say the problems are being sorted out. Without informing Gibson, Monash asks engineer Percy Fairway to be his eyes and ears in Melbourne.

Late in August, Ian Hamilton grants permission to Keith Murdoch to visit the Australian bases on the Gallipoli Peninsula that are now referred to as 'Anzac'. At 30, Murdoch is a remarkable, self-made man who has become one of Australia's most respected journalists. Born into the large family of a Scottish Presbyterian clergyman in Melbourne, he has overcome a humiliating childhood stammer to become friends with the country's most powerful political figures: he and his father have regularly played golf with Prime Minister Andrew Fisher. He is now Managing Editor of the United Cable Service in London, housed in the same building as the *Times*.

Murdoch spends only four days at Gallipoli, but speaks to British correspondent Ellis Ashmead-Bartlett, who has been there since the landing. Ashmead-Bartlett tells him the whole campaign has been an almighty shambles, and Murdoch knows a headline when he hears one. This story is one of the most important in the history of his country.

He sends home emotional reports that glorify the Anzac efforts and savage the British leaders who sent the young heroes to their doom. Ashmead-Bartlett, seizing the opportunity to beat the military censors, pens a letter for Murdoch to pass on to Britain's Liberal prime minister Herbert Asquith, outlining the incompetence of the British military leaders. Gallipoli is 'the most ghastly and costly fiasco in our history since the Battle of Bannockburn', he writes. The only reason any progress has been made is due to the 'superlative gallantry of the Colonial Troops and the self-sacrificing manner in which they threw away their lives against positions which should never have been attacked'.[22] Bean says this 'brilliantly written' account is 'overstating the case as Bartlett always does', but that 'a great deal of it' is unanswerable.[23]

Murdoch agrees to deliver the letter, but as he heads back to London, a British officer in Marseilles, who has been tipped off about the letter's content, confiscates it. Murdoch decides to write his own.

By early September, only about 300 of the original 4000 men of the 4th Brigade who boarded the transport ships in Melbourne remain at the front. There have been reinforcements, but even most of them are sick, wounded or dead.

On 13 September the brigade is finally given leave on Lemnos. Monash says 'it's about time' somebody began to ask questions about the treatment of Australians in 'Tommy' hospitals, and that someone should hang for 'gross mismanagement'. He himself is suffering from an attack of dysentery and a recurrence of his lumbago, though he is given much better care than most of his soldiers.

He takes full advantage of his rank and its special privileges, delighted when the 'French Naval Commander-in-Chief nearly broke himself in two, bowing and bending when I was introduced to him'. 'It makes a lot of difference my being a General', he says; '… it's that little bit of gold gimp on the gorget patches that does the trick'. There is always a special boat, a special gangway lowered, and a special right of way.[24]

Monash sends McGlinn and four other officers for a complete rest in Alexandria, while he finds the bright sun on Lemnos 'genial and comforting'. He is able to switch off among the rolling hills and meadows, dotted with sheep 'the size of poodles', and windmills, 'the sails turning around lazily in the gentle breeze'. Conscious as ever of his weight, he starts doing 16-kilometre walks and takes an artillery officer's charger for rides to the town of Kastro and then to the ancient hot sulphur baths of Therma, where he and Locke lounge about in an orchard eating pomegranates, grapes, figs and quinces.[25] It is a welcome change after more than five months of bully beef, hard biscuits, bacon and jam.[26]

'Did somebody say there was a war on somewhere?' he muses; '… one would never dream that, close by, there are twenty millions of men fighting and killing and maiming each other'.[27]

Monash thinks about his garden at Iona, and the spring crop of roses, lilacs and Virginia creepers, the pansy borders, and the bougainvillea and all the bursting colours he hopes will now be covering his pergolas.[28] He talks constantly about gardening with his batman, Corporal William Thomas Dawson, a forever-fussing 37-year-old tailor from Ballarat, who spent 15 years in the reserve militia before the war.[29] Dawson is always going on about how when the general gets home to Toorak he should plant some walnut trees, which are everywhere on Lemnos and which Dawson grew with great success as a young man at Olinda, on Melbourne's outskirts.

'He is my thoroughly devoted slave,' Monash says, 'who would mother me if I would let him.' Monash demands instant obedience from his troops and, with the destinies of thousands in his hands,[30] 'the old man' or 'Brig', as they call him, won't tolerate argument. Yet he finds Dawson 'absolutely the clumsiest, unhandiest man I have ever met … He spoils every job he touches, is hard of hearing – never remembers anything, is untidy – although perfectly honest, he is a habitual fibber, or rather bluffer – in short he is almost everything a good batman ought not to be – yet I have not the heart to send him about his business.'[31]

Monash takes the opportunity on Lemnos to catch up on the reading material sent by Walter and Lou – the *Weekly Times, Sphere* and *Punch* – and to absorb all the correspondence from Jim Lewis his friend W.E.L. (Ernest) Wears and Felix Meyer. News that the latest fashion item in Melbourne is the soft felt hat known as 'the Monash' makes him chuckle. Several of his old female friends write regularly, including Ada (Krakowski) Benjamin. He is reunited with Annie Gabriel's son Gordon,[32] an enterprising and courageous mining engineer, now a corporal in the 1st Light Horse at Gallipoli, and helps him gain promotion. It seems a lifetime ago that Monash thought about running away with Gordon and his mother to make a new life.

In a letter from England, his old friend from Melbourne Billie Card reminds Monash of the time he marched four or five girls up the 'Bogong or the Geebung mountain ... to see the largest gumtrees in Victoria'. 'Don't you dare think how many years ago that is,' she writes, 'just get on with your bomb-throwing.'[33]

In total, Monash spends nine uncomfortable days as camp commandant on Lemnos, in the village of Sarpi, wrestling with red tape, sorting out slow mail and trying to solve the problems of disorganisation, black markets and the unavailability of tents, horses and canteen stores.[34] But the time away from the battle zone gives him some breathing space to assess the lessons from Anzac.

For a military commander, 'the great essential', he says, 'is to entirely suppress all personal considerations, and to take no notice of one's losses'.

There is the definite tactical objective, and that is all-important – to capture a hill or seize a road ... and whether it costs 100 or 500 men to do it, the great point is to *do* it, to reorganize ready for the next move. If one stops to count the cost or worry over the loss of friends, or the grief and sorrow of the people at home, one simply could not carry on for an hour. The moment a man becomes a casualty ... he must be ruled out completely, as if he never existed – get him away, get him out of sight, forget all about him – pick your man to take his place, and go right ahead with the work in hand. There is absolutely no other way ... it is the *whole* secret of successful leadership in war.[35]

In London, Keith Murdoch sends his 25-page, 8000-word damnation of the Gallipoli campaign to Andrew Fisher, giving him the details straight and plain, 'as if you were by my side, as in the good days'. He tells Fisher that the Prime Minister's fears over what is happening to the Australians on Gallipoli 'have been justified' and that the campaign has been 'a costly and bloody fiasco'. He praises Monash's night march as 'one of the most glorious efforts of the Dardanelles', adding that while there is 'a disposition to blame Monash for not pushing further in' during the August offensive, Murdoch has been over that wild countryside of the Sari Bair range himself and cannot see 'how even as much as he did could have been expected'.[36]

Overall, the campaign 'is undoubtedly one of the most terrible chapters in our history',[37] Murdoch says, with 'raw, untried troops, under amateur officers, homesick and apprehensive', who were packed like sardines for the disastrous landing. He writes of mistakes, mismanagement, misdirections and misery. Ian Hamilton, he says, has a lot to answer for.

'The conceit and self complacency of the red feather men are equalled only by their incapacity', he writes. 'Along the line of communications, especially at Mudros, are countless high officers and conceited young cubs who are plainly only playing at war ... appointments to the general staff are made from motives of friendship and social influence.'[38]

Fisher, who is already in declining health, can't help but feel a sense of guilt over putting Australian troops under such shoddy command, and with Billy Hughes breathing down his neck, his political life soon ends. Herbert Asquith and the members of his British Cabinet opposed to continuing the Dardanelles campaign use Murdoch's comments as a rallying cry in England and publish his letter as a State paper.

Words prove mightier than the sword and Ian Hamilton's military career ends in humiliation.

When Hamilton is recalled to London in mid-October, Monash is in Egypt on a three-week rest, travelling with Locke and four other officers. The loss of a powerful ally upsets him, but he insists he has never felt better.

He tells Walter Rosenhain that while letters from Australia continue 'to express grave misgivings about my nervous stability' and hint that a breakdown is inevitable, his temperament will not allow it. 'As time goes on I get steadily more and more indifferent to all the influences which are calculated to unnerve and upset one's mental equilibrium. It is merely a question of adaptability to a new environment ...'[39] He tells Vic that he overcomes his anxiety after the first few hours of battle, 'and the noise and clamour affects one no more than the noise of a busy city square after one has lived there for a few days. Mine was never an excitable temperament and one has only to keep cool, and think out one's problems and tasks and the work of fighting soon becomes perfectly ordinary and humdrum.'[40]

Of his three weeks in Egypt, he spends five days in Cairo and the rest of the time luxuriating at the Savoy Palace Hotel in Alexandria, where meals are 'daintily served'. He visits the wounded, checks on convalescents, confers over reinforcements and inspects his brigade transport.[41] With his fellow officers he goes to music halls, the local Folies Bergère, cinemas, a boxing match, and the Cairo version of the Moulin Rouge, which he calls a 'sick show'.[42] He spends two days with Sa's son Eric Simonson, a 21-year-old engineering student newly arrived from Melbourne, but steers clear of Cairo's Jewish community, lest he be 'roped in' for religious ceremonies.

While in Cairo he receives a telegram from Birdwood that he has been appointed a Companion of the Order of the Bath, as have Hooky Walker, Jim McCay and all four of Monash's battalion commanders. Yet he is miffed when he hears that Guy Russell is to be knighted, and complains that New Zealand honours its military men more than Australia does. He asks McCay to cause a ruckus.

In Cairo's Mousky market he sips Turkish coffee, smokes a hookah (water-pipe) and haggles with a shopkeeper over the price of silks for Vic and Bert. 'I don't know whether I've been had or not, and don't care,' he writes to Vic, 'so long as you are a little pleased.'[43]

In Alexandria, he says a firm hand is needed to deal with shirkers – though he finds none among his 4th Brigade there. Drinks are banned after 8.30 p.m. and officers are forbidden to go joyriding with ladies in military vehicles. Monash sends Bert a shoe from his horse Tom, 'a very fine, faithful animal who has served me well', and asks Bert to have the souvenir suitably mounted on a plush base, because Tom will not be coming home due to Australia's quarantine laws.

On 1 November Monash attends the ceremony marking the departure of Hussein Kamel, Sultan of Egypt, on the Royal Train from his summer palace in Alexandria to his winter home in Cairo. It is as grand as anything Monash has ever seen, with the station covered in purple carpets, patrolmen in brilliant white, officers in black and gold with red fez, guards of honour in royal blue with white putties on their legs and white gloves, and their commander on a magnificent white Arab stallion. The sultan is dressed simply in a suit, black tie and fez.

'When I was presented to him he remarked: "*Ah, Australien! Je vous fais mes compliments, mon cher general.*" A pretty compliment was it not to be congratulated on being Australian?'[44]

*

The 4th Brigade has been rebuilt to about 2000 men and heads back from Lemnos to Gallipoli on 5 November. One man is killed on the way by a stray bullet.

Delayed while waiting for a ship, Monash arrives back at the peninsula three days later. He is commanding his position from a kilometre and a half of trenches along Bauchop's Hill and makes his headquarters in a hillside olive grove. The Turks are about 400 metres away across a valley. The enemy fires a constant stream of bullets over the roof of what eventually becomes a 'commodious cabin', with a stove made from an old oil drum and a flue made from biscuit tins. Though he is in constant danger of being shot he sends home a packet of acorns for the Iona garden from the holly oak, 'the prickly scrub with which these hills are covered, and which has inflicted many an unkind scratch on hands, arms and bare knees'.[45]

The Anzacs have been on Gallipoli for seven months and, his spirits having been revitalised by time away from the war zone, Monash again finds it 'all very interesting and very exciting'. 'It is astonishing how good humoured our men and the Turks are toward each other, and the Turks are real sports … the men in the front trenches often play off jokes with each other – such as putting up dummies to be fired at, or pretending to charge – and they chaff and jeer at each other pleasantly.'[46]

At noon on 13 November, Monash assembles with the other brigade commanders to meet Birdwood at Anzac Cove's North Beach, and together they gaze out to sea as a tiny boat threads its way between the destroyers, barges, punts and submarines. At about 1.40 p.m., Birdwood, in his trademark slouch hat, marches alone along to the end of the jetty, where he meets 'a very tall officer in plain service khaki' who is accompanied by a 'very small retinue' of three officers and an orderly.

As this stately figure walks up the pier, he is recognised by other soldiers and Anzacs come from everywhere to surround and cheer him.

'It was the great Field Marshal Earl Kitchener of Khartoum himself', Monash gushes. 'I happened to be the first Australian to whom he spoke and he said: "I have brought you all a personal message from the King, he wants me to tell you how much he admires the splendid things you have done here.'"

Kitchener is escorted through Monash Valley and climbs Walker's Ridge to see the war zone first hand. He says little, and slips away as quietly and as secretly as he arrived 'into the mists of the Aegean Sea'.[47]

Rumours abound that the Allies will soon evacuate.

Monash has a rush of blood. Harry Chauvel and William Holmes,[48] who had led the first troops into New Guinea and is now commander of the 5th Brigade, are given command of the 1st and 2nd Divisions after Hooky Walker is wounded by machine-gun fire and James Legge invalided with illness. Monash believes that he deserves to be the senior AIF officer. He raises his concerns with Godley, and the day after Kitchener's visit drafts a polite letter to Chauvel outlining his grievances. 'I have my aspirations', he writes, 'and like every other man a desire to have my activities employed in the widest possible sphere.'[49]

He decides not to send the letter, but writes to Senator Pearce for a ruling and dashes off a note to McCay asking for his support. He only manages to stoke the ire of Birdwood, who tells him: 'The Army Corps commander deprecates the assertion by officers of their claims to appointments which are filled by selection. The seniority and claims of all eligible officers are fully considered before a decision is made.'[50]

Relations will stay frosty. Monash remains peeved, but gets back to work, preparing his brigade for the twin enemies of an approaching cold, wet winter and the high explosive shells the Germans have promised to their Turkish allies.

Karl Roth arrives at Gallipoli with the 4th Field Ambulance on 23 November, and Monash is aghast at the state of his cousin and childhood pal, now a 'frightfully filthy object'.[51] But he tells Karl that if he cleans himself up he'll recommend him for a promotion because of his pharmacy background. Before long, Tante Ulrike's problem child is a sergeant dispenser.[52]

With Monash supervising the engineering, the Anzacs dig tunnels into vertical cliff faces, with kitchens and sleeping quarters branching off under the ground. By night they are like kangaroo shooters, stalking their prey, pot-shotting a sniper here and there, and taking a few prisoners when they can.

On 28 and 29 November Monash is laid low with 'epidemic jaundice', living off rice, arrowroot and cornflower. The temperature on Gallipoli suddenly drops 20 degrees Celsius and a snowstorm envelops the whole peninsula, freezing even the sponges and flannels. The cold is even worse for poor 'Johnny Turk',[53] Monash says, because the enemy is not as well equipped and the really harsh weather is due in a few weeks.

The Anzacs put many of the Turks out of their misery. Monash's tunnelling system means his men can move around their position in relative safety, while firing machine-guns at the Turks from openings in the earth that are virtually invisible and just wide enough for a barrel. 'Then rat-tat-tat-tat-tat ... and the Turks run like rabbits for cover – at least those whom we miss – but we don't miss many, for our gunners are very, very keen.' On one day his No. 14 machine-gun unit takes 30 Turkish prisoners in one group.[54]

Monash also sends out 'listening patrols' at dusk to spy on the Turks, noting 'time, direction, objective, numbers and movements', then follows that initiative on subsequent evenings with 'fighting patrols', and 'surely enough, three times out of four, the silly Turk comes out at exactly the same time by exactly the same route.' When they are near enough the Australian boys 'let them have a shower of bomb' and then go out to collect the spoils – rifles, ammunition, equipment and occasionally a wounded prisoner. 'It is astonishing how small our losses are in these very daring encounters ... a week passes without anyone being killed.'[55]

*

Rumours that the Allies will retreat from Gallipoli infuriate Monash. He has set his teeth on seeing this thing through and feels certain that all the talk of evacuation spreading like a virus is just idle gossip. 'The Anzacs would sooner die on the Peninsula', he says, 'than abandon the territory which it has cost so much blood to win, and which holds the graves of our dead.'[56] He reads reports in British newspapers that quote politicians describing the Dardanelles campaign as 'a dreadful mistake and a hopeless failure'.[57] His blood boils.

If it has been a 'dreadful mistake', he says, 'and I very much doubt it, it has been the fault of the Statesmen themselves and not of the Army ... Had we not attacked the Turk on his own ground, and held his army here, it is certain that England would have had to fight for Egypt.'[58] Still the rumours persist.

General Sir Charles Monro[59] takes over the command of the Mediterranean Expeditionary Force from Hamilton. Birdwood now heads up the Dardanelles Army under Monro, while Godley is given command of the Australian and New Zealand Army Corps and Russell the New Zealand and Australian Division.

On 6 December Birdwood travels from his headquarters on Imbros to inspect Monash's intricate tunnelling system, and compliments him on what he says is now the 'admiration of the whole Peninsula'. Yet Monash is well aware that the Anzacs' heavy toll of 'sickness and debility and physical exhaustion' has been 'directly due to the awful and comfortless conditions of living ... in an absolutely wild and barren tangle of mountains with nothing behind us but the blue Aegean'. He says his men do not 'grouse', though, and cheerfulness and good spirit are 'their most outstanding military virtues' in spite of the severity of their privations.[60] It is almost possible to imagine that the Empire has abandoned them to their fate.[61]

It hasn't.

Monro has been at Gallipoli for just three hours when he announces it is time to call the whole thing off.[62]

Without Monash's knowledge, Kitchener reluctantly agreed to the evacuation plans on 22 November and Westminster approved them on 7 December. Five days later, the 'stupendous and paralysing' news hits Monash like a 'thunderbolt from a clear blue sky'. He anticipates howls of 'rage and disappointment' when the men find out 'what is afoot and how they have been fooled', and he wonders aloud 'what Australia will think at the desertion of her 6000 dead and her 20,000 other casualties'.[63] He anticipates the retreat will be every bit as dangerous as the landing.

A conference of the commanders decides that the Anzacs will bluff their way out of Gallipoli in stages. Two-thirds of the army will be taken away in trickles, leaving the other third to dash to waiting boats on the beach in the dead of night. The first stage will see men and equipment taken off, consistent with the activity of a garrison preparing for a purely defensive winter campaign.[64] Monash admits it is 'an absolutely critical scheme which may come off quite successfully or may end in frightful disaster'. But orders are orders, he says. 'I need not say I feel very unhappy.'[65]

The evacuation of Gallipoli begins after sunset on 13 December.

Five hundred men of the 15th Battalion and about 100 others pack up and make their way across the Aegean on barges at two hours' notice. The following day Monash supervises the packing of stores, grenades, bombs, picks, shovels, sandbags, food supplies and ordnance gear. The heavy guns will be left to the last.

'It is curious and interesting', he observes with an engineer's eye, 'to watch the machine unwind itself as methodically and systematically as it was originally wound up.'[66] The postal organisation and field hospital are disbanded, along with the mule train of supplies. Tins of bully beef and hard biscuits replace fresh meat, bread and communal cooking. Monash begins plotting the rearguard action to be fought by the best of his men from the 13th and 16th after the bulk of the troops have left.[67]

By 16 December the Anzac garrison has been reduced from 41,000 to 26,000. Monash tells his men that under the plans put forward by Brudenell White, the 26,000 men are to hold the lines 'against at least 170,000 Turks (10 Divisions) until the second last day and on the very last day we shall have only 10,000'.[68]

The Anzacs continue to trickle away from Gallipoli, and the nights of 18 and 19 December are chosen for the final mass evacuation. The officers have their final divisional conference and take 'mutual farewells of each other', and Birdwood comes over from Imbros and goes along the whole kilometre and a half of Monash's line shaking hands with all the officers and expressing the hope that they will come out of it alive.

Monash plans to stay with his men until the very last, and has chosen 170 'diehards' – 'the most gallant and capable men in the Brigade' – for the last dash at 2 a.m. on 20 December. They will be supported by a few 'good athletes' in the front trenches who will provide covering fire for 10 minutes before 'making for the beach at best possible speed'.[69] Each one of the 170 diehards is presented with a card showing the exact time he is to leave and exactly what he has to do, 'whether to carry a machine-gun or its tripod, or its belts – or to throw a bomb'.[70]

The men pay their respects at the graves of their mates, and McGlinn heads to the beach at mid-afternoon to prepare to disembark with 800 troops at 9 p.m. He will take with him the records of the campaign, which he and Monash plan to turn into a history of the brigade.

That afternoon Monash is talking to his best typewriting clerk outside his brigade office when the unfortunate soldier is shot straight through the calf, the projectile just missing the bone. The Anzacs are still shooting back, and have even devised a device for firing a rifle automatically. It is done by allowing a tin to slowly fill with water until it overbalances, falls and jerks a string, which pulls the trigger. Monash has 10 of the .303s fixed in just such a way, to be set off by the last men to leave and designed to fire at five-minute intervals. 'In this way the enemy will think we are still in the trenches, after we have got a mile away.'[71]

Late at night on the 18th, 'everything is normal, just the usual sniping, and occasional bombs and bursts of machine-gun fire'.

The Turks bombard the beaches as usual on the night of 19 December, but the weather is perfect for the Anzacs' final escape: the sea and air calm, the sky cloudy, foggy and dull, with a little drizzle, 'so that everything in the distance is dim and blurred'. By 8 p.m. there are only '5000 troops in the whole of Anzac, thinly holding the front line against 170,000 of the enemy. If the Turks only knew it.' The navy bombards Helles to give the impression that another attack is imminent, and an English plane buzzes over Anzac Cove in the moonlight, keeping Turkish reconnaissance pilots at bay.

'The next hour will be decisive', Monash writes in his journal: '... we shall have succeeded in withdrawing the great bulk of the Army Corps without any loss – a wonderful piece of organization, beyond any doubt. If it succeeds, it will be due to splendid preparation on the part of the leaders, and splendid and intelligent obedience on the part of the men.'[72]

At 9 p.m. Monash's last patrol reports that the Turks still suspect nothing. The enemy is digging trenches and putting out wire as though nothing has changed on the Anzac lines. But Monash feels the worst strain he's ever experienced over the next few hours,[73] with every explosion and every crack of a rifle suggesting the start of a mass Turkish attack.

By 10 p.m. Monash has left for the beach with 425 men, leaving his 170 diehards, among about 2000 Anzac soldiers, to hold the line. He forgets the leather case that contains his diary of the evacuation and the orders that he was told to destroy but instead plans to keep as a souvenir. He sends an aide back two and a half kilometres to retrieve his bag. Monash's talent for embellishment will lead him to claim years later that he ran back himself.[74]

He is on the Aegean by midnight as down the little gullies behind him come groups of six to a dozen men, 'like so many rivulets which flow into the main stream'. The last man is 'in every case an officer, closing the gully with a previously prepared frame of barbed wire',[75] or lighting a fuse that an hour later will blow up a tunnel to prevent the Turks from giving chase.

There is no haste, no running, 'just a steady, silent tramp in single file, without any lights or smoking'. Every yard brings the men nearer to safety. With perfect timing the marching lines arrive at the Brighton, Anzac, Howitzer and North Beaches almost at the same instant, 'like so many ghostly figures in the dim light'. They then march onto their respective jetties, sandbags deadening the sound of their marching feet. They board the 400-man motor barges known as 'beetles', crowding in together, the general pressed up against the private. The only sound is the buzz of the beetle engines.

There is a momentary pause to make sure no one has been left behind. Then, at 1.55 a.m., Monash's last man gets away, leaving just the toppling tin cans to fire the rifles.

'We had succeeded in withdrawing 45,000 men, mules, guns, stores, provisions and transport … without a single casualty and without allowing the enemy to entertain the slightest suspicion. It was a most brilliant conception, brilliantly organized, and brilliantly executed.'

The evacuation of the Anzacs has been the most successful operation of the whole campaign. It has been planned to perfection by Brudenell White, whom Monash describes as not just 'a charming good fellow' but 'far and away the ablest soldier Australia has ever turned out'.[76]

The last engineer officer on shore joins the terminals of an electric battery to fire three enormous mines that, with an ear-splitting explosion and huge sheets of yellow flame, blow up the tunnels underneath Russell's Top. 'A couple of hundred Turks must have gone up in the air, but nothing could be seen except a volcano of dust', Monash says.

'Thus dramatically with the bullets whistling harmlessly overhead, we drew off in the light of the full moon, mercifully screened by a thin mist – and so ended the story of the Anzacs on Gallipoli.'[77]

Chapter 18

I recognize the disadvantages I had to labour under to get to where
I now stand ... there is the question of religion, and the question
of parentage, and it is rather gratifying, in spite of these very solid
handicaps ... to have got the honour and status of my present rank.
I am wondering what my enemies out home will be saying.
MONASH AFTER BEING GIVEN COMMAND OF THE 3RD DIVISION AIF[1]

This beastly war is getting to be rather a bore and not nearly
so much fun as building bridges, or touring around the world,
or tending roses in my garden.
MONASH AFTER LEARNING HIS WIFE HAS CANCER[2]

THE TURKS have held on to their peninsula at an enormous
cost. Yet Monash maintains that Gallipoli has not been a
complete disaster.

'It failed only in that it did not achieve its full objective,' he
will argue for the rest of his life, 'from a strategic point of view it
was of great importance. If it had not been engaged on Gallipoli
the Turkish army would have been a serious menace to the Allies.
Not only was the Gallipoli campaign a strategic victory, but as
the builder of the AIF tradition it was alone worthwhile. Only
20,000 Australians were engaged on Gallipoli, but the deeds of

that little band were a never-failing inspiration to the 300,000 Australian soldiers who followed.'[3] Monash says the charge on Gallipoli will be remembered as 'one of the most famous events in history – putting into shade such events as the "charge of the Light Brigade" at Balaclava'.[4]

The invasion has kept the Turkish forces pinned down, stopped them from providing reinforcements in other parts of the conflict, and so weakened their army that they are no longer a major power in the war. He claims it has also prevented a massive operation for control of Egypt and the vital shipping lanes of the Suez.

Three weeks after the Anzac withdrawal, Cape Helles is also evacuated. The death toll from the eight months of fighting is staggering. The Turks number their casualties from defending their homeland at 251,309, including 86,692 dead. Australia lists 8709 killed, New Zealand 2701, Britain 21,255 and France 10,000.[5] Australia's resolve as a nation has been tested for the first time under the most ferocious conditions and not found wanting. The characteristics of bravery and mateship will fuel the legends already being nurtured in the ruins of a military defeat.

Monash sends home his long report of the evacuation in what he calls a 'diary-letter', and Mat types up copies that thrill readers, including Katie and Alfred Deakin. Monash has injected himself into the final scenes of the evacuation, even though he left the beach five hours before the last men off the peninsula. It is this talent for seizing the spotlight that critics such as Bean will use against him.

Vic sends the diary to Colonel Hall and his censors, asking for permission to publish it, but permission is denied even though the *Argus* also mounts pressure on the bureaucrats. Instead the *Age* runs an account of the evacuation penned by Monash's old friend Dr John Springthorpe, who enlisted in the Australian Army Medical Corps with the rank of lieutenant colonel and interviewed Monash after the withdrawal.

Monash's daring tale stands in stark contrast to lingering criticisms from Bean and others such as Birdwood that he let down his gallant comrades after the 1st Division and the Light Horse had fought so hard at Lone Pine and the Nek. Birdwood says that while Monash has 'certainly done well', 'looks after his Brigade' and is an 'excellent organizer … I cannot look upon him as a leader in war'.[6]

The prevailing criticism is that Monash should have driven his exhausted troops harder at Sari Bair during the August offensive, even though, in their distressed condition, he would only have been driving them to the slaughter. Monash has undoubtedly saved the lives of many of his Anzacs by avoiding suicidal risks, but Bean says the 50-year-old brigadier is too old, too indecisive and too worried about pushing his own reputation.

'Sleepy old John Monash – cautious if ever a man was',[7] he writes, claiming that Monash shows great care in his preparations, but has 'defects in his leadership'.[8] His brilliance flashes at times, but he is 'one of the worst sort of men' for the kind of attack needed on Sari Bair, and the 'want of success' of the 4th Brigade 'can't be accidental, every time'.[9]

Yet Monash has shown physical and mental resolve that is beyond question, and an 'indomitable will', according to White,[10] staying the distance as a commander while others such as Chauvel, White and Sinclair-Maclagan all needed lengthy breaks.

The portly McGlinn, who marched the brigade's diehards into camp on Lemnos after the evacuation, remains a lifelong fan of his commander, writing to Vic that he is 'one of nature's noblemen' and 'one of the whitest men God ever put breath into'.[11]

Christmas 1915 is a surreal time for the Anzacs after the horrors they have endured. Some have already left Lemnos for Egypt, while the winter sun, bathing the green fields, rejuvenates Monash and others who remain. At last they are able to move about freely, without the constant whistle and thud of the sniper.

Yet Vic and Bert inform Monash of a plan to visit him in Egypt for a couple of months and he tells them it is 'simple madness' because there is fighting everywhere: 'the Mediterranean is alive with German submarines, so is the Channel and in England there is the constant terror of the Zeppelins'.[12]

As 1916 nears, Monash is given the North Atlantic liner, the *Cardiganshire*, to move some of his 4th Brigade and other units from Lemnos to Egypt, along with 300 horses and 80 mules. He mounts cannons and machine-guns around the ship, and 20 riflemen at each end of the hurricane bridge, hoping that 'Mr Submarine will come along and get the warm reception we have prepared for him'.[13]

The ship reaches Alexandria just on dawn of 31 December and then, travelling by train through the next night, the men reach Moascar, across the railway line from the oasis of Ismailia, a 'beautiful little town with lovely gardens, avenues and plantations – chiefly inhabited by French canal officials'. The weary troops, 'lame ducks ... all in rags'[14] form a rough camp in the sandy desert a few hundred metres from the Suez Canal, but Monash is able to have a hot bath at Ismailia's French Club and dines there a couple of times a week. He organises a 'pukka Brigade parade and march past' for General Sir Archibald Murray,[15] the new commander-in-chief of the Middle Eastern force, but concedes as he begins the arduous task of regathering, reorganising and re-energising his troops that he is now 'working with blunted tools'. 'Instead of a newly raised, experienced and competent body of regimental officers, I have only the remnants – mostly war weary.'[16]

Monash's low spirits plummet further on 19 January when John Gibson cables him seeking his consent for Vic to undergo a major medical operation. Vic had only been promising to visit Monash for the sake of morale and without letting on to her husband, she has become desperately ill. While still corresponding with him in good cheer, she has spent most of the past few months bedridden. Monash doesn't even know the nature of her illness, and when the operation goes ahead Monash is in the dark for days about the outcome, which causes him deep distress. Monash asks Birdwood and Godley about the possibility of returning to Melbourne to be with Vic and Bert, but they tell him the War Office will not allow it because of the 'sacrifice of honour' involved.

In this Egyptian desert, a world away from his seemingly helpless loved ones, the uncertainty over his wife's condition intensifies the private pain he feels over the fate of so many of his countrymen. Against his strongest instincts, he becomes forlorn and morose as he looks about at his ragged troops. He suspects that he is only preparing a few thousand more Australians for 'some fresh scene of slaughter', to 'get blown into little pieces, or get holes drilled into themselves, for the honour of Australia and the good of posterity'.[17]

He remains the guardian for his extended family even on foreign shores. He tries his best for Karl Roth, but his wayward cousin succumbs to the bottle again and there are suspicions he is pinching morphine. He is hospitalised with cystitis, tremors and 'mental trouble (mild)' and repatriated. He dies just a month after returning home.[18]

However, other members of Monash's extended family prosper. Aubrey Moss,[19] the son of Vic's brother Jack, is already a staff sergeant and about to be commissioned as a second lieutenant. Sa Simonson, whose husband Max is suffering dementia, writes often to Monash asking him to look out for her boys Eric and Paul.[20] Eric becomes one of Monash's aides, and by February 1916 he and Paul are both commissioned officers. Monash also helps Bert's friend Gershon Bennett, a young dentist, gain a commission in England.

Vic survives her operation and Monash is beside himself with 'relief and joy'. Not until two weeks after the procedure does her surgeon Rothwell Adam tell Monash that she has uterine cancer. Because of her morbid fear of the condition that killed her mother, Vic has not been told of the exact nature of the illness. Yet she is recovering remarkably well, and Dr Adam tells Monash the prognosis is good.

Vic cables Monash to tell him 'You were the only man I ever loved', and Monash asks for an urgent message from the surgeon if there is any change in her condition. He is careful in writing to Vic and to her relatives about mentioning the cancer in case the word shatters her fragile nerves.

And he says to hell with the War Office. If his wife's crisis becomes 'real and urgent and great',[21] Monash will return home whether the generals and politicians like it or not.

Monash has left his Turkish enemies behind at Gallipoli, only to find new and powerful ones in his path.

The massive wave of volunteers coming into the AIF after Gallipoli, inspired by the stories of Australian courage, results in a huge program of reorganisation. As secret agents and reconnaissance pilots investigate the Sinai Peninsula for signs of enemy troop movements,[22] two Anzac corps are established, with Birdwood and Godley as the commanders.

More than anything since the convict system, Gallipoli has taught the Australians to distrust British leadership. More than ever the Anzacs are determined not to be used as fillers for British divisions. The decision is made to split battalions so that they are rebuilt with a mixture of veterans and new recruits. Sixteen hundred of Monash's battle-hardened veterans from the 4th Brigade[23] are transferred to the new 12th Brigade, but Monash shrewdly retains his HQ officers, his battalion commanders Cannan and Pope and his machine-gunners and signallers:[24] men with the specialised skills that require time to learn. Another 4000 recruits who arrive from the Egyptian bases at Heliopolis and Zeitoun boost his remaining 2000 troops. The 4th Brigade becomes a 'much larger and complex command'.[25] The New Zealanders form their own division, which means that the New Zealand and Australian Division, which included the 4th Brigade, is disbanded.

Birdwood will have charge of the 1st and 2nd Australian Divisions and the New Zealanders under Guy Russell. Godley will have the 3rd, 4th and 5th Divisions.

Monash attends a dinner to farewell the rest of the New Zealand and Australian Division at the New Zealand headquarters. It is followed by a campfire concert at which a haka is performed in his honour, and he falls about laughing as he watches the doctor and chaplain 'stripped and tattooed in war paint'.[26] He is sad to farewell General Russell, whom he calls a 'splendid chap', but with deficiencies as a leader.

The 4th Brigade will become part of the 4th Division in Godley's corps. Monash is not thrilled. While he thought Godley had some charm at their first meeting, it has worn off long ago. All the army corps staff hate the big man now just as the New Zealanders loathed him, because 'he belongs to the Army Clique, which holds all militia officers in contempt as *mere amateurs*'. He has done Monash's brigade 'very well, and for that I am grateful [but] … while in a formal way he is very dignified … he has not that urbanity and tact which makes a man really liked by his Staff and Commanders'.[27]

Herbert Cox will command the 4th Division. Monash tries to hide his resentment over missing out by telling Vic that it's not a job he would like because 'the worry and responsibility I now have are more than enough', and that he has resolved not to canvass for promotion. Actually, he is seething. 'If Australia chooses to let her forces be exploited to find jobs for unemployed senior British officers, that is not my affair',[28] he snorts.

Monash writes to McCay, telling him he is furious at missing out on one of the divisional postings. 'Surely Australia won't stand this!' he thunders. 'I am the only Australian Brigadier who has served continuously throughout the campaign, without a single day's absence from duty; and have secured three "mentions" and have been recommended for special distinction … there will be at least two, if not three, commands of Australian Divisions vacant very shortly, and it is surely not an unreasonable aspiration, that in the light of my training and services, I should be selected for one of them.'[29] He tells Vic that Pearce called Birdwood, asking that 'White or I might get' the 4th Division, 'but Birdwood preferred to entrust it to Cox – a Kitchener man and an old Indian colleague of Birdwood's'.[30]

Vic is now well on the way to recovery, and he asks her to cultivate a friend in Billy Hughes, who has become Prime Minister following the resignation of the deeply stressed Andrew Fisher. 'He is one of the Wallabies [a member of Monash's bushwalking Wallaby Club] and I like him very much. It may help me for you to be chummy with Mrs Prime Minister', he writes, adding that it wouldn't hurt his prospects for advancement if she could get some more praise for him in the Melbourne press.

In north-eastern France, the German 5th Army mounts a massive attack on hills north of Verdun-sur-Meuse. The Battle of Verdun will rage all year, with close to a million casualties and 300,000 deaths.

Late in February Monash's brigade moves 45 kilometres west to Tel-el-Kebir, scene of a great battle three decades earlier between the British and Egyptians. When Cox, who has temporary command of the Australian Provisional Formations, takes a few days' leave, Monash is left in temporary command of 40,000 men, six infantry and six artillery brigades. He says the 'worry of running the show ... is very great indeed', and he will be glad when Cox gets back so he can confine himself just to his own brigade work. Perhaps he protests too much.[31] He is always trumpeting the performance of his men and uses the interstate rivalries in his brigade to promote excellence and efficiency.

Walker and Legge are given command of the 1st and 2nd Divisions and McCay the 5th after George Pearce insists Birdwood appoint more Australians to command their own troops. Pearce asks Birdwood to strongly consider the claims of Chauvel, Monash, Holmes and White.[32] Chauvel is given command of the Anzac Mounted Division under Birdwood, who considers Holmes too inexperienced and White too valuable as a staff officer.

Monash is 'a man of very considerable ability', Birdwood says, 'and with good administrative powers', but he has not shown Birdwood 'that resolution which is really essential'. There is also 'among a considerable number of the force a great feeling against him on account of what they consider his German extraction'.[33] Legge has already warned Birdwood that because of Monash's German connections, promoting him would be 'very inadvisable'.[34]

Monash is dismayed to lose McGlinn to McCay's staff, but quickly replaces him with Major Jim 'Dolly' Durrant.[35]

Rumours around Tel-el-Kebir are as plentiful as grains of sand, and the junior officers think they know more about the Allied plans than even the generals. There is talk that soon the Anzacs will move to England, France, Salonika, Mesopotamia or even India.

In mid-March the 1st and 2nd Divisions begin leaving for the muddy trenches of France. With only a few hours for Monash and Durrant to prepare, the 4th and 5th Divisions are ordered to immediately replace them in defending Egypt and Suez from a potential Turkish advance, even though Monash says there is not a Turk 'within 50 miles of the canal'.[36]

At 4 a.m. on 26 March, Monash leads the 'first flight' of 6000 men, along with horses, vehicles and a train of 250 camels on a three day, 72-kilometre march across the desert to Serapeum, halfway along the Suez Canal and about 15 kilometres south of Ismailia.

The convoy stretches for almost 7 kilometres. The men carry full packs and ammunition through the desert furnace. The combination of recent double inoculations,[37] heat, flies, dust, a meagre water ration and chafing new boots trudging through soft sand becomes apparent on the first day's slog of 23 kilometres to El Mahsama. Because of the cruel heat, Monash orders the men to march from 4 a.m. and to rest during the blistering hours from 11 to 3.

At the end of the second day's 27-kilometre journey to Moascar, the main body of the men arrives to the tune of marching bands, but New Zealand troops are called on to help about 100 Australians in distress. On the final 22-kilometre leg to Serapeum, nerves are frayed and tempers stretched. Monash is infuriated by the heat and the disorder and those infernal flies, telling some of the limping soldiers as they near Serapeum that his sisters could do as well. He barks at others for diving into the Suez before they reach their destination. Some of the men curse him under their breath.[38]

Serapeum is the most horrible place Monash has ever known, 'unbearably hot'. Although there is usually a cool breeze at night, all it really does is lift the desert sand and form clouds so dense that Monash cannot see for more than 50 metres.

Dust and sand cover everything – man, beast and food – in a thick layer. The heat is so intense that the men can train only in the morning and late evening, and though they are not in fear of Turkish snipers or constant attack as they were at Gallipoli, the flies and sandflies are relentless, blistering the skin and rattling the nerves. Monash tells Vic how grateful he is for the green fly netting she has sent him.[39] He is hopeful the war will be won within a year.[40]

More than ever, he longs to be back at Iona with his family, and on 8 April, the date of his 25th wedding anniversary, he cables Vic with a tender message of undying affection. Bertha writes to her father saying that 'sometimes I could just cry and cry, for wanting you back so badly'.[41]

Five days later, Monash witnesses what to many of the men seems like Armageddon. The sun and sky are blotted out for 20 hours by a ferocious wind known as the *khamseen*. At 7 a.m. the calm of the cool morning is broken by gusting winds from the south-west carrying sand and stones. By noon the winds have formed a giant twister, a whirling dervish of sand and gravel hundreds of metres tall. One building after another is torn apart and tents fly into the sky like sheets of paper. Wild-eyed horses scream in terror and strain at their ropes. Men blinded by the storm walk into wagons, and one is knocked over and killed by the steam train that supplies the camp. There is nothing for Monash and his troops to do but huddle together for safety in the remaining tents 'gasping, choking, eyeballs inflamed, chests raw with coughing',[42] until finally on the following noon, the hail of storm and pebbles calms, leaving a trail of devastation.

The wind remains hot and strong when Monash rides out of the camp on his horse Tom and heads for Serapeum's No. 1 railway siding and a short break beside the Nile. Tom is still panicked by the weather, and it takes Monash two hours to coax him along the 8 kilometres to the railway, where hundreds of soldiers are busy hauling sand off the line so the trains can move again. After hours of painstaking work by these soldiers, Monash finally takes his seat in the carriage for a slow, eight-hour journey to Cairo, 160 kilometres away. He arrives bedraggled, weary and wheezing from a chest infection. He collapses into bed, utterly spent, and sleeps for 11 hours.[43]

The desert storm has done nothing to dampen Monash's ambition, though, and while McCay has filled him in on the 'network of intrigue and the squabbles between the War Office and the Commonwealth Government'[44] over higher appointments among Australian generals, promotion is always on his mind. He tells Vic: 'if they want me to command a Division they know where to find me'.[45]

Monash is particularly feisty. A portion of his frontline raids an advanced enemy post, capturing 33 Turks and an Austrian officer, with the loss of only one man. Monash has started reading a bestselling verse novel, *The Songs of a Sentimental Bloke*, by the poet C.J. Dennis and the chaplains in Serapeum have been using the storyline about a roughneck being smoothed out by marriage as the subject for Sunday sermons.[46] But the book's good humour does nothing to brighten Monash's mood when he wades in 'hot and strong' to reform the Australian mail system in Cairo, telling the slackers there that they are all sitting around 'like a lot of mummies'.

He returns to Serapeum for a visit by Sir Archibald Murray and Edward, the Prince of Wales. Monash's men put on a 'star turn', despite being war-weary and longing for home. The whole brigade demonstrates its skills in the desert with displays involving rifles, bayonets, real grenades and machine-guns. Monash preens. 'The old Commander in Chief was mightily pleased and said so.'[47]

Monash presides over the first Anzac Day ceremony for his men. The whole brigade is turned out at 6.45 a.m. Every man who served at Gallipoli wears a blue ribbon on his right breast, and every man who took part in the landing on the first day wears a red one as well. There is a dignified service. The brigade's massed band plays Handel's 'Dead March' before buglers play the 'Last Post'.

The rest of Anzac Day is a holiday, with cricket matches in the morning, and in the afternoon a swimming carnival featuring 15,000 men lined up for a kilometre and a half north of the Serapeum pontoon bridge on both sloping banks of the Suez, 'one teeming mass of naked humanity'.[48] Prince Edward 'heartily' enjoys the festivities, including a skit on the Gallipoli landing that Monash finds 'screamingly funny'.[49] In the evening there are mess dinners and band concerts and the men wish each other many happy returns 'of this famous day – *Our Day*'.[50]

Monash is constantly impressing his superiors, especially Cox. The pair are now getting on famously as Monash prepares his men and the rest of the 4th Division to follow Birdwood's and Godley's troops out of this 'dreadful desert' to the 'cold and wet' of France, which right now seems so much more inviting.[51] Cox has 20,000 Australians in the 4th Division under his command and realises that he could command them much more efficiently with Monash's help. He also realises that Australian soldiers are very different in temperament from the British Tommies: more likely to chafe at harsh discipline and quicker to demand a fair go. The British hierarchical system does not work on men raised on principles of egalitarianism, thumbing their noses at toffs in a new and free society.

Cox has always listened with rapt attention[52] as Monash addresses his men, and at a meeting of divisional commanders on 29 April, Cox calls on Monash to address the gathering. Afterwards, Monash believes he has made a 'great impression'.[53] Yet the following day Cox risks alienating his Australian commanders by condemning the performance of 46-year-old Lieutenant Colonel Leslie Tilney[54] of the 13th Battalion. Tilney has a bad heart, and has never recovered from the dysentery and hepatitis he contracted on Gallipoli,[55] but is popular with his men. Monash holds him in high regard too.

Tilney complains to Monash about Cox's behaviour and tells him he wants to take the matter higher, to Godley. Monash tells Tilney he has a case, but manages to tactfully placate him. He writes to McCay and McGlinn, though, telling them that Cox's actions show the danger of 'putting Australian troops under a Divisional Staff who wholly misunderstand the Australian attitude and temperament'.[56]

Monash believes leadership should always be based on merit.

From almost the earliest days of the war violence was done to a deep rooted tradition of the British Army, which discouraged any promotion from the ranks. The Australian Imperial Force changed all that. Those privates, corporals and sergeants who displayed, under battle conditions, a notable capacity for leadership were earmarked for preferment. They afforded to all its men a tangible and visible proof of the recognition of merit and capacity, and their example was always a powerful stimulus to all their former comrades.

There was thus no officer caste, no social distinction in the whole force. In not a few instances, men of humble origin and belonging to the artisan class rose, during the war, from privates to the command of Battalions. The whole Australian Army became automatically graded into leaders and followers according to the individual merits of every man, and there grew a wonderful understanding between them.[57]

On 3 May Cox writes to Birdwood, saying that if it is 'desirable to put in a local product' as a divisional commander, 'I should like to say that I am prepared to recommend Monash be given a trial. He is a very able man … very tactful and his judgment is reliable. Any little weaknesses which appeared when he was in command of the Brigade at Anzac would not count so much in a Divisional command. He seems to me to have "come on" very much.'[58]

Birdwood prefers Harry Chauvel. For starters, Chauvel is not a Jew, and there are not the same vicious rumours surrounding him as those that still circulate about Monash. Still, Chauvel is needed for the Mounted Division in the desert campaigns.

Monash is slightly wounded by a piece of shrapnel from a demonstration of the new Stokes Mortar on 8 May, but a week later is again temporarily in charge of the 4th Division when Cox is taken ill. Monash finds the role is 'anything but a picnic … with a good deal of rushing around and hard riding' to check on his 25-kilometre-wide frontline and troops scattered across a wide area.[59] Yet others are impressed.

While conceding that he cannot pretend that Monash is as qualified to command a division 'as a trained officer',[60] Godley writes to Senator Pearce on 31 May to say Monash is deserving of a trial and will do well if he has 'really good, well trained staff officers to help him'.[61] Birdwood then gives his recommendation to Pearce and to Governor-General Munro Ferguson on 6 June.

By then, Monash is on his way to Marseilles, still unaware that he is to be promoted. He and 3200 of his troops have sailed from Alexandria on the *Transylvania* at daybreak on 2 June. The other 2800 of his brigade, along with the brigade's horses and vehicles, are aboard two large transatlantic liners, the *Canada* and the *Havreford*.

On a return journey, the *Transylvania* is sunk by a German U-boat, with the loss of 412 lives, mostly Allied troops.[62]

Monash thinks the war in France will be a doddle compared with Gallipoli, where the Anzacs were cooped up within 100 metres of the enemy lines.[63] While at sea he receives the news about the Battle of Jutland, the greatest naval battle up to that time.

British admiral John Jellicoe, commanding 151 British, Australian and Canadian ships, waged war off the Danish coast with 99 German ships under the command of Reinhard Scheer. Almost 10,000 men died, and 25 vessels were sunk, though both sides claimed victory.

A few days later, British morale takes a massive blow when Kitchener, the face of the British military, drowns along with 600 others after his ship hits a German mine off Scotland's Orkney Islands.

Monash and his men enjoy a trouble-free journey, with not a single sighting of a submarine, and they reach Marseilles on 7 June. France is paradise after the desert. Monash finds his way to a railway compartment reserved for him and Durrant, and they put their feet up as French gardens and rivers fly by.

They finally reach Paris at 8 a.m. on 8 June. Monash's troop trains will not arrive in Calais for at least a day or two, so he and Durrant go sightseeing.

The Paris of 1916 is very different from the city of light that Monash, Vic and Bert visited back in 1910. Now there is 'a sombre air over the whole city and very large numbers of people in black'.[64] The Eiffel Tower and the Louvre are closed, but Monash and Durrant still visit the Place de la Concorde, Napoleon's Tomb and the Musée Grévin. They see a review at the Folies Bergère, but to Monash's chagrin, drinks stop at 9.30 p.m. and the avenues are deserted by 11. The next day they head to the Gare du Nord for the train to Calais, to be reunited with the brigade, waiting a little further on. First, though, they are confronted with a trainload of veterans from the bloodletting at Verdun, who are farewelling their womenfolk at the station as they return to the killing fields.

Monash and Durrant journey to Calais, then Bailleul, 80 kilometres inland, and finally nearby Erquinghem-Lys, where Monash's brigade headquarters is established in a two-storey mansion among 'spring foliage, herbage, flowers and crops galore'. Six of his horses are killed by German shelling but he manages to save Tom, Dick and Harry.[65]

Monash traverses the area in a new, fast Daimler car, finding billets everywhere for his officers and warning his men that with French soldiers — husbands and fathers — away at the front, the Australians are to take no more than a 'brotherly interest' in the French women. There are sniggers all round as Monash's brow furrows. Monash and his driver are soon racing in the Daimler down the narrow lanes to dine with Birdwood and White at the magnificent Château de la Motte-aux-Bois, which Birdwood has commandeered as his base.

It is a world away from the privations of Gallipoli or the desert, but overhead is the noise of the German and Allied guns and of aerial dogfights, though most of the civilians left in the area seem oblivious to the fighting. Before long, Monash is again in the thick of it. Just 200 metres from where he is sleeping, the Germans bombard a Romanesque church, obliterating it and killing an old woman and two sappers in the process.

General Douglas Haig begins preparations for Britain's Somme Offensive under Henry Rawlinson's[66] 4th Army. More than a million soldiers will be killed or wounded in this campaign.

Haig decides to use raiding parties all along the front as diversions to cover the main attacks. Monash, whose brigade is defending a 3-kilometre front, is ordered to prepare his men for a night offensive, and is given help in readying them by Brigadier General William Holmes, whom he regards as 'a real good fellow'.[67] Monash selects 'Jacka's Mob', the 14th Battalion, to pick their best men for the lightning raid, under the immediate control of British lieutenant colonel George Jackson,[68] a veteran of guerrilla raids in the Boer War. Monash and Jackson spy out the terrain on 19 June as plans are made to attack the German line on 2 July, 24 hours after the beginning of the Battle of the Somme.

As Monash plots out the manoeuvre, he is also intrigued by rumours, backed by Jackson, that he will soon be given command of a new 3rd Division, being raised from new Australian recruits, and that approval of this appointment has been received from Australia.[69]

Monash was born in this bluestone cottage in Dudley Street, West Melbourne in 1865. The house has since been demolished. *(Australian War Memorial, H17218)*

Baby John with mother Bertha in November 1865. *(Monash family collection)*

The little general aged three. *(William Davies & Co. Photographers / National Library of Australia)*

Monash as a teenager in 1880, about to make his mark on the world. *(Stewart & Co., Melbourne, National Library of Australia manuscript collection MS 1540, Deakin family photograph album)*

Colour Sgt. John Monash, standing far left with the University Company, Victorian Rifles in 1885. His great friend Sgt. George Farlow is standing next to him. *(Monash University Archives, image number 1416)*

The pleasant, plucky and married Annie Gabriel, with whom a young Monash fell in love. *(Monash family collection)*

Monash with his daughter Bertha and father Louis.
(Monash University Archives, image number 1902)

Vic and four-year-old Bertha in 1897.
Vic and Monash had recently reconciled
after a separation that lasted almost
a year. *(Monash family collection / National
Library of Australia)*

Monash supported his large extended family. Even though he faced his own financial battles, he paid for his sister Lou to travel to England to marry Walter Rosenhain. At her farewell aboard the *Weimar* in September 1901 are, back row: Minnie Behrend, Monash, Herman Roth, Sophie Roth, Vic, Mat Roth; middle row: Mat Monash, Lou Monash, Tante Ulrike Roth; front row: Elsa Behrend, Bert Monash. *(Monash family collection / National Library of Australia)*

Monash was building bridges around Victoria and mending them at home throughout the 1890s. He and Vic (far left) pose with workmen on the Fyansford Bridge on the outskirts of Geelong in 1898. Foreman Chris Christensen is second from the right. *(Monash University Archives, image number 202)*

Albert Boldt died, pinned under his traction engine, after Monash's new King's Bridge in Bendigo collapsed during testing in 1901. *(University of Melbourne Archives, UMA/I/6203)*

Monash was a picture of contentment with Vic and Bertha in London during their luxury European vacation in 1910. *(Monash family collection / National Library of Australia)*

Just before heading off to war, Monash took the opportunity to lead a group of hikers up Mount Buffalo in October 1914. It was one of his favourite places on earth and he was not sure he would see its majestic vistas again. *(Monash family collection / National Library of Australia)*

The sight of soldiers marching through the streets of Melbourne was a common one during the Great War. On 17 December 1914 Monash led his 4th Brigade down Collins Street as they prepared to ship out. *(Harold Paynting Collection, State Library of Victoria, H91.40/388)*

Monash (left) and McGlinn were unkindly known as Tweedledum and Tweedledee by their men as they visited the sights of Egypt before facing the arduous climbs on Gallipoli. Monash went on a strict fitness regime when the fighting began. *(Newspix)*

Keith Murdoch was one of the most powerful figures in Australian journalism. *(National Library of Australia, MS 2823, Papers of Sir Keith Arthur Murdoch)*

War correspondent Charles Bean became Monash's greatest critic but later called him Australia's greatest soldier. *(George Lambert / Australian War Memorial, ART07545)*

Colonel Monash's Headquarters, 4th Australian Infantry Brigade, at Anzac. Monash is in the centre with McGlinn to his right. *(C.E.W. Bean / Australian War Memorial, G01187)*

The winter on Gallipoli was ferocious. Australian artillery men put many of the under-equipped Turks out of their misery. *(T.P. Bennett / State Library of Victoria, H83.103/355)*

The Western Front was an endless vista of devastation. Here Australian soldiers clear the road near the Cloth Hall in Ypres, Belgium. *(Frank Hurley / Mitchell Library, State Library of New South Wales, A1404004)*

The dead and wounded are everywhere on the fields of Flanders around Ypres. *(Hubert Wilkins / State Library of Victoria, H37630/10)*

Monash relied on double-decker London buses to transport his men in northern France after Ludendorff launched his Spring Offensive in 1918. *(Australian War Memorial, E01102)*

Monash presents the Victoria Cross to Sgt Bill 'Rusty' Ruthven in Camon, France on 13 July 1918.
(Donated by the Herald & Weekly Times Limited / State Library of Victoria, H38849/5550)

Monash (seated) with his two Aides-de-Camp and the Camp Commandant at the Australian Corps Headquarters in Bertangles, 20 July 1918. Left to right: Captain Aubrey Moss, Major Walter Berry, Camp Commandant, and Captain Paul Simonson. Moss and Simonson were Monash's nephews. *(State Library of Victoria, H42579)*

Troops of the 5th Australian Infantry Brigade, Australian Artillery and tanks waiting for the second stage of the attacks at Warfusee-Abancourt, near Amiens in northern France, on 8 August 1918. *(Hubert Wilkins / State Library of Victoria, H37630/30)*

French Prime Minister Georges Clemenceau (in the brown suit) travelled to the front lines in July 1918 to tell Monash (sixth from the left) and his men that France would never forget the 'great deeds' of the Australians. Tom Blamey has his foot on the step. *(Australian War Memorial, P03631.212)*

Monash found war repellent, 'every day filled with loathing, horror, and distress … the loss of precious life and the waste of human effort'. Here, dead Germans litter a trench on the Hindenburg Line as Monash's forces surge ahead near Ronssoy in September 1918. *(Hubert Wilkins / State Library of Victoria, H37630/28)*

With a lifelong love of theatre, Monash put on a grand show at Bertangles when King George V travelled to France to award him his knighthood. *(Australian War Memorial, EO3895 and EO2964)*

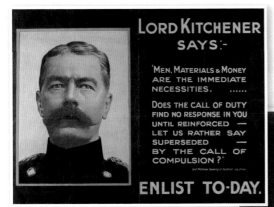

Lord Kitchener was the face of the British military until his death by drowning in 1916. *(David Allen & Sons / State Library of Victoria, H30304)*

General William Riddell Birdwood bristled as Monash superseded him on the Western Front. *(Australian War Memorial, P03717.009)*

Monash rose to power on the Western Front under the direction of Britain's Commander-in-Chief, Field Marshal Douglas Haig. Here Haig (at left), speaks with French Commander-in-Chief General Joffre and British Prime Minister David Lloyd George.

Monash and Bertha visited countless war graves during their tour of the battlefields in 1919, sending photos home to the relatives of dead soldiers. *(Len Woolcock / State Library of Victoria, H82.288/15)*

Below, Monash sits for his portrait in the studio of the artist James Quinn in London in 1919; and, at right, is captured by John Longstaff in this three-quarter length portrait. *(State Library of Victoria, H32848, H3154)*

Flanked by Bertha and an ailing Vic, Monash is greeted by a stern-faced Governor-General Ronald Munro Ferguson after arriving home from the war to cheering crowds on Boxing Day 1919. Vic has only weeks to live. *(Monash family collection / National Library of Australia)*

Four generations of the Monash family were photographed at Iona in 1926 for Tante Ulrike's eighty-fourth birthday. From left: Bertha, David Bennett, Tante Ulrike, Monash and John Monash Bennett. *(Monash University Archives, image number 1432)*

Monash and Lizzie Bentwitch on holiday at Mount Buffalo. They never married, despite their passionate relationship that lasted for almost fifteen years. *(Alice Manfield / State Library of Victoria, H2003.97/33)*

The last ride. Monash leads the 1931 Anzac Day march on his dappled grey charger. At sixty-five his health was already in serious decline. *(Australian War Memorial, A03451)*

Australia's greatest soldier: the statue of Monash near the Shrine of Remembrance in Melbourne is a permanent memorial to his intellect and determination. *(Grantlee Kieza)*

Monash saw the Shrine as a lasting tribute to the sacrifice made by Australians in the Great War. *(Newspix)*

Michael Monash Bennett with a bronze statue of his great-grandfather unveiled at Monash University's Clayton campus in Melbourne in April 2015. The 3-metre sculpture was created by Peter Corlett OAM. *(Eugene Hyland / Newspix)*

On 26 June Birdwood confirms that Pearce, Munro Ferguson and Billy Hughes have agreed. He realises his appointment has only come about because of the Australian Government's insistence on appointing an Australian. Yet it is the high point of Monash's career.

Now, as he prepares for an attack on the German line in the Bois Grenier sector, he just has to make sure he lives long enough to savour it.

As the British shell the German line in preparation for the massive attack on the Somme, Monash spends four days going over plans and practising his raid. He takes his men to La Rolanderie Farm, where a replica is made of the German trenches based on intelligence reports, and where his raiding team of 83 men and six officers can go through a full dress rehearsal for their attack.[70] Ballarat farmer Lieutenant Harold Wanliss,[71] who has not yet seen action but looks like a great leader in the making, is chosen to command the raiding party as they set off from the village of La Houssoie. Monash requests a barrage of 3700 shells to cover the men as they move forward and follow-up fire from the trench mortar crews. The plan is for the mortar fire to destroy the barbed-wire defences of the Germans, and for Wanliss's raiders, armed with revolvers and coshes, to quickly gather intelligence and create maximum carnage in the trenches before escaping.

On the night of 2 July, Monash gives the signal to advance and the initial mortar attack hits a German wiring party of 10 men as the Australians cross No Man's Land. But when the raiders reach the enemy wire they find four rows still intact: the mortar fire has fallen in the open space between the entanglements. The German machine-gunners have been waiting and the Australians are easy prey. Monash loses contact with the leaders because of signal rocket failure.

Lieutenant Archibald Harvey, a Bundaberg bank clerk, shouts, 'Come on Australia', but is wounded while hacking through the wire, as is Lieutenant John Roderick, and Lieutenant Robert

Julian, a Geelong ironmonger, is killed. Corporal Richard Garcia, a Melbourne farrier wearing a luminous watch Monash has given him for night fighting, is shot through the shoulder and thigh but survives. Wanliss takes a machine-gun bullet in the mouth but, wounded again in the neck, arm and stomach, he leads 25 men over the bodies of the fallen.

The trenches are almost empty by the time the raiders arrive. They club five Germans and hurl some grenades; 'uppercut everyone about' is the way Wanliss describes the close-quarter combat in boxing parlance.[72] But the enemy fire from beyond is overwhelming, and the Australians retreat to orders of 'Out, out', only to suffer more casualties on the way back as they take cover in a canal. Monash says Wanliss deserves a VC but he gets a Distinguished Service Order instead.

As the men come in Monash takes a roll call and finds that every officer has been hit, and that there are 38 casualties in total. Nine men have not returned. Bean writes that only the thorough training of the men saved them from a complete disaster, and that, 'like most other hurriedly organized attacks with inexperienced troops, this operation, in spite of much gallantry, did more harm to the raiders than to the enemy'.[73] The artillery boys nickname the whole shemozzle 'Monash's Muddle'.

Monash tells Walter Rosenhain that some of his scouts and wounded threw themselves on the barbed wire to form a bridge for the others,[74] but it is a gross exaggeration, just like Monash's claim that the Australians killed more than 50 of the enemy.[75] The next night the Germans hit back hard, so that after less than four weeks in France, Monash has suffered 300 casualties and is utterly exhausted from sleepless nights and 'multifarious administrative' duties.

Monash still believes that the war in France is 'child's play' compared with Gallipoli,[76] but Rawlinson's 4th Army suffers 57,470 casualties on the first day of fighting on the Somme. The battle and the movement of Cox's 4th Division to the Somme delay Monash's promotion to lead the 3rd Division as a major general. Finally, on 15 July, he hands over his 4th Brigade to former Charters Towers schoolmaster Colonel Charles Brand.[77]

Not all of Monash's men are sad to see him go.

Lieutenant Tom Chataway will write that many were in favour of the change of commanders because Monash 'had always been a very distant man' and Brand mixed more with the men, placing their comfort 'before that of vigorous discipline'.[78] But McGlinn sees Monash's promotion as a slap in the face 'to those miserable curs' who plotted against him, all those who dismissed his abilities, or spread rumours about him being a German spy or looked down upon him because he is a Jew. Lieutenant Louis Isaac Goldstein, a pearl cleaner from Broome who has served with Monash since Gallipoli, tells his chief, 'there isn't a man amongst us who does not love and respect you. I will never forget you at Monash Gully during those strenuous days of Pope's Hill and Quinn's Post … you were so fatherly and considerate.'[79]

Monash has led his men through grim times, learning to love them in their life-and-death struggles.

He is now leaving them for London to take up his new command, and in the darkest days of war he will soon be in love again.

Chapter 19

Dear Mother,
The time is near at hand for a great offensive and should I fall, I will
be proud to know I did so in the cause of Righteousness and Justice.
This will be a great blow to you but cheer up. Dad, I have kept your
wishes, neither smoked nor taken liquor. Give my regards to all the
boys and girls. So goodbye for a short time.

PRIVATE HENRY WILLIAMS, 19, OF COLLINGWOOD, WHO DIED SOON
AFTERWARDS FROM WOUNDS SUFFERED IN THE BATTLE OF FROMELLES ON
19 JULY 1916[1]

Of course, a Major General commanding a fighting division is a
quite tremendous person ... wherever one goes people stare and
follow one about.

MONASH ON HIS PROMOTION, 22 JULY 1916[2]

A S SOMBRE AS PARIS was, it is a carnival compared with
London when Monash arrives there. Or at least that's the
way he describes it to Vic and Bert as he warns them about sailing
to Europe to rejoin him.

At night all of London is in absolute darkness, he says: every
window screened, no streetlights, no lamps on cars, train windows
shuttered. Accidents are frequent and transport is chaotic. In the
daytime large crowds gather around Waterloo and Victoria Stations

to meet trainloads of wounded and broken men, 'coming in all day and every day – miles and miles of motor ambulances full of bandaged men', women weeping and wailing, and crowds with ashen faces in a fit of panic. In the hotels there is no life, no laughter, no colour. Museums and galleries are closed for the duration, grand hotels have become hospitals and food is at famine prices.

He tells his family that as much as he wants to be with them again as soon as possible, it is suicidal to risk a visit to England with the Germans continuing their submarine attacks and with London in the grip of the Zeppelin raids as the Germans pour fire from the sky. Even if they made it to England, 'it would be a horrible, uncomfortable experience, full of terror and anxiety'.[3] The *Lusitania* has gone down off the coast of Ireland with nearly 1200 deaths, and by the end of the war the U-boats will have sunk as many as 5000 ships.

Despite the grim picture Monash paints to his family, London does have its delights for a major general on the loose, thousands of miles from home. He attends the theatre even if the crowds are down, visits Westminster Abbey and orders smart new uniforms from Burberry. He starts wearing the red armlets of a divisional commander, 'and this attracts even more attention than the gold peaked cap and gorgets, and ribbons'.[4]

Monash spends 10 days with Walter and Lou at their home, Warrawee, in Kingston upon Thames in Surrey. He revels in family life again, especially playing with the three Rosenhain girls, Mona, Nancy and Peggy, who are in awe of him. Thirteen-year-old Mona kisses a photo of Monash every night before falling asleep and writes to him often. He plays the piano, inspects Walter's laboratory and rekindles his sparring matches with his brother-in-law over the chessboard. Walter gives Monash increasingly complex jigsaw puzzles and Monash outlines a system guaranteed to win at roulette. Walter trumps him again by exposing its flaw.

Monash also looks up Lizzie Bentwitch. It is six years since they last saw each other, and he is a far more exciting and attractive man than she remembers. His boots are shined to a mirror finish with the Kiwi polish Vic has mailed to him, and his uniform, with all the flashes of gold, suits his swarthy looks. Monash is watching his diet more seriously than ever, and at 51 has shed more than 20 kilograms from the 100-kilogram bulk that made him a figure of fun to his critics back in Melbourne. He is no longer a Tweedledum in tight pants, but instead has a presence befitting one of the King's most important soldiers. His face is thinner, and while it may have a few more wrinkles than Lizzie recalls, Monash himself feels younger and fresher than he has for years despite the workload and responsibilities.[5] Lizzie can sense his virility.

Monash takes her to tea and regales her with stories of his many adventures and heroic acts, though she is so voluble he sometimes struggles to get a word in sideways. When Lizzie finally pauses to draw breath, he tells her that he and McCay are the only citizen officers in the whole Empire to hold the lofty rank of major general.

He finds Lizzie marvellous company, especially after what he has lived through in the 15 months since landing on Gallipoli. She seems much more outgoing without Vic on the scene, and together they go to the theatre three times. Monash has not seen his own family for a year and a half, and Lizzie is such a good listener, more submissive than Vic and disinclined to argue.

On first glance they appear an odd couple: Monash the cerebral intellectual; Lizzie with her loud dress sense, slightly scatty mannerisms and incessant chatter. But perhaps opposites attract. She will take him home – which for her is a series of luxury hotels – to show him the miniature portraits she paints. He will compliment her talent. He will confide in her more every time he comes to London. It is so long since he has had real female company and Lizzie helps him to forget, momentarily, all the horrors he has seen.

Before long they are lovers.

On 21 July Monash travels to his new base at Larkhill on Salisbury Plain, near Stonehenge, and rents a manor house on a property called Collins Farm at nearby Durrington. He will live here with his senior administrative officer, Englishman Lieutenant Colonel Harold Mynors Farmar, and Farmar's family.

A Gallipoli veteran, Farmar is from a well-connected if poor family and attended Sandhurst free of charge on the recommendation of Queen Victoria herself.[6] Monash delights in playing with the Farmar children, Susan, Hugh and little Mary, who will become a bestselling novelist.[7] Farmar's wife Violet tells Vic that Monash is just the most wonderful company, someone 'who would cheer up any house by his sunny ways and delightful conversation'.[8]

After four days Monash moves permanently to his new headquarters by the River Avon, in rolling countryside very much like that he remembers motoring through between Daylesford and Ballarat. The meadows surrounding his home are a carpet of wild flowers of all colours.

He still has occasional struggles with lumbago and uses aspirin to kill the pain, but is now free of rheumatism. He continues to smoke heavily, using the Capstan full-strength, brown-label pipe tobacco Vic sends him, but every day he undertakes long, hard walks and rides with Eric Simonson to inspect his troops. He does callisthenics and stretching exercises and lifts dumbbells in preparation for the biggest battles in the history of Australia.

The lush countryside along the Avon is a stark contrast to the devastation occurring beside the Somme in northern France.

On 19 July, a few nights after Monash sailed for England, Australia suffered the worst 24 hours in its history, with 5533 casualties, including 2000 deaths, at Fromelles.[9]

Though he was not wounded himself, Colonel Harold Pope, who gave his name to a hill at Gallipoli and was a popular leader with a confident manner and kind eyes, fell asleep from exhaustion the next afternoon. After Jim McCay tried to wake him without success, he accused Pope of being drunk and sent him home in disgrace. Monash tries to console his old comrade but says there is nothing he can do to rectify the situation. Pope is eventually given another command.[10]

Meanwhile Monash has his own concerns. Instead of the 4th Brigade's 6000 men, Monash now commands 20,000, equipped with 3000 horses, 4000 mules, 64 artillery guns, 192 machine-guns, 18 cars, 82 trucks and 1100 wagons. His troops include headquarters staff, artillery, engineers, infantry, a squadron of cavalry, a medical department, a supply department, a cyclist corps and depot units. His staff officers include George Jackson; Hobart-born Major Guy Wylly VC, an officer in the Indian Army;[11] and Duntroon-trained Major George Wootten.[12] His four brigadier generals are Alexander Jobson,[13] an accountant who until recently was writing a financial column for the Sydney *Sun*, Walter McNicoll,[14] the first principal of Geelong High School, Colin Rankin,[15] a Queensland cane farmer and politician, and Harold Grimwade,[16] a pharmacist and businessman. His division will be under the control of Sir Henry Sclater's[17] Southern Command.

Monash and Jackson go on an inspection tour of the 9th, 10th and 11th Brigades – the 33rd to 44th Battalions – and Monash is ecstatic about the standard of his men, 'a very mixed but very fine lot'. Some are the sons of peers, while others have been promoted from the ranks. It will be a pleasant and agreeable job, he reasons, to turn them into a 'fine fighting Division', because they are the finest Australian soldiers he's ever seen 'and their soldierly bearing and behaviour are simply splendid'.[18]

But while his men are 'equal in every way in physique and bearing, to the earlier Divisions', they are largely novices and will have to be trained thoroughly to become a cohesive unit. There are still equipment shortages, no single brigade has met till they reached England and some battalions have never been together before, all in one place. 'Officers didn't know their men, and vice versa. The men had no rifles or bayonets, and had never seen a Mills bomb, or dug a trench, or seen a Vickers or Lewis machine-gun, or a Stokes mortar. All they had learned to do was stand up straight in rows and behave themselves. All the bayonet fighting they had been taught in Australia had to be unlearnt.'[19]

Still, as Monash spends hours riding about on horseback to supervise his troops and their preparations, he realises that most of them are 'men of standing', including his nephews Eric Simonson and Aubrey Moss – known as 'Mo' and 'Arf a Mo' for their moustaches – prominent Sydney barrister Edwin Brissenden, who is a corporal working as a clerk at divisional HQ, and Professor Harold Woodruff, the Director of the Veterinary School at Melbourne University. 'There are a great many master tradesmen,' Monash adds, 'owner farmers, miners, professional men and several members of parliament.'[20] Sergeant Charlie McGrath and Quartermaster Sergeant Alfred Ozanne[21] are the Federal Labor members for Ballarat and Corio respectively, while Lieutenant Ambrose Carmichael[22] is the former New South Wales Treasurer. Monash decides, though, that one of the MPs, Colin Rankin, is only in the job because of his political connections and that he is not up to scratch. He says the 11th Brigade has been 'grossly mismanaged' under Rankin and replaces him with Cannan, but only after a spirited battle with AIF bureaucrats in London.[23]

Monash is floored by the death in France of little Harry Cathie, a 24-year-old bank clerk who is the son of his old landlord from Gipps Street. While it grieves him 'beyond words', he writes that 'it is no use fretting about our losses in this war. We all have to suffer, some more, some less, it is part of the price we have to pay for past and prospective happiness. There is nothing to do except to hold up one's head, and go on, cherishing in kindly memory the many who have fallen.'[24]

Vic writes to tell her husband that Charles Smith of the *Argus* has called Monash 'the finest soldier I ever saw'.[25]

Almost as soon as Monash's promotion is made official in mid-August, he faces war on a new front. There is a proposal to tear apart the 3rd Division for redistribution to other units devastated at Fromelles and at Pozières, where Annie's son, Corporal Gordon

Gabriel, has been awarded the Military Medal for bravery. Gordon will eventually return to Melbourne with a bullet wound in the bum, a lieutenant's uniform and an English wife.

Despite the rumours that Monash's division will be chopped up, he goes 'full speed ahead' with his men's training. When 2800 of them are taken to reinforce other divisions devastated in France he protests that 'men are now being torn asunder, who enlisted together'.[26] He asks Julius Bruche, now at AIF headquarters on London's Horseferry Road, to send the best possible replacements, but before any more of his men are marched out of Larkhill, Haig intervenes to keep the 3rd together.

Billy Hughes tells Australia the nation must send 70,000 more troops to win this war. He wants to push through conscription, which Britain and New Zealand have already adopted, and organises a referendum on the issue for 28 October.

Under his command, Monash expects his 3rd Division to stand out from all others. To make his troops distinctive he orders that the flaps of their slouch hats be turned down so that the brim is flat all round. He sends hundreds of men for specialist training, and organises the digging of 2000 metres of trenches at Larkhill for practice. In mock battles, soldiers attack with air and artillery support and then occupy their positions for days on end, in preparation for the real thing. They practise marching in gas masks through No Man's Land and finding billets in local villages, as they will have to do in France and Belgium.

He complains that his men are being 'inspected to death',[27] with visits from his commanding officer General Sclater; the Chief of the Imperial General Staff, General Sir William Robertson;[28] the Inspector of Infantry, Major General Sir Francis Howard;[29] and the Commander-in-Chief of Home Forces, Field Marshall Lord French,[30] looking 'old and worn and lifeless' after the recent battles in France.[31]

He is much more welcoming when attractive women come to visit. He even hosts an afternoon tea with cakes, jellies and flowers on 1 September for Lady Birdwood and Lady Moore, wife of Brigadier General Sir Newton Moore, the former premier of Western Australia. He is quite taken with Janetta Birdwood, who despite having a 16-year-old son looks about 25, is 'very sweet and unassuming' and takes 'a girlish delight' in everything as Monash escorts the ladies around the camp.[32]

That same month, Germany's new supreme army commander, Paul von Hindenburg, and his deputy chief of staff, Erich Ludendorff, tour the frontlines at the Somme and Verdun. Hindenburg was grieved that his soldiers 'hardly ever saw anything but trenches and shell holes ... for weeks and even months'. In these dispiriting conditions, he notes, German soldiers have 'to renounce that mighty spiritual exaltation which accompanies a victorious advance ... How many of our brave men have never known this, the purest of a soldier's joys?'[33]

The Schlieffen Plan to overrun France with Germany's 'race to the sea' is now bogged down in a long, horrific trench war of attrition in France and Belgium that is slowly eroding the German spirit. Germany will lose nearly three-quarters of a million men, killed or wounded, over the next few months in France and Flanders. Ludendorff already knows his army is at breaking point.

The 4th Brigade has performed brilliantly around Pozières under former schoolmaster Charles Brand, and Monash is determined to have his 3rd Division reach that lofty standard. With the number of arms being turned out by British factories, he feels the Allies will soon have enough firepower to smash their way into Germany.

Monash dines with the Sclaters in Salisbury on 12 September and, perhaps at Monash's prompting, Lord French promises to ask King George to visit Larkhill to inspect the division before the weather becomes 'too cold'.[34]

Fifteen days later the King is on his way.

Monash has rehearsed his men so thoroughly there can be no slip-ups, and he has 27,000 of them – the 3rd Division, plus

Australian and New Zealand training battalions – waiting on Bulford Field, 7 kilometres outside Larkhill. If they march in a column Monash estimates it will take the men five hours to pass His Majesty, but instead he has them packed in, 100 men to every 10 paces. Even then the march takes two hours. The King is due to arrive at 11.15 a.m., but even though there are five roads to the field, Monash has so many men now that the first units have to head to the assembly ground at 7.15 a.m.

Monash has come a long way from his days herding goats in Jerilderie, and is delighted that a man from the *Times* as well as Springthorpe from the *Age* are there to cover the royal visit. Monash has invited the Rosenhains down too, of course, and they look on with pride.

'I suppose it does not happen to very many people to have the privilege and pleasure of spending two-and-a-half-hours continuously … with the King of so mighty an Empire,' Monash says, 'and talking with him the whole time on a footing of perfect freedom.'

George V arrives from the Bulford train station on a magnificent black horse, an Australian waler he has bought in India. The King is dressed in khaki like Monash, but with the badges of a field marshal on his shoulders. He is accompanied by two equerries, as well as a standard bearer carrying a small Royal Standard on a lance, and one mounted servant in a black top hat and long black coat. Beside him are General Sclater and an aide.

The King rides up to Monash and his flagstaff. A much bigger Royal Standard is unfurled and flutters in the breeze as Monash gives the Royal Salute and 27,000 bayonets flash together into the 'present arms'. Sixteen massed bands – almost 400 musicians – strike up 'God Save the King'. Monash has always loved parade and pomp, and this is a glorious moment for him on an otherwise overcast day.

Then the King trots towards Monash and Monash trots towards him, swooning. George V extends his hand as he comes near, and with 'a cheery winning smile' and 'in a deep clear vibrating voice' says, 'How do you do, General? I am so very glad to be able to come down to see you all. It is the first time I have been able to see Australian troops in England.'

As they head down the line of men, nearly 3 kilometres in length, the King asks, 'You used to command the 4th Brigade didn't you? They've done awfully well – I hear you were at Gallipoli all the time, that *was* splendid.'

Monash, the relentless social climber, finds the monarch 'chatty, and breezy, and merry all the time'. The King tells him he has been in Melbourne twice and that it was a fine city, and asks him all sorts of questions about the comfort of the men and about guns and wagons.

At the end of the 3rd Division line, the King looks back over the vast array of men and tells Monash, 'Well, General, I heartily congratulate you. It's a very fine division. I don't know that I've ever seen a finer one.' Monash nods politely in appreciation but inside he is beaming.

He and the King continue riding together until the very end of the line, and as George canters towards the saluting point for the march past, Monash and his staff gallop across to the front of the parade, with Eric Simonson at the front, followed by Jackson, Farmar, Monash and Grimwade. Then Monash turns back to join his sovereign. The march past takes nearly two hours to pass the King, who talks constantly to Monash as the men file by, jumping from subject to subject – rifles, clothing, artillery, hats, the French, weather, tanks – breaking off occasionally to mutter, 'Splendid, splendid.'

He has inspected a million and a half men since the war began, he says, and tells Monash that no one could have built such a force except 'Lord K'. Kitchener had his critics, but by Jove, the King says, he was the man to build an army.

'You know, General,' the King starts, 'if we win this war ...'

But Monash, quick as a flash, cuts him politely off with a raised eyebrow. '*If* we win?'

'Oh yes, we'll *win* right enough,' the King replies with a laugh as he throws his head back, 'nobody need make any mistake about that.' He says his cousin the Kaiser has made an awfully big mistake. 'Those stupid Germans! They started out to smash the British Empire! Smash it to pieces! And look, just *look*.'

With a sweep of his arm towards the mass of marching men, the King, 'with shining eyes', tells Monash, 'See what they've really done? They've made an Empire of us.' The colonies have put forward 600,000 men to defend the great traditions of Britain and her Empire. 'Marvellous, marvellous!'

George asks Monash if he met his son the Prince of Wales in Egypt, and tells Monash that the Prince wrote to his father to say 'how good all you Australians had been to him'.

George tells Monash, 'It makes a lump come in my throat, to think of all these splendid fellows coming all those thousands of miles; and what they have come for.'

When the procession is finally over the two men ride side by side to Bulford Station a kilometre and a half away, and Monash has the men drawn up 100 deep, breaking into mighty cheers and raising their hats on bayonets. The horses are terrified but behave themselves.

The train is ready for departure in just one minute. His Majesty turns to one of his equerries, Lord Wigram, to say, 'Splendid timing wasn't it, Clive, the general couldn't have timed it more beautifully could he?'

Then the King dismounts, gives his horse a lump of sugar and shakes hands with Monash and his staff.

He invites Monash to the palace as soon as he can get away.

'Now goodbye, General,' he says as he steps onto the royal train. 'Thank you very much.'

As soon as the King is gone it rains on Monash's parade. The heavens open and all 27,000 men are soaked on the 7-kilometre slog back to Larkhill.[35]

*

Monash sends Vic a piece of Virginia creeper from his garden, a copy of Charles Dixon's painting of the Gallipoli landing and two pieces of the aluminium framework from a Zeppelin, 'the Aerial Monster', that has been shot down over Essex and given to Walter to assess.[36]

He spends four days in London visiting the War Office to work out the supply chain for his men, but also goes to the National Gallery, which is the only one open, and stays at the palatial Cavendish Club in Mayfair[37] as an honorary member. He catches up with Lizzie Bentwitch, visits the theatre four times with her and dines at the Cheshire Cheese. He strolls through Richmond Park with the Rosenhains.

He tries on new uniforms, orders a new chamois vest and underpants for the looming winter in France, and organises 20,000 new leather vests for the division.[38] He petitions the War Office successfully for a supply of new warm blankets for all the horses, at a cost of £1500. It is a struggle for him though to get enough for 'the poor brutes' to eat. There are shortages of hay, chaff and oats throughout England.[39]

On 7 October 1916, while stationed near Bapaume on the Somme, Adolf Hitler, having been promoted to lance corporal and working as a dispatch runner well back from the front, receives a severe wound to the leg after a shell blast. He is sent to convalesce at a hospital at Beelitz,[40] near Berlin.

During his recovery he visits Berlin and is enraged by what he sees as a defeatist attitude developing in the wake of crippling food shortages, and among striking workers who simply cannot go on.

It is all the fault of the Jew, he tells himself. It is always the Jew. And the Bolshevik.

Birdwood visits in October and says Monash is getting on 'capitally'.

Later that month, Monash calls a meeting of his brigadiers to give them the honest truth about this war. He hates everything about warfare but he hates losing even more. He shelves the sensitivity of the artist and the compassion of the high-minded intellectual, and temporarily forgets about playing with small children and writing home with little jokes about life on the front. This war is all about killing Germans, he says. He tells the brigadiers that the Australian soldier heading to France must be a ruthless killer, because that is the only way to end this war. The Hun is to be exterminated, and Monash wants his officers to adopt a 'callous state of mind'. He urges them to 'hypnotise themselves' into a state of indifference against 'loss and death and bloodshed'. Loyalty on the battlefield is paramount.

'It is mighty easy being loyal to a man who is your superior when you agree with him, and he does what you expect him to do, and you are pleased to be with him,' Monash tells his audience. 'But the loyalty we want is loyalty to the man when you think he is unnecessarily severe, critical or wrong, when he is adopting a course of action which you feel and know to be incorrect. That is the only kind of loyalty that is worth a damn. But there is a tendency to criticise. Wipe it out gentlemen … It creates a bad spirit which leads to inefficiency and failure in battle.'[41]

The Germans know they are 'for it' now, Monash says; they 'have begun to squeal good and proper and during the next few months they will fight and scratch and bite as they have never done before'.[42]

Billy Hughes's referendum on 28 October fails, even though Hughes declares that everyone who doesn't vote for conscription wants Germany to win.

In Germany, Hindenburg and Ludendorff insist that all Germans aged from 16 to 50 must take part in compulsory military service. They demand a 100 per cent increase in the manufacture of ammunition and trench mortars, and a 300 per cent increase in artillery and machine-guns.

*

On 21 October Monash receives the Companion of the Most Honourable Order of the Bath (CB) at Buckingham Palace. The King presents it to him 'in his usual, chatty, informal way',[43] and Monash celebrates with a weekend at Surrenden, the 2000-hectare Kent estate of Sir Henry Dering, a baronet who serves as Monash's assistant provost marshal. Monash and the other guests spend the Saturday shooting rabbits, pheasant and partridge on land that had been in the Dering family for 1000 years. Monash finds the shooting cruel 'but very fine sport'. On the Sunday he tours the house, admiring the priceless artworks by van Dyck, Gainsborough and Holbein.

On 6 November, 120 generals watch as 2000 of Monash's men explode a whopping 2300-kilogram mine and then fortify the massive crater that it leaves.[44] Monash then lectures the assembled officers on this aspect of modern warfare, and afterwards calls the exhibition 'a veritable triumph for me'.[45]

Then, on 13 November, Monash turns out the men as a complete force, in a column stretching for 24 kilometres. He wants each man to know he is part of something huge and unstoppable. Snow has begun to fall, heralding the coldest winter in Europe in 30 years, and the 3rd Division keeps warm with movement.

At 5 a.m. on 21 November, the 3rd Division begins the first leg of its journey to Southampton on 87 trains, each with about 30 carriages. From there, over six days, ships will take them to Havre and Rouen. Monash tells Vic that Sclater has called his men the best-trained division that has left England since the first full-time soldiers headed for the front in 1914. 'You should just have heard the men cheering as train after train went out today',[46] he says.

Yet there are still problems to be sorted. Monash castigates the 43rd Battalion as the worst performed of his men, and Grimwade's artillery batteries are staying behind for more training.

But on 24 November Monash and his staff leave Charing Cross, bound for Folkestone and then Boulogne. Monash is plotting the destruction of all German resistance.

Chapter 20

*I hate the business of war and soldiering with a loathing that I
cannot describe – the awful horror of it, the waste, the destruction
and the inefficiency. Many a time I could have wished that wounds
or sickness, or a breakdown of health would have enabled me to retire
honourably from the field of action.*

MONASH ON THE THOUGHT OF BECOMING A FULL-TIME SOLDIER,
MARCH 1917[1]

*I have recently confirmed six death sentences … in some clear case of
cowardly desertion the law should take its course. One single execution
will stop the rot.*

MONASH ADVOCATING THE FIRING SQUAD FOR DESERTERS, JULY 1917[2]

THE TEMPERATURE is below freezing even at midday as
Monash makes his headquarters at Steenwerck, 25 kilometres
north of the French city of Lille. The 3rd Division has charge
of the Armentières sector of Flanders and is part of Godley's II
Anzac Corps under the 2nd British Army of Sir Hebert Plumer,[3]
a near-60-year-old with white hair and a walrus moustache.

Immediately upon arriving, Monash visits the frontline,
6 kilometres away. He and Eric Simonson pay their respects at
the grave of Harry Cathie, one of about 100 tucked in behind
hedges at a place called Wye Farm. The Hun has been quiet of

late, Monash tells his officers, but the Australians will soon start annoying their enemy.

Monash moves into a château complete with electric lights and hot running water that is already occupied by Captain Plouvier of the French Army. The Plouvier family make room for Monash, Farmar, Simonson and Jackson and their batmen. The house has three baths, so Monash can relax with a good soak when not getting shot at. Junior officers, grooms and drivers are housed in garden huts. Monash is well within earshot of the heavy German guns but tells Vic he is safe from attack apart from 'aeroplane bombs'.[4] An enemy plane is brought down on his first day in charge.[5]

He now commands 8 kilometres of the 150-kilometre British line, and has military and civil jurisdiction over two large towns, a dozen smaller villages and hundreds of hamlets. His command stretches back more than 30 kilometres from the front and takes in Bailleul, which has a fine officers' mess, and Armentières, now virtually a burned-out ghost town. Armentières is about the size of Geelong, Monash says, 'but with much finer buildings' which 'Fritz' bombs every day, so that the streets are deserted, and rows and rows of three-storey houses now stand like skeletons with roofs gone, windows shattered and their fronts blown out. Of the 30,000 who once lived there, only about 5000 have stayed, and merely because they are too poor to escape.[6]

On 12 December 1916, German Chancellor Theobald von Bethmann-Hollweg,[7] with Kaiser Wilhelm's approval, informs the Reichstag that Germany is prepared to enter into preliminary peace negotiations. It is just a ruse, though: the Kaiser wants to cause a backlash in his enemies' backyards, later admitting: 'we've got the English and the French governments in a nice predicament, trying to explain to their people why they don't make peace'.[8]

Hindenburg and Ludendorff force a return to unrestricted submarine warfare on 9 January 1917 and cause the dismissal of the Chancellor and other opponents of this policy. They plan to maintain the Prussian military elite's dominance over German society.[9] Hindenburg calls the Battle of Verdun – which has raged for most of the year, with 300,000 deaths – the 'beacon light of German valour', and he and Ludendorff retain a blind faith that their men can somehow still conquer the Western Front.

But as Monash looks about at the 'pathetic' scenes of destruction throughout Flanders, he predicts: 'Kaiser Bill is up against it at last, and he knows he's going to get it good and plenty.'[10]

Monash complains that the work of a divisional commander is 'very strenuous' and 'difficult to do properly',[11] but other Australian divisions fighting in the bloody Somme mock the 3rd's lack of battle action and call them 'The Neutrals' or 'The Deep Thinkers'.[12]

Birdwood visits Steenwerck on 17 December and stays two days, driving about, chatting to hundreds of the men, and especially seeking out those who were at Gallipoli. He tells Governor-General Munro Ferguson that Monash has proved to be a tremendous success and is 'quite a Napoleon in his language',[13] and that his men are the most disciplined of all five Australian divisions. Godley, Monash's commander, backs Birdwood, claiming the 3rd is the best division he's seen 'as regards smartness, discipline and general appearance', and that Monash is 'proving himself to be as capable and excellent a Divisional Commander as he was a Brigadier'.[14]

On 21 December, Haig arrives looking old and grey, having presided over half a million deaths of his men so far. He is a favourite of the palace even though the new British Prime Minister, David Lloyd George – like Billy Hughes, raised in Wales – has a disdain for his leadership.

Much to the annoyance of his men, Monash puts on a parade for Haig in the deep freeze, turning out his reserve brigade and detachments from all other units of the division for inspection in cold, hard rain. Haig has heard glowing reports about this Australian commander who so impressed the King, and calls him 'a clever Australian of Jewish type'.[15] He has been told Monash is an auctioneer in private life, but has him confused with Canadian general Arthur Currie.[16]

Haig and Monash ride together for the march past, and at the end Haig puts his arm around Monash's shoulder and tells him: 'You have a very fine Division. I wish you all sorts of good luck, old man.'[17] It is a rare gesture of warmth from a military commander of few words and long silences whose critics regard him as a butcher, sending masses to their doom.[18]

For six months, the main responsibility of the 3rd is defending its 8-kilometre line, which has become virtually impassable after winter snowfalls turn Monash's domain into a lake of mud. He can't leave the château without getting covered in slush from head to toe. The roads cannot cope with the wear and tear from men and machines, and before long the mud is ankle-deep in most places and in some parts up to the knees. Carts, wagons and automobiles splash through as best they can, but transports can't get within 3 kilometres of the front. It's even worse in the trenches, with streams and canals blocked and the whole country flooded, so that many of the soldiers are knee-deep for days on end in cold, icy mud and water. Everyone suffers from chilblains that are too severe even for the usual cures of whale oil, turpentine and other lotions.[19] Monash issues a card of instruction to his men on how to deal with trench feet, a condition that can necessitate amputation. The Australians are also hit with mumps, with as many as 300 men a week reporting ill.

Much of the division's work, beyond the fighting, involves securing the rows of trenches that support the frontline: keeping them drained, or trying to; repairing buildings after shelling; patching and building roads; and maintaining their supply of food, ammunition and heating fuel coming from the rail line at Steenwerck. The town's railhead is busier than the Spencer Street goods yard, with 2000 soldiers, 118 huge motor lorries and hundreds of mule-drawn wagons working every day in the mud and then heading out onto the narrow, congested country roads.

Monash implements anti-aircraft defences, wireless stations and a carrier pigeon dispatch service, complete with six lofts. There are also salvage stores, a building program to house more troops and a small hospital to treat minor illnesses.

He organises large communal baths made from brewing vats, and each day 2000 men, 20 at a time, wash away the mud, filth and lice infestations – while symbolically scrubbing away the horrors of war – to don clean boots, fresh underwear and fumigated uniforms, although usually patched and threadbare.[20] Monash has a supply of 6000 rubber gumboots, with 3000 in use at any one time, and he has a team collecting and replacing the used boots and socks with fresh ones on a daily basis. Two hundred local girls are employed in laundries, washing and ironing, working in steam so thick it seems impenetrable.

Much of the distribution of food to the cold and hungry men on the front is done at night for safety reasons, with the supplies carried on the backs of their comrades because the trenches are not wide enough for wagons. In boxes lined with straw, hot food and drinks – Oxo, coffee and cooking pots full of porridge and stews – are carried forward through the muck to the cold and hungry men. They cannot cook themselves lest their smoke draw enemy fire.[21]

Back from the line, Monash uses electric power from the tramways to light the empty factories and mills that are used to house most of his soldiers. In the engineering lecture theatre of a large technical school, the Ecole Professionnelle, he sets up a 500-seat cinema run by the Olympic swimmer Frank Beaurepaire, who is now with the YMCA after being invalided out of the AIF following a bout of appendicitis.[22] Monash makes Beaurepaire Sports Secretary and Amusement Manager, and also starts a pantomime company backed by the military bands. This is 'not an amateur show', Monash insists; these soldiers are 'real *artists* and their performances a high-class musical treat, staging operatic scenes, and putting on their numbers with full orchestral accompaniment and all the adjuncts of scenery, good lighting and appropriate costumes'.[23] All of the performers have their turn on the frontline, and one of the leading 'ladies' even performs with a piece of shrapnel in his neck.[24]

'It bucks the men up a lot,' Monash says, 'after a six-day tour in the trenches.' Many of the songs and jokes are directed at Monash and Godley but Monash, who attends once a week, says they are quite respectful and in good taste, and 'the men simply roar with delight'.[25]

Monash establishes his battle headquarters in the basement of the school amid a maze of telephone and telegraph wires and 27 interpreters. Although the kilometres of boggy terrain and rows of trenches and barbed-wire entanglements ensure there can be no massed attack from either side, there is constant sniping, regular raids and frequent shelling by artillery and mortar. In Armentières, Monash has artillery hidden away in factories, houses, schools and churches, so that it is impossible for the Germans to locate the source of their torment day and night.

He tries to relieve his frontline battalions every six days and limits the amount of continuous front trench duty for each man to a maximum of 48 hours in every 12 days.[26] The rest of the time they can rest or perform other duties in the supply chain. The complex system of trenches means it is at times possible for patrols from either side to enter and move for some distance along parts of the opposing trenches, only to find them empty. Snipers bag two or three Germans a day.

Back from the frontline, the 3rd Division are also responsible for policing their area, and while Monash insists his own men are 'thoroughly well disciplined', they and 50 gendarmes guard 400 German prisoners, direct traffic that can be 'more congested than Flemington Road on Cup Day',[27] catch spies, arrest looters and shut down the sales of illegal alcohol that seem to be conducted in every second house. The gendarmes also have to evict prostitutes, though not all the men are happy to see them go. There are large numbers of men guarding ammunition dumps, and the water pumping plant in Armentières.

Monash says much of the success of his command is due to picking the right men for the right jobs.[28]

On Christmas Eve and Christmas night, Monash's 33rd Battalion go on the attack while their general is getting ready for a 'very jolly little dinner' at the Château de la Motte. It is his third Christmas away from Vic and Bert, but Monash makes the most of the situation, dining on pheasant, champagne and liqueurs. The guests include a princess, a baroness, a countess, a prince, Generals White, Russell and Godley, and cavalry commander Sir Edmund Allenby. By 'common consent', no one mentions the war.[29]

Back at the front, though, no one can ignore it.

On New Year's Eve, a raid by the 11th Brigade runs into heavy machine-gun fire, and on 9 January the 39th Battalion make another raid, killing some Germans but suffering the loss of a Ballarat chemist named Lieutenant Wallace Gordon Jewkes. He gets the drop on five Germans, who put their hands in the air, yelling 'Comrade', but when Jewkes gets closer to take them prisoner, one of the Germans shoots him through the head. All five of the enemy are immediately cut down. 'It was a lesson to our boys', Monash says, 'to take no chances in the future.'[30]

Temperatures plummet to minus-9 Celsius and the sun is not visible for a week. The whole country is frozen hard. The mud becomes solid rock. Streams, drains, ponds and ditches are all masses of solid ice. Taps don't work.

The shelling and shooting continue.

On 28 January, more than 200 men from the 10th Brigade fight their way to the third German trench, despite heavy losses. Monash's front is widened to 11 kilometres.

By the end of the month, the 3rd Division has suffered more than 600 battle casualties, but has also landed its own damaging blows by men 'who were just magnificent'.[31] Brudenell White tells Monash: 'A respect for you which began in 1902 has gone on steadily increasing.'[32]

On 3 February 1917, Monash moves his headquarters a few kilometres south to the village of Croix-du-Bac.

Birdwood tells him, erroneously, that the AIF men voted against Hughes's conscription plan, and Monash will later be aggrieved to learn Minnie Behrend has embarrassed Vic by calling out to her while marching in an anti-conscription parade through Melbourne.[33]

Monash already has a collection of souvenirs to bring home: a Mauser pistol, a machine-gun barrel and a red and blue German field service cap with a hole in the middle. He anticipates he will soon have many more, with preparations going on throughout France on 'a stupendous scale' for 'very big events in the early Spring'.[34] The British are building hundreds of kilometres of railway lines and transporting 450,000 tons of food and ammunition to the front every week.

Monash begins preparations of his own for a raid that Bean will call 'the most important ever undertaken by Australians'.[35]

Throughout February, the 3rd Division launches five more battalion attacks and fends off three from the Germans. The Australian raiders leave behind leaflets in German telling the enemy to surrender, because things are about to go from bad to worse for them.[36] Monash is preparing his men for their biggest assault yet. It is to be undertaken on 27 February at Houplines, and will involve 824 men of the 10th Brigade, 20 of them officers, led by Lieutenant Colonel Charles Davis, a 'calm and invariably courteous' Bendigo barrister.[37]

Monash writes the orders and supervises the rehearsal. Smoke and poison gas shells will be used in the early bombing at 9.40 p.m., three hours before the raid begins. He rightly believes it will confuse the Germans into thinking that gas is present whenever they see smoke.

The gas is dispensed with when the final bombardment comes, but many Germans are still rushing for their gas masks and their defences are hampered. The raiders, wearing steel vests and carrying wire cutters, make their way across No Man's Land by the light of flares, backed by heavy artillery that forms a box barrage around the target area. The artillery is so accurate that one of the raiders says he could have toasted bread against it.

The raiders spend 35 minutes occupying the 800-metre line of the 23rd Bavarian Infantry Regiment, penetrating to the third trench. They kill as many as 200 of the enemy, take 17 of the luckier ones prisoner and capture a machine-gun, a searchlight and other valuable equipment.[38]

The raid is deemed a great success, although 30 Australians are killed and more than 100 are wounded, including Captain William Symons, who was awarded the Victoria Cross at Lone Pine.[39] Haig sends Monash a congratulatory telegram. Plumer comes down to decorate 35 men for bravery, and with Godley paying rapt attention, Monash lectures to his battalion and company commanders on his new methods of attack. Godley says it is the best lecture he has ever heard.[40]

Monash has his feet up 1200 kilometres away in the French Riviera on 13 March when 25 of his men from the 11th Brigade are killed raiding the German line.[41] Even though they are backed by the 2nd British Army's mobile artillery section, known as the 'Travelling Circus', the mission is a disaster, with the German trenches hardly entered.

Godley has given Monash a fortnight's leave, and Monash has left Alexander Jobson in temporary command, believing that while the Sydney accountant is 'far from being as efficient' as Monash would like, Jobson's 'active mind and great industry' compensate for his lack of military experience.[42] Monash is able to turn off the horrors of war like a tap and direct his mind to replenishment. He is in picturesque Menton in the south-east corner of France, looking out over the deep blue Mediterranean instead of the thick brown Flanders mud. He travelled down by car with Eric Simonson through a heavy snowstorm as far as Amiens, where he observed that the cathedral looked every bit as grand as it did in the painting of it at home in Iona. He spent four days in Paris and dined again at Maxim's, although the privations of the war are such that the waiters are now women – imagine that! He took in a revue at the Casino de Paris before journeying on to Marseilles and Toulon, and finally Menton. He has seen more sun here in a day than he did in weeks at Steenwerck, and has been sucking in the delightful smells of orange, lemon and olive.

Monash has been travelling incognito as a tourist, forgoing the chance to meet the Prince of Monaco, and instead thrills to *The Barber of Seville* at Monte Carlo's casino. The highlight is Elvira de Hidalgo as Rosina, her most famous role. 'She is a graceful little brunette,' Monash says, 'and although her voice has no great volume, it is the most exquisitely tuned and trained voice I have yet heard. She could not rise to Melba's pathos and swaying emotion, but in the lighter music of Rossini, I think she does as well.' Most of the grand hotels in Monte Carlo have become drab hospitals or convalescent homes, but there is nothing to spoil his view of the Maritime Alps or the seaside villages. All the time Monash is impressed by the politeness and egalitarian attitude of the French and their fighting men: '... both white and black ... from the exquisite of the Parisian Boulevards to the coal black Senegalese ... the majority are magnificent looking men, smart and soldierly'.[43]

The Allied Army in France is a 'glorious army', he tells Vic: 'its camaraderie, its prestige, its spirit and endurance, its morale and confidence are wonderful. It is an Army – British, Australian, Canadian and French – united in a bond of fellowship, such as there never was before in all history, and it is something to have lived for ... to have held a high command in such an army.'[44]

Monash is now the senior AIF commander on the Western Front. Legge has fallen badly out of favour with Haig and Birdwood over the poor performance of his 2nd Division at Pozières, and Monash finds Legge 'lazy and pedantic and quarrelsome'.[45]

Birdwood takes the opportunity when Legge is stricken with the flu to send him home. He is replaced by Sandhurst graduate Brigadier General Nevill Smyth,[46] who led the 1st Australian Infantry Brigade at the Battle of Lone Pine and received a Victoria Cross in the Sudan 20 years earlier.

McCay has also performed poorly on the Somme, and when he is granted medical leave for his neuralgia, Birdwood moves him sideways. He will eventually command the AIF depots in England.

Talbot Hobbs,[47] a Perth architect with 24 years' military experience as an artillery man, replaces him in commanding the 5th Division. Monash first met Hobbs as an engineer during his stay in the west all those years ago. William Holmes takes over the 4th Division from Herbert Cox, who having spent much of his career in India, has suffered badly through the European winter.[48]

Monash still wants more recognition. Upset that he did not receive a mention in dispatches in 1916, and worried that it might affect his standing, he asks Godley to praise him to Pearce. Godley tells him that the mention in dispatches only applies to soldiers serving on the Western Front at the time, and 'you can't have it both ways ... training and raising a new Division in England and at the same time be mentioned for fighting in France'.[49]

Monash wants the kudos rather than a career. Despite his seniority among Australian generals, he has no intention of soldiering beyond an armistice. The very idea of life in the military is anathema to him and he hates the whole bloody business of war. He tells Vic his only consolation over his involvement in the present conflict is 'the sense of faithfully doing my duty to my country, which has placed a grave responsibility on me; and to my Division, who trust and follow me, and I owe something to the 20,000 men whose lives and honour are placed in my hands ...'.[50]

Once his duty is done, he says, he'll turn his back 'once and for all on the possibility of ever again having to go through such an awful time'. If there were some administrative role in a peacetime Australian army of the future, he'd consider it, provided he had 'the freedom of an independent citizen', and only if it became necessary for his family's bread and butter. 'I have fought all my life for personal independence, and shall not give up what I have won, except as a last resort.'

He is aghast at Vic's suggestion that they let out Iona and move into something smaller. His one great wish, he says, is to be back in Toorak with her; Iona is the 'ideal home in which to spend our declining years in great personal ease and comfort'. Having devoted so many years to building up his fortune and establishing a comfortable home, it is a 'bitter thought' that someone else might live there.

'I wonder can you realize the deep yearning I feel for a few months' *peace* and quiet life, within the portals of my own home. To be rejoined to it and to you and Bert is my constant daily longing, and the extinction of that hope would make my present life of turmoil and strife and horror, almost unbearable.'[51] Vic sends him her photograph to put beside his bed and he tells her it is 'perfectly wonderful how you keep so young ... if I were not in love with you already, I am certain I should fall in love again'.[52]

By 23 March, Monash is back amid the 'mud and slush and cold winds and bare trees and bleak expanse of Flanders'.[53] As soon as he returns from the Riviera his divisional commanders meet to discuss plans to take the Messines Ridge in order to deny the German 4th Army the high country south of Ypres. He says it will give 'the Boche as nasty a knock as he has had yet anywhere'.[54]

On 26 March Monash's front is extended to 12 kilometres, to take in Ploegsteert Wood and Hill 63. America is now on the brink of entering the war after repeated U-boat attacks on her ships, and the German armies on the Somme have made a tactical retreat to the Hindenburg Line, a 140-kilometre defensive line between Arras and Laffaux, on the River Aisne, with a division every 7 kilometres. The withdrawal is called Operation Alberich, after the malicious dwarf of Richard Wagner's *Der Ring des Nibelungen*. The move has been designed to shorten the

German front and make their positions easier to defend. The troops employ a scorched-earth strategy as they depart – levelling villages, poisoning wells, chopping down trees, blowing up roads and bridges, and putting bombs and booby-traps in ruins and dugouts.[55]

At this point Monash becomes embroiled in a bitter political imbroglio back home after one of the parliamentarians in his division, Quartermaster Sergeant Alfred Ozanne, is given a medical discharge. Ozanne, the Federal Labor member for Corio, sought medical leave for nasal surgery as the division was about to embark for the war in France, and Monash was advised, perhaps erroneously, that this was Ozanne's way of seeking to avoid the bullets. Prime Minister Billy Hughes, leader of the Nationalist Party, has guaranteed that 'khaki seats' occupied by politicians at the front will not be opposed. But with the April Federal election looming, Hughes takes the opportunity to discredit Labor member Ozanne. Monash is asked to submit a report on Ozanne's case and replies that he believed the parliamentarian was virtually a deserter.[56] Without Monash knowing what is afoot, Hughes arranges publication of Monash's report, under Monash's signature, and the newspapers cut loose with headlines of 'Shirker or Deserter'[57] and 'If Guilty, Liable to Death'.[58] Ozanne's reputation is shattered, and he loses his seat to Hughes's candidate, Sergeant John Lister. Monash's reputation suffers too. One staff-sergeant based in Geelong is reprimanded for calling Monash 'a damned liar' at a public meeting to support Ozanne and Dr William Maloney, the Labor member for Melbourne, refers to Monash at public meetings as 'the cowardly German general',[59] The Federal Opposition Leader Frank Tudor, the Labor member for Yarra, says it is a 'cowardly thing' to stab Ozanne in the back. 'Why should Major General Monash have sent out a cable message concerning the affair five months after it had occurred,' he asks, 'and on the eve of a general election? It was done only for a political purpose.'[60] Ozanne sues the *Geelong Advertiser* newspaper for £5000 damages after it claims he was liable to the death penalty. His barrister, Joan Lazarus, later Australia's first female Queen's Counsel, tells the court that her client has not only lost his seat but has also been held up to public hatred, ridicule and contempt.[61] But Ozanne loses the case and is ordered to pay costs. He declares himself bankrupt.[62]

Monash has little sympathy for Ozanne, but a heavier burden is the thousands of young lives in his hands. His frustration rises every time he has to write letters to his soldiers' next of kin. On 6 April he pens a letter to Mrs Elsie Urquhart, whose husband Bill, a tiny 46-kilogram draughtsman, was killed on Christmas Eve and buried in Armentières. He gives Elsie his 'sincerest sympathy' for such 'a cruel blow' but he hopes she will be consoled by the fact that her husband, a lance corporal and bugler, 'played the part of a brave man, and that he fell nobly doing his duty in the defence of his country'.[63] Monash writes many similar letters, and also receives some from distraught family members. One Queensland widow, who has lost two sons in the war, writes begging him to withdraw her third boy from the line. Another writes to say of her son 'that please remember he is all I have'. He writes to Birdwood asking him to look into some of these cases.[64]

All of them have their effect on Monash. In letters to his friends and family he questions any notion of war's nobility. War 'is not a business in which one can take any pride or pleasure or even pretend to', he tells John Gibson back in Melbourne. 'Its horror, its inefficiency, its unspeakable cruelty and misery has always appalled me, but there is nothing to do but to set one's teeth and stick it out as long as one can.'[65]

He has written to Gibson because he is aggrieved that neither Gibson nor Percy Fairway has written to him in six months about the business he's left behind. Gibson has fallen out with Vic, after he reduced the pay of a clerk, who told Vic that her husband's company was being mismanaged. Monash has told Vic that Gibson 'is at heart the very best fellow I have ever met' and that it is a 'cruel injustice' to Gibson to suggest he does not have the Monashes' best interests at heart.[66] He tells Gibson that he is eternally grateful to him for the work he has done in his absence, but that Gibson will have to hold the reins of the company for a while longer, because Monash is 'living and moving every hour of the day and night in the midst of most tremendous events'.[67]

In an attack on the village of Bullecourt on 11 April, Holmes's 4th Division manages to penetrate the Hindenburg Line, but suffers more than 3300 casualties, with 1170 Australians taken prisoner: the largest number captured in a single battle throughout the war.[68] Many of the prisoners were treated abhorrently, starved and beaten and used as slave labour. During the course of the war, 310 Australian prisoners of the Germans, or about one in 12, died in captivity.[69]

The use of British tanks as cover for the infantry is a catastrophe – in Monash's view, partly due to the 'mechanical defects of the Tanks … partly to the inexperience of the crews'.[70] While tanks burn on the battlefield like lifeless dinosaurs, Major Percy Black, who started out as a private at Gallipoli, yells out to his men, 'Come on boys, bugger the tanks!'[71] as he leads a charge. He is shot through the head. His body is never found, despite a wholehearted search by his mate Harry Murray.

Between 9 and 12 April the sky all around Monash's headquarters is lit as though by a 'monster bushfire', and the earth trembles at continuous heavy cannon blasts.[72] Four divisions of the Canadian Corps battle three divisions of the German 6th Army in the opening stages of the Battle of Arras. French and British assaults around the Aisne will follow.

Monash moves his headquarters back to Steenwerck to prepare for what he calls the 3rd Division's big 'stunt', codenamed Magnum Opus.[73] After five months, he is able to relinquish control of the Armentières sector but more than ever he is ready for a fight. He is in the best physical shape he has been in for more than 20 years; his waist is now 37 inches and he can squeeze it down to 31½. Everyone tells him he looks 'hard as nails', and he feels 'young and vigorous and full of punch'.[74]

The Battle of Messines will be undertaken by Plumer's British 2nd Army, with 100,000 men to take the Wytschaete–Messines Ridge, the high ground south of Ypres. Winning the ridge is vital to the Allies' plans to launch a larger campaign east of Ypres.

There are three corps assigned to the objective: the British IX and X Corps and Godley's II Anzac, which contains Monash's 3rd Australian, the 25th British and the New Zealand Division. The 4th Australian Division are to be used as reinforcements.[75]

II Anzac will strike east and north-east from Hill 63 and Ploegsteert through Messines. Monash receives detailed proposals from his three brigade commanders – Cannan, whom he rates highly, McNicoll, who is 'a bit dour and acidy', and Grimwade, who has done 'great things' with his artillery. He then sits down to devise the attack in minute detail for each battalion, right down to the role of some platoons and even sections.[76] The plans come to resemble those of an enormous raid, rather than the kind of grinding offensive common to the war. Bean later concedes Monash's plans have 'an amount of thought and care far beyond that ever devoted to any other scheme of operations produced by a staff of the AIF'.[77]

As Monash waits for the battle to begin, he visits about a dozen glasshouses that remain intact at Steenwerck, admiring the ferns, mosses, maidenhair, pansies and fuchsias. He puts some of the flowers in a box to send to Vic as his writing table shakes with the blast of guns in the battle for Fresnoy, east of Arras.[78]

Monash visits General Arthur Currie, the portly knock-kneed auctioneer and failed Vancouver real estate investor with whom Haig confused him. Currie's men have just taken Vimy Ridge in the Battle of Arras and Monash calls it 'a truly astonishing feat'.[79] They exchange notes. Currie, according to two historians, is 'tall, wide in the beam, with his [belt] worn high over his paunch', and has a 'jowly, morose face'.[80] But his clear ideas on combat are impressive.

Monash is also visited by the twin daughters of his landlady from Croix-du-Bac, grieving the recent death of their father in Verdun but still able to make Monash laugh with their impressions, in fractured English, of Monash ordering his batman Dawson – or 'Dosson' as the girls pronounce it – to fetch his hat and stick.[81]

Monash clears his head every morning for the work ahead with a brisk walk around the garden of the château, and decorates his room with photos Vic sends him of Iona and his garden.

They make him think long and hard about the country he is fighting for. He rejoices in the success of Harry Chauvel in the Middle East and the talk that Chauvel will be made a lieutenant general in charge of a mounted corps in Egypt.

'Imagine an Australian rising to the rank of a corps commander?' he says.[82]

Monash constantly studies aerial photographs of the landscape around Messines, and sends out 36 circulars on the planned manoeuvres. The machine-gunners' instructions come in seven parts. Each brigade practises its attack in a training area, and two large models are set up of the battlefield showing in miniature the trenches, wire entanglements, streams, roads and ruins.[83]

Monash's troops are busy making roads, building tramways and railways, forming ammunition dumps, making gun emplacements and camouflaging them, laying a complex system of underground cables and fixing machine-gun positions.[84] The timetable for a co-ordinated burst of artillery, machine-guns and mortars has been planned to the second. Tunnellers have prepared huge mines to explode underneath the German defences. British fighter planes dogfight with the Germans to stop any reconnaissance.

Plumer visits on 15 May and again on 18 May to go over the plans. Godley meets with his divisional commanders. Haig arrives six days later and remarks that Monash is 'a clear headed determined Commander' who has thought of every detail.[85] All is done with the precision of civil engineering construction.[86] Monash has prepared carefully but he knows it is the German reaction that will determine whether the battle is a brilliant success or 'a bad hammering': 'attack always has everything against it, the defence always everything in its favour'.

'Whatever happens I have every confidence in the men, and I know they have in me. It just needs a bit of luck that's all.'[87]

The 3rd Division's operational orders for the Battle of Messines are issued on 27 May.

Night raiding parties suffer heavy casualties, but drag German prisoners back to the Anzac line for interrogation on the preparedness of the enemy.

On the eve of the great attack, Monash reminds his men of the cruelty of the Hun and how the Germans treated the prisoners they took at Bullecourt. His soldiers are to show no mercy.

Haig tells Monash that he has 30 per cent more firepower than has ever been used in war before, with 1500 field guns and 700 heavy guns,[88] a cannon for every 6 metres of front. Over 10 days, three and a half million shells, including poison gas shells, are fired at the enemy. The guns destroy every landmark in their way. Sides of mountains are blown apart and villages flattened.[89] The Germans do not have the same resources, but on the night of 3 June they pump an avalanche of gas bombs into Ploegsteert Wood, causing bedlam among the artillery there.

On the morning of 5 June, a German airman drops a bomb on an ammunition train of II Anzac at one of the specially built railheads at Bailleul, and carriages explode throughout the day. Seventeen similar trains arrive as replacements.[90]

The Germans know that a great attack is coming – the captured prisoners verify it – but the constant shelling confuses them as to the exact time of zero hour.

On 6 June, the night before the attack is to begin, Monash cannot sleep because of 'the excitement, mosquitoes and noise'.[91] The largest of the exploding mines, at Spanbroekmolen, has taken six months to dig and contains 41 tons of ammonal in a tunnel 27 metres deep.[92] Plumer's chief of staff, General Tim Harington, tells the press: 'Gentlemen, we may not make history tomorrow, but we shall certainly change the geography.'[93]

Monash's eight attack battalions prepare for their role in the offensive. They will be on the right flank, with Guy Russell's New Zealanders on the left.

Monash's men start their 5-kilometre approach through Ploegsteert Wood, but as many as 2000[94] are overcome by toxic fumes as the whine of flying gas shells fills the air and they burst all round. Some men are killed or wounded by flying nose-caps, or by the high explosive or incendiary shells that accompany the gas. Even though the Australians have won praise for their training using gas masks, they struggle to breathe, weighed down by ammunition, arms and equipment. Wounded and gassed men stumble about or are blown apart. Officers have to remove their masks to give orders. Mules and horses choke violently and gasp piteously for air.

The success of the operation depends on having the men in position 200 metres from the enemy at zero hour, 3.10 a.m. on 7 June. They press on and finally reach their position, where water has been placed for them. Some, exhausted, fall asleep for a few minutes.

At 3.05 the first tinge of dawn creeps over Messines. At 3.09, bleary eyes struggle to see the seconds tick down on their luminous watches.

At 3.10 a.m. the Canadian tunnellers hit the detonator switches.

The whole landscape explodes, one deafening roar after another.

Over the course of 20 seconds 19 mines go up, causing 'huge bubbles, swelling, mushroom-shaped, from the earth', then bursting 'to cast a molten, rosy glow' on the clouds of smoke they create.[95]

Ten thousand German troops are instantly annihilated by what seems like a massive rolling earthquake. The mine at Spanbroekmolen forms the Lone Tree Crater, 76 metres in diameter and 12 metres deep. Four of the mines are exploded in front of Monash's 9th Battalion, who charge through the dust and smoke, catching the Germans in a state of panic.

The 9th and 10th Brigades have to cross a small stream of the Douve River in No Man's Land that runs round the southern edge of Messines Ridge. Monash has calculated that it will be unfordable, and his lead battalion on that flank, the 40th, lays a number of small bridges. The following battalion, the 38th, crosses and seizes the southern shoulder of the Messines Ridge on the flank of the New Zealanders.

Monash has studied the aerial photos of every trench, wire entanglement, gun placement and machine-gun battery. The operation itself is 'child's play', he says, compared with the 'nightmare march' to get to the start line.[96]

The Germans have no chance. Lieutenant William Garrard, a Hobart schoolmaster, says he has never seen a people so demoralised: the terrified enemy, emerging from their foxholes and dugouts, are cowering and cringing like beaten animals.[97] The only real resistance comes from machine-gunners who fire on the 33rd Battalion, under Ballarat Gallipoli veteran Lieutenant Colonel Leslie Morshead.[98] Rifle grenades silence them.

Private John Carroll[99] of that battalion is awarded the Victoria Cross after charging a German trench and bayoneting four men. He then notices a comrade in difficulty and goes to help, killing a fifth German. Then he single-handedly attacks a machine-gun team, killing three of them and capturing the gun. Later, with two of his comrades buried by a shell, he manages to rescue them in spite of heavy shelling and machine-gun fire.

The first stage of the attack is over by 4.10 a.m., as the devastated countryside becomes more and more visible by the light of dawn. The New Zealanders occupy Messines. At 5.03 a.m., with the sun up, the second phase begins and the 9th and 10th Brigades reach their allotted positions in half an hour. The 37th Battalion is attacked supporting the New Zealand assault towards the German-held Oosttaverne Line, but Captain Robert Grieve[100] will also be awarded the VC after destroying two German machine-guns despite heavy fire and a sniper's bullet in the shoulder.

Under Monash's direction, the division readies for a counter-attack by readjusting artillery, mortar and machine-guns, and putting out more barbed wire. Monash lowers the congestion of men in the forward lines to reduce casualties from German artillery. By nightfall on 7 June, he believes his position is 'absolutely secure' on his new lines.[101] The next day the 10th Brigade suffers severe casualties from shelling but continues on to Potterie Farm, and the Germans pull back another 1600 metres.

Haig visits Monash on 9 June and Madame Jeanne Plouvier, his landlady from the chateau at Steenwerck, photographs the pair shaking hands. Haig confirms his original impression of Monash: '(evidently of Jewish descent) and by trade head of a Ferro-Concrete firm. He is a most practical and capable commander, and has done well.'[102] Godley writes to Pearce to praise Monash's brilliance,[103] and Bean will write that the 3rd Division has been altogether admirable in showing a 'spirited yet controlled advance in precise accordance with plan, in spite of the powerful effort of the German artillery to crush this flank during the approach march and afterwards'.[104] Monash is not impressed with Bean's summation of the battle, though, calling his reporting 'the apotheosis of banality' and his language 'silly tosh'.[105]

The 3rd Division is finally relieved on 12 June and the whole operation hailed a monumental success, with far fewer casualties than expected. It has been a powerful blow against the Germans: Erich Ludendorff admits it has cost the German Army dearly and drained German reserves from the Arras and Aisne fronts, which allows the French Army breathing space.[106]

However, Monash makes an example of the 37th's commanding officer, Walter Smith, relieving him of his command for 'considerable disorganisation' and a lack of leadership and energy. 'Under the stress of fighting, he personally lost control and grasp ... I do not feel disposed to risk the success of future operations by a repetition ...'[107]

Monash estimates he has fired more than £1 million worth of bombs and ammunition.[108] His division has taken 314 prisoners, including four officers, and captured 11 field guns, 27 machine-guns and 10 trench mortars.[109]

The severity of the fighting that the 3rd faced on its southern flank is reflected in the fact that II Anzac Corps has suffered more than half the 26,000 casualties incurred on the British side, and 4000 of them are from Monash's division. Most are men who were gassed and will later rejoin their units. About 600 have been killed. But Monash tells Godley a considerable amount of killing was done to the Germans in their front and support lines, both with the bayonet and via bombs in the dugouts.

A few days later, with the landscape around him in utter ruin, Monash sits at his writing desk and pens a note to Harold Farmar's seven-year-old daughter Susan, who has just sent him a photo of herself with her siblings, Mary and Hugh:

> Well, thank you very, very much; and also for the love you sent. How is the pony? … Tell Hugh that there are such a lot of very pretty butterflies here in France, and some lovely white moths.
> My kindest regards to your Mummie and Auntie Violet.
> Your friend
> John Monash[110]

Monash moves to Bailleul, but the fighting continues all around, and Paul Simonson's two batmen are killed as he leads his company in an attack on the Oosttaverne Line. When the Germans begin shelling the town of Nieppe, Monash sends in troops to evacuate 1400 old people, invalids and children, and to extinguish large fires in several factories.[111] Lieutenant Phil Schuler, a young journalist, dies from bullet wounds to the face, throat, arm and leg.[112] He covered the fighting at Gallipoli for the *Age*, which is edited by his father Frederick, before deciding to enlist.

'He was a most promising officer,' Monash tells Vic, 'I am deeply sorry for Schuler's parents.'[113]

General Robert Broadwood,[114] of the British 57th Division, who has taken over the Armentières section from Monash, is killed by a shell on 21 June, while walking with two of his staff in what Monash considered a safe place, and where he had often inspected his own batteries.[115]

Monash and Eric Simonson pay a visit to the Tank Battalion and have a long ride in one of those 'very wonderful and very terrible machines'.[116] Monash is then given leave and takes a 'delicious 10 days in London', preceded by a 'nerve-wracking' crossing of the Channel, in a fleet of fast steamers guarded by destroyers and seaplanes on the lookout for U-boats.

Food is in short supply in London, but there is plenty of entertainment, and for his 52nd birthday Eric and Paul Simonson take him to see the Melbourne Grammar School old boy Oscar Asche in his record-breaking musical *Chu Chin Chow* at His Majesty's. Monash also goes to see the opera *Aïda*, and takes Walter and Lou to watch the Gladys Cooper farce *Wanted: A Husband*. He thinks it might cheer Lou up, because she is perpetually sour, the high prices and shortage of food doing nothing for her mood.[117] He tells his youngest sister that happiness comes from within, and that 'you must try – you must really – to cultivate a placid temperament, and put yourself under a strong discipline so as not to allow outside happenings to worry, irritate and arouse you'.[118]

He and Lizzie Bentwitch celebrate his birthday privately, at a Chelsea restaurant close to the Thames. He is careful to keep their meetings secret from Walter and Lou. Monash and Lizzie have a good laugh at Madge Titheradge in *General Post*, and at a revue called *Bubbly* starring Teddie Gerard and Shirley Kellogg.[119]

At 10.30 p.m. on 7 July, Monash watches an air raid from his suite at the Prince's Hotel in Piccadilly. The attack is all over in just three minutes, and the biggest 'noise and excitement' is that made afterwards 'in the newspapers'. Still, he continues to tell Vic that London is no place for her. He goes shopping in Bond Street for pearls for Vic. And for Lizzie.

He travels to Larkhill to visit McCay, who tells Monash that he has become an 'old man' and will no longer be any good for active service. Monash finds his old friendship 'strongly revived' during his few hours with his school rival, and comments that despite 'the adverse repute in which [McCay] seems to be universally held', he shows all 'his old clearness of grasp and power, and was as nice and amiable and friendly as it was possible for any one to be'.[120]

During Monash's time in London, General William Holmes,[121] Commander of the 4th Division, is killed by a German shell while showing the Premier of New South Wales, William Holman, the ground won at Messines. Monash is distressed by the death of a man he considered 'a real good fellow'; his distress is accentuated by a spat only a few days earlier, when Holmes took offence over what seemed a trivial breach of military etiquette. The King's uncle, the Duke of Connaught, was inspecting a parade of the 3rd and 4th Divisions in Bailleul's town square when Monash presented the 4th Brigade's Gallipoli VC recipients, Harry Murray and Bert Jacka. Holmes fumed that Monash was trying to upstage him, and that Monash had 'abruptly interposed' himself and made the presentation without Holmes's permission or consent.[122] Holmes rejected Monash's explanation that Godley had motioned for him to do so, and said he would take the matter higher. He does not live to see the outcome.

Sinclair-Maclagan takes over the 4th, leaving Monash and Chauvel as the only Australian-born divisional commanders.

Monash returns to Bailleul to be given command of II Anzac for three weeks, in the absence of Godley and Russell. Under increased shelling, he moves his headquarters a few kilometres back, where he entertains Haig again and readily accepts the field marshal's praise. Birdwood tells him that Haig has a very high opinion of him and has gone out of his way to express it, something that is rare from Haig.

Monash suspects that there is 'some change afoot' over the higher commands. 'There have been vague rumours for some time in well-informed circles of a contemplated regrouping of the Australian forces', he tells Vic, and there is talk Birdwood may get an army command, leaving a corps command for Monash. 'As I am senior Australian officer in France, the gossips have naturally coupled my name with these rumours.'[123]

For more than a year, Prime Minister Billy Hughes has been pushing for an Australian corps to be commanded by an Australian, and the feeling from government and within the AIF has intensified during 1917.

In London, Keith Murdoch has won powerful and influential friends, including the newspaper tycoon Lord Northcliffe, and 'almost every important member of the Asquith Government'.[124] According to Bean, Murdoch is now the intermediary between Prime Ministers Hughes and Lloyd George; 'moreover, Hughes [relies] almost exclusively upon Murdoch's advice as to the political interests of himself and his party among men and officers of the AIF'.[125] After heavy Australian losses at Bullecourt and Fromelles, Murdoch and Andrew Fisher, now the British High Commissioner, cable Hughes to urge him to maintain his rage against the British Government, and to fight for an Australian corps. Murdoch and Bean tell Lloyd George that the one great motive of the Australian people in this war is nationalism.

Meanwhile, Monash busies himself with the administrative work of a corps commander from his new base, inside a medieval tower in the village of Ravelsberg. He's proud that discipline in his 3rd Division is an example to the rest of the corps, but he approves six death sentences for men of the 4th Division convicted of cowardice or desertion, and is aggrieved when they have to be commuted to 10 years' jail because the Australian Government will not condone executions in the AIF. He complains to Plumer about it, and resolves to write to Pearce to 'strongly urge' that in clear cases of 'cowardly desertion' firing squads be used. 'One single execution will stop the rot,' he says.[126]

He remains impressed by the French soldiers, and assures Vic that they are not 'short and of poor physique' the way they may be portrayed at home. 'This does apply to the Belgians,' he says, 'but the French are for the most part tall, handsome and graceful and if short, are usually very sturdy. The same cannot be said of most of the English raised regiments.'[127]

Almost immediately, though, Monash has weightier matters to occupy him. The victory at Messines has set the ball rolling for Haig's massive British offensive at the Passchendaele Ridge near Ypres, designed to grind down German resistance, shut down their supply chain at the Roulers railway junction and secure the Belgian coast all the way to Holland. Passchendaele will become known as the Third Battle for Ypres. It is a controversial plan but Haig finally gains approval from the British Government even though there will be little support from the French, whose armies are temporarily racked by rebellions. A huge Allied bombing campaign begins around Ypres on 15 July.

Two of Monash's brigades, the 9th and 11th, are assigned subsidiary roles as part of the 2nd Army's feint at Lille, a diversionary battle for the real assault around the ridges of Passchendaele. They are to be part of an attack 20 kilometres to the south at Warneton and for 18 days, the 11th Brigade works on a new system of trenches, with water up to their waists and under heavy shelling. The battle is launched in earnest on 31 July. The Germans have held the strategic ground at Windmill Ridge as the 9th Brigade under finance writer and brigadier, Alexander Jobson, made a series of attacks, but just before dawn on 31 July, the 11th takes the ridge, suffering 550 casualties. One of the casualties from the attack is Brigadier Jobson, whose nerves are shot. Monash tells him that as divisional commander his duties 'involve many painful and disagreeable tasks' and out of 'motives of sincere regard ... and in terms of the utmost candour' Jobson is finished.

'My dear Jobson,' Monash writes, 'I have regretfully come to the conclusion that the stress of the last few weeks has told so heavily upon you, that it has seriously impaired your efficiency as a Brigade Commander ... I have lost confidence in your ability to see this thing through [but] ... I particularly do not wish to do anything harsh and least of all to have to say anything officially which may reflect upon you hereafter.'[128] Jobson is allowed to resign with dignity.

Monash though is going from strength to strength.

He uses triplanes flying at just 150 metres to chart the progress of his infantry, with an observer in each plane sketching the layout then dropping it back over headquarters. The reports arrive an hour faster than by any other means.[129]

Monash orders his men to take as many prisoners as possible. Farmar later recalls a private who has been so affected by the order that he turns up at divisional headquarters, saying, 'You Mr Monash? You wants some Fritzies? Well, I've brought you two', and pointing to a pair of bedraggled Germans nearby. Monash ferries the soldier back to the front in his car.[130] Another time Farmar recalls an inspection by Haig when a chubby Jewish officer is thrown by his horse during the preparations. That night, as is customary, Monash reads out the weather report, beginning with: 'A heavy dew fell this morning.' Monash and his men then fall about with laughter.[131]

Despite the 11th Brigade taking Windmill Ridge, Plumer is still critical of aspects of the attack, saying that for some commanders it was their 'first experience of semi-open warfare carried out on a wide front and they showed clearly that such operations require even more attention to details than those usually described as trench warfare'.[132] In reply, Monash writes a long review outlining his strategies for attack and defence against counter-attacks. On 9 August the 3rd Division is relieved, and Monash is happy to let Sinclair-Maclagan's 4th Division take charge. Although Haig and Plumer issue orders for Monash's men to be regrouped into full battle strength with the addition of 3000 more fighting men as soon as possible, most of the division moves to Bléquin and Lumbres near seaside Boulogne for six weeks' training and reorganisation in 'beautiful rolling country, mostly in beautiful autumn sunshine'.[133]

First, though, Monash takes the opportunity to climb to a vantage point on the Belgian peak Scherpenberg at dawn to see the second phase of the fighting at Ypres, an artillery spectacle across a 25-kilometre line to the sea that is 'magnificent and terrifying, putting into the shade the most terrible lightning and thunder storm ever witnessed. The whole country simply trembled.'[134]

The British advance on Ypres becomes bogged down in torrential rain, and plans will eventually be drawn for Plumer's army to begin another campaign in the same area.

Monash moves his headquarters to the Château d'Hervarre near Fauquembergues, 40 kilometres from Boulogne, and his men revel in their time away from the front. Birdwood has not been in favour with the War Office since the drowning of Kitchener, his great ally, and there is more talk that all the senior English brass at II Anzac Corps under Godley will be replaced with Australian commanders.

Paul Simonson takes over as Monash's senior aide after Eric decides to join the Australian Flying Corps, but before he leaves, Eric drives Monash over the plains of Picardy to inspect the troops. They can only get 'third rate accommodation at exorbitant prices', and the surf at Dieppe is nothing like Manly or Sandown, but the countryside is glorious. Monash tells Vic that if the Russians had not imploded on the Eastern Front the war would be over by now, but that it won't be much longer 'given the immense American effort is still to come'.[135] The Americans had declared war on Germany four months earlier but their numbers in Europe are still a trickle. The great American military wave is building, though, and about to be unleashed.

Monash tells his family not to worry about Eric in the air force, as flying is now much safer than motoring and the planes are very stable. In a misguided attempt to comfort them, he relates a story about a two-man Australian fighter crew who were killed by the same bullet. Their plane flew for '100 miles [and] safely landed but with both pilot and observer killed. The machine had flown for about three hours, all by itself … and had made a smooth safe landing … That will show you how reliable the modern machines are.'[136]

The rumours about the Australianisation of the AIF at the expense of British officers prove correct, and Monash is forced to relinquish Harold Farmar to the 35th Division. Farmar tells Monash that he will always be grateful for the 'inspiration of loyal devotion' Monash has given him during their 14 months together, and that under Monash's command he has realised that the 'poorest instrument will respond unexpectedly well with a master touch'.[137] Later he will say that Monash is 'a genius', instilling confidence in every man in the division, but that despite his superb brain he remains a man 'of most humble mind', bringing all involved in a project into his confidence, giving every man a share in a job and the responsibility for his part.[138]

Monash and George Jackson make the most of their break from the action. They visit a camouflage factory just north of Boulogne where hundreds of French and Chinese women create items to disguise the Allied troops, things that look like shattered trees but are really observation posts made of iron surrounded by branches, telegraph poles that are really periscopes, fake haystacks that are gun pits, even papier-mâché models of soldiers' heads to draw German fire. Monash lunches with the daughters of Sir Arthur Lawley, the late Governor of Western Australia. One is a maid of honour to the Queen, and both are army nurses, spending nine hours a day in operating theatres.

He pays a visit to the machine-gun depot at Camiers, but admits that it's really just an excuse for an outing to the famous watering hole Paris-Plage, where everything is designed on the 'most luxurious and extravagant scale' and 'all the shops appear to cater only for the wealthiest classes'. At a military horse show he is seated between 'two very pretty women': the Marquise d'Armaille, the president of the show, and the Duchess of Westminster, 'young, and very beautiful with golden hair and large blue eyes', who is running a hospital in the local casino. Monash has them giggling when he tells the Marquise she is speaking French 'like a machine-gun' – so fast he can't follow.[139]

On 22 September, Haig motors 40 kilometres north from his headquarters at the Château de Beaurepaire near Etaples in a convoy of two Rolls-Royces – he always travels with a spare car in case his breaks down. He watches Monash parade 12,000 of his men at Blequin, inland from Boulogne. Naturally, Monash says the parade is a 'brilliant success', and the field marshal stays chatting to him and his senior officers for an hour.

Haig likes the cut of this man, and invites Monash to dinner with two of his generals behind locked doors at his headquarters, to discuss the continued plans for Passchendaele and the role Monash might play.[140] Haig tells Paul Simonson, 'Your uncle is a great man.'

Monash then hosts Matron Kellett[141] and a dozen of her nurses, most of whom have been tending to the Anzacs since they first arrived in Egypt. The following day he visits their No. 25 General Hospital in the coastal village of Hardelot Plage and is introduced to the wife and two daughters of the French aviator Louis Blériot, who has a villa nearby. Blériot had accelerated the arms race in Europe back in 1909 when he became the first man to fly across the English Channel, proving that England was now vulnerable to attack from the air.

Now, in the skies above France there is the constant buzz of fighter planes, Allied and German, dog-fighting and flying low for reconnaissance. Baron Manfred von Richthofen and his comrades Hermann Göring and Ernst Udet are like hungry eagles swooping on prey. But 60 kilometres north, near Ostend, the Germans lose one of their fighter pilots on 5 September, when Lieutenant Franz Pernet's Albatros is shot down and crashes into the sea. Pernet's body washes ashore in the Netherlands weeks later.

He is Erich Ludendorff's stepson, and the seemingly aloof and unflinching general begins to understand the intense pain felt by so many families on both sides.

In one of Franz's last letters, he wrote to Margarethe Ludendorff: 'Mother, you can't imagine what a heavenly feeling it is when all the day's fighting is successfully over, to lie in bed and say to oneself before going to sleep "Thank God you have another 12 hours to live".'[142]

Chapter 21

*[Monash's] ambition makes him an underground engineer: he has
the Jewish capacity of worming silently into favour without seeming
to take any steps towards it, although many are beginning to
suspect that he does take steps ... Besides we do not want Australia
represented by men mainly because of their ability, natural and inborn
in Jews, to push themselves.*
C.E.W. BEAN, OFFICIAL HISTORIAN OF THE AIF[1]

*The town of Ypres, once a marvel of medieval architectural beauty, lies all
around us ... For three years it has been dying a lingering death and
now there is nothing left of its fine streets, its great square, its cathedral,
the historic Cloth Hall ... but a charred collection of pitiable ruins.*
MONASH ON THE EFFECTS OF GERMAN BOMBING[2]

THE RATS AND MICE are rampant down here in the
tunnels beneath the ancient town of Ypres. It is cold and
dank, and the smell of decay is enough to make Monash retch.
Above ground, the wreckage of what were once grand medieval
buildings and spires, founded upon the wealth of cloth-weaving,
topples into dust day after day. Monash estimates it has cost the
Germans much more in ammunition to destroy Ypres than it cost
the Flemish to build it.

The once ornate town is in ruins, yet strategically it remains vital to both sides in the war, because what's still left stands precariously between the Germans and the Channel ports.

Monash makes his new headquarters in a series of underground chambers near the Menin Gate, safe from the constant shelling. He will live beside the rats for three weeks.

Above the tunnels the traffic is chaotic – busier, he says, than Elizabeth Street, Melbourne, after the last race on Melbourne Cup day. Soldiers in tin helmets heading to the front, Chinese coolies, heavily laden mules, convoys of motor lorries, dispatch riders on motorbikes, generals in limousines, horses and wagons, motor ambulances, traction engines pulling huge howitzer cannons, and every now and then a Royal Flying Corps automobile carrying aeroplane parts, all move at a snail's pace in both directions through the rubble, in 'a never halting, never ending stream'.[3]

The 3rd Division has arrived in Ypres on 1 October after having marched 80 kilometres inland from Bléquin and nearby Lumbres over five days for an intended assault by the two Anzac corps on 6 October. The Allies have already made massive strikes in the area, in the Battle of the Menin Road Ridge, starting on 20 September, and the Battle of Polygon Wood, which began six days later. Now Plumer wants to take the Broodseinde Ridge, which is a barrier to further attacks eastward. The Anzacs will join the massed attack of the 2nd and 5th Armies. Plumer has ordered 'bite-and-hold' tactics, grabbing limited objectives that can be held against German counter-attacks.

With winter looming, the operation is brought forward to daybreak on 4 October. Monash has just three days to make his preparations and bring his assault troops into their positions for this, the Third Battle of Ypres. There will be 12 Allied divisions attacking, and the four Anzac divisions will be side by side in the frontline for the first time. Despite his scorn for Monash's flashiness, Bean will concede that his men 'look magnificent'.[4]

On 3 October, the day before the attack, there is heavy rain and squalls. Monash tells his troops that if the Germans charge first, they are not to go forward to meet them, but should hold their positions and let the artillery kill all the Huns it can; the infantry will then pick off the survivors.

That night, the Anzacs take refuge in shell holes in drizzling rain. With Keith Murdoch and Charles Bean watching and taking notes from a ridge just behind the Australian line, Monash's two attacking brigades, the 10th and 11th, have to make their way through the slush across the sodden Zonnebeke Valley, as most of the temporary duckboard bridges have been blown apart by shelling.

The Anzac attack is set for 6 a.m., but in the half-light the Germans send up occasional white illumination flares. Bean says that in the mist they look 'dull and glazed like fishes' eyes'.[5] The Germans have been planning their own attack for 6 a.m., codenamed Operation Hohensturm, and at 5.20 a.m. they begin sending up sheafs of yellow flares 'like a bunch of grapes'. A few minutes later they begin a huge artillery barrage that makes a noise like great empty biscuit tins banging about.[6]

One in seven men from the 1st and 2nd Divisions is killed or wounded in the initial bombing. The ground is so wet that the exploding shells send up steam rather than dust. Half an hour later, the Allied barrage responds, but as the Anzacs continue their advance they find Germans charging out to meet them with fixed bayonets.

The 43rd Battalion are hit by machine-gun fire from a concrete pillbox near Zonnebeke Station, but together with the 37th they make it over a crest and into the next valley, from which the Gravenstafel Spur rises. This is the first objective for Monash's troops.

Firing a Lewis machine-gun from his hip, Castlemaine-born foundry worker Lance Corporal Wally Peeler[7] of the 37th Battalion wipes out four German machine-gun posts in an hour, killing 30 enemy soldiers.[8] The 37th and 43rd Battalions dig in, while the 38th and 42nd move forward.

Parties of the 11th Brigade go about gathering prisoners along the railway line in 'swarms beyond all previous experience of the

AIF, rounding them up from every pillbox and other shelters'.[9] The 41st and 44th Battalions are temporarily halted by wire in the bog. The 40th Battalion from Tasmania comes in for withering blasts from 10 machine-guns, which stall their advance, 270 metres from their objective on the ridge. Olympic sculler and Military Cross recipient Captain Cecil McVilly,[10] from Hobart, already wounded, is shot again directing his troops. He somehow survives.

With McVilly out of action, Sergeant Lewis McGee,[11] an engine driver with a young wife and daughter, takes his handgun, races alone to the nearest concrete pillbox 50 metres away, shoots the machine-gun crew and takes the remaining soldiers in the garrison as prisoners.[12] McGee has recently been recommended for a commission, and no wonder, as he then races back to his men and leads his platoon, to take control of their side of the Broodseinde Ridge. They line up 300 prisoners along the way.

By 9.15 the 3rd Division is digging, under the cover of its artillery, what Bean calls 'perhaps the most complete and accurately-sited front and support lines ever made by Australians in battle'.[13] The decaying corpses of British soldiers killed here three years ago are still visible. Some members of the 41st chance their luck and continue 200 metres past the objective to the Kerselaarhoek Cemetery, but are immediately ordered back after Monash rebukes their brigadier, Bull Cannan, fearing that they will be caught by friendly fire.[14] Lewis McGee and Walter Peeler will both be awarded the Victoria Cross.

Five thousand German prisoners are taken along the whole front. Bean interviews one of them, a brigade commander, who is being fed cups of tea to help ease the discomfort from a bullet wound in his arm that is gushing blood. The Australians chop off his shoulder straps as souvenirs.

'Your men are funny,' the German officer tells Bean. 'They rob while they fight.'[15]

Despite a heavy toll of casualties, the exercise at Ypres has been a magnificent success for Monash, and Passchendaele beckons.

He cables Melbourne with the words of Haig: 'GREATEST BATTLE OF WAR.'[16] It is the first significant victory for the AIF, and Monash declares 'there has been no finer feat'[17] in the campaign.

The Germans call it a 'black day',[18] and Ludendorff says it has been 'extraordinarily severe' on Germany, causing 'enormous losses', 35,000 casualties and as many as 25,000 deaths.[19] The fighting has taken a heavy toll on the Allies as well: 20,000 casualties for the gain of about 1000 metres. The Australians number their dead or wounded at 6423 and the New Zealanders at 1853.

Monash's 3rd Division has suffered 1810 casualties, or just over a quarter of its troops sent into battle, but Monash is keen to go again immediately. Plumer, who prefers to take small, manageable bites, applies the brakes. Monash hands over his captured territory to the British 66th Division on 7 October and withdraws his infantry to prepare for a follow-up strike.

'Great happenings are possible in the very near future,' Monash tells Vic, 'as the enemy is terribly disorganized and it is doubtful if his railway facilities are good enough to enable him to re-establish himself before our next two blows, which will follow very shortly, and will be very severe … my next objective will be Passchendaele.'[20]

Plumer and Harington tell Monash that what he has done has been extraordinary, that none of the other divisions on the Western Front could have marched for five days and then on three days' notice 'carried out so big a task so completely and with such perfect synchronisation and small losses'.[21]

Haig now wants to strike again at Passchendaele on 9 October, but the rain continues. It becomes like a cloudburst on 8 October, and a weather report says a tempest is hurtling towards Flanders from the west of Ireland.

Haig now makes the most questioned decision of his career: rolling the dice in the belief that the enthusiasm of the men will be able to overcome the horrific conditions. He decides to wager all the human poker chips he has and drive the Allies on, regardless of the weather. Godley supports him but Plumer, Harington and Birdwood – who knows his men are exhausted – want to wait for clear skies. Yet Haig insists that the Germans will crumble with just a little more pressure.

The approaches to Passchendaele are like a swamp, but Haig orders two cavalry divisions to be within a day's march of the battlefront, with the rest of the Cavalry Corps, less one division, ready to follow.[22]

Drenching rain continues, and when Nevill Smyth's 2nd Australian Division joins the Allied attack on 9 October, across a 12,300-metre front from south of Broodseinde to St Jansbeek, they look like men who have been buried alive and dug up again.

The attack will be known as the Battle of Poelcappelle, after a village on the front controlled by General Hubert Gough's British 5th Army.[23] Heavy casualties are suffered on both sides. Advances made are lost to German counter-attacks in the heavy rain. The men are tired and slow, every step an act of dragging one stuck foot out of the mud. Machine-guns jam, mud has to be scraped off shells before they can be fired, carrier pigeons are too wet to fly. It is impossible to obtain decent aerial photographs.

Even on the roads, hundreds of pack mules constantly flounder in deep shell holes, which are impossible to detect under the covering of thick, slimy mud. Many animals are shot when they can't get out quickly. Often men are dragged out of the mud minus their boots and breeches. The water is so toxic that many vomit after going under.[24]

Haig still has plenty of men to use as collateral, and on 12 October he tries his luck again. Monash's 3rd Division, with the New Zealanders on their left and the 4th Division on their right, set out for the First Battle of Passchendaele and a proposed 2000-metre advance. The operation is to be performed in three stages, and the soldiers are given a timetable of six and a half hours that requires a faster speed in the mud than could be achieved in the dry. Monash pleads for a 24-hour postponement,[25] but Haig is insistent that every hour's delay gives the Germans breathing space the Allies can't afford.

Bean interviews Haig on the eve of the battle, in surroundings far different from the mud flats in front of Passchendaele where Australians will soon be dying. The two men sit in gilt-edged Louis XVI chairs. Haig tells Bean that the Australians have some wonderful commanders, and he is especially impressed with Monash, 'a very solid man' who has 'made a great success of everything he has touched'.[26] Bean almost chokes. He knows Haig is thinking of an Australian corps, and as capable as Monash might be, Bean does not want a pushy Jew in the top job.

Bean tells Haig that Birdwood is doing a marvellous job already as the corps commander, and the Australians trust him. It would be a pity to change the order of things. Haig tells him the plan is to have an Australian as the commander of an Australian corps. Bean tells him if that's the case, Bean's hero Brudenell White is the 'greatest soldier we have by a long way'.[27]

Crown Prince Rupprecht of Bavaria, the German commander at Passchendaele, looks out at the teeming deluge in front of him and writes in his diary: 'Most gratifyingly – rain; our most effective ally.'[28] The tents for Monash's two attacking brigades do not arrive in time, so on the night of 10 October his men have to sleep in the open near Potijze, east of Ypres, sheltering under waterproof sheets, or pieces of old iron or timber. Ammunition is scarce because of the weather and many of the heavy guns become bogged on the way to their positions. The artillery fire will be inadequate. General Gough tries to have the attack put off, but Haig is insistent.

Monash's 3rd Division is to march on the Passchendaele Ridge and take a position 400 metres further on. His 10th Brigade will have to negotiate the flooded stream of the Ravebeek Valley. The 38th Battalion, carrying a flag to fly from Passchendaele church, is tasked with capturing the village.

The march to the attacking line starts at 6 p.m. on 11 October, and at 3 a.m. the men arrive for zero hour in the cold and dark and heavy rain.

At 4.20 a.m. the rain stops, to be followed by a light fall of British shells on the German positions: a salvo that is hardly any protection at all for the advance that begins at 5.25 a.m. The 9th Brigade goes forward in utter confusion, trapped by the sticky mess underfoot and defenceless against machine-gun reprisals. Some of the men of the 10th Brigade even drown as they wade along trying to take cover, from one shell hole to the next. Each stretcher case requires 16 bearers, in relays of four each, over a distance of almost 4000 metres.[29]

The 9th Brigade's Captain Clarence Jeffries,[30] a mining surveyor from Wallsend, New South Wales, distinguishes himself throughout the day, rushing one concrete pillbox, capturing four machine-guns and 35 prisoners, and then leading his company forward under extremely heavy enemy fire to take another machine-gun emplacement and capture two guns and 30 more prisoners. His actions earn him a Victoria Cross. He is killed later in the day.

About 20 men, mostly from the 38th Battalion, reach the Passchendaele church at the edge of town, but lacking support they are forced to withdraw.[31] So too are the men of the 4th Division who make it to their objective on the Keiberg Spur.

Monash, directing operations from Ypres, where even the tunnels are luxury compared with the mud, is delighted with the early reports coming from the battle as his men reach their objectives and send back 351 prisoners. As the day goes on, though, the reports become less frequent and more alarming. Two reconnaissance planes are brought down and messages are delayed by the weather. Shortly after midday the 40th Battalion starts sending messages back by a flashing lamp from a captured pillbox, saying that the casualties have been heavy. The two recent Victoria Cross recipients, Lewis McGee and Walter Peeler, have both been shot: Peeler in the right arm and McGee, fatally, in the head.

The 36th Battalion sends back messages of distress by pigeons, which somehow get through the storm.[32] Monash arranges for artillery support, but the field commanders are already bringing back their devastated troops – or what's left of them. Guy Russell's New Zealand Division has been annihilated, unable to overcome the Ravebeek mud, the dense wire that has just been laid and the relentless machine-gun fire. In terms of lives lost it is the worst day in New Zealand's history, with 845 dead among the division's 2735 casualties. Monash tallies 3199 casualties in his 3rd Division, while the 4th Division counts 1000.

Writing from his tunnel, and defying the censors as he usually does, Monash tells Walter Rosenhain that just eight days after his great triumph at Broodseinde, Passchendaele has been a tragedy. But the plan 'was fully justified', he says, 'and would have succeeded in normal weather conditions' because his men and the New Zealanders are first-class soldiers. With 48 hours' preparation instead of 24 they could have done it, he says. The weather has been so bad that there has been 'no flying and no photographing, no definite information on the German re-dispositions, no effective bombardment, no opportunity of replenishing our ammunition dumps ... [yet] Higher Command insisted on going on ...'.[33]

As far as Monash is concerned, his men are now being put into the 'hottest fighting' and being 'sacrificed in hair-brained [sic] ventures',[34] and there is no one in the War Cabinet to lift a voice in protest.

Funerals keep Monash busy for the next few days.

On 16 October, he is at the grave site of his friend Major William Adams DSO,[35] at the Ypres Reservoir North Cemetery, just behind the burned-out ruins of the great Cloth Hall. The overworked Chaplain George Percival Cuttriss begins his eulogy with:

Here where thou liest, there is no sound of war
Nor any echo of the Huns' fierce hate.[36]

The 3rd Division holds its position around Ypres until the men can be relieved, and according to Bean they are 'shelled to hell'.[37] The Germans send over bombardments of high explosives, mixed with exploding canisters of 'sneezing gas' (diphenyl chlorarsine). Ludendorff calls it the *Maskenbrecher* (mask breaker), because it makes it hard for the victims to keep their respirators on, and the attack is then followed by a wave of mustard gas (dichlorethyl sulphide). Over four nights, the valleys behind the Anzac lines are drenched with toxic fumes, causing hundreds of choking, blistered casualties.

Monash says Australia's interests in the war are suffering badly because it is not represented in the War Cabinet.[38] His 3rd Division comes under the temporary control of Canadian General Currie, who, with much more time to prepare than the Australians, finally takes Passchendaele on 10 November.

More than 15,600 Canadians are killed or wounded among 275,000 casualties suffered under British command in the fight to eventually take Passchendaele. The Germans tally 220,000 killed or wounded.

Ludendorff writes that the suffering on both sides at Passchendaele has been worse than eternal damnation:

> Enormous masses of ammunition, such as the human mind had never imagined before the war, were hurled upon the bodies of men who passed a miserable existence scattered about in mud-filled shell-holes. The horror of the shell-hole area of Verdun was surpassed. It was no longer life at all. It was mere unspeakable suffering. And through this world of mud the attackers dragged themselves, slowly but steadily, and in dense masses. Caught in the advanced zone of our hail of fire they often collapsed, and the lonely man in the shell-hole breathed again. Then the mass came on again. Man fought against man, and only too often the mass was successful.[39]

Passchendaele has devastated Australia's infantry divisions in France, taking out more than half their ranks. Of the 55,000 casualties suffered by the two Anzac corps in 1917, 38,000 of them have been sustained around Ypres. With Billy Hughes's first referendum for conscription having failed and enlistment in Australia dwindling, the AIF will now have to rely on the return to duty of men who have been wounded or sick.[40]

Headquarters insists that Monash's 3rd Division, after all they have been through, not march the 80 kilometres back to Bléquin, but travel instead by bus and train on 22 October. The troops rest there for three weeks, but meanwhile Monash is busy fighting his own private battle.

Hughes has referred the request for the formation of an Australian army to the Imperial War Cabinet, and Haig is again asked to consider the issue. Monash says that behind the push is 'a sense of Nationhood, vaguely formed early in the war, and steadily crystallizing in the minds both of the Australian people and of the troops themselves, that all the Australian Divisions should be brought together under a single leadership'.[41]

Using the Canadian model as a guide, McCay reasons that the Australians could have a commander in the field and a general officer commanding in London. McCay wants the desk job and asks for Murdoch's assistance in getting it.

As he declared to Haig, Bean wants Brudenell White as the Australian commander in the field. He first met White in Melbourne in September 1914 and liked him straight away. Born at St Arnaud in Victoria's mallee country, White lived on pastoral stations in Queensland, around Gympie, Charters Towers and Gladstone, and went to exclusive schools in Brisbane. He is the modest Anglo-Saxon outdoor hero that, for Bean, typifies Australia. He is a Christian too. White has sparkling blue eyes, a wide and ready smile and a gracious manner. 'From the first word,' Bean writes, 'I felt he was my friend.'

Bean has always been a careful, thorough journalist, painstaking in his facts, but there is a sense of hero worship in his regard for White, and a touch of envy and the casual racism of his time in his disregard for the proud, intellectual Monash.

To Bean, White is an organisational genius, modest and paternal, while Monash is always swelling his chest and puffing himself up with pride, 'trying to make out the best case for himself after the event'.[42] In fact so egotistical is Monash, Bean claims, that 'he accepts any pretty story which is put up to him' and has no grasp of what is really going on at the front – 'never has had'. Bean claims that Monash favours only the commanders who stroke his ego, while any who challenge his ideas fare badly.[43]

Monash simply won't do as Australian commander in chief, Bean says, Brudenell White, meanwhile, is everything Bean sees in an Australian hero; his modesty and charm have worked wonders on the reporter. 'Monash for an Australian Commander in Chief we cannot have', Bean continues. 'He is not the man. White would do, but not Monash.'

Bean hates the fact that Monash has what he calls the 'ability, natural and inborn in Jews, to push themselves,' Bean says Monash and Rosenthal both show the irritating quality in abundance, and that Rosenthal is even worse than Monash.[44]

Rosenthal, an architect, is actually Anglican, and has designed many churches around Australia,[45] but Bean has let posterity know his feelings. He will soon spread the word.

Despite Bean's criticisms, Monash's prestige grows at the front and at home. Even Bean concedes that Monash 'has great lucidity in grasping what has to be done and explaining it'.[46] Monash says he tries to bring systematic order in the face of carnage, whether it be working his ambulances like a cab rank, organising the ammunition supplies or keeping track of the huge laundry lists. Whether it is fighting or feeding, Monash says, 'I strive to introduce similar systematic methods and order, so that there shall be no muddling, no overlapping, no cross purposes, and everybody has to know exactly what his job is, and when and where he is to do it.'[47]

Murdoch, who was unimpressed by Monash's strategies before Messines and Broodseinde,[48] has sent a report to the Melbourne

Herald saying that the men of the 3rd swear by his leadership.[49] Even the fact that Monash prefers to give cold and weary troops soup, Oxo and coffee instead of standard-issue rum, because alcohol causes more trouble than good, does not seem to dent his popularity. Chaplain Cuttriss describes Monash as a 'born leader' and 'a popular and painstaking officer', and remarks on 'the rousing and prolonged cheering'[50] that greets Monash whenever he addresses his men. This despite the fact that Monash admits he is 'very firm and very strict' with his orders and that 'everybody who does not work up to time, and come up to scratch, usually does not get a second chance with me'.[51] Back in Australia returned officers such as Pope, Locke and Professor Woodruff are constantly talking him up.

Haig tells the War Office that an Australian corps of five divisions is unworkable, and that he is considering forming a second Australian corps under Monash; White should be tested in charge of a division before further promotion. But the heavy losses at Passchendaele have so weakened Australia's forces that when Haig meets with Birdwood and White on 29 October 1917, he decides that another corps is not feasible. They suggest the 3rd Division leave II Anzac and join the Australian Corps, and the 4th be temporarily withdrawn and used as a reserve. All AIF divisions are to be commanded by Australians.

It doesn't hurt Monash's reputation that Vic and Bert have made good friends with Billy Hughes, and that their neighbour in St Georges Road is Bob Garran,[52] the Prime Minister's solicitor-general and confidante.

On 1 November Haig finally decides that all Australians will go into one corps under Birdwood.[53] An Australian commander will be chosen later. The brims of the 3rd Division's felt hats, which Monash has ordered to be worn flat, become slouch hats again that day.[54]

'So the name ANZAC disappears, "2nd ANZAC" as a Corp name disappears and "First ANZAC" becomes the "Australian Corps"', Monash explains. Haig is 'obdurate' that there be only four divisions and Monash, unaware that Birdwood once suggested breaking up Monash's division because it was the least experienced, boasts that with one division having to go, 'mine was universally regarded as the best of the five'.[55]

The corps is to be transferred for the winter to the now quiet but still boggy Messines, where the 3rd distinguished itself five months ago. They have dinners and parties to commemorate the end of II Anzac Corps, and Godley throws Monash 'a splendid farewell banquet', though Monash is relieved to be out from under the lanky Englishman's command.[56]

Birdwood goes on leave and Monash is made temporary corps commander.

A mammoth spring offensive is being planned by the Germans, and almost a million of their men – 48 divisions – are being moved to the Western Front following the Russian Revolution and the surrender of Russia's forces. There seems no better time for the Germans to mount a massive attack on the Allies, as the Americans are still not at full strength and the French troops have been rocked by a series of mutinies involving 3000 court martials and 43 executions. The Germans have suffered horrific casualties since the start of the war while the Allies are confident that the Americans will eventually turn the war in their favour. Yet, they are not prepared for the great offensive forming in the mind of Erich Ludendorff.

On 11 November Monash moves from the Château d'Hervarre back to his old lodgings in Steenwerck, which he rates as his most comfortable home in France despite the absence of most of the antique furniture and expensive paintings, which have been put away for safe keeping.[57]

On the same afternoon, 100 kilometres south-east in Mons,[58] Ludendorff, now effectively Germany's supreme military commander, travels to the headquarters of Crown Prince Rupprecht for a meeting with Germany's senior military officers to discuss plans to punch a hole through the Western Front with the Spring Offensive. Ludendorff admits that Germany is outgunned and outnumbered, but says it still has enough resources and the will to score one mighty finishing blow.

The weather becomes bitterly cold and all of Flanders is covered by a hard frost. The dry cold is not as harsh as Melbourne in June, but Monash admits that men 'who have to lie out all night in the snow' are not as fortunate as he is, in the big house by the fire.[59]

Raids continue on both sides. Monash directs successful night attacks by the 39th and 40th Battalions on 30 November and 1 December respectively. He is delighted by a commendation from Henry Rawlinson, now commanding the 2nd Army, since Plumer has been given charge of the British Expeditionary Force on the Italian Front. Plumer wanted to take Monash and the 3rd with him to Italy, but Haig said they were too valuable in France.[60]

Monash has enough spare time to read the works of O. Henry, although some of the American officers arriving in France tell him that the old west has changed and the days of the 'cowboy and the bronco buster are over'.[61] He sketches the church at nearby Neuve Eglise and its wintry surrounds to send back to Iona. He also sends his pantomime troupe to entertain Matron Kellett and the nurses at No. 25 General Hospital at Hardelot Plage and travels across for a sumptuous thank-you dinner. He is enthusiastic that the Australian soldiers will support Billy Hughes's second plebiscite for conscription on 20 December. They do, but the majority of Australian voters don't.[62]

There is some friction between Monash and Brudenell White over the divisional artillery, but the mild-tempered White tells him that 'I daresay that we will find our views are not much at variance'.[63] That same day, 5 December, Walter McNicoll is given temporary command of the 3rd Division as Monash and Paul Simonson cross the Channel. Monash embarks on two weeks' leave, a large part of which he will spend in the arms of Lizzie Bentwitch. He has a new lounge suit of grey tweed and Lizzie thinks he looks absolutely wonderful. Monash writes home to Vic to say that walking around London incognito is a wonderful feeling, and that it is 'quite delightful to be jostled and edged into the gutter by crowds of young second lieutenants and Tommies'.

Privately, he is happy not having to return salutes constantly, or risk being recognised with a woman who is not his wife. However, he is excited by a mention in dispatches for the sixth time, and that the *Times* carries a report that includes his name. Women take no notice of him, he says, when he is not wearing the decorations of a general.[64]

He and Lizzie, though, have already begun to form a deep and lasting attachment that will become a tangled web. He has not seen Vic in three years and it has been a long, lonely and cruel war.

The time Lizzie and he spend together makes him remember his days as a young man cutting a dash with the eligible young ladies of Melbourne. He makes the most of it, and will later use his experiences for a piece of licentious writing he calls the 'Gulston' narrative.

Parting with Lizzie is difficult, but he returns to France on 19 December, only to find that the 3rd Division, which was relieved on 16 December and given a month's rest, has been called back to Armentières. There is unpredictability over the Portuguese troops following an uprising against the government in Lisbon.

That week, at the Kaiser's headquarters in the spa town of Bad Kreuznach, Wilhelm II holds a meeting with Ludendorff, Hindenburg and General Mustafa Kemal, now Turkey's military leader. Ludendorff is pressing ahead with his idea for a great surge against their enemies.

In Steenwerck, Monash busies himself organising new defences and trying to make his men as comfortable as possible. The Australian General Strike of 1917 holds up the arrival of their Christmas treats, but Monash arranges for every man in the 3rd Division to receive 250 grams of pudding and a little festive cheer, with a great Christmas pantomime by the 'Anzac Coves' lasting two hours and soldiers forming a line of chorus 'girls'.

He welcomes a group of Japanese officers and entertains three American divisional commanders and their staffs, who stay with him at the château for six days. 'They are very new to the game, and have a lot to learn.'[65]

On Christmas Day, the festive mood sours when Birdwood and White criticise some of Monash's rear defensive work, and Monash spends most of what has been planned as a jolly afternoon writing out a justification for his tactics. Two days later, after a 'heart to heart', he and White patch things up. Criticism is not what Monash expects after a year of success.

On New Year's Day, Birdwood calls Monash to tell him he is to receive a knighthood. And not just the KCMG[66] that McCay gets, but the higher honour of Knight Commander of the Bath, which will also go to Hooky Walker and Talbot Hobbs.

At home in Melbourne Mat does a little war dance in celebration that her brother has finally got the better of McCay.[67] Monash telegraphs McCay with 'most cordial congratulations from his oldest friend';[68] Birdwood confides to him that McCay is livid with jealousy but has received more than he deserves.[69]

Monash tells his friend Felix Meyer that to exercise the command of such men as the 3rd 'is an honour far greater than can be accorded by the grant of any titles. The troops consist of the very flower of our Australian youth; from every point of view they are magnificent.' He says they have slaved under him for a long time 'to learn the art of war' and then 'fought like veterans'. They have never had a failure, he says, and are one of the few divisions that Haig 'jealousy guards as his Corps d'elite and which he employs in battle only for the most crucial enterprises ...'.[70]

Monash sends his 'heartiest congratulations' to the newly titled Victoria, Lady Monash, who he claims is now the third-ranking woman in Australia after Lady Munro Ferguson and the Chief Justice's wife, Lady Madden.

'My darling', Vic writes back. 'Best love. Wonderful man. What a genius you are. Jewish community gone mad, off their heads. K.C.B.!!!' There is nothing more she could wish for, she says, as her two greatest ambitions in life were a title and dinner at Government House. Her loving husband has given her both.[71]

Monash tells Vic that all his hard work has been for her, and that his pleasure at the knighthood 'has been far more on your behalf than on my own. We started from small beginnings – but it has been from the first my ambition to provide for you the utmost that life can give. The two essentials for that were money and position and the one without the other would have been very little use.'[72] They can now live in 'dignified comfort' for the rest of their lives, though as Vic is forever telling him, 'one cannot ever have too much money'.

If his life is spared, Monash tells her, he plans to come home and continue his service to Australia. Of course, the university will want him, probably even as chancellor, and the government will offer him some sort of top military position, because 'they simply cannot, on my record, afford to pass me by'. There will be so many big job offers, he says, the hardest part will be deciding which ones to accept and which to reject.

Monash admits his letters can be 'monstrously egotistical', 'but I suppose – like the male peacock before the pea-hen – one may be permitted to do a little strutting before one's own wife …'.

And Vic should not discount the very real possibility, he warns, that he might soon be made a State governor. Victoria Lady Monash, as he delights in addressing her, might soon be an 'Excellency!!'[73]

At her hotel, Lizzie Bentwitch is thrilled for Monash as well, and she wants to see him as soon as she can so they can celebrate together.

Vic can have all the titles in the world. Lizzie has her man.

Chapter 22

GERMAN ARMY HEADQUARTERS, AVESNES, NORTHERN FRANCE, 21 JANUARY 1918

We'll just blow a hole in the middle. The rest will follow of its own accord.
GERMAN COMMANDER ERICH LUDENDORFF EXPLAINING THE PLAN FOR
OPERATION MICHAEL, THE INTENSE BOMBARDMENT OF THE ALLIES[1]

Thank Heavens – the Australians at last.
GENERAL WALTER CONGREVE AFTER MONASH ARRIVES
WITH REINFORCEMENTS FOLLOWING THE START OF GERMANY'S
SPRING OFFENSIVE[2]

THE GERMANS call it *Vernichtungschlact* – the battle of annihilation, one monumental attack that will neutralise the enemy and change the whole course of the war.[3]

It is the one chance for the increasingly desperate and mercurial Erich Ludendorff to turn German hopes around. He still has the Blue Max medal at his throat, a fierce stare etched into his hard face and a hatred for the cowards who call for peace. He remains fully focused on victory, and to hell with the cost.

Those in his inner circle wonder if their *Führer* is going mad. The British naval blockade has caused mass starvation in Germany, and the lack of quality food for both man and beast results in constant suffering. Influenza, dysentery, typhus, tuberculosis and scurvy ravage an enervated, depressed population. Without proper fodder, farm animals produce inferior meat and milk. German livestock counts reach all-time lows, and those that survive are usually emaciated.[4] Crime becomes rampant as people steal simply to eat, and the longer Germany starves the more its ardour for war dwindles.

On the frontlines soldiers' rations are reduced, and those who are given new uniforms find them ill-fitting and inadequate against the cold and wet. Bandages are in such short supply that crepe paper is used to dress wounds. In Germany's occupied territories every available source of metal – kitchen utensils, doorknobs and household fixtures – is melted down to make weapons and ammunition. Church bells and organ pipes are requisitioned, even plumbing from German homes. Crucial army equipment – motor transport, aircraft and tanks – is in short supply. Pack animals are skin and bone.[5] The pre-war death rate of children under 15 has doubled.

Yet Ludendorff still holds fast to the warrior spirit of the Prussian military. When British tanks first appeared on the Somme two years ago, he claimed the best weapons against them were 'coolness, discipline and courage'. The only reason the huge ponderous machines had any success at all, he reasoned, was because of 'tank panic'. By the start of 1918, Germany still has only five tanks of a crude design, while the British are making thousands.[6]

Ludendorff believes that the fall of Russia has transformed the war. In his mind, the great influx of German forces from the Eastern Front will give the Fatherland the balance of manpower. With more than 4 million men at his disposal, the Germans will have the advantage in numbers for the first time. He plans a massed attack along the River Somme in March, to separate the English and French forces and create a gap through which the Germans can surge so as to reach the Channel ports.

With more and more Germans deserting in the face of hopelessness, or being infected with the spirit of revolution spreading out from Russia, Ludendorff knows he has to act fast. He orders his commanders to compile a complete array of plans for an attack across the whole German front.[7]

On 21 January he summons his most senior generals to his headquarters in the snow-covered woods at Avesnes in northern France and finalises his plan for a series of huge onslaughts, starting with Operation Michael against the British 3rd and 5th Armies on both sides of Saint-Quentin, and on a front extending from Arras to the River Oise.

The Prussian Army occupied the fortress at Avesnes after the Battle of Waterloo in 1815, and from there marched towards Paris. Ludendorff believes Avesnes is the ideal place to plot this new triumph.[8] When Prince Rupprecht asks Ludendorff what the operational objective of 'Michael' will be, Ludendorff tells him it will be simply to blow a hole in the middle and come what may.

He plans a five-hour tornado of high explosive shells mixed with poison gas. During the lightning bombardment more than 1.1 million shells will be fired from 6600 cannons and 3500 mortars. If Ludendorff's plan succeeds, the British defences will be immobilised, and the Germans will be able to capture the rail link at Amiens, march to the Channel ports and force the British back to the sea, leaving the defence of Paris in tatters.

All winter his best men train as stormtroopers, implementing a new strategy in which heavily armed soldiers, supported by mortars and flame-throwers, will charge deep into hostile defences slashing holes for the infantry.[9] Ludendorff insists he wants only men 35 or younger who are full of the Prussian warrior spirit, the *furor teutonicus*.[10]

At the beginning of 1918, as the 3rd Division rests up during another wretched winter of rain, snow, sleet and wind, Monash lectures his men on the wickedness of the Hun, the Germans' brutal treatment of Australian prisoners, the gutless sinking of the *Lusitania* and the execution – no, make that *cold-blooded murder* – of the saintly British nurse Edith Cavell, who saved the lives of wounded men from both sides but was killed by a German firing squad, despite international pleas for mercy, for helping Allied prisoners escape Belgium.

As Monash moves about the troops in his work outfit – a crumpled khaki uniform and worn boots, usually with the spurs upside down as a nod to the egalitarianism of the Australian soldier and the fact that the battlefield recognised grit rather than meticulous appearance – he could pass for a sergeant in the transport unit. To the Australian soldiers in France, he is becoming one of them.

As well as receiving a Christmas parcel from Vic and Bert, complete with shaving stick, toothbrush, toothpaste, nail cleaner, nail brush and boracic powder,[11] Monash welcomes more and more American officers to his base. By the end of 1917 there are 100,000 American troops in France. By May, 318,000 are due, with another million planned before August. Monash tells Vic their effort 'will be on a very potent scale, and if Italy holds out, and if France does not also have a psychological breakdown which some people fear, I think one can safely speculate upon a termination of the war not later than the coming summer …'.[12] With Hughes's second plebiscite having been defeated, the number of Australian troops is now 'well on the down grade, and it is only a question of which side will be exhausted first'.[13]

On 27 January the 3rd Division is moved back to the line at Ploegsteert, east of Messines, where they maintain an 8-kilometre front. Monash immediately begins harassing the Germans with major raids on the edge of Warneton.[14] On 10 February, 200 men from the 37th and 38th Battalions kill 102 Germans and capture 33. On 3 March, 235 men from the 9th Brigade take 11 prisoners and claim to have killed 50. Monash, speaking German, interrogates many of the prisoners himself – separately, so there is no collusion between them – and says he has definitely established the important fact 'that whether the Boche intends to launch a great offensive in the West, or not, he certainly has no intention of doing so on the front of the Australian Corps'.[15] The Australians are just too fierce.

He tells Vic that his time is so limited now with all the demands of a divisional commander, and so many people to see – journalists, other commanders, distinguished officers, secretaries, clerks, orderlies and messengers – that he often has to get out of bed or interrupt his meals to sort out some problem. There are 'always some loose screws somewhere that want tightening up, and some stiff bearings that want oiling, and the furnaces need constant stoking, or else the fire will go out'.[16]

He draws up plans to capture Warneton with two brigades in a night-time operation,[17] lectures on military intelligence and writes a pamphlet on machine-gun tactics. He experiments with smoke bombs to blind enemy machine-gunners, and on 26 February gives a three-hour lecture to divisional officers stressing that the next great German offensive will provide the opportunity for a counter-strike that could end the war.[18] He still likes to exercise his mind on subjects other than battle tactics, and in the course of preparing for what may be the greatest battle in human history, he sends away for the Pelman System of memory training, labours over the intricate jigsaw puzzles Walter Rosenhain sends him, and subscribes to the *Times*, *Punch* and *La Vie Parisienne*.

Monash loses his valuable aide George Jackson, who is promoted to command the 87th Infantry Brigade, and he is given Carl Jess, his staff officer on Gallipoli, who is now a lieutenant colonel. Jess is the second of Monash's aides who has a German background, the other being Major George Wieck.[19] Bean raises a wary eyebrow.

Jackson writes to Monash to say that he wishes Monash were in command of his new division, because the general there is a 'dangerous madman … please burn when read'.[20] Years later Jackson will say that while Monash always had a bad habit of praising himself and his men too much, he was 'delightful' to work with. Far-seeing, he had the methodical, precise approach of an engineer who studied aerial photographs and plans more thoroughly than any other commander, and was also a man big enough to change his mind when needed.[21]

When Percy Abbott, Commander of the 12th Light Horse Regiment and Federal member for New England, visits Monash for three weeks at Birdwood's request to see how a division should be run, he too is impressed. Abbott calls Monash one of the 'brainiest' and 'biggest' men he has ever met, with 'a big grasp of his job and his ever watchful eye on everything'.[22]

On 9 March, the 3rd Division is again taken out of the frontline, and Monash and Paul Simonson head to Paris for three weeks' leave, driving down in a 'splendidly fitted up' Vauxhall limousine, after Monash finds out that other divisional commanders are 'not so squeamish' as he has been about using government cars and petrol for their pleasure. With Paul hammering the accelerator, they cover the 300 kilometres 'in the astonishing time of under five hours', and spend the next three days taking in the sights of the capital, with Monash acting as tour guide for his nephew.

They are in the theatre on 1 March when the Germans launch an air raid. A hundred people are killed nearby, but patrons in concert halls throughout Paris stand to sing 'La Marseillaise'. 'This is another of the Boche's miscalculations,' Monash says, 'he thinks he will terrify the French nation into submission.'[23]

Erich Ludendorff hopes to terrify the Allies into a retreat as he works 17-hour days and begins to position hundreds of thousands of men and millions of shells for Operation Michael, Germany's first major offensive in the west since Verdun 13 months earlier. It is Germany's last hope for an end to the war that does not involve the white flag. Hindenburg tells his stormtroopers: 'Muscles tensed, nerves steeled, eyes front! We see before us the aim: Germany honoured, free, and great! God will be with us to the end.'[24]

Blissfully unaware of Ludendorff's exact plans, Monash leaves Paul in Paris and heads to the Riviera again: staying in the same room at Menton's Hotel Regina where he was a year ago, walking the beach in blissful idleness, 'lolling about' in the sunshine.[25]

Matron Kellett writes to Monash about rumours he will be given command of the Australian Corps. It puts an extra spring in his step as he maintains his now-rigorous fitness regime with long invigorating walks in the nearby hills. He reads George Bernard Shaw's critique of Wagner, which he calls 'brazen revolutionary cynicism' but 'very clever and ingenious'. Even though he is dismayed that he can't try his roulette system in Monte Carlo's casino – where soldiers of all ranks are forbidden to gamble – he goes there to see a performance of the new opera *Maître Manole*, by Raoul Gunsbourg, 'with a brilliant orchestra and cast'.[26]

That performance, though, is nothing compared with the show that the maestro of German artillery, Colonel Georg Bruchmüller,[27] prepares at dawn on 21 March 1918, as thousands of guns are trained on the Allied positions south-west of Saint-Quentin. Seventy-two divisions from three German armies are to be hurled against the battle-weary British – the 14 divisions of the 3rd Army under Julian Byng and the 12 divisions of the 5th Army under Hubert Gough. The 3rd Army is holding a 45-kilometre front, while the 5th is the weakest link, thinly stretched along 67 kilometres in front of Amiens.

The British have known for weeks that a mass attack is coming, thanks to aerial photographs and information supplied by German deserters. The Germans have built new supply roads. Shell craters have been turned into trench mortar batteries. Heavily laden trucks and horse-drawn wagons have been seen heading into Saint-Quentin from the east, and German officers have been observed studying British lines. The Kaiser's royal train has arrived near Avesnes.[28]

But it's the *intensity* of the attack that catches everyone by surprise on this foggy spring morning of 21 March. Having rehearsed his movements perfectly, Bruchmüller unleashes hell right on the stroke of 4.40 a.m., in the biggest single artillery attack ever seen. The Germans guns fire together all along the front of the British lines: 4000 field guns, 2600 heavy guns and 3500 trench mortars.

For five hours, high explosive shells, shrapnel and gas hit the British troops in a great cacophony of destruction. To many of the soldiers it seems like the end of the world. The German gunners have never fired faster, or in such a frenzy. The British troops who aren't killed by the blasts or left choking and reeling by the gas are in a state of shock at the unearthly noise and force of the continuous explosions.

Heavy shells hit the rear positions 5 kilometres back, destroying Allied artillery and supply lines, while the trench mortars, smoke canisters, mustard gas, chlorine gas and tear gas rain down on the forward trenches. The whole countryside looks like one enormous cloud of smoke and fire.

Like some demonic vision, 72 German divisions then surge forward through a thick fog, filled with a mixture of anger, bloodlust and elation at a looming victory.

By the end of the day, the Western Front has been shattered. There are nearly 20,000 Allied troops dead and 35,000 wounded. After the second day the 5th Army is in retreat. The 3rd soon follows. The stormtroopers advance 22 kilometres in a single day: a milestone not seen in the west since 1914 when the Germans had stormed through Belgium and northern France.

Behind the slow trudge of British defeat, the sound of advancing German guns gets ever closer. On 24 March the town of Bapaume falls as the German tidal wave rolls on towards the sea, pushing the thin line of British soldiers ever closer to the shore.

Royal Flying Corps pilots trying to stop the German advance with aerial bombing raids report that from every town in the vicinity huge plumes of smoke rise to 2500 metres. Refugees flee covered in powdery dust from the smoke and explosions.

British officers are told to use their revolvers if necessary to check panic among their troops. Before long the attack costs the British 177,739 casualties, with 75,000 taken prisoner.

On 24 March Ludendorff writes: 'Within a period of three days … the English Army suffered the greatest defeat in British history.'

His joy is short-lived. That night his wife takes a phone call from the Luftwaffe. Margarethe Ludendorff's second son, Erich

Pernet, has just been shot out of the sky and killed between Amiens and Saint-Quentin – just like his brother a few months ago.

Margarethe collapses with shock and never really recovers. From that moment, as he sends thousands of men to their deaths, Ludendorff becomes obsessed with finding his favourite stepson's body.[29]

On the same day, Monash is on a train heading back to the front, preparing his body and mind for a pivotal moment in the history of the world.

Last night he was luxuriating by the Côte d'Azur, and about to travel on a sightseeing journey to San Remo in Italy with General Rosenthal, commander of his 9th Brigade, who has been recovering in Menton after being gassed. Monash had just seen the evening newspapers, which gave him the first details of Ludendorff's great offensive, and he was considering what should be done when an urgent telegram arrived from Carl Jess telling him that the 3rd Division has been ordered to the front.[30]

Monash and Rosenthal board the train at 8.30 a.m. on Sunday 24 March. Because of the battles raging, they spend nearly 24 hours travelling before reaching Paris, which has just been shelled for the first time by a long-range German gun 120 kilometres away. Paul Simonson meets them in a car at the crowded, chaotic Gare de Lyon and they go 'bowling at a great rate' to Amiens, to find the town in a state of turmoil after a barrage of bombing has caused the civilian population to flee.

All around there are 'war-worn, mud-spattered, excited and starved looking troops of all kinds', struggling to get back to their units and rejoin the fight. The overworked railway staff have gone days without sleep and are in a state of 'almost mental paralysis'. At Amiens Station Monash receives news from Jess that while marching to Ypres the 3rd Division has been re-routed, and is now at Blaringhem. The men are about to travel by train to Doullens, 25 kilometres north of Amiens, to act as reserves for X British Corps.

After travelling for more than 30 hours, Monash meets an omnibus full of his officers and NCOs, who have arrived ahead of the rest, in Doullens. Streams of soldiers and stragglers pour through from the east with 'the most hair-raising stories' that the Germans have overrun the Somme. 'Viewed from this locality,' Monash tells Vic, 'it almost looked as if the whole British Army in this part of the world was in a state of rout.'[31]

The news of the German triumph is so alarming that the Allied High Command does its best to keep it quiet so as not to create panic. Divisions in reserve such as the 3rd have to rely on rumour, Monash says, 'which was always unreliable, and partly upon severely censored communiqués, framed so as to allay public anxiety. Nothing definite emerged from such sources, except that things were going ill.'[32]

All Allied telegraph and telephone communications have been cut, and it is difficult to find any information on where the various headquarters are located. Monash races to Blaringhem to gain a clearer picture of the German attacks. He arrives at 7 p.m. on 25 March, after spending a day and a half travelling. He sees off his division as they depart by train for Doullens, and finally manages to get some shut-eye. The next day, 26 March, he is asked to help occupy the line between Arras and Albert.

Monash travels back to Doullens, where there are 'brilliantly uniformed French and British officers' everywhere and a fleet of motor-cars in the town square. He doesn't know it yet, but a crucial meeting of senior Allied politicians and generals is taking place here, to which he is not invited.

They all want to halt the German advance, but for different reasons: the French are concerned about protecting Paris, the British more worried about the ports. Haig suspects the French general Philippe Pétain[33] is in 'a funk' and has lost his nerve, while Pétain fears the British will be herded into the Channel. French Prime Minister Georges Clemenceau is appalled by Pétain's pessimism, while French general Ferdinand Foch[34] tells the gathering: 'We must fight in front of Amiens, we must fight where we are now … we must not now retire a single inch.'[35]

Haig pushes for Foch to be promoted above Pétain, and the veteran of the Franco-Prussian War of nearly 50 years ago is eventually installed as Allied Généralissime, the supreme Allied commander.

While the commanders inside the meeting come to a unified purpose, outside Monash sees a state of 'almost indescribable confusion' on the streets of Doullens. Wild-eyed English soldiers and panicked civilians stream westward towards the coast, with their belongings in 'wheelbarrows, hand carts and farm wagons'.[36] All of them look starved and broken with fatigue, the women, young and old, dressed in their mourning black.

Bean later writes: 'For as far as the eye could see, especially along the road from the south-east, came carts lurching with towering loads, precious mattresses, bedsteads, washstands, picture frames, piled together with chairs, brooms, saucepans, buckets, the aged driver perched in front upon a pile of hay for the old horse; the family cow – and sometimes calves, or goat – towed behind by a rope or driven by an old woman or small boys or girls on foot. One old man, whose wife was too sick to walk, was wheeling her before him in a barrow.'[37]

British heavy artillery and transports are also in retreat, with great howitzers rumbling past the Australian soldiers and streams of Tommies shouting: 'You're going the wrong way, Digger, Jerry will souvenir you.'[38]

Monash has little regard for any of the British. 'These Tommy Divisions are the absolute limit,' he tells Vic, 'bad troops, bad staffs, bad commanders.'[39]

By a stroke of good fortune, Monash reaches Doullens Station just as his men from the 9th Brigade are disembarking with their commander Rosenthal and a portion of the 33rd Battalion. A British military policeman waving a Webley revolver is trying to control the crowded traffic at the station crossroads.

The Town Major of Doullens – the officer responsible for local defence[40] – rushes up to Monash to tell him that German armoured cars have broken through at Hébuterne and that the German cavalry is just 16 kilometres away. The rumours are just that: an 'example of the condition of chaos that reigned supreme'.[41]

Monash orders Rosenthal to man the defences, ready for any attack. He races 10 kilometres east to Mondicourt to meet McNicoll and some of the 10th Brigade. McNicoll collects 'many hundreds' of the fleeing English soldiers, 'and by very direct methods' forces them to join his own troops.[42] Monash sets up his headquarters at Couturelle and establishes signal communications with the British X Corps at nearby Frévent. He then issues orders for the grouping of his three brigades.

At 9 p.m. a dispatch rider delivers him orders to join the 7th Corps in the little abbey town of Corbie. No sooner has that rider roared off into the night than another arrives with news that the 7th has abandoned Corbie because of heavy shelling, and is now on the move to Montigny-sur-l'Hallue, about 30 kilometres to the south along the road to Amiens.

Monash takes off for there just after 10 p.m., accompanied by four of his staff and two dispatch riders, with 'two motor-cars and two motor cycles, in black darkness, on unfamiliar roads congested with refugee traffic'.[43] With what Bean calls 'his usual forethought', Monash has with him representatives of all departments of his staff to deploy his orders quickly: Major Wieck (general staff), Captain Clarence Pyke (administrative staff, and a professional tea-taster in his former life),[44] Major Wilfred Vickers (medical staff)[45] and Major Ron Hamilton (commander of the divisional signal company).[46]

It takes two hours to cover the 30 kilometres, and when Monash gets to Montigny he comes across about 500 of the 7th Corps who have fled Corbie. They have taken refuge in a bare salon of 'stately proportions, in a deserted château by the roadside'. They are 'sitting very disconsolately … practically wringing their hands, as all the Divisions of the Corps had been biffed badly that day'.[47] All their untouched luggage is piled in the corridors.

The only two soldiers who seem to have their wits about them are the 7th's commander, Lieutenant General Walter Congreve, and his brigadier, Alexander Hore-Ruthven,[48] both Victoria Cross recipients. They are poring over maps by the flickering light of a candle, and as Monash walks in, Congreve exclaims: 'Thank Heavens – the Australians at last.'[49]

That line will become a favourite greeting between Monash family members of future generations.

Congreve tells Monash that at 4 o'clock his troops were holding a 10-kilometre line between Bray-sur-Somme and Albert when the German stormtroopers crashed through. What is left of his three divisions is falling back rapidly, after four days without food or sleep.

'The enemy is now pushing westwards,' Congreve says, 'and if not stopped tomorrow will certainly secure all the heights overlooking Amiens. What you must try and do, Monash, is get your Division deployed across his path. The valleys of the Ancre and the Somme offer good points for your flanks to rest upon. You must, of course, get as far east as you can.'

Congreve says he knows of a line of old trenches that are still in good condition, running from Méricourt-l'Abbé towards Sailly-le-Sec, and Monash should occupy them, if he can't get further east.[50] The rapid withdrawal of the British in the area has left a 16-kilometre gap, virtually undefended, with a clear run to Amiens between the Ancre and the Somme. Monash needs to plug the hole before the Germans flood through.

He puts the first two arriving battalions of the 11th Brigade on either side of the road from Bray to Corbie. His 10th Brigade takes over the sector north of the road, and the 9th Brigade stays in reserve at Heilly on the Ancre, near what will be his new headquarters at Franvillers.[51]

Sinclair-Maclagan soon arrives at the Château Montigny and Congreve orders him to bring his 4th Division into a position of support on high ground in a bend of the Ancre. He drives on to Château Baizieux. Sinclair-Maclagan's chief general staff officer,

Lieutenant Colonel John Lavarack,[52] is already there, having passed a brigade of British siege artillery in retreat.

'You Australians think you can do anything,' the British commander says to Lavarack, 'but you haven't a chance of holding them.'

'We're going to stand and fight,' says Lavarack, 'you Poms should stay with us.'

The British brigadier has a rethink.

'Right you are,' he says, and the retreat is immediately halted.[53]

It is now 1 a.m. on 27 March, and Monash realises that everything depends on 'quick decision and faultless executive action'. He finds a working telephone in the Château Montigny and avails himself of three large buses from General Byng of the 3rd Army,[54] to ferry more of his men from Doullens to Franvillers.

He and his staff work all night, 'considering and settling all detailed arrangements'.[55] There is barely time to shut his eyes before Monash is on the move again with Paul Simonson and a staff officer to Franvillers, where the buses are yet to appear. Despite his own weariness, Monash issues detailed, meticulous directions warning his men that 'the Boche attacks up valley and hollows and is quick at finding a gap. He gets his [machine-guns] forward and uses them in enfilade [in a volley of fire along a wide axis]. His infantry wait at 600 yards for the M.G.s to get to work. The next 48 hours are regarded as critical.'[56]

Bean later writes that Monash's orders show his 'great powers of grasp and of lucid exposition at their best – the officers to whom they were read at the time recognised with a flash of pride, the "old man's" masterly touch. The situation that called for each phase of action was clearly explained, and the action then crisply ordered.'[57]

An hour of suspense follows. Franvillers has been evacuated of civilians, and on the high plateau beyond the Ancre Valley there is smoke and fire as the Germans drive back the few British cavalry troops trying to delay the avalanche.

'You can imagine my state of mind while waiting there,' Monash tells Vic, 'not knowing how long it would take any of my Infantry to arrive.' By the light of a torch, Wieck and Pyke copy Monash's intricate battle plans to give to the troop commanders when they finally make it to Franvillers.

Monash continues watching the German cavalry wreaking havoc in the distance south of Morlancourt on this crisp, clear morning. A sigh of overwhelming relief escapes from him just after 8 a.m., as 60 London motor buses, all crowded with Cannan's 11th Brigade and overflowing with guns and ammunition, lumber along the narrow road towards him in 'a miracle of good management'.[58]

The Somme country is utterly familiar to the other four divisions fighting here, but even though the 3rd, the youngest of the corps, has distinguished itself in Flanders, it has yet to taste war here. That will soon change.

British cyclist patrols are on the high ground, looking out across the Ancre Valley to the south-east. Lines of communication have been re-established and they are reporting on the German advances between the Ancre and the Somme.[59] The men of the 11th Brigade have barely had any sleep in 48 hours, but they quickly form up and march down the steep, winding road to the little village of Heilly, and then across the Ancre and the defensive line 4 kilometres away.

By 10 a.m. buses start arriving with the first two battalions from McNicoll's 10th Brigade, and by 11 a.m. they bring Rosenthal's 9th. Hour after hour the buses come. Despite their fatigue the men march on, 108 paces to the minute,[60] to meet the Germans. Their heads are erect and they march with the 'swing and precision of a Royal review parade'.[61] This will not be the slow, unrelenting grind of trench warfare. This will be blood and thunder out in the open on the Somme.

There is not a man here, Monash knows, who does not fully grasp the situation.

The whole responsibility of ending the German onslaught has fallen to them.

On the road to Franvillers and Heilly, the 3rd Division meets cheering, tearful crowds. The French people's saviours have come at last!

Women who last night saw the German artillery's fire scorch the sky like sheet lightning over the nearby hills burst into tears and shout: *'Vive l'Australie!'* Villagers who have fled their homes turn back at the sight of the khaki uniforms and slouch hats.

In Heilly, when the march of the leading battalion is temporarily halted, one Digger sits cleaning his rifle by the side of the street and tells a local woman that there is no need to run any more. The Australians have arrived and there are many of us. *'Fini retreat, Madame,'* he says in the best French he can muster. *'Fini retreat beaucoup Australiens ici.'*[62]

A lieutenant of the 5th Division later recalls: 'Old men and womenfolk … pressed around telling us that now the *bons Australiens* had arrived they would not depart.'[63]

Bull Cannan reckons he has never seen his men so intent on cleaning their rifles and Lewis machine-guns: 'Not if they could help it would the Germans get through to these old folk and children who placed such evident trust in the AIF uniform.'[64]

By 2 p.m. on 27 March, Monash has six battalions – more than 5000 men – in position. The 44th Battalion are the first Australians to march into Corbie, ordered to guard the Somme bridges until the 9th Brigade arrives.

All afternoon the Germans appear over the skyline, trying to work forward in the folds of the ground and sneak up the gullies. But they meet well-directed Australian rifle fire and suffer heavy losses. Towards nightfall the German attempts to continue the advance die away.[65]

By 6 p.m. Monash's artillery begins to arrive, and an hour later Congreve and Monash confer by telephone. Monash directs the 9th Brigade to the right along the Ancre.

By 10 a.m. the next day, 28 March, Monash tells Birdwood that his position 'is quite secure against all but an attack on a grand scale', and that while the men are very sleepy, 'every hour that we are left unmolested is improving their condition'.[66] The steadfastness of the Australians has 'an astonishing effect in stiffening up everybody on both flanks. The tendency to run has been checked; people begin to regain confidence.'[67]

Sinclair-Maclagan's 4th Division to the north has been engaging the Germans for more than 24 hours and is pushing their attack back at Dernancourt. After two days' hard travelling, his 12th Brigade is settling down for a rest at Senlis-le-Sec when orders come to move 3 kilometres to Hénencourt. Weary but ready for a fight, they march on, and as they top a nearby hill, to the left they see the whole panorama of battle before them.[68] The town of Albert, its cathedral tower rising high above the surrounding buildings, lies in a hollow, shrouded with a grey mist, 'red shell bursts and the smoke of many fires'.[69]

All over the countryside there are shells exploding, heavy artillery guns blazing, mounted cavalry charging, wounded men stumbling from the frontline, Red Cross vehicles racing along the narrow roads. Warplanes buzz overhead and three aeroplanes are down in the field in flames.

At Hénencourt, where there is hardly a building intact, the brigade wheels left up the Albert–Amiens road as shells hail down all around. Hares are fleeing across the fields and a terrified, riderless horse, its flanks covered in blood, bolts through the procession of men.[70] Another shell blows a group of Australians apart and sends a Lewis machine-gun flying 7 metres into the air.

The crisis of the 4th Division at Dernancourt is momentarily halted, and near there Monash's 38th Battalion assists the British 35th to fend off another German attack. Monash wants to fight fire with fire, and visits Cannan and McNicoll to discuss a raid by daylight patrols.

At the suggestion of General Foch, Congreve gives Monash the green light for an attack towards the high ground west of Morlancourt. It will come in waves at 4 p.m. and 7 p.m. on 28 March, with two leaps, each of 1000 metres. It is a hurried attack, conceived with the need to strike quickly, and by men still inexperienced in open warfare.

McNicoll, not expecting much opposition and despite having been badly wounded in a frontal attack at Kirithia on the Gallipoli Peninsula, adopts similar tactics for the 40th Battalion, without adequate artillery support and on level ground in front of the German guns. They are shelled almost immediately.

There is a breakdown in communications, and the 41st Battalion, who were supposed to support them, believe they are not to move until dusk. Bean recalls that the 40th 'advanced under a storm of rifle and machine-gun fire', which, 'though less fierce than that whirlwind of Gallipoli, was nevertheless very deadly'.[71] The Australians are forced to take cover in an old line of trenches.

The 42nd and 43rd Battalions decide to advance behind more cautious patrols, but are met with bursts from at least six machine-guns. The nightmare finishes with a gain of about 1000 metres and with 300 casualties.

Bean questions Monash's otherwise meticulous preparations: 'With what strength each brigade should attack, and how its troops should be disposed, appears to have been left by Monash to the discretion of the brigadiers but ... that prudent and normal procedure was not accompanied by close consultation ...'[72]

Monash orders his artillery brigades to cross the Ancre and take up positions in the angle between that river and the Somme. The next day, 29 March, a raiding party from the 38th Battalion shoots down 30 Germans on a scouting mission.

Then, just before noon on 30 March, the Germans mount a counter-attack on the new Australian positions under heavy but ill-directed artillery fire. Eight hundred metres from where the 11th Brigade is entrenched, large numbers of advancing German artillery, 'like a large crowd dispersing after a football match',[73] appear from Sailly-Laurette, heading over a slope towards the flats.

In the middle of their advance is a weary, frightened mule, laden with ammunition. The bewildered creature is immediately shot and goes rolling down a hill. Hundreds of German soldiers soon follow it. Within 10 minutes their advance is in chaos. German officers try to rally their men, but every attempt only brings a fusillade of .303 bullets. Within half an hour, every German has either been hit or run for cover. After the sun goes down that evening the anguished sounds of wounded men crying for stretcher-bearers can be heard all night.

Monash estimates – over-estimates most likely – that 3000 have been killed.[74] 'We simply slaughtered the enemy wholesale', he says. 'After an hour, the whole attack had petered out.'[75]

The 3rd Division now links with the 4th to secure the British front north of the Somme, and together with the 5th Division and the New Zealanders presents a powerful barrier to any further German ambitions. Though it has begun disastrously, the success of Monash's advance causes him to write to Jackson that it is a 'splendid illustration of the old doctrine which you and I have so often preached, that any sort of plan was better than no plan at all, and all that was wanted … was some clear definite plan communicated promptly'.[76]

After more than a week of hard fighting the wheels fall off the German steamroller. The mighty force that Ludendorff ignited on 21 March is now all but spent. The hungry, disillusioned Germans, who have been fighting and marching for more than a week and are now meeting stubborn resistance, limp on slowly.

Fighting continues south of the Somme and Monash has to send Rosenthal's 9th Brigade, whose 'mere presence … seemed to stiffen up everybody'.[77]

Major General Richard Mullens, who commands the British 1st Cavalry Division, writes to Monash to thank him 'for your most valuable and encouraging support and assistance, especially on the 30th March, when we had a hard fight to keep the Boche out of our position … it was a very real relief to know that I had your stout-hearted fellows on my left flank … Your order for the placing of your heavy guns and batteries so as to cover my front was of very real assistance, and incidentally they killed a lot of Huns.'

Monash tells Birdwood that the arrival of Australian troops 'has had an extraordinary effect in steadying the whole line and in giving confidence to a lot of people who had become very "windy"'.[78]

The Germans continue to probe for openings. On 1 April Monash reaches the 11th Brigade just 10 minutes after three of its officers are killed by shellfire.

He says the whole problem south of the Somme is due to the failure of the 5th Army. General Gough, its commander, is dismissed on 4 April.

To guard the bridges in Corbie and Aubigny, Monash is assigned the 15th Brigade under the 'outspoken, impulsive, excitable'[79] 'Pompey' Elliott,[80] who will become Monash's great ally.

On 4 April, the Germans launch an assault by 15 divisions and capture the town of Le Hamel. They prepare to take Hill 104 on the march to Villers-Bretonneux, but are held back by the Australians, with the 4th Division distinguishing themselves again around Dernancourt. The Germans will come again, but Hindenburg later admits that it is all in vain. 'Our strength was exhausted, the Great battle in France was over!'[81]

Bean concludes that Operation Michael, which began in such a blaze of fiery success for Ludendorff, lost its sting when the advancing Germans encountered the 3rd and 4th Australian Divisions in the last days of March.[82] The Australians held a sector vital to the defence of Amiens, and refused to buckle against an attack that Churchill will later call 'the mightiest military conception and the most terrific onslaught which the annals of war record'.[83]

In the brief interludes between shellfire attacks, Monash continues to dictate letters home to relieve his stress: 'it is astonishing how one learns to do a number of things simultaneously', he tells Felix Meyer. The writing, he says, keeps 'one's mind elastic and one's thinking machinery cool'.[84]

Monash is just as busy with the logistics of his personnel as he is with plotting their victories. With all their animals and machinery and guns, his force of 20,000 stretches for more than 30 kilometres if they are marching together. It takes as many as 20 villages to house them all and 32 trains to carry them.

He has found it pays to closely consider the psychology of both his enemy and his own men in deciding how to keep morale high in times of crisis: whether to appeal to patriotism, revenge or self-preservation. The best way to carry out his command is to 'erect optimism into a creed for myself and all my brigades … and secondly to try and deal with every task and every situation on the basis of simple business propositions. Differing in no way from the problems of civil life, except that they are governed by a special technique. The main thing is to always have a plan, if it is not the best plan, it is at least better than no plan at all.'[85]

Continued shelling on Franvillers forces Monash to move his headquarters into a 'very fine old Louis XI Chateau' 10 kilometres west at St Gratien, where the Comte de Thielloye makes the Australians 'very comfortable'. Having 'received the most flattering congratulations from everyone that matters', Monash feels 'highly elated' about his situation.[86]

Even with smoke and fire all around them, the French countryside is a breath of fresh air for the Allied soldiers, so long bogged down in trenches. There are wide, green fields and crops waving in the breeze, and fresh food everywhere – poultry, pigs, sheep, cows, milk and rich grain and wine stores. An innkeeper in Doullens, about to flee the town, gives his stock of wine to the 42nd Battalion. On another occasion men fill their water bottles with fine vintages, one later commenting that there is nothing more refreshing after a hard day's marching and fighting 'than sweet red wine, especially as our water was generally bad'.[87]

There is widespread looting of abandoned homes and shops, though Monash insists the British are the main culprits, coming across stores of wine and causing 'some very regrettable scenes … but I quickly had all the villages policed with good stout Australians and we readily restored order'.[88] After a British officer is allegedly caught leaving Corbie with a cart full of looted champagne, Pompey Elliott, full of his typical bombast, orders that anyone caught doing the same is to be publicly hanged in the market place.

In a move rarely seen from other commanders, and which makes the French authorities 'exceedingly grateful',[89] Monash organises a systematic collection of valuables and produce that will be safeguarded by the French authorities: wool from the Riebmont mill worth £87,694; 100 tons of grain and forage; 214 head of cattle; and boxes of clocks, tableware, linen and curtains that might otherwise have been souvenired.

Ludendorff finally calls off Operation Michael on 5 April, but continues attacking with smaller raiding parties. The Allies have suffered a quarter of a million casualties and lost 1300 heavy guns and 200 tanks, but whatever gains the Germans have made mean little, as they have not been able to take Amiens or Arras.[90]

British and French factories are working overtime to make more weapons and the Americans are now coming in their millions. Germany has suffered 239,000 casualties in just two weeks, many of them the elite shock troops who require months of specialist training to replace. The German war chest is just about empty.

'Nowhere have any Australian units given an inch of ground', Monash says, 'and the Boche has battered himself unavailingly against the Australian wall.'[91] He laments that many of the British divisions haven't been worth the cost of their uniforms.[92] That is evident, he reckons, in what is happening up north in Flanders, where Ludendorff, having drawn the British back to defend Amiens, has mounted another major offensive called Operation Georgette, initiating the Battle of the Lys. Steenwerck, Armentières and Ploegsteert are now in flames, because, Monash says, 'those rotten Portuguese and those bad Tommy Divisions' were left to guard the area and 'let the Boche walk back in'.[93]

Monash is not alone among Australian commanders in talking up the achievements of his men and himself in halting Operation Michael, but he wins no favours with men like Bean, especially as the 3rd Division has only really faced a small portion of the massive German attack, which was concentrated south of the Somme.

Despite Monash's triumph in his sector, 12 April is 'Altogether ... a distressing day'. Lieutenant Owen Lewis, the 21-year-old son of Monash's old engineering mate Jim Lewis, is killed when his plane comes down in flames near McNicoll's headquarters at Heilly. Monash has seen a lot of Owen before his death. After the crash he speaks to Owen's older brothers Keith and Athol, both lieutenants in Monash's corps, but they are too dazed to do anything. Lieutenant Colonel John Milne, a Queenslander with a broad Scottish accent,[94] is also killed by shellfire: the third of Monash's commanding officers to die in France. In the last few weeks Milne has led two important raids on German defences: near Warneton, and at Villers-Bretonneux.[95] Monash admits it is hard to 'keep up one's spirits but it has got to be done, for if the Divisional General were to start to despair, and wring his hands, the Division would go to pieces in just 10 minutes'.[96]

Monash perfects a tactic the Anzacs call 'peaceful penetration': advancing the Australian line incrementally, with offensive patrols to gather prisoners, conduct reconnaissance and to occupy the enemy's outpost line. The repeated harassment of the Germans and constant encroaching into their space causes further erosion of the enemy's shaky morale.

The 3rd conducts raids on three out of every five days in April. In some units, it is treated as a competition, to see who can capture the most prisoners. They force the German frontline back 1600 metres at Morlancourt.

But the Germans keep fighting. For three hours on 17 April, commencing just before dawn, they pump poison gas shells into Villers-Bretonneux and nearby Bois l'Abbé at a rate of one every two seconds. Both towns are drenched in toxic fumes, clothing is soaked, skin blistered and eyes burned. The shelling resumes the next day and Monash's 33rd Battalion suffers 271 casualties.

Three days later, on 21 April, Monash races over to Cannan's 11th Brigade headquarters at Morlancourt Ridge for a sight to behold. The young German flyer Baron Manfred von Richthofen, known as the Red Baron for his brightly coloured triplane, has just been brought down with a single bullet through the heart.

Richthofen had been chasing a Sopwith Camel piloted by Canadian rookie Wilfrid 'Wop' May, for the German's 81st aerial kill, at about 11 a.m., when he flew low over a battery of Australian machine-guns. Another pilot, Canadian Captain Arthur 'Roy' Brown, was hot on Richthofen's tail. A bullet tears up through his body, yet Richthofen still has enough control to make a rough landing in a field beside the Bray–Corbie road, near the village of Vaux-sur-Somme. As Sergeant Ted Smout[97] of the Australian Medical Corps reaches him, Richthofen whispers his last word: '*Kaputt.*'

Nearby, Australian soldiers are already ripping apart Richthofen's upturned Fokker triplane for souvenirs. The angle of trajectory suggests he was killed by one of three Australians, Cedric Popkin, Snowy Evans or Robert Buie.

The following day the baron is buried with full military honours in the cemetery at Bertangles, and his squadron is taken over by Hermann Göring. Richthofen's personal effects are afterwards dropped over the German lines with a message of condolence by the Royal Air Force.

Monash sends pieces of the red fabric of Richthofen's plane and its wooden propeller home as souvenirs. He calls Richthofen 'undoubtedly the most successful and brilliant of all the German fliers'.[98]

On 24 April, the Germans capture Villers-Bretonneux, which just a few weeks ago the Australians fought so hard to defend. The attack is spearheaded by the few new tanks they have even though they now see them as essential to a modern war. The battle is the first involving tank-against-tank fighting: three British Mark IVs against three German A7Vs. Amiens is once more under threat after, Monash says, the 'Tommies' have again been 'biffed out of town'.

It is 'the same old story', Monash says.[99] The Australians had done the work to secure the town, but after his 9th Brigade had been withdrawn to rest, the area was taken over by the British 8th Division, decimated by earlier fighting.

Bill Glasgow's[100] 13th Brigade and Pompey Elliott's 15th begin a night attack to recapture the town. With the British in support, the 15th strike from the north and the 13th from the south, meeting at the town's eastern edge. Though vastly outnumbered, the Australians surround the Germans and drive them from Villers–Bretonneux and the adjacent woods on Anzac Day. Lieutenant Clifford Sadlier[101] of the 51st Battalion, a commercial traveller from Subiaco, is awarded the Victoria Cross after mounting a grenade attack. Sergeant Andrew Fynch,[102] a Melbourne plasterer who will die in a few weeks, recalls that 'with a ferocious roar and the cry of "Into the bastards, boys"', Pompey Elliott's 59th Battalion was down on the Germans 'before the Boche realised what had happened. They screamed for mercy but there were too many machine-guns about to show them any consideration. Each man was in his glee and old scores were wiped out two or three times over.'[103]

Hindenburg will later agree with Monash that the efforts of the 13th and 15th Brigades, in 'their magnificent feat ... in the early hours of Anzac Day 1918' finally destroyed the 'German hopes of a decisive victory'[104] and was the turning point of the war.

As the sun rises on the third anniversary of Anzac, Monash looks down upon the Australians, in full possession of the town, as nearly 1000 German prisoners are marched past his château.[105]

'When the Germans [first] attacked they got an awful bump,' Monash explains, 'and for the first three weeks he poured out blood like water to shift us.'

Monash calls the retaking of Villers–Bretonneux the 'finest thing yet done in the war, by Australians or any other troops', and says that 'the people in England, the English troops and officers, and finally the War Office itself, is beginning to realise that the Australians are the best troops in the whole Empire'.[106]

They have also realised that Monash is the best commander the Australians could have.

Villers-Bretonneux remains in Allied hands for the rest of the war.

Erich Ludendorff is told of the discovery of a fresh grave near Nesle with an English marker that says 'Here rest two German pilots'. He has his stepson's body exhumed and buried at Avesnes before arrangements can be made for its transfer to Berlin.

The war has 'spared me nothing', he says, and before long he is walking out during staff meetings, his mind elsewhere.[107] His junior officers sometimes find him weeping. Soon a psychiatrist urges a move from Ludendorff's cramped quarters in Avesnes to Spa in Belgium, where the German commander can undertake walks and breathing exercises. As long as Ludendorff appreciates the beauty of life, the psychiatrist tells him, he will feel much more relaxed and at peace.[108]

On 29 April, at his château in St Gratien, Monash shares a glass of wine with another German flier shot down nearby.[109] The pair might just as easily be toasting Monash's success, and the mentions the Australians are finally receiving in the British press for their achievements in France. As the spring sunshine summons blooms of daisies, dandelions, buttercups, daffodils, tulips and blue and white violets in great vivid carpets across the swathes of countryside that have not been scoured by explosives or poison gas, Monash's standing is blossoming like never before.

After months of scant press coverage because British correspondents have been discouraged from writing about Dominion successes at the expense of their own troops, the *Daily Telegraph* and the *Times* start telling British readers all about the Australians' valour. Haig sends a dispatch 'which – though tardily – acknowledges the work done by our three divisions here in stopping the enemy from getting Amiens'.[110]

For the next couple of weeks, the 3rd Division remains in place – sniping the Germans, bombing them with artillery and mortars, or sending over poison gas canisters. Cannan's 11th Brigade leads the way in bringing in prisoners to be interrogated, 300 of them, many glad to be out of the shooting gallery at last and unafraid to reveal German plans. Monash oversees four 'miniature battles'[111] by the 9th and 10th Brigades in rapid succession, starting on 30 April, and on 3 May Rosenthal leads the 9th to the right of Morlancourt to steal several hundred metres of precious dirt. Two nights later, the 9th Brigade captures 200 prisoners and 15 machine-guns in an advance that extends the 3rd Division's line 800 metres across an area almost 2 kilometres wide.

'Congratulations have been pouring in',[112] Monash says, but hardly has he finished dictating the sentence when the 34th Battalion is forced to abandon another mission and 300 casualties are sustained. Monash carefully analyses what has gone wrong, after so much earlier success, and attributes it to confusion and indecision all round.

He moves his resting headquarters to Allonville while the 3rd Division is relieved by the 2nd. He sits for the artist John Longstaff, who is painting his portrait for the Australian War Museum. He assembles 10,000 men for an inspection by Haig on 17 May, and a photographer flies high above his headquarters to capture the moment for posterity. The commander-in-chief calls it 'altogether a most inspiring sight', remarking that the Australian soldier is a far different individual now from when he first came to France, 'both in discipline and smartness'.[113]

Monash's ears tingle at the praise.

As Haig sits astride his charger, watching the pride of Australia's fighting force and their inspirational leader, he has already agreed to plans for Monash to become Australia's greatest soldier.

John Monash is about to be honoured like no Australian officer before him: with command of the Australian Corps – more than 166,000 fighting men – which he describes as the finest 'Corps Command in the British Army'.[114]

Chapter 23

*To be the first native born Australian Corps Commander is something
to have lived for, and will not be forgotten in Australian history ... for
all practical purposes I am now the supreme Australian Commander,
and thus at long last, the Australian nation has achieved its ambition
of having its own Commander-in-Chief.*
MONASH ON REACHING THE TOP OF THE AUSTRALIAN MILITARY[1]

*Yes – Monash will get there – he must get there all the time on
account of the qualities of his race; the Jew will always get there.*
ARTIST WILL DYSON ON MONASH'S PROMOTION, QUOTED BY
WAR CORRESPONDENT C.E.W. BEAN[2]

THE NEWS that Charles Bean has been dreading hits him
right between the eyes with such a sickening thud that the
usually unflappable reporter is flummoxed. He has covered this
war since Gallipoli, but few of the horrors he has witnessed have
shocked him like the news that Monash is being given the top
position in the Australian Army.

Not only has Brudenell White been passed over, but Bean's
hero is leaving the corps altogether. Birdwood is planning

to take over Gough's re-formed British 5th Army while also retaining an administrative position as the AIF's General Officer Commanding. White is going with Birdwood as his chief of staff, because White is a brilliant organiser and Birdwood isn't. The GOC AIF is the senior Australian position, but it's administrative. The real soldiering – battle orders and strategy – is handled by the Corps Commander, and that's Monash.

Bean is stunned. All of what he sees as Monash's gaudy self-promotion, his cheap and garish advertising, has paid off, at the expense of a general Bean sees as a much more modest and deserving man, representing the paternal Victorian values of Bean's Australia. The war correspondent is convinced that nearly everyone in the Australian hierarchy believes, as he does, that White is by far the most brilliant soldier Australia has produced.[3]

Monash had been hearing the rumours of his promotion for months. They were so loud among the senior officers in the AIF that on 26 March George Jackson even wrote to congratulate him. Monash, though, dared not believe it until he heard the news with his own ears. McCay, who had continually trumped Monash at school, was also angling for the top job, but Birdwood told Senator Pearce that McCay was unpopular and that his command would implode. When McCay had once approached Birdwood about usurping Monash at the 3rd Division, 'Birdie' told him he didn't want McCay ruining the 3rd 'like he had ruined the 5th'.[4]

On 12 March Birdwood wrote to Pearce telling him that Monash:

> … has commanded first a brigade and then a division in this force without I think a day's intermission since our training days in Egypt in Jan. 1915. Of his ability, there can be no possible doubt, nor of his keenness and knowledge. Also, he has had almost unvarying success in all the operations undertaken by his division, which has, I know, the greatest confidence in him. I am aware, of course, of the feeling there was against him in Australia … owing to, I

understand, his German origin, but this has, I think, been entirely lived down as far as the AIF is concerned, by his good work ... I do not think we could in justice overlook in any way his undoubted claims and equally undoubted ability to fill the appointment.[5]

Finally, on 12 May, Birdwood tells Monash that he has recommended him to the Australian Government as the new commander of the Australian Corps. Haig has backed him too. Monash will become a lieutenant general, with five major generals and 25 brigadier generals under his command.

He tells Vic that 'the appointment will give me a unique and unimpeachable standing both in England and Australia'. Overcoming the prejudices brought about by 'certain disabilities of ancestry and religion' is a ground 'for pardonable pride to have achieved such a status', and he has the 'greatest possible confidence' in his ability to make a success of such a vital role. He can't help but boast that his corps is the largest of the 20 in France, and 'its prestige and renown stands much higher than that of any other Corps'.

His command is 'more than two and a half times the size' of the French Army under Napoleon at the battle of Waterloo. And his artillery is 100 times more powerful than Wellington's. He lets that sink in.[6]

He receives congratulatory messages from Hobbs, Rosenthal, Cannan, Godley and Smyth, as well as the deluded McCay, who claims that only ill health kept him out of the running for the job.[7] Pompey Elliott is overjoyed, but McGlinn warns Monash that 'a crowd in London' at AIF headquarters are 'yelping' that he gives preferential treatment to other Jews.[8] Theodore Fink writes to Keith Murdoch to tell him that most Australians are happy with the appointment, though Monash 'has his enemies'.[9]

Four days after informing Monash of his appointment, but with the news still to be made public, Birdwood summons Bean into his office at the magnificent château of the Marquis de Clermont-

Tonnerre at Bertangles, a few kilometres north of Amiens. The château is a little brother to the Palace of Versailles: three storeys of white stone, a slate roof, an 80-metre façade and stunning grounds with double-storey outbuildings and manicured gardens dominated by mighty chestnuts and copper beeches.[10] It is a long way from the dugouts of Gallipoli. Bean half expects to see Louis XVI or Marie Antoinette in the gardens, but instead the place is alive with the business of modern war: sentries in crisp khaki uniforms, motorcycle dispatch riders waiting for their orders, Birdwood's new Rolls-Royce parked on the gravel drive, and the Australian flag and Union Jack flying proudly in the breeze.

The opulence only makes Birdwood's news that much more painful. As the colour drains from Bean's face, Birdwood explains that White, Monash and Hobbs were all in the running for the top job, but Hobbs's credentials couldn't match those of the other two. While everyone knows White has 'great capacity', there is no way Birdwood could pass over Monash. Bean says the loss of White – quiet and reserved, an Anglican son of the Australian bush – in favour of a Jewish intellectual businessman who loves the opera is 'a very great blow'.[11] The journalist suggests Birdwood should have a rethink.

Bean believes that White embodies Australia's frontier spirit, while Monash approaches war like an engineering project. His campaigns are not so much about heroics as they are about detail. Even though General Congreve says Monash is the best divisional commander he has met on the Western Front, and that Monash's reputation stands 'well in the opinion of every British general under whom he had served',[12] Bean is certain Birdwood and Haig have got it wrong. Monash would be much better suited to the GOC job in London, Bean thinks, and anyway, that workload will be too great for Birdwood, even with White by his side, if Birdwood is also to lead the 5th Army. Bean leaves astonished and aggrieved by what he sees as Birdwood's monumental blunder.

The next day, 17 May, as Haig is inspecting Monash's troops, Bean is in Querrieu, 10 kilometres north-east of Amiens, talking with the war artist Will Dyson, the English-born journalist Fred Cutlack and the photographer and adventurer Hubert Wilkins.[13] Bean 'blurts out' the news about Monash to his astonished audience.

'There was immediately a great consternation,' Bean later recalls. The group had been discussing the relative merits of the modest White, 'who does not advertise', and Monash, who never tires of self-praise. The way Bean remembers it, Dyson says that White's reluctance to push himself forward is a weakness, but that he still prefers a modest man to one who 'insists on … insinuating himself into the front rank'. Being a Jew, Dyson suggests, Monash is bound to get what he wants. 'I'm not sure that because of that very quality Monash is not more likely to help win this war than White,' Dyson is reported as saying. 'But the manner of winning it makes the victory in the long run scarcely worth the winning.'[14]

Do Bean and Dyson really feel that winning the war will be a hollow victory if their preferred choice is not the commander? In any case, the pair resolve that if White will not push himself forward, they will do it on his behalf whether White likes it or not.

They feel they owe it to him.

To Bean and Dyson, White is the sort of man who does his job regardless of accolades or reward. If the credit comes, so be it, but he does not seek glory for himself.[15] Not like that trumpet-player Monash, always making a noise about his successes. Even Birdwood concedes that Monash is not slow in putting all his wares on the counter.

Bean dashes off the 'straightest and strongest telegram' he can to Senator Pearce,[16] telling him that the Australian Government simply cannot afford to lose General White because he is quite simply the 'Greatest Australian Soldier.'[17]

Bean is no longer an impartial observer; he plans to change the mind of the Australian Government any way he can. In his mind he knows more about these military matters than the generals.

Later he grudgingly concedes that Monash has an 'almost Napoleonic skill in transmitting the appearance of his capacity', and that 'in some respects [he is] an outstandingly capable commander' – 'but ... though a lucid thinker, a wonderful organiser, and accustomed to take endless pains, he had not the physical audacity that Australian troops were thought to require in their leaders and it was for his ability in administration rather than for tactical skill that he was then reputed'. Moreover, he says, a few of those who knew both Monash and White 'doubted whether Monash's judgment would be as resistant as White's to the promptings of personal ambition or whether he was as well equipped to overbear a wrongly insistent superior or the strain of a great disaster'.[18] He was not seen at the frontlines the way that Birdwood was, preferring to be at his desk, studying reports, planning, directing, organising, commanding. Birdwood instead was forever bobbing up between bullets here and there, to slap backs and shake hands with troops from Albury to Zeehan. Bean is quick to point out that in fact 'it was averred against Monash' at Gallipoli 'that he was seldom seen in the front line, the complaints from Quinn's Post where the problems were toughest and the danger greatest, being sometimes bitter'.[19]

Bean sets out to rescue White.

On 18 May, as the Australian Government approves the recommendation of Monash in the absence of Billy Hughes, who is sailing to England via North America, Bean and Dyson brave the Channel crossing to see Keith Murdoch in London. They want his help in ensuring White is made the corps commander. Murdoch is the best-connected journalist in Australia and they believe he can exert the necessary political leverage to see their plan through. Though still just 32, Murdoch wields enormous power and influence and, well aware of Monash's organisational brilliance, is only too willing to help Bean's cause to see Monash made the GOC.

Bean and Dyson convince Murdoch that their views 'represent those widely held in the AIF'.[20] Murdoch sends a cable to Hughes telling him some officers 'claim that in operations strategy and understanding of Australians [White] is much superior to Monash whose genius is for organisation and administration and not akin to the true AIF genius of front line daring and dash'.[21]

Hughes, despite twice trying to force conscription on Australia, appears to know little about what is really happening at the front, and places reliance on the advice of Murdoch, who with a word can influence senior military positions. Hughes cables Pearce urging him to postpone the Birdwood–Monash decision until he reaches London, but the telegram arrives too late and Monash's promotion goes through.

Murdoch then sends a cable to the Sydney *Sun*, saying there is a 'strong unanimous view' that Monash is likely to become 'the supreme administrator' in London, while White will become the Corps Commander. The Official Censor blocks the report.

While all the political gamesmanship goes on in London, the war continues in France, with Monash's peaceful penetrations continuing to advance the Allied line. Monash says his first task as corps commander is to 'secure complete domination' over the 'thoughts, action and policy' of his senior commanders, so that they and all the men under them have 'a sense of responsibility to themselves, their commanders, their comrades, their men, their country and their cause'. He does it through constant conferences, lectures and addresses.

Quick and clear decisions are the key. While Monash demands that set pieces be adhered to because the artillery needs to know exactly where the infantry is in front of them, he also encourages commanders in the field to use their initiative in fluid battles. Officers on the spot have a far greater idea of the immediate demands, he says, than a general back at headquarters. A mistake made in good faith rarely brings a rebuke beyond a quiet explanation later of what might have been done instead. Monash also orders his commanders to withdraw men with long service records who are suffering from shellshock, or what will be called 'post-traumatic stress' by later generations.

On 19 May 1918, the 2nd Division attacks the Germans holding the village of Ville-sur-Ancre, gaining more than 900 metres. The village is defended on all sides by machine-guns, but after a burst of shellfire these are rushed before the German gunners can return to their posts. Small parties of Germans hold out, shooting at the advancing Australians from behind the ruins, only to have the walls blown apart around them by Lewis gun bullets or by bombs. Much of the fighting is at close range with revolvers, like a Wild West shootout.[22] Sergeant Bill 'Rusty' Ruthven,[23] a wood machinist from Collingwood, rushes around like a terrier chasing rats. He disables a machine-gun post with a Mills grenade and then leaps in among the stunned Germans, bayoneting one and capturing the machine-gun. He is rushed by some of the enemy coming out of a shelter, but wounds one and captures six others. Then, armed with a revolver, he starts chasing Germans on foot. He rushes an enemy position and shoots two men who refuse to surrender, then single-handedly captures the whole of the garrison, taking 32 prisoners.[24] Ruthven receives the Victoria Cross and is eventually promoted to lieutenant.

After the fighting stops, two Australians who have never been in combat before are playing a piano they find in a little cottage. As they thump away on the ivories for 20 minutes with renditions of musical hall songs and 'Waltzing Matilda', the cellar flap door suddenly opens and a German sergeant major crawls out with 10 other men. The Germans put their hands up in surrender. The Australians don't know for a while who is more embarrassed.[25]

The Australians suffer 418 casualties on the day, but they capture 45 machine-guns, cause 800 German casualties and take 330 Germans prisoner.

On 22 May, the 3rd Division is back in action, taking over from the 4th at a new base at Glisy, halfway between Amiens and Villers-Bretonneux. Monash works closely with the local French divisional commander and his corps commander, who are 'right good fellows'.[26] He has tunnels dug deep into the 'wet, stuffy and smelling surroundings' as a defence against the heavy shelling, which he finds 'very disconcerting'.[27] Bean visits Monash in his underground base and, while still believing White to be the superior commander, can't help but be impressed by Monash's organisational skills and the construction of his headquarters: there is a terraced veranda for offices 'with deep dugouts leading off them for living rooms'.[28]

Three days later, on 25 May, the Germans launch another massive gas bombardment in the area with 18,000 shells. The 11th Brigade cops the brunt of it, and Hubert Wilkins, who goes up to photograph the gassed men, estimates there are 700 of them so burned or blistered they require medical attention.[29] The surrounding ground, drenched in poison, has to be evacuated.

But though the air is putrid for miles around, Monash's chest swells with pride as he plans to hand over the 3rd Division to Jack Gellibrand[30] on 28 May and take over from Birdwood two days after that.[31]

He walks about to confer with his men, by his side a captured German Doberman that the Diggers are teaching English and which everyone takes turns petting.[32] Monash and Henry Rawlinson even take time to attend a replica of an Australian country race meeting that Grimwade organises at Abbeville in glorious sunshine, complete with 30 licensed bookmakers toting money bags and clerks calling out the odds, as well as booths, marquees, a grandstand and a judges' box.

Monash calls it feeding his troops on victory.[33]

Then, on 27 May, the race to the English Channel ports begins again as Ludendorff launches his third great offensive, Operation Blucher. The Germans charge across the Aisne and reach the Marne, just 100 kilometres from Paris. Again, the French are driven back in despair.

The story goes that French troops on the retreat at Lucy-le-Bocage warn a US marine commander that he should retreat too.

'Retreat?' says Captain Lloyd Williams, of Berryville, Virginia. 'Hell, we just got here.'[34]

*

The Australian Corps has now been thoroughly Australianised. Bill Glasgow is taking charge of the 1st Division, still fighting at Hazebrouck in Flanders under Hooky Walker. Glasgow is from a family of Queensland graziers, even if his father-in-law, a Federal politician, was born in Frankfurt.[35] Architects Rosenthal and Hobbs are in charge of the 2nd and 5th Divisions respectively; Gellibrand, a Tasmanian orchardist, has the 3rd. Sinclair-Maclagan, who has command of the 5th, was born in Scotland, but qualifies as an honorary Digger, being 'whole-heartedly Australian' according to Monash, after having served in the Australian military for 17 years.

The promotion of Gellibrand and Glasgow is a bitter blow to the volatile Pompey Elliott, who writes a scathing letter to Brudenell White. For the rest of the war Elliott nurses a grudge.

On 30 May Monash informs the 3rd Division that he is taking command of the whole corps, with the rotund, hard-working Brigadier General Tom Blamey as his chief of staff. He tells his men that leaving them after watching their magnificent work for the past 19 months 'is naturally a severe wrench for me', and that 'I find it quite impossible to give adequate expression to my feelings of gratitude towards all ranks'.[36]

Far from getting a little respite from his heavy workload, though, Monash now finds himself not just fighting against the political machinations over his appointment but also 'confronted with responsibilities which ... exceeded sixfold those which I previously had to bear'.[37] He is now giving orders to the other divisional commanders who have been his colleagues, and has to consider their personalities and temperaments as subordinates.

He moves into the château at Bertangles along with his two aides-de-camp, Paul Simonson and Aubrey Moss. The château is only a few kilometres from the tunnels of Glisy, but a world away with its elegant grandeur and opulence. Monash gets to know the old marquis, who still lives there but who is miserable despite the majesty of his home. His son has been killed just days earlier.

By 2 June, Bean fears that the game is up. At Bertangles, he interviews Brudenell White, who tells him that the outgoing Birdwood has been an inspiring leader who first displayed his courage to the Australian troops at Gallipoli. He says that unlike many of the other British generals, 'General Birdie' treated Australians as 'human men' and related to them man-to-man, despite his rank.[38] 'Birdie' understands that the Australians have a different view of discipline from British soldiers, and he has always been willing to fight those above him to better the lot of those below.[39] His administration has been absolutely fair too, White says, but he has never been much of an organiser and White can't remember him ever drawing up plans for attacks that were actually carried out.

Bean's eyes light up. Monash is an organiser, and Bean knows that Birdwood recognised early Monash's 'peculiar capacity for organising and training … the great care and capacity with which his arrangements were made … and at times [the] brilliance [that] flashed through, astonishing those who observed it'.[40]

Bean writes to 'Dear Murdoch' that the Australian team has dropped its best player – in cricketing terms, 'its [Victor] Trumper', he says – in favour of Monash, 'a very capable man' but a lesser player nonetheless, in the mould of 'a Clem Hill or a [Warren] Bardsley'.[41] He says that as Monash is 'there now and further charge would do no good, as things are, I intend to work loyally by him.' For now.

Monash knows that Hughes remains undecided about the GOC role, and on the same day, after consulting with Birdwood, Monash writes to the Prime Minister asking him to suspend judgment on the issue, and make up his own mind about Monash's capabilities with a visit to his troops in France. 'Upon every ground and in the best interests of the AIF,' Monash implores Hughes, 'the present organisation should be left undisturbed.'[42]

On 3 June, Ludendorff's Operation Blucher, like Operations Michael and Georgette before it, comes to a shuddering halt. The Germans have sacrificed another 100,000 men.

But while Ludendorff's troops have little energy left to fight, Murdoch and Bean keep pressing their attack.

Three days after Ludendorff calls off his latest assault, Murdoch writes to Monash telling the new lieutenant general that while Monash has his 'personal esteem', Murdoch believes Monash's real genius lies not on the battlefield but in the 'higher sphere' of administration and policy. If Monash takes the job of GOC, Murdoch suggests, he might gain yet another promotion to full general – just one rung below field marshal – and his appointment 'would be the solution to many of our country's difficulties'. Surely it's an offer worth considering, he urges. Murdoch reminds Monash that he is reporting for 250 newspapers.[43]

Monash replies politely to the young journalist but tells Birdwood: 'It is a poor compliment both for him to imagine that to dangle before me a prospect of promotion would induce me to change my declared views and for him to disclose that he thinks I would be a suitable appointee to serve his ulterior ends.'[44]

Monash drafts another letter to Murdoch, which he first sends to Birdwood, explaining why he wants to prove himself as corps commander, telling the journalist: 'You and your friends believe my abilities are mainly administrative, you probably think that a non-professional soldier is unlikely to be a good commander, that in the past I have been a figurehead controlled by professional staff officers.'[45]

Birdwood tells Murdoch that the pressman might have the clout to eventually get his way and have Birdwood removed from the GOC post, but 'I warn you I shall make a hard fight before I die'.[46]

On 7 June at Aubigny, just outside Villers–Bretonneux, a German shell explodes at the feet of a little, old Digger named Private Henry Gibb, of the 14th Battalion. When the smoke and cloud of red dirt finally clear, Henry's comrades rush to gather the many parts of his body together so he can have a decent burial. His son, Harry Gibb, himself a big-gun man with Monash's 7th Field Artillery Brigade, is shown the grave[47] and a headstone is fashioned that lists Henry's age as 45.

A few months later, at Darlinghurst in Sydney, Agnes Gibb, Henry's wife of nearly 33 years, receives a parcel of his personal effects, to wit, 'one notebook, pair of spectacles (damaged) and a silver wrist watch and strap'.[48] She informs the AIF that Henry lied on his enlistment forms. His birth certificate says he's 60 years old, but he is probably 63[49] when he dies – making him the oldest soldier to die fighting for Australia in the Great War.

That other 'Little Digger' Billy Hughes arrives in London on 15 June, with his deputy Joseph Cook, now also the Navy Minister, ready to sort out the Monash controversy. He is met by his former boss Andrew Fisher, now the British High Commissioner, and by McCay, for some unknown reason still confident he will oust Birdwood for the GOC administrative job in London.[50] Monash has already written to Bean to say it is unreasonable to expect him not to take command of the Australian Corps when Haig and so many others have faith in him, and that Haig would have given him charge of another corps had the Australian role not become vacant.[51]

Bean is not fazed.

On 16 June he and Murdoch visit Hughes at the Regents Park house that the British Government has lent to the Prime Minister for his stay. Hughes declines to stay at the Savoy, where Joseph Cook is lodging, in case large hotels are targeted by Germany's Gotha bombers.

Bean finds the increasingly deaf and cantankerous Hughes sitting with an amplifying device on the table to help him hear. The small, frail man looks much older than his 55 years. He is pale and blue around the lips and has traces of facial eczema. Hughes's son Bill[52] won a Military Medal for courage at Messines a year ago and fought around Villers-Bretonneux, but today Bill's father looks perpetually nervous.

He brightens up at the prospect of an argument. He asks Bean straight what he thinks of Birdwood. Before Bean can answer, Hughes tells him that Birdwood has never struck him as a man of great intellect, whereas White and Monash do, and he knows Monash has great abilities, while Birdwood relies more on 'the social arts' to win favour. Birdwood is a popular chap and he works hard at it. Hughes is still thinking about this whole Monash business, he tells Bean, and the decision must be made only in consideration of what is best for the whole force.[53]

Bean thinks he knows exactly what is best for the force and the men in it: Brudenell White. The men are 'safe with White', he says. Bean knows how White orchestrated the evacuation of Gallipoli without a single loss of life. To him, Monash is a different story altogether. How could Monash possibly inspire the men with his 'very ordinary ideals'? To Bean, Monash is all about looking good and having his ears tickled. No. He is not the man. For the Australian troops, for the Australian nation to flourish, Brudenell White must be given the supreme command.[54]

Monash writes home of this 'very serious intrigue', telling Vic that he will have to discuss the whole thing 'very thoroughly' with Hughes, but warns that 'I suppose I shall have to do whatever the Commonwealth Government finally decides as being best for Australia … but I am at present hoping that I shall be left undisturbed in this very fine command'.[55]

While Bean focuses on his own agenda, Monash is more concerned with winning a war. His peaceful penetrations have been successful, but across the vast western face of Europe the advances have only been small. There has been no Allied offensive of any great size since Passchendaele eight months ago.

Monash plans a vivid demonstration of the fact that there is still plenty of kick left in the Empire's Army and he wants the Australians to have the first shot.[56] Some of his larger cannons already have a range of 20 kilometres, but he is anxiously awaiting the arrival of high-velocity guns designed to blow up railway stations 32 kilometres away. The big guns weigh 190 tons and are mounted on railway carriages with 16 axles.[57]

Monash travels around to brief his commanders in the Rolls-Royce Birdwood has left him. It flies the Australian flag, and when he travels through territories occupied by French, American or British troops there is 'a tremendous lot of saluting, and turning out of guards ... and all sorts of traffic, both road and rail, is held up to clear the road for me'.

Monash expects to be treated regally, to be saluted by all those underneath him. While Birdwood had the common touch, and would chat with soldiers of all ranks and vocations, laying a reassuring arm on their shoulder, Monash can be aloof, abrupt and short-tempered with his subordinates. He wants to shake up the all-too-cosy atmosphere at his headquarters.[58] He says that despite the increased anxiety, workload and responsibility, 'the power and authority which I now wield, are ... most satisfactory to me'.[59]

He and Blamey visit the commander of the British Tank Corps, Hugh Elles, and Brigadier General Anthony Courage of the British 5th Tank Brigade, who give the Australians demonstrations of the newest machines. Elles is still being hailed for his work at Cambrai, where he led 350 tanks against the Germans.

Monash wants to launch an attack to recapture Hamel. It lies on a spur between two hills and Monash sees it as important for strengthening the Australian line. But the attack is conditional upon an increase to his artillery and some additions to his air resources, which at the moment stretch to 20 aircraft that are used mostly for reconnaissance. Monash tells his officers the plans are top secret, though he has no qualms about flouting the censorship laws by revealing all in a letter to Walter Rosenhain, at the very time when his brother-in-law is under surveillance as a German living in England.[60]

On 21 June, Monash submits a battle plan to Rawlinson, commander of the British 4th Army, titled 'HAMEL OFFENSIVE'. He has marked in blue on a map the proposed objective line that will straighten and shorten the Australian position and eliminate the German bulge into the 6-kilometre Allied front.

Monash, Gellibrand and Sinclair-Maclagan have met several times to discuss straightening the line. The attack also will deepen the Australians' forward defensive zone, improve their jumping-off position for future operations, advance their artillery south of the Somme and deny the Germans observation ground near Vaux-sur-Somme. Monash plans a combined-arms approach, incorporating artillery, infantry, aircraft and tanks. It will become known as the Battle of Hamel.

He tells Rawlinson the push will be primarily a tank operation, with at least one and preferably two battalions of tanks to be employed alongside four infantry brigades, 'totalling, say, 7500 bayonets'. General Courage suggests a tank attack in three waves, with smoke shells to hide their advance from German lookouts on the Morlancourt heights opposite the Somme.

Yet Blamey, Sinclair-Maclagan and Brigadier General Walter Coxen,[61] commander of the Australian Corps Artillery, convince Monash that his reliance on tanks alone is still too experimental. Australian troops have bitter memories of the great mechanical monsters. At Bullecourt a year ago, the tanks failed badly and the 4th Division suffered enormous casualties.

Monash knows it will not be easy to restore confidence in the mobile fortresses. So he decides to utilise a creeping barrage, in which the artillery moves slowly in front of the advancing infantry, giving them protection, and with the tanks advancing beside the troops. Monash gains extra artillery pieces from the British.

The new Mark V tank has not seen action yet, but Monash knows it represents a great advance in warfare. 'The epicyclic gearing', he later explains, the greater power of its engines and the improved balance of its whole design give it 'increased mobility, facility in turning and immunity from foundering in ground even of the most broken and uneven character. It could be driven and steered by one man, where it previously took four; and it rarely suffered suspended animation from engine trouble.'[62] It is faster too, able to reach almost 8 kilometres an hour.

Monash buses 'battalion after battalion of the 4th, 6th and 11th Brigades of Infantry' to Vaux, a village tucked away in a quiet valley, north-west of Amiens, where his men can spend all day making friends with these great 29-ton machines. The infantry are taken for joyrides, and are allowed to clamber all over the 2.5-metre-tall monsters, inside and out, and even help to drive them. Platoon and company leaders meet dozens of tank officers face to face, and they argue each other to a standstill over every aspect of the machines.

'I had formed the theory that the true role of the Infantry was not to expend itself upon heroic physical effort,' Monash will recall, 'nor to wither away under merciless machine-gun fire, nor to impale itself on hostile bayonets, nor to tear itself to pieces in hostile entanglements but, on the contrary, to advance under the maximum possible protection of the maximum possible array of mechanical resources, in the form of guns, machine-guns, tanks, mortars and aeroplanes.'[63]

Set-piece exercises are designed and rehearsed over and over again. Grenades are hurled at the tanks. Red flags mark enemy machine-gun posts, real wire entanglements are laid out to show how easily the tanks can mow them down, real trenches are dug for the tanks to leap and straddle and strafe with fire.

The tanks throw themselves upon targets, and, pirouetting round and round, Monash says they can blot out enemy machine-gun posts 'as a man's heel would crush a scorpion'.[64] Before long, the Diggers become friends with the tanks and even have pet names for each one.

Vic and Bert take a holiday with Sa Simonson in the rural quiet of Bendigo, while for two weeks, at the same time every day before dawn, Monash has his men firing high-explosive gas and smoke shells at the German line. He is conditioning the enemy to expect a regular barrage. He wants them to instinctively don gas masks when the real attack begins so they will have much of their effectiveness dulled.

Monash will use 60 tanks to break through the barbed wire and run straight over machine-gun posts, and also to carry food, water and extra ammunition to the advancing infantry, thus replacing 1200 men who might otherwise be killed trying to bring vital equipment to the soldiers across No Man's Land.

Aircraft will fly low to drown out the noise of the tanks as they approach, to confuse the Germans. For a week before the attack the aircraft fly low over Vaire Wood and near Lamotte-Warfusée, dropping flares, as if searching for German troop concentrations. Like the constant gas shelling, Monash wants to use the continual aircraft presence to confound the enemy over the Australians' true purpose.[65]

Monash will also employ aircraft to drop ammunition to his advancing troops. Previously it has required two men to carry one ammunition box, holding 1000 rounds, which a machine-gun can expend in less than five minutes. Carrying parties have to travel up to 5 kilometres across the open, exposed ground and back. Casualties among ammunition carriers are always substantial. At Monash's suggestion, young Captain Lawrence Wackett,[66] of the Australian Flying Corps, perfects an idea first used by the Germans, to drop boxes of bullets by parachute throughout the offensive. The task will be carried out by the Royal Air Force's No. 9 Squadron.[67]

Rawlinson suggests that American involvement in a set-piece attack alongside the Australians will give the Americans experience and strengthen the Australian battalions, which have been weakened by casualties and falling recruitment.

On 24 June, Monash calls Birdwood to hear the latest on his new position. Birdwood has met with Hughes and Fisher, and it did not go especially well. Fisher was scathing in his assessment of Monash's capabilities. Birdwood put him straight before stressing to Hughes that he had complete confidence in Monash, as did Rawlinson and Plumer.[68]

Monash puts his case to Pearce. General Talbot Hobbs also writes to the senator, saying Monash is very much a 'fighting leader' respected by all in the AIF.[69]

Murdoch visits Birdwood to inquire whether he sincerely believes that Monash is up to scratch as a corps commander and Birdwood is vehement. 'Of course,' he declares, 'he can do it much more ably than I.'[70]

Monash feels the pressure of the intrigues to remove both Birdwood and himself 'going on apace' and taking all sorts of subtle forms. 'This crowd strongly desire to displace Birdwood', he tells his wife, '… they have already started a propaganda to make it appear that he will be too busy as an Army Commander to attend to AIF work … they have started an attempt to attack my capacity to command the Corps, and are putting about a propaganda that Brudenell White, being a permanent soldier, would be better fitted for this job.'

He tells Vic that because of the loss of prestige, he cannot relinquish the corps command until he has made a success of it, and 'I propose therefore to fight them on their own battleground'. Rawlinson and Haig are his trump cards. But with his battalions practising on tanks every day for a major battle, he declares in something of an understatement: 'It is a great nuisance to have to fight a pogrom of this nature in the midst of all one's other anxieties.'[71]

At the same time as Monash is preparing his artillery and infantry to work in cohesion, Bean is writing out a memo for Hughes listing Monash's faults. The next day he writes to Brudenell White, who by now is getting a little embarrassed by all the reporter's fawning.

'You know and I know,' Bean starts, 'and Gen Birdwood knows and everyone knows, that our men are not as safe under Gen. Monash as under you. You know that no one will safeguard them against a reckless waste … of life … as you can or would.'[72]

White pens a polite reply to Bean but tells Monash: 'In case there is any suspicion lurking in your mind, may I say once and for all and very definitely that if the conspirators in this matter do happen to be General White's friends, they are not acting at the suggestion or with the approval of General White.'[73]

Yet Monash is too preoccupied with his battle preparations for now to devote more thought to the matter. On 26 June Rawlinson obtains permission from Haig to go ahead with the offensive: the prospect of victory justifies the cost of casualties that will weaken the Australian line. Two days later Monash draws up an agenda for his conference with his divisional commanders, listing 118 items they can thrash out.

On the same day, Corporal Phillip Davey,[74] an Adelaide horse driver with the 1st Division, comes under heavy fire at Merris, near Armentières. His commander is dead and his comrades pinned down by a German machine-gun, but Davey destroys the enemy crew with grenades and turns the gun back on the Germans. He is badly wounded, but is awarded the Victoria Cross.

Davey was invalided home from Gallipoli, but returned to his unit in France in 1916, before being accidentally wounded and then gassed. In January 1918 he received the Military Medal at Warneton in Belgium, crawling into No Man's Land under heavy fire to rescue a badly wounded comrade.[75] His brother Claude, serving in the same battalion, received the same award the previous year, only three months before he was killed at Bullecourt. Another brother, Richard, also received the Military Medal. Two other Davey brothers enlisted as well, the youngest at 15.

For the first time in history, US troops will fight under a foreign commander as Major General George Bell Junior[76] promises Monash eight American companies[77] – 2000 men – from the 131st and 132nd Infantry Regiments of the 65th Brigade.

The final corps conference for the battle is held at Bertangles on 30 June. Over four and a half hours, 250 officers discuss with Monash an agenda now stretching to 133 items. Every element of his plans is analysed, from the issue of gas masks to that of reserve machine-guns. Every officer is encouraged to speak his mind and to raise his concerns.

From Monash's own interrogations of German prisoners he knows that Hamel and the two woods just south of it are being guarded by 2790 German infantrymen, with 2860[78] in reserve. The Germans are disillusioned and dispirited.

Monash chooses Sinclair-Maclagan to head his attack and gives him five brigades, three in attack and two in defence. To the south, the 6th Brigade is to penetrate 1000 metres and form a defensive flank almost to the Roman road that runs to Villers-Bretonneux. In the centre, the 4th Brigade is to take Vaire Wood and Hamel Wood. In the north the 11th Brigade is to take Hamel.[79]

The date for the attack is fixed as 4 July, American Independence Day: an acknowledgment of the importance of the American contribution.

Billy Hughes has great political sense and limitless gumption but his timing is awful.

Three days before Monash is about to launch his major offensive on Hamel, Hughes and Cook, unaware of the secret plans, arrive in France, and along with Birdwood, proudly wearing his slouch hat, head out to see the troops on the line, some of whom are about to risk their lives against machine-gun fire and cannons. Hughes wants to gauge the opinions of Monash's fellow officers about their commander[80] before heading to an inter-Allied war council at Versailles.

Monash has to give Hughes and Cook a guided tour of the front for two days and try to prepare for an imminent battle at the same time.

The Prime Minister's party arrives in France on 1 July, and after an overnight stay at Crécy, heads to Bertangles. Monash is ready for them.

Just as he had done in England when parading for the King, Monash has his troops arranged in a grand display. The men preparing for the Hamel attack are lined up in their brigades in the forests near their camps so the German aeroplanes on patrol cannot spot them. Bean is as nervous as the young soldiers about to go into battle. He knows he and Murdoch also face their own war when Hughes confronts them over their support for White as the AIF commander.[81]

Hughes and Cook both take turns standing on a box making rousing speeches to the men as Monash stands to one side puffing on one of his ever-present cigarettes. Hughes looks like an angry, big-eared gnome as he tells them that they are fighting for the sake of freedom, to keep alive the concept of a free world and to save Australia from 'the Prussian domination'. He is so proud of them, he says – proud that they have willingly offered up their lives on behalf of their country.[82]

Joe Cook tells the men about the repatriation scheme, the best in the world, he says, to bring them home after the war. As Cook speaks, flapping his arms about and yelling at the top of his voice to be heard by the men at the back, Hughes lies on the ground on his stomach behind Cook. He is weary from lack of sleep and from the long journey, and he chews on a stalk of grass, staring into the faces of the young men and boys about to risk their lives on the frontline. Hubert Wilkins works the movie camera as Hughes looks at the soldiers intently, as though his eyes are trying to burrow through to their very souls. These youngsters are about to march into a wall of German machine-gun bullets and cannon blasts and the Prime Minister knows many of them will perish. But here they are laughing at Joe Cook's corny jokes as if they were at a picnic under gum trees back home.

Monash will recall that the speeches by Hughes and Cook do much to 'hearten and stimulate' the men for what lies ahead.[83]

At about 5.30 p.m., Hughes mounts a gun carriage to speak to a West Australian battalion in full battle dress. As he speaks he finds the constant stream of shells flying overhead 'a little disturbing to the necessary flow of oratory' and asks a major standing beside him if he could tell them to 'let up a little'. The major tells him that the bombs are actually coming from the Germans aiming for Monash's headquarters a kilometre away, and there's not much he can do about it for the moment.

Hughes and Cook visit 5th Division headquarters at St Gratien and 2nd Division headquarters at Camon, and are taken to see the 11th Brigade, the 4th, the 6th and finally to the Australian Flying Corps No. 3 Squadron at Flesselles. At each of the division headquarters Hughes takes the commander aside to talk about Monash's abilities.

He has lunch with Hobbs and Bruche, two of Monash's great supporters, and Hughes and Hobbs have a long private discussion afterwards. All of the commanders vouch for Monash as a great leader. The only one Hughes doesn't meet is White's friend Gellibrand, who is already causing headaches for Monash by feuding with Walter McNicoll, commander of Gellibrand's 10th Infantry Brigade.

Monash finds it hard to have a private word with the Prime Minister, but when he does get Hughes aside he tells him 'quite frankly' that he would regard his own removal from the corps command as 'a degradation and a humiliation'.[84] Just like Ulysses S. Grant's in the American Civil War, Monash believes, a general's success is best achieved with a lack of political interference.

Hughes gives Monash a political reply, laying a soothing hand on the general's shoulder and coming in close to tell him: 'You may thoroughly rely upon your wishes in this matter receiving the greatest possible weight.'[85]

Monash outlines to Hughes his plans for the attack on Hamel, telling him they will involve 'the least cost in human suffering' possible: about 300 casualties including walking wounded.[86]

To Hughes this immediately stamps Monash 'as an outstanding figure of World War 1', the only general he has known closely who gave due consideration to the human cost of battle. 'He was no swashbuckler, nor was his plan that of a bull at a gate', Hughes later recalls. 'It was enterprising without being foolhardy, as was to be expected of a man who had been trained as an engineer and had given profound study to the art of war. Monash always understood thoroughly the ground he was to fight on. Maps lived for him.'[87]

Watching on, Bean can only hope that Monash somehow trips up and falls flat on his face. Instead the new commander can't put a foot wrong.

Hughes is seriously rattled by all the praise he hears for Monash from the other Australian generals. He tells Murdoch that he hasn't met one person – not one – who doesn't think Monash should be the man in charge. Murdoch replies that Hughes only met the commanders Monash wanted him to meet and of course they were all going to support their mate. That was Monash's plan. But Hughes has heard and seen enough. When he and Cook climb into their car for the drive to Paris, Bean knows that it's checkmate. Monash has won again and Bean concedes that he feels 'pretty blue'.[88]

Hughes will eventually offer Monash whatever job he wants: GOC in London or the corps command. Monash stays with his men and Birdwood maintains his administrative role.

'So much for our high-intentioned but ill-judged intervention', Bean writes many years later.[89] The bluff and outspoken Colonel Thomas Dodds, Birdwood's deputy adjutant general, calls him 'an irresponsible pressman'.[90] In response Bean tells Dodds that Monash has used 'all sorts of clever well hidden subterranean channels' to try to get Birdwood's job, but years later will write, 'I do not now believe this to be true.'[91]

As far as White is concerned, Birdwood has made the right decision.

'Monash was my senior and an abler man', he tells Bean much later. 'I could not see on what grounds he could be passed over without injustice … I felt strongly at the time that Birdwood chose rightly and events and time have strengthened that opinion.'[92]

On 4 July, a day to inspire the American troops under his command, Monash sets about proving it.

Chapter 24

A WHEAT FIELD OUTSIDE HAMEL, NORTHERN FRANCE, ZERO HOUR, 3.10 A.M., THURSDAY, 4 JULY 1918

*A perfected modern battle plan is like nothing so much as a score for
an orchestral composition, where the various arms and units are the
instruments, and the tasks they perform are their respective musical
phrases. Every individual unit must make its entry precisely at the
proper moment, and play its phrase in the general harmony.*
MONASH ON HIS ROLE AS A MILITARY CONDUCTOR[1]

*We knew you would fight a real fight, but we did not know that from
the very beginning you would astonish the whole Continent with
your valour ... I shall go back tomorrow and say to my countrymen:
'I have seen the Australians; I have looked into their faces ... I know
that these men ... will fight alongside us till the freedom for which we
are all fighting is guaranteed; for us and our children.'*
FRENCH PRIME MINISTER GEORGES CLEMENCEAU, ON MEETING
MONASH'S TROOPS AFTER THE BATTLE TO TAKE HAMEL[2]

THEY LIE MOTIONLESS on a still dark night in the long
grass and among the tall stalks of wheat that soon will be
ready for the summer harvest. There are 7000 Australian Diggers
and 1000 American Doughboys, bayonets fixed, waiting quietly
for the command to attack. Some have taken the opportunity

to sleep after what, for some, will be their last meal. Others are wide awake, their hearts racing so fast they can almost hear the drumbeat in their heads. A thick fog, unusual for this time of year, floats all around the men and they know that this will make it even harder for the Germans to see them coming.

At the same time every morning for a week, aeroplanes have been flying low over this area to create a noisy diversion, and artillery pieces have fired great volleys of smoke bombs and the best mustard gas the French can provide.

The same thing has happened on this morning of American Independence Day, but now there is a lull in the violent cacophony, as though the maestro Monash is building all the pieces of his grand symphony to the cannon-blast crescendo of Tchaikovsky's *1812 Overture.*

The infantrymen made their final preparations last night, each man receiving 220 rounds of ammunition and a pair of grenades. Each soldier carries either a pick or a shovel and every second man carries a flare. Officers have been instructed to use wireless messages from captured positions. There was a second hot meal late in the night for those who could stomach food before the gunfire begins.

The 60 tanks began rumbling to their starting line from Fouilloy and Hamelet, a kilometre and a half away, at 10.30 p.m., and by 1 a.m. were in position, another kilometre and a half behind the front. Their movement was covered by the constant harassments of the night flying squadron.[3] Once in position, the tanks were met by guides from the infantry, who helped the tank commanders mark the tracks to the infantry battalions with tape, so they can find them in the dark.[4]

At 2.50 a.m. the tank commanders restart their engines as a night-bombing air squadron blasts away at Hamel and the valley beyond, dropping 350 11-kilogram bombs. Monash has studied aerial photographs microscopically and knows the location of the enemy placements exactly.

At 3.02 a.m., eight minutes before zero hour, the harassing fire begins as the tanks begin to roll on and into the darkness. Pompey

Elliott's 15th Brigade makes a diversionary attack north of the River Somme, launching a 'feint' against Ville-sur-Ancre to draw German fire. Monash's artillery sends over smoke shells without the gas towards the defences around Hamel, and as he predicts there is a rush behind the German lines for the protective masks.

The Australian commander has timed the tanks to advance 720 metres in eight minutes to reach the start line for the Australian infantry. If they can do it, he says, the battle is already won, and the fighting should last no more than 90 minutes. He has told his troops that this battle will be like a grand symphony and timing is everything. 'Old Monash talks too much,' Rawlinson has said, 'but [he] is very good at the preliminaries.'[5]

But not everything goes like clockwork for the master conductor. In war, it rarely does.

There is a last-minute change foisted upon Monash that will call for all of his nerve, bombast and cunning. As he is plotting out the battle down to the minutest detail, at the same time as juggling the demands of the Prime Minister, he is also faced with the prospect that the whole attack will be derailed. Because of the secrecy necessary, it isn't until 2 July that anyone informs the American commander, a southern gentleman named 'Black Jack' Pershing,[6] and his fiery aide-de-camp Captain George S. Patton[7] that American soldiers are taking part.

Pershing has already received widespread criticism for his reliance on frontal assaults, which have resulted in unnecessarily high numbers of American casualties, and he is also uneasy about being the first American commander to allow his troops to fight under a foreign general. At first he orders the withdrawal of 1000 of the Americans, who are 'loud in their lamentations'[8] because they are itching to get a crack at the enemy. Their removal causes a major reshuffle of Monash's personnel, especially for the 11th Brigade, which now has to attack with 2200 men instead of 3000.[9]

Then at 4 p.m. on 3 July, just 11 hours before the attack is due to commence, Monash is at the 3rd Division's headquarters at

Glisy, on his daily round of visits to his commanders, when a call from Rawlinson knocks the wind from him.

No American troops, *at all*, are to be used the next day.[10] Pershing now fears his men are not sufficiently well trained to take part.

Monash is enraged. The withdrawal of 2000 men, 25 per cent of his force, on the eve of battle is a critical blow to such a finely tuned strategy. He tells Rawlinson that if the Americans withdraw at such a late hour he will cancel the whole fight. Rawlinson tells him that Haig has approved Pershing's directive.

Monash has to think quickly. He has to win this administrative battle before any attack on Hamel can take place.

Monash asks Rawlinson to meet him in an hour at Sinclair-Maclagan's headquarters, which have been dug out of a quarry in a wood close by at Bussy-lès-Daours.[11] As Monash heads over there in the Rolls-Royce a scowl adds more lines to his weathered face. He resolves to 'take a firm stand' and press his views as strongly as he dares, 'for even a Corps Commander must use circumspection when presuming to argue with an Army Commander'.[12]

When Rawlinson arrives with his chief of staff Major General Archibald Montgomery[13] at 5 p.m., Monash tells them that 'the whole of the Infantry destined for the assault at dawn next morning, including those very Americans, [is] already well on its way to its battle stations'.[14]

Rawlinson is 'very much upset'.[15]

'The Americans are in their positions now and are ready to fight,' Monash continues; 'if they are ordered out now no Australian will ever fight beside an American again. We are risking an international incident.'[16]

Monash will write that Rawlinson has a 'charming and sympathetic personality' but that he knows the 2nd Army commander is really gun-shy and malleable. Monash can bend him with a reasoned argument and the force of his personality. Two years ago Rawlinson earned heavy criticism at the Battle of the Somme, where the British suffered 60,000 casualties and 20,000 dead on the first day.

Monash tells him straight.

First, it is already too late to withdraw the Americans. Second, if the Americans don't participate the battle is off. Third, unless the order comes directly from Haig the fight will go ahead as planned, and fourth – and you'd better hurry up, General Rawlinson – unless that order comes by 6.30 p.m. it will be too late to stop the attack.

Rawlinson is unnerved. As Monash suspected, the British general is indecisive and worried about making another critical error.

He tells Monash that he agrees with him, he really does, but Monash must obey Haig's direction. 'You don't realise what it means,' Rawlinson exclaims, 'do you want me to run the risk of being sent back to England? Do you mean it is worth that?'

'Yes I do,' Monash says. 'It is more important to keep the confidence of Australians and Americans in each other than to preserve even an army commander.'[17]

'But orders are orders,' Rawlinson says, with a tone of desperation.

'Haig would not have given such an order,' Monash says, 'if he had known that it meant the abandonment of the battle.'

Then he plays his ace, saying that it is prudent for a 'commander on the spot to act in the light of the situation as known to him, *even* to the extent of disobeying an order'.

Rawlinson says he'll make contact with Haig, and after repeated attempts to raise general headquarters from Bussy he is told that the field marshal is on his way back from the war council at Versailles.

Rawlinson realises that while Monash is under his command, he is also a great favourite of Haig and the King. To go against Monash could be far more dangerous than to allow him to go ahead with the battle.

He promises to make a decision by 6.30 p.m. and Monash knows he has already won the first round. He goes ahead with the preparations as planned and the men take their places as ordered, moving in the dark like shadows.[18]

Rawlinson finally reaches Haig at 7 p.m. and the commander-in-Chief says the 1000 Americans *are* to take part in the fight just as Monash has ordered.

After Rawlinson departs, Monash outlines every last detail of the battle to war correspondents Bean, Murdoch and Fred Cutlack; standing before a map and without notes, he rattles off every move and counter-move, 'names of battalions and everything'. With a half-smirk he tells them how he outwitted Rawlinson, knowing that Haig would be in his motorcade of two Rolls-Royces, heading from Versailles to his base at the Château de Beaurepaire outside Montreuil, 230 kilometres to the north. Monash says he knew all along Haig would not be back in time to cancel the attack, even if he wanted to.[19]

A few hours later, the aircraft start creating their diversion and the tanks begin to roll. At his château, Monash retires early, his work done, but when Walter Coxen rises to head to the front and supervise his artillery that morning he sees Monash slowly walking the 130 paces of the gravel drive from his front stairs to the château's 200-year-old iron gates. Monash stops occasionally to look at the luminous face of his watch and listens to make sure every instrument is joining the symphony at precisely the right time – the British tanks, the RAF planes, the smoke shells fired from Australian and British cannons and mortars, the Australian and American infantrymen. In front of Hamel, German soldiers are putting on their gas masks believing that this regular harassment will soon be over.

At 3.02 a.m. on 4 July the black sky lights up with the sound of hundreds of cannons that are hiding the low rumble of 60 tanks on the move. Soon the tanks will be beside the infantry, the whole line of soldiers rising as one, lighting cigarettes, slinging rifles over their shoulders[20] and moving up to the line of artillery shells, which will then creep further forward.

In the distance, the village of Hamel is already on fire.

Monash goes inside his office to plan the next stage of his masterpiece.

The artillery barrage is on target, mostly. The field guns rain down shells 200 metres in front of the infantry as they creep forward through the mist, although many of the advancing men do not wait for the monstrous tanks. Howitzers and heavy cannons fire their projectiles further into the German line.

At half a dozen points, the guns fire short, and their first shells catch some of the Americans and Australians as they wait in the wheat fields. In the confusion, as Australian shells cause thick chalky clouds of dust to erupt amid the fog, Corporal Mick Roach, a mining labourer from Copeton near Inverell, is killed by shellfire when trying to turn around a platoon of over-eager Americans who are rushing straight into a target area for the artillery. A dozen men from Australia's 15th Battalion are killed by stray shellfire near Pear Trench.

At the same position, Private Harry Dalziel,[21] a locomotive fireman on Queensland's Cairns–Atherton line,[22] is part of a two-man Lewis gun team. Here, the artillery fire has caused little damage to the German position and the tanks have not arrived to break the wire. Harry's comrades encounter blazing attacks from several German Maxim machine-guns behind thick wire entanglements. Harry helps his mate load a fresh drum of ammunition into the Lewis gun and then, armed only with a revolver, charges one of the posts, killing two of the Germans with his handgun and another with a knife, but sparing a boy who he reckons has fought bravely. Part of Harry's trigger finger is blown off, but even though blood spurts in all directions he keeps fighting, twice racing across open ground under heavy enemy artillery and machine-gun fire to grab ammunition dropped by parachute. Even with his wounded hand he busily fills magazines for the Lewis gun until a bullet blows open his skull[23] and his brain is exposed. He is given little chance of survival, but he defies the odds, and will soon have a broad, if somewhat lopsided, smile on his face when George V places on his breast the thousandth Victoria Cross to be awarded.[24]

At Pear Trench some of the enemy hold up their hands, shouting, '*Merci Comrade*', and offer the Australians 'watches of different makes, gold and silver leaf wrist watches of beautiful designs'.[25] Elsewhere in the trench, at least one German machine-gunner continues to fire until a party of Queensland troops reaches him. Although some of the Germans hold up their hands, others throw grenades. The Queenslanders kill every last one of them, at least 40 men.[26]

At Vaire and Hamel Woods, uncut entanglements delay the 16th Battalion from Western Australia. Machine-gun fire kills their captain, so Lance Corporal Thomas 'Jack' Axford, a labourer at the Boulder City Brewery in Kalgoorlie, takes matters into his own hands, throwing grenades as he charges the machine-gun post. He jumps into a trench, kills 10 men with his bayonet and takes six of the lucky ones prisoner.[27] After also receiving the Victoria Cross, Axford admits: 'I must have been mad.'[28]

During a halt in the action as the artillery creeps up, a lieutenant of the 14th Battalion hears two men discussing the recent Fitzroy–Carlton game.[29]

As the greying dawn gives way to the sun, the tanks become much more effective in better light, firing grape-shot – small metal balls in canvas bags, like massive shotgun blasts – against pockets of resistance. Often the tanks simply drive straight over German machine-gun posts, flattening them like a housewife's iron, then reverse back and forward over the enemy, to make sure they are all dead.

Under Monash's direction, four of the tanks are used to cart supplies. On just one machine there are 133 coils of barbed wire, 450 pickets on which to hang it, 45 sheets of corrugated iron, 50 petrol tins filled with water, 150 trench mortar bombs, 10,000 rounds of ammunition and 20 boxes of grenades.[30] The tanks also ferry wounded troops and German prisoners back to the Australian line. None of the tanks is lost in the battle and only three are temporarily disabled. The Royal Air Force delivers 111,600 bullets in parachute drops.[31]

Coming up through the centre of the attack, Lieutenant Ted Rule is with the 14th Battalion as they dig a support trench while bullets fly from an unseen enemy. Rule asks a tank commander to waddle his machine over to investigate. A white flag is raised, but when the Australians go across to take prisoners they are fired on. A shell from the Australian barrage kills Rule's batman and another Australian soldier is shot through the head. Germans are seen running for their lives but Rule finds more in two dugouts. He orders them out, only to find they are a group of terrified boy soldiers no more than 14 or 15 years old.

'We could not kill children', he says. 'With a boot to help them along they ran with their hands above their heads back to our lines.'[32]

Monash has planned for the battle to take 90 minutes. It takes 93 and is over before 5 a.m. Using the common tactics of the war to that point, it might have lasted for weeks, months even, with much greater casualty rates.

'No battle within my previous experience, not even Messines, passed off so smoothly', Monash says. 'It was the perfection of team work.'[33]

By the end of the offensive more than 2000 Germans are dead and 1600 have been taken prisoner. Brigadier General Evan Wisdom[34] of the 7th Brigade calls them 'the poorest lot I have seen', guessing that the enemy is now holding its lines with its weakest men, worn down by the constant harassment of peaceful penetration.

The spoils of war are stretched out across half a hectare of captured ground: two anti-tank machine-guns, 177 machine-guns, 32 trench mortars and a new anti-tank gun in the form of a gigantic bipod-supported rifle with a .530 calibre bullet. The Allies have suffered 1400 casualties, 1062 of them Australian, and a combined 800 deaths: a low figure by the standards of this wasteful war.[35]

Congratulations pour in from Allied commanders and politicians, and even though Bean is still trying to undermine Monash, he will later write: 'Hamel was ... a trial of a surprise offensive carried out with John Monash's methods of infinite care in co-ordination ... Haig, who on July 1st had visited Monash to talk over the coming operation, noted: "Monash is a most capable commander, who thinks out every detail of any operation and leaves nothing to chance".'[36]

Monash has every reason to feel proud of himself, but his gift for exaggeration shows itself again when he writes after Hamel that the battle was:

> ... the first offensive operation, on any substantial scale, that had been fought by any of the Allies since the previous autumn. Its effect was electric, and it stimulated many men to the realisation that the enemy was, after all, not invulnerable, in spite of the formidable increase in his resources which he had brought from Russia. It marked the termination, once and for all, of the purely defensive attitude of the British front. It incited in many quarters an examination of the possibilities of offensive action on similar lines by similar means – a changed attitude of mind, which bore a rich harvest only a very few weeks later.[37]

This is not really true, because the British counter-attacked at Ypres, and the French, under General Charles 'The Butcher' Mangin, displayed a devastating counter-punch against the Germans only a few weeks ago in the Matz Valley, using four divisions and 150 tanks, more than twice the number Monash has used. As Rawlinson steps up to take much of the credit for Hamel's success, Monash likewise stretches the truth by later saying 'it is undeniable and unchallengeable that the whole conception of the battle ... rested upon my own unaided efforts ...'.[38]

By the standards of the Great War, Hamel has been a minor battle, but its execution has been a tremendous victory for the

Australian Corps, and has proved that Monash, a general with modern ideas for a modern war, is the best man to lead it.

After the battle, Ted Rule's battalion celebrate their success with 'four ladies of easy virtue' in a village north of the Somme. At 5 a.m., with the tanks and the troops having overrun Hamel, Monash relaxes at Bertangles and waits for confirmation that his precise timetable has been thoroughly successful. As the light dawns on the greatest day of his military career, he sits down in his office and begins to sketch a pencil portrait of Billy Hughes's chauffeur to send home to Vic and Bert. He says drawing keeps his nerves 'cool and steady'[39] and helps him think.

Soon Haig will publish a brochure for distribution to the whole British Army, containing the complete text of Monash's orders, and a full and detailed description of the whole of the battle plans and preparations; a lesson to everyone on how to win a war.

'No fighting operation that the Corps has ever undertaken', Monash declares, 'has been more brilliantly, cleanly and perfectly carried through.'

'The psychological effect ... was electric and startling. People came from far and near to hear all about it and find out how it was done.'[40]

At the Supreme War Council at Versailles, the Prime Ministers of England, New Zealand and the dominion of Newfoundland all ask Billy Hughes to telegraph their heartiest thanks and congratulations to Monash. The French leader Georges Clemenceau,[41] still known as 'Le Tigre' despite his 76 years and declining health, starts directing a secretary to send his congratulations also, when, no, he decides to thank the Australians in person.

The following Sunday, the ancient prime minister, together with his aide General Mordacq,[42] drives 110 kilometres north from Paris to Sinclair-Maclagan's headquarters at Bussy.

In the afternoon, a few of the Australian troops wait in the quarry to receive this 'Great Old Man' of France with his long white drooping moustache, who arrives wearing a neat brown three-piece suit, bow tie and small crumpled felt hat.

He is greeted by Monash, Rawlinson and Sinclair-Maclagan. A few officers and men of the 4th Brigade arrive on the scene straight from the trenches, still in fighting kit and covered in mud. A small circle of officers and men forms round Clemenceau, who takes off his hat and addresses the men in English as best he can, though he is panting from the effects of emotion and asthma. Hubert Wilkins, who was shot in the right arm while photographing the battle three days earlier, captures the scene in colour.

Clemenceau asks to be excused for his 'bad English', but says how much he wants to thank all of the men there for their success in the battle, and 'for coming all those thousands of miles across the seas to fight for La Belle France'.

'France will never forget your great deeds and what she owes to Australia.'[43] He speaks of freedom for the children of France, and of the heroic feats Australia has performed on the ancient battlefields of Europe and the great work she has done in creating her own nation. He speaks of liberty, equality and fraternity.

A Digger in the background, covered in dirt, yells out: 'Three cheers for France', and Sinclair-Maclagan leads the cheering as a tear springs to the eye of Le Tigre.

While Clemenceau moves through the circle of Australians to shake their hands, the 4th Division band strikes up 'La Marseillaise'. Clemenceau stands straight and still and salutes. After the last note of the French anthem the old man rushes to embrace the bandmaster.[44]

Just three days after taking Hamel, Monash submits a plan for a major attack on the Monument Farm orchard, better known as Monument Wood, that will smooth out a bulge in the Australian line south-east of Villers-Bretonneux.

Instead, Rosenthal's 2nd Division makes a full-scale battle unnecessary as they push the line forward 1000 metres using night raids.

On the night of 13 July, Rosenthal's 26th Battalion from Queensland comes into the conflict zone. Shortly after midnight they push 100 metres down the Stamboul Trench and erect a barricade opposite the south-western corner of the orchard. At 6 a.m., covered by the fire of two Stokes mortars and Lewis guns, they attack a German position, only to be met by Germans throwing king-size stick grenades that are packed with extra explosives. The Germans are overpowered. The left company of the 26th sends out patrols south of the railway and gradually Monument Wood is taken.

Inside the captured territory, stuck in a deep shell crater, is a disabled German A7V *Sturmpanzerwagen* tank, known as 'Mephisto', one of only 20 ever built by Daimler-Benz. It is painted in a grey-green camouflage scheme and is decorated with a picture of the devil running off with a British tank under one arm. Mephisto saw action along with 13 other similar tanks supporting the infantry at Villers-Bretonneux in April.

Brisbane schoolteacher Major J.A. Robinson,[45] commander of the 26th, orders that Mephisto be dragged further back into the Australian line to prevent it from being retaken by the Germans. On the night of 22 July 1918, the 26th, using two vehicles from the British 1st Gun Carrier Company, move forward with artillery support and air cover, then dodge return German fire and gas attacks to drag the great beast out of its hole.

It is the first German tank to be captured by the Allies.

The Queenslanders scratch their names into Mephisto's armour and paint the AIF's rising sun emblem on it.[46] The British tell the Aussies they will keep it for the Imperial War Museum, but the boys of the 26th reckon Australia has already given the Poms too much of its very best. Before the British can take possession of it, Mephisto is put on a ship destined for Australia with some of the soldiers who captured it.

It will remain in the possession of the Queensland Museum from that point on.

*

On 15 July, as the 26th is celebrating its success at Monument Wood, Monash tells Vic that he is proud as punch, because he is 'very much now in the limelight'.[47]

He spends two days entertaining a mission bound for Australia headed by Albert Métin,[48] a French cabinet minister who gave up his labour portfolio at the outbreak of war to serve as a private on the front. Monash finds him 'a very fine man', and also says Métin's colleague General Paul Pau,[49] who lost an arm in the Franco-Prussian War of 1870, will appeal 'most strongly to the Australian public' because of his 'charming personality'.[50] Pau will have to carry the extra load of the mission when Métin dies in San Francisco, en route to Sydney, aged just 47. The cause of death is listed as a stroke brought on by war stress.

Monash is invited to celebrate Bastille Day with the local governor, the Prefect of the Somme. Amiens is in ruins, but there is a banqueting room untouched in the bombed-out *hôtel de ville* (town hall), as big as Melbourne's own. The Prefect has a long guest list of dignitaries, including French politicians and military men, the British war correspondent Philip Gibbs and the Olympic bronze medallist Major Neville Lytton,[51] whose grandfather, Lord Lytton, wrote so many of Monash's favourite novels.

Monash makes his first speech in French to the assembled diners. Of course, he says afterwards, his little discourse was 'quite successful'.[52] Monash is on a roll.

Chapter 25

*Viewed from a high vantage point and in the glimmer of the breaking
day, a great Artillery barrage surely surpasses in dynamic splendour
any other manifestation of collective human effort.*
MONASH ON OPENING FIRE AT THE BATTLE OF AMIENS[1]

*August 8 was the black day of the German Army ... Everything I
had feared, and of which I had so often given warning, had here, in
one place, become a reality.*
ERICH LUDENDORFF ON HIS DECISIVE MOMENT OF THE WAR[2]

MONASH HAS SCORED A STINGING blow at Hamel,
and two weeks later the Allies follow it up with an even
more telling strike against Ludendorff's advancing forces around
the river near Reims, 130 kilometres north-east of Paris.

Now effectively the ruler of Germany, Ludendorff starts a
diversionary battle east of Reims on 15 July as the first step of
a massive thrust against Haig's men in Flanders. The German
salient, powered by a quarter of a million soldiers, comes so close
to Paris that cannon blasts can be seen, along with fire on the
horizon.

But Allied reinforcements pour in as, more than ever, the
Great War becomes a numbers game. On 18 July, French general

Mangin ensures Ludendorff's attack on nearby Soissons will be Germany's last great push of the war. Mangin counters with the support of British and Italian troops as well as Americans, whose 85,000 infantrymen include segregated Negro fighters known as the Buffalo Soldiers. Mangin has 100,000 more troops than Ludendorff, and his air power is five times greater than the 210 aeroplanes in the sky for Germany. The French also have more than 2000 cannons and nearly 500 tanks,[3] with many of them the new two-man Renault FTs that are fast and manoeuvrable.

In three weeks of fighting Germany suffers 168,000 casualties, with 56,700 deaths. More than 27,000 officers and men have been captured, most surrendering willingly rather than fighting to the death. The Allies regain most of the territory lost to Ludendorff's great spring attacks, and the victory triggers their 'Hundred Days Offensive' that will eventually result in the German surrender.

As the bad news of the defeat reaches Ludendorff's headquarters in Avesnes, the chest of the Prussian warlord deflates and he seems to shrink in front of his men.

In a state of panic, he turns on Hindenburg.. Then he attacks his own staff for failing in their assessment of the German fighting forces.[4]

The Allies prepare to rock the reeling German command with another monstrous blow in the Battle of Amiens as they push east towards Albert and Moreuil. It will always be the subject of conjecture just who came up with the idea for the campaign, though it seems certain that Monash, Rawlinson and Haig all had similar ideas for many months.

Haig and Rawlinson had been planning a great offensive since April, and in mid-May Foch asked Haig about the possibility of a major Anglo-French fightback south of the Somme, which Haig then outlined to Rawlinson on 23 May.[5] It was a plan that involved constant renewal of the attack, with British and Canadian divisions leapfrogging tiring soldiers as the assault continued. Birdwood and White drew up secret plans for Rawlinson, but the idea was shelved after Ludendorff mounted another of his colossal raids, codenamed Operation Blücher-Yorck, on 27 May around the Aisne River, which resulted in the Germans taking 50,000 prisoners and getting to within 56 kilometres of Paris.

The success of the Australians at Hamel, and the continuing effectiveness of the peaceful penetration raids in proving that the Germans are increasingly dysfunctional and dismayed, later encourages Rawlinson to dust off his plans for the great Allied offensive. He amends them to focus on an even bigger British involvement[6] and formally submits them to Haig on 17 July. They are approved two days later, and on 21 July Rawlinson calls his corps commanders together at the 4th Army's headquarters at Flixicourt, 20 kilometres west of Bertangles.

The plans are top secret, and though Monash says 'never was a secret better kept', he admits that 'an observant enemy agent … might well have drawn a shrewd conclusion that some mischief was brewing' with the arrival at Flixicourt of 'a quite unusual procession of motor-cars, ostentatiously flying the Canadian and Australian flags and the red-and-white pennants of two other Corps Commanders'.[7]

Present are Monash, Rawlinson, General Currie from Canada, General Butler of the British III Corps,[8] General Kavanagh of the Cavalry Corps,[9] and senior officers of the Tank Corps and the air forces of France, Britain and Australia.[10]

Rawlinson unfolds the outline of the whole plan, and details are discussed at great length among the commanders as they forge an attacking arrowhead led by the two citizen soldiers, the now trim and stylish Monash, and the shop-worn Currie. There is nothing flamboyant about Currie, but his soldiers worship this grim-faced commander, who cares for his troops and who spreads the motto 'Pay the price of victory in shells – not lives'.[11]

The broad arrowhead attack is vital, Monash says. 'It would be bad tactics to drive into the enemy's front a salient with a narrow base, for such a salient would make our situation worse instead of better, affording to the enemy the opportunity of artillery attack upon it from both its flanks as well as from its front. The salient must therefore be broad based in relation to its depth, and the base must ever widen as the head of the salient advances.'[12]

Monash wants to reduce his front from 17 kilometres to 7, with the Somme as the northern edge and the Péronne railway at the south. He also asks that Glasgow's 1st Division be brought back from Flanders so that all Australian field units in France will be under one command for the first time in the war. The Australians, numbering 53,000, and a similar-sized body of Canadians[13] will mount the bulk of the attack in two central corps, carrying out the main advance.[14] Rawlinson plans the first wave as a creeping barrage, the second as an attack under mobile artillery and the third as a process of destroying the German fortifications.

The Canadians are to operate on Monash's right, and even further south, the First French Army under General Debeney[15] is to form a defensive flank for the Canadians. Monash initially baulked over the French involvement, saying that while 'The French are irresistible in attack as they are dogged in defence ... whether they will attack or defend depends greatly on their temperament of the moment'.[16]

The British III Corps is to form a defensive northern flank for the Australians. Haig insists that the Cavalry Corps must also play a major role in following the attack, despite Monash's disregard for the old ways of war.[17]

Rawlinson assigns the two colonial commanders their frontages and gives them a free hand in battle tactics. Monash realises that Ludendorff is contemplating no further offensive operations in the Somme Valley and that the condition of the whole German 2nd Army offers 'every temptation to us to seize the initiative against it'.[18]

On 24 July, Foch tells Haig and Rawlinson to proceed. Monash consults with British tank expert 'Boney' Fuller,[19] a small and weedy colonel who in earlier days was intrigued by mysticism and was an associate of the occultist Aleister Crowley. Fuller will be called the 'Wacko Genius of Armoured Warfare' – 'Irascible, overbearing, argumentative, condescending, a fan of woo-woo occultism and, ultimately, a Nazi sympathizer'[20] – but he knows tanks and their capabilities.

With Fuller's support, Monash argues for an extended objective to make sure his men can destroy the heavy German guns. Monash and Blamey then sit down to thrash out details for their corps, broadly following their tactics of combined penetration at Hamel. Birdwood calls Blamey 'an exceedingly able little man, though by no means a pleasing personality',[21] but Monash is not worried about his offsider's abrasiveness, saying Blamey has 'a mind cultured far above the average, widely informed, alert and prehensile' with 'an infinite capacity for taking pains'.[22]

As the battle plans take shape Monash also has to act as peacemaker, sorting out a major dispute between his 3rd Division commander Gellibrand and the 10th Brigade's Walter McNicoll. Gellibrand says McNicoll is argumentative and inefficient, and McNicoll says Gellibrand is a bully. McNicoll asks for a transfer or permission to resign,[23] but Monash smooths things out for a while, though he will split them in October.

Monash's administrative head is Brigadier General Robert Alexander Carruthers, a veteran of the Indian Army and an old friend of Birdwood's. Monash finds him likeable but lazy, and would have given Bruche the job except for Birdwood's complaint that one general with a German name is more than enough for the corps. Monash thinks Birdwood's logic is 'stupid in the extreme'.[24]

Bean, who doesn't know that Paul Simonson and Aubrey Moss are Monash's nephews, writes that, like Napoleon, Monash is 'loyal to his clan'. His personal staff is Jewish, Bean says, 'and the men honoured him for this loyalty'.[25]

With the battle imminent, Monash asks Rawlinson for leave in London, so he can see Lizzie. He arranges publicity for the trip to assuage any fears the Germans might have about an imminent attack, but he makes no mention of whom he will be visiting. A destroyer is on standby at Dover, in case Monash receives a coded message from the War Office for an immediate return.[26] Despite the constant improvements in aircraft, he is not prepared to take his chances flying back, not with Hermann Göring and Manfred Richthofen's crazy brother Lothar still prowling the skies over France. Haig makes sure the Germans know that he is also taking a break from the front, heading to the golf links at the sea-swept resort of Le Touquet, not far from his headquarters at Montreuil.

Monash leaves Bertangles on Tuesday 23 July, takes a boat from Boulogne to Folkestone and is then chauffeured to the Prince's Hotel, where Lizzie awaits. They spend the evening together and have lunch the next day.

On 25 July he and Lizzie attend the Playhouse in Charing Cross, where Gladys Cooper is starring in another farce, *The Naughty Wife*. The next night they are arm in arm at the Gaiety Theatre to see the musical *Going Up*, about a daring young aviator who wins the hand of a high-society girl.[27]

Monash visits the War Office in Horse Guards Avenue every day, undertakes press interviews in which he talks up the exploits of his men, poses for photographers and for the artists John Longstaff and James Peter Quinn, though he finds sitting for them for half an hour at a time very tiring work. He also spends time with the Rosenhains. He is summoned to Buckingham Palace to receive his knighthood on 31 July and invited to the official opening of Australia House on 3 August, but fails to keep either appointment.

The coded message arrives at his hotel on Sunday night, 28 July.

He kisses Lizzie goodbye the next morning and heads back to Bertangles by train, ferry and car.

He writes home to Vic that he spent virtually the whole time in London on 'official business at AIF headquarters' at Horseferry Road. 'I had practically no leisure at all,' he explains, 'and could devote no time at all to amusements or sightseeing.'[28]

*

The next morning, 29 July, Monash and Blamey go over the battle plans that their general staff have prepared. Monash picks the proposal he prefers, then shuts himself up in his office, and makes revisions and masses of notes about supplies, movement and auxiliary forces.

Two days later Monash meets with his five divisional commanders, goes over the plans and calls for questions as Haig visits and tells the men he has absolute trust in their corps commander.

Monash is given a free hand to plot the field and heavy artillery, and the positions for the tanks, the armoured cars and the cavalry brigade. He tells his men that troops destined for battle must be kept in the highest physical condition. This means good food, comfortable housing and adequate rest. A couple of weary days and sleepless nights will play havoc with the fighting trim of even a crack battalion, he notes. So the daily stages of the journey must be short, and the day's supplies must arrive punctually to ensure hot, well-cooked meals.[29]

Meanwhile, Billy Hughes suspects that the British Government is holding its men back while waiting for more Americans to arrive, and is consequently overtaxing the Australians. Lloyd George is aiming for re-election in December and wants to appease a population angry that their sons are being slaughtered. Hughes does not want to sacrifice any Australians as compensation. He demands the power of veto over the use of Australians in battle. Haig ignores him.

The first day's objective for the Australian troops is an advance of 9 kilometres, with the first 3 in a creeping barrage. The attack is set for 10 August, but Foch wants to maintain pressure on the Germans following the French triumph on the Marne and he convinces Haig to bring the battle forward to the morning of 8 August.[30]

The Germans are to be taken by surprise just as they were at Hamel. The Canadian Corps, with four infantry divisions, has moved to Amiens without the Germans realising. The tanks are to arrive at the last possible moment. Advances in range-finding for the artillery and the use of high-quality aerial photographs mean that the first shots from 2034 British field guns and howitzers will immediately hit their target. The French offer 1606 guns in support.[31]

After studying all the aerial photographs, Rawlinson's artillery chief Major General Charles Budworth says 504 of the 530 German guns can be neutralised with the first salvo at zero hour, 4.20 a.m. There will be as many as 115,000 Allied bayonets going against 36,000 Germans[32] in the 2nd Army of General Georg von der Marwitz.

There will also be 625 British aircraft and 1104 French planes, many of them dropping smoke bombs, against just 365 German machines. Including supply vehicles, there will be 634 tanks, the giant Mark Vs that had been so effective at Hamel, a longer version that can carry 15 infantrymen as passengers and the new, lighter, faster Mark A Whippets. The Australian Corps front will be 7 kilometres wide.

More conferences are held on 2 and 4 August, and on the 5th Monash explains to Bean that once through the German lines the Australians have the option of either capturing the railway at Chaulnes or destroying the German heavy guns. Monash intends to go for the guns and put the railway station out of operation later. The Canadians will press on in the attack if there is to be further exploitation of their position while the Australians hold the captured territory.

On 4 August, near Soissons, Lance Corporal Adolf Hitler is awarded the Iron Cross First Class for his enthusiasm as a regimental dispatch runner behind the lines. The medal is usually awarded for acts of bravery, and there are voices of protest from several officers that a 'rear-area pig'[33] delivering messages several kilometres from danger is receiving such an honour. But Lieutenant Hugo Gutmann[34] puts up a fight for Hitler's work to be recognised.

Gutmann is a Jew. In 1937 the Gestapo arrest him but friends from his old regiment help him escape the Holocaust for a new life in America. Gutmann changes his name to Henry G. Grant and becomes a furniture salesman in St Louis, Missouri.

Most of the Diggers are kept in the dark about what is really happening in the first week of August. Monash tells his officers to make sure their men are well rested: 'no football, no wandering – but sleep'.[35] Because of the secrecy surrounding the attack, most of the Australians are only able to work on preparations after the sun goes down. The printed warning 'KEEP YOUR MOUTH SHUT' is added to their service and pay books.

Officers are ordered to stop visiting the front trenches and no one is to be seen studying maps or using field glasses. A prohibition on daylight transport hampers the artillery, but eventually the guns are dragged to their placements and camouflaged. More than 300,000 artillery shells along with machine-gun ammunition, grenades, flares and rockets have to be carted by truck, horse and mule in the few dark hours of the European summer.[36]

Such is the tight security surrounding the plans that when 300 Tommies are captured in a German counter-attack at Morlancourt and a few Australians taken in a raid, none of them knows anything about the looming battle. But on 6 August the Germans spy about 100 tanks massing on the road from Ailly to Morisel, and some captured Royal Air Force officers tell the Germans under interrogation the next day that a big attack is being planned. They just don't know when.

Monash will use four divisions for attack and keep Glasgow's newly arrived 1st Division in reserve 'to exploit any successes gained upon the first day, or else to take over and hold defensively the ground won, if the assaulting Divisions should have become too exhausted'.[37] The 2nd and 3rd Divisions will carry out the first phase, with the fresh troops of the 4th and 5th leapfrogging them as the battle progresses.

Monash concedes the plan is risky. The leapfrog attack has never been used by whole divisions before and it increases the already large amount of preparatory work. But if successful it will 'aid deep penetration' into the heart of the German defences 'by reducing the stress and fatigue imposed on troops'.[38]

> 'On no previous occasion in the war had an attempt ever been made to effect a penetration into the enemy's defences at the first blow, and on the first day, greater than a mile or two ... But the task I had set myself was not only to reach, at the first onslaught, the whole of the enemy's Artillery positions, but greatly to overrun them with a view to obliterating, by destruction or capture, the whole of his defensive organizations and the whole of the fighting resources which they contained, along the full extent of my Corps front.'[39]

One brigade of cavalry for the Australian sector and two cavalry divisions in the Canadian sector move into position from Amiens. Tanks are hidden in forests. Monash's great fear is that the enemy will withdraw to another position before the attack, ruining all of his detailed preparations. He also has doubts about the British on his left flank, north of the Somme. III Corps is a mixture of inexperienced recruits and worn-out veterans who performed miserably at Villers-Bretonneux. They have been assigned tough country, with ravines and woods, where the river loops around the village of Chipilly and where the Germans hold the peninsula called the Chipilly Spur.

Monash insists that General Butler keep III Corps moving until they take the spur. Two days before the attack he tells Sinclair-Maclagan to have the 4th Division make a defensive flank just in case the Tommies let him down.

Bean will recall that no matter who really devised the great attack, the elaboration to the men 'was immensely important' and that Monash 'applied to it his full power of minute forethought, immense care, and *pellucid* exposition, and even in this night march the men felt that whatever might lie in front, all was right behind them'.[40]

*

Monash writes to each of his men:

Corps Headquarters,
August 7th, 1918.
TO THE SOLDIERS OF THE AUSTRALIAN ARMY
CORPS.
For the first time in the history of this Corps, all five
Australian Divisions will to-morrow engage in the largest
and most important battle operation ever undertaken by the
Corps.

They will be supported by an exceptionally powerful
Artillery, and by Tanks and Aeroplanes on a scale never
previously attempted. The full resources of our sister
Dominion, the Canadian Corps, will also operate on our
right, while two British Divisions will guard our left flank.

The many successful offensives which the Brigades and
Battalions of this Corps have so brilliantly executed during
the past four months have been but the prelude to, and the
preparation for, this greatest and culminating effort.

Because of the completeness of our plans and dispositions,
of the magnitude of the operations, of the number of troops
employed, and of the depth to which we intend to overrun
the enemy's positions, this battle will be one of the most
memorable of the whole war; and there can be no doubt
that, by capturing our objectives, we shall inflict blows
upon the enemy which will make him stagger, and will
bring the end appreciably nearer.

I entertain no sort of doubt that every Australian soldier
will worthily rise to so great an occasion, and that every
man, imbued with the spirit of victory, will, in spite of
every difficulty that may confront him, be animated by no
other resolve than grim determination to see through to a
clean finish, whatever his task may be.

The work to be done to-morrow will perhaps make heavy demands upon the endurance and staying powers of many of you; but I am confident that, in spite of excitement, fatigue, and physical strain, every man will carry on to the utmost of his powers until his goal is won; for the sake of AUSTRALIA, the Empire and our cause.

I earnestly wish every soldier of the Corps the best of good fortune, and a glorious and decisive victory, the story of which will re-echo throughout the world, and will live for ever in the history of our home land.

JOHN MONASH,

Lieut.-General.

Cmdg. Australian Corps.

That same day, Erich Ludendorff, trying to assuage his own fears, assures his men that their defensive positions are now stronger than ever. Yet he is no Monash when it comes to inspiring them: 'To my regret the existence of despondent outlooks and rumours has been established and their source traced to Supreme Headquarters. The Oberste Heeresleitung [OHL or Supreme Army Command] is free from despondency ... it prepares stout heartedly to meet the challenges that are to come.'[41] Privately, he admits that the troops are no longer shouting 'hurrah' but are instead 'depressed down to Hell'.[42]

On the afternoon of 7 August the German artillery begins to shell a small plantation about 800 metres north of Villers-Bretonneux, landing bombs in the middle of 18 hidden supply tanks belonging to the 4th and 5th Divisions. They were only parked there the night before, and are loaded to capacity with rifle ammunition, Stokes mortar bombs and petrol. Fifteen of the tanks are destroyed.

That night 19-year-old Gunner James Ramsay Armitage, from Camden near Sydney, lies motionless along with more than 100,000 other men in readiness for zero hour.

'It was utterly still', he later recalls. 'Vehicles made no sound on the marshy ground ... The silence played on our nerves a bit. As we got our guns into position you could hear drivers whispering to their horses and men muttering curses under their breath, and still the silence persisted, broken only by the whine of a stray rifle bullet or a long range shell passing high overhead … we could feel that hundreds of groups of men were doing the same thing – preparing for the heaviest barrage ever launched.'[43]

The regular bombardment comes from the Australian line just before dawn so the enemy will not suspect anything unusual. Then what Monash calls 'a strange and ominous quiet' descends on the darkness. It is only when the explosion of a stray German shell causes hundreds of heads to peer out from trenches, gun pits and underground shelters that the countryside becomes alive and the hidden mass of men is revealed.

Under a heavy mist, made thicker by smoke bombs, the infantry waits, hushed, for the signal to advance. The roar of tank engines grows louder as the drone of hundreds of aircraft overhead masks their advance. Soldiers from the fresh-faced boy to the middle-aged father check that their bayonets are firmly locked, that their steel helmets will not be easily loosed. Pioneer groups grab their picks and shovels for the road-mending work; engineers take up their explosives, primers and fuses.

Some of the Diggers pray. Others are already crawling quietly on their bellies to get closer to the start line for when the artillery barrage begins.

Ludendorff, sleeping at Avesnes, still has no idea that an immense assault is about to rain down on his 2nd and 18th Armies, in the very area where the Germans slaughtered Gough's 5th Army five months earlier.[44]

At Bertangles, Monash has asked the Australian camp commandant Major Walter Berry to wake him before 4 a.m. Together the two Scotch College old boys walk the gravel drive and back again as Monash checks his watch, with the noise of the shells in the distance, the drone of aircraft above.

At 4.15 a.m. they stand on the steps of the château and count down the seconds. Inside, telegraph operators sit by their instruments with their message forms to hand, bracing themselves for the rush of signal traffic. Dozens of staff officers spread their maps and stand with coloured pencils to mark the battle's progress.

Out on the line, men who will fight with machine-guns rather than pencils whisper to their assistants to stick close with the ammo. Others toting Stokes mortars sling their weapons over their shoulders and make sure their comrades have haversacks full of cartridges. Company and platoon commanders, runners by their sides, nervously watch the seconds tick down. They put their whistles to their lips ready to start the life-and-death race.[45]

In hundreds of artillery pits across the Allied front, the heavy guns have been loaded. Sergeants check the range for one last time, and the section officer counts down the last seconds: 'A minute to go. Thirty seconds. Ten seconds. Five, four, three, two, one …

'FIRE!!'

With a roar like a giant volcano exploding, 3640 guns of the British 4th Army and the 1st French Army[46] are fired simultaneously. An hour before dawn, the eastern horizon lights up[47] as though some great power switch has been flicked, then every man and every tank begins the charge.

The artillery shakes the landscape. The field is speedily covered with a cloak of dust, smoke and flames.

Berry turns to Monash. 'Sir, this is a most wonderful day for you.'

'No, Berry,' Monash replies, 'it is a very wonderful day for Australia and history will bear this out.'[48]

Then Monash walks slowly up the stairs into his office.

Blamey has his feet on his desk, smoking a fat cigar without a care in the world. As thousands of Australians charge into the Germans, he says: 'Sir, I have nothing to do, so we can wait while they count thousands of prisoners.'[49]

*

Pigeons carry news from the battle to the lofts at Bertangles. The telephone and telegraph operators feverishly take notes. Aeroplanes drop messages close by and a team of cyclists races them to Monash, often just a few minutes after they are written.

The news is all good.

Practically all the infantry in the 4th Army has attacked in the same formation. There was some confusion at the start owing to the fog, but scouts went ahead of the leading battalions acting like beaters on a pheasant shoot,[50] pointing out where trouble spots needed to be flattened out by the tank crews.

The Germans panic. In most cases, whenever the tanks come near, the Germans leap out, raise their hands above their heads, and wait to be collected and have their belongings ransacked. Some of the Germans already have their watches off to save time. Before long, lines of shellshocked prisoners, grateful to escape with their lives, are being marched back to the Australian lines.[51]

Throughout the first phase of the battle there is hardly any stubborn resistance, and Bean calls the advance 'the most bloodless ever made by Australian infantry in a great battle'. The Canadians, to the right of the Australians, have similar success.

Monash sends a note to Rawlinson: 'Everything going well at 6.45 a.m. Heavy ground mist facilitating our advance, but delaying information. Infantry and Tanks got away punctually. Our attack was a complete surprise. Gailly Village and Accroche Wood captured. Enemy artillery has ceased along my whole front. Flanks Corps apparently doing well.'

Ninety minutes later he writes: '... no doubt that our first objective green line captured along whole Corps front including Gailly, Warfusée, Lamotte and whole Cerisy Valley. Many guns and prisoners taken. Infantry and Artillery for second phase moving up to green line.' And before long it is: 'The Huns never knew what hit them ... not so much a defeat as a stampede.'[52]

The 'open warfare' phase begins at 8.20 a.m. The mist suddenly rises from the plain in front of Villers-Bretonneux like a vast stage curtain, revealing a panorama that the Allies have waited four years to see.

Across the valley all the way to the Somme the Germans are on the run. Allied tanks roll on, Austin armoured cars drive into Lamotte-Warfusée, teams of horses drag heavy guns into place for more shelling, other horses lie dead beside the road, cavalrymen trot about ready to charge on into captured territory.

Lieutenant Alf Gaby,[53] a Tasmanian-born farm labourer from the West Australian bush, is leading an attack near Villers-Bretonneux when he tackles a machine-gun garrison single-handed with just his revolver, driving the crews from their guns and taking 50 prisoners. He is awarded the Victoria Cross. Posthumously. A sniper kills him three days later.

A tank lightens the load for the 14th Battalion at Morcourt, where the men raid cellars full of telephones, typewriters and maps, and take 300 prisoners. Further south, in the heavily wooded Morcourt Valley, the 13th finds an officers' mess stocked with fresh grapes and eggs, good pre-war cigars and a pay office with a money box that is blown open to reveal 25,000 marks.

Captain John Geary, a miner from Meekatharia, Western Australia, jumps on one of the German horses and takes it for a gallop – the cheers of his mates dying with him when he is promptly shot in the head.[54]

The Australians cart away 173 large cannons and blow many others to pieces. Near the village of Vauvillers, a squadron of cavalrymen attacks three trains. Two of the locomotives steam off, but the third is bombed by a Sopwith Camel from the Royal Air Force, and the locomotive crew evacuates. On board the smoking train is a weapon of mass destruction that will become known as the Amiens Gun. The barrel alone weighs more than 40 tons and has an 11.2-inch (28-centimetre) bore. It has been used to shell Amiens, 23 kilometres away. The gun is so big it rests on two great bogie carriages, each on eight axles, and has 20 carriages behind it for its giant ammunition, a workshop and living quarters for the crew.[55] The Amiens Gun will be exhibited in Paris before finding a permanent home outside the Australian War Memorial.[56]

Monash sends more messages to Rawlinson.

10.55 a.m.: 'Fifteenth Battalion has captured Cerisy with 300 prisoners. Advance to red line going well.'

11.10 a.m.: 'Have taken Morcourt and Bayonvillers and many additional prisoners and guns.'[57]

At the same time, four armoured cars head towards the village of Framerville. Two encounter a procession of horse-drawn transport wagons and open fire on the animals and the drivers. Further on they shoot the drivers of three artillery gun carriages, causing the horses to bolt. A lorry driver is also shot and his vehicle blocks the road.

In one of the armoured cars is Lieutenant Ernest James Rollings,[58] a 25-year-old Welsh policeman serving with the 17th (Armoured Car) Tank Battalion which had been attached to the Australian Corps. Rollings is searching for a corps headquarters. He uncovers a house used as an office by the Germans. Inside there are reams of papers scattered all around, some torn to shreds, as though the occupants have just fled.

He stuffs all the papers he can into sandbags. Many of them contain plans for Germany's Hindenburg Line defences. Rollings sends off a carrier pigeon to Monash letting him know about his success and nails a small Australian flag he has been given above the door of the German HQ.[59]

The Australians also souvenir 100 Iron Crosses ready for issue and come back wearing them 'all over their anatomy – in many cases, in the most undignified places'.[60]

Monash continues sending messages to Rawlinson:

12.15 p.m.: 'Hobbs has captured Harbonnières and reached blue line final objective on his whole front.'

1.15 p.m.: 'Australian flag hoisted over Harbonnières at midday to-day. Should be glad if Chief would cable this to our Governor-General on behalf of Australian Corps.'[61]

The only real bump comes, as Monash feared, when the British III Corps find themselves in a rut on the Chipilly bend, under heavy fire from German artillery across the Somme. But Sinclair-Maclagan follows Monash's plan to form a defensive flank as far as the Bray–Corbie Road, and by 1.30 p.m. the third phase of Monash's plan is complete.

By nightfall the Australians have suffered just 2000 casualties but have 8000 German prisoners.[62] The Canadians have gathered in at least as many. Bean says the 'almost perfect co-ordination of all the services' is the outstanding feature of the battle, 'and the main responsibility for the organisation … [lies with] General Monash'.[63]

Rawlinson is impressed with 'the discipline and high organising capacity of the Australian Corps … The Canadians have done splendidly and the Aussies even better – I am full of admiration for these two corps.'[64]

Yet when Lloyd George announces the success of the attack in the War Cabinet the next day, Billy Hughes is furious to learn that Australians were involved without his knowledge.

In Avesnes, Ludendorff has his head in his hands and mutters that this is '*Der schwarze Tag*' – the Black Day of the German Army.

Hindenburg calls it 'our first great disaster'. He says that there is now universal disappointment among German generals that the war seems to have no end 'in spite of all our victories'. The defeat has 'ruined the character of many of our brave men'. He notes that in the shower of pamphlets being scattered by Monash's airmen, the Allies write 'that they did not think so badly of us [and] everything would soon be right again and we could live together in peace, in perpetual international peace'.[65] All the Germans have to do is give up.

Ludendorff summons his divisional commanders and stresses that the disaster is not his fault. They report to him behaviour from the troops that he says 'I should not have thought possible in the German Army'. Large groups of German soldiers have surrendered to single troopers or isolated squadrons. Retiring troops, meeting a fresh division going bravely into action, have shouted to their comrades to surrender because they were only prolonging the war. The officers in many places have lost their influence and allowed themselves to be swept along with the rest. Just like young Adolf Hitler, Ludendorff attributes the defeat of the great German warrior 'to the spirit of insubordination and the atmosphere which the men brought back with them from home'.

As well as the 8000 prisoners, Monash's soldiers have taken a corps and a divisional headquarters, and collected what Ludendorff considers 'documents of inestimable value'. The Allies now have a clearer sense of Ludendorff's difficulty in finding reserves.

The German commander says it is a further reason why the Allies should 'pursue the offensive without respite'.[66]

And pursue they will. Monash writes that a hole has been driven 'on a width of nearly [20 kilometres], right through the German defence', and has 'blotted out, at one blow, the whole of the military resources which it had contained'.[67] Germany will now have to throw into the gap troops and guns hastily collected from every part of its front, making every other point along its defences that much weaker.

At Bertangles Julius Bruche congratulates Monash. It is the most sweeping advance the Allies have ever enjoyed on the Western Front. Rawlinson's 4th Army has moved ahead by 12 kilometres. And the Australians and Canadians have done the bulk of the work.

Bruche will recall that without any sort of conceit, Monash says quietly, 'Yes, it's been a wonderful day, Julius, it's been wonderful.'[68]

Ludendorff is surprised the Allies don't press on with their attack with the same vigour the following day, 9 August, but the Australians have been stunned by the rapid capitulation of the Germans. The plan has always been to free Amiens from the threat of the German guns and to fortify the objectives gained. Rawlinson, Monash and Currie are not prepared for the immediate opportunities given them to press on.

Bean, who has never commanded an army or been in a battle, says it is 'a classic example of how not to follow an attack',[69] and, when surveying the apocalyptic vision of smouldering fire and death with Keith Murdoch, he notes that Monash 'always plays for safety ... he is the last leader in the world ever to take the responsibility of getting beyond his flanks'.[70] Monash has captured the German guns, and for now that is good enough for him.

Montgomery, Rawlinson's chief of staff, later admits the attacks of 9 August were disjointed, and says everyone was so busy congratulating everyone else on their share in the victory that valuable time was lost in preparing for an advance the next day. 'I have no doubt that lives could have been saved,' Montgomery says, 'and a more satisfactory advance made on the 9th if the attacks of the various divisions had been properly co-ordinated.'[71]

When the battle becomes one of constant open warfare rather than one from entrenched positions, communication to headquarters becomes difficult. Signal wire, scarce at the best of times, is often broken by tanks, and the advancing artillery is frequently out of touch.

Consequently, the Germans counter-attack and the Australians suffer heavy casualties. Pompey Elliott is shot in his well-padded left buttock, but continues to direct his men as he stands on a prominent mound with his trousers around his ankles and underlings tending to his backside. There are catcalls about the 'massive magnitude of his posterior', and one of his colonels says that seeing 'Pompey with his tailboard down having his wound dressed' is one of the great sights of the war.[72]

On 10 August, Monash persuades Rawlinson to let him carry out his original intention of operating on both sides of the Somme Valley. General Butler of III Corps is replaced by Godley. The Chipilly Spur is taken by an English regiment led by the AIF's 1st Battalion.

Sinclair-Maclagan is able to withdraw his defensive flank, and at 4th Division's headquarters the next day Monash confers with him and Gellibrand about a simple solution to the German fightback. He wants to trap the Germans across two sharp bends of the Somme, with the 13th Brigade attacking north of the river on the Bray–Corbie Road and the 10th coming from the south along the old Roman road. Monash plans a night-time tank attack in support of the infantrymen for only the second time in the war,[73] believing the noise will spark terror among the enemy. 'The German', Monash tells his commanders, 'is in a condition of great confusion, and we have only to hit him without warning and roll him up.'[74]

North of the river, the plan works brilliantly under former real estate agent Brigadier General Sydney Herring, commanding the 13th Brigade.[75] However, south of the river the operation under Gellibrand and McNicoll fares badly, as the brigade is hit by aerial bombardment and anti-tank guns. The Germans, though, are gradually outflanked and overrun, and pushed back beyond Méricourt and Proyart.

The following day there is even more success.

'The enemy fought hard and determinedly to retain Lihons,' Monash writes, 'and in some parts of the line the battle swayed to and fro. But before the morning was well advanced, we had taken possession of the whole of the Lihons Knoll, of Auger Wood, and of the villages of Lihons and Rainecourt, while the Canadians had passed through Chilly just south of the railway. All that afternoon the enemy made repeated counter-attacks, particularly directed against Lihons and Rainecourt; but they were all successfully driven off by rifle and machine-gun fire without the loss of any ground. It was a great feat to the credit of the First Australian Division, and ranks among its best performances during the war. Some 20 field-guns and hundreds of machine-guns were captured.'

Monash knows little about sport away from the racetrack, but he knows the Australian Corps has changed the goalposts in warfare. 'Such a battle, with such results, would, in 1917, have been placarded as a victory of the first magnitude', he will recall. 'Now, with the new standards set up by the great battle of August 8th, it was reckoned merely as a local skirmish.'[76]

On 11 August, Winston Churchill, Minister of Munitions for just three weeks, calls first thing to congratulate Monash on his splendid success. Then, at 11 a.m., Haig arrives in his Rolls-Royce with the Chief of the General Staff, Sir Henry Lawrence. Next Julian Byng, Commander of the 3rd Army, turns up, and Haig calls a conference then and there.

Much to Monash's delight, the chief won't hear of Monash's withdrawing from the meeting. In fact, during the course of the meeting all the generals frequently ask Monash for his opinion.[77]

Monash has planned to meet his divisional commanders at Villers-Bretonneux at 2.30 p.m. and Haig says he would 'very much' like to come up and meet them all personally. Then at noon Rawlinson calls to say that Marshal Foch is coming up as well, to give fresh orders on tactical policy over the next few days. Foch decides to have an army conference at Villers-Bretonneux, too.

And so at 2.30 p.m., under a wide bunch of trees on the western outskirts of Villers-Bretonneux, Haig, Monash, his divisional commanders and all their staff sit down together, with great maps spread on the grass in front of them. On one side of the road is a large wire cage containing 3000 German prisoners taken in the preceding 24 hours, and all around the men are streams of soldiers heading towards the front to strengthen the Allied position.

Haig starts to make a speech and says, 'You do not know what the Australians and Canadians have done for the British Empire in these days', and then the stern face of the British military starts to crack and he chokes on his words and tears roll down his face.[78]

In due course, Generals Rawlinson, Currie, Kavanagh, Godley, Elles, Henry Wilson[79] and Lionel Charlton[80] of the 5th Brigade Royal Air Force all arrive. Rawlinson has hardly started to expound his ideas when three more limousines pull up bearing Clemenceau, Foch and the French Finance Minister Louis-Lucien Klotz.

'This completed the gathering,' Monash tells Vic, 'met literally by *pure chance* on the actual battlefield and on a site which will live forever in Australian history ... I was personally, naturally – with General Currie – the leading figure in the show, for everybody was highly complimentary and marvelled at the completeness of our success.' Monash calls the result 'stupendous'.[81]

On the same day, at Lihons, Alf Gaby VC has his head blown off by a sniper.

The next day, at Birdwood's request, George V arrives at Bertangles at 3 p.m. to invest Monash with his knighthood. Monash has had only 24 hours' notice, and spent most of the preceding day bathing in the glow of Haig's teary commendations. But he is able to gather 600 of his finest troops for a guard of honour, lining the long drive at Bertangles, from the iron gates with their coat of arms to the steps of the château's forecourt. His staff drag in as much war spoil as they can: several hundred big guns, howitzers, machine-guns, German transport vehicles, even searchlights, 'all arranged most artistically to line the whole great quadrangle of the chateau'.[82] Monash also has a movie camera present and Hubert Wilkins as the official photographer for his great day.

Bean, who looks like he just ate a bad egg, angers Simonson and Moss by telling them the whole show is 'a lot of nonsense', and that Wilkins, exhausted from covering the battle, has more important assignments than photographing this malarkey.[83]

Despite Monash's brilliant battle successes and the rolling wave that is now the AIF, Bean still can't get over the snubbing of White in favour of a man who he suspects is not out for Australia 'but for his own credit'. Bean only has to look around at the pomp and ceremony Monash has arranged for himself at this French palace.[84]

Nothing changes Bean's mind as Monash puts on a show for his King. George V inspects the troops briefly, and has a few words with each of the divisional commanders and with Paul Simonson, but according to Bean takes 'not the least interest in the Diggers'.[85]

Monash has waited all his life just for this moment. All the study, all the concentration, all the social climbing, all the planning, and once more he is about to create history. He is informed that the last time a British monarch knighted a soldier in the field was during the Battle of Dettingen in Germany in 1743. The King back then was George II.

In the centre of the forecourt are a small table, a plush footstool and a sword. As his warplanes circle overhead, Monash places his right knee on the footstool and kneels before his King, who taps his right shoulder with the sword. George V is about to tap his left shoulder when Monash rises halfway through the ceremony, catching the King by surprise. He hasn't got time to kneel again before the King taps his left shoulder. Some of the 600 soldiers behind him break out in laughter. Monash bristles.

After the hasty ceremony, Lieutenant General Sir John Monash farewells the monarch and calls for 'Three cheers for His Majesty', but the Diggers, having already worked all day dragging Monash's war trophies into the château grounds, are only half-hearted.

'Come on!' Monash implores them as the King climbs into his limousine, but the men show as little enthusiasm for the King as he showed for them.

There has been disagreement ever since Amiens over who came up with the idea that knocked all the fight out of Germany: was it Monash, Haig or Rawlinson?

Monash writes home to say it was definitely him: 'Towards the end of the third week in July I propounded certain proposals to Sir Douglas Haig in the nature of a counter-offensive on a very large scale', he tells Vic. 'The Field Marshal was quite favourable but could not give authority for the plan without first of all consulting Generalissimo Foch.'[86] He later tells Bruche that while he was 'the prime mover' he was undeserving 'of the whole credit'.[87]

Blamey reckons he and Monash came up with the plan over afternoon cups of tea.[88] The following August Monash asks Blamey to help him find the letter they drafted to Rawlinson outlining the great offensive, and until 1928 he is still asking the Australian War Memorial if they can find his blueprint in their archives.

Journalist Fred Cutlack later remembers that while Rawlinson had the final say over Amiens, the 'plan and the organization of the attack were indubitably Monash's'.[89] And even Bean says that after Monash inspired victory at Hamel, 'there could be no doubt that it was the activity of the Australian Corps that prompted both Haig and Rawlinson in July to have the Somme project adopted. It is in his efforts to impress on Rawlinson the chance created by the activity of the "Diggers" that Monash's claim to a share in origination of the scheme really lies.'[90]

Five days after the King's visit, Keith Murdoch interviews Monash at Bertangles. He shows Monash Hubert Wilkins's photograph of Monash receiving his knighthood. Monash affects a note of surprise, saying Bean must have arranged for Wilkins to be there and that he knew nothing about it.

Bean can only laugh when Murdoch tells him the story. It confirms much of what he thinks about the Commander of the Australian Corps.

'The old poser!' he snorts.[91]

Chapter 26

*And so you think you're going to take Mont St Quentin with three
battalions! What presumption! However, I don't think I ought to stop
you! So, go ahead, and try and I wish you luck!*
GENERAL HENRY RAWLINSON ON HEARING OF MONASH'S MOST
AUDACIOUS SCHEME[1]

*The men were great ... but greatest of all perhaps was their
Commander ... a rare compelling personality, whose dark flashing eyes
and swarthy face might have seemed more in keeping with some Asiatic
conqueror than with the prosaic associations of the British Army.*
ARTHUR CONAN DOYLE, BRITISH AUTHOR, ON MEETING MONASH[2]

EVER SINCE THE EVACUATION of Gallipoli, Monash has
rarely been seen on the frontlines, but he is still very much a
casualty of the war. He is not taking the same physical risks as the
men in battle, but despite his stoic exterior and confident talk, the
stress has taken a heavy toll. His weight has plummeted to just
72 kilograms, and it is not all down to his strict diet. Long periods
of time glued to his desk have forced him to forgo regular walks,
and while he still does his dumbbell exercises every morning, the
tension is evident in the wrinkled skin hanging loosely on his face
and in the tremors of his hands.[3]

He sleeps little and spends most of his waking hours in deep thought. Every time he and Blamey drive somewhere, there are long periods of silence as 'The Old Man' tilts his head forward and allows the machinery of his brain to run undisturbed.[4]

He is preoccupied with how to hustle[5] the Germans beyond the great bend of the River Somme, where it turns sharply south at Péronne, and to the north, where the excavations for the Canal du Nord, 'already wide and deep', form 'a tactical obstacle of some significance'.[6]

He knows the river and canal will form natural fortifications when winter comes, and perhaps prolong the war into the next year. Already Winston Churchill has told Haig that July 1919 will be the turning point for the war, as the Americans will be at their full strength.[7] But Monash wants a quicker finish.

Following the success of Monash's August assaults, Kaiser Wilhelm summons his major political and military leaders to the Belgian resort town of Spa on 14 August. Crown Prince Rupprecht writes that 'our military situation has deteriorated so rapidly that I no longer believe we can hold out over the winter; it is even possible that a catastrophe will come earlier ... The Americans are multiplying in a way we never dreamed of.'[8]

Ludendorff says Germany must maintain its submarine attacks, and that he still has the power to turn things around. 'In the course of the war I have been compelled five times before to withdraw troops, but only in the end to beat the enemy,' Ludendorff says. 'Why should I not succeed in doing that a sixth time?'[9] He proposes that a 'strategic defensive' could exhaust the Allies as they try to break through.[10]

Ludendorff has been under psychiatric care for some months. Berlin's renowned Dr Hochheimer has found a man in deep mental turmoil, almost a caricature of a Prussian general, with his close-cropped white hair and permanent glare behind the monocle. His orders are almost constantly barked in a shrill voice that suggests panic.[11]

More than 2 million German soldiers have already been killed in this war, but the Kaiser, in his role as Germany's figurehead, concludes the conference by saying there will be no offer of peace until 'the time is right'.[12] Ludendorff agrees.

Haig and Rawlinson plan another major attack on 15 August, to push the Allied front 2.5 kilometres east from Lihons to the line between Roye and Chaulnes. The Canadians and the French will lead the assault, with the Australians making up a flank.

Arthur Currie speaks out against it, though. Ludendorff has brought in every reinforcement he can to stabilise the German position and Currie's aerial photographs show a marked increase in German entanglements. Rawlinson can't get his artillery ready in time, or summon enough tanks to cover those lost, and the battle is cancelled. Currie moves his Canadian troops to Arras, 50 kilometres to the north.

The Australian Corps now has a 14.5-kilometre front to defend from north of the Somme to the Amiens railway, and Monash asks Rawlinson to either shorten the front or give him more men to replenish those in dire need of rest. Rawlinson provides another British division in reserve, two Canadian divisions and an American regiment, and for a time Monash commands 208,000 men.[13]

There are murmurs from within 4th Division that they have done more work than the others, and Keith Murdoch reports there is talk of a mutiny inside the 4th Brigade: threats that the Diggers will simply sit down and refuse to fight the next time they are 'asked to go into some show'.[14]

More than ever, Monash has to utilise his skills of man management; he will recall that 'each Division had to be kept employed until the last ounce of effort, consistent with speedy recovery, had been yielded'.[15] For all of his operations, he organises buses to collect his men when they are near exhaustion: 'it is a matter of pride to the Australian Corps that even amid all the stress of these busy fighting months of August and September' relief operations are 'carried out with precision'.[16]

Raids continue. On 18 August Monash sets the 6th Brigade an objective beyond Herleville, but they lose 177 men, including six who end up buried under a cross that says, in German, 'Six Unknown Australians'.[17]

The following day Rawlinson goes through plans with Monash for the next big wave of Allied attacks. The British 3rd Army will attack along the Albert–Arras railway, with the New Zealanders going in to reclaim Bapaume.

A general Allied offensive is planned for 23 August across a front of 60 kilometres. Rawlinson and Monash are tasked with taking Bray on the northern bank of the Somme, and Chuignes and Herleville among other villages on the south.

Bill Glasgow's 1st Division is given the toughest job. Backed by just a dozen Mark V tanks, the men have to advance more than 2000 metres, crush one machine-gun post after another and seize the valley, the woods and the edge of the plateau beyond Herleville.[18]

Monash's battle conference on the 21st is especially long, as Glasgow's 1st Australian and the British 32nd Divisions, about to be launched together south of the Somme, are not familiar with his battle tactics and are strangers to each other. But, using the same methods of attack that were employed so decisively at Hamel, involving infantry, artillery, tanks and aircraft, the two divisions deliver what Bean calls 'one of the hardest blows ever struck by Australian troops'[19] to win the Battle of Chuignes.

At a kilometre-wide forest called St Martin's Wood, Glasgow's 2nd Brigade encounters 20 machine-guns firing a wall of bullets across a 90-metre front. But the tank commanders know exactly what to do. After a desperate fight, they literally crush all resistance and chase off any other defenders.[20]

At nearby Madame Wood, moon-faced West Australian Lieutenant Laurie 'Fat' McCarthy[21] refuses to be pinned down by machine-gun fire. McCarthy has been full of fight since growing up in the Christian Brothers orphanage at Clontarf in Perth. Back in 1914, he had a battle to convince sceptical recruiting officers that he was a crack shot, even though three fingers on his left hand had been lost to a lumberyard saw.[22]

McCarthy landed on Gallipoli as a private and, fulfilling Monash's ideal that men be promoted on merit, worked his way through the ranks, winning the rare Croix de Guerre with palm for his courage on the Somme in 1917. Now, at Madame Wood, McCarthy goes on a rampage, assisted by Sergeant Fred Robbins, a locomotive cleaner from Murray Bridge, South Australia.

McCarthy is credited with killing 20 Germans and taking another 50 prisoner. His captives are so impressed with his daring that they pat him on the back,[23] and when McCarthy is awarded the Victoria Cross, the British newspapers refer to him as the 'Super VC'.[24]

About 3 kilometres to the north at Herleville, Lieutenant Donovan Joynt,[25] a 'chirpy cock sparrow of a man', 'short and dark, with twinkling grey eyes',[26] faces a dangerous predicament. He's a Melbourne Church of England Grammar School old boy who has worked in an accountancy firm, laboured on a steamer off Cairns, and dug potatoes on Flinders Island. He knows how to adapt.

Joynt is with his batman Private Thomas Newman, a blacksmith's striker from Melbourne, when they come upon a company of the 6th Battalion sheltering in a sunken road and under heavy fire from Plateau Wood. Joynt manages to 'ginger up' the troops and get them moving out of harm's way. Newman suffers a throat wound from a shell burst, and Joynt binds the wound with a tourniquet while trying not to strangle him.

Then, as he and four others scout out a way through the heavily defended wood, they come upon a party of Germans. Joynt raises his revolver and they throw up their hands. Before long, Joynt has 100 prisoners all handing over their wristwatches. The wood is taken without a single Australian casualty.

Three days later Don Joynt suffers a severe wound in the thigh but he is well enough to receive his Victoria Cross the next year at Buckingham Palace. Don's brother Gerald was 34 when he was killed at Polygon Wood in Belgium in 1917 but Don lives to 97.

By dusk on 23 August, 'the whole Chuignes Valley was ours', Monash later recalls. The Germans have retreated to the wasteland from previous battles on the Somme, now 'broken and ruined country'. The 1st Division has suffered about 1000 casualties, but Monash later says, 'I had the satisfaction that night of contemplating a victory far greater than I had calculated upon.'[27]

'We took that day 21 guns and over 3100 prisoners from 10 different regiments. The slaughter of the enemy in the tangled valleys was considerable, for our Infantry are always vigorous bayonet fighters … it was a smashing blow.'[28] The combined operation of the British 3rd and 4th Armies that day collects 8000 prisoners,[29] most of them so dispirited that Monash is sure Germany cannot hold out much longer.

Near the ridge called Froissy Beacon, the Australians seize another monstrous naval gun. It has a 15-inch (40-centimetre) bore and has been bombarding Amiens with projectiles weighing almost a ton. The whole weapon weighs almost 500 tons and Monash calls it 'the largest single trophy' won during the war.[30]

Haig can see the finish line of this war and tells his generals to dig in the spurs, and that 'the most resolute offensive' is needed. 'Risks which a month ago would have been criminal to incur ought now to be incurred as a duty.'[31]

The next morning, north of the Somme, Gellibrand's 3rd Division takes Bray and is going so fast it can't stop. Twice Monash sends orders that Gellibrand must wait and let III Corps take the lead, but by the time the orders arrive Gellibrand's Australians have already resumed the attack.

South of the Somme, Monash has driven three German divisions back 2.5 kilometres. North of the river Gellibrand has Bray; Byng's 3rd Army has captured Albert and the New Zealanders are nipping at Bapaume. Gellibrand's engineers are busy rebuilding bridges systematically destroyed by the fleeing Germans. Monash wants the bridges restored as quickly as possible so a great wave of Allied troops can lead the hunt.

The 1st and 4th Divisions suffer gas shelling during the German retreat and Monash gives them a three-week break. The 1st has captured Cappy and advanced its line to the western outskirts of Foucaucourt, while the 3rd Division has Suzanne. Monash has a tour de force[32] in mind for them in the near future and wants them well rested.

He now looks to force a German retreat across the river at Péronne, where the Somme presents a barrier almost a kilometre wide, with its broad marsh, studded with islets that are overgrown with rushes. The river threads its way in numerous channels between them. 'The marsh itself is no more than waist-deep,' Monash tells his men, 'but the flowing water is too deep to be waded.'[33]

The French Army takes over the whole of Monash's front, which extends south of Lihons, and are tasked with holding it against counter-attacks. On 25 and 26 August, Monash meets with Rosenthal and Hobbs, whose 2nd and 5th Divisions are about to go on the attack again. He plans a major assault on 27 August, but Haig insists he mark time for a month so that the 4th Army's depleted stock of tanks can be restored. The Australians are told to concentrate on smaller raids to ensure the corps is as strong as possible for the big battle looming.

Monash, in the flush of victory, says he is 'greatly embarrassed' by what he sees as a 'go slow' order, and will complain that it did 'not take into account the reserve of striking power which remained in the Australian Corps, even after the past 18 days of continuous fighting'.[34]

Yet Monash spots 'all the loophole necessary' to follow his own strategy when Rawlinson tells him, 'Touch must be kept with the enemy.'

'It was sufficient to justify an aggressive policy on my part,' he later says. 'There followed a merry and exciting three days of pursuit; for the enemy was really on the run.'[35] Monash orders the 2nd and 5th Divisions to maintain constant pressure and 'advance by infiltration',[36] but avoid fighting that might involve heavy losses.

The aggressive pursuit by Monash's men compels the Germans to fight constantly and to withdraw in disorder, abandoning guns and huge quantities of ammunition.[37] During their retreat, though, the Germans use their machine-guns to full advantage, and their skill with the Maxim guns is the only real obstacle to Monash's rapid advance.

> These tactics were not unexpected by me, and I had an answer ready. Defying the whole traditions of Artillery tactics in open warfare, I insisted upon two somewhat startling innovations. The first was to ... put the guns under the direct orders of Infantry Commanders to immediately engage fire with machine-gun nests delaying the Australian advance. The second was to insist that all artillery batteries carry 20 per cent of smoke shell ... [it] proved of inestimable value in blinding the German machine-gunners. A few rounds judiciously placed screened the approach of our Infantry, and many a machine-gun post was thereby rushed by us.[38]

At Fargny Wood, Bernard Sidney Gordon,[39] a cooper's machinist from Beaconsfield, Tasmania, earns a Victoria Cross after single-handedly wiping out an enemy machine-gun, and capturing 63 prisoners and six other machine-guns practically unaided.[40]

By nightfall on 29 August, every German west of the Somme between Péronne and Brie is a prisoner.

The Australians have reached the Somme near Péronne, and Monash now sees the opportunity for them to win a fluid battle as long as they can take the heavily fortified Mont St Quentin, a 100-metre rise about a kilometre and a half north of the town. Mont St Quentin gives the Germans a commanding view of the valley below and they have a battery of machine-guns on the Bouchavesnes Spur.

'I wanted, more than anything else,' Monash later says, 'that this should be an exclusively Australian achievement.'[41]

He initially proposed direct crossings of the Somme at Halle and Brie on 28 August and a frontal attack on Mont St Quentin, but realising that it would be 'criminal folly' for the Germans not to blow up every bridge they can in their retreat, he puts into action a scheme that has been 'vaguely forming' in his mind.

Monash wants to make the Somme useless as a defensive barrier and force Ludendorff to retreat to the Hindenburg Line,[42] from which the Germans launched the Spring Offensive on 21 March.

As they come over a crest near Péronne, all three of Monash's divisions south of the river see the old town below, the moat caused by the merging of the Somme and Cologne, and further back the ramparts and towers of the 17th-century fortress, three wooded hills, and the wide brow and scrubby top of Mont St Quentin, standing like a sentinel 'guarding the northern and western approaches to the town'.[43]

As soon as the Australians begin to approach Péronne they are plastered with shell bursts. On the 2nd Division's front the woods are still held by eager machine-gunners. One of them hits the short, stocky and much-loved Olympic swimmer Lieutenant Cecil Healy,[44] who won a gold medal at Stockholm.[45] Healy is pointing out to his comrades the position of the machine-gun when another burst of bullets kills the only Australian Olympic champion to die on the battlefield.[46]

The next day, 30 August, Monash meets with Rawlinson, Blamey and Rawlinson's chief of staff Archie Montgomery and outlines his plans for three battalions to take Mont St Quentin. Rawlinson is more than sceptical but he knows not to underestimate Monash, given the success of his recent raids and wishes him luck, because he'll need it. And perhaps a little magic.

As a young man, Monash impressed his friends with card tricks and illusions and now he is about to perform his greatest sleight of hand in rendering the Somme 'useless to the enemy as a defensive line'.[47]

He has Gellibrand drive the 3rd Division hard north of the river, especially the 10th Brigade, whom he wants to push on past the bend at Cléry, protecting the bridges the Australians are repairing behind their front and allowing the assaulting troops to come at Mont St Quentin and Péronne from the north. Even for Monash the plan is audacious. He plans to keep the momentum of victory rolling even though his men are exhausted.

Three battalions from Rosenthal's 5th Brigade, the 17th, 19th and 20th, with the 18th in reserve, are given the task of taking Mont St Quentin. At the start of the war the three attacking battalions had a combined force of 2700 men. Now they have fewer than 900. Having been on the move for days on end, and without the protection of tanks, they are now being asked to take a heavily fortified vantage point famous across the Western Front[48] that is being manned by Ludendorff's crack troops, the Second Prussian Guards Division.

Bean later says the task was 'in some ways the most formidable ever faced by Australian infantry'.[49] Monash admits it will take an extraordinary effort: the terrain is mostly open and 'exposed in every direction to full view from the heights, sloped gently upwards towards the commanding knoll'. Cover is scarce, and the few ruins of brickfields and sugar refineries dotting the landscape have all been taken over by the Germans as places of resistance.[50] There is good reason for Rawlinson's scepticism.

But Monash is ever the conjurer. The British 32nd Division will create the illusion of an assault from south of Péronne to divert attention from the real charge coming from the north.

Zero hour is set for 5 a.m. on 31 August, and Bean suspects that 'few officers or men in the tired companies' believe they have any chance of success. There is not even a hot meal that night, but the 18th Battalion bring up dry rations. An issue of rum arrives at 3 a.m. and some of the men ask for seconds.

As the dark sky surrenders to the light, an artillery barrage lands a kilometre and a half in the distance, five brigades of field artillery hammer a trench low on the mount, and four brigades of heavy cannons blast the summit and flanks. Towards the fire charge the brave few hundred. Monash has told the attacking battalions to 'scream like bushrangers', to make as much noise as they can and thus make a few hundred voices sound like a few thousand.

'Each trench was rushed with a cheer whether occupied or not', Bean writes. 'Many contained Germans who had run till they could run no more and were too breathless and frightened to speak.'[51] Hundreds of prisoners, all without wristwatches, and a colonel who has had his smart riding breeches stolen[52] pour back to the Australian lines. The speed of the attack and the combined use of rifle grenades and Lewis machine-guns cause the Germans to either flee or throw up their hands.

The 20th Battalion takes the Bapaume road north of Mont St Quentin and then enters the village of Feuillaucourt. The 17th charges into Mont St Quentin village. 'Casualties slight,' is the message, 'troops awfully bucked.'

A sniper pumps a bullet into the head of tiny milk carter Private Alex Barclay, from Leichhardt, Sydney, who at 152 centimetres and 47 kilograms is not much of a target. The bullet shatters Barclay's helmet and parts his hair, but 75 years later he will still be able to laugh about it, saying: 'I thought I had been hit by an axe.'[53]

By 8 a.m., Rosenthal sends a message to Monash that the Australian flag is flying from Mont St Quentin. Monash will later claim that when he calls Rawlinson the general is at first 'incredulous' but then tells him that Monash has changed the 'course of the war'.[54]

The Australians are not yet at the top, but they're close.

Monash sends in reinforcements to back Rosenthal's attacking battalions, who are 3 kilometres in front of the other men and severely outnumbered. Monash wants to exploit their success before the chance is lost. At 8.35 a.m. he tells Gellibrand by phone that casualties no longer matter, that 'we must get Bouchavesnes Spur and protect General Rosenthal's left', whose 'flanks are in the air' and who are 'undoubtedly fatigued'.

Monash is angered when it takes 10 hours for the exhausted 14th Brigade to make the trek 12 kilometres across the river for an attack on Péronne. He says later that the 5th Division's commander Talbot Hobbs 'is an attractive little man, and a very good commander in some ways but he lacks the drive necessary for an operation of this sort'.[55] Hobbs complains that Monash is pushing the men too hard, and while Monash admits 'I was compelled to harden my heart', he says he has to 'insist that it was imperative to recognise a great opportunity and to seize it unflinchingly'.[56] Monash senses that the war could turn on this battle and he drives the men to their very limits of exhaustion. He cares about his soldiers but perhaps he cares about winning even more.

Private George Cartwright,[57] a London-born sheep station labourer from Elsmore in northern New South Wales, doesn't have to be told twice. For his actions at Road Wood, south-west of Bouchavesnes, he is recommended for the Victoria Cross after taking out a machine-gun post with such daring that his comrades stand up and cheer.[58]

The Germans are still not done, though. They manage to regroup and launch a ferocious counter-attack from their vantage points. The battalions that fought so hard to raise the Australian flag on Mont St Quentin don't have the numbers to fight back, and are forced down the hill.

Major Don Coutts, a 28-year-old doctor from Boort, in northern Victoria, sets up a makeshift hospital in Lost Ravine, a deep cutting in the unfinished Canal du Nord. His new surgery is full of dust and the lingering stench of poison gas shells. For 52 hours straight, five of them in a gas mask, he performs emergency surgery. At 10.30 p.m. on 31 August he amputates a man's arm at the shoulder and another man's leg through the right thigh. With a razor.[59]

The next day, 1 September, the 23rd and 24th Battalions of the 6th Brigade attack Mont St Quentin again in driving rain, a task so daunting that they liken it to throwing peas at a whale.[60] The 14th Battalion attacks Péronne and Gellibrand's 3rd Division goes after the Bouchavesnes Spur.

Six Victoria Crosses are awarded for remarkable courage in the face of machine-gun fire over the next 24 hours, and five of the men live to receive their medals.[61] About a kilometre and a half south-west of Mont St Quentin, a runner for the 23rd Battalion, Robert Mactier,[62] is killed after he earns a VC for wiping out two machine-gun posts and taking 40 prisoners. He leaves all his worldly possessions to his aged mother Christina back on the farm at Tatura, Victoria. She and her husband receive a visit from a local clergyman bearing a brief telegram about his death, but four months later Robert Mactier Senior has to plead with the Defence Department to find out some information 're our dear boy'.[63] Finally Mrs Mactier receives a photograph of her son's gravestone at the Hem Farm Military Cemetery and a badge given to the mothers of fallen soldiers.

After more fierce fighting in the rain, the 6th Brigade retakes Mont St Quentin on 1 September. Gellibrand takes 400 prisoners on Bouchavesnes Spur, and in nearby Anvil Wood a German battalion commander and 200 of his men are marched back to the Australian lines by two privates. The Australians cross the moat to enter Péronne and subdue the Germans firing at them from cellars.

With the bullet wound in his backside still healing, Pompey Elliott dodges machine-gun fire to lead the men of his 15th Brigade across a steel girder onto the ramparts of a partially destroyed bridge. In his haste he treads on a loose beam, and with a mighty splosh falls into a deep canal. He has trouble clambering up the steep sides. Dripping from head to foot, he then directs his battalion commanders to go through Péronne and attack Flamicourt.[64]

The next day the 43rd Battalion's Lance Corporal Lawrence Weathers,[65] a New Zealand-born undertaker from Parkside,

South Australia, takes 180 prisoners with repeated grenade attacks, to end a stand-off in a web of trenches at Allaines in the mount's shadow. He is also recommended for the Victoria Cross, though he is killed less than a month later before receiving it.[66] His brother Tom died on Gallipoli.

Ludendorff orders his troops back to the Hindenburg Line 20 kilometres east. All the territory won by Operation Michael six months earlier is now lost, and to the north the Canadians have broken through the Drocourt–Queant Line, the northernmost section of the Hindenburg Line near Lens.

Ludendorff is weeping more loudly and more often.

Much of the credit for the victory at Mont St Quentin must go to Monash's tactical brilliance and his skill in finding the right men for the right job. It was a risky battle, but the alternative was to do 'nothing and attempt nothing', which would have been 'the worst of bad generalship'.[67] He tells Vic there is the touch of Stonewall Jackson's 'sudden onslaughts' about the attack, 'but of course, on a very much larger scale'.[68]

He gives much of the credit to Rosenthal, 'a massive man, whose build belies his extraordinary physical energy ... an egregious optimist, incapable of recognising the possibility of failure'. But Monash knows it was not Rosenthal, nor he, getting shot at, and that the victory is 'due firstly and chiefly to the wonderful gallantry of the men ... and the sheer daring of the plan'.[69]

Bean eats humble pie. This triumph, he says, 'is held by many Australian soldiers to be the most brilliant achievement of the AIF ... within Australian experience of the Western Front it was the only important fight in which quick, free manoeuvre played a decisive part. It furnishes a complete answer to the comment that Monash was merely a composer of set pieces.'[70]

More than once Rawlinson calls the taking of Mont St Quentin the finest single feat of the war, and says that it was 'not only a tactical victory deserving the highest praise, but it was strategically of first importance, for it broke the Somme line of defence …'.[71]

Haig doesn't seem to have the same degree of appreciation. A couple of days after the victory at Mont St Quentin, a party of editors and newspaper proprietors from Australia visits the front. The Commander-in-Chief doesn't say much about one of the most heroic feats of the war. Nor does he talk much about all the VC winners, or the 3000 Australian casualties. Instead he lectures the dumbfounded newspapermen about the grave need for extending the death penalty to Australian soldiers.[72]

Chapter 27

I put it plainly that [the Australian soldiers] are by nature and instinct sportsmen, and that they would refuse to go on playing any game in which their scores were not put up on the scoring board.

MONASH THREATENING BRITISH HIGH COMMAND OVER THE LACK OF RECOGNITION FOR HIS TROOPS[1]

[Monash] was right to work his troops to the extreme limit of their endurance ... At such times victory often goes to the troops that hold out longest, withstanding strain, toil or exhaustion in perhaps unbelievable degree and for an unbelievable time.

BEAN ON MONASH'S RUTHLESS DRIVE TO THE FINISH LINE[2]

AS THE EUROPEAN WINTER approaches, Monash has Ludendorff on the run and Bean right where he wants him. Squirming. The war correspondent fears that Monash, now revelling in the glory of one massive hit after another, will try to make *him* a casualty of the war too. 'Sleepy old John Monash' is now a raging bull.

The Australians are tottering from the German counter-punches but they are still in better shape than their staggering enemies. As part of a mighty Allied force, they continue pursuing the Germans through the rolling countryside along a trail of a dozen burning villages left in the wake of Ludendorff's retreat.

The rapid Australian advance means Monash is packing up and moving headquarters from one place to the next every few days. He left the grand château at Bertangles for Glisy, and is now in Méricourt, in a dilapidated mansion that was occupied by a German commander only 10 days ago. He has to be close enough to the front for his telephone wires to reach his men as they limp towards the German defences along the Hindenburg Line.

Known to the Germans as the Siegfriedstellung, the line is a series of defensive positions stretching for more than 100 kilometres from Arras in the north to Laffaux, near Soissons, in the south, with Saint-Quentin somewhere in the middle.[3] In places the fortifications are 9 kilometres wide as the Germans erect what they see as an Ally-proof fence of trenches and fortifications protected by barbed wire and machine-gun posts, with underground bunkers virtually impervious to artillery.

The tension between Monash and Bean simmers. Bean wishes he had Murdoch's pluck.

Bean does not have the forceful personality of Murdoch, who looks Monash dead in the eye and tells him straight what he thinks, whether Monash likes it or not. Murdoch is such a strong character, and so influential, that the general is wary of getting on his wrong side. 'Monash has less respect for me,' Bean complains, and he tells Murdoch that he is afraid Monash would like to see him sent back home.[4]

Among the war correspondents in France, Bean and Murdoch lead the newspaper campaign to ensure that the Australian effort is duly recognised. The two pressmen have recently engaged in a spirited debate with Brudenell White, who supports Haig's view that the triumph should be portrayed as a British victory with help from its Dominions.

Murdoch fights the point strongly, and Bean tells White that Australia must always give due credit to its fighting men. He says Australia is a long way from Britain, and America is the powerful ally that could really help the young nation if it were attacked. Looking wisely to the future, Beans suggests Australia should do its best to forge its reputation in America. After all, having powerful and dependable American allies may one day ensure Australia's existence in any future conflicts in the South Pacific.[5]

Billy Hughes also wants more recognition for the Australian forces. He eyes the best seat possible at the negotiating table when the world is eventually carved up at a peace settlement.

On 6 September Monash summons Bean to Méricourt and the fire is burning behind the general's dark eyes. He lectures the war correspondent about journalism. He has two clippings of Bean's press reports sitting on his desk and a deep frown gouged into his forehead. He is not happy with Bean's coverage of recent Australian victories, saying the correspondent is merely reporting what he sees and not the whole story of what is happening in the background. Monash 'said something about lack of imagination', Bean later recalls. Monash tells Bean he wants the colour and the creativity of an Ashmead-Bartlett. His men are heroes, after all, and Monash wants them portrayed with a 'lavish hand'. A dash more excitement in the articles appearing back home would do wonders for morale, he says, and increase the enthusiasm to end this war quickly.[6]

And it's not just Bean's reporting that riles the general. Bean, Murdoch and Hughes, who has been based in London since June, have all highlighted the triumphant march of the AIF and the heroism of the VC recipients, but the British press and the War Office have largely ignored them.

Monash says the question of adequate recognition for the AIF and the other Dominion troops is 'a very burning one'.[7] He says German propaganda has tried to portray Lloyd George 'climbing to victory over the corpses of Canadians and Australians and putting them in wherever the fighting has been hottest'.[8] As a result the British have erred by not only 'suppressing references to the deeds of the Australians, but also exaggerating, to the disadvantage of the Australians, the work done by other troops'. Monash is livid that the London papers have been attributing the successes at Villers-Bretonneux and Mont St Quentin to the

Tommies, who he says 'are brave enough' but 'simply unskilful', and being led by 'young men … from office stools in the English cities'.[9]

He makes a 'very serious remonstration' over the lack of coverage for the Australians to Rawlinson, Henry Wilson, the Chief of the Imperial General Staff, and the *Times* correspondent Perry Robinson, who rarely goes to the frontline but writes his reports based on information provided by the British Army.[10] 'Unless the performance of the Australians is justly placarded,' Monash warns them, 'I will not hold myself responsible for the maintenance of their fighting spirit.'[11]

The Australian troops believe that because of their astonishing success the British are using them more often than their own troops, and as the spearheads for the most dangerous tasks.[12] Brigadier General Charles Brand says after his 4th Brigade snatched a costly victory from a difficult situation 'left by the failure of English troops', his men were growling: 'Whatever we do they'll say *they* won the battle; next time we'll let them win it.'[13]

Just like Monash, the soldiers are boosted by praise and 'certainly do appreciate, and expect, laudatory and complimentary and inspiring messages'. Monash posts congratulatory notes and whatever press reports he can on platoon noticeboards to raise morale.

Before long, he says, his remonstrations have 'an astonishingly successful result' after three separate groups of journalists visit the corps.[14] Soon he is sending home cuttings from the British press,[15] which 'has latterly given us quite generous recognition'.

He preens over mentions of his own name.

'Everybody that matters here fully recognises that my appointment was justified. Never, in Birdwood's time has the Corps had such a series of brilliant successes with such small losses.' The way Monash tells it, Birdwood confided to him that 'It would be quite impossible either for the Imperial Government or the Australian Government properly and adequately to reward my [Monash's] services'. His men are also beginning to recognise 'the value of competent generalship and to have confidence in it. They now at least appear to realize that there are other things that matter beside the gallantry of the troops, which would count for nothing if the battles were badly planned.'[16]

With Birdwood's GOC role in London still being dangled before him, 'the day is not too far distant when the force of circumstances may compel me to accept this higher appointment – while on the one hand that would mean a further promotion and a further increase in status, it would deprive me of the kudos of a fighting commander in the field'.[17]

Some of Monash's battalions that once numbered 1000 men are now down to 150, and Bean, for one, says that if the fighting keeps going like this, before long there won't be an AIF at all.

Monash dismisses all that. His men aren't tired, he says, 'just a little footsore',[18] and six days' rest and a bath are all that is needed to restore his divisions' 'elasticity'. He isn't about to let Bean know that winning is all that matters to him now.

Later he will write that it was essential that the Australians 'should be called upon to yield up the last particle of effort of which they were capable', and that he 'was compelled to disregard the evident signs of overstrain'.[19]

Arthur O'Connor, a journalist for the London *Weekly Dispatch*, visits Monash, and describes him as 'a strong man ... somewhat rugged with alert yet kindly eyes' who speaks 'quietly, deliberately, unhesitatingly' and who is 'intelligent, original, democratic ... [and] *ruthless*'.[20]

While his commanders tell Monash that the men are exhausted, he asks Rawlinson for three days leave in Paris for himself. He plans to dine at Maxim's again and take in the opera. He has had just six days off in six months.

Permission is denied. He understands the frustrations and fatigue of his men.

*

Continuing their chase west, on 7 September the Australian infantry reaches the outer defences of the Hindenburg Line, a desolated landscape of old British trenches infested with thistles and strewn with barbed wire for kilometres along the approaching ridges. This was the British frontline before the Spring Offensive, and the Germans roared through here behind their massive artillery barrage. Now it is the first stage of the German line, which stretches west through tangles of trenches and barbed wire for 7 kilometres either side of the Saint-Quentin Canal.

The barbed wire is everywhere and runs in all directions – 'cleverly disposed', Monash says, 'so as to herd the attackers into the very jaws of the machine-guns'.[21]

The part of the Hindenburg Line that Monash will target runs either side of the canal between the towns of Bellicourt and Bellenglise 5 kilometres to the south. The canal, built by Napoleon more than a century ago, is a daunting barrier, with vertical sides 15 metres high and water too deep to wade stretching across 10 metres. There is barbed wire on both banks.

On 10 September, Rawlinson and Monash pore over plans of the whole Hindenburg Line, provided by the discovery by Ernest Rollings and other intelligence gathering, and begin plotting a two-stage assault to break through the last barrier to an Allied victory.

For the effort now being demanded, Monash stops appealing to his men's patriotism and instead appeals to their pride.

He tells them they are the greatest soldiers in the world and they must maintain that tradition. Constant blows are shattering the enemy and he wants the Australians to keep landing them as long and as hard as they can while the Germans are wobbling.

The 1st Division, bussed in from their rest area in Amiens, start raiding that afternoon, opening up small wounds in the German armour.[22] There are at least four defensive positions where the Germans can make their stand, stretching from the British lines in the east, across the canal to the main Hindenburg Line beyond.

The Germans intend to keep their pursuers at bay for at least a few weeks longer then bunker down for the winter.[23]

The next day, 11 September, Monash again moves his headquarters, this time into a camp of huts built into a wood between Belloy-en-Santerre and Assevillers, just before the Somme. On 12 September Billy Hughes arrives with another party of English journalists and editors, including Lord Burnham, owner of England's *Daily Telegraph*. Bean describes Burnham as 'a rather talkative, smooth, diplomatic but capable Jew'.

Hughes asks Monash to provide a separate château for the party. Bean suspects it is because Hughes doesn't want Monash to hog the limelight by talking about himself all the time. Instead, Monash says they will have to stay at a hotel in Amiens. Bean needles Monash at every opportunity; the ginger-haired correspondent now tells the general that if he put in a tenth of the effort that he put into his knighthood ceremony he could have accommodated everyone at the château in Méricourt. Bean seems surprised that Monash becomes 'very angry' with him.[24]

On that same day, 12 September, America's commander 'Black Jack' Pershing leads his troops – all 550,000 of them, with the backing of 48,000 Frenchmen and 1500 aeroplanes – against the retreating 5th Army of Georg von der Marwitz at St Mihiel.[25]

Pershing's hot-headed protégé George Patton is put in charge of two battalions of light Renault tanks. Arriving on the heights near Essey, he finds soldiers taking cover in shell holes as enemy fire kicks up fountains of dirt all around them. Strolling nonchalantly out in the open is General Douglas Macarthur.[26] Patton trots over to chat, in a meeting of two monumental egos.

Macarthur later claims Patton flinched at one of the explosions and looked annoyed with himself. 'Don't worry, Colonel,' Macarthur said snidely. 'You never hear the one that gets you.'[27]

Patton, the grandson of a Confederate colonel killed in the Civil War, writes home: 'Dear Papa ... When the shelling first started I had some doubts about the advisability of sticking my head over the parapet, but it is just like taking a cold bath, once you get in, it is all right … vanity is stronger than fear …'[28]

Hughes complains to Murdoch that Monash is too stubborn and is wearing out his men. 'He sees only one thing,' the Prime Minister tells the journalist. 'He wants to fight on. He wants to be there at the finish.'[29]

Without consulting Monash, Hughes orders 6000 of the original Anzacs to be sent home for two months' leave. Some of them have been fighting for four years with little rest and have aged a decade, but because of the great distance to Australia they have not been able to visit home in the same way as the British, French and German soldiers.

On 12 September Birdwood is ordered to send home 800 Australians immediately. Most of them are from the 1st and 4th Divisions, and are needed for the upcoming attack on the Hindenburg Line. Hughes tells Monash that all Australian Corps troops must be withdrawn from the war by early October, and he also wants them to winter out of the cold, in the south of France or in Italy.

Monash is taken aback. Blamey will recall the military chief's confrontation with the Prime Minister as being like an Alsatian going after a bantam rooster.[30] Pompey Elliott, who fears his brigade will be dismantled, will later say, 'If Mr Hughes had been in the pay of the Germans, he could not have dealt us a more paralysing stroke.'[31]

According to Bean, Monash 'demurred that the needs of the campaign might render it impossible to withdraw the Corps when the weather broke'.[32]

Hughes tenses. 'They *must* be out of the line by the date mentioned,' he replies, 'and your *position*, General, depends upon this.'[33]

But while Hughes is sure of the Australian Government's approval of his plan, he is wary of Monash's growing standing, and fears that by cabling to Australia he might have the decision overruled by Cabinet.

Eventually Monash is able to keep 350 of the 800, but he and Rawlinson have already decided that after the preliminary attacks on the Hindenburg Line, the Australians will fight just one more battle[34] before resting for the winter and winning the war in 1919.

Some of the men want to stop fighting right now.

About 60 soldiers in Pompey Elliott's 59th Battalion go on strike. They are relieved on 14 September after a week of continuous strain, and have no sooner fallen asleep when they are called out to continue the chase. Three platoons refuse, and their officers support them, saying that a strike is the only way to explain their weariness to their commanders.

Elliott looks into the drained, dusty faces of the tired men and thinks hard about what to say. The usually volatile general says he understands their concerns, as he's been fighting alongside them the whole way – but if they rejoin the fight he will speak up for them as soon as possible.

The men think for a moment about how far they've come and how far they must now go to victory. They grab their guns and bayonets.

Monash knows that with Hughes pulling out his troops at one end and with others falling from fatigue at the other, he must do something drastic as the great battle looms. He informs Rawlinson that he needs reinforcements. He is given America's 27th and 30th Divisions – 50,000 rookies. Once again the soldiers under his command number almost 200,000.[35]

Over a cup of afternoon tea at Monash's headquarters on 13 September, 'quite informally', as he recalls, the Australian commander sits down with Rawlinson to decide on their campaign. Also present are the Englishman's two other corps commanders – General Butler, who has been recalled to lead III Corps, and General Braithwaite, Ian Hamilton's former chief of staff on Gallipoli, now leading IX Corps.

Rawlinson decides to attack the Hindenburg Line on 18 September. For Monash it will be the 'most arduous, the most responsible, and the most difficult' of any plan he has undertaken.[36]

The first phase is an attempt to capture the Hindenburg Outpost Line, also called the Hargicourt Line. Braithwaite will attack in the south, Monash in the middle and Butler to the north.

One of Monash's big concerns for what will be known as the Battle of Epehy is that he has only eight tanks, despite the fact that 'General Elles's repair workshops, manned largely by Chinese coolie mechanics, had been working night and day'.[37] Monash once again plays a conjuring trick and has his men build dummy tanks from hessian, paint, wire, nails and battens. Men compete to make the most realistic dummy and the best efforts are dragged out before dawn so the enemy can see them.[38]

Monash also doubles the machine-gun resources of his two battle divisions by bringing up the complete machine-gun battalions of the 3rd and 5th Divisions, so that he has 256 Vickers guns on a frontage now reduced to 6.5 kilometres. It gives him a dense machine-gun barrage, 250 metres ahead of the infantry.

The British 3rd and 4th Armies and the 1st French Army will attack on a front of 27 kilometres from Holnon to Gouzeaucourt. Rawlinson's attack will have a frontage of 18 kilometres, with Monash in the centre.

Monash's two divisions have to advance about 4.5 kilometres, and will do it in three stages: first hitting the Germans on the old British front, then advancing to the line that the British used as an outpost, and finally taking the Hindenburg Outpost Line.

On 16 September, after Monash holds a meeting of his commanders in a YMCA marquee erected near Sinclair-Maclagan's headquarters, Rawlinson writes in his diary: 'I am pretty sure that the Aust & IX Corps will do their jobs but am not so confident about III Corps ... If they make a mess of this show I shall have to talk seriously to Butler for it will be his fault.'[39]

*

On the rainy, foggy morning of 18 September, at 5.20 a.m., an hour before sunrise, four undermanned attacking brigades from the 1st and 4th Divisions set off for the heavily fortified German defences under a supporting artillery barrage. The brigades are drenched to the skin and slipping on the clay surface beneath them.

At the village of Le Verguier, Sergeant Maurice Vincent Buckley[40] earns a Victoria Cross by rushing at least six enemy machine-gun positions, capturing a field gun, and taking nearly 100 prisoners. With fewer than 20 casualties, the 16th Battalion takes 450 prisoners – more than its own number of fighting men – and snares 60 machine-guns, five field guns and two anti-aircraft guns. Frightened Germans run past an officer of the 11th Brigade, saying, 'Which way?' to be locked up.[41]

One German battalion commander later says the Australian machine-gun attack 'was absolutely too terrible for words. There was nothing to be done but to crouch down in our trenches and wait for you to come and take us.'[42]

Before 10 a.m.,[43] the Australians have possession of the old British lines, and are heading to the Hindenburg Outpost Line overlooking Bellicourt and the canal a kilometre in the distance.[44]

'I could hardly have dared to hope', Monash will write, 'that a trench system of such considerable strength, which had defied the 5th Army for so long, would fall into our hands so easily as it did.'[45]

Bill Glasgow's 1st Division pushes on without a break, and before nightfall has overwhelmed the garrison of the Hindenburg Outpost Line along its front. Sinclair-Maclagan's 4th Division fights to within 450 metres of that line.

The troops are exhausted, all movement is in full view of the enemy, and the wet ground is difficult. They rest until dark and the artillery peppers the enemy's defences. At 11 o'clock that night, the 4th attacks again and, after severe fighting, also captures the whole of its objective.

In the early hours of the next morning, Private Jim Woods, a fruit grower born in Two Wells, South Australia, astonishes his comrades with an extraordinary act of bravery, holding off a German attack with hand grenades until an important position can be secured. Woods, who receives a Victoria Cross, fought a tough battle just to enlist because of his small stature, but he is all heart.[46]

The 6800 Australians fighting that day take 4300 prisoners. In reporting on the battle to Haig, Rawlinson says German officers will no longer face the Australians.[47] Neither of the British Corps has reached its objectives.

The Australians suffer 1260 casualties[48] and the 11th Battalion loses its most popular man, Kiwi-born Captain Wally Rewi Hallahan, who was due to marry an English nurse in two days. He distinguished himself at Gallipoli and in subsequent campaigns, surviving two wounds and earning the Military Cross and Military Medal. He was one of those selected in the first wave to head home under Billy Hughes's enforced holiday. Wally had farewelled his mates, and sent his sister Grace in Kalgoorlie a postcard from England, as he prepared for the voyage home.

Then he was recalled for one last effort in France. He was given a less dangerous role, mopping up just after daylight in the wake of the initial charge, but was struck by a shell and killed about an hour into the battle. He has bequeathed all his property to his sister. A year and a half later she receives two khaki shirts, a pair of pyjamas, two pairs of socks, a scarf, a pair of spurs, a wallet, photos, a collar and tie, a map case, and some handkerchiefs to cry into.[49]

But it has been a great victory, Monash says. If the weather remains favourable he predicts that the Germans will be out of France by Christmas – maybe not Belgium, but definitely France. With some luck the war might be over early in 1919.[50]

'The Hindenburg outpost line had been vanquished. From it we could now look down upon the Saint-Quentin Canal, and sweep with fire the whole of the sloping ground which lay between us and the canal, denying the use of that ground to the enemy, and making it impossible for him to withdraw the guns and stores which littered the area. There is no record in this war of any previous success on such a scale, won with so little loss.'[51]

As feared, General Butler *has* made a mess of his attack, and three days after the first assault his III Corps has still not caught up with Monash. Butler tries daily attacks but is beaten back every time. He decides to make another assault with his four tired divisions and a few tanks at 5.40 a.m. on 21 September and asks Monash if he will take responsibility for the southern 450 metres of Butler's area. Monash reluctantly agrees, and at 10.30 p.m. on the 20th warns the 1st Division that they have to go again.[52]

The order comes at a turbulent time. General Glasgow has just arranged to relieve the tired troops of the 1st Brigade when he tells them they have to fight some more. Some of the men say they are not getting a fair deal and are being put in to do other people's work. There is still widespread feeling that the Australians, as well as fighting on their own front, are being called on to make good the British failures.[53]

The Australian soldiers are all volunteers, and some now see the AIF as an annoying employer,[54] like the great pastoralists of western Queensland who drove the shearers to a mass armed strike. One hundred and nineteen men of the 1st Battalion refuse to fight and walk to the rear, leaving just 10 officers and 84 men to go forward. Captain Hayward Moffat, a grazier from Longreach who survived a gunshot wound to the face at Gallipoli, dies during the fighting that day.

Mutiny is punishable by death, and last year France shot 43 French soldiers[55] for the crime. Monash has softened in his attitude to the firing squad, though. All 119 men are tried for desertion, not mutiny, and 118 are found guilty and sentenced to up to 10 years at Dartmoor Prison in Devon.[56] Monash, though, knows what they have already been through and does not confirm the sentences. Instead the men are kept under arrest in France. After the Armistice Monash and Hobbs will ask Glasgow, who has jurisdiction over the Division, to remit the sentences but

Glasgow refuses. He has none of Monash's public-relations savvy. When Hobbs eventually succeeds[57] Monash as corps commander, he pardons the men and they are sent home.

The spirit of rebellion festers. The timing of the British High Command is rarely good, and now with dwindling numbers in each brigade the generals want to reduce the number of battalions from four to three. Monash realises the importance of streamlining the Allied forces and is happy that it will mean an extra 30 Lewis machine-guns for each battalion – but he also knows the harm it will cause to fraying morale. With the battle for the Hindenburg Line just ahead, Monash and his commanders reluctantly agree to strike off the 19th, 21st, 25th, 37th, 42nd, 54th and 60th Battalions.

To many of the men the decision is like a family break-up; their battalions are bands of brothers. Lieutenant Colonel Charles Story, a fine officer from Victoria's Mornington Peninsula, is so angry about the fate of his 37th that he ignores military protocol and goes over the head of his brigadier, writing a letter condemning the decision to Gellibrand, Monash and Birdwood, and pointing out the deficiencies in other battalions that he says should go instead. Story is relieved of his command, but his attitude is infectious.

On 22 September the men of the 37th are on the parade ground, and obey every command except the final one to join their new battalions. Brigadier General Walter McNicoll tries to talk sense into them, but while the officers reluctantly obey an order to fall out, followed by the sergeants, one corporal and one private, the ranks again refuse.

The remainder are told that if they don't join their new units that afternoon, they will be posted as absent without leave and arrested. The men decide to remain as one battalion, a seasoned corporal becomes their new commander and they march back to their huts. A medical aid post is re-formed by the orderlies, and church parade for the next day arranged with the padre. Rations are smuggled from other units, which suddenly lose boxes of food from the back of wagons.

Most of the other outgoing battalions launch the same protests on 24 and 25 September, though Pompey Elliott is able to threaten, berate, cajole and finally plead with his 59th Battalion and convince them to merge with the 60th. At first he says the protest leaders will be executed, and that one in 10 of the mutineers will be shot at random. When that doesn't work, he tells them how much Australia needs these brave fighting men.[58]

The soldiers of the 25th Battalion tell their brigadier, Evan Wisdom, that it is their unanimous wish to go into the next battle as their own distinct battalion and to be given the hardest task. All the resisting battalions also say they want to fight, but with their identity unchanged.

Monash and Gellibrand meet representatives of the 37th; Monash says he is doing 'a thing unprecedented in military annals' in holding an informal conference with them, 'but I realise that the AIF is different from any other army in the world'.[59] He confers with Rawlinson and his divisional commanders, and asks that the disbanding be deferred for two weeks. Haig agrees. The announcement is received with 'deafening cheers' but Pompey Elliott is now disgusted that his men obeyed but the others have been given special treatment.[60]

None of the mutineers is punished. And Monash figures that with any luck they will all have fought their last battle before long. He has used tact and charm to get his way, but was never about to let the soldiers get the better of him. He is still in control. To destroy the Hindenburg Line he needs shock troops who are focused on victory rather than their personal grievances.

The old British trenches in front of the Hindenburg Line have been taken but the main line behind the canal is still guarded by row after row of entanglements and machine-gun posts. A kilometre further back is a reserve line of positions, then another 3 kilometres back is a final line called the Beaurevoir Line, just west of the village of the same name.

Monash devises a plan for his men to cross a mound above an underground canal tunnel, in effect a land bridge. The mound begins just south of Bellicourt and runs for 5 kilometres north to Le Catelet. The covering over the tunnel will allow him to move tanks and huge numbers of men without worrying about water hazards.

He faces several major problems, though. Butler's III Corps is still 1000 metres from where it should be. Monash was hoping to sidestep his Australian divisions into the area held by III Corps and attack from there, but Butler's failure means a change of plan. Monash will now use the raw American recruits to attack alongside the tanks, charging 3.6 kilometres to take the main Hindenburg Line and the reserve line. The two Australian divisions will then come through and take the final Beaurevoir Line. Next Butler's III Corps and Braithwaite's IX Corps will charge through the gap and spread out on both sides, as though from a sprinkler head, to widen the front, envelop the Germans and squeeze all the fight out of them.

Rawlinson makes a slight adjustment to Monash's plan, insisting that the attempt on the Beaurevoir Line not be made until the results of the prior stages have been assessed. Monash also widens his frontage from 5.5 kilometres to 9 kilometres so as to minimise casualties from flanking fire. There will be an attack south of the tunnel across the water, and Braithwaite selects the 46th Division of IX Corps to cross the canal opposite Bellenglise using rafts made from petrol tins, ladders, collapsible boats and lifebelts sent from Boulogne.

Butler will only be entrusted to use III Corps to guard the Americans' left flank. In consultation with the American commander George Windle Read and the British tank commanders Elles and Courage, Monash assigns Sinclair-Maclagan, at the head of 217 men from the 1st and 4th Australian Divisions, to bring the Americans up to speed on the Australian methods and the technical language used for the orders and maps of the Australian Corps.[61] Monash has spoken to the

American generals for three hours, 'with blackboard and chalk, maps and diagrams',[62] explaining his methods. Some things are lost in translation.

Monash makes his plans for the attack on 29 September, believing the Americans can do what Butler couldn't and take the positions in front of the tunnel. It's a gamble, and 'contrary to the policy which had governed all my previous battle plans, in which nothing had been left to chance'.[63]

Now Butler's failure to advance his III Corps threatens Monash's whole mission.

On Saturday 27 September, at 5.30 a.m., 2000 men[64] from Monash's 27th American Division set off in the fog to carry out a preliminary attack with a creeping barrage, smoke shells and 12 tanks. They aim to establish a suitable 'jumping off' line in preparation for the full-scale assault on the Hindenburg Line in two days. The plan is to capture key points in the trench system: the Knoll, Quennemont Farm and Gillemont Farm. The intended advance is a little less than a kilometre over a 2-kilometre-wide frontage.

Some of the Americans make it to the ridge overlooking the canal tunnel, but most get lost or shot. The soldiers have only 18 officers with them, and before long 17 of them are killed or wounded. In the swirling clouds of smoke and fog and gas, the leaderless men become disorganised targets. Rather than clean out the trenches, they advance, leaving the German machine-gunners still firing from behind them. Many are still out in the field the next day, just 24 hours before Monash is to start a creeping barrage to signal the mass attack. The Americans report 1500 casualties.

Monash now faces an extraordinary dilemma.

The rest of the Americans preparing for the major advance on the Hindenburg Line are nowhere near the designated start line.

If Monash employs the artillery barrage from the start line as planned, two American divisions will be advancing for about 1000 metres through open ground with no artillery cover. If he brings the artillery back to cover them, the Americans already sheltering out in the trenches likely will be killed.

For one of the few times in his military career, he is confused and uncertain.

He asks Rawlinson to postpone the attack until 30 September,[65] but Rawlinson says absolutely not. Other armies will be launching attacks at the same time along the line from Verdun to Flanders. In any case, Rawlinson says he is 'quite prepared for a partial failure at this point', and says Monash should do his best to pursue the original plan, 'in spite of this difficult situation'.[66] Rawlinson will give the Americans extra tanks to help them fight their way to the start line on time for the artillery barrage.

The Australians receive a visit from Arthur Conan Doyle – 'a great, square bulldog of a man with a kindly face', as Bean describes him. The author's son Kingsley was wounded on the Somme,[67] and Conan Doyle tells the soldiers he is proud to have the same blood as theirs running through his veins. The men cheer, but Monash is in a low mood.

While Monash had shown a ruthless streak in driving his weary men on to victory, the idea of cutting down his Allies with 'friendly fire' or giving others no protection at all, makes him ill. When Haig arrives at Monash's headquarters the commander-in-chief finds Monash in 'a state of despair', with so many lives on the line and such uncertainty over their fate.

Haig tells him not to worry because it is 'not a serious matter'.[68]

Erich Ludendorff was expecting to be in Paris by now, with the German flag flying from the Eiffel Tower and the German people gorging themselves on French food and wine. Instead the meat ration at home has been cut further to just 125 grams a week, the bread allowance is not much better and the mood of the people is worse than Ludendorff has ever known it. Germans were happy to go hungry with a glorious victory in sight, but few are willing to starve to defeat. Revolution is in the air.

Ludendorff is now at the Hotel Britannique in Spa, the German Command's new headquarters. It is situated in heavily wooded mountains south-west of Liège, the city Ludendorff pummelled in the opening days of the war.

Dr Hochheimer, Ludendorff's psychiatrist, has advised Germany's commander to perform deep-breathing exercises, sing folk songs and contemplate the delicate beauty of roses in the garden. It should make Ludendorff feel better as he wreaks devastation across Europe, but the German commander can find little solace in these activities. Monash and the Allies are scraping away at the outer layers of his armour north of Saint-Quentin, the 1st and 3rd British Armies are creating havoc around Cambrai, the Canadians have Bourlon Wood and Plumer's 2nd Army is pushing out from Ypres. Much further south, the French and British, backed by a large Greek army, are driving north into Bulgaria. The Australian Light Horsemen are about to take Damascus.

On 28 September, Ludendorff rages at his staff and at Hindenburg, and blames the Kaiser for all of Germany's woes. He becomes ever more hysterical.[69]

When he hears that Spanish flu has broken out in the French Army he claps his hands together and says it is Germany's last chance.[70]

'We still hold Alsace and Lorraine,' he says, 'we're still in control of Belgium, and we're still occupying part of France. We can still paralyse their will to fight.'

Just before 4 p.m. there is a knock at the door. An army clerk salutes and stands to attention. 'An urgent message, General.' He hands a note to Ludendorff.

The general reads just a few words, and suddenly it seems as if he has swallowed cyanide. His heavy jowls quiver.

'This can't be true,' Ludendorff splutters. He throws the message down. 'We have been stabbed in the back.'

As Ludendorff begins to rant, an officer picks up the paper to read that 17 Bulgarian divisions at Salonika have surrendered to a French general.

Ludendorff marches up and down the room, shaking, clenching his fists and throwing his arms about wildly.

He begins to babble.

Then he starts to foam at the mouth. His face turns ghostly white. His eyes roll towards the back of his head; his body goes stiff.

Ludendorff crashes to the floor with a force that shakes the room.[71]

Monash tells Bean and Murdoch on 28 September he has grave doubts that the Americans will reach their objectives. The disastrous fighting on the 27th has shown him that they are 'very unprepared and untrained'. Always suspicious, Bean suspects Monash is 'hedging against a possible defeat in which case he would be able to throw the blame on to the Americans'.[72]

Monash sends a rain of mustard gas and explosives shells over the Hindenburg Line all night, and at 5.55 p.m. on 29 September, backed by a bombardment of a thousand cannons, Monash's two American divisions set off en masse to the positions they were aiming for two days ago. The 27th Division has to do it without a creeping barrage, but will have 34 tanks in support. Close behind are the Australian pioneers and American engineers ready to repair roads to facilitate the massive troop movements.[73] No other forces except the signal service are to pass Monash's start line until zero hour for the mass attack at 9 a.m., by which time the Americans should be in position.

The American commanders have told Monash their men can do the job without the artillery barrage by stealing through most of the ground up to the official start line before zero hour. But Bean will soon write that 'the most brilliant battle plan that Monash ever drew ... broke down largely through his underestimation of the human element'.[74] He has seriously overestimated the ability of the young Americans to perform like battle-hardened veterans.

By 7.05 a.m., news arrives that the 30th Division has crossed over the tunnel on time and that the 27th has passed the Knoll on the Hindenburg Outpost Line.

The 30th, which has a creeping barrage in support, takes Bellicourt on the Hindenburg Line. The 5th Australian Division is to leapfrog them here and push through to the reserve lines further on. But once again the American mopping-up work of eliminating machine-gun posts is lax, and the 5th is delayed before advancing to take Nauroy at 12.20 p.m. There are many Doughboys lying dead in the trampled wheat fields. Gellibrand's 3rd Division becomes mixed up with the stalled 27th Americans, who are more than a kilometre behind to the north.

Some of the tanks of the 27th are disabled by British 'plum pudding' bombs in an old minefield; others are disabled by anti-tank guns. Some run into sunken roads and deep trenches and are unable to be extracted. Most of the heavy German fire is coming from the positions that Butler's III Corps failed to take – the Knoll, Quennemont Farm and Gillemont Farm.

Small parties of Americans heading back to the rear and away from the chattering machine-guns, hidden by smoke and fog, meet advancing Australians from Gellibrand's 40th Battalion and tell them 'they did not know what had happened except that they had failed: they had lost their way in the smoke, were without officers, and did not know what to do, and were anxious to find anyone who could tell them'.[75] Photographer Hubert Wilkins finds a trench full of Americans, sitting quietly as Germans throw stick grenades at them. The Americans think the grenades are harmless used shells.[76]

Gellibrand goes forward to see what's delaying his men and encounters machine-gun fire. He returns, certain that the 27th Americans can't reach their objective. At 11 a.m. Monash receives an airman's report that the American 30th Division has made it through to the Hindenburg Line and the machine-gun fire is coming from isolated pockets they have failed to mop up. Monash orders Gellibrand to attack the pockets of resistance, but without his three brigades of artillery, for fear of hitting the Americans ahead of them.

Gellibrand hesitates and Monash bullies him. Gellibrand is convinced the airman has got it wrong, and that the 'pockets' are actually the Hindenburg Line and the Americans aren't within cooee of it. Monash and Blamey insist that the 'air report in question must be credited'.[77]

Yet Gellibrand is proved right.

Major Blair Wark,[78] a Bathurst-born quantity surveyor from McMahons Point in Sydney, who received a Distinguished Service Order at Polygon Wood a year ago, comes to the rescue of at least 200 Americans from the 117th Infantry Regiment on this morning.

Moving ahead of his troops in the face of heavy fire, Wark hails a passing tank near Bellicourt like it is a London cab, and with it captures two machine-gun posts. He then collects the leaderless Americans near the tunnel entrance. He organises his new recruits into a cohesive fighting force and together they take the village of Nauroy by 11.30 a.m., collecting 40 prisoners as well. Wark then organises a party of troops to capture a battery of German 77-millimetre field guns firing on his rear companies. He captures four guns and 10 more prisoners, and with just two men in support takes another 50 captives near Magny-la-Fosse. Wark's actions earn him a Victoria Cross.

Monash has little time for the British Tommies, but while his assault totters, Braithwaite's 46th (North Midland) Division, backed by a huge artillery barrage, defies the fortified machine-gun positions and the sheer vertical drops into the shallow water to cross the Saint-Quentin Canal. The men, mostly from the mining villages around Derby and Nottingham, swim, wade or float across and then charge at the German trenches with their bayonets.

As the Germans are about to blow the Riqueval Bridge, nine soldiers from the North Staffordshire Regiment, led by Captain Arthur Charlton, drive off machine-gunners in a trench guarding it, and keeping an important lifeline open for the attacking troops.[79] Rawlinson's 4th Army takes 5300 prisoners for the day, the North Midlanders capturing 4200 with the loss of 800 men. They also penetrate 5.5 kilometres into the German defence.

In a chamber dug into the southern entrance of the Saint-Quentin Canal tunnel at Bellicourt, Australian soldiers come upon a discovery that immediately becomes the talk of the Western Front. Inside is a room littered with mutilated German bodies, one of them sitting in a cooking cauldron.

For months there have been reports in Australian and British newspapers that the Germans are boiling down their dead to extract glycerine for making ammunition.[80] Trainloads of bodies are said to be taken to human boiling-down works.[81] Anti-German sentiment is so strong that the reports ring true, and the sight of this dead German in what becomes known as 'The Devil's Kitchen' only confirms them.

An investigation soon proves that the room is actually the soldiers' kitchen, and that a shell exploded during the fighting, killing all the unfortunate men. One of the Germans was blown into the pot by the force of the blast.

At the Hotel Britannique in Spa, Ludendorff has had a fitful night after his collapse. At 6 p.m. yesterday evening, he told Hindenburg that Germany must now ask for an armistice.[82]

Now, on 29 September, he meets with Hindenburg and Foreign Secretary Paul von Hintze. Ludendorff says responsibility for the war will have to be spread as widely as possible. The meeting decides there will have to be a 'revolution from above', a change of power in Germany.

They go to see the Kaiser staying nearby and recommend that rather than fall into the clutches of England or France, Germany should adopt US President Woodrow Wilson's 'Fourteen Points' plan for peace. Germany will fare better at the bargaining table, they say, if it presents itself as a democracy.

The Kaiser's cousin Prince Max of Baden is installed as the new chancellor. Ludendorff and Hindenburg start looking for scapegoats.

*

For the first time since Passchendaele a year ago, Bean returns from a battle that has gone wrong.[83] The 27th Division loses 5000 men over three days but Rawlinson has little sympathy for the confused Americans being cut down in what he says is a 'state of hopeless confusion'. 'It is their own fault', he writes.[84]

Monash, fatigued, frustrated and in a temper, is just as harsh, telling Bean the next day: 'Well you see what I expected might happen has happened. The Americans sold us a pup. They're simply unspeakable.' Blamey does not give the Americans much of a chance to grieve either, swearing like 'a bullock driver' at one of the American divisional commanders over the incompetence of his men.[85]

Despite Monash's anger, the attack of 29 September is far from a disaster. It has only gained a few hundred metres but it has made huge inroads into the German defences. Rather than a straight line of gains as Monash was hoping, the progress has been diagonal, but it has been progress nonetheless.

The southern attack has had the most success around the tunnel entrance at Bellicourt. Further north Gellibrand eventually takes Gillemont Farm. The Australian and American troops then push the Germans off Quennemont Farm and the Knoll.

The outpost line has fallen, but the main Hindenburg Line is still being defended by nightfall. Monash decides to scrap his original plan. Rather than press on eastwards, Gellibrand's and Talbot Hobbs's respective reserve brigades, the 9th and 14th, will swing around and attack the Hindenburg trench system in a north-easterly direction, to take Bony and the northern end of the tunnel. Gellibrand will have to advance without heavy artillery because of the Americans in front of him.

Pouring rain falls on the night of 29 September, making a subsequent advance even harder the next morning. Everybody is drenched. It is the start of what Monash calls 'a day of intense effort, slow and methodical hand-to-hand fighting, in a perfect tangle of trenches, with every yard of the advance vigorously contested'.[86]

Nerves are frayed on the frontline and on the telephone. Again, Monash and Gellibrand argue repeatedly. Monash berates the Tasmanian orchardist for not reporting the loss of tanks, for attacking on a narrow front, for not having a divisional reserve – for not doing better. He considers Gellibrand 'more a philosopher and student than a man of action … with a tendency to uncertainty'.[87] He wants Gellibrand to mount a frontal attack under an artillery barrage, but Gellibrand insists that it's the wrong move given the German positions. He says a flank attack would be better. Monash tells him to do as he's told.

Then Monash rings back to say Gellibrand is right. The next day he apologises for his behaviour. 'Time and again,' Gellibrand will recall, 'I was right in my reports and inferences and disbelieved.'[88]

Gellibrand's men advance 900 metres, and by nightfall the Allies are inching towards their goal over hard-won territory. Monash tells them progress will 'depend upon the tenacity and skilful leading of the front-line troops', with reliance more on the bayonet and the hand grenade than artillery. It is, he says, 'in a peculiar degree, a private soldier's battle'.[89]

During the 55th Battalion's attack near Bellicourt, Private John Ryan,[90] a small, thin railways labourer from Tumut with a smiling face 'burned a deep mahogany brown',[91] captures a German position with grenades and bayonet in an action that leaves him wounded. Ryan is recommended for a Victoria Cross, though Australia will be less appreciative of his courageous service in years to come.[92]

By noon on 1 October, Gellibrand's 10th and 11th Brigades are in Bony and the Fifth Division reports the capture of Joncourt on the edge of the Beaurevoir Line. Patrols are attacking Le Catelet village and a rise called the Knob. Braithwaite's IX British Corps force the Germans to abandon any hope of holding the tunnel.

By nightfall all isolated parties of Americans and their wounded have been brought in.

The next day Rawlinson tells Monash he has done brilliant work, and sends him a note saying he should go on leave 'with delight at all you have done'.[93] Monash still has tremors in his hands, but he will not leave the conflict until the Hindenburg Line is taken.

He writes to his old friend John Springthorpe: 'At times when I feel very tired, I am tempted to hope that it will be the last serious work I shall ever do in my life.'[94]

After three days of what Monash calls 'a stiff fight', the Australians have 3057 prisoners and 35 enemy cannons. The 3rd and 5th Divisions report 2600 casualties and Monash has Rosenthal's 2nd Division bussed in from Péronne to take up a position just west of the Hindenburg Line.

He will attack the Beaurevoir Line tomorrow.

Having been eroded from about 6000 men to 2500, Rosenthal's 5th and 7th Brigades begin this new attack at 6.05 a.m. on 3 October. They have endured heavy gas shelling during the night, but make the most of their limited numbers by fighting ferociously across a frontage of 5.5 kilometres. One captured German officer remarks: 'You Australians are all bluff. You attack with practically no men and are on top of us before we know where we are.'[95] Monash says Rosenthal's brigades have delivered an 'astonishing performance … fighting under open and exposed conditions'.[96]

Lieutenant Joe Maxwell,[97] a 22-year-old apprentice boilermaker from Newcastle, was fined £20 for brawling with civilian and military police in London a year ago, and is even feistier when it comes to the enemy. Having started as a private at Gallipoli, he has received the Military Cross and Bar and a Distinguished Conduct Medal for bravery in Flanders and France. After 3 October he adds a Victoria Cross to his collection. Maxwell opens fire on a Maxim gun position with his revolver and leaps into a trench. His revolver is now empty but the Germans surrender anyway.

Maxwell then approaches a group of Germans who want to surrender, only to find that some of their comrades don't. Twenty

Germans surround him and take him prisoner. Maxwell tells the Germans they are making a big mistake and that the Australian artillery will blow them to 'smithereens'. The Germans say they will fight on. Soon enough, an artillery shell lands in the trench and bodies fly everywhere. Maxwell, taking advantage of the confusion,[98] draws an automatic pistol concealed in his respirator,[99] shoots two of the survivors and makes his escape.

Later in the day, when Maxwell crosses the Beaurevoir Line, he sees an Australian with a severe head wound. He stabs a rifle with fixed bayonet into the ground next to the soldier so stretcher-bearers will spot him, but two days later when Maxwell passes the same spot he sees the wounded man still there, still clinging to life but wrapped in the overcoat of a dead German lying beside him.

'The German apparently seeing his end was near', Maxwell later recalls, 'had taken off his coat to cover the Australian, whom he thought had a chance.'[100]

The Beaurevoir Line falls on 5 October.

Overnight, Germany's new chancellor Prince Max of Baden sends a telegram to President Woodrow Wilson in Washington, D.C., requesting peace talks. But the process for peace is a slow one.

Monash decides to withdraw the 2nd Division, which has lost 1000 men, and send in the two American divisions, which have been reorganised and rested. They can't move in yet, so Monash agrees to one last request from Rawlinson: to push the line still further east with another day's fighting. The battle is really an afterthought.

Monash decides to attack the village of Montbrehain, once home to 900 people, on a plateau dominating the surrounding countryside. Most of the inhabitants have been evacuated, but some elderly couples, women and children still huddle in cellars there.

Rosenthal's 2nd Division carries out the attack in what will be Lieutenant General Sir John Monash's last military campaign.

The 21st and 24th Battalions are selected for the battle. Some of the men are surprised that after six days of continuous fighting on the Hindenburg Line, the Australians are being called upon again instead of being granted leave.

Bean questions the necessity of it, and wonders about the planning, because it is the kind of attack 'that most Australian leaders had come to dread … the driving of a narrow egg-shaped salient into the German position on the high ground'.[101] Bean suspects Monash is trying to wring one last success out of his men before Billy Hughes sends many of them home.[102]

At 6.05 a.m. on 5 October, the two battalions dash off towards Montbrehain and work their way through the village to its eastern outskirts. Leading the way are Captains Austin Mahony[103] and Harry Fletcher,[104] who have been 'bosom friends'[105] for years. They went to school together, trained as teachers together, taught at the same school for a time and shared a flat in the Melbourne suburb of Northcote. On Sundays they would set out together for church before branching off, Fletcher to the Methodist 'kirk' and Mahony to Roman Catholic mass.[106]

After the Gallipoli landing, they enlisted together and had consecutive serial numbers: Mahony 1056 and Fletcher 1057.[107] They both sailed on the troopship *Euripides* in May 1915 and fought together in the closing stages of the campaign for the Dardanelles. They were together at the start of the Battle of Amiens in 1918, and in the great chase across the Somme. Now they are fighting together in what will become the last battle of the Australian infantry in the Great War.

A Bendigo-born building contractor, Captain George Ingram[108] will receive the 60th and last Victoria Cross awarded to an Australian in this war. Under the cover of a Lewis gun, Ingram leads his platoon in a fierce firefight, capturing nine machine-guns and killing all 42 Germans who occupied the line. Ingram kills at least 18 himself, but he's only getting started. Soon his company is besieged by at least 40 machine-guns spitting bullets from a quarry. Again Ingram leads the charge, diving in among the guns, shooting six Germans and forcing 30 men to surrender. Still he isn't done. He brings down a machine-gun crew firing from a cellar ventilator and takes another 30 prisoners.

Germans in other parts of the village keep shooting. About an hour into the battle, a Ballarat student named Lieutenant John Foster Gear, who has risen through the ranks and just received a Military Cross, is shot through the head by a sniper while trying to direct a tank against a machine-gun post.

As Mahony's men move through the village and the Germans retreat, old people and a few young girls creep out from their hiding places to rejoice. One old man wanders up the street shouting: '*Anglais, bon! Bon!*'

At about 8 a.m. Mahony takes a machine-gun bullet through the head. It takes him four days to die. At 9 a.m. a 77-millimetre shell fired from a field gun towards a tank kills Harry Fletcher.

The mates who have survived so much together die together, far from home.

The Australians advance their line a kilometre and a half but suffer 430 casualties. Some of their best and brightest fall at the final hurdle.

The Mahony family run a notice in their local paper:

For Freedom's Cause.
MAHONY.–On 5th October, Captain J. Austin Mahony, M.C. (dear old Dick), dearly loved second eldest son of Mr. and Mrs. J. Mahony. Hansonville, loved brother of William P. (A.I.F), Eileen (Sister Mary of St. Martin), Maurice, Mollie, Ray, Aggie, Francis, Alice, and little Mona ... pal of Capt. Harry Fletcher, Eaglehawk. Age 24 years. He wore the white flower of a blameless life.[109]

A few weeks later one of Mahony's aunts writes to the French general Paul Pau. She says her whole family is broken-hearted especially Mahony's mother, 'to think that on the eve of peace, he was called away'. Austin was 'such a good true boy', she says and with that in mind would the general be so kind as to make sure that his grave is kept clean?[110]

Elsewhere along the Hindenburg Line, the Allies smash down the barricades.

Birdwood's 5th Army is about to liberate Lille. The British 1st and 3rd Armies, with Kiwis and Canadians at the head, march on Cambrai. Plumer's 2nd Army and the Belgian Army are trampling the Germans around Ypres and heading towards Ostend and Bruges. French forces backed by more than a million Americans chop through the Argonne.

Monash finally orders the 2nd Division out of the frontline. There will still be some fighting units attached to British armies, and Australian pilots still taking to the skies, but for the most part, without yet realising it, the Australians have finished their work.

It will be a happy Christmas. The war is all but over.

Monash writes that since the Australians were called in to help turn back the Spring Offensive on 27 March they have captured 29,144 prisoners. Since the Battle of Amiens on 8 August they have liberated 116 towns and villages. By his calculations, per man the Australians have claimed more than double the prisoners, territory and guns of their British counterparts, and in the battles to overthrow Germany the Australian Army Corps has 'played an important, and in some of them a predominating, part'.[111]

From 8 August to 5 October, his total battle casualties were 21,243, including 4998 killed. He later figures that was 'extraordinarily moderate, having regard to the strenuous nature of the fighting, the great results achieved, and the much higher rate of losses incurred by Australian troops during the previous years of the war'. He says the period under his watch 'was the least costly period, for Australia',[112] even though his men were used as shock troops for most of the time.

He writes to tell Defence Minister Pearce that after a good rest, the AIF will have 50 battalions ready to start their own Spring Offensive in 1919.[113]

On 5 October, Monash and Paul Simonson leave France bound for London, shaking hands and accepting the congratulations of Birdwood and White along the way to Boulogne. They arrive in London the next day, and Monash asks the now Brigadier General Thomas Dodds[114] to provide him with a car and absolute privacy for the next few days.[115] Not even Billy Hughes is to call.

Monash is both elated and exhausted, and he wants some time to relax in a plush hotel and celebrate with Lizzie Bentwitch.

He is proud of his men and of himself.

Never one to downplay success, he writes home to Vic to say 'the story of the Corps ... is one which I do not think is equalled in the whole annals of war, throughout history'.[116]

Chapter 28

PRINCE'S HOTEL, JERMYN STREET, PICCADILLY, 8 OCTOBER 1918

In the course of time it will dawn upon the Australian nation that the activities of the Australian Corps were by far the biggest factor in the reversal of the fortunes of the Allies in this war.
MONASH ON THE AUSTRALIAN ROLE IN THE GREAT WAR[1]

Perhaps the strongest testimony to his capacity is the distance he went in spite of a tremendous compound handicap of prejudice, due partly to his Jewish origin, partly to the fact he was an 'amateur soldier' ...
LEADING WAR HISTORIAN LIDDELL HART[2]

HOW DO YOU COME DOWN after seeing thousands of men die; after watching towns being blown apart? How do you sleep in silence when you are conditioned to hear the constant whistle and boom of flying shells; and rifle shots and screams in the dark?

There was an initial euphoria of victory, but now not even Monash's reunion with Lizzie can drag him out of a deep malaise. For his first few days in England, Monash feels 'dull and dispirited and not very well'.[3] He often goes incognito in civilian clothes, especially when he is with Lizzie, to avoid scandal. Occasionally, like a magician pulling off a surprise, he loves to see soldiers slowly recognise his swarthy features, leap to attention and salute.[4]

He spends 7 October in the countryside with Lizzie, and the next night visits the theatre with her in the West End, but the plays they see together over the next few nights bore him. How could they hope to match anything like the human drama, the pulsating action and heartbreaking pathos that he has experienced over the last few years?

Monash is also troubled that his blossoming relationship with Lizzie is heading for disaster. Constantly having to deceive Vic in his letters home stabs him with pain.

Despite his requests to be left alone, on 9 October Monash meets with Billy Hughes, who congratulates him on his marvellous performance and asks him to write an account of the corps's achievements. Monash can't wait to highlight Australia's successes, and by extension his own. He will send a similar message to Defence Minister Pearce to the one he sent Vic, telling him that 'the performance of my five Divisions and Corps troops has not been surpassed in the whole annals of War', and that 'the work of the Corps was the dominating factor' in 'compelling' the Germans to flee to the Hindenburg Line and then sue for peace. Other troops helped 'materially', he concedes, 'but I am able to assert without contradiction that the performance of the Australian Corps ... far transcends the performance of any similar body of troops on the Western Front'.[5]

Later Monash writes that the success of his corps:

> ... depended first and foremost upon the military proficiency of the Australian private soldier and his glorious spirit of heroism ... The democratic institutions under which he was reared ... the instinct of sport and adventure which is his national heritage, his pride in his young country, and the opportunity which came to him of creating a great national tradition, were all factors which made him what he was. Physically the Australian Army was composed of the flower

of the youth of the continent. A volunteer army – the only purely volunteer army that fought in the Great War ... His adaptability spared him much hardship ... To light a fire and cook his food was a natural instinct. A sheet of corrugated iron, a batten or two, and a few strands of wire were enough to enable him to fabricate a home in which he could live at ease ... The Australian is accustomed to teamwork. He learns it in the sporting field, in his industrial organisations, and in his political activities. The teamwork, which he developed in the war, was of the highest order of efficiency. Each man understood his part and understood also that the part, which others had to play, depended upon the proper performance of his own.[6]

Of course, Monash's success has also been aided by the years of hardships that the Germans endured, and his triumphs have coincided with their fading strength. His battle campaigns at Hamel and Mont St Quentin were, nevertheless, brilliantly conceived, and according to the 13th Battalion historian, 'We always knew that [Monash] would do everything to save the lives of men.'[7]

Over the next few days Monash meets with Hughes and his wife Mary at Australia House and at their house in Regents Park. He helps John Springthorpe prepare a series of laudatory articles for the *Age* on the AIF triumphs and the 'Monash Method'.[8] The self-praise improves his mood. Perhaps because of the prejudice he has always felt and the fear that he will never be given true recognition for his efforts, he tells his old friend: 'I do frankly put forward to you, the claim that the success of the Corps, as a fighting machine, has been, in its totality, very largely due to my own efforts.'[9]

Charles Bean, still thinking Monash is too showy but well aware of his organisational skills, also visits Hughes and tells him he should put Monash in charge of the massive repatriation of the AIF to Australia.

As Bean recalls it, Hughes wants Birdwood because he is 'a man of kindness'. Monash is 'far more capable' but is 'out for himself all the time; like a Jew, showy'; Hughes wonders if he has the 'kindliness or the humanity' to deal with repatriation. 'Do you think he is human enough?' Hughes asks Bean. Bean replies that while Monash might be out for himself, his planning on the Western Front was superb. He must get the job. Putting Birdwood in charge would be a 'catastrophe'.[10]

Now that Monash has proved himself in the field he has 'less compunction' in relinquishing command of the corps to take the GOC role in London, but he senses Birdwood is reluctant to go, a situation that makes Hughes 'very angry'.[11]

Monash does some sittings for two portraits being painted by Longstaff and says those who have seen the three-quarter-length work, intended for Vic, 'admire it greatly'. He predicts a full-length portrait for the Art Gallery of New South Wales, featuring himself against a backdrop of a devastated Europe, will be 'really magnificent'.[12]

Louis Montagu, also known as Baron Swaythling, and his wife Gladys, of the Goldsmith and Rothschild banking families, have Monash to lunch at their London house with other prominent British Jews. Swaythling tells him that he is opposed to the growing Zionist movement in Britain and the talk of setting up a Jewish State in Palestine. He suspects it could lead to trouble with the Arabs.

Monash eventually signs a letter to London's *Morning Post*, along with Swaythling, Major Lionel de Rothschild and other prominent Jews, repudiating 'any connection between Jews and Bolshevism', and declaring the Bolsheviks and Bolshevism as 'dangerous in themselves and as false to the tenets and teachings of Jewry'.[13]

At other times, Monash dines with the Antarctic explorer Major Douglas Mawson, now involved in the supply of high explosives and poison gas to the Allied troops, and with his old commanding officer Major General John Stanley, who at 67 has become 'pompous and stodgy'.[14]

The Rolls-Royce is procured to drive Monash down to the grand Elizabethan mansion Cobham Hall in Kent, which is home to the former England cricket captain Ivo Bligh, now Earl of Darnley, and his wife Lady Darnley. Her Ladyship was once known as Florence Morphy, and is the daughter of the police magistrate at Beechworth who worked overtime during the Kelly Gang's reign of terror. Part of Cobham Hall has been turned into a convalescent home for 40 officers and Monash spends a good part of the day lifting their spirits.

The earl has a tiny urn on his writing desk that his wife and her girlfriends gave him years ago in Melbourne when England beat the Australians there. It contains the ashes of a cricket bail, and is now the trophy for Test matches between the two countries. Monash tells the Blighs that he was in the crowd to welcome home the 'Demon Bowler' Spofforth and the other Australians after they beat England nearly four decades ago.

Lizzie is not invited when Monash takes his first ever girlfriend Clara Stockfeld to lunch. Monash and Clara look into each other's eyes and wonder what might have been if Mat had not been with them taking the train into the city from Elsternwick Station 34 years ago. Back then, Clara was the Queen of Hearts, 'a chit of a girl', and he was a sweet-faced boy she called Jack'o. Time has not diminished her fondness for Monash and she reminds him of the kindness of his whispered conversation with her.

'I have blessed you for it often,' she says.[15]

Monash is just as compelling when addressing a large crowd. He gives several press interviews, and along with the British Foreign Secretary, Arthur Balfour, is a guest speaker at the Dominions Luncheon Club at the Savoy, in an event sponsored by New Zealander James Mills, flush with cash after the sale of his Union Steam Ship Company to P&O. Navy Minister Joe Cook is there too, along with Billy Hughes's right-hand man Bob Garran, Monash's neighbour in Toorak.

Naturally, Monash tells Vic later, *he* is the star of the show. Balfour announces that the Empire will retain the Pacific colonies captured from Germany, but he speaks in a 'somewhat ponderous style' and the audience listens for an hour with polite indifference as he goes on and on and then some.[16]

When it's Monash's turn, he jumps up, adopts a 'breezy, whirlwind style' and tells the audience the war will be over within weeks. His speech is 'punctuated with rounds of cheers and laughter',[17] he tells Vic, and afterwards Balfour says to him, 'My God, Monash, if only I could talk like that!'[18] Garran tells him the speech was magnificent.

Monash has become a celebrity like few Australians before or since. The restless yearning for fame and adulation he had as a young man have come to fruition in a way that surpasses the wildest fantasies of his youth.

He is awarded the French Croix de Guerre with palm, the Belgian Croix de Guerre and the Belgian Order of the Crown.[19] He reminds General George Read that the Americans should give him their Distinguished Service Medal,[20] and he becomes a Knight Grand Cross of the Order of St Michael and St George,[21] reckoning that in Australia only Governor-General Munro Ferguson and Joe Cook have such an alphabet to their credit.[22] He even works on the design for his own coat of arms, featuring the Southern Cross, a bridge symbolising engineering, the Lion of Judah, the compasses of King Solomon, a sword enclosed in a laurel wreath and the motto 'For War and the Arts' in Latin.

On 18 October, as Germany fights on lamely while considering President Wilson's ceasefire proposals, Rawlinson asks Blamey, still in France, when the AIF will be ready to fight again. Hughes has ordered the Australians out of the war for the winter but his demands are falling on deaf ears with the British. Blamey tells Rawlinson the men will be ready to go again in two months. The Australian soldiers have astonished the world with their recent efforts and are resting in a lush and peaceful area beside the Somme between Amiens and Abbeville, where the birds have started to sing again.[23]

Just two days later Rawlinson calls back to say the Australians must be ready to fight in a week. Blamey and Hobbs visit Rawlinson and convince him to give them another week, taking the start date to early November. The two Australians say they still need more time. They write to Monash, asking him to step in urgently. The 1st and 4th Divisions are nowhere near ready, and with one mutiny already, the men will regard the new orders as a broken promise from Hughes.

Monash, who still can't get rid of the tremors in his hands, asks Hughes to act. He and the Prime Minister decide to make urgent representations to Sir Henry Wilson, Chief of the General Staff and Lloyd George's principal military adviser. Hughes tells Wilson that the Australians have done more than their share but Wilson is angry that Hughes has promised the men a European vacation when the war is still to be won.

Late on 27 October, Monash arrives back in France to once again fight for his men.

Erich Ludendorff's mind is oscillating from one extreme to the other. He feels suffocated by the Americans' demands. He hoped Germany would be in a powerful position to negotiate when arms were finally laid down, but he sees the German Government as cowards, acquiescing to everything the Americans want. The last straw is when Germany agrees to stop its submarine warfare on 20 October.

'It was the deepest blow to the army, and especially to the navy', he later says. 'The injury to the morale of the fleet must have been immeasurable. The Cabinet had thrown up the sponge.'[24]

He returns to his former belief that somehow Germany might pick itself off the canvas and fight back from its impossible situation. Those who are rushing to peace, Ludendorff says, are selling out his country.

On 24 October Ludendorff declares that the conditions for peace are unacceptable, and without consulting the German

Government he tells his armies they must fight on. Two days later the German Government asks the Kaiser to demand Ludendorff's resignation.

The Prussian warlord slinks back to his hotel room in Spa, lies on the bed next to his wife and thinks back to the power of the German Army at its height, and that glorious night in 1914 when his muscles stiffened as he bombarded Liège. 'There I had found my manhood',[25] he later says.

Then Erich Ludendorff, the old Prussian warlord, dons a pair of blue sunglasses, covers his face with fake whiskers and scurries off to neutral Sweden. He leaves his devastated country to sort out the mess.[26]

Birdwood has started to take a severe dislike to Monash after being usurped at the top of the Australian Corps. But he joins forces with him to petition Haig that the Australians are in no condition to resume a war that is almost over, and in which they have done the bulk of the heavy lifting in recent months.

Haig is insistent but says the battered 1st and 4th Divisions of Glasgow and Sinclair-Maclagan will only be called upon in an emergency. Monash writes to Dodds in London asking him to tell Hughes that he has done all he can, but Hughes has already acquiesced. In some ways Monash is happy to be going back to the frontline, because he wants the Australians to share in the momentous event when Germany finally caves in.

He sets up his headquarters at Eu, on the mouth of the Somme, and moves with his staff into an annexe of the château of the Comte d'Eu but it's only a temporary home. He summons his divisional commanders on 1 November and tells them to prepare for a move to the front.

The Prince of Wales is to join his staff for six months and Monash expects to be given a large slice of Germany to administer after the Armistice.[27] As he awaits orders, Monash shows the visiting Springthorpe around the deep scars of the European battlegrounds, starts his regular walks again, visits coastal Dieppe and attends a conference with General Ivor Maxse, British Inspector of Training.[28] On 5 November the corps is ordered to the front, and Monash makes preparations to rejoin the flickering fight and set up a new base at Le Cateau.

That same day, President Wilson informs Germany that armistice discussions can begin based on his 'Fourteen Points', but that an armistice must be secured through Marshal Foch, the Allied Supreme Commander. Three days later six representatives of the German Government arrive at Compiègne, France, 80 kilometres north of Paris, to begin the peace process.

'In case they do not at once accept,' Monash writes to Vic, 'it is the intention to go on hammering the enemy ... to meet this contingency my Corps is again moving up into the line.'[29]

The following day, as striking masses march on Berlin, the German Government collapses and the Kaiser flees to Holland, the only country that will take him. Germany is declared a republic on 9 November. The new regime wants peace as soon as possible.

From his hiding place in Sweden, Ludendorff writes to his wife to say that if he ever regains power in Germany there will be no mercy for those who betrayed the Fatherland. With an 'easy conscience', he says, he would have the instigators of peace hanged 'and watch them dangle'.[30]

Lance Corporal Adolf Hitler is of the same mind. He is in a military hospital in the Pomeranian town of Pasewalk, recovering from the effects of a British mustard gas shell, which temporarily blinded him on 14 October, near Ypres. The inflammation of Hitler's mucous membrane and eyelids slowly abates and the 'piercing' in his eye sockets diminishes, so by early November he can at least make out the broad outlines of doctors, nurses and other patients, even of the three young Jewish radicals who come into his ward and try to convert the patients to Bolshevism.

Then on 9 November an elderly pastor, 'all a-tremble', arrives at the hospital to inform the sick and wounded that everything is lost: Germany must now throw itself upon the mercy of the Allies.

Hitler is so shocked that 'everything went black before my eyes'.[31] He is blind again as he totters and gropes his way in the darkness back to his bunk. He digs his head into his pillow, and with a pain and sadness he has never felt before he begins to cry tears of grief. And rage. Adolf Hitler vows revenge on the world.

Psychiatrist Edmund Forster, chief of the Berlin University Nerve Clinic, is called in to examine the little lance corporal and give an explanation for the recurrence of his blindness. Dr Forster concludes that it is all in the mind. He says Hitler is 'a psychopath with hysterical symptoms'.[32]

On 10 November, Monash prepares for a move closer to the front and a new headquarters at Le Cateau, a château previously occupied by Crown Prince Rupprecht and once by Field Marshal John French,[33] who in 1914 commanded the Battle of Mons from here. Badly.

The 1st and 4th Divisions have already started moving to the frontline, but the following morning, 11 November at 5.10 a.m., in a railway car at Compiègne, the Germans sign the Armistice, to take effect at 11 a.m. that day. The war continues all along the Western Front until that precise time, and there will be 2000 casualties from both sides on the final day of fighting as men hope to say they fired the last shot of the Great War.[34]

Monash travels down in the Rolls-Royce from Eu to Le Cateau, passing one rejoicing town and village after another – Villers-Bretonneux, Harbonnières, Péronne and Cambrai – although much of the journey is through a 'desert ... devastated by the war'. When he arrives at his château he finds it also ravaged by the senseless fighting; most of the windows have been shattered, all the tapestries and paintings have been stolen and the retreating Germans have used the mirrors of the grand state rooms for revolver practice. Mines are still exploding randomly all around the countryside weeks after being laid, corrosive acids eating away at the fuses. Monash finds it 'an extraordinary prostitution of scientific ingenuity'.

The château is 'cold and cheerless', but Monash figures that a march into Germany at the head of the victorious Australian occupation forces soon will lift everyone's mood.[35]

The Australians only get as far as Charleroi in Belgium, though, when Foch decides that they need go no further.

On 13 November Monash is summoned to a meeting with Hughes in London on the 18th. Brudenell White has already started a Demobilisation and Repatriation Branch, but Hughes surprises Monash by telling him that he wants Monash to replace White as the director-general. With the war over, getting the troops home is now the most important task in the army. Birdwood will remain as GOC of the AIF. Monash tells Vic that with the fighting over, the new job will be much more enjoyable than sitting beside the Rhine for a few months with nothing to do 'among a famine stricken population'.

'Naturally, if I were not wanted here any longer, I should prefer to be allowed to return at once to Australia. But I can hardly refuse an appointment which is the very highest that the Commonwealth has to offer.' It's a huge undertaking, which he suspects will bring him into contact 'with large numbers of very influential officials'.[36]

White is keen to stay on and be part of the great return, but Monash wants his own men involved, and he suggests his old comrade go home. Bean says his hero is 'deeply hurt',[37] but adds that Monash probably thought White would want to go home after so long away.[38] If there is any ill feeling between the two generals it doesn't last.

On 20 November Monash tells Vic and Bert that the coast is finally clear of German submarines and there is nothing to stop them from coming to London. He figures he might be based there for as long as 20 months looking after the demobilisation.

He stresses, though, that Vic and Bert should wait a few months until the English spring before travelling.[39] It will make it a more pleasant voyage, and privately he knows it will also give him more time with Lizzie. He is aware that he will have to sit down with Lizzie at some stage for a long talk, but for now he simply wants to enjoy the afterglow of victory with a woman he has grown to love.

His relationship with Vic has been stormy since their courting days, but Monash has written to her and Bert diligently since sailing for Egypt, doing his best to ease their fears over his safety and boost their morale. He is a master at lifting the spirits of all those around him, even if they are thousands of kilometres away.

Vic tells him he is now a household name in Melbourne. 'You are loved by everyone, officer, soldier and civilian. You are such a wonderful man',[40] she gushes.

Lizzie is of the same opinion.

Monash is not the first soldier to have strayed while away from home, but Lizzie and Monash enjoy each other's company so much and are so often together in the theatre or at restaurants or at Monash's apartment that Lizzie dares to dream that their relationship might become permanent. She pushes Monash to make the break.

Monash tells Lizzie he loves her but that Vic has been his wife for nearly 30 years, in sickness and in health, and he can't leave her. Not now. He writes in his diary of Lizzie's demands and that it has meant 'final refusal of extremes'.[41]

He knows theirs will be a painful break-up.

Monash calls a conference of his senior officers in Le Cateau and tells them of his promotion. Hobbs will take over as commander on 28 November and he will pardon the 118 convicted deserters. The corps gives Monash a farewell dinner and Hobbs tells him how helpful Monash has been to him throughout the war, 'in times of difficulty or stress'.[42] The Australian artist Lieutenant Arthur Streeton says dining beside Monash at Le Cateau, and being told not to rise for anyone, is one of the great honours of his life, and Monash is 'undoubtedly the greatest brain in Australia'.[43]

Most of the officers seem to revere Monash, even if many of the Diggers find him remote and aloof, like the big boss of a corporation.

Yet some generals bristle that the spotlight seems to be shining on just one man after the war, when they all played a part. In later years Brudenell White will claim Monash was 'over-praised', while Gellibrand, perhaps still smarting from his commander's rebukes, will call him an 'ego-optimist' who 'suffered from a sense of great mental superiority over all of us' and favoured the weaker commanders.[44]

Monash's artillery commander Walter Coxen, though, is astounded by the brain 'visualising and marshalling requirements to the minutest detail, in the proper order of sequence'. Monash's chief engineer, Cecil Henry Foott,[45] calls him 'a fine man, a fine soldier', and is proud that he could satisfy the master engineer with his own work. Bull Cannan says Monash is the greatest man he knows.[46]

Other senior officers such as Blamey, Elliott, Grimwade, Morshead and McNicoll are of a similar mind. Sir Basil Liddell Hart, later a leading British war historian, will speculate that if the war had lasted much longer Monash might have succeeded Haig as commander-in-chief of all the British forces: 'He had probably the greatest capacity for command in modern war ... He, more than anyone, fulfilled the idea which gradually developed in the war – that the scale and operations required a "big business" type of commander, a great constructive and organising brain. His views were as large as his capacity ... His grip of situations silenced all doubters and compelled the admiration of even the most critical professional soldiers.'[47]

Even Bean will eventually concede that Monash was 'our greatest military leader'.[48]

Monash has built the reputation of his corps on democratic principles and promotion on merit rather than privilege of birth. He realises that his success as a general rested on the bravery and tenacity of every private upwards, and that the Australian soldier, 'by his military virtues, and by his deeds in battle, has earned for himself a place in history which none can challenge'.[49]

Before leaving the Western Front, Monash and Paul Simonson visit Brussels and nearby Waterloo, studying the ground on which the forces of Napoleon and Nelson fought to a bloody end.

The pair finally depart on 30 November, leaving behind so many terrible memories.

Though always a loyal servant to his superiors, Monash later admits that he found Field Marshal Haig 'technically speaking, quite out of his depth' regarding the immense resources in his hands. Monash was at first 'quite dismayed' at Haig's ignorance about the 'composition in detail of his own formations', but believed Haig's great talent was to stay 'calm, resolute, hopeful and buoyant, in the face of apparently irretrievable chaos and disaster'.[50] Haig of course was not fighting hand to hand in the trenches himself.

As far as the war was concerned, Monash feels that the best thing about it is that it is over. 'From the far-off days of 1914, when the call first came, until the last shot was fired, every day was filled with loathing, horror, and distress', he admits.

'I deplored all the time the loss of precious life and the waste of human effort. Nothing could have been more repugnant to me than the realisation of the dreadful inefficiency and the misspent energy of war ... the thought always uppermost was the earnest prayer that Australia might for ever be spared such a horror on her own soil.'[51]

Chapter 29

*Never can there be questions about Monash's brain. It is there, a
living, searching, strong intelligence, breeding ideas, and judging
them shrewdly. His motto is Action, and his energy already pulsates
through the demobilisation scheme.*
JOURNALIST KEITH MURDOCH ON MONASH'S REPATRIATION WORK[1]

*Monash thinks he won the war and tells everyone so! He might be
very useful but a terrible self-advertiser.*
WILLIAM BIRDWOOD, TURNING ON HIS FORMER COMRADE[2]

MONASH STARTS HIS NEW JOB on 1 December in a
smart office in Victoria Street, only a few hundred metres
from Westminster Abbey. Never mind that it's a Sunday; that has
never stopped him from working before.

Despite his great workload, when he returns to England
Monash is swept up in what he calls 'the blare and blaze of fame',[3]
feted as a military genius. Royalty and big business all want to
meet him. Hamilton, Churchill, Hughes and Birdwood all
praise him in their speeches at the Australian and New Zealand
Luncheon Club.

On 11 December he is at the Albert Hall to see the British
Empire Boxing Tournament for army and navy personnel, which

features some of the world's best professional fighters and where a cheering crowd of 10,000 men back from the front are keen to see fighting of a different kind.

While Monash is sitting in a private box with a number of senior Australian officers, Prince Albert – later King George VI – arrives to present a trophy on behalf of his father to the winning team. The prince, just back from his posting with the Royal Air Force in Nancy, arrives in the stadium just as British heavyweight champion Bombardier Billy Wells scores a points decision over America's former world middleweight champ Eddie McGoorty.[4] Monash is summoned to enjoy the fights beside Albert and the Austrian-born Prince Louis Mountbatten, who has recently changed his name from Battenburg.

Monash later tells Vic that he spent the rest of the evening in the Royal Box, and that while the Australians did not win the trophy they finished 'very high on the list'. The Australians actually finished sixth behind the British Army in a field of nine, but Monash can always put a good spin on Australia's fighting effort. 'Prince Albert is a real jolly boy,' Monash writes, 'full of fun.'[5]

Monash has 160,000 Australians to send home safely and wants them all treated 'with the greatest consideration, as men who had done their work were entitled to be'.[6] Using the preliminary ideas of Brudenell White and Dodds, Monash conceives a broad plan within three days, and heads back to Le Cateau for a quick conference with brigade commanders.

Hughes tells Monash that he doesn't mind if the demobilisation process is a slow one, because a flood of soldiers returning to Australia could mean high unemployment, but Monash wants the men back home as soon as possible. Hughes attacks Monash on 20 December for going too fast, but Monash sticks to his guns, and the next day writes in his diary 'final disappearance of tremors'.[7]

This time Murdoch backs Monash, writing in his dispatch on 21 December that the general is the driving force in making the government surrender. 'Twelve days ago General Monash walked into bare, dusty rooms in Westminster. Now ... the old building hums with life ... Carpetless floors, plain deal tables, hard work. Graphs are on the walls, not telling of casualties and battle strengths now, or of locations for units, but of movements home ...'[8]

Monash tells Murdoch that he plans to give Australia 'spiritual momentum', with brave men returned home in good condition equipped for industrious lives. The men will be sent home on the basis of first come, first go, and of family responsibilities and assured employment back home. Monash arranges the troops into groups of 1000 for each ship and organises them into separate units as they wait to leave. His main problem is finding enough vessels for the task, given that the Indians and Canadians are also heading home, but George Pearce leaves Melbourne at the end of January to help sway British Cabinet ministers into providing all the resources they can.

On the night of 27 December, Monash and Hughes bask in the bonfire of the vanities at the State banquet for President Wilson at Buckingham Palace.

Sitting with Lord Burnham, Kipling, Churchill and Louis Botha, Monash listens intently as George V says it is a truly historic night to welcome the first President of the United States to visit England, almost 150 years after that nation became independent from Britain, and that with shared values and 'common ideals' both countries will work to see these principles extended 'for the good of the world'.[9] When Wilson rises to speak about America's love of freedom and how that love can influence the aspirations of mankind, Monash notes that Wilson's 'mobile face and hands' are a study to watch.

Cigars and cigarettes are served at the table. Monash has five minutes speaking with the King and Wilson but 10 minutes with Queen Mary, and they chat about Prince Edward's time at corps headquarters. 'She was most enthusiastic in praise of Australia and her soldiers, many of whom she had met at Windsor Castle.'[10]

*

Hughes and Joe Cook head to Paris to meet with 68 other international delegates for five months of negotiations over what will become the Treaty of Versailles. Hughes resumes hostilities as soon as he arrives, telling President Wilson that he speaks for '60,000 dead Australians' and he wants his fair share of reparations from the Hun.[11] Wilson sees Germany as an important trading partner and wants to rebuild it as a democracy; Hughes wants to hang the Kaiser and take German New Guinea as compensation. The President calls the Prime Minister a 'pestiferous varmint',[12] but the Little Digger gets most of what he wants.

In London, as Monash sets to work on the demobilisation, he wins friends and influences people wherever he goes. He has drafted a brochure called 'Demobilisation of the AIF: Things Which Australian Soldiers Ought to Know', and arranges lectures at Le Havre for all the men leaving France.

He takes a service flat in the West End, and despite his constant invitations to lunch and dinner with English high society, stays fit by walking to most of his appointments or taking the Tube. For rushed trips or longer distances, he requisitions the AIF's Rolls-Royce and driver, despite Hobbs's protests, and even ponders how he could take the car back to Melbourne as a souvenir. He presides over 1200 dancers at a corroboree to celebrate Australia Day. He writes he is 'Ironized by all'.

Although he lost his religious faith in his university days he has never turned his back on his heritage. On the field he provided for the dietary needs of Jewish soldiers as best he could, and recalls that in times of crisis he would tell himself: 'Remember you are a Jew and that if you muck it up our people will be blamed for it.'[13]

He is hailed by the Jewish community throughout England as a Hebrew warrior in the mould of Joshua and 'our modern Judas Maccabeus'.[14] He has become a hero, not just for helping turn back the Germans, but also for rising above prejudice. Vic writes to him that 'most people I hear are so sorry that we are Jews, and that both you and I had moneylenders for Fathers, etc. I jolly soon had that corrected.'[15]

Even Birdwood puts in the boot. Increasingly disgruntled with the rapid rise of his former subordinate over his head, Birdwood writes to Governor-General Munro Ferguson to say that Monash is an extremely capable man but 'had the faults of his race', and that he had never got on with him 'for five minutes'. He objects to Monash's 'ways and methods'.[16] Munro Ferguson agrees, saying that Monash 'cannot laud his offensives in the field apparently except at the expense of all other Divisions'.[17] Munro Ferguson may even feel threatened. There is talk that Monash will be made Governor of Victoria,[18] and possibly even replace Munro Ferguson as Governor-General. He has already left Birdwood in his wake.

Others who have served beside him retain their old prejudices against his race. Rawlinson has great regard for Monash's ability but has never liked him personally, perhaps because of the praise Monash wins. He will later call Monash 'a clever, slippery, creepy, crawly Jew'.[19] Colonel Jackson, an action man, writes that Monash would not go anywhere near the frontline. 'He was, as you know a Jew, and I have only met one Jew who was physically brave.'[20]

Monash donates his Gallipoli sword to a fund for the families of war correspondents killed in the fighting, and tells audiences that 'the Hebrews formed an exceptionally high proportion of all ranks in the Australian military forces'.[21] The British writer Israel Zangwill says Monash should be made Governor of Palestine.[22] Mat writes to Monash to say, 'If you have done nothing else I hope that you will have helped to remove some of the prejudices against Jewish folks.'[23]

At a dinner given by the Maccabean Society in London's Oxford Street on 4 March 1919, Monash tells his audience, including Birdwood and White, that he finds himself 'the object of considerable curiosity' because he belongs to the Jewish race, and because before the war he did not belong to the 'profession of arms'. Yet he puts forward the best picture of Australia he can, saying, to considerable applause, that in his native country such a thing as religious discrimination is unknown. In his recollection there has never been an obstacle of any kind placed in the way of any Australian Jew in regard to career. Is it any wonder, he asks, that, remembering the sufferings and hardships of his race in other lands, he and so many other Jews of Australia should have been ready when the call came to serve their country?[24]

He takes great care with his appearance, has regular face massages and manicures, and, often with Lizzie by his side as a 'friend', dines with London's prominent Anglo-Jewish families: the Rothschilds, the Montefiores, the Swaythlings. He visits synagogues, and speaks at the farewell for the Australian Jewish chaplain Jacob Danglow at the home of Joseph Herman Hertz, Britain's Chief Rabbi.[25] He pumps the hands of all 400 boys of the Jewish Lads' Brigade at Aldgate in the East End,[26] and chairs a lecture at the Jewish Historical Society at which he is proclaimed 'the Greatest Jewish Warrior of modern times'.[27] He joins the League of British Jews, speaks at meetings to establish a Jewish war memorial and later donates £250 to its cause.

Gentiles clamour for him too.

He is a regular at the Naval and Military and other exclusive clubs. The press baron Lord Northcliffe, General Gough, the Earl and Countess of Selborne and Viscount French all entertain him. Lady Northcote, widow of Australia's third governor-general, takes him under her wing and sends him gifts of pheasants. He is made an honorary life member of the Eccentrics Club and the Savage Club. He is an honoured guest at the Smeatonian Society of Engineers, the Overseas Club, the Lyceum Club, the Ladies' Victory Festival and the British Empire Club, and lectures to the Dynamicables on 'Engineering in War'. He breaks bread with Lord Burnham at the Marlborough Club and forms a friendship with Viscount James Bryce, the historian and politician whom Monash regards as one of the 'most amazing personalities I have met'.[28] He is made an honorary member at Lord's and ushered into the Royal Enclosure at Ascot after asking Churchill for a pass.

*

Vic and Bertha receive free passage to Britain from the Australian Government and leave Melbourne on the RMS *Osterley* on 21 March, unaware that Monash and Lizzie are like newlyweds in London.

For the last four years, Vic and Bert have lived each day on tenterhooks, hoping not to receive a visit from their rabbi with a telegram saying that General Monash has made the supreme sacrifice for his country. Monash has written to them dutifully trying to assuage their fears, but at the same time he has been acutely aware of Vic's fragile health. She has already had one operation for uterine cancer, and there is always the thought that it might return. Despite the fact that Monash has seen destruction close at hand on the battlefield, Vic has come closer to death than he has amid the peaceful climes of moneyed Toorak.

They bickered long and often during their days of struggle, and even in prosperity at Iona, but the distance of four years and four months between them and the reliance upon carefully considered correspondence have promoted a cordiality that did not always exist when they were face to face.

Monash looks forward, very much, to seeing his family again, and knows that once and for all he has to put an end to Lizzie's talk of a permanent relationship.

On 4 April he and Lizzie attend a dinner dance together to mark the closing of the Officers' Club at 138 Piccadilly. It is their last night out together at a formal function, and they soon have what he calls a 'serious scene re future'.[29] Monash tells it to Lizzie straight, but she is determined to stay with him, even if she must remain in the shadows.

Monash is having serious discussions 're future' on other fronts. He has no need for money, but the Victorian Government, through their representative, the academic Sir James Barrett, sounds him out about the role of Chief Commissioner of the State Railways. Monash tells Barrett that he does not want to surrender his personal freedom with a government role, though he might consider being made Commander-in-Chief of the Australian Army.[30] He writes to Acting Prime Minister William Watt hinting at something along those lines.[31] The only reply is silence, and Monash's resentment towards the Australian Government and Billy Hughes boils.

There is no greater advertisement for Australia in England than the man who has orchestrated the corps's greatest victories. On 25 April Monash and Hobbs lead a triumphant Anzac Day march of 5000 Australian troops with bayonets fixed through London, from Buckingham Palace to Australia House on the Strand.

The War Office has tried to stop the parade because of a proposed march by overseas troops on 3 May, but Monash will not hear of Anzac Day being ignored. Birdwood has to be content with a place on the saluting platform at Australia House alongside Hughes, Haig, Chauvel, Pearce, Churchill and Prince Edward.

Monash tells his men that the 7-kilometre march will last only an hour and a quarter, but reminds them that they represent 'the great and immortal Australian Army Corps. Every man should try and look as he ought to feel, proud of his division and the Australian Army.'[32] Thousands of others, including many of the soldiers' comrades, some now 'limbless men' in wheelchairs,[33] assemble along the route, cooeeing and cheering, while others are perched on the great stone lions in Trafalgar Square. Above the parade, the Australian Flying Corps performs loops and rolls in two huge Handley Page bombers and 12 smaller aircraft. Lizzie watches with pride from Monash's headquarters in Victoria Street.

Hughes tells the crowd that Australia's future will be built upon the 'foundation laid on Anzac Day, when Australia was born on the shores of Gallipoli'. The Australians who fought on Gallipoli and in France and Palestine have earned the right to be called the bravest of the brave.[34]

A week later, Monash rides behind Chauvel in the march of the overseas troops, and he will lead Australians still remaining in France in the great Victory Parade for Allied forces in Paris in July.

*

On 29 April, Vic and Bertha sail into Plymouth. Monash has travelled down from London to meet the ship at the earliest possible point.

There are many tears when the family is reunited. Bertha is a grown woman now, all of 26, while Vic looks smaller and far less robust than she did when Monash farewelled her at Port Melbourne.

Bertha can hardly believe the change in her father in the 52 months since he left Melbourne. She tells him he looks 'marvellously fit', and the change in him from roly-poly businessman is 'positively absurd'. She doesn't tell him, though, that he also looks much older than she remembers. His face has been scoured by the horrors his eyes have seen, and what is left of his hair is greying.

Monash sails with his family to the London docks at Tilbury, enjoying some idle time as he thinks about how he will sort out the situation with Lizzie, who is there to greet them in London alongside the Rosenhains.

As far as Vic knows, Monash and Lizzie are just good friends, though they do spend a lot of time staring at each other. Monash ferries Vic and Bertha and their trunks in the Rolls-Royce to an apartment in the high-rise Queen Anne's Mansions in Westminster and announces their arrival in the *Times*, in keeping with what is expected of a knight of the realm.

The London social whirl almost makes Vic dizzy. She has always craved social prestige and now, thanks to her 'wonderful husband', she is invited into a world of privilege and prominence she has scarcely imagined.

The Godleys, Hamiltons and Rawlinsons entertain them, even though Rawlinson dislikes Monash. They dine with Vic's old friend Mary Hughes while her husband is duelling with Woodrow Wilson in Paris. They go to see *Chu Chin Chow* at His Majesty's and Monash finds it as delightful as the first time he saw it with the Simonson boys.

All the partying wears Vic out. She has to stay in London when Monash takes Bertha on a four-day visit to the battlegrounds of France and Flanders. Father and daughter leave Folkestone on a boat to Boulogne on 16 May. Bertha had been over the French countryside nine years ago during the family's European vacation, but she is startled by the obvious difference the war has made. She has her father's gift for organisation, recording everything in a 14-page report called 'My Trip with Dad to France – May 1919'. She takes four photos at Bertangles, 'where [Dad] received his knighthood', and more photos where 'Dad explained the importance of the high ground at Villers-Bretonneux'. They visit the destroyed bridges over the Somme, 'the ruins of the great gun of Chuignes … the ruins of Hamel village … reached Amiens, called on the town mayor'.

They see gangs of German prisoners and visit the graves of dear friends, taking photographs for appreciative relatives. 'Reached the summit of Mont St Quentin,' Bertha writes, 'saw the wire entanglements …'[35]

After Monash and Bertha's return to London, Vic and Monash attend balls, the Ascot races and the jubilee dinner of the Royal Colonial Institute on 24 May.[36] They have a private viewing of Longstaff's portrait of Monash at the Royal Academy, and on 29 May all three Monashes are at Buckingham Palace when he receives his Grand Cross of the Order of St Michael and St George. There is a royal garden party, and a private lunch with the King and Queen, and Prince Albert and Princess Mary. Vic is beside herself. Such pomp. Such extravagance. In June they travel to Oxford and Cambridge, where Monash is awarded honorary degrees in law.

Back at Westminster, Vic suggests the Monashes take Lizzie out to dinner. After all, she has been Vic's great friend for so many years. So Lizzie becomes their regular dining companion as the Monashes become a party of four.

Monash is uncomfortable and stressed. The constant deception, the sly glances, fray his nerves in a way Erich Ludendorff's battle plans never could.

＊

The repatriation process has started well, with Hughes bullying the British into giving him 16 ships in December 1918. Early in the New Year some of the 3rd Division's artillery go on strike, and Monash tells Gellibrand to remember that the war is over and to lighten up on the men. Monash has to maintain a hard fight, though, to sustain the momentum behind the soldiers' return.

In April he tells Murdoch that 'it has been a tough and bitter battle between me and the Shipping Controller', and that the British official has 'adopted every sort and kind of subterfuge, and every species of bluff' for the contest. But 'I have now got the Shipping Controller absolutely beaten, have created such a pool of troops in England, and have secured such a rapid rate of delivery from France ... that by no possibility can the Shipping Controller now catch up to me ... I am not giving him any rest. And scarcely a day passes that I do not deliver an attack upon him from a new angle.'[37]

While men wait to go home, some take advantage of the opportunity to travel around France and Britain, which was one of the incentives for enlisting in the first place.[38] A few hundred Australian servicemen serve in Russia as part of a British force fighting Bolsheviks, and some light horsemen help suppress an Egyptian revolt.

But as many as 40,000 Diggers take part in a program Monash supervises called the AIF Education Scheme, in which soldiers gain practical Non-Military Employment − or Non-Military Enjoyment, as it becomes known.[39] Monash sees it as an important transition from the killing fields back to civilian life. While most are employed on farms or in factories or shops, almost 13,000 men gain formal qualifications from British educational institutions: hundreds pass accountancy and civil service exams, while others matriculate. Monash considers it vital to building Australia's skills base.

By June more than half of the AIF has headed for home, and most of the rest will leave by July. Monash is big enough to apologise personally when mistakes are made, such as when one gunner is packed off without his English wife and children,[40] but overall the repatriation has been another triumph for his businesslike approach to any task.

Hughes set Monash 18 months for the job, but Monash has it beaten in eight. Eleven months into the program and all the Australians are heading home.

Monash is delighted when Bert becomes engaged to her long-time friend Captain Gershon Bennett, a Melbourne dentist.[41] It is a new chapter in Monash's life, and from 8 August, the anniversary of the Australian Corps's great battle in front of Amiens, he also begins work on Chapter One of his recollections of the AIF's phenomenal success. They will eventually be titled *The Australian Victories in France in 1918*.

Murdoch is involved in negotiations for serial rights for the book with the Melbourne *Herald* and the Sydney *Sun*, but Monash eventually accepts an offer of £1100 from the publishers Hutchinsons to deliver 115,000 words. The book will be serialised in the *Sunday Times* in England and in the Sydney *Mail*. Monash eventually earns about £2000 from the book – or enough to buy two villas near the beach at St Kilda if he so desires.[42] He spends little more than a month writing – from seven to midnight every night and most afternoons – but only sees proofs of the early chapters. He asks Walter Rosenhain to steer the rest through to publication.

The book bombs in Britain, where it is seen as Australian propaganda and sells fewer than 1000 copies, even though Monash is careful not to slate the English soldier as he did in his private correspondence. In Australia it sells all 5000 copies printed, doing particularly well in Melbourne, despite a hefty price tag of 27s 6d. Three years later Lothian publishes 7000 copies of a cheaper version that also sells well.

Monash sees the book as an opportunity to prevent Birdwood from stealing some of his glory. He suspects his old commander is working to undermine him, and is furious when Birdwood usurps him at Amiens to present the massive 15-inch cannon captured by Monash's corps. He also fears that Birdwood has a plan to beat him to Australia and become chief adviser to the Australian Army.

In Melbourne, Victoria's premier Harry Lawson has established the State Electricity Commission to assess the merits of brown coal reserves in the Latrobe Valley, as opposed to various hydro-electric schemes being proposed to light the State. Robert Gibson,[43] the younger brother of Monash's business partner John Gibson, is one of the commissioners.

Two of the SEC's foremost advisers are the Antarctic explorer and geologist Edgeworth David[44] and the commission's chief engineer H.R. Harper,[45] who have both seen the power of brown coal at work in Germany.[46] They ask Monash to delve even deeper, with an intelligence operation into the workings of German electricity.

Monash has one of the best men from his corps, Major Edric Noel Mulligan, a mining engineer from Double Bay in Sydney, assemble a squad to infiltrate the Fortuna mine outside Cologne and other German coal centres. They are told to beg, borrow or steal, if they have to, everything they can on new technologies.

Mulligan comes through, and even brings back a working model of a machine to make briquettes. Monash writes a report on the operation, and that November the commissioners recommend using brown coal reserves at Morwell to fuel a power station.[47] The Victorian Parliament approves the idea and brown coal becomes the prime energy source in the State.

Monash attends the farewell banquet for Hughes at Claridge's Hotel and is at Paddington Station to see him off on 8 July, though he is less than enthusiastic when he wishes the Prime Minister *bon voyage*.

By September 1919, James Barrett and John Springthorpe are making inquiries about a senate place for Monash at the looming Federal election. Springthorpe approaches both Hughes and

George Fairbairn, a Victorian senator for Hughes's Nationalist Party. Monash is only half-hearted, because he is reluctant to serve in any government under Hughes, but when Pompey Elliott becomes a Victorian Nationalist senator later in the year, Monash believes Hughes has slighted him again.

Pearce arranges for Birdwood and Monash to sail home on the same ship, the RMS *Ormonde*. Birdwood is planning a triumphant tour of Australia, but the plan is for him to stay in Perth while Monash is feted in Melbourne.

Monash goes to great lengths in his final interviews in London to thank the British authorities who helped with repatriation, and the British people for their hospitality towards the Diggers. The *Times*, in farewelling him and Birdwood, says: 'Sir John Monash is the very type of a scientific soldier who possesses a genius of organisation. He is one of the most striking examples that the war produced of latent military ability in modern civilian life. Australia has reason to be proud of both …'[48]

Monash is glad to be going home but glum about leaving Lizzie. He does not want to be parted from the woman he has grown to love. He and Vic have been back together for only a few months but the old clashes of temperament have already resurfaced. Monash admits he is 'very sad at going away', and on the morning of his departure there are distressing, furtive phone calls to Lizzie's number, Mayfair 2157, and a lot of pleading from the woman who has stolen his heart.

Finally the *Ormonde* sets sail for Australia on 15 November 1919, almost five years after Monash led the 4th Brigade onto the transport ships bound for Egypt.

The trip home is excruciating. Monash has sore teeth and gums, and being in constant close proximity to Birdwood creates a pain somewhere else. The ship has hardly passed Portsmouth when he starts to miss Lizzie. His low mood adds fuel to the tensions between him and Vic. They bicker some more. Monash feels lonely, dispirited and miserable,[49] feelings he did not experience in Lizzie's company.

Vic is miserable too, with nausea and back pain. By the time they reach the Indian Ocean, Monash is asking for help from the ship's doctor, who recommends seeing a specialist when they reach Melbourne.

The *Ormonde* arrives in Fremantle on 19 December and, preoccupied with Vic's health, Monash takes a place in the background as Birdwood puts on a show for the cheering crowds, waving his slouch hat from the deck. Harry Murray VC, the local hero, is the real crowd favourite, though. While Monash sets the foundation stone for a Jewish war memorial in King's Park, Murray is chaired through Fremantle.

'Murray typifies the hero stuff that was in the Aussie army,' Perth's *Daily News* reports, 'Birdwood, the genius of leadership, and Monash the big organising brain that was behind the great machine called the AIF.'[50]

On 24 December, the Monashes arrive in Adelaide and go ashore only for five hours to meet Premier Archibald Peake and his cabinet. Vic is feeling worse than ever, but her smile returns for Christmas at sea, and in the early morning of a gloriously sunny Boxing Day, the *Ormonde* finally steams into Port Melbourne.

A huge crowd, including veterans of the North Melbourne Battery, is on hand to welcome Monash, but Billy Hughes is conspicuous by his absence. Charles Brand, the former 4th Brigade commander, escorts the Monashes and Gershon Bennett to a steamer that takes them to St Kilda, where, just before 10 a.m., thousands more are waiting to cheer Melbourne's military marvel.

A band strikes up 'Home, Sweet Home'. Almost all of Monash's senior staff are there to greet him. Vic and Bertha are presented with bouquets. Vic puts on her best smile to match the radiant weather, but she feels terribly unwell.

Monash tells the crowd that he would have to 'be made of steel' not to be overwhelmed by such a magnificent welcome. The *Argus* reports that 'every returned man appeared determined to have the honour of shaking General Monash by the hand', and then suddenly 'a few enthusiastic young fellows lifted the general on their shoulders' and carried him up the St Kilda Pier to a waiting car as the crowd roared.[51]

To the *Hebrew Standard*, Monash is the type of exceptional general created by exceptional circumstances. 'Neither Caesar, nor Cromwell, nor Smuts was a professional soldier; yet they rose to the very top and they determined the results of great military operations. Sir John Monash was the conspicuous example of this type among the Australians. It might be said of him that he had trained himself to be fit to do anything in life … He has brought honour, not only upon himself and upon his country, but also upon Jewry.'[52]

The *Age* calls him 'Australia's Greatest General', 'a man of action' and 'a born tactician'.[53]

The Monashes are driven through cheering crowds from St Kilda to see Governor-General Munro Ferguson, who is not about to express his true feelings about Monash on this glorious day. The Monashes drive on past Flinders Street Station and more cheering crowds in Swanston Street before arriving at the Menzies Hotel. Vic is now ashen and goes straight to bed.

While she rests, Monash changes out of his uniform to visit friends and relatives he hasn't seen for five years. He calls on his cousins, the Roths, and Tante Ulrike, the last link with his father, and visits Jim Lewis's mother, who helped him greatly after the loss of his own. She can't stop saying how proud she is of his achievements. Then he goes to Iona and breathes in the garden air, which he has yearned for ever since he drove out of the front gate in 1914.

The Monashes spend two weeks at the Menzies as their base for public engagements but Vic is constantly sick. She rallies enough for them to attend the theatre on New Year's Eve, but afterwards she is greatly fatigued.

When they finally move back to Iona Vic rarely leaves her bed, and is visited by three specialists. Despite Vic's love of a society function, she is not well enough to savour the adoration the public now has for the Monash family. Instead, Bertha accompanies her father to the many homecoming receptions in his honour.

There is a civic reception for him at the Melbourne Town Hall on 12 January 1920 at which the cheering lasts for several minutes, and so many other appointments full of adulation that he tires of them. He cancels afternoon tea with Munro Ferguson, but manfully smiles through the civic reception for Birdwood on 20 January and the dinner that evening at Government House.

He finds time to fight some more, leading a protest five days later at the grave of John Batman, the founder of Melbourne, over plans to move Melbourne Cemetery from the Victoria Market site. Bureaucracy, Monash says, is 'desecrating hallowed ground' and 'obliterating monuments to the heroes of the past'.[54] The council doesn't listen.[55]

Vic's condition worsens and Monash realises that it is far worse than he imagined. The doctors don't have the heart to tell her the cancer has returned.

In the middle of February, they inform Monash that it is only a matter of time. He writes to Walter Rosenhain to say that he is 'in a delirium of constant worry and anxiety'.[56]

Then a sword is plunged straight through his heart when he receives an anonymous letter claiming to be from an old soldier, warning him that a general 'said all over Melb. a year ago that your wife and her sister are whores and that you are a beastly dog of a Jew'.[57] He and his family have heard worse.

Monash has given Vic everything she ever dreamed of in life: a title and dinner at Government House, even a place at the table with the King and Queen at Buckingham Palace.

But he can do nothing for her now except provide her with a full-time nurse and tell her that she is the love of his life.[58]

Lady Victoria Monash dies at Iona on 27 February, aged just 50.

Her husband, who saw death almost every day of the war, is stunned by the speed of her passing. He has been hoping to enjoy the peace and tranquillity of the post-war years with Vic in the paradise he has created at Iona. Instead, Iona has become Paradise Lost.

Rabbi Abrahams, who married Monash and Vic nearly 30 years ago, conducts her funeral ceremony at Brighton Cemetery on

1 March. Vic's headstone will bear tributes in both English and Hebrew.

Monash receives hundreds of messages of sympathy from around the world, and the newspapers laud Vic's fundraising work on behalf of the Friendly Union of Soldiers' Wives and the Purple Cross charity for the welfare of horses sent to the war.[59] *Table Talk* says: 'She will be deeply mourned by a large circle, for all those who really knew her, or were associated personally with her in any way, realised the beauty of her character. She was a beautiful woman, with a low, sweet-speaking voice, and a slow, gentle utterance, which seemed but typical of the lovely nature within. She had always something pleasant and gracious to say … Miss Bertha Monash, who was her mother's constant companion, inherits much of her sweet nature.'[60]

Over the next few weeks, Monash finds that the best defence against the numbing grief and the inevitable feelings of guilt is the same thing that has propelled him all his life.

He stays busy.

Chapter 30

*Adopt as your fundamental creed that you will equip yourself
for life, not solely for your own benefit, but for the benefit of the
whole community.*

MONASH AFTER BEING MADE VICE-CHANCELLOR OF
MELBOURNE UNIVERSITY[1]

*He would be up at daybreak. Every minute of each 24 hours had
been planned the night before with the same meticulous care he had
once planned his battlefield. There was no field of human endeavour
into which he did not delve.*

MONASH'S GREAT GRANDSON, MICHAEL MONASH BENNETT[2]

JOHN MONASH IS NOW THE MOST popular man in
Australia, a war hero who has walked with kings and princes
but is recognised by the Diggers 'as being dinkum'.[3] But Billy
Hughes still refuses to offer official recognition for Monash's
extraordinary leadership and Monash becomes increasingly
bitter towards him and the Federal Government. He believes
that the Prime Minister fears being overshadowed and claims
Hughes has 'behaved in a most discourteous and shabby manner
towards me, and I find it quite difficult to be even polite to
him'.[4]

Following the treaty of Versailles, Britain is quick to reward its army and navy chiefs. Field Marshal Haig is made an earl and given a cash gift of £100,000, the equivalent of 500 years of toil for the average Australian worker.[5] Field Marshal French, whose command was a series of blunders, receives £50,000; Plumer, Rawlinson and Byng £30,000; and Birdwood £10,000.[6] Rawlinson is made a baron and Birdwood a baronet.

Monash receives a letter saying he can keep his sword.

'So he came back to Australia,' *Smith's Weekly* says, 'which tooted its trumpets around Birdwood, and forgot its own soldier.'[7] Of course, Monash, as a rich man living in a mansion, has come out of the war in much better shape than most Australian servicemen, many of whom have returned scarred for life, mentally and physically, only to join the ranks of the unemployed or to struggle on soldier settlement blocks until the Great Depression wipes them out altogether.

Just a week after Vic's death Monash is laying the foundation stone for the Scotch College Memorial Hall[8] and joining the building fund for the school's new site at Hawthorn.[9] Two weeks later he is reluctantly beside Birdwood at Melbourne University, wearing robes over their khaki, as they receive honorary doctorates in law.[10] At the opening of the Federal Parliament for 1920, Governor-General Munro Ferguson tells his audience: 'I record with pleasure the visit to Australia of General Sir William Birdwood, who commanded the Australian forces with such distinction throughout the war.'[11] Monash doesn't get a mention.

Currie writes from Canada that Birdwood's presence alongside Monash suggests that Australia does not want too much honour to be placed on an Australian.[12] The *Nation*, the journal of the Returned Soldiers' National Party, complains that Monash, 'perhaps the greatest citizen soldier the world has seen', is made to 'appear the lesser man' by Birdwood's presence, even though Monash 'was infinitely greater than Birdwood'.[13]

Some parliamentarians want to redress the situation.

On 30 March, in the stately confines of the Federal Parliament in Spring Street, Melbourne, Arthur Rodgers, the member for Wannon in western Victoria and a rising young politician in Hughes's government, decides it's time to speak up. Rodgers rises from his chair, clears his throat and expresses his regret that Australia has 'not adequately voiced its appreciation of the great services rendered by Sir John Monash'. His generalship, Rodgers says, 'had been one of the features of the war' and while Rodgers is not asking that the government's gratitude be 'manifested in pounds, shillings and pence', Australia 'should certainly raise some monument to his magnificent work'. There are calls of 'hear hear', but not from Hughes. Rodgers carries on, telling the chamber that Monash 'had won the foremost position of any Australian who went to the battlefield', and he hoped there would be some speedy recognition in some tangible form of the services he had rendered. 'Hear, hear.'

Then George Maxwell, the member for Fawkner[14] and founder of the Shakespeare Society at the University of Melbourne, rises to say that at the very least, Monash should be called to the House and thanked.[15]

He isn't.

A week later the government announces that while it recognises Monash's 'great capacity', it is 'not likely that he would be offered a permanent military position'. The government expresses its hope that some arrangement will be made whereby the Commonwealth might still retain his counsel.[16] The Americans and Canadians promote Pershing and Currie but the Australian Government makes no gesture of gratitude to Monash, awards him no honours, gives him no promotion and offers him no military job. All his medals and awards come from overseas. Perhaps Monash is simply too big now for the Australian Army, who can only pay Chauvel £1500 as inspector-general.

Instead Monash becomes what McGlinn calls a 'national possession',[17] answering reams of correspondence, unveiling monuments and honour boards and comforting the bereaved families of those who attend. He is asked endlessly to speak or to write or to lend support, to become a patron of countless causes, to open fetes and exhibitions, to sign his autograph, to give interviews.

He wades through copious letters from ex-Diggers begging for work or a handout, or just voicing their frustrations at having come home to a country where life is harder than ever. Some wonder what the hell they had their legs shot off for or why their mates died. Monash helps where he can, cancelling a loan for one ex-soldier, giving handouts to others, finding work for some.

Monash also helps to solicit donations for the YMCA, whose work assisted his men so much on the Western Front. He speaks at the local branch of the League of Nations Union and encourages Chauvel and White to join. Monash had planned to accept official invitations from the New South Wales and South Australian Governments but begged off following Vic's death. He makes only one official visit, to Ballarat, where he sees the avenue of honour and then speaks at a dinner at Craig's Hotel, telling the audience that if he had been given one-tenth of the resources at Gallipoli which he had subsequently in France, 'we would have been able to turn back the Turkish army in three months'.[18]

He joins the Prahan branch of the RSL,[19] the nearest to Iona, and in August is with Victoria's premier Harry Lawson at the laying of the foundation stone at Anzac House in Collins Street, urging Australians everywhere to band together like his men on the battlefield to make a better country.[20] He becomes vice-president again of the Boy Scouts Association and lectures on behalf of the Australian War Memorial. He considers running for president of the Returned Sailors and Soldiers' Imperial League but eventually withdraws because he does not want to get involved in faction fights.[21] He becomes president of a group to adopt and assist Villers-Bretonneux and supports the Australian Children's Society to help unmarried British women with babies fathered by Australian soldiers.

Monash remains on the board of Luna Park and Wiltshires and becomes chairman of directors of Melbourne Hotels Ltd, a company backed by the Sydney entrepreneur Arthur Rickard to take over the Grand Hotel and rename it the Windsor.[22] He also becomes chairman of directors of the National Portland Cement Co. and of the Maria Island and Development Co., which aims to find new sources of cement. He and John Stanley join the board of the Atlas Assurance Co. The boardroom offers are too good to resist and are pouring in, £100 to £300 at a time.[23]

On 17 April Monash is a special guest at the annual commencement ceremony at the university and is glad that Birdwood is in Sydney.[24] In May, the government holds a ceremony to thank 70 representatives of the Army and Navy, including Monash, at Parliament House. But when the Prince of Wales arrives in Melbourne soon after, Monash is not one of the official invitees and watches the arrival from the crowd in Swanston Street.

He concedes he no longer has any official capacity, but privately notes that 'if those in official authority have the bad taste to ignore me on important public occasions, I can only leave the matter for the judgement of the public'.[25] The snub is explained as an oversight and Monash is soon at all the official parties for the Prince and among 200 official guests when the Prince lays the foundation stone at Canberra for a new capital.[26]

The snubs continue, however: a few months later, Monash and his officers are ignored in a military review of the demobilisation process. 'I could hardly imagine that my name was intentionally omitted,' he writes, 'but it is significant that I have received no recognition whatever for my demobilisation work, nor a word and not a line, either from the Minister of Defence, or the Prime Minister, or the Government.'[27] The anniversaries of Hamel and Amiens pass without official mention, and Colonel Morshead, having had his career terminated by the AIF and struggling on a 9000-hectare soldier settlement block near Quilpie in Queensland, writes that Monash is the victim of 'jealous and petty treatment'.[28]

Senator Pompey Elliott reflects on the situation by saying that Monash's leadership was in stark contrast to the British generals he had served under, whose legacy was 'the melancholy spectacle ... of rotting corpses forming the edge of the enemy's impregnable wire'. Elliott, who is becoming increasingly depressed post-war, blames lousy commanders for the disasters on Gallipoli, Bullecourt and Passchendaele and says Monash was the only general who saw the futility of so many attacks and protested against their application.'[29]

William Watt, Billy Hughes's treasurer, is one of Monash's supporters. Early in March 1920, Watt offers Monash the position of director-general of the Institute of Science and Industry on a salary of £4000 a year, more than double that of the highest paid public servant in the country. It will take six months for the necessary legislation to be passed, Watt says, and while Monash waits he can head a royal commission into taxation. But within weeks Hughes sends Watt to London on Commonwealth business and then to the July conference on reparations in Spa. Watt, fearing Hughes is trying to get rid of him, quits as treasurer, complaining that he is being treated like 'a telegraph messenger'.[30] Monash writes to Watt complaining of his own treatment at the hands of Hughes's government.[31]

In late April, Senator Pearce suggests a new offer, with Monash combining the science post with a senior place on the Council of Defence but the government doesn't follow through and after a fruitless wait Monash feels 'sorely humbugged'. He busies himself arbitrating a wage dispute between shipowners and marine engineers.[32]

Monash's concrete and construction businesses suffered while he was fighting the war and in June, the entrepreneur and inventor Walter Hume offers him £10,000 for the Concrete Constructions Co., an offer Monash can't refuse. He now becomes a director of yet another business, Hume Pipe Co. (Aust.) Ltd, the major manufacturer of reinforced concrete pipes in the nation, a position that earns him about £350 a year. Monash sells his shares in the Reinforced Concrete Co. to Gibson for £6000, to be paid over five years.

*

On 28 June 1920, William McBeath, a powerful businessman and financial adviser to the Commonwealth, asks Monash if he'd be interested in another job, as general manager of the new State Electricity Commission. The Commission was formed a year ago, but is still little more than an idea in the minds of politicians and bureaucrats. Monash knows the SEC well, having involved himself in the industrial espionage of Germany's coal production on its behalf a year earlier. There are three commissioners, Robert Gibson, George Swinburne, a former Victorian Cabinet Minister and engineer, and Professor Thomas Ranken Lyle, from the University of Melbourne. They tell premier Harry Lawson that Monash is the perfect man to spark the project into life. Swinburne whets Monash's appetite for his civic duty when he tells him:

> There is nothing I have ever been connected with which opens up such possibilities of good in the community and where one's work could be made of immense constructive value ... Morwell, with proper organisational thought and skill, will during the next five years be a monument to the men who tackle it and affords an outlet for organising ability, engineering skill in several departments, town planning, legal practice etc that no other scheme in Australia presents. To me it is an intellectual treat ... It will be a substantial pleasure to be actively associated with you.[33]

The salary of £3000, increasing to £5000 as soon as the Commission turns a profit, seals the deal. Monash negotiates a seven-year contract that makes him the Chairman of Commissioners. He can only be sacked by an Act of Parliament.

By the middle of 1920 Monash is again reorganising all his war records and correspondence at Iona and making recordings on a dictaphone for his secretary. The hall and main passage of his home contain his war trophies: a piece of the propeller from Richthofen's plane, a box of Iron Crosses taken on 8 August, a German machine-gun, a bottle of soil from Gallipoli and shoulder straps – his scalps – representing 200 German regiments. His staff comprises a chauffeur, gardener, cook and maid.

Monash has started an art collection that will eventually include the works of John Longstaff, Hans Heysen, Arthur Streeton, Tom Roberts, Thea Proctor, Jessie Traill, Norman and Lionel Lindsay, Walter Withers, Dora Messon, Ester Paterson, A.E. Newbury, E. Phillips Fox, J.J. Hilder and the Jewish artist Percy White (born Peretz Witofski in Lithuania). He will study their brilliance while listening to his gramophone recordings of Wagner, Beethoven, Mozart, Mendelssohn and Chopin, the music refreshing his senses so that he can plough into more work.

Bertha and Gershon Bennett set a wedding date in 1921 and agree to share the huge house, which has more than enough room for everyone. Gershon still calls Monash 'Sir'.

Monash also thinks about married life again. He has not been without female company since his teenage years and his diary suggests that as well as his affair with Lizzie in England there may have been other liaisons in Egypt and Paris.

While Vic's passing rocked him for a while, he is now looking to make a new life with another partner.

In his vast library, which contains thousands of books – everything from Dickens (*David Copperfield* is his favourite) to Ellery Queen, Thackeray, Bulwer-Lytton, George Eliot, Conan Doyle and Walter Scott – Monash also has a fully itemised collection of indecent photographs and cheap pornography. He orders these curiosities from overseas catalogues and sometimes from Sydney under an assumed name. Once, before the war, some of his purchases were found and destroyed by a customs official. His library contains the works of sex researcher Havelock Ellis, other books on the study of phallic worship and sado-masochism, the Kama Sutra and the writings of de Sade and

Casanova.[34] Perhaps the collection is only of intellectual interest, perhaps not.

Monash is not long a widower when women begin courting this heroic, intellectual and wealthy knight of the realm. The queue includes an actress, a young Jewish university graduate and a sculptor. But Monash's heart was broken months before Vic's death, when he said goodbye to Lizzie in London. Now he plans to heal it. He writes to Lizzie in London and tells her that he is still aching for her.

She says she will come to him straight away.

While Monash has won favour with the Victorian Government for its huge electricity project, his advice is not always adopted. Three of his officers from the war, Gellibrand, Bruche and McNicoll, are candidates for the chief commissionership of the Victorian police. Monash supports Bruche and tells Premier Lawson that Gellibrand is a poor administrator and that appointing him would be a mistake.[35] Gellibrand gets the job but it does not go well, and Monash laments that 'they could not have chosen a more unsuitable man'.[36]

Monash's years tramping through the Australian bush have instilled in him a love for the natural world and he backs James Barrett's campaign to make Gippsland's Mallacoota Inlet a fish sanctuary. He writes of the 'great flights of pelicans, swans, ducks, dabchicks and numerous other native birds' and of the quiet waters 'teeming with every kind of aquatic life'. Could the needs of a few fishermen, he asks, justify the surrender of such a beautiful place.[37]

He never forgets his origins either, intervening in two cases in which Australians of German birth, just like his late parents, are to be deported. Just as Dr Max Herz, a Sydney orthopaedic surgeon, is about to be expelled from the country, Monash asks Bob Garran for assistance and Herz is allowed to stay. But Monash can't save 54-year-old Dr Eugen Hirschfeld, a Queensland physician and former legislative councillor. Hirschfeld was born in Milicz, where Monash's grandfather had studied bookbinding, and has been in Australia since 1890. He is married to Annie Saddler, whose father, V.J. Saddler, was Monash's old boss. Despite his groundbreaking medical research at the University of Queensland, the fact that Hirschfeld was the German consul at the outbreak of war sees him interned and deported in 1920. In 1923, Monash is still trying to help him, and writes to Prime Minister Stanley Bruce. While he has tried to do the State some service, Monash points out, this is the first time he is asking for any kind of favour in return.[38] But Bruce isn't listening. Hirschfeld goes to America and practises in Allentown, Pennsylvania, before he is finally readmitted to Australia in 1926, a year after his son Franz is elected Rhodes scholar for Queensland. The Queensland RSL is vehement in its protests against the readmittance[39] but Monash sends them an olive branch, saying he would be the last man to permit any kind of treachery on his watch but that 'the days of war hysteria are over, and one should bring to bear on such a question, a spirit of fair play and charity'.[40]

Lizzie Bentwitch slips quietly into Melbourne aboard the P&O liner *Naldera* on 23 September 1920. Bertha is furious, believing that her father has betrayed Vic's memory. The Rosenhains side with Bertha. Walter Rosenhain writes to ask what Monash sees in the woman, who he claims is 'an unscrupulous liar'. He warns his otherwise shrewd brother-in-law that 'a designing woman may be more difficult to deal with than … a Hindenburg system'.[41] Walter reckons Lizzie even lies about her age, claiming she's 40 when she is much older. Monash procures her birth certificate, which shows that she is indeed 46 but he reasons it's a woman's right to lie about her age. He defuses Walter by saying the situation is in hand and there will be 'no undesirable outcome'.[42]

Bertha is harder to convince and warns Monash that if 'that woman' moves into her mother's house she will be moving straight out. Monash values the relationship with his daughter too much ever to marry his lover, who arrives in Melbourne with what *Punch* calls 'a very English accent [and] trunks full of fascinating fripperies that have a Continental flavour'.[43] When the *Bulletin* speculates on the likely marriage of 'a front-rank war-knight, a widower'[44] Monash writes a fiery response denying it and informing the magazine that the report has greatly distressed his family.[45]

Monash accommodates Lizzie at a variety of luxury digs: the Windsor, Cliveden Mansions and the Oriental Hotel. She doesn't seem to mind his family's treatment of her nor the fact that his love for her is conditional. He calls Lizzie 'Ell' and they dine regularly at the Menzies, impervious to all the gossip. She is his constant companion at social events if not family gatherings, and sometimes he has to demand invitations for Miss Lizette Bentwitch to official functions. She vacations with him in Perth, Hobart and Mount Buffalo.

A week after Lizzie's arrival, Monash takes his place in a temporary office for the SEC in the Tramways Building in Bourke Street and sets out to conquer what he hopes will be a 'big and strenuous job'.[46]

Victoria's electricity supply is in a mess. There is only enough black coal to supply the Victorian railways; all other electricity depends on black coal from New South Wales. Monash's task is to develop open-cut mining of brown coal in the Latrobe Valley, build the plants to generate and transmit power across the State, and provide both cheap electricity and inexpensive briquettes for domestic and industrial fuel.

Almost a century later his great grandson will marvel at Monash's enterprise and efficiency:

At night he would spend an hour around the fire with the family, reading aloud from his wealth of literature. Half an hour of each day was spent in his garden at Iona, tending his roses and training his flowering creepers. Astronomy attracted him. At the foot of the garden he erected a platform for a powerful telescope, and on clear nights he could often be found following the course of Jupiter or Saturn or the Moon … He had one of the most comprehensive early gramophone collections. It was said that, in the middle of all his work and his worries, he would go into the piano room and play for half an hour – and then emerge (I quote) "like a giant refreshed" to tackle all his problems.[47]

Elizabeth Taylor, his private secretary (who calls him Poppa),[48] is dazzled by Monash's mind and his manners, saying later that 'Nothing can rob me of those 11 years I spent in his service'.[49]

By November 1920 Monash convinces Cabinet to build an eight-storey building for his offices at the corner of William and Little Flinders Streets (now Flinders Lane), with material supplied by the Reinforced Concrete Co. Monash also receives approval to build the town of Yallourn to operate the power station. Cabinet passes legislation for a £1.43 million loan to the SEC, which will be his budget.[50] The task is a giant conundrum, like one of the intricate jigsaws that Walter set for Monash during the war to keep his brain firing. It combines administrative, financial and engineering problems and he will again call on his Herculean force of will to get his way.

His first offensive is against Harold Clapp,[51] the new Chairman of the Commissioners of Victorian Railways, whose salary of £5000 makes him Australia's highest paid public servant. The Railways has its own generating station and is selling surplus power, a situation Monash finds intolerable. He negotiates with Clapp and the minister in charge of the commission, Arthur Robinson,[52] for the Railways to take its power from the SEC. Monash and Robinson both built business empires on the back of free trade, but for this enterprise they want State socialism and a monopoly on both the wholesale and retail of electricity in Victoria.

Monash's second offensive comes on 16 December 1920 before a select committee of the Victorian Parliament, which meets in the Exhibition Building. Monash has told the Parliament that the proposed hydroelectricity scheme at Kiewa should be developed but only as a complement to the brown coal furnaces being planned for the Latrobe Valley. George Michell,[53] a long-time friend of Monash's, is a consultant to both the commission and the Victorian Hydro Electric Co. He tells the committee that Monash had misled the members over the costs of the brown coal plans and Kiewa.

Michell should have said nothing.

Monash squashes his old friend like a tank hitting a machine-gun post. The old general is 'a brainy Hercules', says committee member Frederic Eggleston[54] while Michell becomes 'a blinking, timid scholar'. Monash stands over the softly spoken scientist 'like a colossus'.[55] After a verbal pummelling that lasts less than 30 minutes, Michell has no argument left.

Only a few weeks before, Monash has qualified as Australia's first Doctor of Engineering from Melbourne University after submitting 'Australian Victories in France in 1918' as a thesis on the subject of engineering applied to modern warfare.[56]

To celebrate, Monash, Bertha and Gershon take a 10-day holiday, journeying west in the family's new Buick with the Monash monogram on two of the doors. They visit the Grampians and Mount Gambier. Lizzie is not invited. Monash's health has suffered with the increased workload and the family tensions, but gradually he will pick up from his 'chronic state of lassitude and abdominal discomfort', disordered digestion, lumbago and rheumatic pains.[57] He takes 'abdominal antiseptics', changes his diet and starts regular exercise with classes from the Bjelke-Petersen School of Physical Culture, which was started in a Hobart Gymnasium in 1892 by the uncle[58] of the long-time Queensland Premier.

The gymnastics classes give Monash the kick he needs to insist that German technology be used at Yallourn, even though there is still widespread repugnance over using their ideas with 60,000 war dead from Australia.

Construction begins on the Latrobe River weir and the Yallourn powerhouse that will eventually generate 50,000 kilowatts. Orders are placed for six turbo-generators. Another 15,000-kilowatt powerhouse is planned to run alongside one in the Melbourne suburb of Newport, which is already being fuelled by black coal to supply the railways. Transmission towers begin to line the 200 kilometres between Yallourn and Yarraville. The Bendigo-born Jewish engineer Hyman Herman – who calls Monash 'the ablest, biggest-minded and biggest-hearted man I have ever known'[59] – is sent to Germany to further explore brown coal technology.

On 24 January 1921 Monash jots down some notes on policy and governance for the proposed town of Yallourn, which will be the first Australian example of a model garden town based on the English working villages, though there will be more variation in house design and Yallourn allotments will be much bigger, typically of 1000 square metres. Monash says each home should be large enough for the residents to keep a horse and tend a large garden.

The design of the town is left to architect Alfred Romes La Gerche and the town planner, W.E. Gower. Monash says home ownership is important for workers but at Yallourn it is not yet practicable and for the time being the SEC will have to rent out properties at below market prices and subsidise public facilities. Monash insists that a good teacher be found for the school and that trees not be cut down unless absolutely necessary. But working conditions are still harsh and the Australian Workers' Union becomes increasingly militant over its members there.

On the train from Melbourne to Yallourn, over the next few years, Monash will often sit in the carriage anonymously yarning to strangers about their lives and their aspirations. On arrival at the work site his first question is invariably: 'What can I do to help?' even though he is fighting battles on many fronts. He makes personal donations to the Yallourn RSL and other clubs in the town and writes letters of good wishes to staff members getting married.

On 8 August 1921, he commemorates the victory at Amiens with a dinner at Iona, inviting the eight most senior members of the corps and their wives as well as the widowed Lady Bridges and his sister Mat. Bertha is the hostess and the men wear dinner jackets without military decorations. Monash sends telegrams to the other generals around Australia and Gellibrand organises a return function for Armistice Day.

Monash tells the electricity commissioners that the plant to make the coal briquettes will have to be made in Germany and that German technicians will have to install it in Yallourn. This does not go down well. The plant is ordered from the Zeitz Co. of Halle but the Federal Cabinet, bombarded by protests from trade unions and the RSL, refuses to allow entry permits for German workers, claiming that under an amendment to the Immigration Act, 'persons of German parentage and nationality are classed as prohibited immigrants' until 1925.[60] Monash is convinced the ban is because of his ever-widening rift with Billy Hughes and says the whole future of Victorian electricity rests on the decision. Hughes finally relents in March 1922[61] and a German construction engineer and five foremen from the Zeitz Co. arrive in August.

Soon, Monash is involved in another crisis. Early samples of the brown coal around Morwell showed a moisture content of between 45 to 48 per cent and, on those figures, orders were placed in England to build the great powerhouse boilers. But a new seam of coal shows moisture content of between 65 and 68 per cent. There is more water in the coal than coal. Frederic Eggleston says that if the project were being funded by private enterprise it would be abandoned. Monash tells everyone involved to keep stumm and Arthur Robinson manages to delay informing Parliament until 1923,[62] when plans are well underway to redesign and modify the boilers and devise new ways of drying the coal on the way to the furnace.

*

Powerful opposition grows to the SEC from rural interests, local councils and private power companies, who have no desire to be swallowed by a new Monash army rolling across the State. Gradually, Monash brings some of his enemies around. He builds a transmission line from Geelong to Warrnambool so that the power already being generated by the Melbourne Electricity Supply Co. can reach more distant markets; he announces the hydro and irrigation scheme, Sugarloaf-Rubicon; and he starts work on transmission lines from Yallourn.

Gradually the SEC wins over local councils, promising cheaper power to more homes, even if Monash manages to convince the government to employ tariffs for more remote regions, saying that a flat rate for power across the State will be disastrous.

But the Melbourne City Council sets up an Electrical Defence Committee[63] to protect its interests and starts a huge leaflet drive of anti-SEC propaganda. It also hires journalists to dig up dirt on Monash. Again Monash sees them off, with another select committee backing the SEC and Monash's claims that present electricity supply in Victoria is an exercise in wastefulness.

The committee finds that Monash and his staff 'are evincing the keenest interest to ensure that the country districts will be enabled to benefit by the undertaking at the lowest possible price, and at the earliest date'.[64]

Monash tells Walter that the committee had found 'overwhelmingly' in favour of his views and that within a few hours the government had 'passed no less than five new Acts of Parliament, greatly extending the powers of the Commission ... had I failed to carry parliament and the press with me, it would have been a serious injury to my personal prestige ... Now that I have had my fight and overthrown my enemies, it is hardly probable that there will be any recrudescence of this trouble in the future.'[65]

Monash becomes not just the commission's commander-in-chief but its most popular tour guide as well, talking up 'the greatest engineering undertaking in the Southern Hemisphere' in all corners of the State.[66] He has to survive a series of attacks from the *Age* over the use of foreign machinery on what the paper calls a 'needless white elephant', at which Monash's 'megalomania' and 'needless bombast' is creating runaway expenditure. He is careful to make an ally of Keith Murdoch, now the editor of the *Herald*, and regularly leads tours of the Yallourn site for the press and various VIPs on a special train from Flinders Street. Dressed in a plain suit, gumboots and puffing on his pipe, Monash develops a showman's flair, opening the furnaces to show visitors to Yallourn the great heat being generated and occasionally pretending to push in critics of the scheme to laughter and applause. Monash promises that Melbourne will have electricity from Yallourn by the middle of 1924.

One of those taking his tour is the editor of the *Sydney Morning Herald*, Charles Brunsdon Fletcher,[67] who writes:

> Sir John is ... neither tall nor physically impressive. He is a Jew at first glance, and typical in face and feature. A short, thick-set man, he does not carry any of the advantages which one associates with fine soldierly presence; but one knew that here was no boaster ... He was in the middle of a remarkable monument to his daring and skill as an engineer at Yallourn, but he did not say, 'Look around' as though he were asking for an acknowledgement. For an hour and more I heard him giving facts and figures which paralysed the imagination, but he made no more of them than to convey certain definite conclusions ... The mind which had grasped at the certainty of victory on the battlefields of France in 1918 was now ... demonstrating the assurance of victory on a vast scale in Australia along the lines of peaceful development. It was the man of action grappling with a great practical problem ... Then it was that one began to study his hands. They were so strangely out of harmony with his body, but so curiously expressive of the soul within him. I could see his forebears of more than 2000 years back,

as prophets and Jewish leaders of the Maccabean type, hold up just such hands in adjuration or command – the hands of a man of genius ... This, then, is the man who came back to Australia to be slighted by political leaders for whom he was too strong, but to be held in respect and esteem by returned soldiers everywhere ... Now that I have seen him and spoken with him, have asked questions and received answers, have watched him with his subordinates, and have studied his ways with ordinary folk, I am quite satisfied. Australian problems on the largest scale have at least one man capable of solving them; and his energy and resource ought to be our greatest immediate asset.[68]

Monash's complexion 'is reddish-brown and a little florid' and he has a curious way of standing when observing or in conversation, 'with chin thrust forward and head hunched'. The voice is normally quiet and contained, 'the accent neutral – if anything educated Australian rather than educated English, his charm powerful and his manner highly courteous'. He is at first reserved and dignified but visitors find him 'warm, genial, homely, unassuming, approachable, human, decent, gentle'.[69]

Monash writes references and pushes the causes of McGlinn and Morshead and other men who become generals, Alan Vasey,[70] Iven Mackay[71] and the future governor-general, Lord Casey.[72] He sends money to the Rosenhains to help pay for his nieces' education, pays for the Roths to have a comfortable life and occasional holiday, and supports his widowed sister-in-law Belle after Sa Simonson, her last surviving sister, passes away.

He sometimes loans his car for disabled children to be taken on outings and occasionally makes use of his membership of the Metropolitan Golf Club (he was introduced by John Gibson in 1921), although he is more interested in the walk than the score.

When Monash is not working on bringing electricity to as many Victorians as he can, he devotes large amounts of time and energy to building a memorial for fallen comrades that will become Melbourne's Shrine of Remembrance.

In 1920 a State advisory committee on war memorials had recommended an arch of victory over St Kilda Road, but after Monash joined an executive committee it was decided on a more impressive tribute the following year. Monash is appointed chairman of the assessors for an architectural competition for a building that he wants to reflect Australia's collective grief rather than any celebration of victory. Architects Phillip Burgoyne Hudson, a former lieutenant, and James Hastie Wardrop, a Military Medal recipient, win the competition with a design inspired by the Mausoleum of Halicarnassus, one of the seven wonders of the ancient world.[73] Monash is captivated by the concept on a site near the corner of St Kilda Road and Domain Road, but Murdoch's *Herald* begins a campaign against what it calls a 'Tomb of Gloom', arguing that the £25,000 required could be better spent on a memorial hospital or homes for war widows.

Monash is careful to tread carefully around Murdoch because his SEC can ill afford any more enemies and for a time the shrine proposal grinds to a halt. Plans are put forward instead for a city square with a cenotaph at the top of Bourke Street. Monash won't give up without a fight, though.

Jewish communities increasingly look to Monash as their spokesman, even though he is only a cultural Jew and even needs advice about how to observe many of the holidays. He knows that to reject their invitations and requests would be to disrespect his heritage, and so on 22 March 1921 he presides over the welcome of Joseph Hertz, Chief Rabbi of the British Empire.

A month later, Bertha marries Gershon Bennett in the drawing room at Iona with Rabbi Danglow performing the ceremony.[74] The happy couple make their home at Iona. Monash joins the board of management at the St Kilda Hebrew congregation but warns Danglow he is unlikely to attend many meetings. Still, he becomes more interested in religion with his advancing age and observes Yom Kippur each year, at least as far as staying home from the office. Fasting is asking too much, although he eats a fairly bland diet centred on porridge, boiled mutton and soused herring. From 1925 he attends Yom Kippur at the synagogue with a borrowed prayer book.

When the increasingly erratic Senator Pompey Elliott refers to the war hero Lieutenant Colonel Eliezer 'Lazar' Margolin in the house as 'an illiterate Polish Jew',[75] Monash springs to the defence with a letter to the editor of the *Argus* the next day, declaring that 'the implied calumny is ridiculous' and that Margolin is 'a gallant, cultured gentleman of fine physique and engaging personality ardently loyal to Australian soldiers and ideals'.[76] In 1926 Monash is asked to open the Judean League's communal hall in Carlton, only to be pleasantly surprised that it will be known as Monash House. Under the influence of Lizzie and Lieutenant Colonel Margolin, Monash also changes his mind on Zionism and comes to support a moderate form, backing the British and the League of Nations in recognising Palestine as the Jewish homeland and facilitating migration there. Lizzie's British cousin Norman Bentwich[77] becomes the Attorney-General in Palestine, eventually surviving an assassination attempt from a young Arab. From 1920, when Monash chairs a public meeting in Melbourne by the visiting British Zionist Israel Cohen,[78] there is even talk that he might succeed his old commanding officer Lord Plumer as British High Commissioner in Jerusalem.

On 10 May 1922 at Iona, Monash welcomes his first grandson, John Monash Bennett, into the world. John will be followed by David in 1924 and Elizabeth (Betty) in 1926. Monash dotes on his grandchildren, the great general giggling with the babies, giving them piggy back rides, playing hide and seek and performing magic tricks, sometimes giving the babies their bottles. He teaches 'the kiddies', as he calls them, to read and to play draughts and to farm silkworms. Bertha says his patience with the children is 'inexhaustible'. He takes them on outings and gradually centres his life on them, spends less time at the office and more at home, surrounded by his loved ones, his artworks, his vast library, his classical records and the thousands of books in his libraries, the ones with the red dot on the spine having been personally signed by some of the world's great authors. He keeps a cellar almost exclusively of Australian wines but drinks it rarely, preferring a pre-dinner Scotch with 'Gersh'. He rarely touches beer and prefers tea to coffee. Although he is a regular at the theatre with Lizzie he avoids as many social functions as he can, in favour of nights around the fire reading aloud and solving the *Herald* crossword.

Mat visits him most Sundays, watching him working in the garden or in his workshop. She writes him a note saying: 'My dear big John, I can never thank you enough for all you have done ... but for you I should have gone under long ago.'[79]

Monash is fascinated by what he sees through the 80mm Zeiss telescope in the Iona garden, remarking that it is not so much the location and identification of the 'heavenly objects' which intrigues him, but rather the 'algebraical and mathematical processes which their location involves'. There is no relaxation that can compete, he says, with dabbling 'in algebraical and trigonometrical formulae'.[80]

From 1922 Monash begins to offload many of his properties, believing that Melbourne house prices are inflated and will eventually crash. Being the landlord of ex-diggers also embarrasses him, especially when they protest over rent rises while he is sitting in splendour at Iona. A group of Richmond activists condemns him for exploiting the poor. In 1922 he has the best financial year of his life, earning £6665, and by 1924 calculates his net worth at £63,000. He begins transferring assets to Bertha to avoid the inevitable death duties. Victor Wischer, with whom he quarrelled over a cricket bat when they were 12, is now his solicitor. Monash buys land in Bertha's name at Olinda, Heathmont and Mount Eliza.

He is called upon to record a message for Thomas Edison's 75th birthday as the representative of Australia. He lends his support to the National Geographic Society, the Victorian Society for the Protection of Animals, the Big Brother Movement, the Royal Colonial Institute, the Society of Australian Authors and the Egypt Exploration Society. He sends money to help Annie Gabriel, who has moved back to Sydney with Fred.

Monash becomes a part-time vice-chancellor at the University of Melbourne on 2 July 1923. The other nomination is James Barrett but Monash's lifelong fear of losing an election forces the chancellor Sir John MacFarland to arrange a private meeting of the University Council and take an informal vote. It is a close run thing. The more conservative elements of the council raise their eyebrows at the Lizzie Bentwitch situation, but Monash has enough numbers to force Barrett to withdraw.[81] Monash immediately twists the arm of Victoria's treasurer, Sir William McPherson, to increase the government's annual grant from £30,000 to £45,000 to help with new buildings for schools of Arts, Anatomy, Agriculture and Botany. He becomes acting chancellor for a year from March 1925 while MacFarland is on extended leave. He persuades Robert Gibson to provide a grant from the Commonwealth Bank. He hosts a dinner at the Menzies Hotel in 1926 for the Governor-General with the aim of convincing 10 businessmen to provide a library fund of £20,000 and for the Melbourne City Council to take over maintenance of the university grounds. Monash tells the audience that if the university does nothing but teach it is no different from a high school; it has to instil intellectual longing, so that men might grasp all the possibilities being offered by a civilisation on the 'threshold of great discoveries'.[82]

With Gershon Bennett's help, Monash is also instrumental in establishing the School of Dentistry and he examines 'Job' Bradfield,[83] the man who will build Sydney Harbour Bridge, for his doctorate of engineering from the University of Sydney.

*

Senator Pearce still hopes Monash will be the executive officer on the advisory Council of Defence, but after Japan signs the Washington Treaty stifling an arms race in February 1922, the Australian Government pares down the armed forces. Japan it seems, no longer poses a threat.

The Sydney newspaper and tobacco magnate Hugh Denison is mortified, however, and in his *Sun* newspaper, among the first Australian dailies to carry news rather than advertising on its front page,[84] calls on Monash to revitalise the Australian Army.[85] Brigadier General Bertie Lloyd[86] encloses the clipping when he writes to Monash the next day, telling him that while the government is blind to the dangers it faces, Monash is 'our foremost organiser'. 'Our ship of defence is perilously near the shoals,' he writes, 'and a storm is brewing – there is no one else for the helm.'[87]

Monash, now more interested in electricity than artillery, tells Lloyd it would be a 'very thankless job'.[88] Soon, however, Monash shows he is very much a commander-in-chief when needed.

Gellibrand had resigned from the Victorian police in 1922 after the government had ignored his recommendations for reform. On 2 November 1923, more than half of Melbourne's police go on strike over poor pay and harsh treatment. They are immediately sacked and just as soon hoodlums run riot through Melbourne in 'unparalleled lawlessness',[89] smashing jewellery store windows and looting. One mob drags people off a tramcar and derails it.[90] About 200 people are injured in brawls. William Brunton, Melbourne's Mayor Elect, forms a Citizens Protection Committee and 500 special constables are sworn in under police commissioner Alexander Nicholson. Premier Lawson convenes a meeting with Monash, Elliott and Major General John Forsyth and tells them that the government is 'very grim and determined' and it is to be 'a fight to the finish'.[91]

Monash takes charge, explaining to Attorney-General Arthur Robinson: 'I got the following organisation going … I told Elliott to go to the Town Tall and organise the specials … I told Forsyth to act as the connecting link between Elliott and Nicholson …

Nicholson did nothing whatever.' Realising the 'paralysis of the police organisation', Monash creates his own organisation independent of the police based on military lines.[92] McCay rings to volunteer. Monash warns the public to stay out of the city. Cabinet approves the recruitment of as many as 5000 men[93] and Monash and McCay organise them on a five-battalion basis with mounted, foot and motor police using maps and coloured pins as though Melbourne had become a battlefield in northern France. By 6 November, Melbourne Cup day, order is restored.

Three days later, Monash hands control to McCay and boards a train to Sydney to open another memorial. Yet again, he has presided over an astonishing victory.

Chapter 31

JEWISH MEMORIAL HALL, DARLINGHURST ROAD, SYDNEY, 11 NOVEMBER 1923

Anzac Day stands for everything we hold dear. There are some who would like us to forget the day, and what it stands for, but we, who know the great sacrifice made by those who fell, can never let the day die. It is Australia's national day. It is the day above all days when Australia should pay tribute to those who gave their all.
MONASH'S ANZAC DAY MESSAGE, 1927[1]

Could one resist a personality at once so strong and forceful, yet so simple and loveable; a man whose humility and modesty combined with a strength of character almost colossal, made him dear to all who knew him?
FRANK MCKENNA, SECRETARY OF THE PRIME MINISTER'S OFFICE[2]

HAVING SORTED OUT THE CHAOS of the police strike, Monash heads to Sydney to open the Jewish War Memorial Hall in Darlinghurst.[3] He asks his hosts not to publicise the event, declaring he is tired of the adulation and publicity, though he doesn't complain too bitterly when Premier George Fuller and Justice Judge John Cohen – president of the Jewish War Memorial Committee – greet him at Central Station along with a large press contingent and a crowd of cheering spectators.[4]

At the opening of what becomes known as 'The Maccabean Hall' on 11 November, Monash says fellow Jews will look to the building 'to keep the Jewish people together, especially the younger generation, and prevent the regrettable drift of those who are leaving the religion of their fathers'.[5]

The next night Monash tells an audience at Sydney Town Hall that a similar apathy exists in the Australian Government towards defence and that it could find no room for him any more. The situation is dire:

Look at our air force … it is a sham. We have not enough ammunition to last our artillery for more than a few hours. We could not maintain a battle for a full day. I do not think we have any Mills bombs. I have never seen a tank in Australia. I know I will be peppered for this, but I want the opportunity of telling you people straight the position. The AIF used to listen to me and trust me. I hope the people of Australia will do so. To those of us who know the game by bitter experience the question of this equipment is a deplorable thing, as is the training that is going on. We realise that if trouble came we should not have adequate equipment to put into the hands of our men.

Monash is just warming up.

Lots of people in these days are talking from platforms that there is no necessity for defence in Australia; that there is going to be no more war; that we have the League of Nations and such shibboleths. Is there any man who has read history who believes anything of the kind? Of course, the human race is evolving to better things, and sooner or later we shall succeed in finding palliatives to make war rarer, perhaps, but that we will ever succeed in preventing war I am one who does not believe.

Scaling back the military because there is now a League of Nations, he says, is like 'deciding that we will have no more burglaries, and then dismissing the police force'.[6] The threatened closure of the Royal Military College, Duntroon, he warns, would destroy Australia's last hope of defending herself. Later he confides to Bert that the old fort at Queenscliff would stand no chance against the new Japanese cruisers.

On Anzac Day 1924, the Victorian Branch of the RSL hires Melbourne Town Hall for a banquet, having voted that 'suitably recognising the services to Australia of Sir John Monash' be the first business of the incoming State Council. 'Mighty Monash',[7] as one paper calls him, is loudly cheered into the hall.[8] Ernest Turnbull, the Victorian president, says Monash has won 'a place in the temple of the Immortals',[9] and Senator Brigadier General Edmund Drake-Brockman, representing the Commonwealth Government, says Monash's achievements are still 'not yet properly appreciated by the people of Australia'. Some day, he says, the people of the whole world will recognise that thanks to Monash, the war ended at least a year before it otherwise would have. Monash's orders during the latter stages of the war are no 'taught in the army schools of Great Britain as models of strategy'.[10]

Monash rises to more loud cheering and is visibly moved. He tells the audience their applause is the most severe ordeal he has ever faced. All the glory belonged to the men who had put their life on the line, he says. War is rotten and no soldier wants to experience another.[11]

Early in June 1924, Monash has a trial switch-on at Yallourn for visiting railways commissioners. He delivers a speech about this mighty undertaking and the cohesion needed to bring such an engineering masterpiece together and then gives the signal to an operator to power up. The operator pulls the switch and there is an almighty bang from the boiler-room – followed by a painfully long silence. Without a blink, Monash looks at his watch and says,

'Gentlemen, we are now long overdue at the briquetting works.' He sends an apology to the operator for putting him under too much pressure. On 15 June, the first generator finally begins work, powered by the brown coal from the great open cut mine that leaves a huge heap of overburden called Mount Monash on the landscape. The next day power crackles down the line through seven suburban sub-stations to Melbourne. Monash, the master of timing, has kept his word and delivered the power as scheduled. In November Yallourn briquettes, cheaper and more efficient than firewood, come into production for retail sales.

Monash finds time for other work as well. He advises the Australian Government on the building of a new cruiser[12] and also backs the calls from Australia's military leaders to increase spending on the now threadbare armed forces. Prime Minister Stanley Bruce subsequently announces a five-year defence program to appease some of their concerns.[13]

He also gives free advice to the Melbourne Cricket Ground on how to increase their crowd capacity to give all 75,000 patrons a good view. He suggests changing the playing surface to a circle. The idea does not go down well at the Melbourne Football Club but Monash admits he is not really a sports fan.[14]

On 8 September 1924 Monash begins heading a three-month royal commission into the police strike. He condemns the strikers for their dereliction of duty but also lambasts Commissioner Nicholson for not acting on the genuine grievances of his men. There had been 'a painful absence of tactful handling of many suburban and provincial constables',[15] he says, which was the root cause of the problem. He advises that the sacked officers should be reinstated. What was needed more than anything was an able chief commissioner and he eventually persuades Tom Blamey to take the job. Blamey becomes a central figure, along with other senior military men such as the rising star Edmund 'Ned Herring'[16] in the secret paramilitary society, the White Guard, 'ready to act swiftly and suddenly against communist subversion'.[17]

*

In September 1924 Monash also becomes president of the Australasian Association for the Advancement of Science at the request of Edgeworth David and the naturalist Baldwin Spencer.[18] He becomes the country's official spokesman for scientific development for the next two years and lobbies hard for more funding for research. He also becomes the Australian council member of the Institution of Civil Engineers (London), lobbying the government on legislation for engineers and architects. George Swinburne thinks Monash is spreading himself too thin but it is Swinburne who suffers a breakdown at the end of 1924. The electricity commission persuades him not to retire but instead to sail for Germany and report on the latest brown coal developments.[19]

On 19 January 1925, while on board the RMS *Orama*, Swinburne writes an angry letter denouncing inefficiencies at Yallourn, condemning Monash for spending too much time in Melbourne and not enough at the site. There is too much pipe smoking going on around head office, he says.[20] Monash coolly assesses the attack. Rather than dash off a reply he waits a full six months before asking Swinburne to permit him 'equal candour' in the hope that their discussions would 'in no way impair our friendship or cordial personal relations'.

Swinburne's letter, he says, has caused 'considerable consternation ... and a very extreme vexation' with 'no coating to the pill' and has made Monash labour 'under a sense of injury and embarrassment'. All the problems of inefficiency raised by Swinburne were being addressed. Monash is more worried about the role of Frederic Eggleston, the new minister in charge of the commission. He calls Eggleston 'a carping critic, accepting our explanations with obvious reservations'. As to his basing himself in Melbourne rather than Yallourn, Monash says it is just like in his days on the Western Front, setting up his HQ where everyone knows where to reach him at a moment's notice and where he can make informed decisions with a 'complete' picture of what is going on.[21]

Anzac Day is established as an annual national event in 1925 on the 10th anniversary of the Gallipoli landing. The commemoration falls on a Saturday. Nine days earlier, Pompey Elliott, the chief organiser of the march on behalf of the RSL, asks Monash to lead the procession, along with Chauvel and representatives from the Navy and Air Force. Monash says he does not want to take any 'prominent position' but will assemble with the Diggers and walk as one of them. Eventually, however, he allows Elliott to persuade him to take the chief role at the head of the parade, with about 6000 men behind him. Rather than wear his uniform, Monash wears a suit with an umbrella under his arm, and looks rather chuffed.[22] The crowd breaks into applause when he enters the Exhibition Building for the commemorative service presided over by the new Governor-General Lord Forster and Prime Minister Bruce. And there is hearty applause when Bruce says: 'Let us hope that we are approaching the time when the whole of our people will recognise that Anzac Day is the greatest day in our national history.'[23]

Monash takes charge of the Anzac Day Commemorative Council and soon Victoria passes an Act that makes 25 April not only a public holiday but a sacred one like Good Friday, with the closure of cinemas and theatres and a ban on the sale of liquor.[24] The next year a crowd of 12,000 marches on a Sunday. Arrangements are made with the Commercial Travellers Club to transport the large number of disabled soldiers and Monash is persuaded to march in uniform with full regalia, sword, medals and decorations. This time he speaks first at the Exhibition Building telling the crowd that more than ever Australia needed the wartime spirit of comradeship, that 'the living had a duty to the dead'.[25]

On 8 August 1925 Monash invites about 20 officers, this time without their wives, to Iona to commemorate Amiens. Gellibrand, now back in Hobart and soon to become the Federal Member for

Denison, hosts a similar function at which guests toast 'The King, Fallen Comrades and Our Leader and the Men He Led'. Brudenell White describes these annual get-togethers, where the old soldiers drink a ferocious rum and brandy punch, as a 'potent (mark the word) means of cementing ties' and preserving their fellowship.[26] Pompey Elliott still remains sullen about missing out on a divisional command and his mood grows continually more morose.

Monash's last official role for the Australian military is in September 1925, when Chauvel invites him to Duntroon as Blamey conducts a tour for senior officers. 'I soon found myself quite at home in the work,' he tells Bertha, 'and although feeling at first a little rusty, have found no difficulty in speedily taking a position of authority, and laying down vital principles. Chauvel is deplorably slow, weak and hesitating [Monash can't help himself], and carries no weight. He soon deferred to me and let me take the leading role in the discussions.'[27]

At Yallourn, ballooning expenditure puts Monash and the SEC under more heavy bombardment. In its first year of operation the Commission makes a greater loss than expected because the government has cut back on extensions of the power supply that would have been profitable. Monash tells the Rosenhains that 'My big job ... is not a bed of roses. While the works and schemes are developing to my own satisfaction, and to the undoubted overwhelmingly great benefit of the community, there is little thanks for it ... We have a nasty way in this country of levelling criticisms and abuse, and doubt upon all leaders and higher workers.'[28]

On 29 July 1925 the commission, fearing that the government might veto further development at Yallourn, asks for a formal inquiry into the SEC turning a profit and an American, Willits H. Sawyer, from Columbus, Ohio, is appointed to head the investigation in December. On 23 December, Monash addresses Parliament to receive his funding allocation and informs the chamber that a German named Emil Gaudlitz has offered to buy the Victorian electricity enterprise if the State lost faith in it.[29] What the SEC needs, he says, is further expansion, not cost cutting. Sawyer eventually judges the enterprise to be financially sound and says that he can 'hardly conceive a higher type of citizenship and personality devoted to public duty' than he has found among Monash and his fellow commissioners. When Eggleston loses his seat in April, Monash is delighted, saying it would be 'impossible to get a worse Minister'. Eggleston hits back by blaming some of the commission's problems on Monash's 'ruthless egotism'.[30] He is one of Monash's few critics during this post-war twilight period.

By 1927 the commission is profitable. 'Thus are the critics and croakers being confounded,' Monash tells the Rosenhains. 'But no one will ever know the hard fight it had been, both to conquer the stupidity of ignorant Ministers and Parliamentarians, and to flog my organisation into efficient functioning.'[31] The solution to nearly all his problems is 'German methods, policies and machinery'. 'You can imagine the degree of hostility and opposition engendered by such a course of action. Nothing but my war prestige would have sufficed to justify the purity of my motives, and I doubt if anyone else could have battled through ...'[32]

Monash's organisational brilliance shone like a beacon through the Australian landscape of the 1920s. He had transferred his acumen for the battlefield seamlessly to the boardroom. Politics seemed the logical destination for a man capable of such management on a vast scale. Billy Hughes had dashed Monash's political aspirations in 1919 but Stanley Bruce made overtures to him about joining his Federal Government in 1923. Monash, though, was committed to the SEC and wanted to see the job through to the very end. Again, in 1925 Bruce urges him to stand for the Senate alongside Pompey Elliott, who is now showing severe signs of what will later be called 'post-traumatic stress disorder', but Monash gives him the same answer. His own politics are those of a self-made businessman and engineer, material gains based on technological advancements and free enterprise. All men should receive fair wages and good workers should be paid well. Parliamentary democracy is the secret to freedom, he says, and the British system of government and law are unsurpassed. He believes in a White Australia policy and that moderate protectionism is justified in a country struggling after the loss and maiming of so many men. He despairs that more Australians are interested in sport and jazz than education and technology, and complains that in recent years his country seems to have 'less culture, less art, less music, less scientific achievement, and more of everything that is sordid ... While our population is increasing, and our prosperity is increasing so is our vulgarity ... our want of discipline.'[33]

Monash occasionally takes on work for the Federal Government, publicising Commonwealth loans and entertaining officers from the visiting navies of France, Britain, America and Japan. He is constantly called on to give speeches and at Iona in 1926 hosts one of his favourite organisations – the Beefsteak Club, a social dining group of about 20 academics and doctors.

He lectures them on leadership in war, explaining that:

The capacity to form judgements, rapidly and soundly, is, I believe more temperamental than intellectual. A successful leader must be unemotional to the extent of being callous to the external influences which evoke joy or sorrow, elation or despondency; he must be indifferent to praise or blame; he must have the capacity to persevere calmly and dispassionately with the business in hand ... he must be patient to a degree. He must have determination and steadfastness of purpose of a very high order. He must have an exalted confidence in himself and in the correctness of his judgement, amounting to an intellectual arrogance.[34]

The most critical of all the tasks of a leader, however, he says is the 'creation and maintenance of the morale of his men', infusing by example that devotion to the cause. Those who served or worked under him will say that perhaps Monash's greatest gift as a leader is to define a problem in simple terms and reduce complex difficulties into manageable problems.

Sometimes, however, he gets things woefully wrong.

When Hindenburg is elected President of Germany in 1925, beating the challenge of the increasingly eccentric Erich Ludendorff (now out of hiding in Sweden), Monash reassures readers of the *Herald* that 'fears of a revival of a warlike spirit in Germany are grossly exaggerated ... Germany is militarily powerless for the next quarter of a century.' Later he voices his opinion that the aeroplane will have little influence on modern war.

Monash and Lizzie spend hours together at the theatre, in smart restaurants and the luxury hotels where she lives. They pose together, as man and wife, for the artist Agnes Paterson and the work is exhibited by the Victorian Artists' Society.[35] Meanwhile, tongues wag over Lizzie's unpopularity at Iona. *Truth* newspaper asks why Monash doesn't marry the 'pleasant-faced Jewess who sits behind a large ostrich fan',[36] while *Smith's Weekly*[37] writes of 'the troublesome daughter' thwarting their true love. Lizzie is on his arm at nearly all 17 first nights of the Grand Opera season in 1924 and the eight Kreisler concerts of 1925 and helps organise the visits from Sydney of Henri Verbrugghen's orchestra. Often Monash sits with the musical score on his knee, following the conductor with the same keen eye that once surveyed Mont St Quentin. He continues to support Gregan McMahon's theatre society and Allan Wilkie's Shakespearean society and entertains the Bundaberg soprano Gladys Moncrief with a lunch at the Windsor.

In November 1926, more than 1000 members of the Australian Workers' Union at Yallourn go on strike, demanding a 44-hour week.[38] The briquetting plant is closed immediately. The impasse lasts three weeks until, with Melbourne about to face severe power restrictions, the dispute is finally resolved when Monash agrees to cut some work on Saturdays. On 20 March 1927 another strike hits: workers down tools, accusing a foreman of using bullying tactics. Large areas of Melbourne are without power for three days and Monash draws up a plan for volunteer labour to run Yallourn in case of future emergencies. He consults with Jack Holloway,[39] the Trades Hall secretary, about resolving future disputes through agreed channels. Holloway calls Monash 'one of the greatest men I ever met … the really great men were those who could spare time and inclination to do little human acts which others would brush aside'.

'He wanted cheaper heat, light and power for all Victorians,' Holloway says. 'He believed that every home, even the poorest in the State, should be able to afford a full range of appliances and the electricity to run them.' Holloway recalls the time two young kitchen hands at the Naval and Military Club were charged with pinching a piece of cheese rind and a ham bone 'not worth six pence' and were in the city watch-house, terrified of fronting court. Monash went out of his way to get the charges dropped.[40]

But by the mid 1920s, Monash begins to complain about stress, nerve strain and lumbago. His backaches are worsened when he ricks it moving a washing machine. His weight fluctuates, too, as high as 87 kilograms before he brings it down to just over 70. By 1927 he begins to suffer high blood pressure.

Brudenell White is given charge of organising the 1927 royal visit by Prince Albert and his wife Elizabeth for the opening of the new Parliament House in Canberra. Albert is the Duke of York and will become King George VI. Elizabeth is upset that they have to leave their baby daughter – the future Queen Elizabeth II – back in England, but Albert wants to see and be seen by the greatest number of Australians possible.

The royal visit to Melbourne coincides with Anzac Day and with Monash at the helm this will be a march like none before.

The night before the march, at an RSL dinner held in Anzac House in Collins Street, Monash speaks to his audience about a matter, which he says is close to his heart. To him the proposal for an Anzac square at the top of Bourke Street is out of the question and the only design worthy of a Shrine of Remembrance is that from the architects Hudson and Waldrop. Monash already has reinforcements at the ready. His supports include town planner Kem Kemsley[41] and Wally Peeler VC; other backers, scattered around the hall, rise, as arranged, to applaud and cheer Monash's comments.

The following day, almost 30,000 men, with Monash leading, take to the streets in the Anzac march while as many as half a million people line the route, waving flags and cheering. Behind Monash, blinded soldiers are driven in cars and behind them march more than 40 Victoria Cross recipients. Melbourne has never seen such a huge mass of people gathered for one event.

Brudenell White is awestruck, telling Monash: 'I never expect to see again in my lifetime such an impressive ceremony.'[42]

Monash joins Prince Albert at the temporary cenotaph in front of Parliament House to take the salute and then, at the Exhibition Building, tells the crowd that the Anzac march had grown from a 'small beginning until it had reached the mighty demonstration' seen this day. It was on this day 12 years ago, he says, that the flower of Australian youth, on the cliffs of Gallipoli, performed a memorable feat of arms, which instantly welded the people of Australia into a nation.

Australia's death toll from the war was more than 60,000, and everyone present has friends and comrades 'in the host', he says. There are many in the crowd who have survived the stress of war, but now it is the duty of all Australians to remember the spirit of mateship, loyalty and energy in building a great nation.

Monash says he hopes that the people of Australia will keep sacred the memory of this day 'for all time'.[43] The cheers are almost deafening.

Monash presses on with his Shrine of Remembrance, backed by the RSL, Legacy, the *Age* and *Argus*. Murdoch's *Herald* holds out, saying that the shrine is too severe, stiff and heavy, but Monash counters that it is 'dignified, noble, appealing and eminently suited as a memorial of great service and sacrifice, without that ridiculous note of victory and conquest which characterised the memorials of the barbarian past'.[44]

Monash gets his way. Even though Premier Ned Hogan says he would prefer to spend the £25,000 on a memorial hospital, Victorian Governor Lord Somers lays the foundation stone for the shrine on Armistice Day 1927. Monash takes over the construction, employing Fairway and the Reinforced Construction Co., who give him a good price. He rejects the idea that there should be statues of him, White and Chauvel, but supervises the public appeal for shrine funds, writing to other wealthy businessmen and admonishing the Victoria Racing Club for not digging deeper.

At a time when most soldiers only want to forget the horrors they saw during the war, Monash wants the shrine and Anzac Day to remind them of the comradeship and sense of nationhood that their service forged. He was their leader, he told them, but together they were an unbeatable team.

'Leadership counts for something, of course,' he says, 'but it cannot succeed without the spirit, élan and morale of those led. Therefore I count myself the most fortunate of men in having been placed at the head of the finest fighting machine the world has ever known ...' Yet he still wouldn't mind a bit of praise. 'Hardly a military leader of the war has escaped criticism,' he adds, 'but I am happy in the knowledge that I have never had to meet any criticism of my tactical leadership.'[45]

In February 1929 he is invited to take part in unveiling the Martin Place cenotaph in Sydney, where again the old Diggers give him three cheers.

As Monash's health begins to decline his sense of finality draws him ever nearer to his Jewish roots. In October 1927 he accepts the role of honorary president of the Australian

Zionist Federation,[46] but on the condition that he will only be a figurehead, lending moral support but not time. A letter to all Australian Jews seeking recruits is distributed the following year under his name. But, ever the military man, his greatest loyalty will always be to King and Country. When Anglo-Arab police interfere with Jewish worship at the Wailing Wall in Jerusalem,[47] prompting anti-British protests, Monash writes to Rabbi Israel Brodie,[48] who has succeeded Rabbi Abrahams at the Melbourne Hebrew congregation.

'While I in common with every Jew have the utmost sympathy with the unfortunate sufferers,' he says, 'it is quite another matter for me to be associated, however indirectly, with any action of any body of British citizens which seeks to express publicly any sentiments critical of or hostile to the British authorities.'[49]

To Monash, religion is one thing, but patriotism quite another.

The thirst for knowledge remains at the foundation of Monash's whole being, the power of his mind still a rare force even as he begins to decline physically. His whole life has been about making the most of whatever talents he had and whatever opportunities came his way, creating opportunities when none presented themselves. In his 1982 biography, Professor Geoffrey Serle theorised that if Monash was a genius, 'it was his "infinite capacity for taking pains" (a trait Monash had ascribed to Blamey) which made him so'.

He was not a polymath, but a man with a wide general knowledge; he in fact struggled for years academically. He was not a brilliant mathematician, his engineering was sound but not extraordinary, his practice of law was confined to narrow fields. His greatness was achieved by 'cultivating to a super-pitch of excellence the ordinary talents and virtues; a retentive memory, energy and capacity for hard work, concentration, orderliness, common sense, power of logical analysis, attention to detail, fine judgement' and a mild spirit that allowed him to work well with colleagues even when under great strain.[50] Eric Simonson said

Monash was a man 'without caprice' who in his deliberations 'had a calm serenity and patience'.[51] Even when he was surrounded by enemies he got the job done.

Addressing the Scotch College speech day at Melbourne Town Hall in 1928, almost half a century after he had won his first prize there, Monash tells the gathering that:

> There is no such thing as effortless genius or undeserved success. Success is the result of industry and of self-denial. Those who are still young will find that in ... life competition is fierce and relentless, and the reward is obtained by those who are capable. The world depends upon scholars, thinkers, and scientists, and the possibilities of a successful career are inexhaustible to a boy if he is able to carry away with him the rich feast of preparation that he is able to obtain at school.[52]

In January 1929 Monash writes to the Rosenhains to say that because of his heavy workload and constant public demands, he has given up 'all hope' for any privacy or leisure for the rest of his days. The only alternative course is to retire into obscurity but such a move is impossible. He resolves to continue beating onwards against the current. His weight is creeping up again over 82 kilos but he limits himself to a 60-hour working week so he can spend more time with his grandchildren, with Lizzie, and in pursuing his many hobbies and interests. At the close of each day's work at the SEC office, and then again last thing at night, he will plan his day ahead, ready to tick off all tasks great and small when the sun rises. To those who tell him they are 'too busy' for more work, he says there is always time to do one more thing.

But the workload is getting too much and he feels himself burning out. In 1928 Tante Ulrike dies in Caulfield at the age of 86,[53] 60 years after she came to Australia to help Bertha with the new baby 'Johnnychen'. Vic's sister Belle, Colonel Henry Hall, George Swinburne and Douglas Haig all die within a year of each other and John Gibson, Jim McCay and Monash's niece Mona Rosenhain soon after. Monash becomes increasingly aware of his own mortality.

Few things in life hurt him as much, though, as the sudden death at Iona of his grandson and namesake John Monash Bennett, aged six,[54] from a rare flu virus. He had just started at Scotch College. He 'was at school, well, on Friday, and died Sunday morning'.[55] 'No one will ever know how much I had built upon this boy,' Monash tells the Rosenhains. 'He had been my constant companion since his birth ... he was an exceptionally talented lad, and extraordinarily loveable.'[56] Monash tries to write a story of the young boy's life but finds the subject too distressing. Instead he provides funds for a drinking fountain at Scotch's junior school in his grandson's name and establishes a prize in his honour.[57]

He spends even more time with his other grandchildren, David and Betty, playing Charlie Chaplin movies for them on his home projector and building Betty an exquisite two-storey doll's house, complete with electric light, bathroom fittings and staircase exactly to scale. In August 1929 he welcomes another grandson, John Colin Monash Bennett. He also entertains his niece Nancy Rosenhain on an extended holiday in Melbourne.

In September 1929, after Arab massacres of Jewish settlers in Palestine, Monash does his best to placate the many Melbourne Zionists wanting to protest against British control there. At a Town Hall meeting of 2000 people, Monash cools the more radical elements by saying that while they have every right to be bitter, it is no use protesting against the British because 'every Jew who has made his home in the British Empire owes it unbounded gratitude, complete loyalty and profound allegiance'.[58] Despite the slings and arrows he has encountered over his religion from military officials and from men like Bean, he says he was never a victim of virulent anti-Semitism and has never had to speak against it as a problem in Australia. Monash all but tells them that his own success and popularity prove that mainstream anti-

Semitism in Australia does not exist. In fact, the English author Colin MacInnes will argue that 'Monash, by the simple fact of his presence and prestige, made anti-Semitism as a "respectable" attitude, impossible in Australia'. Men who had fought in the war spoke of Monash with 'reverence ... And worshipping him as they did (and through him their own youth and courage) they could never publicly deny the hero they themselves had followed: nor could they deny his people.'[59]

In October 1929, it is rumoured that the now Baron Birdwood, commanding the British Indian Army, will succeed Lord Stonehaven as Australia's next Governor-General[60] as he is the favourite of George V. Monash is talked about as a possibility for the office but it eventually goes to Isaac Isaacs. Monash writes to Isaacs, rejoicing for his fellow Jew in 'this culmination of a great career'.[61] Monash has known all along that his arrangement with Lizzie, which is not exactly kosher, may disqualify him for the highest office in the land. And he doubts that he would have the energy now for such a role. When there are again calls for him to become national president of the RSL, Monash tells the president of the West Australian branch that he is 'a very tired man'.[62]

In any case, he has other pressing concerns. On 24 October a huge share market run on Wall Street in New York ends when the Dow Jones Industrial Average tumbles 9 per cent, sparking two days of panic selling. Five days later, on Black Tuesday, the Dow crashes 23 per cent, sending the world's financial markets spiralling into the Great Depression. At 64, Monash has more money than he could spend in his remaining days, but still he is taking no chances for the mouths that depend on him and the future generations that will follow.

His income falls to £5360 in 1929–30 and after government budget cuts drops again to £4336 the following year. It is still a dozen times the wage of a clerk,[63] but Monash has a morbid fear of ending up broke like his father and grandfather. He has already given Bertha his life assurance policies that are about to mature and he figures he can save £1468 by economising on furniture, clothing, wine, tobacco, gifts, charities and memberships of a dozen societies.

While the Depression does not stop funds for a duplication scheme to expand the electricity commission's network, Monash still has what he calls 'the very disagreeable task' of laying off hundreds of men in a bleak economic climate. Victoria's premier, Ned Hogan, a former farm labourer, timber-cutter, rabbit-catcher and caber-tossing champion, admits that:

Under the very wise guidance of Sir John Monash ... this State enterprise has come out of the dark shadows in which it was staggering for years, and during the very difficult times that we passed through the Commission deserved the sympathy and consideration of the Government and Parliament, but did not get very much of either. I am very pleased indeed to know that the undertaking is now economically sound, and is likely to become a greater asset to the State with the passing of each year. Credit for this very fine result is due to the very able gentleman who is in charge of the undertaking. I think that Sir John Monash has earned the trust and confidence of Parliament, and any Bill which the Government submit on his advice will receive very friendly consideration from me and my party.[64]

Monash works well with John Cain,[65] the new Labor minister overseeing the commission, but still has to fight for expansion against 'Governments and Parliaments composed of men of low intellectual calibre, and timorous and narrow vision ... there is never a time when I have not to direct a campaign of publicity, education and persuasion, in order to advance and stabilise each successive step'.[66]

Future Prime Minister Bob Menzies is a young minister in the Victorian Government in 1929, and for all his life will regard

Monash as 'the finest advocate I ever listened to … He was a great advocate who knew how to think, who worked out his thoughts and who could then present them to other people with such compulsion, such persuasion that they began to wonder why they hadn't thought of it themselves.'[67]

Menzies recalled the dread his colleagues felt if Cabinet ever rejected Monash's request. Monash would invade the Cabinet room like he was taking Hamel:

> … we all stood up, we were all in the presence of a man we knew was a greater man than we would ever be … he looked around towards the Premier and he said, 'Well, Mr Premier, I gather that the Cabinet has rejected my proposal.'
>
> 'Well, yes, yes, I think that's right Sir John.'
>
> 'Well,' he said, 'that can only be because they've utterly failed to understand it. I will now explain it.' And he sat there, with that rock like look, and he explained it, and one by one we shrivelled in our places … above all things having done that, he had the force of character, the utter integrity, the persuasiveness of language, the clarity of vision which enabled him to take all the ideas that he had and put them clearly into the minds of other people.[68]

Monash wins plaudits from the other side of politics, too, especially from the rising star of Labor, John Curtin.

Monash had been on hand to welcome the intrepid Australian aviator Bert Hinkler to Melbourne in 1928 and the following year Curtin tells Federal Parliament, while debating defence expenditure, that Monash and Hinkler are both great Australians ignored in their homeland because of those members 'on the other side of the house'.

'Australia's greatest military genius is not actively associated with the defence administration of the Commonwealth …' Curtin says. 'The man who led Australia's army in the greatest war in history could not be found a satisfactory position by the

Ministry when he returned ... [and] one of the greatest aviators in the world ... could not be found a niche in our Air Force.'[69]

Even with his vast workload and commitments, Monash still finds time to back Phil Finkelstein's 1929 Theatre Royal production of R.C. Sherriff's play *Journey's End*, which is set in Saint-Quentin as Operation Michael approaches. The play featured a young Laurence Olivier on its opening night in London but has Reginald Tate in the lead role in Melbourne. In 1930 Monash goes to see the movie version. Around this time, he also sits down to make notes on his life and plans to write his memoirs. He catches up with old friends, writing to Billie Card[70] in California and reminding the now Mrs Bowater of the way they danced in the old days. He writes to Bill Elliott, 'if still alive', telling the schoolteacher who was bailed up by Ned Kelly that he keeps green the memory of his happy boyhood in Jerilderie.

He even forgets about how stand-offish he found Vida Goldstein, now a lauded feminist writer and political force, and sits for an interview with her to run in the *Christian Science Monitor*.

Amid the economic gloom Monash is buoyed by a series of honours.

On Armistice Day 1929, new Prime Minister Jim Scullin[71] announces that Monash and Harry Chauvel have been promoted to the rank of general. Some of Monash's colleagues and politicians believe Scullin should go further and make Monash a field marshal,[72] but Monash is still touched by the gesture and when Scullin writes to congratulate him on the eve of his 65th birthday, Monash replies heartily that 'your letter is the very first of its kind sent to me by any previous Prime Minister, either in his personal or representative capacity'.[73]

Monash also receives the two highest engineering awards on offer. In December 1929 the Institution of Engineers, Australia awards him the Peter Nicol Russell Memorial Medal in a presentation that is broadcast nationally[74] and in June 1931, after many years sponsoring it, he is awarded the Kernot Memorial Medal.

Monash becomes interested in golf again and buys an instructional book by the Australian champion Ivo Whitton. He soon finds, however, that he no longer has the energy to play. In 1930 he finishes a long piece of licentious writing called the 'Gulston' narrative based on his experiences with Lizzie in London from 1917 to 1919, but the vitality of a decade past is now long gone.

In February 1930 he tells organisers that he can no longer march on Anzac Day because the effort stresses him 'very seriously, both physically and psychologically'.[75] Instead he will take a car to the saluting base. He changes his mind at the last minute and marches again but the day leaves him 'in a thoroughly exhausted and nervous condition'.[76]

The next night, at a reunion of his old comrades, he tells them that during these days of mass unemployment and sadness, Anzac Day has a 'deeper significance than appears on the surface'.

> It is true that it is intended as an act of remembrance of our comrades who have gone … but it is something more than that. It is an occasion for elevating the public spirit and public sentiment. We are gathering our citizens together in hundreds of thousands, who have presented to them noble ideas and noble thoughts, and they are animated by common ideals of worthy purpose. Heaven knows we need such stimulation today.[77]

Monash keeps up a hectic schedule. He helps Blamey gain reappointment as Victoria's police commissioner on a salary of £1250, protests to Scullin over a proposed tax on the sale of books and welcomes the British aviator Amy Johnson. He even helps his old critic Charles Bean earn a Doctor of Letters from Melbourne University.[78]

Behind the scenes, many in Australia want Monash to become even busier. As the Depression worsens, Monash fields calls from various radical elements around the country to oust the government and take command of the country the way he had taken command in France.

There are ratbag outfits such as the Knights of the Empire, governed by the 'Supreme Council of King Arthur', the Imperial Patriots, the Order of Silent Knights, the Empire Loyalty League. Father John Graham, a Hobart priest, sends a telegram to Monash imploring him to save Australia the way Mussolini saved Italy[79] and 'Old Digger' writes to the *Bulletin* saying that Monash is one of the greatest organisers the world has ever seen and could save Australia within three years.[80]

More serious proposals come from the prominent architect Kingsley Henderson, the burly businessman Robert Knox and L.N. Roach, the Australian boss of British Dominion Films, who ask Monash and Robert Gibson to lead their movement against the Scullin Government's economic measures.

Monash is horrified, replying that as a public officer he is 'absolutely precluded from any public action or any public declaration of my views' which could jeopardise his standing or his role in important public works. Moreover his ferocious workload in public service since 1914 has 'greatly sapped my vigour and mental elasticity'.[81] At his time of life, he says, he no longer has the capacity for any public responsibility other than those he has already undertaken.

When Monash is nominated by Scullin to represent Australia at the opening of New Delhi, conspiracy theorists propose sinister motives. He soothes the concerns of his old artillery commander Major General Grimwade by telling him that one group in Australia wants him to stay to lead a revolution and 'constitute myself Dictator' while another wants him to stay and suppress a revolution by 'the Communists and red raggers'. 'To suggest that the Commonwealth Government made the appointment in order to get me out of the country, is of course, sheer nonsense.'[82]

When the Sydney journalist Colin Barclay-Smith writes on behalf of Sydney businessmen 'who sit among the ruins of their businesses',[83] begging Monash not to leave the country, he receives a blunt reply:

> What do you and your friends want me to do? To lead a movement to upset the Constitution, oust the jurisdiction of Parliament, and usurp the Governmental power? If so, I have no ambition to embark on High Treason ... the only hope for Australia is the ballot box, and an educated electorate ... If it be true that many people in Sydney are prepared to trust my leadership, they should be prepared also to trust my judgment.[84]

Monash looks forward, very much, to seeing the myriad delights of India, even though he receives an anonymous call that Mahatma Gandhi is plotting to have him poisoned. A large crowd sees Monash off from Spencer Street Station on 14 January 1931. He takes the train to Adelaide to board the *Maloja* with Lizzie. She will accompany him throughout the trip but not to official functions and will not be officially accommodated. In Adelaide, Monash tells reporters that he has faith in the youth of Australia to help restore the country 'to its former position of prestige and prosperity'.[85] In Perth there are the rounds of receptions and speeches and he meets up with Talbot Hobbs, Carl Jess and the reporter Charles Smith, about to be made a director of West Australian Newspapers. After years of almost constant work, Monash finds the journey across the Indian Ocean pleasant and relaxing. He is trackside for the Bombay raes, and he and Lizzie spend two days at Government House in Bombay and three romantic nights at Agra, where they are inspired by the Taj Mahal at moonlight. He hates Benares – 'a disgusting spectacle' and 'a civilisation at its lowest' – but sparks up at the Viceroy's palace in New Delhi, where he meets up again with General Currie, who is there representing Canada. Monash is accompanied by Frank

McKenna from the Prime Minister's Department, who acts as his secretary. He speaks at the opening of the Dominion columns in the new capital. Although he is awestruck by the grandeur of New Delhi, he finds Sir Edwin Lutyens, the 61-year-old architect of the city, 'a silly old man – almost a buffoon'.

Tours of military posts follow along the North West Frontier and through the Kyber Pass into Afghanistan. He sees Colonel Guy Wylly, from his old 3rd Division, and then spends two weeks travelling by train with Lizzie and McKenna through India's south, jotting down his notes on the great disparities of life in this huge, unfathomable nation.

McKenna finds Monash unpretentious and generous, and remembers him giving one of his guides the money to pay for his medical course. Monash is courteous to everyone he meets, although privately he finds the Nizam of Hyderabad 'a dirty little miser', in stark contrast to the Maharajah of Mysore, who presides over a 'wonderful city and state' and gives proof that 'Indians are fully capable of modern government by a benevolent bureaucracy'.[86] He and Lizzie travel through Madras and then spend five days in the hills of Ceylon before sailing on the *Otranto* from Colombo bound for Fremantle on 21 March. They arrive in Western Australia 15 days later.

Monash is hardly back on Australian soil when he hears the gut-wrenching news that Annie Grace Gabriel, his first great love, has died at Ashfield in Sydney on 25 February, aged 66.[87] She had stayed with Fred for more than 40 years in homes in Brisbane, Sydney and Melbourne but she had never stopped loving the handsome young militia officer she had trysted with all those years ago.

There is more bad news. Nellie Melba has also died, two days before Annie, in Sydney from complications brought on by facial surgery in Europe.

And on 23 March, while Monash was at sea, the severely depressed Senator Pompey Elliott killed himself with a stab wound to the arm while being treated as an inpatient in a private hospital in Malvern. He had been admitted to the hospital after trying to gas himself at his home in Camberwell.

The news of the three deaths weighs heavily on Monash.

He follows the tour of India with a series of lectures, declaring that the Empire should be very wary of other revolutionary ideas, too, and especially careful about Gandhi, who was released from jail while Monash was there. India gaining self-rule would be a disaster for Australia, he says, because it would mean a potential enemy 'on our trade route'. 'Gandhi is an ascetic,' Monash tells the Constitution Club in Melbourne. 'He is highly skilled and learned but whether he is sincere or whether he is a humbug I cannot say. One is inclined to think that he is a humbug, because some of his doctrines urge civil disobedience.'[88]

At a civic reception in Perth there are again calls for Monash to do something drastic about the Federal Government to get Australia out of its economic quagmire, but he replies that he has 'no desire whatever to upset the constitution of Australia and find myself up against a brick wall'.[89] The calls for him somehow to overthrow Scullin's government grow even louder from men such as Arthur Streeton[90] and from the Sydney radio broadcaster John Murdoch Prentice, who says he would gladly serve under Monash as dictator.[91]

But Monash is failing fast. For two years doctors have been warning him to watch his blood pressure and he has again shed 6 kilograms under their orders. His memory for important dates is starting to fade and he allows himself to be talked into a series of sensationalist articles on the war for *Smith's Weekly*. The Australian diggers had come under attack in a number of English war books and *Smith's Weekly* decided to cash in with Monash's counter-attack as he labels 'The Australian Army Corps ... the greatest fighting unit of shock troops the world has ever seen'.[92]

Though the articles appeared under Monash's name they were actually penned by ghost writer Eric Baume in a distinctly tabloid style, with all the bluster of a *Boys Own* adventure rather than the formal dignity of Monash's letters or *Australian Victories*.

So readers were given lurid headlines and such fanciful tales as that of Major General Sir Charles Rosenthal or 'Rosey' as he is described 'bustling back across the parapet with three Jerry "kamerads" in a great state of fear. "Take these cows!" he ordered the nearest N.C.O., and at once made a beeline back to his own divisional headquarters. Again at Villers-Bretonneux [Rosey] had an escapade which should certainly have resulted in his court martial. I feel very guilty, as a matter of fact, that I didn't have him arrested. He deliberately crawled out on the mound to have a "look-see." A bullet got him on the point of the thumb, and went far into his arm. Now, a wound of that kind meant a certain Blighty. But as the ambulance coves were getting Rosey on to the stretcher, he appealed to them to send me a message asking that I have him kept in France. You see, he knew very well that I was going to pull off a battle in about a fortnight. And he wanted to be in it ... As far as I remember, Rosey was wounded about eight times. He made it a habit!'[93]

Bean is so dismayed at the florid articles that he writes to Monash to advise him to make it public that the words are not from his pen and that Monash cannot believe 'the stupid, vain myth' that there were no worthy soldiers in the war outside the AIF. Bean says the name of the AIF is being damaged by the tone and 'for the sake of your own reputation, to be cautious in your interviews with the press'.[94]

Monash leads the Anzac Day parade again in 1931 but this time he rides a dappled grey charger and looks old and tired at the head of 23,000 men.[95]

A few weeks later he is forced to admit that he now has a 'disposition – steadily getting worse – to fatigue'.[96] After walking a mile or so, or negotiating the stairs at Iona or tinkering in his workshop he is soon out of breath and has to lie down 'more or less exhausted'. His doctor Sidney Sewell[97] diagnoses 'irregularity of heart action, some dilation, and some valvular leakage'. Sewell prescribes digitalis, massage and regular check-ups.

Monash has to abandon the annual get-together to commemorate Amiens on 8 August but does not stop all commitments, attending the opening of the new Kernot Engineering School and examining a doctoral thesis on engineering.

Sewell and Sir Richard Stawell have recently founded the Association of Physicians of Australasia[98] and Monash consults both of them on 28 August to get the bad news.

He relays it to Walter three days later, telling him: 'I feel it my duty to advise you and Lou of certain developments in regard to my health, which may possibly preclude my writing to you again.'[99] The two doctors fear that Monash now has a growth in his abdomen but his heart is not strong enough for them to operate. He begins putting his affairs in order. 'I feel, of course, rather cast down,' he tells his brother-in-law. There is, after all, still so much work to do, but instead he has to 'shape my course to be ready for any emergency'. He writes a note to himself entitled 'Emergency Action': it includes a reminder to burn all his erotica and to destroy the love letters from Annie Gabriel and Lizzie Bentwitch.

He tries to make the most of the time he has left, attending the University Council meeting on 7 September and the Shrine of Remembrance committee meeting four days later, ticking off everything on the agenda. On 23 September he tells the old Diggers at the 6th Battalion reunion that as much as he loves to be among his old comrades, this will probably be the last time he sees them. There are gasps all around.[100] He apologises to Arthur Robinson that he cannot keep a speaking engagement in mid-October because the slightest stress exhausts him. He writes to Walter Coxen on 29 September to apologise for not having been able to attend Coxen's retirement function.

He sends a cheque to Mat to tide her over for a while. It is now 16 years since he wrote her a farewell letter aboard the *Seang Choon* on his way to Gallipoli. In that letter, he had reminded her of the easy friendship they had enjoyed since their childhood in Jerilderie. As he sailed towards that uncertain fate all he thought about, he said, was his pride in his country and his love for his family.[101] Nothing has changed now, as the twilight of his life fades.

That night Monash has a slight heart attack at Iona and is confined to bed. He has another heart attack a few days later and then pneumonia sets in. Bertha cares for him and she recalls how he wrote to her as he neared the Turkish coast and the waiting guns, telling her that she had always been 'a sweet and loving daughter and my deepest pride'.

'So dearie,' he had said back then, 'I hope – and it is my last wish to you – that your grief at losing me will be tempered by the pride you will be able to feel that your father has done his country some service. My fondest love.'[102]

On the morning of 8 October 1931, at five minutes to 11, Monash lets out a final gasp and is gone. He is just 66.

Dr Sewell informs the press and the news causes a wave of grief and disbelief around the country. Flags fall to half-mast immediately.

'He wanted to wear out rather than rust out,' Sewell explains, adding that Monash had chosen to keep taxing himself despite the warnings and that 'one could not help feel that this was the decision he had the right to make for himself'.[103] The stress of the war had largely contributed to the state of Monash's heart, Sewell says, but Sir John had decided to go out on top.

The tributes are as fulsome as they are predictable, from the King down. The minister in charge of the SEC, John Cain, says Monash's life was 'an inspiration' and that 'the history of Australia would contain no nobler record'.[104] Lou had just received her brother's letter when he passed, and says it was written by a brave man who 'never shirked an unpleasant job in his life'.[105] Even Billy Hughes, now in opposition, says Monash was the 'living embodiment of the spirit of the AIF and all its glorious achievements'[106] while Drake-Brockman, now a judge of the Commonwealth Court of Conciliation and Arbitration, says simply that Monash was the greatest Australian who ever lived.[107] Tributes are paid around Australia and in synagogues in London and Hampstead.

The funeral will be unlike anything Melbourne has ever seen.

Monash's body is taken from Iona to the Queen's Hall in Parliament House, where it lies in state with a military guard from 5 p.m. on Friday, 9 October, in readiness for the State funeral organised for Sunday, 11 October.

A continuous procession of mourners passes the coffin, which is draped controversially in the Union Jack, upon which rests Monash's sword and cap and a small bouquet of flowers from his grandchildren. Hundreds of thousands pay their respects, from the generals to the down-and-outs. People who knew him well mourn alongside those who knew him only as the wise old man who led Australia in its greatest hour. They file by the coffin 'almost without intermission until late in the night'.[108]

The same Sunday, there are 60,000 people at the Melbourne Cricket Ground to see Geelong beat Richmond in the Victorian Football League grand final. The players and officials wear black armbands and the crowd stands for two minutes' silence.[109]

Monash's funeral puts the grand final in the shade. Police estimate more than 300,000 (but some say 500,000) turn out under calm, grey skies to say goodbye to Melbourne's most admired citizen.

At 12.30 p.m., Rabbis Danglow and Brodie conduct a private service inside the Queen's Hall and Chauvel delivers a eulogy. Monash's coffin is carried down the Parliament House steps and placed on a gun carriage as 15,000 men and women of the services march past eight abreast, saluting with their hats over their hearts to the slow, solemn beat of muffled drums. Then, at 2 p.m., to the mournful sound of the 'Dead March in Saul', the gun carriage, drawn by seven horses, begins the 13-kilometre journey to Brighton Cemetery. The returned soldiers lead the procession, many struggling to cope with the walk and the vast crowds pressing in. There is an official military escort along with representatives of the Scotch College Cadets Corps and the Melbourne University Rifles. Monash's riderless charger trots along with boots reversed in the stirrups, followed by officers and brigades, the clergy, official representatives and seven cars laden with flowers.

Lizzie is not invited to participate and instead watches her one true love go past on his final journey from outside the Windsor Hotel, weeping inconsolably with a friend's arm around her shoulder. Above, De Havilland Moths and Westland Wapitis from the RAAF and Aero Club provide an aerial tribute.

Down Spring Street the mourners march slowly, and then into Collins Street, 'where the trees in new leaf add beauty to the scene'.[110] The procession passes the Naval and Military Club, which in earlier days was the German Club, then into Swanston Street and past the Town Hall where Monash once sang in Louis Pulver's Hallelujah chorus more than half a century earlier. Then it is past Flinders Street Station and over the Princes Bridge, which gave Monash his start in engineering and of which he was so proud. They move along to the unfinished Shrine of Remembrance, which is still surrounded by scaffolding. The official escort and main group of mourners stop at the shrine for another service. Chauvel addresses the crowd.

The gun carriage moves on down St Kilda Road, followed by hundreds of cars and many more old Diggers on foot; they are determined to go that extra mile for their commander.

Gershon Bennett's cousin Henry Isaac Cohen says that this is a funeral unlikely ever to be repeated in Australia; it is a tribute to a military commander who was 'patient and gentle, full of worldly wisdom. Simple in his tastes, temperate in his habits', who died as he wished: 'in harness, in the plenitude of his great mental powers, in the height of his fame, beloved of his kith and kin.'[112]

Thousands more line the route through the suburbs, where many of the houses have their blinds drawn as a mark of respect. Paddocks near Brighton Cemetery become large car parks, with about 50,000 people present for the last leg of Monash's final march. The gun carriage stops 90 metres from where Monash will be buried next to Vic. Eight Jewish ex-servicemen, including

Aubrey Moss and Eric and Paul Simonson, carry Monash to the graveside.

As Monash is laid to rest beside his wife, the 'Last Post' is played, followed by a 17-gun salute and the 'Reveille'.

'A prince and a great man has fallen,' Rabbi Danglow tells the mourners. 'We have lost a great national hero, a gallant soldier and pre-eminent citizen. His career began modestly and he grew from strength to strength through his mighty power of intellect and capacity for self sacrifice and his wonderful powers of concentration.

'His name will forever live in the hearts of his people.'[113]

Chapter 32

*When peace comes, and we are free to move about the country, no
doubt the tourist of the future will come to inspect these parts. I
suppose that some day, on some high plateau overlooking Anzac
beach, there will be a noble memorial erected by the people of
Australia, to honour the memory of their fallen dead, who lie
peacefully sleeping in the little valleys all around.*

MONASH WRITING FROM GALLIPOLI[1]

O NE YEAR AFTER MONASH'S death, Miss Lizette M.
Bentwitch places a memorial notice in the *Argus*, an annual
ritual she will perform until her own passing in 1954, when
she is buried in Brighton Cemetery near her soul mate. Her 'In
Memoriam' notice of 1934 declares that love is eternal, 'reaching
far beyond the grave'.[2]

Having already transferred much of his wealth to Bertha,
Monash leaves an estate of £27,053. Most of it, including Iona and
all the artworks and jewellery, goes to Bertha and Gershon. But
he also leaves gifts of £100 each to Walter, Lou and his surviving
nieces, Peggy and Nancy Rosenhain, and provides quarterly
annuities to support Mat (£50), his cousins Mathilde and Sophie
Roth (£50 each) and Elizabeth Bentwitch (£200), 'my friend'.[3]
There are also provisions for regular donations of £50 to Jewish
charities, animal welfare groups and the Salvation Army.

Years earlier, as Monash prepared to fight on Gallipoli, he had
written to Vic to say that the world's home was burning and that

there were now 'at a very low estimate 20 million men engaged in this war'. He predicted it would take 'months or years to quell the racial hatreds, which it has engendered, and make the world again a place in which to wander about in search of pleasure'.[4]

Just 15 months after Monash's death Hindenburg appoints Adolf Hitler as Chancellor of Germany, ushering in a reign of terror and death unprecedented in human history. Using similar attack methods to those Monash perfected at the end of World War I, the Germans over-run Poland in 1939 and then much of Europe with massed waves of tanks, aeroplanes, artillery and stormtroopers. By the outbreak of World War II, most of the Jews of Krotoschin, the home of Monash's father and grandfather, have already left for America or Australia. But the Nazis round up the last 17 Jews still living there and on 16 October 1939 deport them to the ghetto in Lodz for extermination. The synagogue that Baer-Loebel Monasch helped to build is torn apart. The memorial stones in Krotoschin's Jewish cemetery are destroyed.[5]

This second world war will be even more destructive than the first, but once again Australians will punch above their weight, influenced by Monash's example, distinguishing themselves with his mantra that 'the Australian army is proof that individualism is the best and not the worst foundation upon which to build up collective discipline'.[6] Monash's abilities and victories in France in 1918 inspire a new generation of Australian commanders such as his old chief of staff, Tom Blamey.

During his lifetime Monash argued against Melbourne erecting a statue to him, but after his passing many memorials are unveiled, at Yallourn, Scotch College and at the university. Finally in 1950 a life-size statue of him mounted on his charger is unveiled on Linlithgow Avenue near the Shrine of Remembrance.

There are the inevitable comparisons with other great military brains such as Napoleon, although Monash was nothing like the power hungry war chiefs who preceded him.

War correspondent Fred Cutlack, who writes the foreword to Monash's posthumous collection of war letters in 1934 says that while Monash had an extraordinary mind and an ability to grasp the full details of a subject, allied with that was his 'humanity ... his genial kindliness, his wide-ranging and ready sympathy, his abiding love of life'.[7]

Brudenell White says that what gave Monash most gratification was not power, nor pride of place, nor honour at the main table but rather the 'greeting at the end of the day accorded him by a devoted grandchild'.[8] And Gershon Bennett says that while Monash was 'very human, and therefore not without fault', he was the 'gentlest soul' he had ever known, whose greatest love was for children.[9]

In years to come, Monash's name will adorn a local government area in Melbourne, a Canberra suburb, a town in the Riverland area of South Australia, a Tasmanian mountain, an Israeli commune, streets and roads throughout Australia, and a major freeway linking Melbourne's CBD to its south-eastern suburbs and beyond to Gippsland, where Monash spent so many happy times. From 1996 his portrait will be displayed on Australia's highest currency, the $100 bill.[10] When Melbourne opens a second university in 1958, it will be named after the man deemed to be the greatest Victorian who ever lived, a man who made his name on the battlefield but whose abiding passion was for education; a military commander who preferred to build up rather than to tear down. In April 2015, a 3-metre statue of Monash is unveiled at Monash University by the Governor of Victoria, Alex Chernov. It was created by renowned Australian sculptor Peter Corlett and depicts Monash, as a civilian, deep in thought. In 2018 the $100 million Sir John Monash Centre, a major interpretive museum honouring the 290,000 Australians who served on the Western front, will be opened next to the imposing Edwin Lutyens-designed memorial at Villers-Bretonneux.

Monash grew up with the insecurity of an outsider, constantly trying to prove himself as the Jewish son of a German, a part-time soldier in a culture where the British aristocracy still ruled. He sometimes displayed the egotism and vanity of a man from humble origins, who from infancy had been taught that education and application would equip him to climb the ladder of life. At the heart of his very being was a devotion to serving his country to the best of his ability. Bunkered down on Gallipoli, with scenes of awful slaughter all around and not knowing whether he would live or die, Monash wrote home to Vic that 'there can be no satisfaction, in the end, in a life wholly spent in the pursuit of selfish ends'.[11]

From his days as a boy in Jerilderie herding goats and hitching rides with the bullockies, to tramping through the bush and up through the wondrous Australian Alps as a young man, and then fighting beside his comrades at Gallipoli and on the Western Front, Monash had developed a deep affection for the Australian people. He loved his country and appreciated all the opportunities Australia had given him and his family.

To John Monash, it was something to have lived for.

Epilogue

BY the end of 2015, Monash University had five Australian campuses, another in Malaysia and facilities in China, Italy, India and South Africa.

Monash is better known now than when he first sailed for Gallipoli more than 100 years ago.

Each year, General Sir John Monash Scholarships are awarded to as many as 15 outstanding graduates from Australian universities who demonstrate leadership skills and have a plan for a better Australia. The scholarships enable them to undertake Masters or Doctoral degrees at leading universities overseas.

Monash's daughter Bertha Bennett continued her father's devotion to public service – raising funds for the Alfred and Royal Dental Hospitals. Gershon Bennett ran a successful dental practice after the Great War but enlisted again in World War II and became a colonel and Deputy Director of Dental Service, based in Darwin. He died in 1955 aged 62. Bertha died 24 years later aged 86.

Their eldest surviving son, David Monash Bennett, feeling burdened by the weight of expectation as he walked through the Monash Gates each day at Scotch College, did his best to hide his family connection and served as a private in the 2/23 Battalion AIF in New Guinea and Borneo.

With an honours degree in history from Melbourne University, he became headmaster of the experimental ERA – Education Reform Association – school at Donvale in Melbourne's East.

The co-educational secondary school, which opened in 1971 with six staff members, allowed its 89 students to wear casual clothes and sit in on meetings with teachers and parents to decide school matters. David resigned under duress the following year after a disagreement with the school council.

A member of the Fabian Society, which aims for 'greater equality of power, wealth and opportunity', he became an education commissioner under Labor Prime Minister Gough Whitlam, attempting to improve schooling in Aboriginal communities. He died in 1984, aged 59.

His sister Betty Durré, also a member of the Fabian Society, earned degrees in science and education from Melbourne University and became a high school chemistry teacher. She taught at the Swinburne College of Advanced Education between 1966 and 1986 and died in 2006 aged 79.

Colin Monash Bennett, the youngest of Bertha's children, became a leading Australian journalist. He wrote for the *Age* from 1950 until 1980, served as the paper's film critic for 25 years, and became an influential figure in the encouragement of Australia's own movie and TV industries.

Monash's sister Mat devoted her last few years to charitable work and died at Iona aged 69. An accomplished linguist, she was decorated by the French Government for her interest in French culture. Monash's youngest sister, Lou Rosenhain, died in 1942, eight years after her husband, Walter.

Lizzie Bentwich kept up her vigil, honouring Monash until her death at a private hospital in Toorak in 1954 at the age of 81. Each year on the anniversary of his death she placed a notice in the *Argus* and put flowers on his grave. She is buried in Brighton Cemetery, close to her lover and his wife.

Fred Gabriel, Monash's great rival in love, died only months after Annie in 1931, in the Sydney suburb of Summer Hill. They had been married for 47 years.

Tom Blamey juggled his roles as Victoria's police commissioner, leader of the clandestine anti-communist White Army and commander of the 3rd Division in the militia, which he undertook in 1931. He was forced to resign as police commissioner in 1936 after giving a false statement in the investigation into the shooting of a police officer.

He was promoted to lieutenant general a few weeks after the outbreak of World War II and given command of the 6th Division and then command of the AIF. In March 1942 he became Commander-in-Chief of the Australian Military Forces. Reporting to Douglas MacArthur during fighting in the South Pacific, Blamey made enemies in his own ranks with his forceful character. MacArthur called him a 'sensual, slothful and doubtful character but a tough commander likely to shine like a power-light in an emergency. The best of the local bunch'.[1] John Curtin said of his abrasive ways: 'when Blamey was appointed the Government was seeking a military leader, not a Sunday School teacher'.[2] After the war, Blamey was involved in another anti-Communist group, 'The Association'. Prime Minister Bob Menzies appointed him field marshal in 1950 and Blamey died in 1951 at the Repatriation General Hospital, Heidelberg, aged 67. His State funeral was almost as large as Monash's.

William Birdwood may have been overtaken by Monash on the Western Front but he outlived him by 20 years. After his tenure as Commander-in-Chief in India he was appointed Baron Birdwood of Anzac in 1938. Birdwood died at Hampton Court Palace in 1951.

Ian Hamilton lived until the age of 94, long enough to see his Anglo-German Association, which he founded in 1928, fail to improve relationships between the two old enemies. The harsh penalties imposed by the Allies on Germany caused a festering resentment that fuelled an even more catastrophic war.

Billy Hughes was Prime Minister until 1923 and had another run at the top job in 1939, when he lost narrowly to Menzies. He was a feisty attorney-general from 1939–41. He died at his home in Lindfield, Sydney, in 1952 aged 90, while still a Member of Parliament. It is said 450,000 people lined the streets to say goodbye.[3]

Brudenell White quit the military during the funding cuts of 1923 and became the first chairman of the Public Service Board. He was recalled to active duty in 1940 but was one of 10 people – three of them cabinet ministers – killed when an RAAF Lockheed Hudson II bomber crashed near Canberra on 13 August the same year.[4] He was 64.

Ewen Sinclair-Maclagan returned to duty with the British Army after World War I, commanding the 51st Highland Division. He retired in 1925 and died in Dundee, Scotland, in 1948, a month short of his 80th birthday.

Charles Rosenthal, wounded twice on Gallipoli and again on the Western Front, became an alderman of Sydney Municipal Council from 1921–24, was the Nationalist Member for Bathurst in the NSW Parliament from 1922–25 and a member of the Legislative Council in 1936–37. Despite his successes, he was declared bankrupt during the Depression and in 1937 accepted the post of administrator of Norfolk Island, which he held until 1945, supervising tree-planting and conservation of the old convict buildings. He died in 1954 at Green Point on the New South Wales Central Coast.

After John 'Jack' Gellibrand's term as the member for Denison in Tasmania ended in 1928, he returned to farming, first in Tasmania and then from 1936 at Murrundindi, near Yea, north-east of Melbourne. He died there in 1945 aged 73 and was buried in Yea Cemetery.

Thomas 'Bill' Glasgow became a Nationalist Senator for Queensland, serving from 1920 until 1932. He was Minister for Home and Territories and later Defence. During World War II he was Australia's first High Commissioner to Canada. He died in Brisbane in 1955 aged 79.

After returning to Perth, architect Talbot Hobbs designed the West Australian War Memorial in Kings Park, and again led the 5th Division from 1921–27. He died of a heart attack at sea while sailing to the unveiling of a war memorial designed by Sir Edwin Lutyens at Villers-Bretonneux. He was 73.

Alexander Godley lived to 90 and died in an Oxford nursing home. After the Great War he was Commander-in-Chief of the British Army of the Rhine, occupying the vanquished territory, and in 1923 he was promoted to general. Knighted in 1928, he was Governor of Gibraltar for five years until 1933.

Albert Jacka VC started an electrical appliance business in St Kilda and was elected mayor for 1930–31. The Depression ruined him. He became a commercial traveller with the Anglo-Dominion Soap Company but died in 1932 of chronic nephritis, aged 39.

Harry Murray VC became a grazier after the war. In 1927 he left his wife to marry her niece. At the outbreak of World War II he became commander of the 26th Militia Battalion based in Townsville. In 1954 he shook the hand of Queen Elizabeth in Brisbane. Murray died in 1966, aged 85, after a car accident near Condamine, Queensland.

Portly Paddy McGlinn, Tweedledum to Monash's Tweedledee at Gallipoli, returned to Australia in March 1920 and was made a brigadier general in July. He went back to work as an engineer at the Post Master General's office and died in 1946 aged 77.

Carl Jess, another of Monash's staff officers, was promoted to major general in 1935 and knighted four years later. As chairman of the Department of Defence's Manpower Committee, he greatly increased the size of Australia's militia before the outbreak of World War II. His elder son, Carl McGibbon Jess, a lieutenant in the 2nd AIF, was killed in action at Tobruk in 1941. His surviving son John David Jess was a member of Federal Parliament from 1960–72.

Carl Jess died in 1948 aged 64.

Charles Bean returned to Gallipoli in 1919 with the Australian Historical Mission, which uncovered the bones of light horsemen, still lying where they fell. Bean's six volumes of the official history of the war were published between 1921 and 1942. More than once he declined a knighthood. Bean was instrumental in the creation of the Australian War Memorial.

He died in 1968, a few weeks short of his 89th birthday.

Keith Murdoch's power and influence continued to grow through a chain of newspapers and radio stations. He backed Joseph Lyons and his United Australia Party to oust Prime Minister James Scullin in 1932. Murdoch was knighted the following year. In 1942 he became chairman of the Herald group and then bought control of a company that, among other interests, published the weekly *Mail* in Adelaide. The company was called News Limited. Murdoch died at Cruden Farm, Langwarrin, in 1952 aged 69. His son Rupert turned News Limited into an international media giant.

Mustafa Kemal became Prime Minister of Turkey in 1920 and, after Turkey was proclaimed a republic on 29 October 1923, became the nation's first president. He was in office for 15 years until his death aged 57 from cirrhosis of the liver. He is credited as the driving force behind the modernisation of his country. In 1934 the Turkish Parliament awarded him the surname Atatürk, meaning 'Father of the Turks'.

A year after appointing Adolf Hitler chancellor of Germany, President Paul von Hindenburg succumbed to lung cancer at his home in Neudeck, East Prussia, in 1934. He was 86. The day before Hindenburg's death, Hitler visited him. Suffering from dementia, Hindenburg thought Kaiser Wilhelm II had come to see him and called Hitler 'Your Majesty'.[5]

Erich Ludendorff also suffered delusions.

At Hitler's prompting, Ludendorff took part in the failed Beer Hall Putsch to seize power in Munich in 1923. The following year, he was elected to the Reichstag representing a coalition of the German Völkisch Freedom Party and the Nazis. He served until 1928, when he became something of a recluse with his second wife, Mathilde, a prominent philosopher and psychiatrist.

They founded Germany's Society for the Knowledge of God and spread conspiracy theories without let-up. Mathilde claimed the Dalai Lama was the power behind the Jews and that together they were trying to undermine Germany through Communism, Catholicism, capitalism and Freemasonry.[6]

Ludendorff became a worshiper of the Nordic god Wotan and grew to hate both Jews and Christians, although when he died in 1937 it was at a Catholic hospital at Munich, surrounded by the Sisters of Mercy.

Ludendorff had also grown to hate Hitler in his final years. After Hindenburg made Hitler Chancellor, Ludendorff told the ancient president, 'This accursed man will cast our Reich into the abyss and bring our nation to inconceivable misery. Future generations will damn you in your grave for what you have done.'[7]

Endnotes

Chapter 1

1. Field Marshal Viscount Montgomery of Alamein, *A History of Warfare*, George Rainbird Ltd, 1968, p. 264.
2. Monash to his wife Vic, 16 May 1915.
3. David Lloyd George, *War Memoirs of David Lloyd George, Volume 6*, I. Nicholson & Watson, 1936, p. 3424.
4. *Argus* (Melbourne), 27 December 1918, p. 4.
5. W. Warren Wagar, *H. G. Wells: Traversing Time*, Wesleyan University Press, 2004, p. 147.
6. Ryan A. Davis, *The Spanish Flu: Narrative and Cultural Identity in Spain, 1918*, Palgrave Macmillan, 2013, p. 6.
7. *Daily Observer* (Tamworth, NSW), 31 December 1918, p. 2.
8. *Advertiser* (Adelaide), 17 December 1934, p. 16.
9. Prince George was killed in the crash of a flying boat during World War II. His brother Prince Albert later assumed the title King George VI.
10. *Brisbane Courier*, 28 December 1918, p. 7.
11. Scott Berg, *Wilson*, Simon & Schuster, 2013, p. 438.
12. Michael Paterson, *Winston Churchill: Personal Accounts of the Great Leader at War*, David & Charles, 2005, p. 150.
13. The official figure is 8709. From awm.gov.au.
14. *Argus*, 5 May 1919, p. 7.
15. David Gilmour, *The Long Recessional: The Imperial Life of Rudyard Kipling*, Farrar, Straus and Giroux, 2002, p. 250.
16. Rabbi Raymond Apple, *Journal of the Australian Jewish Historical Society*, June 1993, vol. XI, part 6.
17. Monash diary, 31 December 1882.

Chapter 2

1. Birdwood to Australian Governor-General Ronald Munro Ferguson, 25 February 1915, Novar Papers, Munro Ferguson Collection, National Library of Australia.
2. On 9 February 1801 the Austrians signed the Treaty of Lunéville, ending the war on the continent.
3. 'Dov Bear Monasz' printing press in Krotoshin', from masechet.blogspot.com. au/2012/07/dov-bear-monasz-printing-press-in-krotoshin.html. Leibush's name in German was written 'Loebel-Herz'.
4. In their everyday life, Jews named Dov in Europe during this period were usually known as 'Ber' – meaning 'bear' – in Polish or 'Baer' in German. Monash's grandfather also gave his name as Bar Loebel Monasch. From Alexander Beider, *Handbook of Ashkenazic Given Names and Their Variants*, Avotaynu, 2009, p. 25.
5. James 2:23, King James Bible.

6. Baer-Loebel Monasch, 'The life, labours, joys and sorrows of B.L. Monasch: Bookbinder, printer, publisher and innkeeper of Krotoschin in the province of Posen', translated from Monasch's original text in German by Peter J. Fraenkel, *Australian Jewish Historical Society Journal*, vol. 10, no. 7, November 1989, p. 647.
7. Joseph Marcus, *Social and Political History of the Jews in Poland, 1919–1939*, Walter de Gruyter, 1983, p. vii.
8. According to *Encyclopaedia Judaica*, the Polish troops, engaged in a war with Sweden in 1656, committed the massacre on the orders of Stefan Czarniecki, a Polish national hero. 'Krotoszyn', by Shimshon Leib Kirshenboim and Danuta Dombrowska, *Encyclopaedia Judaica*, Ed. Michael Berenbaum and Fred Skolnik, Vol. 12. 2nd ed. Detroit: Macmillan Reference USA, 2007, pp. 373–374.
9. 'The life, labours, joys and sorrows of B.L. Monasch', pp. 647–663.
10. Geoffrey Serle, *Monash*, Melbourne University Press, 1982, p. 1.
11. Julie, Marie, Isidor, Louis, Charlotte, Julius, Rosa, Ulrike, Max and Adolph survived Baer. Daughter Klara died of consumption, Hanchen and Helene from cholera.
12. Also called Chumash.
13. Dr Joseph Johlsohn (1777–1851), a German Bible translator and son of a rabbi.
14. *Monatsschrift für die Geschichte und Wissenschaft des Judenthums* was published from 1851 until 1939.
15. 'The life, labours, joys and sorrows of B.L. Monasch', pp. 647–663.
16. Heinrich Graetz (1817–1891).
17. Klara died in 1846. Baer wrote: 'It was her misfortune that her mother was too weak to suckle her and she had to be fed by a Polish wet-nurse. This was probably the cause of her consumption and her early death. At the age of two we had to give up this good, beautiful and dear child.'
18. Robyn Annear, *Nothing But Gold: The Diggers of 1852*, Text Publishing, 1999. The ships were *Hero, Himalaya, Brilliant, Sarah Ann, Statesman* and *Kate*.
19. *Argus*, 28 May 1867, p. 2.
20. melbournesynagogue.org.au.
21. The synagogue was built on the rear of a 500-square-metre site now occupied by 472 Bourke Street.
22. James C. Docherty, *The A to Z of Australia*, Rowman & Littlefield, 2010, p. 201.
23. Ann Galbally, *Redmond Barry: An Anglo-Irish Australian*, Melbourne University Press, 1995, p. 34.
24. *Argus*, 13 August 1855, p. 1.
25. Serle, *Monash*, p. xv.
26. *Argus*, 12 August 1856, p. 10.
27. *Ibid.*, 6 April 1857, p. 8.
28. Melbourne's Exhibition Building stood on the site now occupied by the Royal Mint.
29. *Argus*, 25 August 1859, p. 8.
30. Reminiscences of A. Behrend, from Monash Papers.
31. germanaustralia.com.
32. Jack Pollard, *Australian Cricket*, Angus & Robertson, 1982, p. 363.
33. The English tour was a huge success. The touring side beat the Melbourne XVIII at the MCG before a total crowd of 45,000 that availed itself of 500 cases of beer. The Englishmen eventually played 13 scheduled matches and two scratch games.
34. *The Gold Diggers* is now in the National Gallery of Victoria, Melbourne.
35. 'The life, labours, joys and sorrows of B.L. Monasch.'
36. Szczecin was then known as Stettin.
37. Monash Papers, Series 2.
38. *Ibid.*
39. Ulrike was born in 1842.
40. Monash Papers, Series 2. Also on the voyage was a young Welsh Jew, Emilia Aronson, who after marrying Charles Baeyertz became a world-famous Christian evangelist.

41. Reminiscences of A. Behrend, Monash Papers.
42. Birth notice for John Monash in *Argus*, 28 June 1865, p. 4.
43. *Argus*, 16 May 1868, p. 4. Martin died on 9 March that year, at Homburg vor der Höhe, aged 57.
44. *Ibid.*, 1 April 1867, p. 7.
45. *Ibid.*, 28 March 1868, p. 4.
46. Monash to Will Steele, 24 July 1884.
47. Monash Papers, Series 2.
48. *Argus*, 14 March 1939, p. 10.
49. Monash Papers, Series 2.
50. *Argus*, 3 August 1872, p. 5.
51. Monash Papers, Series 2. Box 113.

Chapter 3
1. *Jerilderie Herald and Urana Advertiser* (NSW), 28 November 1913, p. 1.
2. John Monash notes in Monash Papers, Series 2.
3. Bradford to Monash, 13 June 1917.
4. From *Women of the West*, a poem by George Essex Evans (1863–1909).
5. *Sydney Morning Herald*, 13 July 1869, p. 2. The town's name was then spelled 'Narandera'.
6. Naturalisation date, 10 March 1871, from *New South Wales, Australia, Certificates of Naturalization, 1849–1903*.
7. *Narandera Argus and Riverina Advertiser*, 7 October 1932, p. 4.
8. *Wagga Wagga Express and Murrumbidgee District Advertiser*, 3 January 1872, p. 4.
9. Said to be the world's longest creek at more than 300 kilometres.
10. *Albury Banner and Wodonga Express*, 30 October 1931, p. 10.
11. *Sydney Morning Herald*, 16 February 1877, p. 1.
12. *Jerilderie Herald and Urana Advertiser*, 6 June 1918, p. 2.
13. *Ibid.*, 31 October 1913, p. 1.
14. *Illawarra Mercury* (Wollongong), 10 May 1864, p. 2.
15. *Australian Town and Country Journal*, 5 August 1876, p. 10.
16. *Western Star and Roma Advertiser* (Toowoomba), 1 July 1922, p. 5.
17. Justin Corfield, *The Ned Kelly Encyclopaedia*, Lothian Books, 2003, p. 140.
18. *Jerilderie Herald*, 22 April 1948, p. 3.
19. *Ibid.*, 5 February 1931, p. 1.
20. *Albury Banner*, 30 October 1931, p. 10.
21. Monash to William Elliott, 27 May 1892.
22. *Ibid.*, 6 June 1922.
23. *Herald*, 17 October 1931.
24. Monash to his cousin Leo Monasch, August 1882.
25. *Herald* (Melbourne), 17 October 1931.
26. jerilderie.nsw.gov.au/tourism/our-history/sir-john-monash.aspx.
27. *Sun News-Pictorial* (Melbourne), 2 December 1926. p. 7.
28. Kane to Bertha Monash, 20 March 1876; biographical details from Graham J. Whitehead, *The Rev Henry Plow Kane: School Master and Vicar*, Kingston historical website, localhistory.kingston.vic.gov.au/htm/article/428.htm.
29. *Sydney Morning Herald*, 16 February 1877, p. 1.
30. Elliott to Monash, 23 September 1885.
31. 'William Elliott, Australia's Greatest Son', *Albury Banner and Wodonga Express*, 30 October 1931, p. 10. The school moved to Hawthorn in 1906.
32. *Ibid.*
33. *Ibid.*
34. *Jerilderie Herald*, 25 July 1913, p. 1.
35. germanaustralia.com.

36. *Herald* (Melbourne), 17 October 1931.
37. Bertha Monash to John, 26 January and 1 February 1882.
38. From the 1839 play *Richelieu*.
39. From the 1830 novel *Paul Clifford*.
40. *Argus*, 27 January 1934, p. 11.
41. *Ibid.*, 9 May 1942, p. 2S.
42. Public Record Office Victoria, VPRS 4966 Consignment P0 Unit 1 Item 5 Record 1 Document: Jerilderie Letter.
43. *Sun News-Pictorial* (Melbourne), 2 December 1926, p. 7.
44. *Table Talk*, 18 April 1929. In the 1940s reports appeared in the Australian press quoting Monash as saying that he was in Jerilderie when the Kelly Gang raided the town in February 1879, though Monash was actually at school in Melbourne at the time. (See *Argus*, 9 May 1942, p. 2S.)
45. Monash to his brother-in-law Walter Rosenhain, 27 March 1911.
46. Monash to his father, 1878.
47. 'Australia', by Meyer Samra, Israel Porush, Yitzhak Rischin and William D. Rubinstein, *Encyclopaedia Judaica*, Ed. Michael Berenbaum and Fred Skolnik, Vol. 2., 2nd ed. Macmillan Reference USA, 2007, p. 682.
48. L.E. Fredman, 'Levien, Jonas Felix Australia (1840–1906)', *Australian Dictionary of Biography*, adb.anu.edu.au/biography/levien-jonas-felix-australia-4016/text6369, published in hard copy 1974.
49. Australia won the first Test and the Centenary Test at the MCG in 1977, 100 years later, by the identical margin of 45 runs.
50. Maurice Brodzky, *Historical Sketch of the Two Melbourne Synagogues … Together with Sermons Preached*, A & W Bruce, 1877, p. 51.
51. Raymond Apple, *The Great Synagogue: A History of Sydney's Big Shule*, University of New South Wales Press, 2008, pp. 188–189.
52. Monash to Louis Pulver, 8 September 1885.
53. On Saturday, 2 February 1878 (*Argus*, 1 February 1878, p. 4).
54. Monash in an undated letter to his father, 1878.
55. Louis Monash to John, 23 July and 8 October 1878.
56. Myers later moved to Hollywood and worked as the Jewish consultant on the 1916 epic *Ben Hur*. His daughter Carmel became a celebrated leading lady opposite Rudolf Valentino and Joan Crawford.
57. John Monash to Louis, 10 July 1878.
58. *Ibid.*
59. Louis Monash to John, 23 July 1878.
60. Albert Behrend to Monash, 13 July 1878.
61. *Argus*, 14 October 1878, p. 7.
62. Two men charged with Ellen – her son-in-law William Skilling and a neighbour, Bricky Williamson, who probably played no part at all in the matter – were each given six years.
63. *Argus*, 18 December 1878, p. 9.
64. *Jerilderie Herald*, 18 July 1913, p. 1. As related by Joe Byrne to schoolteacher Bill Elliott.
65. Also known as the Woolshed Inn.
66. *Jerilderie Herald*, 25 July 1913, p. 1.
67. *Ibid.*, 5 September 1913, p. 1.
68. *Ibid.*, 12 September 1913, p. 1.
69. *The Jerilderie Letter* first appeared in *Adelaide's Register News-Pictorial*, 29 September 1930, p. 17.
70. *Jerilderie Herald*, 28 November 1913, p. 1.
71. *Ibid.*, 2 January 1914, p. 1.
72. Baer died on 13 March 1879 (masechet.blogspot.com.au/2012/07/dov-bear-monasz-printing-press-in-krotoshin.html).
73. The wedding was 3 April 1879 (*Argus*, 5 April 1879, p. 1).

74. *Jerilderie Herald*, 19 September 1918, p. 3.
75. Monash to his cousin Leo Monasch in Minnesota, 15 February 1882.
76. Monash Papers, Series 2.
77. *Ibid.*
78. *Argus*, 31 December 1879, p. 7.
79. *Ibid.*, 1 January, 1880, p. 5.
80. From Melbourne School of Engineering, eng.unimelb.edu.au/about/history/timeline/1880s.html.
81. Later Lieutenant General Sir James Whiteside McCay (1864–1930).
82. *Argus*, 17 December 1880, p. 3.
83. Morrison to Monash, 5 January 1881.
84. Monash to Louis Monash, 28 January 1881.
85. Serle, *Monash*, p. 23.
86. *Herald* (Melbourne), 17 October 1931.
87. Miles Pierce, *Early Electricity Supply in Melbourne*, from the 3rd Australasian Engineering Heritage Conference 2009, ipenz.org.nz/heritage/conference/papers/Pierce_M.pdf.
88. *Australasian*, 9 July 1881, p. 5S.
89. *Argus*, 17 December 1881, p. 10.
90. Serle, *Monash*, p. 21.
91. Monash diary, 27 January 1882.
92. Leo Monasch was the son of Baer's oldest son Isidor, who migrated to Minnesota. Census records sometimes also record the surname of Leo and his brother Gustav as 'Monash'.
93. John to Leo Monasch, 15 February 1882.
94. Bertha to John, 26 January 1882.

Chapter 4
1. Monash diary, 18 August 1884.
2. Monash to his friend Will Steele, 15 April 1883.
3. Monash to Eva Blashki, 26 July 1886.
4. Guérin became the first woman to graduate from an Australian university when she gained her Bachelor of Arts in December 1883.
5. Monash diary, 6 March 1882.
6. Monash to Will Steele, 15 April 1883.
7. Louis Monash to John, 15 July 1881, 28 February 1882, and 6 March, 26 March and 13 April 1882.
8. *Argus*, 20 August 1932, p. 6.
9. John Monash to Louis, 26 July 1882.
10. Ecclesiastes 9:10, King James Bible.
11. Commonplace Book, Monash Papers, Series 14.
12. Monash to Pulver, 8 September 1885.
13. The *Australian Dictionary of Biography* reports that during a séance in Canada led by John Saunders, Walker burned himself with the phosphorus he used to make illuminated writing. Saunders helped extinguish the fire but died from tetanus three weeks later as a result of the burns he also suffered. F. B. Smith, 'Walker, Thomas (1858–1932)', *Australian Dictionary of Biography*, adb.anu.edu.au/biography/walker-thomas-4789/text7975, published in hard copy 1976.
14. *Australasian Sketcher with Pen and Pencil*, 1 July 1882, p. 199.
15. Monash diary, 1 May 1882.
16. *Ibid.*, 27 June 1882.
17. *Ibid.*, 31 July 1882.
18. *Ibid.*, 13 September 1885.
19. *Ibid.*, 28 April 1889.
20. He also used the alias Julian Thomas.

21. Monash diary, September 1883.
22. *Ibid.*, 13 August 1882.
23. *Ibid.*, October 1882.
24. space.com/3366-greatest-comets-time.html.
25. Monash diary, 25 November 1882.
26. *Argus*, 1 December 1882, p. 9.
27. Edward Bulwer, Lord Lytton, *Kenelm Chillingly*, Hunter, Rose and Company, 1873, p. 155.
28. Monash Papers. Series 11. Box 205.
29. Elliott resigned his job as the Jerilderie headmaster to buy the paper three years later. *Australian Town and Country Journal*, 28 February 1885, p. 16.
30. Monash diary, 31 December 1882.
31. Monash to Arthur Hyde, 9 January 1883.
32. Monash to Will Steele, 13 February 1883.
33. *Ibid.*
34. *Ibid.*
35. Arthur Hyde to Monash, 28 March 1883.
36. Monash to Leo Monasch, 9 May 1883.
37. Monash to Will Steele, 15 April 1883.
38. Monash to Leo Monasch, 9 May 1883.
39. Monash to Sweet, 20 March 1913.
40. *Argus*, 15 August 1883, p. 8.
41. Monash diary, 20 August 1883.
42. *Ibid.*, 14 September 1883.
43. *Ibid.*, 2 October 1883 and 29 December 1883.
44. Jim Lewis, a former Scotch College student. In Lewis's notes contained in Monash Papers.
45. Monash Papers, Kate Lewis notes.
46. *Argus*, 3 June 1884, p. 7.
47. *Melbourne University Review*, Issue 1, 26 July 1884.
48. Later Governor of South Australia.
49. John to Leo Monasch, 27 June 1887.
50. The corps was formed on 28 August 1884 – from *Young Victoria: A monthly journal of the Scotch College Boys*, 17 September 1884, p. 18.
51. His service officially began on 27 July.
52. *Argus*, 15 October 1884, p. 5.
53. *Melbourne University Review*, 26 July 1884.
54. Monash diary, 10 August 1884.
55. George Farlow notes, Monash Papers.
56. Monash diary, 16 August 1884.
57. *Ibid.*, 18 August 1884.
58. Monash to Will Steele, 12 October 1884.
59. Monash diary, 12 October 1884.
60. *Ibid.*
61. *Ibid.*, 7 February 1885.
62. *Argus*, 19 January 1885, p. 5.
63. Monash diary, 17 January 1885.
64. *Argus*, 24 January 1885, p. 5.
65. Monash diary, 5 February 1885.
66. *Ibid.*, 14 February 1885.
67. Argus, 21 February 1885, p. 9.
68. *Ibid.*, 14 February 1885, p. 5.
69. Monash diary, 19 June 1885.
70. *Ibid.*, 14 February 1885.

71. *Town and Country Journal* (Sydney), 4 April 1885, p. 12.
72. *Argus*, 18 June 1885, p. 8.
73. Serle, *Monash*, p. 47.
74. museumvictoria.com.au/collections/themes/2352/p-blashki-sons-melbourne-victoria. Phillip Blashki fathered 14 children. His wife, Hannah, had four by her first marriage. In later years he designed cricket's Sheffield Shield. His son Myer became a leading artist, using the name Miles Evergood.
75. Monash diary, 19 June 1885.
76. *Ibid.*, 19 June 1885.
77. *Ibid.*, 27 June 1885.
78. Deakin to Monash, 25 July and 6 August 1885.
79. Bryan Egan, 'Springthorpe, John William (1855–1933)', *Australian Dictionary of Biography*, adb.anu.edu.au/biography/springthorpe-john-william-8610/text15039, published in hard copy 1990.
80. Monash diary, 26 August 1885.
81. *Ibid.*, 4 September 1885.
82. *Ibid.*, 6 September 1885.
83. *Ibid.*, 16 September 1885.
84. *Ibid.*, 4 September 1885.
85. *Ibid.*, 16 September 1885.
86. Monash to Jim Lewis, 25 October 1885.
87. Monash to his future wife Victoria, 7 December 1890.
88. *Australasian* (Melbourne), 24 October 1885, p. 5S.
89. Monash to Rose Blashki, 7 December 1885.

Chapter 5
1. Monash diary, 18 August 1886.
2. Michael Cannon, 'Munro, David (1844–1898)', *Australian Dictionary of Biography*, adb. anu.edu.au/biography/munro-david-4270/text6903, published in hard copy 1974.
3. *Argus*, 22 August 1885, p. 12.
4. *Ibid.*, 28 August 1885, p. 5.
5. *Australasian Sketcher*, 16 December 1885, p. 195.
6. Percy Grainger became a world-renowned composer. His lifelong obsession with sado-masochism may have been caused by Rose Grainger's harsh discipline.
7. Monash to Jim Lewis, 25 October and 24 November 1885; Lewis to Monash, 31 October and 22 November 1885.
8. Monash diary, 28 July 1886.
9. *Ibid.*, 4 September 1885.
10. *Ibid.*, 28 July 1886.
11. *Argus*, 23 March 1885, p. 6.
12. Monash to Jeanette Blashki, 4 June 1886.
13. Monash to Rose Blashki, 14 February 1886.
14. Monash to Jeanette Blashki, 4 June 1886.
15. Monash to Eva Blashki, 13 September 1885.
16. Monash to Will Steele, 8 December 1888.
17. *Argus*, 7 July 1886, p. 4.
18. Monash to Leo Monasch, 11 January 1887.
19. Monash diary, 28 July 1886.
20. Monash to George Farlow, 26 July 1886.
21. Monash to Eva Blashki, 26 October 1885.
22. Monash diary, 2 August 1886.
23. Monash to Eva Blashki, 26 July 1886.
24. Monash diary, 25 January 1887.
25. Monash to Eva Blashki, 7 October 1885.

26. *Ibid.*
27. Monash diary, 18 August 1886.
28. Janice N. Brownfoot, 'Goldstein, Vida Jane (1869–1949)', *Australian Dictionary of Biography*, adb.anu.edu.au/biography/goldstein-vida-jane-6418/text10975, published in hard copy 1983.
29. *Ibid.*
30. Monash diary, 18 August 1886.
31. Farlow to Monash, 6 June 1887.
32. Monash diary, 26 August 1886.
33. *Ibid.*, 5 September 1886.
34. *Ibid.*
35. *Ibid.*, 26 September 1886.
36. *Ibid.*, 10 September 1886.
37. *Argus*, 8 September 1886, p. 10.
38. *Table Talk* (Melbourne), 10 September 1886, p. 1.
39. Monash diary, 10 September 1886.
40. Monash to Jeanette Blashki, 23 December 1886.
41. *Argus*, 2 November 1886, p. 1.
42. Mathilde Monash to Monash, 3 November 1918.
43. Monash diary, 29 November 1886.
44. Monash diary, 15 December 1886.
45. Monash to Clara Stockfeld, 19 December 1886.
46. Monash diary, 10 July 1887.
47. The name was changed to Her Majesty's in 1900.
48. George Farlow notes, Monash Papers.
49. Monash to Stockfeld, 29 December 1886.
50. Serle, *Monash*, p. 70.
51. Monash diary, 1 January 1887.
52. Michael Cannon, 'Munro, David (1844–1898)', *Australian Dictionary of Biography*, Australian National University, http://adb.anu.edu.au/biography/munro-david-4270/text6903, published first in hardcopy 1974.
53. Monash diary, 27 April 1887.
54. *Australasian*, 5 February 1887, p. 14.
55. *Argus*, 24 February 1887, p. 8.
56. Monash diary, 21 February 1887.
57. J.B. Lewis note, Monash Papers.
58. *Sun* (Melbourne), 10 February 1933.
59. Monash diary, 6 March 1887.
60. *Ibid.*, 14 March 1887.
61. *Ibid.*, 20 March 1887. Ricardo Burt's daughter Violet died in 1883 (ancestry.com).
62. *Ibid.*, 20 March, 27 March and 19 April 1887.
63. *Ibid.*, 6 April 1887.
64. Monash to Vic, 18 June 1916.
65. *Daily Sketch* (London), 14 July 1919.
66. Monash to Leo Monasch, 13 May 1888.
67. Monash diary, 17 April 1887.
68. *Ibid.*, 21 April 1887.
69. Monash diary, 16 July 1887.
70. *Ibid.*, 16 July 1887. Murphy later became a well-known journalist.
71. *Ibid.*, 11 May 1887.
72. *Argus*, 16 December 1881, p. 5.
73. Farlow to Monash, 6 June 1887.
74. Monash diary, 18 December 1887.
75. *Ibid.*, Monash diary 20 March 1887.

76. *Ibid.*, 27 June 1887.
77. *Ibid.,* 24 June 1887.
78. *Ibid.*, as quoted in Serle, *Monash*, p. 73.
79. In 1944 the hospital was moved to Parkville.
80. Monash diary, 3 August 1887.
81. *Queenscliff Sentinel, Drysdale, Portarlington and Sorrento Advertiser*, 20 August 1887, p. 1.
82. *Bendigo Advertiser*, 16 August 1887, p. 2.
83. Monash diary, 17 August 1887.
84. *Ibid.*, 21 August 1887.
85. *Ibid.*, 20 March 1887.
86. *Ibid.*, 30 August 1887.
87. *Ibid.*, 11 August 1887.
88. *Ibid.*, 11 September 1887.
89. *Ibid.*, 12 October 1887.
90. *Ibid.*, 23 and 26 October 1887.
91. *Ibid.*, 9 November 1887.
92. *Ibid.*, 8 January 1888.
93. *Ibid.*, 18 December 1887.
94. *Ibid.*, 9 November 1887.
95. Monash to Will Steele, 16 September 1888.
96. Monash diary, 15 and 20 November 1887.
97. *Portland Guardian*, 25 November 1887, p. 2S.
98. Monash diary, 12 November 1887.
99. *Ibid.*, 1 December 1887.
100. *Ibid.*, 5 December 1888.
101. *Ibid.*, 29 December 1887.
102. *Ibid.*, 13 January 1888.
103. Monash to Will Steele, 15 January 1888.
104. *Ibid.*
105. Monash diary, 13 January 1888.

Chapter 6
1. Monash to Will Steele, 29 April 1888.
2. *Kerang Times and Swan Hill Gazette*, 24 February 1888, p. 1S.
3. North Melbourne was then known as Hotham.
4. Fellowes later became Chief Constable of Hampshire but died in 1893, crushed by a runaway horse and carriage.
5. Monash to Will Steele, 19 February 1888.
6. Ann M. Mitchell, 'Youl, Richard (1821–1897)', *Australian Dictionary of Biography*, adb.anu. edu.au/biography/youl-richard-4900/text8201, published in hard copy 1976.
7. *Argus*, 23 February 1888, p. 13.
8. Monash to Will Steele, 19 February 1888.
9. Monash diary, 23 February 1888.
10. *Ibid.*, 24 January 1888.
11. *Ibid.*, 8 March 1888.
12. *Sydney Morning Herald*, 13 March 1888, p. 8.
13. Monash diary, 17 March 1888.
14. *Ibid.*, 28 March 1888.
15. *Ibid.*
16. *Ibid.*, 28 March 1888.
17. Monash to Lowe, 5 April 1888.
18. *Ibid.*, 23 March 1888.
19. Monash to Leo Monasch, 13 May 1888.
20. Monash to George Farlow, 14 April 1888.

21. Monash to Munro, 5 April 1888.
22. Munro's reply to Monash, 7 April 1888.
23. Monash to Leo Monasch, 29 November 1889.
24. Monash diary, 18 April 1888.
25. *Ibid.*, 2 May 1888.
26. Monash to Will Steele, 13 May 1888.
27. Monash diary, 6 May 1888.
28. *Ibid.*, 31 August 1888.
29. *Ibid.*, 29 April 1888.
30. Monash to his cousin Karl Roth, 26 September 1889.
31. Monash to Annie Gabriel, 8 December 1888 and Monash diary, 31 December 1888.

Chapter 7
1. Monash diary, 26 January 1890.
2. *Ibid.*, June 1888.
3. *Ibid.*, 1 July 1888.
4. Monash to George Farlow, 22 July 1888.
5. Monash diary, July–August 1888.
6. *Ibid.*, July–August 1888.
7. *Ibid.*, 13 January 1889.
8. *Ibid.*, 25 November 1888.
9. *Ibid.*, 18 November 1888.
10. Monash to Annie Gabriel, (mid-November, undated) 1888.
11. *Ibid.*, 8 December 1888.
12. Monash to Will Steele, 8 December 1888.
13. *Ibid.*, 13 December 1888.
14. Monash to Annie Gabriel, 13 January 1889.
15. Serle, *Monash*, p. 89.
16. Monash diary, 31 December 1888.
17. Monash to Annie Gabriel, 1 March 1889.
18. Monash to Farlow, 17 April 1889.
19. Serle, *Monash*, p. 90.
20. Monash diary, 17 March 1889.
21. Monash diary, 7 April 1889.
22. Monash to Annie Gabriel, 14 April 1889.
23. *Ibid.*
24. Monash diary, 30 April 1889.
25. *Ibid.*, 6 July 1889.
26. Formal submission to O.C. North Melbourne Battery, 20 June 1889.
27. Monash diary, 23 June 1889.
28. Sarah Maria Moss (1864–1923).
29. Isabella Deborah Moss (1867–1928).
30. Monash diary, 23 June 1889.
31. John Buckley Castieau, *The Difficulties of My Position: The Diaries of Prison Governor, 1855–1884*, National Library of Australia, 2004, p. 148.
32. *Melbourne Punch*, 11 April 1872, p. 6.
33. Monash diary, 20 July 1889.
34. *Ibid.*, 14 July 1889.
35. Monash to Annie Gabriel, 10 July 1889.
36. *Ibid.*, 18 July 1889.
37. Monash diary, 20 July 1889.
38. *Ibid.*, 7 April 1889.
39. *Ibid.*, 11 August 1889.
40. Monash to Annie Gabriel, 1 August 1889.

41. Monash diary, 11 August 1889.
42. *Ibid.*, 11 August 1889.
43. Monash to Evie Corrie, 25 August 1889.
44. Monash diary, 23 August 1889.
45. *Ibid.*, 25 August 1889.
46. Monash to Will Steele, 26 August 1889.
47. *Ibid.*, 26 August 1889.
48. Monash diary, 28 August 1889.
49. Monash to Annie Gabriel, 2 September 1889.
50. Monash diary, 8 September 1889.
51. *Ibid.*
52. *Ibid.*, 13 September 1889.
53. Monash diary, 22 September 1889.
54. See Epilogue.
55. Monash to Vic Moss, 21 September 1889.
56. *Ibid.*, 29 September 1889.
57. Monash diary, 30 September 1889.
58. *Ibid.*, 29 September 1889.
59. Sometimes recorded as Dean-Pitt.
60. Monash to Vic, 25 September 1889.
61. *Ibid.*, 3 October 1889.
62. Monash diary, 4 October 1889.
63. *Ibid.*, 5 October 1889.
64. *Ibid.*, 23 October 1889.
65. *Table Talk*, 18 October 1889, p. 8.
66. Monash diary, 6 November 1889.
67. *Ibid.*, 18 November 1889.
68. *Ibid.*, 18 November 1889.
69. *Ibid.*, 26 January 1890.
70. *Ibid.*, 13 April 1890.
71. *Portland Guardian*, 28 April 1890, p. 4.
72. Monash diary, 1 April, 1 July 1890.
73. *Caulfield and Elsternwick Leader*, 31 May 1890, p. 4.
74. Monash diary, 13 July 1890.
75. Monash to Vic, 8 August 1890.
76. Monash Papers. Series 11. Box 205.
77. Vic to Monash, 7 September 1890.
78. Monash diary, 4 November 1890.
79. Monash to Vic, 14 November 1890.
80. *Ibid.*, 14 December 1890.
81. Monash to Max Roth, 24 January 1891.
82. Monash to Karl Roth, 26 February 1891.
83. Monash diary, 5 January 1891.

Chapter 8
1. Monash diary, 29 April 1892.
2. *Evening News* (Sydney), 13 April 1891.
3. Monash to Mat Monash, 12 April 1891.
4. Monash diary, 27 February 1891.
5. Serle, *Monash*, p. 104.
6. *Williamstown Chronicle*, 14 March 1891, p. 2.
7. Monash diary, 7 March 1891.
8. *Australasian*, 11 April 1891, p. 25.
9. Monash diary, 29 June 1891.

10. *Ibid.*
11. *Argus*, 28 June 1890, p. 11.
12. Monash to Mat Monash, 11 August 1916.
13. *Bairnsdale Advertiser and Tambo and Omeo Chronicle*, 19 April 1890, p. 3.
14. Monash diary, June 1891.
15. *Argus*, 7 October 1890, p. 7.
16. Moton David Moss (1857–1906).
17. *Table Talk*, 8 January 1892, p. 10
18. Monash to Dave Moss, 3 August 1891.
19. Monash to Vic, 16 September 1891.
20. Monash to Will Steele, 15 April 1883.
21. *Evening News*, 20 June 1891, p. 3.
22. Monash to Lewis, 10 January 1892.
23. *Argus*, 9 November 1929, p. 3S.
24. Monash to Leo Monasch, 9 September 1893.
25. Monash diary, 13 February 1892.
26. Serle, *Monash,* p. 113.
27. Monash diary, 29 April 1892.
28. *Worker*, 18 November 1893, p. 2.
29. *Australasian*, 16 July 1892, p. 24.
30. Later Sir Leo Finn Bernard Cussen (1859–1933), Judge of the Supreme Court of Victoria.
31. Monash to Vic, 14 September 1891.
32. Monash diary, 1 January 1893.
33. *Argus*, 28 January 1893, p. 1; *Australasian*, 4 February 1893, p. 46.
34. Monash to Leo Monasch, 9 September 1893.
35. *Australasian*, 27 May 1893, p. 46.
36. Monash to Zox, 1 June 1893.
37. *Launceston Examiner*, 25 August 1893, p. 5.
38. *Argus*, 6 June 1893, p. 6.
39. *Ibid.*, 7 September 1893, p. 10.
40. Michael Venn, 'Speight, Richard (1838–1901)', *Australian Dictionary of Biography*, adb.anu.edu.au/biography/speight-richard-4626/text7619, published in hard copy 1976.
41. Monash to Leo Monasch, 9 September 1893.
42. *Argus*, 4 October 1893, p. 5.
43. Monash diary, 19, 24 October 1893.
44. Argus, 8 November 1893, p. 8.
45. *Ibid.*, 23 December 1893, p. 8.
46. Monash to Zox, 20 March 1894.
47. Monash to Thornley, 24 July 1894.
48. Monash to Anderson, 19 June 1894.
49. Monash to Anderson, 19 June 1894.
50. urbanmelbourne.info/forum/the-australian-building-apa-building. The building was demolished in 1980.
51. aholgate.com/manage/enggabiz.html.
52. *Argus*, 28 July 1894, p. 3.
53. Monash diary, 26 July and 1 August 1894.
54. Monash to Farlow, 14 October 1894.
55. Monash diary, 24 October 1894.

Chapter 9
1. Monash diary, 10 November 1896.
2. *Argus*, 7 February 1890, p. 12.
3. *Ibid.*, 11 December 1894, p. 6.

4.   Monash to Dave Moss, 26 October 1894.
5.   Monash to Karl Roth, 2 December 1894.
6.   Cecil Edwards, *John Monash*, State Electricity Commission of Victoria, 1970, p. 19.
7.   Monash diary, July 1895.
8.   *Argus*, 3 May 1895, p. 7.
9.   Monash diary, 13 July 1895.
10. Account of the reunion, Monash diary, 25–28 July 1895.
11. Commonplace Book, Monash Papers.
12. *Age*, 15 May 1895, p. 4.
13. *Argus*, 8 September 1896, p. 7.
14. Monash diary, January 1896.
15. *Traralgon Record*, 11 February 1896, p. 2.
16. *Argus*, 16 March 1896.
17. Monash diary, 12 March 1895.
18. *Ibid.*, 8 September 1896, p. 7. The original verdict had granted them £321 plus £121 in expenses.
19. Monash to Outtrim, 29 July 1896.
20. *Australian Town and Country Journal*, 23 May 1896, p. 45.
21. *Table Talk*, 5 June 1896, p. 13.
22. *Ibid.*, 31 July 1896, p. 14.
23. *Argus*, 20 May 1896, p. 4.
24. *Australian Town and Country Journal*, 23 May 1896, p. 45.
25. *The Australasian*, 25 July 1896, p. 39.
26. Monash to Bruno Monasch, 17 November 1905.
27. Monash diary, 18 November 1889.
28. *Ibid.*, 24 July 1890.
29. *Bendigo Advertiser*, 3 October 1896, p. 5.
30. Monash diary, 10 November 1896.
31. George Farlow notes, Monash Papers.
32. *Table Talk*, 29 January 1897, p. 10.

Chapter 10
1.   Monash to Vic, 18 October 1898.
2.   Elizabeth Bentwitch (1874–1954), generally known as Lizette, Lisette or Lizzie.
3.   *Argus*, 20 August 1900, p. 1.
4.   Monash to Vic, 28 September 1897.
5.   *Argus*, 6 September 1897, p. 8.
6.   Monash to Vic, 28 September 1897.
7.   Monash to Albert Behrend, 27 June 1899.
8.   Monash to Vic, 7 October 1897.
9.   Costa Rolfe, *Winners of the Melbourne Cup: Stories that Stopped a Nation*, Red Dog Books, 2012, p. 78.
10. Monash to Vic, 3 November 1897.
11. Monash diary, 1 January 1898.
12. *Brisbane Courier*, 16 February 1898, p. 7.
13. *Ibid.*, 9 March 1898, p. 6.
14. *Argus*, 18 March 1898, p. 5.
15. D.J. Fraser, *Early Reinforced Concrete in NSW: 1895–1915*, Paper G1173 of the Institution of Engineers, Australia, 19 April 1985.
16. Paul Finn, 'Want, John Henry (1846–1905)', *Australian Dictionary of Biography*, adb.anu. edu.au/biography/want-john-henry-8979/text15801, published in hard copy 1990.
17. Michael Venn, 'Speight, Richard (1838–1901)', *Australian Dictionary of Biography*, adb.anu. edu.au/biography/speight-richard-4626/text7619, published in hard copy 1976.
18. Monash to Vic on 29 August 1898, and Monash diary, 10 August 1898.

19. On 20 August 1898. From *Argus*, 20 August 1900, p. 1.
20. Monash to Vic, 18 October 1898.
21. Monash to Leo Monasch, 1 July 1898.
22. Serle, *Monash*, p. 133
23. *North Melbourne Courier and West Melbourne Advertiser*, 7 April 1899, p. 2.
24. *Argus*, 5 July 1899, p. 7.
25. *Worker* (Brisbane), 22 July 1899, p. 2.
26. *Argus*, 21 July 1899, p. 6.
27. Monash to Gummow, 23 August 1899.
28. *Argus*, 4 August 1899, p. 6.
29. The bridge deal had originally been put together by Anderson and their trainee engineer–draughtsman Arthur Timmins. From aholgate.com.
30. Boer War Memorial (bwm.org.au).
31. *Australasian*, 21 October 1899, p. 33.
32. *Argus*, 15 January 1900, p. 5.
33. Chris Clark, 'Price, Thomas Caradoc (1842–1911)', *Australian Dictionary of Biography*, adb.anu.edu.au/biography/price-thomas-caradoc-8110/text14159, published in hard copy 1988.
34. *Argus*, 15 January 1900, p. 5.
35. André Wessels, *A Century of Postgraduate Anglo Boer War Studies*, Sun Press, 2010, p. 32.
36. *Argus*, 1 February 1900, p. 9.
37. Monash to Albert Behrend, 27 June 1898.
38. Monash to Karl Roth, 28 June 1900.
39. *Argus*, 9 June 1900, p. 6.
40. Monash to Albert Behrend, 1 May 1900.
41. *Argus*, 3 April 1900, p. 4.
42. aholgate.com.
43. *Maffra Spectator* (Victoria), 7 May 1900, p. 2.
44. From Road Bridge over the Tambo River, Bruthen, Victoria, 1901 at www.aholgate.com.
45. *Argus*, 6 October 1900, p. 14.
46. constitution.naa.gov.au.
47. *Argus*, 26 January 1901, p. 13.
48. *Ibid.*, 29 January, p. 6.
49. *Ibid.*, 30 January, p. 7.
50. *Smith's Weekly*, 10 June 1933.
51. *Bendigo Advertiser*, 19 April 1901, p. 2.
52. aholgate.com.
53. *Bendigo Advertiser*, 15 May 1901, p. 2.
54. *Ibid.*

Chapter 11
1. Monash to his sister Lou, 18 November 1902.
2. *Bendigo Advertiser*, 18 May 1901, p. 5.
3. *Ibid.*, 1 June 1901, p. 4.
4. *Argus*, 17 July 1901, p. 8.
5. *Ibid.*, 14 December 1901, p. 16.
6. *Australasian* (Melbourne), 28 September 1901, p. 23.
7. Monash to Walter Rosenhain, 8 January 1918.
8. In 1896.
9. *Bendigo Advertiser*, 4 October 1901, p. 3.
10. *Argus*, 22 December 1902, p. 6.
11. Monash to his sister Lou, 18 November 1902.
12. *Geelong Advertiser*, 26 September 1902, p. 3.
13. *Argus*, 22 September 1902, p. 5.

14. Alfred Graf von Schlieffen (1833–1913).
15. Monash to Lou, 18 November 1902.
16. *Coburg Leader*, 29 November 1902, p. 4 and Serle, *Monash*, p. 146.
17. Serle, *Monash*, p150.
18. *Ibid., p. 151.*
19. Monash to Lou, 30 June 1903.
20. Sir Edward Thomas Henry Hutton (1848–1923).
21. In June 1904.
22. *Bendigo Advertiser*, 10 October 1904, p. 6.
23. *Riverina Recorder*, 12 October 1904, p. 3.
24. Professor W.C. Kernot, 'Introductory Notes on Motor-cars', 1904.
25. Proceedings of Victorian Institute of Engineers, 7 September 1904.
26. Later Dame Mabel Brookes (1890–1975).
27. To Mat Monash, 29 June 1907.
28. Monash to Sandow, 24 December 1908.

Chapter 12
1. Monash to Mat, 23 March 1908.
2. *Ibid.*, 22 February 1908.
3. *Horsham Times*, 29 May 1906, p. 2.
4. *Coburg Leader*, 22 September 1906, p. 4.
5. aholgate.com.
6. Monash to Gummow, 26 June 1905.
7. Monash to Lou, 5 May 1906.
8. Monash to John Gibson, 20 May 1916.
9. *Ibid.*, 1 February 1909.
10. Monash to Mat, 22 February 1908.
11. Later Major General Sir Julius Henry Bruche (1873–1961).
12. Monash to Lou, 5 May 1906.
13. Monash to Mat, 22 February 1907.
14. Lou to Monash, 20 June 1906.
15. Monash to Mat, 23 March 1908.
16. Later Major General Sir William Throsby Bridges (1861–1915).
17. *Argus*, 22 January 1909, p. 9.
18. *Ibid.*, 15 March 1909, p. 7.
19. Monash to Mat, 22 February 1908.
20. *Argus*, 12 April 1909, p. 7.
21. *Ibid.*, 13 August 1909, p. 4.
22. S.F. Rowell, 'Bruche, Sir Julius Henry (1873–1961)', *Australian Dictionary of Biography*, published first in hardcopy 1979.
23. *Ibid.*, 11 January 1910, p. 4.
24. Field Marshal Horatio Herbert Kitchener, 1st Earl Kitchener (1850–1916).
25. naa.gov.au.
26. *Argus*, 10 January 1910, p. 8.
27. Monash to Walter Rosenhain, 5 May 1906.
28. Allom Lovell Sanderson Pty Ltd and Heritage Group, Victorian Public Works Department, *State Library and Museum of Victoria Buildings, Conservation Analysis*, Melbourne, 1985, vol. 1, p. 39, referring to *Argus*, 23 April 1906.
29. aholgate.com.
30. *Argus*, 7 April 1910, p. 9.
31. *Age*, 6 February 1909.
32. Peebles to Monash, 23 September 1909.
33. *Punch* (Melbourne), 5 August 1909.
34. *Argus*, 8 January 1910, p. 6.

35. Vic to Monash, 13 January 1910.
36. *Argus*, 17 January 1910, p. 7.
37. *Ibid.*, 10 January 1910, p. 8.

Chapter 13
1. John Russell Young, *Men and Memories: Personal Reminiscences*, vol. 2, F.T. Neely, 1901.
2. *Advertiser* (Adelaide), 17 October 1931, p. 8.
3. aholgate.com/marriv/oceanwrf.
4. *Singleton Argus*, 24 May 1910, p. 4.
5. Alice Keppel became great-grandmother to Camilla Parker-Bowles, now Duchess of Cornwall.
6. Jane Ridley, *Bertie: A Life of Edward VII*, Random House, 2012, p. 458.
7. Barbara Tuchman, *The Guns of August*, Bantam Books, 1982, pp. 15, 28–31.
8. *Ibid.*, p. 28.
9. Monash to Mat, 24 July 1910.
10. *Ibid.*, 6 June 1910.
11. Monash to Walter Rosenhain, 27 March 1911.
12. *Argus*, 12 November 1913, p. 1.
13. Monash to Lou, 21 November 1910.
14. Monash to Walter Rosenhain, 2 January 1911.
15. *Ibid.*
16. Monash to Lou, 12 July 1911.
17. *Ibid.*
18. aholgate.com.
19. *Argus*, 8 February 1911, p. 5.
20. *Geelong Advertiser*, 7 January 1911, p. 8.
21. *The Catholic Press*, 30 March 1911, p. 10.
22. *Kalgoorlie Miner*, 15 April 1911, p. 4.
23. Serle, *Monash*, p. 181.
24. *Reveille* magazine, 1 May 1937.
25. Monash to Schultz, 30 July 1911.
26. Monash to Mat, 13 May 1912.
27. Monash to George Higgins, 20 March 1912.
28. *Table Talk*, 26 November 1925, p. 7.
29. Monash to Leo Monasch, 6 June 1912.
30. Monash to Walter Rosenhain, 15 September 1911.
31. Monash to Mat, 22 June 1912.
32. *Ibid.*, 22 June 1912.
33. Monash company records, 2 April 1911.
34. J. R. Poynter, 'Baillieu, William Lawrence (Willie) (1859–1936)', *Australian Dictionary of Biography*, adb.anu.edu.au/biography/baillieu-william-lawrence-willie-5099/text8517, published in hard copy 1979.
35. The building was demolished in 1974. From Professor Erik Eklund, 'Melbourne and mining history', monash.edu, 10 September 2012.
36. Monash to Eric Simonson, 8 January 1910.
37. Claude Grahame-White and Harry Harper, *The Aeroplane in War*, Bell & Cockburn, 1912.
38. Hugh Driver, *The Birth of Military Aviation: Britain, 1903–1914*, Boydell & Brewer Ltd, 1997, p. 139.
39. *Sydney Morning Herald*, 17 August 1912, p. 4.
40. *Australasian*, 22 June 1912, p. 67.
41. Later Sir George Foster Pearce (1870–1952). He served as Senator for Western Australia from 1901 to 1938.
42. Later General Sir Henry George Chauvel (1865–1945).

43. Geoffrey Serle, 'McCay, Sir James Whiteside (1864–1930)', *Australian Dictionary of Biography*, adb.anu.edu.au/biography/mccay-sir-james-whiteside-7312/text12683, published in hard copy 1986.
44. Later General Sir Cyril Brudenell Bingham White (1876–1940).
45. Monash to Jim McCay, 12 November 1912.
46. Monash to Julia McCay, 25 November 1912.
47. *Table Talk*, 18 July 1912, p. 24.
48. *Barrier Miner* (Broken Hill), 2 August 1913, p. 3.
49. *Geelong Advertiser*, 24 September 1913, p. 4.
50. Vic to Monash, 26 May 1913.
51. Sir Robert Randolph Garran (1867–1957).
52. *Varsity Engineer*, December 1913.
53. Lecture, 10 October 1913, Monash Papers.
54. Monash note, 9 November 1913.
55. General Sir Ian Standish Monteith Hamilton (1853–1947).
56. *Independent* (Footscray), 24 January 1914, p. 2.
57. *Argus*, 10 February 1914, p. 6.
58. *Ibid.*, 14 February 1914, p. 18.
59. *Ibid.*
60. Hamilton to Monash, 14 February 1929.
61. *Age*, 5 March 1914, p. 10.
62. Monash to Bruche, 26 March 1914.
63. *Catholic Press* (Sydney), 9 July 1914, p. 19.
64. *Freeman's Journal* (Sydney), 9 July 1914, p. 12.
65. *Argus*, 8 July 1914, p. 12.
66. *Advocate* (Melbourne), 18 July 1914, p. 37.
67. Monash to Lou, 26 June 1913.
68. Max Hastings, 'Royal love birds whose blind arrogance cost 15 million lives', *Daily Mail Australia*, 7 September 2003.
69. Shane Maloney and Chris Grosz, 'Archduke Franz Ferdinand and the platypus', *The Monthly*, May 2011; *Sydney Morning Herald*, 22 May 1893, p. 6.
70. telegraph.co.uk/history/world-war-one/10930863/First-World-War-centenary-the-assassination-of-Franz-Ferdinand-as-it-happened.html.
71. Timothy Snyder, *The Red Prince: The Fall of a Dynasty and the Rise of Modern Europe*, Random House, 2009, p. 79.
72. Frederic Morton, *Thunder at Twilight: Vienna 1913–1914*, Da Capo Press, 2013, p. 259.
73. Luigi Albertini, *The Origins of the War of 1914*, Oxford University Press, 1965, p. 35.
74. Frederic Morton, *Thunder at Twilight*, p. 260.
75. Sean McMeekin, *July 1914: Countdown to War*, Icon Books, 2013.
76. *Weekly Times*, 4 July 1914, p. 33.
77. Gordon Martel, *The Month that Changed the World: July 1914*, Oxford University Press, 2014, p. 81.

Chapter 14

1. *Jewish Herald* (Victoria), 18 December 1914, p. 5.
2. *Weekly Times*, 18 July 1914, p. 53.
3. *Argus*, 4 August 1914, p. 9.
4. thefirstshot.com.au.
5. *McIvor Times and Rodney Advertiser* (Heathcote, Victoria), 6 August 1914, p. 2.
6. The announcement is made at 11 p.m. on 4 August, London time.
7. navyvic.net/news/newsletters/july2014newsletter.pdf.
8. A.W. Jose, *Official History of Australia in the War of 1914–1918*, published 1920 to 1942, vol. ix, p. 547.
9. A.M. Robertson, *War in Port Phillip*, Nepean Historical Society, p. 2.

10. *Ibid.*
11. Monash to Gustav Monasch in Minnesota, 19 October 1914. Leo's sons, Stanley and Jerome Monasch, eventually enlist with the American forces.
12. Monash to Karl Roth, 26 September 1914.
13. *Argus*, 24 October 1913, p. 1.
14. War service record for Karl Chaskel Roth (1869–1916), National Archives of Australia.
15. *Ballarat Courier*, 24 September 1914, p. 4.
16. Officially called the Pour le Mérite.
17. *Advertiser* (Adelaide), 16 September 1914, p. 7.
18. *Evening News* (Sydney), 5 November 1914, p. 5. William Malcolm Chisholm, the elder son of Dr William Chisholm, of Macquarie Street, Sydney, was born on 25 February 1892.
19. Spee was killed three months later along with two of his sons when the Germans lost four ships and 2200 men in the Battle of the Falkland Islands.
20. Letter (undated) from Leading Stoker William Kember to Dr F.A. Pockley, from acms. sl.nsw.gov.au/_transcript/2012/D12285/a4895.htm.
21. Six Australians in total die on the mission.
22. Bill Gammage, *The Broken Years: Australian Soldiers in the Great War*, Melbourne University Publishing, 2010.
23. *Geelong Advertiser*, 24 September 1914, p. 3.
24. Later Lieutenant General James Gordon Legge (1863–1947).
25. C.E.W. Bean Papers, AWM. Folder 138.
26. *Gippsland Mercury*, 2 October 1914, p. 7.
27. *Punch* (Melbourne), 17 September 1914, p. 29.
28. Monash to Mat Monash, 2 October 1915.
29. *Table Talk,* 3 December 1914, p. 6.
30. G.F. Pearce, *Carpenter to Cabinet*, Hutchison, 1951, pp. 124–125.
31. *Argus*, 29 October 1914, p. 7.
32. MacFarland to Monash, 23 December 1914.
33. Later Brigadier General John Patrick McGlinn (1869–1946).
34. Later Lieutenant General Sir Carl Herman Jess (1884–1948).
35. *Argus*, 21 October 1914, p. 9.
36. *Hebrew Standard of Australasia* (Sydney), 23 October 1914, p. 9.
37. *Weekly Times* (Victoria), 24 October 1914, p. 10.
38. *Advertiser*, 9 November 1914, p. 7.
39. *Brisbane Courier*, 18 November 1914, p. 7.
40. *Bendigo Advertiser*, 14 December 1914, p. 7.
41. *Jewish Herald*, 18 December 1914, p. 5. Among the Jewish soldiers present are the names Monash, Cohen, Isaacson, Jona, Rosenfield, Jacobs, Freadman, Tallenstein, Fryberg, Simons, Solomon, Buttel, Bloom, Benjamin, Levy and Sloman.
42. *Jewish Herald*, 18 December 1914, p. 5.
43. oztorah.com/2011/03/rabbi-jacob-danglow-a-profile.
44. *Jewish Herald*, 18 December 1914, p. 5.
45. *Bendigo Advertiser*, 14 December 1914, p. 7.
46. *Argus*, 18 December 1914, p. 8.
47. *Ibid.*
48. *Ibid.*
49. *Ibid.*
50. John Robertson, *Anzac and Empire: The Tragedy and Glory of Gallipoli*, Hamlyn Australia, 1990, p. 35.
51. *Argus*, 18 December 1914, p. 8.
52. *Monash*, Serle, p. 494.
53. *Argus*, 22 December 1914, p. 7.
54. *Ibid.*

55. Later Field Marshal Sir William Riddell Birdwood (1865–1951).
56. General Sir Alexander John Godley (1867–1957).
57. *Jewish Herald*, 1 January 1915, p. 11.
58. *Barrier Miner* (Broken Hill), 5 February 1915, p. 4.
59. *Argus*, 3 February 1915, p. 9.
60. Monash to Vic, 13 February 1915.
61. Michael Komesaroff, 'Brewis, Charles Richard Wynn (1874–1953)', *Australian Dictionary of Biography*, adb.anu.edu.au/biography/brewis-charles-richard-wynn-5352/text9049, published in hard copy 1979.
62. *Argus*, 3 February 1915, p. 9.
63. Monash to Vic, 24 December 1914.
64. *Examiner* (Launceston), 5 February 1915, p. 6.
65. naa.gov.au/naaresources/documents/Cousins-in-Arms.pdf.
66. The Australian transports were: A29 *Suevic*; A30 *Borda*; A32 *Themistocles*; A33 *Ayrshire*; A34 *Persic*; A35 *Berrima*; A36 *Boonah*; A37 *Barambah*; A38 *Ulysses*; A39 *Port Macquarie*; A40 *Ceramic*; A42 *Boorara*; A43 *Barunga*; A44 *Vestalia*. A41 remained in Albany for repairs after a fire in the coal bunkers. *Barunga* stayed behind with engine problems on the day of the departure. A31 *Ajana* joined the convoy from Fremantle on 2 January 1915. The New Zealand transports were: HMNZT *Knight of the Garter*, HMNZT *Willochra* and HMNZT *Verdala*. (From flotilla-australia.com.)
67. Gordon de L. Marshall and Les Douglas, *Maritime Albany Remembered*, Tangee Publishing, 2001, p. 4.
68. Monash to Vic, 25 December 1914.
69. *Ibid.*, 18 January 1915.
70. Vic to Monash, 11 and 23 January 1915.
71. William Morris (Billy) Hughes (1862–1952).
72. Vic to the editor of the *Argus*, 12 January 1915, p. 7.
73. *Argus*, 4 February 1915, p. 7. Charles Patrick Smith (1877–1963) covered the Gallipoli campaign until he was invalided to Egypt in September and in later years became a director of West Australian newspapers.
74. *Ibid.*
75. National Archives of Australia.
76. *Argus*, 8 February 1915, p. 8.
77. Monash to Vic, 18 January 1915.
78. Monash to Pearce, 13 March 1915.
79. Monash to Vic, 17 and 26 January 1915.
80. *Ibid.*, 29 January 1915.
81. A.G. Butler, *The Australian Army Medical Services in the War of 1914–1918*, Australian War Memorial, 1938, p. 64.
82. Monash to Vic, 25 March 1915.
83. *Ibid.*, 2 February 1915.
84. *Ibid.*, 13 February 1915.
85. *Ibid.*, 15 January 1916.
86. Birdwood to Ronald Munro Ferguson, 25 February 1915.
87. Godley to Defence Minister George Pearce, 30 March 1915.
88. Monash to Vic, 10 February 1915.
89. Monash relating Godley's comments to Vic, 13 February 1915.
90. Monash diary, 14 February 1915.
91. Monash to Vic, 27 February 1915.
92. Monash diary, 3 March 1915.
93. Monash Papers, Box 80.
94. Locke (1894–1962) became a major general during World War II.
95. Charles Smith to Vic Monash, 11 June 1917.
96. Charles Edwin Woodrow Bean (1879–1968).

97. Later Sir Keith Arthur Murdoch (1885–1952).
98. Bean, *Official History*, vol. i, p. 137.
99. *Ibid.*
100. Monash to Vic, 25 March 1915.
101. *Ibid.*, 30 March 1915.
102. *Ibid.*, 5 April 1915.
103. *Ibid.*, 22 March 1915.

Chapter 15
1. Monash to Vic, 16 May 1915, published *Argus*, 10 July 1915, p. 19.
2. Speaking to the men about to attack Hamel. C.E.W. Bean diary, 2 July 1918. From AWM 606/116/1 June to Sept 1918. p. 12.
3. C.E.W. Bean reporting in *Bendigo Advertiser*, 20 March 1915, p. 9.
4. Lieutenant General Sir Harold Bridgwood Walker (1862–1934).
5. A.J. Sweeting, 'Walker, Sir Harold Bridgwood (1862–1934)', *Australian Dictionary of Biography*, adb.anu.edu.au/biography/walker-sir-harold-bridgwood-8954/text15749, published in hard copy 1990.
6. Monash to Vic, 8 April 1915.
7. Now more commonly spelled 'Moudros'.
8. Monash to Vic, 14 April 1915.
9. Group Captain Keith Isaacs, RAAF (ret.), 'Wings over Gallipoli', *Defence Force Journal, Gallipoli 75th Anniversary 1915–1990*, no. 81, March–April 1990, p. 7.
10. Michael Lawriwsky, *Return of the Gallipoli Legend: Jacka VC*, Harlequin, 2011.
11. Alfred Herbert Love diary, January to 25 April 1915, MS 9603, State Library of Victoria.
12. L.M. Newton, *The Story of the Twelfth: A Record of the 12th Battalion, AIF During the Great War of 1914–1918*, 12th Battalion Association, 1925, p. 58.
13. Monash to Vic, 24 April 1915.
14. *Ibid.*, 25 April 1915.
15. *Evening Post* (Wellington, New Zealand), 26 October 1915, p. 7.
16. Sir Ian Hamilton, *Gallipoli Diary, Volume I*, George H. Doran, 1920, p. 126.
17. Later Major General Ewen George Sinclair-Maclagan (1868–1948).
18. Hugh Dolan, *36 Days: The Untold Story Behind the Gallipoli Landings*, Pan Australia, 2010, p. 301.
19. Alfred Love diary.
20. Les Carlyon, *The Great War*, Picador, 2007, p. 129.
21. Bean, *Official History*, vol. i, p. 252.
22. Generalleutnant Otto Liman von Sanders (1855–1929).
23. Mustafa Kemal Atatürk (1881–1938).
24. anzacsite.gov.au/2visiting/walk_11turkish.html.
25. Frank Walker, 'Bravery of first Anzac to hit the beach at Gallipoli', *Sun-Herald* (Sydney), 17 April 2005. Duncan Chapman died at Pozières, France, in 1916.
26. Lawriwsky, *Jacka VC*.
27. Monash to Vic, 25 April 1915.
28. Bean, *Official History*, vol. i, pp. 256–257.
29. Later Captain Albert Jacka VC, MC and Bar (1893–1932).
30. Alfred Love diary.
31. John (Jack) Simpson Kirkpatrick (1892–1915). He enlisted in Perth as John Simpson, probably because he did not want to use his real name, as he had deserted from the merchant navy five years before.
32. Diary of Irish Guards captain Aubrey Herbert, 10 May 1915.
33. Monash to HQ, NZ and A Division, 20 May 1915.
34. *Ibid.*
35. General Sir Ian Hamilton, *Gallipoli Diary Volume 1*, George H. Doran, 1920, p. 143.
36. *Ibid.*

37. Patrick Balfour, Baron Kinross, *Atatürk: The Rebirth of a Nation*, K. Rustem, 1981, p. 78.
38. Alfred Love diary.
39. Michael Lawriwsky, *Return of The Gallipoli Legend: Jacka VC.*
40. *Ibid.*
41. Monash diary, 26 April 1915.
42. Later Major Percy Charles Herbert Black (1877–1917).
43. Later Lieutenant Colonel Henry William (Harry) Murray VC (1880–1966).
44. Lawriwsky, *Jacka VC.*
45. Bean, *Official History*, vol. i, p. 500.
46. Locke war diary, Monash Papers, AWM. Series 3.
47. Alfred Love diary.
48. Later Brigadier General Henry Normand MacLaurin (1878–1915), promoted posthumously.
49. *Australasian*, 27 April 1935, p. 8.
50. Les Carlyon, *Gallipoli*, Pan Macmillan, 2001, p. 222.
51. Francis Duncan Irvine (1875–1915).
52. Glenn Wahlert and Russell Linwood, *One Shot Kills: A History of Australian Sniping*, Big Sky Publishing, 2014, p. 31.
53. Ion Llewellyn Idriess, OBE (1889–1979), later a prolific Australian author.
54. Wahlert and Linwood, *One Shot Kills*, p. 29.
55. *Argus*, 28 July 1915, p. 9.
56. *Sun* (Melbourne), 22 August 1925.
57. Margetts letter, 23 May 1915, Australian War Memorial.
58. *Evening Post* (Wellington, New Zealand), 24 September 1915, p. 7. Frederick Walter Skelsey (1881–1956).
59. Monash to Vic, 16 May 1915.
60. Bean, *Official History*, vol. i, pp. 597–598.
61. Carl Jess diary. Imperial War Museum.
62. John Laffin, *Damn the Dardanelles!: The Story of Gallipoli*, Doubleday, 1980, p. 76.
63. Bean, *Official History*, vol. i, p. 281.
64. *Ibid.*, p. 598.
65. *Daily News* (Perth) 12 July 1915, p. 6.
66. Monash to Vic, 16 May 1915.
67. Later Field Marshal Sir Thomas Albert Blamey (1884–1951).
68. Bean diary, 3 May 1915.
69. *Ibid.*
70. *Ibid.*, 3 December 1917.
71. Bean, *Official History*, vol. vi, p. 205.
72. Later Major General James Harold Cannan (1882–1976).
73. Monash official report, 12 May 1915, Monash Papers.
74. Private Frank T. Makinson, Makinson letter diaries, 10 April 1915 to 3 January 1916, Frank T. Makinson Collection, State Library of New South Wales. Makinson, a solicitor's managing clerk from Neutral Bay, Sydney, enlisted at the age of 35 and embarked from Melbourne on the *Ulysses* with Monash on 22 December 1914. He served in the 13th Battalion at Gallipoli, and was killed in action in France on 29 August 1916.
75. Monash diary, 17 May 1915.
76. Monash to Vic, 14 May 1915.
77. *Ibid.*, 30 May 1915.
78. *Ibid.*, 16 May 1915.
79. *Ibid.*, 18 July 1915.
80. *Ibid.*, 16 May 1915.
81. *Ibid.*
82. *Ibid.*, 8 and 14 June 1915.
83. Monash to Bert, 7 June 1915.

84. *Ibid.*
85. Sir David Orme Masson (1858–1937).
86. Monash to Professor David Masson, 14 June 1915.
87. Monash to Vic, 27 May 1915.
88. *Ibid.*, 16 May 1915.
89. *Ibid.*, 30 May 1915.
90. Roland Perry, *The Australian Light Horse: The Magnificent Australian Force and Its Decisive Victories in Arabia in World War I*, Hachette, 2010.
91. Later Baron Richard Gavin Gardiner Casey (1890–1976) Governor-General of Australia 1965–1969, Australian Treasurer 1935–1939.
92. Bridges's horse Sandy, stabled in Egypt when the general was killed, was the only Australian Waler horse to return from World War I. Strict quarantine rules meant that 11,000 horses in the Middle East were sold to the British Army as remounts for Egypt and India, while others were destroyed. Sandy lived at the Remount Depot at Maribyrnong, before being put down in 1923 because of ill health.

Chapter 16
1. Monash to Vic, 31 May, 3 June 1915.
2. *Ibid.*, 18 July 1915.
3. Mehmed Esad Pasha (1862–1952), also known as Mehmet Esat Bülkat.
4. *Bendigonian*, 12 August 1915, p. 27.
5. Michael Lawriwsky, *Hard Jacka*, Harlequin, 2011.
6. Keith George Wallace Crabbe (1894–1915).
7. Bean, *Official History*, vol. ii, pp. 149–150.
8. Edward J. Erickson, *Ordered to Die: A History of the Ottoman Army in the First World War*, Greenwood Publishing Group, 2001, p. 87.
9. Monash diary, 19 May 1915.
10. Alec Jeffrey Hill, *Chauvel of the Light Horse: A Biography of General Sir Harry Chauvel*, Melbourne University Press, 1978.
11. Monash to Bert, 6 June 1915.
12. Monash diary, 21 May 1915.
13. Monash to Bert, 6 June 1915.
14. *Herald* (Melbourne), 9 October 1931.
15. Monash to Vic, 21 May 1915.
16. *Ibid.*, 27 May 1915.
17. Monash to Bert, 7 June 1915.
18. Granville John Burnage (1858–1945).
19. D.V. Goldsmith, 'Burnage, Granville John (1858–1945)', *Australian Dictionary of Biography*, adb.anu.edu.au/biography/burnage-granville-john-5433/text9215, published in hard copy 1979.
20. *Reveille* magazine, 1 September 1939.
21. Walter Rosenhain to Mat Monash, 3 November 1915.
22. *Argus*, 10 July 1915, p. 19.
23. *Kalgoorlie Miner*, 28 July 1915, p. 6.
24. *Ibid.*
25. Monash to Charles Smith, 3 June 1915.
26. *Argus*, 14 June 1915, p. 9.
27. Monash to Vic, 25 September 1915.
28. *Ibid.*, 18 July 1915.
29. Bob Courtney (Senior Curator of Heraldry and Weapons, Australian War Memorial), 'Anzac: Gallipoli marksman', Joint Imperial War Museum–Australian War Memorial Battlefield Study Tour to Gallipoli, September 2000, archive.iwm.org.uk/upload/package/2/gallipoli/pdf_files/Gallmark.pdf.
30. Brian Tate, 'The assassin of Gallipoli', *Courier-Mail* (Brisbane), 24 April 1993.

31. John Hamilton, *Gallipoli Sniper: The Life of Billy Sing*, Pan Macmillan, 2008, p. 6.
32. On 26 August 1915. From National Archives of Australia.
33. Wahlert and Linwood, *One Shot Kills*, p. 48.
34. Later Lieutenant General James Gordon Legge (1863–1947).
35. Gavin Souter, *Lion & Kangaroo: The Initiation of Australia*, Sun, 1992, p. 223.
36. Later Major General Sir Andrew Hamilton Russell (1868–1960), known as Guy.
37. Monash to Vic, 18 July 1915.
38. Brigadier General Francis Earl Johnston (1871–1917).
39. Later Major General Harold Edward Elliott (1878–1931).
40. Monash to Vic, 20 June 1915.
41. *Ibid.*, 27 and 30 June 1915.
42. Vic to Monash, 9 July 1915.
43. The others promoted were Frederic Godfrey Hughes, Granville de Laune Ryrie, Ewen Sinclair-Maclagan and Henry MacLaurin (posthumously). From *Argus*, 29 July 1915, p. 7.
44. *Argus*, 5 August 1915, p. 6.
45. Walter Rosenhain to Mat Monash, 20 October 1915.
46. Captain Charles Stuart Cunningham to Monash, 24 July 1915.
47. *Argus*, 18 August 1915, p. 8.
48. Monash to Vic, 4 July 1915.
49. Bert to Monash, 24 August 1915.
50. *Ballarat Courier*, 12 June 1915, p. 5; *Jewish Herald*, 30 July 1915, p. 6.
51. Monash to Oscar Behrend, Albert's son, 18 February 1916.
52. Monash to Vic, 18 July 1915.
53. *Ibid.*
54. *Ibid.*, 4 July 1915.
55. Joseph Lievesley Beeston, *Five Months at Anzac*, Angus & Robertson, 1916.
56. Monash to Vic, 18 July 1915.
57. *Ibid.*, 5 July 1915.
58. Later Lieutenant General Sir Thomas Ralph Eastwood (1890–1959).
59. Percy John Overton (1877–1915).
60. 'A "duty clear before us," North Beach and the Sari Bair Range, Gallipoli Peninsula, 25 April–20 December 1915', from anzacsite.gov.au/download/dutyclear75.pdf, p. 24.
61. Charles Bean diary, April–May 1915, AWM38 3DRL 606/5/1, p. 34.
62. Monash to Vic, 16 August 1915.
63. Lieutenant General Sir Frederick William Stopford (1854–1929).
64. Monash to Vic, 30 July 1915.
65. General Sir Herbert Vaughan Cox (1860–1923).
66. Monash to Bertha, 8 May 1915.
67. Lieutenant Colonel William Garnett Braithwaite to Monash, 4 August 1915.
68. Operations of August 6 and 7, from Australian War Memorial 3DRL/2316, Monash Personal Files Book 6, 3 August – 7 August 1915 RCDIG0000592.
69. *Sun*, 11 October 1931.
70. *Ibid.*
71. Monash to Vic, 6 August 1915.
72. *Ibid.*
73. Address delivered by Monash to 4th Brigade officers and NCOs, 6 August 1915.
74. Bean, *Official History*, vol. vi, pp. 205–206.
75. Monash to Vic, 5 September 1915.
76. Carlyon, *Gallipoli*, p. 380.
77. Bean, *Official History*, vol. ii, p. 584.
78. Peter Pedersen, *Monash as Military Commander*, Melbourne University Press, 1985, p. 92.
79. Monash to Vic, 16 August 1915.
80. Bean, *Official History*, vol. ii, p. 576.

81. *Ibid.*, p. 585.
82. Monash to Vic, 16 August 1915.
83. Bean, *Official History*, vol. ii, pp. 588–589.
84. Lieutenant Colonel Leslie Edward Tilney (1870–1937).
85. Monash to Vic, 16 August 1915.
86. Ashley Ekins (ed.), *Gallipoli: A Ridge Too Far*, Exisle Publishing, 2013, p. 134.
87. Bean, *Official History*, vol. ii, p. 591.
88. Monash to Vic, 16 August 1915.
89. *Ibid.*
90. *Ibid.*
91. Ekins (ed.), *Gallipoli: A Ridge Too Far*, p. 133.
92. *Ibid.*, p. 134.
93. John Robertson, *Anzac and Empire: The Tragedy and Glory of Gallipoli*, Cooper, 1990, p. 105 (from Allanson's diary and papers, Imperial War Museum, London).
94. Robert Rhodes James, *Gallipoli*, Batsford, 1965, p. 272.
95. *Ibid.*
96. In his 16 August 1915 letter home, Monash wrote: 'The Indian Brigade came up on our right, but did not do nearly so well. When they lose their officers – as they did heavily on this morning – the men are rather helpless – altho' they are fine soldierly fellows.' The letter was published in F.M. Cutlack (ed.), *War Letters of General Monash*, Angus & Robertson, 1934, which Cutlack said showed the egotism of 'the old chap' (Monash). Allanson made no mention of the alleged incident when appearing before the Dardanelles Commission in 1917, nor did he mention it when discussing incompetent commanders of the August Offensive with C.E.W. Bean.
97. Ekins (ed.), *Gallipoli: A Ridge Too Far*, p. 134.
98. Bean, *Official History*, vol. ii, p. 653.
99. Monash diary, 7 August 1915.
100. Ekins (ed.), *Gallipoli: A Ridge Too Far*, p. 137.
101. Bean, *Official History*, vol. ii, p. 664.
102. *Ibid.*, p. 656.
103. Ekins (ed.), *Gallipoli: A Ridge Too Far*, p. 137.
104. Later Lieutenant Colonel John Murray Rose (1865–1948).
105. Bean, *Official History*, vol. ii, p. 662.
106. *Ibid.*, p. 664.
107. Ekins (ed.), *Gallipoli: A Ridge Too Far*, p. 137
108. Bean, *Official History*, vol. ii, p. 663. Some of the men subsequently died in Turkish prison camps.
109. Papers of Senator George Pearce.
110. Later Lieutenant Colonel Legge (1896–1940).
111. Monash to Vic, 16 August 1915.
112. *Ibid.*, 12 August 1915.
113. *Ibid.*, 16 August 1915.
114. *Ibid.*, 5 September 1915.
115. *Ibid.*, 30 August 1915.
116. *Ibid.*, 9 to 10 October 1915.

Chapter 17
1. *Ibid.*, 5 September 1915.
2. *Ibid.*, 16 August 1915.
3. *Ibid.*, 9 to 10 October 1915.
4. *Ibid.*, 4 October 1915.
5. *Ibid.*, 30 August 1915.
6. Monash diary, 9 August 1915.
7. Monash to Vic, 5 September 1915.

8.   *Ibid.*
9.   *Ibid.*, 15 January 1916.
10. *Ibid.*, 5 September 1915.
11. *Ibid.*, 25 September 1915.
12. Monash lecture to officers, October 1916, Monash Papers. AWM. Series 3.
13. Monash to Godley, 24 August 1915.
14. Monash lecture to officers, October 1916.
15. Monash diary, 27 August 1915.
16. Monash to Walter Rosenhain, 26 September 1915.
17. Monash to Godley, 28 August 1915.
18. Monash to Vic, 5 September 1915.
19. *Ibid.*
20. *Ibid.*, 20 September 1915.
21. Monash to John Gibson, 8 September 1915.
22. Ellis Ashmead-Bartlett to Herbert Asquith, State Library of New South Wales.
23. Bean diary, 29 September 1915.
24. Monash to Vic, 20 September 1915.
25. *Ibid.*, 4 October 1915.
26. *Ibid.*, 6 December 1915.
27. *Ibid.*, 20 September 1915.
28. Monash to Bert, 2 October 1915.
29. War service record for William Thomas Dawson, National Archives of Australia.
30. Monash to Vic, 6 December 1915.
31. *Ibid.*
32. War service record for Gordon Escott Gabriel (1885–1964), National Archives of Australia.
33. Billie Card to Monash, 5 October 1915.
34. Monash to Colonel Chaytor (later Major General Sir Edward Walter Clervaux Chaytor), 3 October 1915.
35. Monash to Vic, 9, 10 October 1915.
36. Murdoch to Andrew Fisher, 23 September 1915, Murdoch Papers, MS 2823, National Library of Australia.
37. Murdoch to Andrew Fisher, 23 September 1915.
38. *Ibid.*
39. Monash to Walter Rosenhain, 17 October 1915.
40. Monash to Vic, 9, 10 October 1915.
41. *Ibid.*, 13 October 1915.
42. Monash diary, 13 October 1915.
43. Monash to Vic, 19 October 1915.
44. *Ibid.*, 1 November 1915.
45. *Ibid.*, 10 November 1915.
46. *Ibid.*
47. *Ibid.*, 13 November 1915.
48. Later Major General William Holmes (1862–1917).
49. Monash to Chauvel, 14 November 1915.
50. Birdwood to Monash, 25 November 1915.
51. Monash Papers, Series 2.
52. War service record for Karl Chaskel Roth (1869–1916), National Archives of Australia.
53. Monash to Vic, 1 December 1915.
54. *Ibid.*, 6 December 1915.
55. *Ibid.*
56. Monash to Walter Rosenhain, 10 December 1915.
57. *Ibid.*
58. *Ibid.*

59. General Sir Charles Carmichael Monro, 1st Baronet of Bearcrofts (1860–1929).
60. Monash to Vic, 6 December 1915.
61. Monash to Theodore Fink, 11 December 1915.
62. Monash to Walter Rosenhain, 10 December 1915.
63. Monash to Vic, 12 December 1915.
64. The evacuation of Anzac, from anzacsite.gov.au.
65. Monash to Vic, 12 December 1915.
66. *Ibid.*, 15 December 1915.
67. *Ibid.*, 14 December 1915.
68. *Ibid.*, 16 December 1915.
69. *Ibid.*
70. *Ibid.*, 18 December 1915.
71. *Ibid.*
72. *Ibid.*, 19 December 1915.
73. *Age*, 1 February 1916. p. 7.
74. *Register News-Pictorial* (Adelaide), 26 April 1929, p. 30.
75. Monash to Vic, 20 December 1915.
76. Monash to Bert, 22 April 1916.
77. *Ibid.*, 20 December 1915.

Chapter 18
1. Monash to Vic, 18 June 1916.
2. Monash to Billie Card, 27 January 1916.
3. *Argus*, 26 April 1924, p. 16.
4. Monash to Vic, 26 January 1917.
5. Carlyon, *Gallipoli*, p. 345.
6. Birdwood to Munro Ferguson, 26 November 1915.
7. Bean diary, 30 August 1915. AWM38 3DRL 606/10/1, June –Sept 1915, p. 114.
8. Bean, *Official History*, vol. vi, pp. 205–206.
9. Bean diary, 15 and 21 August 1915.
10. *Herald* (Melbourne), 9 October 1931.
11. Vic to Monash, 25 July 1915.
12. Monash to Vic, 23 December 1915.
13. *Ibid.*, 30 December 1915.
14. *Ibid.*, 9 January 1916.
15. General Sir Archibald James Murray (1860–1945).
16. Monash to Vic, 15 January 1916.
17. Monash to Billie Card, 27 January 1916.
18. War service record for Karl Chaskel Roth (1869–1916), National Archives of Australia. Date of discharge 26 June 1916, date of death 21 July 1916.
19. Aubrey Moton Abraham Moss (1887–1944).
20. Eric Laudon Simonson (1894–1954), Paul William Simonson (1895–1966).
21. Monash Papers, Series 2.
22. Monash to Vic, 27 January 1916.
23. *Ibid.*, 5 March 1916.
24. *Ibid.*, 14 February 1916.
25. *Ibid.*, 5 March 1916.
26. *Ibid.*, 15 February 1916.
27. *Ibid.*
28. *Ibid.*, 5 March 1916.
29. Monash to McCay, 11 February 1916.
30. Monash to Vic, 22 April 1916.
31. *Ibid.*, 5 March 1916.
32. Pearce to Birdwood, 4 February 1916.

33. Birdwood to Pearce, 24 March 1916, Bean Papers.
34. Serle, *Monash*, p. 259.
35. Later Major General James Murdoch Archer Durrant (1885–1963).
36. Monash to Vic, 26 March 1916.
37. For typhoid and paratyphoid (Bean, *Official History*, vol. ii, p. 70).
38. E.J. Rule, *Jacka's Mob*, Angus & Robertson, 1933, pp. 36–37.
39. Monash to Vic, 29 March 1916.
40. *Ibid.*, 8 April 1916.
41. Monash papers, Series 2, Box 107.
42. Monash to Vic, 15 April 1916.
43. *Ibid.*
44. *Ibid.*, 8 April 1916.
45. *Ibid.*, 22 April 1916.
46. *Ibid.*, 30 April 1916.
47. *Ibid.*
48. *Ibid.*, 26 April 1916.
49. *Ibid.*
50. *Ibid.*
51. *Ibid.*, 15 May 1916.
52. Bean, *Official History*, vol. vi, pp. 205–206.
53. Monash diary, 29 April 1916.
54. Leslie Edward Tilney (1870–1937). His son Lieutenant Leslie Tilney Junior died as a prisoner of the Germans in 1944.
55. Captain Dr W.J. E. Phillips to Monash, 18 August 1916.
56. Monash to McGlinn, 30 April 1916, Monash to McCay, 10 May 1916.
57. John Monash, *Australian Victories in France in 1918*, Hutchinson & Co., 1920, p. 294.
58. Cox to Birdwood, 3 May 1916.
59. Monash to Walter Rosenhain, 12 May 1916.
60. Godley to Birdwood, 20 May 1916.
61. Godley to Pearce, 31 May 1916, Godley Papers, Australian War Memorial.
62. The wreckage was discovered in 2011 off the island of Bergeggi, Italy, at a depth of 630 metres.
63. Monash to Vic, 28 May 1916.
64. *Ibid.*, 12 June 1916.
65. *Ibid.*, 22 July 1916.
66. General Henry Seymour Rawlinson, 1st Baron Rawlinson (1864–1925).
67. Monash to McGlinn, 18 June 1916.
68. Later Major-General George Hanbury Noble Jackson (1876–1958).
69. Monash to Vic, 24 June 1916.
70. David Coombes, *Crossing the Wire*, Big Sky Publishing, 2011.
71. Harold Boyd Wanliss (1891–1917), promoted to captain in March 1917 and killed at Polygon Wood, Belgium, six months later.
72. Bean, *Official History*, vol. iii, p. 301.
73. *Ibid.*, p. 302.
74. Monash to Walter Rosenhain, 3 July 1916.
75. The Germans claimed they suffered six dead and 46 wounded (Bean, *Official History*, vol. iii, p. 302).
76. Monash to Vic, 18 July 1916.
77. Later Major General and Senator Charles Henry Brand (1873–1961).
78. Lieutenant Thomas Percival Chataway, 'Death rides aboard', unpublished manuscript, quoted in Coombes, *Crossing the Wire*, 2011.
79. Louis Isaac Goldstein to Monash, 16 July 1916. In November 1918 Goldstein changed his name to Louis John Goldie.

Chapter 19

1. Henry Egryn Williams (1897–1916), of the 60th Battalion, died from his wounds on 18 August 1916 in a hospital at Chelmsford, Essex. His letter was dated 17 July, two days before the battle, and was found in his breast pocket (Bean, *Official History*, vol. iii, p. 118).
2. Monash to Vic, 22 July 1916.
3. *Ibid.*, 18 July 1916.
4. *Ibid.*, 22 July 1916.
5. *Ibid.*, 6 November 1916.
6. Patrick Marnham, *Wild Mary: A Life of Mary Wesley*, Random House, 2014, p. 17.
7. As Mary Wesley CBE (1912–2002).
8. Violet Farmar to Vic, 26 September 1916.
9. The number was more than the combined Australian deaths from the Boer War, Korean War and Vietnam War combined.
10. Pope was eventually reinstated as a lieutenant colonel with the 52nd Battalion.
11. Colonel Guy George Egerton Wylly (1880–1962). Born in Hobart, he received the Victoria Cross for bravery in South Africa in 1900.
12. Major General Sir George Frederick Wootten (1893–1970).
13. Brigadier General Alexander Jobson (1875–1933).
14. Brigadier General Sir Walter Ramsay McNicoll (1877–1947).
15. Colin Dunlop Wilson Rankin (1869–1940) held the seat of Burrum in Queensland's Legislative Assembly for 13 years. His daughter Dame Annabelle Rankin became the first woman to enter the Federal Parliament from Queensland.
16. Major General Harold William Grimwade (1869–1949).
17. General Sir Henry Crichton Sclater (1855–1923).
18. Monash to Vic, 30 July 1916.
19. *Ibid.*, 26 October 1916. Monash believes that their bayonet training is totally inadequate for combat.
20. *Ibid.*, 18 July 1916.
21. David Charles McGrath (1872–1934), Alfred Thomas Montgomery Madden Ozanne (1877–1961).
22. Ambrose Campbell Carmichael (1871–1953).
23. Monash memo re: Rankin, 1 August 1916. AWM.
24. Monash to Vic, 11 August 1916.
25. Vic to Monash, 1 August 1916.
26. Serle, *Monash*, p. 268.
27. Monash to Walter Rosenhain, 9 September 1916.
28. Field Marshal Sir William Robert Robertson (1860–1933).
29. Major General Sir Francis Howard (1848–1930).
30. Field Marshal John Denton Pinkstone French, 1st Earl of Ypres (1852–1925).
31. Monash to Vic, 16 September 1916.
32. *Ibid.*, 10 September 1916.
33. Quoted in William J. Astore, 'The Tragic Pursuit of Total Victory: Germany's Unrelenting Offensive that Lost WWI', from historynet.com.
34. Monash to Vic, 16 September 1916.
35. *Ibid.*, 30 September 1916.
36. *Ibid.*, 10 October 1916.
37. *Ibid.*
38. *Ibid.*, 12 October 1916.
39. *Ibid.*, 26 October 1916.
40. Thomas Weber, *Hitler's First War*, Oxford University Press, 2010.
41. Monash Papers, Box 86. AWM
42. Monash to Vic, 16 October 1916.
43. *Ibid.*, 23 October 1916.

44. *Ibid.*, 6 November 1916.
45. Monash diary, 17 November, 1916.
46. Monash to Vic, 21 November 1916.

Chapter 20
1. Monash to Vic, 16 March 1917.
2. *Ibid.*, 26 July 1917.
3. Field Marshal Herbert Charles Onslow Plumer, 1st Viscount Plumer (1857–1932).
4. Monash to Vic, 2 May 1918.
5. *Ibid.*, 26 November 1916.
6. *Ibid.*, 21 December 1916.
7. Theobald Theodor Friedrich Alfred von Bethmann-Hollweg (1856–1921).
8. Quoted in Annika Mombauer and Wilhelm Deist, *The Kaiser: New Research on Wilhelm II's Role in Imperial Germany*, Cambridge University Press, 2003, p. 231.
9. Astore, 'The Tragic Pursuit of Total Victory: Germany's Unrelenting Offensive that Lost WWI'.
10. Monash to Vic, 16 December 1916.
11. *Ibid.*
12. Serle, *Monash*, p. 277.
13. Birdwood to Munro Ferguson, 31 December 1916.
14. Godley to Pearce, 11 December 1916.
15. Field Marshal Sir Douglas Haig diary, National Library of Scotland.
16. General Sir Arthur William Currie (1875–1933).
17. As quoted in Monash to Vic, 21 December 1916.
18. Allan Massie, 'Was Field Marshal Haig a hero or dunderhead?', *Telegraph* (UK), 29 December 2007.
19. Monash to Vic, 21 December 1916.
20. Jessica Bretherton, 'Life in the rear: Estaminets, billets and the AIF on the Western Front, 1916–18,' awm.gov.au/sites/default/files/Life in the rear Edited (CZ)_0.pdf. Letter from Lieutenant David Caldwell to his mother, 12 July 1916, Australian War Memorial, PR83/174.
21. Monash to Vic, 11 January 1917.
22. J.R. Poynter, 'Beaurepaire, Sir Francis Joseph Edmund (Frank) (1891–1956)', *Australian Dictionary of Biography*, adb.anu.edu.au/biography/beaurepaire-sir-francis-joseph-edmund-frank-5175/text8695, published in hard copy 1979.
23. Monash to Vic, 15 March 1918.
24. *Ibid.*, 19 July 1917.
25. *Ibid.*, 11 January 1917.
26. *Ibid.*
27. *Ibid.*, 11 January 1917.
28. *Ibid.*, 11 January 1917.
29. *Ibid.*, 30 December 1916.
30. *Ibid.*, 11 January 1917.
31. *Ibid.*, 15 January 1917.
32. Brudenell White to Monash, 12 January 1917.
33. Serle, *Monash*, p. 269.
34. Monash to Vic, 15 January 1917.
35. Bean, *Official History*, vol. iv, p. 567.
36. Monash to Vic, 12 February 1917.
37. Charles Herbert Davis (1872–1923). From J.K. Haken, 'Davis, Charles Herbert (1872–1923)', *Australian Dictionary of Biography*, adb.anu.edu.au/biography/davis-charles-herbert-5913/text10071, published in hard copy 1981.
38. Bean, *Official History*, vol. iv, p. 566.
39. Later Lieutenant Colonel William John Symons VC (1889–1948).

40. Monash to Vic, 4 March 1917.
41. Bean, *Official History*, vol. iv, p. 568.
42. Monash to Brigadier General Hubert John Foster (1855–1919), Chief of the Australian General Staff, 7 May 1917.
43. Monash to Vic, 14 March 1917.
44. *Ibid.*
45. *Ibid.*, 26 April 1917.
46. Later Major General Sir Nevill Maskelyne Smyth VC (1868–1941).
47. Later Lieutenant General Sir Joseph John Talbot Hobbs (1864–1938).
48. *Brisbane Courier*, 11 October 1923, p. 10.
49. Godley to Monash, 22 June 1917.
50. Monash to Vic, 16 March 1917.
51. *Ibid.*
52. *Ibid.*, 2 February 1917.
53. *Ibid.*, 24 March 1917.
54. *Ibid.*
55. David Bilton, *The Germans in Flanders 1917–1918*, Pen and Sword, 2013, p. 158
56. *Geelong Advertiser*, 19 April 1917, p. 3.
57. *Bendigo Advertiser*, 19 April 1917, p 5.
58. *Geelong Advertiser*, 19 April 1917, p. 3.
59. *Ibid.*, Saturday 28 April 1917, p 3.
60. *Age*, 25 April 1917, p. 11.
61. *Geelong Advertiser*, 14 April 1920, p. 3.
62. *Sydney Morning Herald*, 15 June 1923, p. 5.
63. Monash to Mrs Elsie Urquhart, 6 April 1917.
64. Monash Papers. AWM.
65. Monash to John Gibson, 29 April 1917.
66. Monash to Vic, 16 March, 25 April 1917.
67. Monash to John Gibson, 29 April 1917.
68. awm.gov.au/units/event_110.asp.
69. awm.gov.au/exhibitions/stolenyears/ww1/germany/.
70. Monash, *Australian Victories in France*, p. 49.
71. Jeff Hatwell, *No Ordinary Determination: Percy Black and Harry Murray of the First AIF*, Fremantle Arts Centre Press, 2005, p. 162.
72. Monash to John Gibson, 29 April 1917.
73. Monash to Vic, 19 April 1917.
74. *Ibid.*, 26 April 1917.
75. Dr Andrew Richardson (Historian, Australian Army History Unit), from army.gov.au/Our-history/History-in-Focus/The-Battle-of-Messines-1917.
76. Bean, *Official History*, vol. iv, p. 576.
77. *Ibid.*
78. Monash to Vic, 3 May 1917.
79. *Ibid.*, 15 May 1917.
80. James McWilliams and R. James Steel, *Amiens: Dawn of Victory*, Dundurn, 2001, p. 19.
81. Monash to Vic, 15 May 1917.
82. *Ibid.*
83. Bean, *Official History*, vol. iv, p. 576.
84. Monash to Vic, 19 May 1917.
85. Peter Dennis, *The Oxford Companion to Australian Military History*, Oxford University Press, 1995, p. 405.
86. Monash to Vic, 1 June 1917.
87. *Ibid.*, 19 May 1917.
88. *Ibid.*, 1 June 1917.
89. Bean, *Official History*, vol. iv, p. 582.

90. *Ibid.*, p. 585.
91. Monash to Walter Rosenhain, 16 June 1917.
92. Spanbroekmolen Mine Crater Memorial, Pool of Peace, Belgium, from greatwar.co.uk.
93. General Sir Charles Harington Harington (1872–1940), quoted in Ian Passingham, *Pillars of Fire: The Battle of Messines Ridge 1917*, The History Press, 2012.
94. Richardson, from army.gov.au/Our-history/History-in-Focus/The-Battle-of-Messines-1917.
95. Bean, *Official History*, vol. iv, p. 595.
96. Monash to Walter Rosenhain, 16 June 1917.
97. *Ibid.*
98. Lieutenant General Sir Leslie James Morshead (1889–1959).
99. John Carroll VC (1891–1971).
100. Robert Cuthbert Grieve VC (1889–1957).
101. Monash to Walter Rosenhain, 16 June 1917.
102. John Crawford and Ian McGibbon, *New Zealand's Great War: New Zealand, the Allies and the First World War*, Exisle Publishing, 2007, p. 299.
103. Godley to Pearce, 12 June, 8 July 1917.
104. Bean, *Official History*, vol. iv, p. 681.
105. Monash to Vic, 24 September 1917.
106. John Terraine, *The Road to Passchendaele*, Leo Cooper, 1977.
107. Monash to Godley, 15 June 1917.
108. Monash to Vic, 17 June 1917.
109. Monash to Godley, 26 June 1917.
110. Monash to Susan Farmar, June 1917 (undated).
111. Monash to Vic, 20 June 1917.
112. Mark Baker, 'Schuler's war', *Age*, 23 April 2005.
113. Monash to Vic, 1 July 1917.
114. Lieutenant General Robert George Broadwood (1862–1917).
115. Monash to Vic, 19 July 1917.
116. *Ibid.*
117. *Ibid.*, 11 July 1917.
118. Serle, p. 293.
119. Monash to Vic, 1 July 1917.
120. *Ibid.*, 26 July 1917.
121. General Holmes was killed on 2 July 1917.
122. Holmes to Monash, 26 and 27 June; Monash's reply, 27 June.
123. Monash to Vic, 6 August 1917.
124. Bean, *Official History*, vol. iv, p. 6.
125. *Ibid.*
126. Monash to Vic, 26 July 1917.
127. *Ibid.*, 26 July 1917.
128. Monash to Jobson, 30 July 1917.
129. Monash to Vic, 3 August 1917.
130. Serle, *Monash*, p. 293.
131. *Ibid.*, p. 304.
132. Plumer to Monash, 2 August 1917.
133. Monash to Vic, 24 September 1917.
134. *Ibid.*, 16 August 1917.
135. *Ibid.*, 1 September 1917.
136. *Ibid.*, 17 January 1918.
137. Farmar to Monash, 5 September 1917.
138. As quoted in Vic to Monash, 7 August 1917.
139. Monash to Vic, 10 September 1917.
140. *Ibid.*, 24 September 1917.

141. Adelaide Maud Kellett (1873–1945).
142. Eric Lawson, Jane Lawson, *The First Air Campaign: August 1914–November 1918*, Da Capo Press, 1997, p. 149.

Chapter 21

1. Bean diary, 3 December 1917 (AWM38 3DRL 606/94/1 Nov to Dec 1917 p. 56-57) and 18 October 1917 (AWM38 3DRL 606/91/1 - October 1917, p. 66.)
2. Monash to Vic, 1 October 1917.
3. *Ibid.*
4. Bean, *Official History*, vol. iv, p. 840.
5. *Ibid.*
6. *Ibid.*
7. Walter (Wally) Peeler VC (1887–1968).
8. *London Gazette*, 26 November 1917, Supplement: 30400, p. 12329.
9. Bean, *Official History*, vol. iv, p. 856.
10. Cecil Leventhorpe McVilly (1889–1964).
11. Lewis McGee VC (1888–1917).
12. Bean, *Official History*, vol. iv, p. 865.
13. *Ibid.*, p. 866.
14. *Ibid.*, p. 875.
15. Bean diary, 4 October 1917. AWM38 3DRL 606/89/1 Sept to Oct 1917, p. 16.
16. Monash to Vic, 4 October 1917.
17. *Ibid.*, 7 October 1917.
18. Bean, *Official History*, vol. iv, p. 876.
19. Erich Ludendorff, *Ludendorff's Own Story, August 1914–November 1918: The Great War from the Siege of Liege to the Signing of the Armistice*, Harper & Brothers, 1919.
20. Monash to Vic, 7 October 1917.
21. Monash to Walter Rosenhain, 6 October 1917.
22. Bean, *Official History*, vol. iv, p. 883.
23. General Sir Hubert de la Poer Gough (1870–1963).
24. Bean, *Official History*, vol. iv, p. 906.
25. Monash to Walter Rosenhain, 15 October 1917.
26. Bean diary, 11 October 1917.
27. *Ibid.*
28. On 12 October (Bean, *Official History*, vol. iv, p. 928).
29. Monash to Vic, 21 October 1917.
30. Clarence Smith Jeffries VC (1894–1917).
31. anzacsinfrance.com/1917.
32. Bean, *Official History*, vol. iv, p. 920.
33. Monash to Walter Rosenhain, 15 October 1917.
34. Monash to Vic, 18 October 1917.
35. Major William Affleck Adams (1869–1917). Distinguished Service Order.
36. Spoken by chaplain Reverend G.P. Cuttriss at the grave of Major W.A. Adams, 3rd Australian Pioneer Battalion, from awm.gov.au/collection/RCDIG0000624.
37. Bean, *Official History*, vol. iv, p. 931.
38. Monash to Vic, 18 October 1917.
39. Erich Ludendorff, *Ludendorff's Own Story*.
40. Bean, *Official History*, vol. v, p. 1.
41. Monash, *Australian Victories in France*, p. 7.
42. Bean diary, 3 December 1917, AWM38 3DRL 606/94/1 Nov to Dec 1917, p. 56.
43. *Ibid.*
44. *Ibid.*, 18 October 1917.
45. A.J. Hill, 'Rosenthal, Sir Charles (1875–1954)', *Australian Dictionary of Biography*, adb.anu. edu.au/biography/rosenthal-sir-charles-8268/text14483, published in hard copy 1988.

46. Bean diary, 3 December 1917.
47. Monash to Vic, 21 October 1917.
48. Serle, *Monash*, p. 302.
49. *Herald* (Melbourne), 18 August 1917.
50. G.P. Cuttriss, *Over the Top with the Third Australian Division*, C.H. Kelly, 1918, p. 110.
51. Monash to Vic, 21 October 1917.
52. Sir Robert Randolph Garran (1867–1957).
53. Monash to Vic, 14 November 1917.
54. Bean, *Official History*, vol. v, p. 7.
55. Monash to Vic, 14 November 1917.
56. *Ibid.*, 15 January 1916.
57. *Ibid.*, 14 November 1917.
58. David T. Zabecki Ph.D., *Germany at War: 400 Years of Military History*, ABC–CLIO, 2014, p. 792.
59. Monash to Vic, 28 December 1917.
60. *Ibid.*, 17 January 1918.
61. *Ibid.*, 28 December 1915.
62. Of the 199,677 votes by members of the AIF, 103,789 were for, 93,910 against.
63. White to Monash, 5 December 1917.
64. Monash to Vic, 28 December 1917.
65. *Ibid.*, 30 December 1917.
66. Knight Commander of the Order of St Michael and St George.
67. Mat to Monash, 3 January 1918.
68. Monash telegram to McCay, 2 January 1918.
69. Monash to Vic, 12 January 1918.
70. Monash to Felix Meyer, 3 April 1918.
71. Vic to Monash, 4 January 1918.
72. Monash to Vic, 15 March 1918.
73. *Ibid.*

Chapter 22
1. Michael Carver, *The Warlords*, Pen and Sword, 2005.
2. General Sir Walter Norris Congreve VC (1862–1927). Monash and his staff arrived as reinforcements after the start of Germany's Spring Offensive on the Somme. The quote was relayed in Monash to Vic, 2 April 1918.
3. David T. Zabecki, *Germany at War: 400 Years of Military History* (4 volumes), ABC–CLIO, 2014, p. 1346.
4. David A. Janicki, 'The British blockade during World War I: The weapon of deprivation', studentpulse.com.
5. L.C.F. Turner, *Official History of Australia in the War of 1914–1918*, vol. v, introduction, awm.gov.au/histories/first_world_war/volV_introduction/.
6. Bryan Cooper, *The Ironclads of Cambrai*, Pen and Sword, 2010.
7. David T. Zabecki, *Germany at War*, p. 792.
8. Paul Hindenburg, *Out of My Life*, Cassell Limited, 1920, p. 342.
9. L.C.F. Turner, *Official History*, introduction to volume v.
10. Astore, 'The Tragic Pursuit of Total Victory: Germany's Unrelenting Offensive that Lost WWI'.
11. Monash to Vic, 31 January 1918.
12. *Ibid.*, 17 January 1918.
13. *Ibid.*, 16 March 1918.
14. Bean, *Official History*, vol. v, pp. 44–48.
15. Monash to Vic, 15 March 1918.
16. *Ibid.*
17. He drafted the plans on 22 February.

18. Monash Papers, Box 87. AWM.
19. Later Lieutenant Colonel George Frederick Gardells Wieck (1881–1973).
20. Jackson to Monash, 23 January 1918.
21. Jackson to Liddell Hart, 4 October 1935.
22. Serle, *Monash*, p. 309.
23. Monash to Vic, 15 March 1918.
24. William J. Astore, *Hindenburg*, Potomac Books, Inc., 2014.
25. Monash to Vic, 15 March 1918.
26. *Ibid.*, 17 March 1918.
27. Astore, 'The Tragic Pursuit of Total Victory: Germany's Unrelenting Offensive that Lost WWI'.
28. Ludendorff, *Ludendorff's Own Story*.
29. John Toland, *No Man's Land: 1918, The Last Year of the Great War*, University of Nebraska Press, 2002, p. 57.
30. Monash to Vic, 2 April 1918.
31. *Ibid.*
32. Monash, Australian Victories, p. 21.
33. Later Marshal Henri Philippe Benoni Omer Joseph Pétain (1856–1951).
34. Later Marshal Ferdinand Foch (1851–1929).
35. Peter Pedersen, *Villers-Bretonneux*, Pen and Sword, 2004.
36. Monash to Vic, 2 April 1917.
37. Bean, *Official History*, vol. v, p. 174.
38. *Ibid.*
39. Monash to Vic, 2 April 1917.
40. Bean, *Official History*, vol. v, p. 147.
41. Monash to Vic, 2 April 1917.
42. Monash, *Australian Victories*, p. 24.
43. *Ibid.*, p. 26.
44. Later Major Clarence Abraham Pyke (1888–1956).
45. Later Colonel Wilfred Vickers (1884–1946).
46. Later Lieutenant-Colonel Ronald Garnet Hamilton (1887–1956).
47. Monash to Vic, 2 April 1918.
48. Brigadier General Alexander Gore Arkwright Hore-Ruthven VC, 1st Earl of Gowrie (1872–1955), later Governor of South Australia and New South Wales, and Governor-General of Australia.
49. Monash to Vic, 2 April 1918.
50. Monash, *Australian Victories*, p. 26.
51. Bean, *Official History*, vol. v, p. 157.
52. Later Lieutenant General Sir John Dudley Lavarack (1885–1957) and Governor of Queensland.
53. Bean, *Official History*, vol. v, p. 159.
54. Monash to Vic, 2 April 1918.
55. Monash, *Australian Victories*, p. 27.
56. Bean, *Official History*, vol. v, appendix III.
57. *Ibid.*, p. 177.
58. Monash to Vic, 2 April 1918.
59. Bean, *Official History*, vol. v, p. 154.
60. *Ibid.*, p. 151.
61. Monash, *Australian Victories*, p. 28.
62. Bean, *Official History*, vol. v, p. 177.
63. *Ibid.*
64. *Ibid.*, p. 179.
65. Monash, *Australian Victories*, p. 29.

66. Monash to Birdwood, 28 March 1918.
67. Monash to Vic, 2 April 1918.
68. Bean, *Official History*, vol. v, p. 163.
69. *Ibid.*
70. *Ibid.*, p. 166.
71. *Ibid.*, p. 217.
72. *Ibid.*, p. 215.
73. *Ibid.*, p. 231.
74. The German 18th Division did not compile losses for the day, but in their official history claim to have had 1819 officers and men killed during the whole March offensive. The figure of 3000 may have come from Cannan, who in one report said there were more than 3000 'killed and wounded'.
75. Monash to Vic, 2 April 1918.
76. Monash to Jackson, 2 April 1918.
77. Monash to Vic, 2 April 1918.
78. Monash to Birdwood, 30 March 1918.
79. *Argus*, 24 March 1931, p. 7. The description comes from C.E.W. Bean.
80. Major General Harold Edward 'Pompey' Elliott (1878–1931).
81. Hindenburg, *Out of My Life,* pp. 364–365.
82. L.C.F. Turner, *Official History,* introduction to vol v.
83. Winston Churchill, *The World Crisis*, Hutchinson, 1928, p. 36.
84. Monash to Dr Felix Meyer, 3 April 1918.
85. *Ibid.*
86. Monash to Vic, 2 April 1918.
87. Bean, *Official History*, vol. v, p. 189.
88. Monash to Vic, 2 April 1918.
89. Bean, *Official History*, vol. v, p. 192.
90. C. B. Davies, J. E. Edmonds and R. G. B. Maxwell-Hyslop, *Military Operations France and Belgium, 1918: The German March Offensive and Its Preliminaries*, IWM & Battery Press, 1995, p. 489 (first published 1935).
91. Monash to Vic, 12 April 1918.
92. *Ibid.*, 4 April 1918.
93. *Ibid.*, 12 April 1918.
94. Lieutenant Colonel John Alexander Milne (1872–1918).
95. Betty Crouchley, 'Milne, John Alexander (1872–1918)', *Australian Dictionary of Biography*, vol. 10, Melbourne University Press, 1986, pp. 521–522.
96. Monash to Vic, 12 April 1918.
97. Ted Smout died in 2004 aged 106.
98. Monash to Vic, 23 April 1918.
99. *Ibid.*, 26 April 1918.
100. Later Major General Sir Thomas William (Bill) Glasgow (1876–1955).
101. Clifford William King Sadlier VC (1892–1964).
102. Sergeant Roy Andrew Fynch (1891–1918).
103. Bean, *Official History*, vol. v, p. 603.
104. John Monash, 'Villers-Bretonneux turning point of war', *Advocate* (Burnie, Tasmania), 16 April 1920, p. 1.
105. Monash, *Australian Victories*, p. 37.
106. Monash to Vic, 2 May 1918.
107. G.J. Meyer, *A World Undone*, Random House, 2006, p. 558.
108. *Ibid.*
109. Monash to Vic, 2 May 1918.
110. *Ibid.*, 26 April 1918.
111. Monash, *Australian Victories*, p. 38.
112. Monash to Vic, 7 May 1918.

113. Haig diary, 17 May 1918.
114. Monash to Vic, 14 May 1918.

Chapter 23

1. Monash to Vic, 14 and 31 May 1918.
2. Bean diary, 17 May 1918. AWM38 3DRL 606/111/1 - May 1918, p. 20
3. Paul Byrnes, 'Prime Minister Rt Hon. WM Hughes visits Western Front (1918)', from aso.gov.au.
4. Monash to Vic, 12 January 1918.
5. Birdwood to Pearce, 12 March 1918.
6. Monash to Vic, 31 May 1918.
7. McCay to Monash, 27 May 1918.
8. McGlinn to Monash, 2 July 1918.
9. Fink to Murdoch, 29 May, 19 June, National Library of Australia, MS 2823, Papers of Sir Keith Arthur Murdoch (1886–1952), Appendix 1 Series 1: Correspondence, 1908–1952.
10. Monash to Vic, 14 August 1918.
11. Bean diary, 16 May 1918. AWM38 3DRL 606/111/1 - May 1918, p. 6.
12. Bean, *Official History*, vol. vi, p. 190.
13. Sir George Hubert Wilkins (1888–1958).
14. Bean diary, 17 May 1918, AWM38 3DRL 606/111/1 - May 1918, p. 20-21.
15. *Ibid*, p. 19-20.
16. *Ibid.*, 16 May 1918. AWM38 3DRL 606/111/1 - May 1918, p. 6.
17. *Ibid.,* p. 33.
18. Bean, *Official History*, vol. vi, p. 196.
19. *Ibid.*, p. 205.
20. C.E.W. Bean, *Two Men I Knew*, Angus & Robertson, 1957, p. 172.
21. Murdoch cables, 20 and 21 May 1918.
22. *West Australian* (Perth), 27 May 1918, p. 5.
23. Later Lieutenant William 'Rusty' Ruthven VC (1893–1970).
24. *London Gazette,* 9 July 1918.
25. *West Australian* (Perth), 27 May 1918, p. 5.
26. Monash to Vic, 4 June 1918.
27. *Ibid.*, 4 June 1918.
28. Bean diary, 30 May 1918.
29. Bean, *Official History*, vol. vi, p. 160.
30. Major General Sir John Gellibrand (1872–1945).
31. Monash to Vic, 25 May 1918.
32. Monash to Susan Farmar, 26 May 1918.
33. Monash, 'Leadership in war', address to Beefsteak Club in Melbourne, 30 March 1926, as quoted in Sally Warhaft, *Well May We Say: The Speeches That Made Australia*, Text Publishing, 2014, pp. 81–90.
34. Williams was killed 11 days later. From H.W. Crocker, *Don't Tread on Me: A 400-Year History of America at War, From Indian Fighting to Terrorist Hunting*, Crown Forum, 2006, p. 261.
35. Jacob Stumm was the Liberal Member for Lilley in Brisbane until 1917, his German birth hastening his retirement.
36. Monash, *Australian Victories in France*, p. 41.
37. *Ibid.*, p. 40.
38. Bean's conversation with Brudenell White, Bean diary, 30 May 1918, AWM38 3DRL 606/113/1 May to June 1918 p. 4.
39. *Ibid.*
40. Bean, vol. vi, p. 205.
41. Bean to Murdoch, 2 June 1918.

42. Monash to Hughes, 2 June 1918.
43. Murdoch to Monash, 6 June 1918, Murdoch Papers.
44. Letter drafted to Birdwood but not sent.
45. *Ibid.*
46. Birdwood's letter, mentioned in Bean diary, 10 June 1918.
47. Carlyon, *The Great War*, p. 634.
48. AIF Kit Store to Mrs Agnes Gibb, Darlinghurst, 1 July 1918.
49. Henry James Gibb, from aif.adfa.edu.au.
50. Bean diary, 15 June 1918.
51. Monash to Bean, 11 June 1918.
52. Ernest Morris (Bill) Hughes (1897–1986).
53. Bean diary, 17 June 1918.
54. *Ibid.*
55. Monash to Vic, 18 June 1918.
56. Monash, *Australian Victories in France*, p. 44.
57. Monash to Vic, 8 June 1918.
58. Serle, *Monash*, p. 330.
59. Monash to Lou Rosenhain, 30 June 1918.
60. Monash to Walter Rosenhain, 3 and 22 June 1918.
61. Later Major General Walter Adams Coxen (1870–1949).
62. Monash, *Australian Victories in France*, p. 48.
63. *Ibid.*, pp. 49, 75–76.
64. *Ibid.*, p. 50.
65. Bean diary, 3 July 1918.
66. Sir Lawrence James Wackett (1896–1982).
67. Monash, *Australian Victories in France*, p. 60.
68. Monash Papers, Box 92.
69. Hobbs to Pearce, 27 June 1918.
70. Monash Papers, Box 92.
71. Monash to Vic, 25 June 1918.
72. Bean to White, 26 June 1918.
73. White to Monash, 6 July 1918.
74. Phillip Davey VC (1896–1953).
75. Peter Burness, 'Davey, Phillip (1896–1953)', *Australian Dictionary of Biography*, adb.anu. edu.au/biography/davey-phillip-5892/text10029, published in hard copy 1981.
76. George Bell, Junior (1859–1926) was the son of Union Civil War officer Brigadier General George Bell (1828–1907).
77. Monash, *Australian Victories in France*, p. 52.
78. John Laffin, *The Battle of Hamel: The Australians' Finest Victory*, Kangaroo Press, 1999, p. 66.
79. Bean diary, 3 July 1918.
80. Paul Byrnes, 'Prime Minister Rt Hon. WM Hughes visits Western Front (1918)', from aso.gov.au.
81. Bean diary, 2 July 1918. AWM38 3DRL 606/111/1, June to Sept 1918, p. 11
82. *Ibid,* p.12.
83. Monash, *Australian Victories in France*, p. 55.
84. Monash to Birdwood, 2 July 1918.
85. *Ibid.*
86. *Ibid.*
87. Papers of William Morris Hughes, National Library of Australia.
88. Bean diary, 2 July 1918, p. 12.
89. Bean, *Two Men I Knew*, p. 173.
90. Bean diary, 1 June 1918.
91. *Ibid.*
92. White to Bean, 14 October 1938.

Chapter 24
1. Monash, *Australian Victories in France*, p. 56.
2. *Sydney Morning Herald*, 30 November 1929, p. 13.
3. Bean diary, 3 July 1918. AWM38 3DRL 606/116/1, June to Sept 1918, p. 13.
4. Bean, *Official History*, vol. vi, p. 280.
5. Rawlinson diary, 1 July 1918, Churchill Archives Centre, Churchill College, Cambridge.
6. John Joseph Pershing (1860–1948), born in Laclede, Missouri.
7. Later General George Smith Patton Junior (1885–1945).
8. Monash, *Australian Victories in France*, p. 52.
9. Bean, *Official History*, vol. vi, p. 276.
10. Monash, *Australian Victories in France*, p. 53.
11. *Sydney Morning Herald*, 30 November 1929, p. 13.
12. Monash, *Australian Victories in France*, p. 53.
13. Later Field Marshal Sir Archibald Armar Montgomery-Massingberd (1871–1947).
14. Monash, *Australian Victories in France*, p. 53.
15. Bean diary, 3 July 1918.
16. Monash, *Australian Victories*, p. 53. Monash also related the incident to Bean (Bean diary, 3 July 1918).
17. Bean diary, 3 July 1918, WM38 3DRL 606/116/1 - June - September 1918, p. 18.
18. Bean, *Official History*, vol. vi, p. 281.
19. *Ibid.*, p. 279.
20. *Ibid.*, p. 285.
21. Henry Dalziel VC (1893–1965). He became a sergeant in the Citizen Military Forces after joining in 1933. Businessman Kerry Stokes donated Dalziel's Victoria Cross to the Australian War Memorial in 2010, after buying it and five of his other service medals for $525,000.
22. *Brisbane Courier*, 21 March 1919, p. 7.
23. *London Gazette*, 17 August 1918.
24. On 13 December 1918.
25. Henry Dalziel VC, 'My VC', 6 November 1942, cited at noble.com.au.
26. Bean, *Official History*, vol. vi, p. 290.
27. *London Gazette*, 18 August 1918.
28. P.L. Edgar, 'Axford, Thomas Leslie (Jack) (1894–1983)', *Australian Dictionary of Biography*, adb.anu.edu.au/biography/axford-thomas-leslie-jack-12159/text21787, published in hard copy 2007.
29. Bean, *Official History*, vol. vi, p. 300.
30. *Ibid.*, p. 305.
31. *Ibid.*, p. 308.
32. Rule, *Jacka's Mob*, p. 305.
33. Monash, *Australian Victories in France*, p. 56.
34. Brigadier General Evan Alexander Wisdom (1869–1945).
35. Bean, *Official History*, vol. vi, p. 326.
36. *Ibid.*, p. 332.
37. Monash, *Australian Victories in France*, p. 64.
38. Monash to Bruche, 10 October 1919.
39. Monash to Vic, 4 July 1918.
40. *Ibid.*, 5 July and 8 November 1918.
41. Georges Benjamin Clemenceau (1841–1929).
42. Jean Jules Henri Mordacq (1868–1943).
43. *Sydney Morning Herald*, 30 November 1929, p. 13.
44. *Ibid.*
45. Later Lieutenant Colonel James Alexander Robinson (1888–1971).
46. *Brisbane Courier*, 12 June 1919, p. 7.
47. Monash to Vic, 15 July 1918.

48. Albert Emile Métin (1871–1918).
49. Paul Marie Cesar Gerald Pau (1848–1932).
50. Monash to Vic, 19 July 1918.
51. Neville Stephen Bulwer-Lytton, 3rd Earl of Lytton, OBE (1879–1951). He won the bronze medal at the 1908 London Olympics in Jeu de Paume, also called Real Tennis.
52. Monash to Vic, 15 July 1918.

Chapter 25
1. Monash, *Australian Victories in France*, p. 121.
2. Ludendorff, *Ludendorff's Own Story*.
3. Elizabeth Greenhalgh, *The French Army and the First World War*, Cambridge University Press, 2014, pp. 314–315.
4. McWilliams and Steel, *Amiens*, p. 82.
5. Rawlinson diary.
6. Bean, *Official History*, vol. vi, p. 468.
7. Monash, *Australian Victories in France*, p. 72.
8. Lieutenant General Sir Richard Harte Keatinge Butler (1870–1935).
9. Lieutenant General Sir Charles Toler MacMorrough Kavanagh (1864–1950).
10. Monash, *Australian Victories in France*, p. 73.
11. Bernd Horn and Stephen John Harris, *Warrior Chiefs: Perspectives on Senior Canadian Military Leaders*, Dundurn, 2001, p. 53.
12. Monash, *Australian Victories in France*, p. 70.
13. McWilliams and Steel, *Amiens*, p. 31.
14. Monash, *Australian Victories in France*, p. 73.
15. Marie-Eugène Debeney (1864–1943).
16. Monash, *Australian Victories in France*, p. 70.
17. *Ibid.*, p. 74.
18. *Ibid.*, p. 69.
19. Major General John Frederick Charles Fuller (1878–1966).
20. Stephan Wilkinson, 'J.F.C. "Boney" Fuller: Wacko Genius of Armored Warfare', historynet.com, 9 July 2009.
21. Birdwood to Munro Ferguson, 28 October 1918, Novar Papers, Australian War Memorial.
22. Monash, *Australian Victories in France*, p. 296.
23. Monash Papers, Box 88. AWM.
24. Monash to Walter Rosenhain, 12 July 1918.
25. Bean, *Official History*, vol. vi, p. 208.
26. Monash to Vic, 2 August 1918.
27. Monash diary, July 1918.
28. Monash to Vic, 2 August 1918.
29. Monash, *Australian Victories in France*, p. 77.
30. Alistair McCluskey, *Amiens 1918: The Black Day of the German Army*, Osprey Publishing, 2008, p. 9.
31. James McWilliams and R. James Steel, *Amiens*, p. 24.
32. Bean, *Official History*, vol. vi, p. 606.
33. Dalya Alberge, 'A loner, an object of ridicule and a "rear-area pig": Adolf Hitler according to his WWI regiment', *Daily Mail* (UK), 18 August 2010.
34. Hugo Gutmann, later known as Henry G. Grant (1880–1962).
35. Monash notes, Personal Files Book 20, 31 July to 15 August 1918.
36. Monash, *Australian Victories in France*, p. 101.
37. *Ibid.*, p. 81.
38. Monash to Bruche, 17 October 1919.
39. Monash, *Australian Victories in France*, p. 84.
40. Bean, *Official History*, vol. vi, p. 525.

41. McWilliams and Steel, *Amiens*, p. 93.
42. David Bilton, *The German Army on the Western Front 1917-1918*, Pen and Sword, 2007, p. 72.
43. Gunner J.R. Armitage diary, Australian War Memorial.
44. John Toland, *No Man's Land: 1918*, p. 354.
45. Monash, *Australian Victories in France*, p. 118.
46. Bean, *Official History*, vol. vi, p. 529.
47. Monash, *Australian Victories in France*, p. 121.
48. John Thompson, *On Lips of Living Men*, Lansdowne Press, 1962, p. 142.
49. Serle, *Monash*, p. 347.
50. Bean, *Official History*, vol. vi, p. 529.
51. *Ibid.*, p. 550.
52. Monash, *Australian Victories in France*, p. 123.
53. Alfred Edward Gaby VC (1892–1918).
54. Bean, *Official History*, vol. vi, p. 569.
55. Monash, *Australian Victories in France*, p. 129.
56. The gun's carriage was eventually destroyed but the barrel remains intact.
57. Monash, *Australian Victories in France*, p. 123.
58. Ernest James Rollings (1893–1966), born Hereford, England, died Neath, Glamorganshire, Wales. The *Sunday Express* of 8 November 1931 ran an article entitled 'The man who ended the war ... Where is he?', referring to the discovery of the plans for the Hindenburg Line. The article sparked a hunt through the British Isles. Rollings only admitted he was the man in question after the paper tracked him down. He had been wounded in the head soon after Amiens and went home to resume his work as a policeman in 1921. The newspaper article made him famous. British philanthropist Lady Houston gave him £5000 as a belated gift for his war service and he retired in 1943 with the rank of Acting Chief Constable.
59. Bean, *Official History*, vol. vi, p. 578.
60. Monash to Vic, 15 August 1918.
61. Monash, *Australian Victories in France*, p. 123.
62. *Ibid.*, p. 129.
63. Bean, *Official History*, vol. vi, p. 606.
64. Rawlinson to Clive Wigram, 1st Baron Wigram, Equerry to the King, 28 August 1918.
65. Paul von Hindenburg, *Out of My Life*, Cassell and Company, 1920, p. 392.
66. Ludendorff, *Ludendorff's Own Story*.
67. Monash, *Australian Victories in France*, p. 131.
68. John Thompson, *On Lips of Living Men*, p. 143.
69. Bean, *Official History*, vol. vi, p. 684.
70. Bean diary, 9 August 1918. AWM38 3DRL 606/116/1 - June - September 1918, p. 63.
71. Bean, *Official History*, vol. vi, p. 683.
72. Lecture by Elliott's biographer Ross McMullin, National Library of Australia, 2002, from nla.gov.au.
73. The first had been at Rossignol Wood near Arras in March.
74. Bean, *Official History*, vol. vi, p. 685.
75. Brigadier-General Sydney Charles Edgar Herring (1881–1951), DSO.
76. Monash, *Australian Victories in France*, p. 140.
77. Monash to Vic, 11 August 1918.
78. John Hetherington, *Blamey: The Biography of Field-Marshal Sir Thomas Blamey*, Cheshire, 1954, p. 47.
79. Later Field Marshal Sir Henry Hughes Wilson, 1st Baronet (1864–1922).
80. Later Air Commodore Lionel Evelyn Oswald Charlton (1879–1958).
81. Monash to Vic, 11 August 1918.
82. *Ibid.*, 14 August 1918.
83. Bean diary, 11 August 1918.

84.   *Ibid.*, 7 July 1918 606/116/1 June to Sept 1918, p. 23; 5 August, p. 47.
85.   *Ibid,* 12 August, p 78.
86.   Monash to Vic, 2 August 1918.
87.   Monash to Bruche, 10 October 1919.
88.   Bean diary, 16 September 1918.
89.   F.M. Cutlack, 'August 8: Ludendorff's "Black Day" – What Australians did', *Sydney Morning Herald*, 9 August 1920, p. 8.
90.   Bean, *Official History*, vol. vi, p. 480.
91.   Bean diary, 17 August 1918, AWM 3DRL 606/116/1 June to Sept 1918, p. 82.

Chapter 26
1.   Monash, *Australian Victories in France*, p. 181.
2.   Arthur Conan Doyle, *The British Campaigns in Europe, 1914–1918*, Geoffrey Bles, 1928, p. 205.
3.   Monash diary, 21 December 1918.
4.   *Reveille* magazine, October 1931.
5.   Monash, *Australian Victories in France*, p. 149.
6.   *Ibid.*, p. 148.
7.   Haig diary, 21 August 1918.
8.   Harry R. Rudin, *Armistice 1918*, Yale University Press, 1944, p. 27.
9.   Quincy Howe, *A World History of Our Own Times: From the Turn of the Century to the 1918 Armistice*, Simon & Schuster, 1949, p. 640.
10.   Ralph Haswell Lutz, *Fall of the German Empire, 1914–1918*, Hoover Institution, Stanford University, 1932, p. 455.
11.   Alexander Watson, *Ring of Steel: Germany and Austria-Hungary at War, 1914–1918*, Penguin UK, 2014.
12.   'Deceit used by the high command: An unexpected peace', from firstworldwar.com.
13.   Vernon R. Northwood, with assistance from Gershon Bennett, *Monash*, State Electricity Commission of Victoria, 1950, p. 21.
14.   Bean diary, 18 and 19 August 1918.
15.   Monash, *Australian Victories in France*, p. 146.
16.   *Ibid.*, p. 145.
17.   Bean, *Official History*, vol. vi, p. 722.
18.   *Ibid.*, p. 734.
19.   *Ibid.*, p. 736.
20.   *Ibid.*, p. 740.
21.   Lawrence Dominic (Laurie) McCarthy VC (1892–1975). From *Canberra Times*, 1 May 1965, p. 2, quoted at awm.gov.au/people/P10676502/.
22.   'York's own hero to be honoured', *Avon Valley Advocate* (WA), 10 October 2012.
23.   Robert K. O'Connor QC, Lieutenant Frederick Bell VC Memorial Lecture 2012, from friendsofbattyelibrary.org.au.
24.   'McCarthy – Super VC', *Richmond River Herald and Northern Districts Advertiser* (NSW), 25 July 1919, p. 8.
25.   William Donovan Joynt VC (1889–1986).
26.   Bill Gammage, 'Joynt, William Donovan (1889–1986)', *Australian Dictionary of Biography*, adb.anu.edu.au/biography/joynt-william-donovan-12711/text22919, published in hard copy 2007.
27.   Monash, *Australian Victories in France*, p. 157.
28.   *Ibid.*, p. 158.
29.   Bean, *Official History*, vol. vi, p. 760.
30.   Monash, *Australian Victories in France*, p. 163.
31.   Bean, *Official History*, vol. vi., p. 761.
32.   *Ibid.*, p. 165.
33.   *Ibid.*, p. 175.

34. *Ibid.*, p. 167.
35. *Ibid.*, p. 168.
36. Bean, *Official History*, vol. vi, p. 773.
37. Monash, *Australian Victories in France*, p. 171.
38. *Ibid.*, p. 169.
39. Bernard Sidney Gordon VC (1891–1963).
40. *London Gazette*, 26 December 1918.
41. Monash, *Australian Victories in France*, p. 176.
42. *Ibid.*, p. 177.
43. *Ibid.*, p. 177.
44. Cecil Patrick Healy (1881–1918).
45. With the 1912 4 x 200-metre freestyle team that also included boxing champion and rugby star Harold Hardwick.
46. Bean, *Official History*, vol. vi, p. 783.
47. Monash, *Australian Victories in France*, p. 177.
48. Bean, *Official History*, vol. vi, p. 810.
49. *Ibid.*, p. 809.
50. Monash, *Australian Victories in France*, p. 183.
51. Bean, *Official History*, vol. vi, p. 813.
52. Joe Maxwell VC, *Hell's Bells and Mademoiselles* (revised ed.), HarperCollins Australia, 2013, p. 217.
53. *Canberra Times*, 12 November 1993, p. 6.
54. Monash, *Australian Victories in France*, p. 186.
55. Bean diary, 1 September 1918.
56. Monash, *Australian Victories in France*, p. 193.
57. George Cartwright VC (1894–1978).
58. Bean, *Official History*, vol. vi, p. 819.
59. Michele Bomford, *Beaten Down by Blood: The Battle of Mont St Quentin–Peronne 1918*, Big Sky Publishing, 2012.
60. W.J. Harvey, *The Red and White Diamond: Authorised History of the Twenty-Fourth Battalion AIF*, 24th Battalion Association, 1920, p. 280.
61. Lieutenant Edgar Towner, a farmer from Blackall, Queensland; Sergeant Alby Lowerson, a gold miner from Myrtleford in the Victorian high country; Private William Matthew Currey, a wireworker from Wallsend, New South Wales; Corporal Alexander Buckley, a farmer from Gulargambone, New South Wales; and Corporal Arthur Hall, a farmer from Nyngan, New South Wales.
62. Robert Mactier VC (1890–1918).
63. War service record of Robert Mactier, SERN 6939, National Archives of Australia.
64. Bean, *Official History*, vol. vi, p. 852.
65. Lawrence Carthage Weathers VC (1890–1918).
66. On 26 September Weathers received serious wounds north-east of Péronne during an artillery barrage. He died three days later.
67. Monash, *Australian Victories in France*, p. 188.
68. Monash to Vic, 8 September 1918.
69. Monash, *Australian Victories in France*, p. 177.
70. Bean, *Official History*, vol. vi, p. 873.
71. John Terraine, *To Win a War: 1918, The Year of Victory*, Sidgwick & Jackson, 1978, pp. 128–129.
72. Bean, *Official History*, vol. vi, p. 485.

Chapter 27
1. Monash to Vic, 11 September 1918.
2. Bean, *Official History*, vol. vi, p. 940.

3. Geoffrey Jukes, Peter Simkins and Michael Hickey, *The First World War: The War to End All Wars*, Osprey Publishing, 2013.
4. Bean diary, 2 September 1918. AWM38 3DRL 606/116/1/ June to Sept 1918, p. 115
5. *Ibid.*, 18 August 1918.
6. *Ibid.*, 6 September 1918.
7. Monash to Vic, 11 September 1918.
8. *Ibid.*
9. *Ibid.*
10. spartacus-educational.com/JrobinsonP.htm.
11. Monash to Vic, 11 September 1918.
12. Bean, *Official History*, vol. vi, p. 875.
13. *Ibid.*, p. 876.
14. Monash to Vic, 11 September 1918.
15. Some examples are *Illustrated Sunday Herald*, 22 September; *Observer*, 22 September; *Daily News*, 25 September; *Morning Post*, 28 September.
16. Monash to Vic, 11 September 1918.
17. *Ibid.*, 21 August 1918.
18. Bean diary, 4 September 1918.
19. Monash, *Australian Victories in France*, p. 202.
20. *Weekly Dispatch*, 16 June 1918.
21. Monash, *Australian Victories in France*, p. 217.
22. Bean, *Official History*, vol. vi, p. 887
23. Monash, *Australian Victories in France*, p. 215.
24. Bean diary., 13 September 1918.
25. Marwitz had commanded the 2nd Army at Amiens.
26. Later Field Marshal Douglas MacArthur (1880–1964).
27. James H. Hallas, *Squandered Victory: The American First Army at St. Mihiel*, Greenwood Publishing Group, 1995, p. 138.
28. 'Sep 20, 1918: U.S. officer George S. Patton writes home after Saint-Mihiel offensive', from history.com.
29. Pedersen, *Villers-Bretonneux*, p. 278.
30. Roland Perry, *Monash: The Outsider Who Won a War*, Random House Australia, 2007 p. 418.
31. Ross McMullin, *Pompey Elliott*, Scribe Publications, 2009, p. 488.
32. Bean, *Official History*, vol. vi, p. 879.
33. Bean, *Official History*, vol. vi, p. 879.
34. Bean diary, 16 September 1918.
35. Monash, *Australian Victories in France*, p. 254.
36. *Ibid.*, p. 242.
37. *Ibid.*, p. 221.
38. Bean diary, 18 September 1918.
39. Rawlinson diary, 16 September 1918.
40. Sergeant Maurice Vincent Buckley VC (1891–1921). After he joined the light horse in 1914 and went to Egypt, Buckley contracted a venereal disease, returned to Australia and was declared a deserter after walking out of his camp. In mid-1916 Buckley re-enlisted in the AIF, using the alias Gerald Sexton. He died in a riding accident at Gippsland.
41. Bean, *Official History*, vol. vi, p. 906.
42. Monash, *Australian Victories in France*, p. 223.
43. *Ibid.*, p. 232.
44. Bean, *Official History*, vol. vi, p. 917.
45. Monash, *Australian Victories in France*, p. 232.
46. James Park Woods VC (1886–1963). He stood just 160 centimetres tall.
47. Bean, *Official History*, vol. vi, p. 932.

48. *Ibid.*, p. 931.
49. War service record for Walter Rewi Hallahan (1889–1918), National Archives of Australia.
50. *Argus*, 23 September 1918, p. 7.
51. Monash, *Australian Victories in France*, p. 232.
52. Bean, *Official History*, vol. vi, p. 932.
53. *Ibid.*, p. 933.
54. Steve Meacham, 'Portrait of the Anzacs: Deserters more interested in booze, brawls and sex', *Sydney Morning Herald*, 2 August 2010.
55. historylearningsite.co.uk/mutiny_french_army.htm.
56. Ashley Ekins, *1918 Year of Victory: The End of the Great War and the Shaping of History*, Exisle Publishing, p. 117.
57. On 28 November 1918.
58. McMullin, *Pompey Elliott*, pp. 489–490.
59. Norman Gordon McNicol, *The Thirty-Seventh: History of the Thirty-Seventh Battalion AIF*, John Burridge, 1936, p. 252.
60. Bean, *Official History*, vol. vi, p. 939.
61. Monash, *Australian Victories in France*, p. 244.
62. *Ibid.*, p. 248.
63. *Ibid.*, p. 251.
64. Bean, *Official History*, vol. vi, p. 983.
65. Monash, *Australian Victories in France*, p. 251.
66. *Ibid.*, p. 252.
67. Kingsley Conan Doyle died of Spanish flu on 28 October 1918.
68. Haig diary.
69. David Sinclair, *Hall of Mirrors*, Random House, 2011.
70. Hugh Cecil and Peter Liddle, *Facing Armageddon: The First World War Experience*, Pen and Sword, 2003, p. 59.
71. Barrie Pitt, *1918: The Last Act*, Pen and Sword, 2014, p. 97.
72. Bean diary, 28 September 1918. AWM38 3DRL 606/117/1, p. 5.
73. Bean, *Official History*, vol. vi., p. 958.
74. *Ibid.*, p. 994.
75. *Ibid.*, p. 961.
76. *Ibid.*, p. 962.
77. *Ibid.*, p. 978.
78. Blair Anderson Wark VC (1894–1941).
79. *London Gazette*, 3 October 1919.
80. *Age*, 30 December 1918, p. 6.
81. *Daily News* (Perth) 9 April 1918, p. 6.
82. Ludendorff, *Ludendorff's Own Story*.
83. Bean diary, 29 September 1918.
84. Rawlinson diary, 29 September 1918.
85. Serle, *Monash*, p. 366.
86. Monash, *Australian Victories*, p. 267.
87. *Ibid*, p. 268.
88. Serle, *Monash*, p. 367.
89. Monash, *Australian Victories in France*, p. 267.
90. Edward John Francis Ryan VC (1890–1941).
91. *Sydney Morning Herald*, 25 October 1919, p. 12.
92. Like so many returned servicemen affected by the horrors of war, Ryan found it tough to adjust to civilian life and keep a job. During the Depression he was on the road for four years looking for work, and in August 1935 he walked 160 kilometres from Balranald, New South Wales, to Mildura, Victoria, for a temporary job on the local council. In May 1941 he died of pneumonia aged 51.

93. Birdwood to Monash, 3 October 1918.
94. Monash to John Springthorpe, 2 October 1918.
95. Bean, *Official History*, vol. vi, p. 1021.
96. Monash, *Australian Victories,* p. 277.
97. Joseph Maxwell VC (1896–1967).
98. Robert Macklin, *Bravest: How Some of Australia's Greatest War Heroes Won Their Medals*, Allen & Unwin, 2008, p. 109.
99. Monash, *Australian Victories in France*, p. 309.
100. Maxwell, p. 229.
101. Bean, *Official History*, vol. vi, p. 1033.
102. *Ibid.*, p. 1043.
103. John Austin Mahony (1893–1918).
104. John Harry Fletcher (1893–1918).
105. *Bendigo Advertiser*, 1 November 1918, p. 5.
106. *Ibid.*
107. Mark Day, 'Mates who stood united until the bloody end', *Australian*, 4 October 2008.
108. George Morby Ingram VC (1889–1961).
109. *Bendigo Advertiser*, 26 October 1918, p. 8.
110. War service record for John Austin Mahony, Service Number 1056, National Archives of Australia.
111. Monash, *Australian Victories*, p. 287.
112. Monash, *Australian Victories in France*, p. 262.
113. Monash to Pearce, 3 October 1918.
114. General Thomas Henry Dodds (1873-1943).
115. Monash to Dodds, 2 October 1918.
116. Monash to Vic, 8 November 1918.

Chapter 28

1. Monash to Vic, 8 November 1918.
2. Sir Basil Henry Liddell Hart, *Through the Fog of War*, Random House, 1938, p. 147.
3. Monash diary. October 1918.
4. Thompson, *On Lips of Living Men*, pp. 139–140.
5. Monash to Pearce, 5 November 1918.
6. Monash, *Australian Victories in France*, pp. 293–294.
7. Thomas Alexander White, *The Fighting Thirteenth*, Naval & Military Press, 2009, p. 157.
8. *Age*, 21 February 1919, p. 4.
9. Notes for Springthorpe, 4 October 1918, Monash Papers, Box 92.
10. Bean diary, 13 October 1918, AWM38 3DRL 606/117/1 Sept to December 1918 pp. 9/54
11. Monash to Vic, 8 November 1918.
12. *Ibid.*, 3 November 1918.
13. *Hebrew Standard of Australasia*, 2 January 1920, p. 10. The *Morning Post* letter was published on 23 April 1919. Later Monash would disassociate himself from this anti-Zionist stance.
14. Monash diary, October 1918.
15. *Ibid.*
16. *Argus*, 9 November 1929, p. 3S.
17. Monash to Vic, 3 November 1918.
18. *Argus*, 9 November 1929, p. 3S.
19. Monash to Vic, 3 November 1918.
20. Monash wrote to Read on 24 December 1918.
21. *Cairns Post*, 3 January 1919, p. 5.
22. Monash to Vic, 8 November 1918.
23. *Ibid.*

24. Ludendorff, *Ludendorff's Own Story*.
25. *Ibid.*
26. William L. Shirer, *Rise and Fall of the Third Reich: A History of Nazi Germany*, Simon & Schuster, 1990, p. 34.
27. Monash to Vic, 8 November 1918.
28. General Sir (Frederick) Ivor Maxse (1862–1958).
29. Monash to Vic, 8 November 1918.
30. Margarethe Ludendorff, *My Married Life with Ludendorff*, Hutchinson, 1930, p. 229.
31. Adolf Hitler, *Mein Kampf*, Houghton Mifflin, 1971, p. 204 (first published 1925).
32. John Toland, *Adolf Hitler*, vol. 1, Anchor Books, 1976, p. xix.
33. John Denton Pinkstone French, 1st Earl of Ypres (1852–1925).
34. historyplace.com.
35. Monash to Vic, 8 November 1918.
36. *Ibid.*, 20 November 1918.
37. Bean, *Two Men I Knew*, p. 180.
38. Bean diary, 21 November 1918.
39. Monash to Vic, 20 November 1918.
40. Vic to Monash, 30 November 1918.
41. Monash diary, 15 January 1919. Monash Papers, NLA. Series 5 Box 139.
42. Hobbs to Monash, 8 November 1918.
43. Streeton to Felix Meyer, 11 October 1931.
44. Gellibrand's annotated copy of Monash's *Australian Victories in France*, Australian War Memorial.
45. Brigadier General Cecil Henry Foott (1876–1942).
46. Serle, *Monash*, p. 376.
47. Liddell Hart, *Through the Fog of War*, p. 147.
48. *Sydney Morning Herald*, 10 October 1927, p. 10.
49. Monash, *Australian Victories in France*, dedication page.
50. Monash, 'Leadership in war', as quoted in Warhaft, *Well May We Say*, pp. 81–90.
51. Monash, *Australian Victories in France*, p. 297.

Chapter 29
1. *Herald* (Melbourne), 28 February 1919.
2. Birdwood to Lord Stonehaven, 21 July 1925.
3. Monash to Vic, 17 December 1918.
4. *Examiner* (Launceston), 25 February 1919, p. 3. McGoorty had fought in Australia between 1914 and 1917 and had lost twice to Les Darcy.
5. Monash to Vic, 13 December 1918.
6. *Everylady's Journal*, 6 February 1920.
7. Monash diary, 21 December 1918.
8. *Herald* (Melbourne), 28 February 1919.
9. *Barrier Miner* (Broken Hill), 31 December 1918, p. 4.
10. Monash to Vic, 28 December 1918.
11. *Advertiser* (Adelaide), 12 August 1933, p. 8.
12. Margaret MacMillan, *Paris 1919: Six Months That Changed the World*, Random House, 2002, p. 48.
13. Serle, *Monash*, p. 414.
14. *Jewish Chronicle*, 17 January 1919.
15. Vic to Monash, 30 November 1918.
16. Birdwood to Munro Ferguson, 6 December 1918.
17. Munro Ferguson to Birdwood, 2 May 1919.
18. *Jewish Herald*, 21 March 1919, p. 10.
19. In 1920. Van Badham, 'Michael Gove, the British education secretary belittling Australia's war dead', *Guardian* (UK), 6 January 2014.

20. Jackson to Liddell Hart, 4 October 1935.
21. *The West Australian*, 27 January 1919, p. 5.
22. *West Australian* (Perth), 27 January 1919, p. 5.
23. Mat Monash to Monash, 1 February 1919.
24. *Jewish Herald*, 16 May 1919, p. 14.
25. *Hebrew Standard of Australasia*, 18 July 1919, p. 10.
26. *Jewish Herald*, 8 August 1919, p. 13.
27. *Ibid.*, 13 June 1919, p. 10.
28. Serle, *Monash*, p. 412.
29. Monash diary, 6 April 1919.
30. Monash to Barrett, 22 April 1919.
31. Monash to Watt, 16 May 1919.
32. *Evening News*, 26 April 1919.
33. *Age*, 28 April 1919, p. 7.
34. *Geelong Advertiser*, 28 April 1919, p. 3.
35. Monash Papers, Series 4. Box 130.
36. *Sydney Morning Herald*, 6 June 1919, p. 7.
37. Monash to Murdoch, 15 April 1919.
38. '1918: Australians in France – Home at last – The Australians return', awm.gov.au.
39. Nathan Wise, *Anzac Labour: Workplace Cultures in the Australian Imperial Force During the First World War*, Palgrave Macmillan, 2014, p. 128.
40. Monash to Gunner John George McAdam, 14 May 1919.
41. *Jewish Herald*, 11 July 1919, p. 12.
42. *Argus*, 14 July 1919, p. 2.
43. Sir Robert Gibson (1863–1934) became Chairman of the Commonwealth Bank in 1926.
44. Sir Tannatt William Edgeworth David (1858–1934).
45. Herbert Reah Harper (1871–1956).
46. *Border Watch* (Mount Gambier, South Australia), 30 September 1919, p. 1.
47. *Australasian*, 29 November 1919, p. 38.
48. *Daily Herald* (Adelaide), 20 November 1919, p. 5.
49. Monash diary.
50. *Daily News* (Perth), 19 December 1919, p. 5.
51. *Argus*, 27 December 1919, p. 7.
52. *Hebrew Standard of Australasia*, 2 January 1920, p. 10.
53. *Age*, 26 December 1919, p. 5.
54. *Argus*, 26 January 1920, p. 6.
55. Batman's body was exhumed and reburied at Fawkner Cemetery in Melbourne's north.
56. Monash to Rosenhain, 12 February 1920.
57. The anonymous letter was dated 17 February 1920.
58. *Western Mail* (Perth), 11 March 1920, p. 35.
59. *Daily News* (Perth), 28 February 1920, p. 4.
60. *Table Talk* (Melbourne), 4 March 1920, p. 8.

Chapter 30

1. Monash to Dixon, 3 August 1923, after being appointed vice-chancellor of Melbourne University.
2. Monash's great grandson, Michael Monash Bennett at the 80th Monash Commemorative Tribute, Brighton Cemetery, 9 October 2011.
3. *Argus*, 26 April 1924, p. 16.
4. Monash to Robert Henry Beardsmore, 20 September 1920.
5. What it used to cost, Wages in Victoria, from slv.vic.gov.au.
6. *Narandera Argus and Riverina Advertiser*, 15 August 1919, p. 4.
7. *Smith's Weekly*, 7 August 1920.

8.   *Ibid.*, 5 March 1920, p. 6.
9.   *Australasian*, 13 March 1920, p. 54.
10.   *Argus*, 23 March 1920, p. 6.
11.   *North Eastern Ensign* (Benalla), 5 March 1920, p. 2.
12.   Currie to Monash, 24 August 1920.
13.   *Nation*, February 1920.
14.   He was succeeded as the Member for Fawkner by future Prime Minister Harold Holt.
15.   *Horsham Times*, 9 April 1920, p. 6; *Argus*, 31 March 1920, p. 11.
16.   *Daily News* (Perth), 6 April 1920, p. 4.
17.   R. Sutton, 'McGlinn, John Patrick (1869–1946)', *Australian Dictionary of Biography*, http://adb.anu.edu.au/biography/mcglinn-john-patrick-7359/text12783, published first in hardcopy 1986.
18.   *Argus*, 24 July 1920, p. 19.
19.   Then known as the Returned Sailors and Soldiers Imperial League of Australia (RSSILA).
20.   *Argus*, Melbourne, 23 August 1920, p. 6.
21.   *Ibid.*, 19 April 1920, p. 6.
22.   *Australasian*, 17 July 1920, p. 35.
23.   Monash to Walter Rosenhain, 14 July 1920.
24.   *Argus*, 19 April 1920, p. 7.
25.   Monash to Bainbridge, 10 June 1920.
26.   On 21 June 1920.
27.   Monash to Bruche, 15 September 1920.
28.   Morshead to Monash, 29 May 1921.
29.   *Age*, 28 May 1921, p. 12.
30.   *Worker* (Brisbane), 24 June 1920, p. 14.
31.   Monash to Watt, 1 September 1920.
32.   *Argus*, 26 June 1920, p. 20.
33.   Swinburne to Monash, 30 July 1920.
34.   Serle, *Monash*, p. 498.
35.   Monash to Lawson, 18 May 1920.
36.   Monash to Bruche, 11 August 1920.
37.   Monash to Barrett, 6 July 1920.
38.   Monash to Stanley Bruce, 23 July 1923.
39.   *Queensland Times* (Ipswich), 12 August 1926, p 4.
40.   Monash to Major Herbert Maddock, 2 July 1926.
41.   Rosenhain to Monash, 2 September 1920, also 18, 23 February 1921.
42.   Monash to Rosenhain, 7 December 1920.
43.   *Punch*, 30 September 1920.
44.   *Bulletin*, 2 December 1920.
45.   Monash to *Bulletin*, 14 December 1920.
46.   Monash to Rawlinson, 14 March 1922.
47.   Monash's great grandson, Michael Monash Bennett at the 80th Monash Commemorative Tribute, Brighton Cemetery, 9 October 2011.
48.   Serle, *Monash*, p. 461.
49.   Taylor to Meyer, 11 October 1931.
50.   *Argus*, 15 December 1920, p. 9.
51.   Sir Harold Winthrop Clapp (1875–1952).
52.   Sir Arthur Robinson (1872–1945). As well as becoming Victoria's Attorney-General he was at various times a director of Ford Motor Co. of Australia, International Harvester Co. of Australia, Bank of Adelaide, British-Australian Lead Manufacturers, Australian Deposit & Mortgage Bank, Australian Mutual Provident Society, Central Insurance and the Colonial Gas Association. From Leonie Foster, 'Robinson, Sir Arthur (1872–1945)', *Australian Dictionary of Biography*, National Centre of Biography, Australian National

University, http://adb.anu.edu.au/biography/robinson-sir-arthur-8241/text14429, published first in hardcopy 1988.

53. Anthony George Maldon Michell (1870–1959).
54. Sir Frederic William Eggleston (1875–1954).
55. Eggleston's, Confidential Notes, Australian National University Library.
56. *Healesville and Yarra Glen Guardian*, 13 November 1920, p. 2.
57. Monash to Lou Rosenhain, 10 April 1921.
58. Hans Christian Bjelke-Petersen (1872–1964), born in Copenhagen, Denmark, uncle of future Queensland premier Joh Bjelke-Petersen.
59. Herman to Bertha Bennett (Monash), 9 October 1931.
60. *Morwell Advertiser*, 27 January 1922, p. 2.
61. *Geelong Advertiser*, 10 March 1922, p. 5.
62. *Argus*, 22 November 1923, p. 11.
63. *Argus*, 19 July 1922, p. 14.
64. *Ibid.*, 8 December 1922, p. 8.
65. Monash to Walter Rosenhain, 28 December 1922.
66. *Herald*, 21 September 1921.
67. 'Fletcher, Charles Brunsdon (1859–1946)', *Australian Dictionary of Biography*, National Centre of Biography, Australian National University, http://adb.anu.edu.au/biography/fletcher-charles-brunsdon-6191/text10641, published first in hardcopy 1981.
68. *Sydney Morning Herald*, 3 May 1924, p. 13.
69. Serle, *Monash*, p. 505.
70. Major General George Alan Vasey (1895–1945).
71. Lieutenant General Sir Iven Giffard Mackay (1882–1966).
72. Richard Gavin Gardiner Casey, Baron Casey (1890–1976).
73. Built between 353 and 350 BC at what is now Bodrum in Turkey, it was destroyed by earthquakes from the 12th to the 15th century.
74. *Table Talk*, 14 April 1921, p. 9.
75. *Geelong Advertiser*, 6 May 1921, p. 3.
76. *Argus*, 7 May 1921, p. 18.
77. Norman De Mattos Bentwich (1883–1971).
78. *Jewish Herald*, 20 August 1920, p. 5.
79. Mat to Monash, 18 October 1922.
80. Monash to Eric Oswald Hercus, 3 October 1924.
81. *Argus*, 23 June 1923, p. 20.
82. *Ibid.*, 25 November 1926, p. 12.
83. Dr. John Jacob 'Job' Crew Bradfield (1867–1943).
84. R. B. Walker, 'Denison, Sir Hugh Robert (1865–1940)', *Australian Dictionary of Biography*, National Centre of Biography, Australian National University, http://adb.anu.edu.au/biography/denison-sir-hugh-robert-5955/text10159, published first in hardcopy 1981.
85. *Sun*, 30 July 1923.
86. Herbert William Lloyd (1883–1957).
87. Lloyd to Monash, 31 July 1923.
88. Monash to Lloyd, 6 August 1923.
89. *Sunday Times* (Perth), 4 November 1923, p. 1.
90. Sunday Times (Sydney), 4 November 1923, p. 7.
91. *Mirror* (Perth), 3 November 1923, p. 1.
92. Monash to Arthur Robinson, 9 November 1923.
93. *Argus*, 6 November 1923, p. 10.

Chapter 31
1. *Sydney Morning Herald*, 25 April 1927, p. 9.
2. F.J. McKenna, *Angelus* (the Canberra Parish paper), November 1931.
3. Since 1983, it has been home to the Sydney Jewish Museum.

4.   *Evening News* (Sydney), 10 November 1923, p. 6.
5.   *Sydney Morning Herald*, 12 November 1923, p. 8.
6.   *Ibid.*, 13 November 1923, p. 9.
7.   *Mirror* (Perth), 26 April 1924, p. 1.
8.   *Argus*, 26 April 1924, p 16.
9.   *Geelong Advertiser*, 26 April 1924, p. 7.
10. *Mirror* (Perth), 26 April 1924, p. 1.
11. *Argus*, 26 April 1924, p 16.
12. *Daily News* (Perth), 22 August 1924.
13. *Brisbane Courier*, 21 June 1924, p. 7.
14. Monash to Mackey, 6 January 1923.
15. *Argus*, 6 February 1925, p. 11.
16. Later Lieutenant General Sir Edmund Francis Herring (1892–1982).
17. Geoff Browne, 'Herring, Sir Edmund Francis (Ned) (1892–1982)', *Australian Dictionary of Biography*, National Centre of Biography, Australian National University, http://adb.anu. edu.au/biography/herring-sir-edmund-francis-ned-12626/text22747, published first in hardcopy 2007.
18. Sir Walter Baldwin Spencer (1860–1929).
19. *Age*, 13 January 1925, p. 9.
20. Swinburne to SEC Commissioners, 19 January 1925, SEC archives.
21. Monash to Swinburne, 20 July 1925.
22. *The Maitland Weekly Mercury*, 2 May 1925, p. 14.
23. *Argus*, 27 April 1925, p. 11.
24. *Ibid.*, 14 April 1927, p. 15.
25. *Ibid.*, 26 April 1926, p. 11.
26. White to Monash, 9 August 1927.
27. Monash to Bertha, 16 September 1925.
28. Monash to Lou Rosenhain, 16 July 1925.
29. *Argus*, 23 December 1925, p. 19.
30. Eggleston, Confidential Notes, III, Menzies Library, Australian National University.
31. Monash to Walter Rosenhain, 6 January 1928.
32. *Ibid.*, 27 October 1927.
33. Monash to Walter Rosenhain, 7 December 1923.
34. Monash, Leadership in War: an address to the Beefsteak Club in Melbourne, 30 March 1926; as quoted in Sally Warhaft, *Well May We Say*, pp. 81–90.
35. daao.org.au/bio/agnes-paterson/biography/.
36. *Truth*, 29 August 1925.
37. *Smith's Weekly*, 20 March 1926.
38. *Argus*, 30 November 1926, p. 11.
39. Edward James (Jack) Holloway (1875–1967).
40. *Age*, 27 March 1967, p. 23.
41. Sir Alfred Newcombe (Kem) Kemsley (1896–1987).
42. White to Monash, 26 April 1927.
43. *Age*, 26 April 1927, p. 10.
44. Monash to Premier Lawson, 1 August 1927.
45. *Hebrew Standard of Australasia* (Sydney), 25 March 1927, p. 9.
46. *Ibid*, 7 October 1927, p. 2.
47. *Argus*, 20 December 1928, p. 17.
48. Sir Israel Brodie (1895–1979), later Chief Rabbi of Great Britain and the Commonwealth, 1948–1965.
49. Monash to Brodie, 3 November 1928.
50. Serle, *Monash*, p. 507.
51. *Monash –The Man and His Method*, for radio broadcast. In Monash Papers.
52. *Argus*, 20 December 1928, p. 14.

53. *Ibid*, 4 June 1928, p. 1.
54. *Ibid*, 11 March 1929, p. 1.
55. *Table Talk*, 14 March 1929, p. 70.
56. Monash to Walter Rosenhain, 3 April 1929.
57. *Argus*, 19 December 1929, p. 15.
58. *Jewish Herald*, 12 September 1929.
59. Colin MacInnes, *England, Half English: A Polyphoto of the Fifties*, Faber & Faber, Limited, 2009, p. 187. See also Daphne Anson, *The 'Modern Judas Maccabaeus' Remembered*, elderofziyon.blogspot.com.
60. *Australasian* (Melbourne), 26 October 1929, p. 10.
61. Monash to Isaacs, 30 December 1930.
62. Monash to Collett, 23 April 1931.
63. guides.slv.vic.gov.au.
64. Victorian Parliamentary Debates, v. 178, p. 3402.
65. John Cain (1882–1957) became the 34th Victorian Premier in 1943. He is the only Premier of Victoria whose son [John Cain b. 1931] has also served in that office.
66. Monash to Walter Rosenhain, 3 January 1929.
67. Prime Minister Robert Menzies at the Centenary Service for Monash, Linlithgow Avenue, Melbourne, 11 April 1965.
68. *Ibid*.
69. *Argus*, 7 December 1929, p. 20.
70. Monash to Bowater, 20 May 1929.
71. James Henry Scullin (1876–1953).
72. *Age*, 28 June 1928.
73. Monash to Scullin, 25 June 1930.
74. *Sydney Morning Herald*, 28 November 1929, p. 15.
75. Monash to Brigadier General J.C. Stewart, 12 February 1930.
76. *Ibid.*, 29 April 1930.
77. Sally Warhaft, *Well May We Say… The Speeches That Made Australia,* p. 91.
78. *Argus*, 20 April 1931, p. 5.
79. Father Graham's telegram, 17 March 1931.
80. *Bulletin*, 3 December 1930.
81. Monash to Knox, 12 November 1930.
82. Grimwade to Monash, 16 December 1930, Monash's reply 17 December.
83. Barclay-Smith to Monash 19 December 1930.
84. Monash to Barclay-Smith, 23 December 1930.
85. *Chronicle* (Adelaide), 22 January 1931, p. 52.
86. Monash letters to Bertha Bennett.
87. *Sydney Morning Herald*, 28 February 1931, p. 12.
88. *Argus*, 11 August 1931, p. 6.
89. *Townsville Daily Bulletin*, 2 April 1931, p. 8.
90. *Townsville Daily Bulletin*, 9 February 1931, p. 7.
91. *Reveille*, December 1931.
92. *The Register News-Pictorial* (Adelaide), 9 April 1930, p. 4.
93. *The Southern Mail* (Bowral), 2 May 1930, p. 2.
94. Bean to Monash, 21 May 1930. AWM38 3DRL 606/277/1.
95. *Argus*, 27 April 1931, p. 7.
96. Monash to Walter Rosenhain, 1 September 1931.
97. Sir Sidney Valentine Sewell (1880–1949).
98. John V. Hurley, 'Sewell, Sir Sidney Valentine (1880–1949)', *Australian Dictionary of Biography*, National Centre of Biography, Australian National University, http://adb.anu.edu.au/biography/sewell-sir-sidney-valentine-8388/text14727, published first in hardcopy 1988.
99. Monash to Walter Rosenhain, 1 September 1931.

100. *Sun*, 24 September 1931.
101. Monash to Mat, 24 April 1915.
102. Monash to Bertha, 24 April 1915.
103. *News* (Adelaide), 8 October 1931, p. 1.
104. *Argus*, 9 October 1931, p. 7.
105. Lou Rosenhain to Bertha Bennett, 13 October 1931.
106. *Argus*, 9 October 1931, p. 7.
107. *News*, 8 October 1931, p. 1.
108. *Argus*, 10 October 1931, p. 21.
109. *Ibid.*, 12 October 1931, p. 9.
110. *Ibid.*, 12 October 1931, p. 7.
111. Cohen to Temple Beth Israel, St Kilda, 1931 in Monash Papers.
112. *Argus*, 12 October 1931, p. 7.

Chapter 32
1.   Monash to Vic, 18 June 1915.
2.   *Argus*, 8 October 1934, p. 1.
3.   *Barrier Miner* (Broken Hill), 31 October 1931, p. 8.
4.   Monash to Vic, 8 April 1915.
5.   International Jewish Cemetery Project, International Association of Jewish Genealogical Societies, iajgsjewishcemeteryproject.org/poland/krotoszyn.html.
6.   Sir John Monash, *The Australian Victories in France in 1918*, Hutchinson & Company, 1920, p. 293.
7.   Forward to *War Letters of General Monash*, edited by F.M. Cutlack, Angus & Robertson, 1934.
8.   White to Melbourne Legacy, 1931, in Monash Papers.
9.   Gershon Bennett at Sir John Monash Memorial Oration, 1936.
10. Dame Nellie Melba's portrait is on the obverse side.
11. Monash to Vic, 6 December 1915.

Epilogue
1.   William M. Leary, *We Shall Return!: MacArthur's Commanders and the Defeat of Japan, 1942–1945*, University Press of Kentucky, 2015, p. 34.
2.   *Ibid.*, p. 33–34.
3.   From www.nma.gov.au/primeministers/william_hughes.
4.   *Morning Bulletin* (Rockhampton), 14 August 1940, p. 4.
5.   Joachim C. Fest, *Hitler*, Houghton Miffin Harcourt, 2013, p. 475.
6.   Richard Steigmann-Gall, *The Holy Reich: Nazi Conceptions of Christianity*, 1919-1945, Cambridge University Press, 2003, p. 88.
7.   Ellen Kennedy, *Constitutional Failure: Carl Schmitt in Weimar*, Duke University Press, 2004, p. 16.

Bibliography

John Monash documented his life in meticulous detail. Most of his correspondence is divided between the National Library of Australia and the Australian War Memorial.

The National Library of Australia contains 253 boxes of his material in the manuscript section MS 1884 under the following series:

1. General correspondence: A (letters received), 1879–1931

General correspondence: B (outward letters), 1883–1931

2. Correspondence with particular individuals, 1860–1931

3. Correspondence: special categories, 1918–20

4. Correspondence: World War I, 1915–20

5. Diaries and notebooks, 1879–1931

6. School and university

7. Engineering, 1886–1932

8. Military, 1908–16

9. Arbitration and royal commissions, 1896–1929

10. Subject files, A–Z and souvenir albums, 1801–1931

11. Manuscripts, 1881–1928

12. Scientific matters, 1914–30

13. Travels, 1907–31

14. Press cuttings, pamphlets and other printed items, 1894–1929

15. Photographs and glass slides

16. Death and memorials

Addition 20 January 1983

Addition 15 April 1986

Addition 28 June 1994

APPENDIX 1 Books from Monash's Library taken into the main book stacks, April 1986

APPENDIX 2 Medals, decorations and badges of Sir John Monash transferred to the Australian War Memorial in January 1985

Other works cited include:

Albertini, Luigi. *The Origins of the War of 1914*, vol. 2. Oxford University Press, 1953.

Annear, Robyn. *Nothing But Gold: The Diggers of 1852*. Text Publishing, 1999.

Astore, William J. *Hindenburg: Icon of German Militarism*. Potomac Books, 2014.

Balfour Baron Kinross, Patrick. *Atatürk: The Rebirth of a Nation*. K. Rustem, 1981.

Bean, C.E.W. *The Story of ANZAC from the Outbreak of War to the End of the First Phase of the Gallipoli Campaign, May 4, 1915. Official History of Australia in the War of 1914–1918*. University of Queensland Press, 1941.

Bean, C.E.W. *Two Men I Knew: William Bridges and Brudenell White*. Angus and Robertson, 1957.

Beckett, Ian F.W. *The Making of the First World War*. Yale University Press, 2012.

Beeston, Joseph Lievesley. *Five Months at Anzac*. Angus and Robertson, 1916.

Berg, A. Scott. *Wilson*. Simon and Schuster, 2013.

Bilton, David. *The German Army on the Western Front 1917–1918*. Pen and Sword Books, 2007.

Bomford, Michele. *Beaten Down by Blood: The Battle of Mont St Quentin–Peronne 1918*. Big Sky Publishing, 2012.

Butler, A. G. *The Australian Army Medical Services in the War of 1914–1918*. Australian War Memorial, 1938.

Carlyon, Les. *Gallipoli*. Pan Macmillan Australia, 2001.

Carlyon, Les. *The Great War*. Pan Macmillan Australia, 2007.

Carver, Michael. *The Warlords: Military Commanders of the Twentieth Century*. Pen and Sword Books, 2005.

Castieau, John Buckley. *The Difficulties of My Position: The Diaries of Prison Governor, 1855–1884*. National Library of Australia, 2004.

Cecil, Hugh and Peter Liddle. *Facing Armageddon: The First World War Experience*. Pen and Sword Books, 2003.

Churchill, Winston. *The World Crisis*. Hutchinson, 1928.

Coombes, David. *Crossing the Wire*. Big Sky Publishing, 2011.

Cooper, Bryan. *The Ironclads of Cambrai*. Pen and Sword Books, 2010.

Corfield, Justin. *The Ned Kelly Encyclopaedia*. Lothian Books, 2003.

Crawford, John and Ian McGibbon. *New Zealand's Great War: New Zealand, the Allies and the First World War*. Exisle Publishing, 2007.

Cuttriss, G. P. *Over the Top with the Third Australian Division*. C.H. Kelly, 1918.

Davies, C.B., J.E. Edmonds and R.G.B. Maxwell-Hyslop. *History of the Great War Based on Official Documents, by Direction of the Historical Section of the Committee of Imperial Defence: Military Operations France and Belgium, 1918, vol. 1: The German March Offensive and Its Preliminaries* (1935). Imperial War Memorial and Battery Press, 1995.

Davis, Ryan A. *The Spanish Flu: Narrative and Cultural Identity in Spain, 1918*. Palgrave Macmillan, 2013.

De L. Marshall, Gordon and Les Douglas. *Maritime Albany Remembered*. Tangee Publishing, 2001.

Dennis, Peter. *The Oxford Companion to Australian Military History*. Oxford University Press, 1995.

Docherty, James C. *The A to Z of Australia*. Rowman and Littlefield, 2010.

Dolan, Hugh. *Thirty-six Days: The Untold Story Behind the Gallipoli Landings*. Pan Macmillan Australia, 2010.

Doyle, Arthur Conan. *The British Campaigns in Europe, 1914–1918*. Geoffrey Bles, 1928.

Edwards, Cecil. *John Monash*. State Electricity Commission of Victoria, 1970.

Ekins, Ashley. *Gallipoli: A Ridge Too Far*. Exisle Publishing, 2013.

Erickson, Edward J. *Ordered to Die: A History of the Ottoman Army in the First World War*. Greenwood Publishing Group, 2001.

Galbally, Ann. *Redmond Barry: An Anglo–Irish Australian*. Melbourne University Press, 1995.

Gilmour, David. *The Long Recessional: The Imperial Life of Rudyard Kipling*. Farrar, Straus and Giroux, 2002.

Greenhalgh, Elizabeth. *The French Army and the First World War*. Cambridge University Press, 2014.

Hallas, James H. *Squandered Victory: The American First Army at St. Mihiel*. Greenwood Publishing Group, 1995.

Hamilton, John. *Gallipoli Sniper: The Life of Billy Sing*. Pan Macmillan, 2008.

Harvey, W. J. *The Red and White Diamond: Authorised History of the 24th Battalion AIF*. Published for the 24th Battalion Association by Alexander McCubbin, 1920.

Hatwell, Jeff. *No Ordinary Determination: Percy Black and Harry Murray of the First AIF*. Fremantle Arts Centre Press, 2005.

Hill, Alec Jeffrey. *Chauvel of the Light Horse: A Biography of General Sir Harry Chauvel*. Melbourne University Press, 1978.

Hitler, Adolf. *Mein Kampf* (1925). Houghton Mifflin, 1971.

Horn, Bernd and Stephen John Harris. *Warrior Chiefs: Perspectives on Senior Canadian Military Leaders*. Dundurn, 2001.

Howe, Quincy. *A World History of Our Own Times: From the Turn of the Century to the 1918 Armistice*. Simon and Schuster, 1949.

Jukes, Geoffrey, Peter Simkins and Michael Hickey. *The First World War: The War to End All Wars*. Osprey Publishing, 2013.

Laffin, John. *The Battle of Hamel: The Australians' Finest Victory*. Kangaroo Press, 1999.

Lawriwsky, Michael. *Return of the Gallipoli Legend: Jacka VC*. Harlequin, 2011.

Liddell Hart, Sir Basil Henry. *Through the Fog of War*. Random House, 1938.

Lloyd George, David. *War Memoirs of David Lloyd George,* volume 6. I. Nicholson and Watson, 1936.

Ludendorff, Erich. *Ludendorff's Own Story, August 1914–November 1918: The Great War from the Siege of Liege to the Signing of the Armistice*. Harper and Brothers, 1919.

Ludendorff, Margarethe. *My Married Life with Ludendorff*. Hutchinson, 1930.

Lutz, Ralph Haswell. *Fall of the German Empire, 1914–1918*. Hoover Institution, Stanford University, 1932.

Macklin, Robert. *Bravest: How Some of Australia's Greatest War Heroes Won Their Medals*. Allen & Unwin, 2008.

MacMillan, Margaret. *Paris 1919: Six Months That Changed the World*. Random House, 2002.

Marcus, Joseph. *Social and Political History of the Jews in Poland, 1919–1939*. Walter de Gruyter, 1983.

Marnham, Patrick. *Wild Mary: A Life of Mary Wesley*. Random House, 2014.

Martel, Gordon. *The Month That Changed the World: July 1914*. Oxford University Press, 2014.

Maxwell VC, Joe. *Hell's Bells and Mademoiselles* (revised edition). HarperCollins Publishers Australia, 2013.

McCluskey, Alistair. *Amiens 1918: The Black Day of the German Army*. Osprey Publishing, 2008.

McMeekin, Sean. *July 1914: Countdown to War*. Icon Books, 2013.

McMullin, Ross. *Pompey Elliott*. Scribe Publications, 2009.

McNicol, Norman Gordon. *The Thirty-seventh: History of the Thirty-Seventh Battalion A.I.F.* John Burridge, 1936.

McWilliams, James and R. James Steel. *Amiens: Dawn of Victory*, Dundurn, 2001.

Meyer, G.J. *A World Undone*. Random House, 2006.

Mombauer, Annika and Wilhelm Deist. *The Kaiser: New Research on Wilhelm II's Role in Imperial Germany*. Cambridge University Press, 2003.

Monash, Sir John. *The Australian Victories in France in 1918*. Hutchinson and Co., 1920.

Montgomery, Field-Marshal Viscount of Alamein. *A History of Warfare*. George Rainbird Ltd, 1968.

Morton, Frederic. Thunder at Twilight: Vienna 1913–1914. Da Capo Press, 2013.

Newton, L.M. *The Story of the Twelfth: A Record of the 12th Battalion, AIF during the Great War of 1914–1918*. 12th Battalion Association, 1925.

Northwood, Vernon R., with assistance from Gershon Bennett. *Monash*. State Electricity Commission of Victoria, 1950.

Passingham, Ian. *Pillars of Fire: The Battle of Messines Ridge 1917*. The History Press, 2012.

Paterson, Michael. *Winston Churchill: Personal Accounts of the Great Leader at War*. David and Charles, 2005.

Pedersen, Peter. *Monash as Military Commander*, Melbourne University Press, 1985.

Pedersen, Peter, *Villers–Bretonneux*. Pen and Sword, 2004.

Perry, Roland. *The Australian Light Horse: The Magnificent Australian Force and Its Decisive Victories in Arabia in World War I*. Hachette, 2010.

Perry, Roland. *Monash: The Outsider Who Won a War*. Random House, 2007.

Pitt, Barrie. *1918: The Last Act*. Pen and Sword, 2014.

Pollard, Jack. *Australian Cricket*. Angus and Robertson, 1982.

Rhodes James, Robert. *Gallipoli*. Batsford, 1965.

Ridley, Jane. *Bertie: A Life of Edward VII*. Random House, 2012.

Robertson, John. *Anzac And Empire: The Tragedy and Glory of Gallipoli*. Hamlyn Australia, 1990.

Rolfe, Costa. *Winners of the Melbourne Cup: Stories That Stopped a Nation*. Red Dog Books, 2012.

Rudin, Harry R. *Armistice 1918*. Yale University Press, 1944.

Rule, E.J. *Jacka's Mob*. Angus and Robertson, 1933.

Serle, Geoffrey. *Monash*. Melbourne University Press, 1982.

Shirer, William L. *Rise and Fall of the Third Reich: A History of Nazi Germany.* Simon and Schuster, 1990.

Sinclair, David. *Hall of Mirrors.* Random House, 2011.

Snyder, Timothy. *The Red Prince: The Fall of a Dynasty and the Rise of Modern Europe.* Random House, 2009.

Souter, Gavin. *Lion and Kangaroo: The Initiation of Australia.* Sun, 1992.

Terraine, John. *The Road to Passchendaele.* Leo Cooper, 1977.

Terraine, John. *To Win a War: 1918, The Year of Victory.* Sidgwick and Jackson, 1978.

Toland, John. *Adolf Hitler*, volume 1. Anchor Books, 1976.

Toland, John. *No Man's Land: 1918, the Last Year of the Great War*, University of Nebraska Press, 2002.

Thompson, John. *On Lips of Living Men.* Lansdowne Press, 1962.

Tuchman, Barbara. *The Guns of August.* Bantam Books, 1982.

Von Hindenburg, Paul. *Out of My Life.* Cassell Limited, 1920.

Wagar, W. Warren. *H.G. Wells: Traversing Time.* Wesleyan University Press, 2004.

Wahlert, Glenn and Linwood, Russell. *One Shot Kills.* Big Sky Publishing, 2014.

Warhaft, Sally. *Well May We Say ... The Speeches That Made Australia.* Text Publishing, 2014.

Watson, Alexander. *Ring of Steel: Germany and Austria–Hungary at War, 1914–1918.* Penguin, 2014.

White, Thomas Alexander. *The Fighting Thirteenth.* Naval and Military Press, 2009.

Wise, Nathan. *Anzac Labour: Workplace Cultures in the Australian Imperial Force During the First World War.* Palgrave Macmillan, 2014.

Young, John Russell. *Men and Memories: Personal Reminiscences*, volume 2. F.T. Neely, 1901.

Zabecki, David T. *Germany at War: 400 Years of Military History.* ABC–CLIO, 2014.

Acknowledgements

John Monash likened a modern battle plan to an orchestral symphony, with each instrument playing its essential part. He might have been describing this biography, as so many people had vital roles. I am eternally grateful for their help.

I am most indebted to my publisher, Amruta Slee, who saw the need for a major, unvarnished book about Monash's huge life, a life so important to Australia's history and the shaping of our national identity.

Thanks especially to my editors Emma Dowden, Kevin McDonald and Denise O'Dea, for their patience, diligence and care.

Monash's grandson Colin Bennett, who lived at the general's house 'Iona' for his first twenty-two years, and Colin's son Michael Bennett were unstinting in their support and gave welcome advice and recollections. They realised the inspirational nature of the whole, colourful Monash story with all its twists and turns and insisted on no whitewash.

The Australian War Memorial contains a wealth of Monash material including his war records and I would like to thank Craig Tibbitts, Kelda McManus and Ricky Phillips for helping me.

The great learning institution that bears Monash's name now promulgates his legacy and Karen Rogers from the Monash University Archives was extremely generous in providing rare photographs of the great man, as were Julie Warden and Georgina

Ward from Monash's alma mater, the University of Melbourne.

The State Libraries of Victoria and Queensland were priceless resources.

Finally, I am deeply indebted to Kate Boesen, Kylie Scroope and the wonderful staff of the National Library of Australia in Canberra, who provided me with unlimited access to the diaries, letters, records and photographs compiled by Monash during his extraordinary life. It was an immense delight and privilege to read his most intimate thoughts in their original form; to pore over his correspondence and peer into diaries Monash compiled as a small boy, as a soldier facing Turkish bullets on Gallipoli and as a powerful man with the future of the world upon his shoulders.

Probably no Australian has ever documented a life with the extraordinary, meticulous detail that Monash did. It was as though he knew from childhood that he was destined for greatness. During his sixty-six years he became a shining example of the power of education and application to rise above any circumstance; of setting one's teeth to a task and seeing it through no matter what bombs, bullets or brickbats were hurled along the way.

To be entrusted to chronicle such a monumental life was an honour.

Index

R

railways case 162–64

Rainecourt (France) 482

Rankin, Brigadier General Colin 338, 339

Rankin, James 40

Ravelsberg (France) 372

Rawlinson, General Henry: France 330, 332; commends JM 393; attends race meeting 432; Hamel 438–39, 443, 450–53, 457, 459; JM's appointment to top job 442; Amiens 463–65, 476, 478–79, 483, 486; plans fresh attack 489–90; German retreat 493; Mont St Quentin 495, 500–501; lack of press coverage 505; Hindenberg Line 507, 527, 528; Epehy 510–11, 513; faces mutiny 516; Beaurevoir Line 517, 519; Saint-Quentin Canal 523–24, 525; demands AIF return to war 538–39; entertains the Monashes 555; rewarded 566

Read, General George 538

Read, George Windle 517

rebellion 489, 510, 514–16

recession. *See* financial crises

recruitment 226; *See also* conscription

Red Baron (Baron Manfred von Richthofen) 377, 420

Reed, J.B.A. Benyon 183

Reims (France) 462

Reinforced Concrete & Monier Pipe Construction Co. 185, 188, 195–96, 211, 300, 570, 576, 601

Rennick, Berrie 79–80

repatriation 557

Reserve Gully (Gallipoli) 285, 287

Ricardo, Sidney 35

Richards, Henry 39

Richardson, Joseph Richard 173

Richthofen, Baron Manfred von 377, 420

Rickard, Arthur 569

Rintel, Rabbi Moses 35

Riqueval Bridge 523

River Clyde (steamer) 254

Riviera 402

Roach, L.N. 610

Roach, Corporal Mick 454

Road Wood (France) 498

Robbins, Sergeant Fred 491

Roberts, Field Marshal Earl 218

Robertson, General Sir William 4, 340

Robinson, Arthur 576, 579, 587, 615

Robinson, Major J.A. 460

Robinson, Jess 82, 94

Robinson, Captain Montgomery 224–26

Robinson, Perry 505

Roderick, Lieutenant John 331

Rodgers, Arthur 567

Rollings, Lieutenant Ernest James 478

Rose, Captain J.M. 293

Rosenhain family 91

Rosenhain, Clara 155, 198

Rosenhain, Lou (née Monash, JM's sister): birth 23; after father's death 146–47; writes to her sweetheart 165; and marries him 176–77; Mat stays with 191; JM's visit to England 204–5; War breaks out 227; reception for 230; JM visits 335, 370, 467; JM sends money 582; JM's death 616; death 625

Rosenhain, Mona 335, 604

Rosenhain, Nancy 604, 620

Rosenhain, Peggy 620

Rosenhain, Walter: courts Lou 165; marriage 176–77; Mat stays with 191; JM's correspondence on aircraft 194; JM's visit to England 198, 204–5; JM cultivates 215; JM lends money to 219; War breaks out 227; reception for 230; reports of JM's death 281; JM's mental health 305; French campaign 332; JM visits 335, 370, 467; JM's Passchendaele report 387; JM's memoirs 558; Vic's illness 563; opposes Lizzie 574; JM sends money 582; last years 625

Rosenthal, General Charles: Bean on JM's Jewishness 390; in Italy 405; Operation Michael 408, 411, 415; Morlancourt 423; JM's appointment to command Australian Corps 426; commands 2nd Division 433; Hamel 459–60; German retreat 493; Mont St Quentin 496, 497, 500; Hindenberg Line 527, 528; after the War 627

Roth, Herman 170

Roth, Karl 121, 127, 147, 170, 227, 308–9, 319, 582

Roth, Louis 170

Roth, Mary 227

Roth, Mathilde 170, 620

Roth, Max 21, 64, 127, 137

Roth, Sophie 170, 211, 620

Roth, Ulrike (née Monasz) 19, 20–21, 137, 148, 170, 211, 562, 603

Rothschild family 552

Rothschild, Major Lionel de 536

Royal Air Force's No. 9 Squadron 441

Royal Colonial Institute (London) 556

Royal Geographic Society of Australasia 209

Royal Horticultural Society 84

Royal Society of Victoria 209

Royal Victorian Institute of Architects 182

royal visit 599–600

RSL 568, 591, 605